CONCISE
DUTCH AND ENGLISH
DICTIONARY

. . . this work can be recommended for those about to buy
their first Dutch dictionary or those wishing to bridge the
gap between a "pocket" dictionary and an advanced work.

Modern Languages

TEACH YOURSELF BOOKS

CONCISE DUTCH AND ENGLISH DICTIONARY

Dutch–English/English–Dutch

Peter and Margaretha King

TEACH YOURSELF BOOKS
Hodder and Stoughton

First printed 1958
Fourteenth impression 1986

Copyright © 1958
Hodder and Stoughton Ltd

This volume is available in the U.S.A.
from David McKay Company Inc.,
750 Third Avenue, New York, N.Y. 10017.

ISBN 0 340 26480 2

Printed in Great Britain
for Hodder and Stoughton Educational,
a division of Hodder and Stoughton Ltd
Mill Road, Dunton Green, Sevenoaks, Kent,
by Richard Clay (The Chaucer Press) Ltd, Bungay, Suffolk

INTRODUCTION

About 17,000 words are given in the Dutch–English section, and about 14,000 in the English–Dutch, though the actual number of equivalents is really far greater than this, and certainly enough for everyday use.

Condensation was essential if the maximum amount of information was to be given, and this has been effected by the use of brackets and punctuation.

Brackets. Where brackets occur in a word and its translation, two separate equivalents can be obtained by the inclusion or rejection of the parts in the brackets on both sides :

peril(ous), ge'vaar(lijk) (*n*)

Here, *the symbol "n", used throughout for neuter nouns*, is also placed in brackets, since, of course, it cannot apply to the adjective. Hence

peril, het ge'vaar
perilous, ge'vaarlijk

Similarly, **washing,** was(goed *n*) gives the two renderings : *de was* or *het wasgoed.*

Hyphens placed after Dutch words signify that they can be used as adjectives in composites :

autumn(al), herfst(–)

i.e., the autumn, *de herfst*; autumn (*or* autumnal) weather, *herfstweer*. Likewise foster(-mother), *pleeg(moeder)* implies that the Dutch *pleeg* can be used to form a composite equivalent to any of the English foster-relations (*pleegkind* = foster-child, etc.).

Punctuation between two or more translations is intended to assist in deciding which one is required. Commas have been used between two words that are more or less synonymous ; semi-colons separate literal from metaphorical meanings, the literal being given first, even where that is far less common, and they also separate words of entirely different meaning but the same origin ; colons are used between words of different origin and between different parts of speech. Finally, where an English word can be used as a noun or adjective as well as a verb, the verbal meaning is always given last. Hence in the example—

lead, leiding; eerste plaats, voorsprong; riem; voorbeeld *n*: lood *n* : leiden, ertoe brengen; voor('op)gaan; aanvoeren

the commonest literal noun form is given first (*guidance*), followed by other literal meanings, *first place* (cf. " in the lead ") and the extent of this advance (" a lead of two lengths "), another quite different literal meaning, riem (*the dog's lead*) and then the metaphorical application (*example*). After the first colon the translation of the other English noun of the same spelling, the metal *lead*, is given, followed by the various equivalents of the verb *to lead* (with a condensation, by the use of brackets, of the two verbs *voorgaan*, to lead the way and *voor'opgaan*, to go in front of).

Obviously the final selection from a number of alternative translations must be made by the reader himself, and this can be done with reasonable accuracy only by cross-reference. *Where there is any doubt about the correct Dutch equivalent for an English word, the only safe check is to refer to the Dutch–English section in order to eliminate those Dutch words which do not correspond with the sense of the English word.*

Adverbs have the same form as adjectives in Dutch, so that these are shown separately only where an adverb has no corresponding adjectival form.

Stress marks, denoted by ' immediately preceding the stressed syllable in Dutch words, are given only where the main stress does *not* fall on the first syllable.

Spelling. Inconsistencies in the spelling of Dutch words in the two parts of the dictionary may be encountered. The reason for this is that the official spelling list recently published (1954) introduces a number of changes, chiefly in the spelling of loan-words. Since many of the older spellings are more common than the revised forms in the official list, these commoner spellings are given in the Dutch–English section (though the new spelling may be given too), while the English–Dutch section gives only the revised forms. Further reference to this, and the earlier spelling reform of 1947, is made on p. 13.

CONTENTS

ACKNOWLEDGEMENTS

The authors wish to record their deep regret that illness prevented Mr H. Koolhoven from completing this work, which owes so much to his guidance in the earlier stages, and they are grateful to him too for the use they have made of his Teach Yourself Dutch *in the Teach Yourself series:*

They also express their appreciation to the publishers of Mrs Annie Holch Justesen's Hollandsk Grammatik, *which they strongly recommend for advanced students of the language, for permission to use this work in the preparation of the section on grammar.*

A special word of gratitude is due to Miss A. Huysinga for her extensive advice and reading of the manuscript.

SOUNDS AND SPELLING

THE way in which the vowel sounds in Dutch influence the spelling can be explained much more easily if a distinction is made between open and checked vowels, instead of between long and short. A long vowel is called open (or free), since it can occur anywhere, and in particular at the end of an open syllable. A short vowel can never occur at the end of a syllable, since it is checked by the consonant that follows it, with which it stands in close contact.

Consequently in a word like *poten*, the *o* is open [po·tə], since the two syllables are split between the *o* and the *t*, whereas in *potten* [pɔtə] the *o* is checked because though only one *t* is pronounced, the division between the syllables falls within this *t*, as is shown in the spelling *pot-ten*.

All the diphthongs, whether consisting of long or short elements, are open.

All vowels, whether open or checked, are lengthened by a following *r*.

Open Vowels

[a·]   More open and further forward in the mouth than Eng. *father*. (cf. first element in Eng. *eye*).
     Spelt **aa** in closed syllables, **a** in open syllables.

[o·]   A rounded vowel as in Fr. *beau*. It is particularly affected by a following *r* (as in *oor, toren*), when it tends towards [u·r]. Spelt **oo** in closed syllables, **o** in open syllables.

[y·]   A high front vowel with strong lip-rounding, as in Fr. *lu*. Spelt **uu** in closed syllables, **u** in open syllables.

[e·]   Between Fr. *é* (as in *été*) and Eng. *face*. It is strongly affected by a following *r* when it tends towards [i·r].
     Spelt **ee** in closed syllables, **e** in open syllables, except at the end of a word, when it is spelt **ee** to distinguish it from final *e*, which is pronounced [ə].

[i·]   As in Eng. *see*, but a little shorter (except before *r*).
     Spelt **ie** in closed syllables. In open syllables it is generally spelt **ie**, though in a number of loan words it is spelt **i**. The ending *-isch* is always pronounced [i·s].

[u·]   As in Eng. *cool* but shorter (except when followed by *r*). Always spelt **oe**.

[ø]   Like Fr. *feu* (i.e., with the tongue as for [e·] and the lips tightly rounded).
     Always spelt **eu**.

Checked Vowels

These always occur in closed syllables.

[ɑ]   Between *hut* and *hot*, or like Eng. [ɑ:] (as in *father*) shortened. Always spelt **a**.

[ɔ]   Between *cot* and *caught*. Always spelt **o**.

[œ]   As in *away*, but with the lips slightly rounded. Always spelt **u**.

11

[ɛ]   Between *wet* and *hat* (see below).
        Always spelt **e**, except in a few words loaned from English,
        when it is spelt **a** (*jam, tram, shag*, etc.).

[ɪ]   Between *pit* and *pet* (see below).
        Always spelt **i**.

        The Dutch sounds [ɪ] and [ɛ] fall about half-way between the
        alternative words in the following descending scale:

                        pit (Eng.)
                          pit (Du.)
                        pet (Eng.)
                          pet (Du.)
                        pat (Eng.)

The Neutral Vowel

[ə]   Like the indistinct sound in *away*, and, as in English, always
        unstressed. It can occur in closed or open syllables (hence
        also finally), and is generally spelt *e*, though it also occurs in
        the suffixes -*ig*, -*lijk*: *enig* [eˑnəx], *lelijk* [leˑlək].

Diphthongs

[aːi]   When the diphthongs [aːi], [oːi], [uˑi] are followed by a vowel,
[oːi]   the second element is replaced by a [j]-glide, becoming re-
[uˑi]   spectively: [aːj], [oːj], [uˑj].
        They are always spelt **aai, ooi, oei**.

[ɪˑu]   When followed by a vowel, these diphthongs, which are
[eˑu]   always spelt **ieuw, eeuw, uw**, become [iˑʋ], [eːʋ], [yˑʋ].
[yˑu]

[ɛi]   Between *rite* and *rate*.
        It is spelt **ij** or **ei** according to the origin of the word.

[œy]   This is probably the most difficult Dutch sound for the English-
        man. It falls between the [ʌ] in Eng. *hut* followed by Dutch
        [y] (as in *nu*) and the French diphthong in *feuille*.
        It is always spelt **ui**.

[ou]   The first element is more open than [ɔ], tending towards [ɑ].
        The spelling is either **ou** or **au**, depending on the origin of
        the word.

Consonants and Semi-vowels

    Final consonants are never voiced; i.e., [b, d; v, g, z] become
[p, t; f, x, s] and this has partially affected the spelling, so that *v*,
z never appear at the end of a word.

    The plosives **p, t, k; b, d** are pronounced as in English but with-
out any aspiration. Intervocalic **d** is often dropped in normal
speech, particularly in the West of the country, and replaced by a
[j]-glide (*goede* [guˑjə]) or [ʋ]-glide after u (*oude* [ɔuʋə]).

    The fricatives **f, v** are pronounced as in English, except that **v**
initially passes from unvoiced to voiced or even remains entirely
unvoiced. [ʋ] (spelt **w**) is pronounced like [v] but with no friction.
It is always entirely voiced. When followed by **r** it is pronounced [v].

[z]   Pronounced like Eng. **z**, except that initial **z**, like initial **v**,
        starts slightly unvoiced.

[x]	This is the sound in the Scottish *loch*. It is represented by **ch** and also, at the end of a word, by **g**. The combination *schr* is rarely pronounced [sxr]; the [x] is reduced or dropped altogether, but where this sound [sr] is heard, the spelling will always be *schr*.
[g]	This consonant (written **g**) starts unvoiced [x] and then becomes voiced (cf. initial **v** and **z**), though it is often entirely unvoiced.
[j]	As in *yes*, and often with distinct friction. Always spelt **j**.
[ŋ]	Written **ng** and pronounced as in *long*, never [ŋg] as in *finger*.
[n]	Written **n** and pronounced as in English, except in the ending -**en**, where in spoken standard (i.e., Holland) Dutch it is dropped: *even kijken* [e·və kɛikə].
[l]	l has the same pronunciation as in English, but where it is followed by **f**, **g**, **k**, **m**, **p** in the same syllable a short [ə] separates the two consonants: *elf* [ɛləf].
[r]	The *r* is always trilled in Dutch except at the end of a word, where it is audible only as a weak fricative.

The remaining consonants are pronounced in Dutch as they are in English.

Assimilation

Assimilation plays a very important part in Dutch pronunciation, where any combination of fricatives and plosives must be either voiced or voiceless, so that such a combination as in Eng. *width* is impossible.

The following rules apply where consonants fall together within a word or at the end and beginning of two adjacent words:

1. In combinations of a plosive (in which the air stream is emitted in a staccato explosion) and a fricative (in which the air stream is constant), the plosive decides whether the combination shall be voiced or voiceless:

   opvegen [ɔpfe·gə]   *niet zo* [ni·t so·]

2. A combination of two fricatives is always voiceless:

   grasveld [grɑsfɛlt]   *droog zand* [dro·x sɑnt]

3. An unvoiced next to a voiced plosive becomes voiced:

   uitbarsten [œydbɑrstə]   *op de tafel* [ɔb də ta·fəl]

Spelling

In the older spelling, which was officially revised in 1947, double vowels will frequently be found in open syllables, and *sch* may occur medially and finally even where the *ch* is not pronounced. A further attempt to remove anomalies, particularly in the use of such foreign digraphs as *th* and *ph*, and the plural endings in such composites as *paardenhaar* (horsehair), has been made by the Dutch and Belgian Governments' publication of a *Woordenlijst van de Nederlandse Taal* in 1954. Further reference is made to this list in the Introduction.

The rules of pronunciation which affect spelling can be summarized as follows:

1. Final consonants are always voiceless.

2. Assimilation may change the voicing of two adjacent consonants.

3. Whether an open (long) vowel is written with a double or single letter will depend on whether it falls in a closed or open syllable, and conversely, the consonant after a checked (short) vowel must be doubled if another syllable be added (*man, mannen*; man, men).

4. In words ending in *-isch* the *ch* is not pronounced and the *i* is long [i·s]. The suffixes *-lijk*, *-ig* are pronounced with the neutral vowel-sound [ə], i.e., [lək], [əx].

GRAMMAR
Articles

1. There are two forms of the definite article:

de for the common gender (formed by the coalescence of the older masculine and feminine genders) in the singular and plural.

het for neuter nouns in the singular and *de* in the plural.

de tuin, the garden	*het huis*, the house
de tuinen, the gardens	*de huizen*, the houses

There is one form only of the indefinite article:

een peer, a pear   *een appel*, an apple

het is sometimes written *'t* [ət], indicating its normal pronunciation. *een* is similarly sometimes written (and always pronounced) *'n* [ən].

2. Relicts of the inflected forms of the articles are still used in some names and phrases, e.g.:

Den Haag (The Hague, *meaning* at-the-Hedge)
's nachts (from *des nachts*, of a night, i.e., at night *or* every night)

Nouns

3. The *gender* of nouns is indicated in the dictionary by denoting neuter nouns by the symbol *n*; the remainder may be assumed to be common gender. (See further the Introduction.)

4. There are three plural endings: *-en, -s, -eren*. *-en* is the normal ending:

hand, handen; *huis, huizen*; *man, mannen*; *naam, namen* (for changes in spelling see pp. 12, 14 above)

and

getuige, getuigen (witness(es)), where only *-n* is added.

A number of plurals do not undergo the spelling changes we should expect, with a resultant change in vowel-sound:

dag, dagen (days); *gat, gaten* (holes); *pad, paden* (paths); *spel, spelen* (games); *weg, wegen* (ways); *oorlog, oorlogen* (wars)

and where the vowel itself changes:

lid, leden (members); *schip, schepen* (ships); *stad, steden* (towns) and the suffix *-heid*, plur. *-heden*: *moeilijkheid, moeilijkheden* (difficulties)

Note also:

> *koe, koeien* (cows); *zee, zeeën* (seas); *knie, knieën* (knees)

-s is used for the plural of:

> all diminutives: *huisjes* (cottages), etc.
> all words ending in *-el, -em, -en, -er, -aar(d), -erd.*
> loan-words ending in vowels: *drama's; studies; piano's; cadeaus*
> and a number of other foreign words: *details; romans; trams,* etc.

-eren is added to the following words, all of which are neuter, to form their plurals:

> *ei(eren)*, egg(s); *lam(meren)*, lamb(s); *rund(eren)*, cow(s),
> bull(s); *kind(eren)*, child(ren); *lied(eren)*, song(s); *goed(eren)*,
> stuff, goods; *kalf, kalveren; hoen(deren)*, hen(s); *rad(eren)*,
> wheel(s); *gemoed(eren)*, mind(s); *gelid, gelederen*, joint(s)

also

> *been* (bone, leg), *benen* (legs), *beenderen* (bones)
> *blad* (leaf, page, tray), *bladen* (pages, trays), *bladeren, blaren*
> (leaves)
> *kleed* (cloth), *kleden* (cloths), *kleren* (clothes)

5. Composites ending in *-man* form their plurals with the formal suffix *-lieden* or the less formal *-lui*:

> *werkman, werklui* (workmen); *staatsman, staatslieden* (statesmen)

but

> *Engelsman, Engelsen; Fransman, Fransen*

6. *Singular* forms are used for measures after definite numerals and *een paar* (a few):

> *drie meter; anderhalve liter* (one and a half litres); *vier maal* (four
> times); *een paar keer* (a few times, once or twice); *tien jaar*
> (ten years); *zes uur* (six o'clock)

But the plural is used after adjectives:

> *twee lange jaren* (two long years)

and the plural is always used for:

> *seconden, minuten, dagen, weken, maanden* (months), *eeuwen*
> (centuries, ages)

The following have no plural forms:

> *hoop* (hope); *dank* (thank(s)); *arbeid* (labour); *doel* (aim);
> *lof* (praise); *dood* (death)

7. There are no *case-endings*, except *-s*, (*-'s* after *a, o, u*) for the genitives of names and titles:

> *Jans broer* (John's brother); *Anna's jurk* (Anne's dress); *tantes
> bril* (auntie's glasses)

Otherwise the written genitive uses the preposition *van*, while the use of the possessive pronoun is common in everyday speech:

> *de naam van de man, de man z'n (= zijn) naam* (the man's name);
> *de man van de vrouw, de vrouw d'r (= haar) man* (the woman's
> husband)

The genitive in *-s* is also used for days, periods of the day and seasons, with the meaning *every* or *during*:

> (*'s*) *Vrijdags* (on Fridays); *'s avonds* (in the evening); *'s zomers* (in the summer) (cf. § 2)

and in the formation of many compounds:

> *stadsmens* (townsman); *veiligheidshalve* (for safety's sake)

Relicts of a dative case occur in a few expressions, the commonest of which are given in the dictionary, e.g.:

> *ten dele* (in part); *ter wille van* (for the sake of)

Adjectives

8. These take the ending *-e* before singular and plural nouns of both genders:

> *de laatste tijd* (the last time); *het oude huis* (the old house); *de betere scholen* (the better schools)

They remain uninflected when they follow their nouns or when preceding a singular neuter noun, by itself, with the indefinite article, or with an indefinite pronoun:

> *moederlief* (dear mother); *de zon is warm*; *vorig jaar* (last year); *een oud huis*; *zulk mooi weer* (such lovely weather)

Attributive adjectives are also uninflected when they describe the quality of a person:

> *een groot dichter* (a great poet); *een oud vriend* (i.e., a friend of long standing rather than a person of great age)

Adjectives ending in *-en* are never inflected:

> *de Gouden Eeuw* (the Golden Age); *mijn eigen tijd* (my own time); *verleden week* (last week)

9. Final *f* or *s* after open vowels or diphthongs in adjectives become *v* or *z* when they are inflected:

> *doof, dove* (deaf); *lief, lieve* (dear); *wijs, wijze* (wise)

also

> *half, halve*

but

> *kies(e)* (delicate); *kuis(e)* (chaste); *heus(e)* courteous

10. *Comparatives* are formed by the addition of *-er*. *Superlatives* by the addition of *-st*. They are inflected in the normal way and are used more extensively than in English.

> *trouweloos, trouwelozer, trouweloost* (faithless)

Where adjectives end in *-r*, a *d* is inserted before the comparative ending:

> *ver, verder, verst* (far)

Irregularities:

> *goed, beter, best* (good)
> *veel, meer, meest* (much)
> *weinig, minder, minst* (little, few)

When comparing two persons or things, Dutch uses the superlative:

Dit is het langste van de twee.   This is the longer of the two.

11. Adjectives used substantivally take the inflection *-e*, and *-en* when referring to more than one person:

het beste (the best thing); *de blinden* (the blind)

Adverbs

12. These have exactly the same form as adjectives:

Om goed te zijn moet een boek goed geschreven zijn.   To be good, a book must be written well.

Peculiar to Dutch are the diminutive forms *zachtjes* (softly) and *netjes* (nicely), comparable with the predicative adjectives *netjes*, *frisjes* and others.

The comparison of adverbs is also the same as of adjectives except that *graag, gaarne* (gladly, willingly) borrow from *lief* (dear) for their comparative and superlative forms:

liever (rather) and *liefst* (by preference)

Similarly *dikwijls* borrows from *vaak* (often), *vaker, vaakst*.

The superlative adverb is formed with *het* and the superlative adjective:

wat ik het liefst zou willen, what I should like most

or the simple adjectival form is used adverbially with a qualifying adverb to express the superlative sense:

uiterst zelden, very seldom
hoogst waarschijnlijk, most probably

Pronouns

13. *Personal pronouns.*

AS SUBJECTS	AS OBJECTS AND AFTER PREPOSITIONS
Singular	Singular
1. *ik*	*mij, me*
2. *jij, je*	*jou, je*
u	*u*
gij, ge	*u*
3. *hij* }*die* *zij, ze*	*hem, 'm*} *die* *haar, ze*
het, 't	**het, 't*
Plural	Plural
1. *wij, we*	*ons*
2. *jullie*	*jullie*
u	*u*
gij	*u*
3. *zij, ze*	*hen, hun, *ze*

* *het, ze* (when referring to things) are never used after a preposition:

of it (them), to it (them), with it (them), etc.; *ervan, ertoe* (or *eraan*), *ermee*, etc. (cf. thereof, thereto, therewith)

The written forms are named first; the alternatives are used in speech or quoted speech.

The three forms of the second person express ascending degrees of formality:

> *jij* (*je*), *jullie* are used in addressing animals and between (intimate) friends, by adults to children and by seniors to juniors (in rank or relationship).
>
> *u* is used otherwise (i.e., where the surname or some title, *dokter*, *tante*, etc., is used), and in correspondence the capital *U* is normal.
>
> *gij* (thou, ye) and *u* (thee, you) are used in the Bible, prayer, poetry, ceremonial occasions or formal speeches and in some dialects.

The third person subject-case *die* is frequently used when referring to things which are not neuter:

> *Waar is je fiets?—Die staat thuis.*
> Where is your bicycle?—It's at home.

Otherwise *hij* is used or, where the writer is familiar with the one-time feminine gender of the noun referred to, *zij*.

But *hem* (pronounced [əm]) is generally used in the object case:

> *Waar is je fiets?—Ik heb 'm verkocht.*
> Where is your bicycle?—I've sold it.

14. *Possessive pronouns.*

	Singular	Plural
1.	*mijn, m'n*	*ons* (inflected form *onze*)
2.	*jouw, je*	*jullie, je*
	uw	*uw*
3.	*zijn, z'n* (his or its)	*hun*
	haar, d'r	

ons *huis heeft* **zijn** (*z'n*) *achterdeur in* **onze** *tuin*
our house has its back door in our garden

Independent possessives are formed with the definite article (*de* or *het* according to the gender of the noun referred to), followed by the possessive pronoun ending in *-e* (or *-ne* after *hun*):

> *Dit huis is het onze.* This house is ours.
> *Is deze wagen de hunne of die van jullie?* Is this car theirs or yours?
> (There is no independent possessive of *jullie*.)

15. *Demonstrative pronouns.*

Singular (common gender)	*deze* (this)	*die* (that)
(neuter)	*dit* (this)	*dat* (that)
Plural (both genders)	*deze* (these)	*die* (those)

The genitive *dezer* (occasionally *dier*, of those) is used in certain expressions and to avoid cumbersome constructions:

> *één dezer dagen*, one of these days, in the near future

and the neuter genitives *dezes*, *dies* and datives *dezen*, *dien* (from *dit*, *dat*, respectively) may be encountered in literary writing and a few expressions:

> *en wat dies meer zij*, and so on (*literally*: and whatever more there may be of that)

Note:

> *dit (dat) zijn vrienden van me*, these (those) are friends of mine

Independent demonstrative pronouns are not used with prepositions. *With* (etc.) *this*, *these* is rendered by *hiermee* (etc.); *with* (etc.), *that*, *those* is *daarmee* (etc.) (cf. bottom of §§ 13, 16).

The other demonstrative pronouns are inflected like adjectives, except *zo'n* (*zo'n man*, such a man):

> *dat zijn degenen die ik bedoel*, those are the ones I mean

16. *Interrogative pronouns.*

> *wie*, who; *wat*, what; *welk*, which; *wat voor (een)*, what sort of (a)

Since the genitive *wiens* is formal, the form *wie* + possessive pronoun is sometimes used:

> *Wiens boek bedoelt u?* Whose book do you mean?
> *Wie z'n boek bedoelt u?* (cf. §§ 7, 17)

wat and *wat 'n* are also used in exclamations:

> *Wat idioot!* How ridiculous !
> *Wat is die veranderd!* Hasn't he changed !
> *Wat 'n mensen!* What a lot of people !

As with *het* (§ 12 *passim*), *wat* can never follow a preposition, the forms *waarmee*, etc., being used instead. *Waar* and its propositional suffixes are generally split up:

> *waar denk je aan?* What are you thinking of?

welk is inflected:

> *welk huis*; *welke tuin*; *welke huizen*

wat voor (een) is frequently used where there is no parallel in English:

> *Wat voor een dokter is hij?*⎫
> or *Wat is hij voor een doktor?*⎭ What is he like as a doctor?

> *Wat voor boek heb je gekocht?* What did you buy in the way of a book?

It is often used with the partitive genitive:

> *Wat heb je daar voor lekkers?* That looks nice; what is it?

17. *Relative pronouns.*

> *die*, *dat*; *wie*; *wat*; *welk*

dat (that, which) is used when the noun to which it refers is singular and neuter; *die* (who, that, which) is used in all other cases.

waaraan, waarmee, waarvan, etc., are used instead of *die, dat, wat* + preposition (cf. §§ 12, 13, 16), but *wie* can be used after a preposition when referring to persons:

> *Het boek waarvoor ik een gulden betaalde.*
> or *Het boek waar ik een gulden voor betaalde.*

> The book for which I paid a guilder.

> *Waar ik voor gekomen ben is dit.* What I've come for (*or* about) is this.

> *De jongen waarmee hij naar school gaat.*
> *De jongen met·wie hij naar school gaat.*
> The boy he goes to school with.*

wat is used after the indefinite pronouns *alles, iets,* the demonstrative *dat* and in constructions where any of these is implied:

> *Ik doe alles wat ik kan.** I'm doing everything I can.
> *Dat is precies wat ik bedoelde.* That is just what I meant.

welk (which) is used adjectivally, in more formal writing.

18. *Indefinite pronouns.*

The possessive forms of *men* (one), *iemand* (someone, anyone), *niemand* (nobody), *ieder* (everyone) are *zijn, iemands, niemands, ieders.*

Plurals take *-e* when referring to things and *-en* for persons:

> *alle(n),* all; *enige(n),* a few, any; *enkele(n),* a few; *sommige(n),* some; *andere(n),* others; *verscheidene(n),* and *verschillende(n),* various, several; *vele(n),* many; *weinige(n),* (a) few

When used as adjectives all indefinite pronouns except *wat* and *geen* are inflected like other adjectives:

> *elke dag; ieder jaar; enkele weken*

As in English, *al* precedes the definite article or pronoun:

> *al het water; al mijn boeken*

though *alle* is the normal form of *al de:*

> *alle lucht,* all the air
> *alle huizen,* all the houses

These pronouns are so much a part of Dutch idiom that it is not possible to do more than name a few commoner instances of their application.

men (one) is frequently used where English requires the passive voice:

> *naar men weet,* as far as is known

iemand is used for some *or* any unspecified person:

> *Iemand vroeg of iemand hem ook kon helpen.* Somebody asked whether there was anyone who could help him.

---

* Note that the pronoun can never be omitted in Dutch as it is in English.

but where *anyone* is used with emphasis in English, the Dutch requires *iedereen*, which also means each one, everyone (cf. *ieder* below) :

> *Iedereen zal je de weg kunnen wijzen.* Anyone will show you the way.
> *Iedereen weet dat.* Anyone (everyone) knows that.

iets and *wat* are interchangeable, and can be used with a partitive genitive:

> *Heb je iets gekocht?—Ja ik heb wat lekkers voor je.*
> Did you buy anything?—Yes, I've got something nice for you.

They can also be used in the sense of *somewhat, a bit*:

> *Dit is iets te veel, mag ik wat minder hebben?* This is a bit too much, may I have a little less?

allemaal is used in everyday language to replace *alle* (all, referring to things), *allen* (all, of people) and *alles* (everything):

> *Zij zijn alle (allemaal) te koop*, they are all for sale
> *Wij fietsen allen (allemaal) graag*, we all like cycling
> *Alles moet weg, het moet allemaal weg*, everything must go

A preposition followed by *iets, niets* or *alles* is often rendered by *ergens, nergens* or *overal* + the preposition (*met* and *tot* becoming *mee* and *toe*):

> *Dat herinnert me ergens aan.* ⎫
> *Dat herinnert me aan iets.* ⎬ That reminds me of something.

> *Ik weet nergens van.* ⎫
> *Ik weet van niets.* ⎬ I know nothing about it.

wie and (less commonly) *alwie* are really relative pronouns used indefinitely:

> *(Al)wie dit zag zal het nooit vergeten.* Anyone who saw this will never forget it.

ieder and *elk* can both mean *each* or *every* as adjectives or nouns :

> *ieder (elk) op zijn buurt*, each in turn
> *iedere (elke) keer*, every (or each) time

and as stressed adjectives they also have the sense of *any (at all)*

> *Ieder (elk) huis is better dan helemaal geen huis.* A house of any sort is better than no house at all.

sommige (*n*) means *some* in the sense of a certain number of individual things or persons:

> *Sommigen aanvaardden het, anderen weigerden.* Some accepted, others refused.

enig (*e*) is more restrictive, i.e., it means *some* only in the sense of *a few* or *a little*, hence *any*:

> *Is er enige kans op herstel?* Is there any chance of recovery?
> *Ja, er is wel enige kans.* Yes, there is some chance (but not a great deal).
> *Enigen waren zeeziek.* A few people were seasick.

enkel(e) could have been used in the last example, as also:

> *enkele* (or *enige*) *weken geleden*, some (i.e., a few) weeks ago

enig and *enkel* also mean *only* and *single* resp.:

> *het enige wat ik kon doen*, the only thing possible
> *Er was maar één enkele mogelijkheid.* There was only one (single) possibility.

enkel is also used adverbially, meaning *only*:

> *enkel en alleen*, simply and solely

ander is frequently used in conjunction with *een* [e·n]:

> *een of andere dokter*, some doctor or other
> *Ik moet 't een en ander doen.* I've one or two things to do.

but *met het een en het ander*, with one thing and another.

As a noun referring to a person it means *someone else*:

> *Ik gaf het aan een ander.* I gave it to someone else.

and as a partitive genitive it means *else*:

> *niemand (iets) anders*, no one (something) else

19. **er.** As we have seen (§ 13), English *it, them* (of things) after a preposition is rendered by *er* with the preposition in Dutch. But it is also used as a pronoun meaning *of it, of them* without a preposition when qualified by an indefinite pronoun or a numeral:

> *Zal ik er één nemen?* Shall I take one (of them)?

It can also be used adverbially:

> *Er is iemand voor u.* There is someone to see you.

frequently in passive, impersonal constructions:

> *Er wordt gebeld.* There is a ring at the door.
> *Er is mij gezegd dat . . .* I was told that . . .

er is sometimes omitted when it has already been used in the sentence:

> *Er is wat voor te zeggen.* There is something to be said in its favour.

Numerals

20. *Cardinals.* Units precede tens (e.g., as in English *five and twenty past two*):

> *vierenveertig*, 44
> *honderdzesendertig*, 136

honderd and *duizend* are never preceded by *een* or followed by *en*. An old dative ending *-en* has survived in the use of cardinals:

(*a*) after prepositions—
> *voor zessen*, before six (o'clock)
> *hij sneed het touw in tweeën*, he cut the string in half

(*b*) in constructions *met* + poss. pronoun + cardinal—
> *wij waren met z'n drieën*, there were three of us

(*c*) after *wij, jullie*—
> *jullie vieren*, you four

ongeveer, meaning *roughly* or *about*, (*approx.* is written as *circa* or ±, i.e., *plusminus*) is often replaced by *'n* (*stuk*) *of* in conversation:

> *ik heb er een stuk of drie*, I've got about three of them
> *een week of vijf geleden*, about five weeks ago

Ordinals. With the exception of *eerste*, *derde* and *achtste*, all cardinals from 1 to 19 form their ordinals by the addition of *-de*. The remainder are formed by adding *-ste*, as are also the indefinite ordinals:

> *De hoeveelste is het vandaag?—De tweede (Juli).*
> What is the date today?—The second (of July).

Verbs

21. Dutch verbs fall into three groups: weak, strong and auxiliary verbs. The same parts of the verbs are used in Dutch as in English, i.e., the present and preterite tenses, the present and past participles, the imperative and, of course, the infinitive. The perfect and pluperfect are formed with the auxiliaries *hebben* (to have) and *zijn* (to be), and the future tense with *zullen* (shall, will). The passive mood is formed in conjunction with *worden* (to become) and *zijn*. There is no equivalent of the English progressive tenses.

22. *The infinitive* ends in *-en* or *-n*. The stem is found by taking away the ending.

When the ending is *-en* preceded by a double consonant, or *-n* preceded by a double vowel, one consonant or one vowel is dropped with the ending: the stems of *hebben* and *gaan* are *heb* and *ga*.

When the ending *-en* is preceded by *v* or *z*, the stem ends in *f* or *s*:

> *leven*, to live—stem: *leef*
> *lezen*, to read—stem: *lees*

23. *The present tense* of weak and strong verbs is formed from the stem, the stem + *t* and the form of the infinitive:

staan, stem: *sta*	*geloven*, stem: *geloof*
ik sta (I stand)	*ik geloof* (I believe)
je, u, gij staat	*je, u, gij gelooft*
hij staat	*hij gelooft*
wij staan	*wij geloven*
jullie staan	*jullie geloven*
u, gij staat	*u, gij gelooft*
zij staan	*zij geloven*

When the stem ends in *t* no second *t* is added. (No Dutch word ends in a double consonant): *je, u, gij vecht* (*vechten*, to fight). The interrogative form is obtained by a straightforward inversion, *sta ik*, etc., except that final *-t* is omitted before *je*. Note also:

> *Houd je* (pronounced *hou' je*) *d'r niet van?* Don't you like it?

24. *The preterite or past tense* of weak verbs only (strong verbs are dealt with in § 28) is formed by the addition of *-de* or *-den* to the

stem unless the consonant preceding the ending *-en* in the infinitive **is** unvoiced, when the ending is *-te*, *-ten*:

ik geloofde	*ik praatte* (I talked)
je, u, gij geloofde	*je, u, gij praatte*
hij geloofde	*hij praatte*
wij geloofden	*wij praatten*
jullie geloofden	*jullie praatten*
u, gij geloofde	*u, gij praatte*
zij geloofden	*zij praatten*

25. *The participles.* The present participle of weak and strong verbs and the auxiliaries is formed by the addition of *-d(e)* to the infinitive:

Al huilend(e) viel hij in slaap, Still crying he fell asleep
stromend water, running water
bestaande methoden, existing methods

The past participle of weak verbs only (for strong verbs and auxiliaries see §§ 27, 29) is formed by adding the prefix *ge-* to the stem and *d* or *t*, after it, according to whether the past tense takes *-de* or *-te*. But (see note to § 23) no *d* or *t* is added when the stem ends in *d* or *t*:

gestudeerd; *gereisd*; *gehoopt*; *gepraat*

Verbs with an unstressed prefix do not take *ge-* in the past participle:

(ge'loven), ge'loofd; (be'duiden), be'duid; (veront'rusten), veront'-rust

Verbs with a stressed prefix place *ge-* between the prefix and the verb to form the past participle:

('aanhalen), 'aangehaald: (voor'opstellen), voor'opgesteld ;
but ('voorbereiden), 'voorbereid (because of the second, unstressed, prefix *be-*)

26. *The imperative* singular is the same as the stem; the plural is formed by adding *t* to the stem (unless this ends in a *t*);

lach niet, lacht niet, do not laugh
sta, staat, stand

27. *The strong verbs.* Strong verbs differ from weak verbs primarily in that the vowel of the stem itself changes in the preterite and past participles and the past participle always has the ending *-en*.

There are seven classes of strong verbs which are given below, each group having the same vowels in the preterite and past participle as the example given at the head of the group. Composites are not normally shown, since they follow the same pattern as the simple verbs.

I. Type: **bijten—beet—gebeten**

belijden, bezwijken, blijken, blijven, drijven, glijden, grijpen, hijsen, knijpen, kijken, kijven, krijgen, zich kwijten van, lijden, (ge)lijken, nijgen, overlijden, prijzen, rijden, rijgen, rijzen, schrijden, schrijven, schijnen, slijpen, slijten, smijten, snijden, spijten, splijten, stijgen, stijven, strijden, strijken, verdwijnen, (ver)mijden, verwijten, wijken, wijzen, wrijven, zwijgen.

II(*a*). Type: **bieden—bood—geboden**

bedriegen, gieten, genieten, kiezen, liegen, schieten, verbieden, verdrieten, vliegen; verliezen (verloor—verloren), vriezen (vroor—gevroren).

II(*b*). Type: **buigen—boog—gebogen**

druipen, duiken, fluiten, kluiven, kruipen, ruiken, schuilen, schuiven, sluipen, sluiten, snuiten, snuiven, spruiten, spuiten, stuiven, zuigen, zuipen; *also* spugen, tijgen

III. Type: **binden—bond—gebonden**

beginnen, blinken, dingen, dringen, drinken, dwingen, glimmen, klimmen, klinken, krimpen, ontginnen, slinken, spinnen, springen, stinken, verslinden, vinden, winden, winnen, wringen, zingen, zinken, zinnen

IV. Type: **bergen—borg—geborgen**

delven, gelden, melken, schelden, schenden, schenken, smelten, treffen, trekken, vechten, vlechten, zenden, (ver)zwelgen, zwellen, zwemmen; *also* schrikken

V. Type: **nemen—nam, namen—genomen**

bevelen, breken, spreken, steken, stelen; *also* komen (kwam, kwamen—gekomen)

VI. Type: **geven—gaf, gaven—gegeven**

genezen, lezen, meten, treden, vergeten, vreten; *also* eten (at, aten—gegeten) *and* bidden, (bad, baden—gebeden) liggen, zitten

VII(*a*). Type: **laten—liet—gelaten**

blazen, slapen, vallen; lopen (liep—gelopen), roepen (riep—geroepen), houden (hield—gehouden), houwen (hieuw, gehouwen), wassen (wies—gewassen) (to grow); *also* gaan, hangen, vangen *with preterites in* -i- (ging—gegaan, *etc.*)

VII(*b*). Type: **sterven—stierf—gestorven**

bederven, helpen, verwerven, werpen, zwerven; *also* heffen (hief—geheven), scheppen (schiep—geschapen) (to create)

In addition there are three more like **dragen—droeg—gedragen** :

graven, slaan (sloeg—geslagen), varen

and like **scheren—schoor—geschoren** are:

bewegen, wegen, zweren (to fester) *and* zweren (to swear) (zwoer—gezworen)

The following are irregular:

doen—deed—gedaan	to do
staan—stond—gestaan	to stand
weten—wist—geweten	to know
zien—zag—gezien	to see

A number of verbs have regular weak preterites and regular strong past participles formed by adding ge- to the infinitive:

bakken (bakte—gebakken), bannen, barsten, brouwen, heten, lachen, laden, malen, raden, scheiden, spannen, stoten, vouwen, wassen (to wash), weven, zouten; *also* wreken (wreekte—gewroken)

Finally there are some irregular weak verbs:

brengen—bracht—gebracht	to bring
denken—dacht—gedacht	to think
zoeken—zocht—gezocht	to seek
kopen—kocht—gekocht	to buy
plegen—placht (no p.p.)	* to be in the habit of
durven—durfde or *dorst—gedurfd*	to dare
vragen—vroeg—gevraagd	to ask
jagen—joeg or *jaagde—gejaagd*	to hunt, to chase
waaien—woei or *waaide—gewaaid*	to blow
zeggen—zei, zeiden—gezegd	to say

28. *Strong preterites* are conjugated in this way:

blijven, to remain	*nemen*, to take
ik bleef, I remained	*ik nam*, I took
je, u bleef	*je, u nam*
gij bleeft	*gij naamt*
hij bleef	*hij nam*
wij bleven	*wij namen*
jullie bleven	*jullie namen*
u bleef	*u nam*
gij bleeft	*gij naamt*
zij bleven	*zij namen*

29. *Auxiliary verbs:—zijn, hebben, worden, zullen, kunnen, mogen, willen, moeten.* Note that there is no equivalent of the English auxiliary *do* used

(*a*) in negative constructions—
I do not smoke. *Ik rook niet*

(*b*) in questions—
Do you smoke? *Rookt u?*

(*c*) to emphasize the main verb—
Do take care. *Pas toch op.*

---

* The regular weak verb *plegen, pleegde, gepleegd* means to commit: *hij pleegde een moord,* he committed murder.
Verplegen (to nurse) is also regular

zijn, to be.
An alternative form, *wezen,* is always used where the infinitive is used instead of the past participle:

Ik ben wezen kijken.   I have been to have a look.   (See § 31.)

Present	Preterite	Subjunctive
ik ben	*ik was*	*hij zij,* may he be
je bent	*je was*	*hij ware,* he were
u bent, (is)	*u was*	
gij zijt	*gij waart*	Imperative
hij is	*hij was*	sing. *wees*
wij zijn	*wij waren*	plur. *weest*
jullie zijn	*jullie waren*	
u bent	*u was*	Participles
gij zijt	*gij waart*	pres. *zijnde*
zij zijn	*zij waren*	past *geweest*

hebben, to have

Present	Preterite	Imperative
ik heb	*ik had*	sing. *heb*
je, gij hebt	*je, u had*	plur. *hebt*
u hebt, (heeft)	*gij hadt*	
hij heeft	*hij had*	
wij hebben	*wij hadden*	Participles
jullie hebben	*jullie hadden*	pres. *hebbende*
u hebt, (heeft)	*u had*	past *gehad*
gij hebt	*gij hadt*	
zij hebben	*zij hadden*	

worden—werd, werden—geworden (to become) is conjugated in the same way as other strong verbs.
The remaining auxiliary verbs are conjugated in the same way as strong verbs except in the present tense.

zullen—zou, zouden (no past participle)
kunnen—kon, konden—gekund
mogen—mocht, mochten—gemogen
willen—wilde, wilden—gewild (but, *gij woudt,* cf. would; and in speech, *wou, wou'en*)
moeten—moest, moesten—gemoeten

ik zal, I shall, will	*kan,* can	*mag,* may	*wil,* want	*moet,* must
je, zult, (zal)	*kunt, (kan)*	*mag*	*wil(t)*	*moet*
gij zult	*kunt*	*moogt*	*wilt*	*moet*
hij zal	*kan*	*mag*	*wil*	*moet*
wij zullen	*kunnen*	*mogen*	*willen*	*moeten*
jullie zullen	*kunnen*	*mogen*	*willen*	*moeten*
u, gij zult	*kunt*	*mag, moogt*	*wilt*	*moet*
zij zullen	*kunnen*	*mogen*	*willen*	*moeten*

30. *Compound forms of the verb.*
The perfect tense is formed with the present tense of *hebben* or *zijn* and the past participle of the main verb.

The pluperfect is obtained from the preterite of *hebben* or *zijn* in conjunction with the past participle.

zijn and *blijven* always take *zijn* in the perfect and pluperfect. Otherwise the rule for the auxiliaries is that all transitive verbs take *hebben*. Intransitive verbs take *hebben* when they express a continued action or state; they take *zijn* when they denote a passing from one position or state to another, e.g.:

> *ik heb geslapen*, I have slept; *ik heb gestaan*, I have stood; *de prijzen zijn gestegen*, prices have risen; *hij is vroeg vertrokken*, he left early; *ik ben thuis geweest*, I have been home

cf. also:

> *Wij hebben uren gelopen.* We have walked for hours (continued action).
> *Wij zijn naar huis gelopen.* We walked home (from one position to another).

Accordingly we should expect the transitive verb *vergeten* (to forget) to take *hebben*, whereas it often takes *zijn*, since to **have** forgotten something can imply a condition in the present, cf. *ik* **ben** *het kwijt*, (literally) I am without it, i.e., I **have** mislaid it.

> *Ik heb mijn bril vergeten.* I've forgotten my glasses.
> *Ik ben uw naam vergeten.* I've forgotten your name *or* I **forget** your name.

The future is rendered by the auxiliary *zullen* and the infinitive of the main verb:

> *Hij zal het morgen doen.* He will do it tomorrow.

The present *conditional* is rendered by *zouden* and the infinitive; the past conditional by *zouden* + *hebben* (or *zijn*) and the past participle or, in normal speech, by the pluperfect:

> *Dat zou ik nooit doen.* I would never do that.
> *Dat zou ik geweigerd hebben.* } I would have refused.
> *Dat had ik geweigerd.*

The *passive voice* uses the auxiliary *worden* in the present and preterite and *zijn* in the perfect tenses, both with the past participle. Similarly, the future passives use *zullen* + *worden or zijn* and the past participle.

The complete paradigm of *halen.*

Active	Indicative	
present	*ik haal*	I fetch
preterite	*ik haalde*	I fetched
perfect	*ik heb gehaald*	I have fetched
pluperfect	*ik had gehaald*	I had fetched
future	*ik zal halen*	I shall fetch
future perfect	*ik zal gehaald hebben*	I shall have fetched
present conditional	*ik zou halen*	I would fetch
past conditional	*ik zou gehaald hebben* *ik had gehaald* }	I would have fetched

Imperative
sing. *haal*.   plur. *haalt* (*u*), fetch

Infinitive

| present | (*te*) *halen* | to fetch |
| perfect | *gehaald* (*te*) *hebben* | to have fetched |

Participle

| present | *halend*(*e*) | fetching |

Passive	Indicative	
present	*ik word gehaald*	I am fetched
preterite	*ik werd gehaald*	I was fetched
perfect	*ik ben gehaald*	I have been fetched
pluperfect	*ik was gehaald*	I had been fetched
future	*ik zal gehaald worden*	I shall be fetched
future perfect	*ik zal gehaald zijn*	I shall have been fetched
present conditional	*ik zou gehaald worden*	I would be fetched
past conditional	*ik zou gehaald zijn* } *ik was gehaald*	I would have been fetched

Infinitive

| present | *gehaald* (*te*) *worden* | to be fetched |
| perfect | *gehaald* (*te*) *zijn* | to have been fetched |

Participle

| perfect | *gehaald* | fetched |

The Use of the Verb

31. *The infinitive* is used without *te* after the auxiliary verbs *zullen, kunnen, mogen, willen, moeten* and also after *blijven, doen, gaan, helpen, horen, komen, laten, leren, voelen, zien:*

Hij wil helpen afwassen.	He wants to help with the washing up.
Dat doet me denken.	That reminds me.
Het gaat regenen.	It is going to rain.
Ik moet het laten repareren.	I must have it repaired.

It will be seen in the first and last examples above that an accumulation of infinitives is possible in sentences where the main verb (or a compound future tense) governs an infinitive which is itself followed by another infinitive. The same thing occurs in the perfect tenses, where the past participle is replaced by the infinitive if it governs an infinitive:

Ik had het moeten laten repareren.   I ought to have had it repaired.

The infinitive without *te* is also very frequently used instead of the (singular and plural) imperative:

Niet doen (pron. *nie'doen*) !   Don't do it ! *or* Stop it !
Niet Roken, No Smoking

The infinitive can always be used as a (neuter) noun, often equivalent to the English gerund:

> *Ik houd* (pron. *hou'*) *van zwemmen.* I like swimming.
> *Specialisten in het fabriceren van beddegoed.* Specialists in the manufacture of bedding.

The infinitive with *te* is used after the following verbs where English uses the present participle, the gerund or the infinitive: *komen* (when it implies futurity); *liggen, lopen, hangen, staan, zitten*; *(be)hoeven, (be)horen, dienen* (ought), *plegen, weten* (to know how), *zien* (when it implies to manage); *beginnen, denken, durven, menen,* and a number of others which take the same construction in English (expect, hope, refuse, etc.).

> *Dat moet ik zien te weten te komen.* I must find out about that (somehow).
> *Hij stond met zijn vrouw te praten.* He was (*or* stood) talking to his wife (see § 32).

But *te* is omitted between the infinitives in the group *liggen—zitten* above and a following infinitive:

> *Wij hoorden hier niet te staan praten.* We ought not to be standing talking here.

The infinitive with *te* can be used as a passive attributive adjective:

> *het door ons te betalen bedrag,* the amount payable (to be paid) by us

The infinitive after *om te* is used to express purpose:

> *Zij is naar de stad (gegaan) om boodschappen te doen.* She has gone into town to do some shopping.
> *een doek om mijn fiets (mee) schoon te maken,* a cloth for cleaning my bicycle

and also where some quality or quantity is defined, sometimes implicitly:

> *Het was om te gillen,* It was screamingly funny (literally: it was enough to make anyone scream with laughter)
> *te weinig om te gebruiken,* too little to use
> *iets om te onthouden,* something worth remembering

32. *The use of the present participle.* The present participle can be used as an adjective or as an adverb:

> *drukkend weer,* oppressive weather
> *verbazend snel,* amazingly quick (ly)

It cannot be used to form progressive tenses as in English. These can be rendered in a number of ways:

> I have (had) been living there for years. *Ik woon (woonde) daar al jaren.*
> He was talking to his wife when I entered the room. *Hij stond (zat) met zijn vrouw te praten toen ik de kamer binnenkwam.*
> He was waiting for the train. *Hij wachtte op de trein.*
> She is cooking. *Zij is aan het koken* or *zij is bezig met koken.*
> I shall be going away next week. *Volgende week denk ik uit te gaan.*

Nor can it be used independently:

> Finding it was cold, he put on a coat. *Toen hij merkte dat het koud was, trok hij een jas aan.*

33. *The past participle* can also be used as an adjective or adverb.

34. *The present tense* is used for the present, sometimes for the future, and for expressing continuity from the past to the present time (cf. § 32).

> *Ziet u hem morgen?* Will you be seeing him tomorrow?
> *Hij is al lang dood.* He has been dead for a long time.

35. *The perfect tense* is used when an isolated action is completed, even when the time of the action is stated and English requires the preterite:

> *Vanochtend ben ik vroeg wakker geworden.* I woke up early this morning.

Otherwise the past tenses are used in the same way in both languages, except, of course, that the English imperfect (*I was living, etc.*) is rendered by the Dutch preterite tense (cf. § 32).

Prepositions

36. These are small but fearful hazards in any language, witness the frequent errors by Englishmen in their own language. To give all the equivalents for every Dutch preposition would be no more helpful than to give none at all, and as with all idiom, a dictionary can help only with making a start. The rest must come through familiarity with Dutch usage.

A number of prepositions, e.g., *binnen, door, in, langs, om, op, over, uit, voor, voorbij,* are used adverbially after the object as the prefix of a separable verb of which the main part has either occurred earlier or is omitted as self-evident:

> *zij kwamen de kamer binnen,* they came into the room

but *binnen de kamer,* inside the room

> *hij is de stad in*(*gegaan*), he has gone into town

but *in de stad,* in the town

> *de straat langs,* past or along the street

but *langs de straat,* along the street

> *de heuvel op,* up the hill

but *op de heuvel,* on the hill

> *de stad uit,* out of town

but *uit de stad,* from the town

> *het huis voorbij,* past the house

but *voorbij het huis,* beyond the house

Conjunctions

37. *dat* can never be omitted as *that* often is in English; and it is normally preceded by a comma:

> *Ik wist, dat ik gelijk had.* I knew I was right.

Unlike English, *after*, *before* and *until* are rendered in Dutch by the preposition + *dat*, whereas *now that* is just *nu*:

> after (before, until) I had seen him, *nadat (voordat, totdat) ik hem gezien had*
> now that I've met you, *nu ik U ontmoet heb*

Syntax

If a sentence begins with some word that is not the subject, the subject is placed immediately behind the verb:

> *Ik ga morgen naar kantoor.* ⎫
> or *Morgen ga ik naar kantoor.* ⎬ I am going to the office to-morrow.

niet normally comes immediately after the direct object:

> *Ik gaf hem het boek niet*, I did not give him the book.

When compound verbs are used, the participle or infinitive always comes at the end:

> *Morgen zal ik haar opzoeken.*   I will go and see her tomorrow.

Similarly where the main verb governs an infinitive (with or without *te*):

> *Hij heeft geweigerd mij geld te geven.*   He has refused to give me money.
> *Wij kunnen de kinderen op straat horen spelen.*   We can hear the children playing in the street.

In subordinate clauses the verb always comes at the end:

> *Hij zei, dat hij het niet gedaan had* (or *had gedaan*).   He said that he had not done it.

Prepositions used adverbially (i.e., as prefixes of separable verbs and with *er-*, *daar-*, *waar-*) come as late as possible in the sentence compatible with the above rules for the end position of verbs:

> *Daar wist ik niets van.*   I knew nothing about that.
> *Denk er eens over na.*   Just think it over a while.   (Cf. § 19.)
> *iets waar ik heel weinig van af kon weten* (cf. § 16), something which I could only know very little about

A DUTCH-ENGLISH DICTIONARY

For notes on the use of this dictionary see the Introduction

A

aaien, to stroke
aak, (Rhine) barge
aal, eel
aalbes, red, black *or* white currant
aalmoes, (an) alms
aalmoeze'nier, almoner, chaplain to the forces
aambeeld *n,* anvil
aambeien, piles
aam'borstig, short-winded
aan, at; on; to
aanbeeld *n,* anvil
aanbellen, to ring the bell
aanbesteden, to put out to contract
aanbevelen, to recommend
aanbevelens'waardig, recommendable
aanbeveling, recommendation
aan'biddelijk, adorable
aan'bidden, to worship, to adore
aanbieden, to offer
aanbieding, offer
aanbinden, to tie on
de strijd aanbinden, to join issue
aanblik, sight, spectacle
aanbod *n,* offer
aanbouw: in —, under construction
aanbranden, to burn (in cooking)
aanbreken, to dawn; to open (a bottle); to broach (a cask)
aandacht, attention
aan'dachtig, attentive
aandeel *n,* share, portion
aandeelhouder, shareholder

aandenken *n,* memory; memento
aandienen, to announce
zich laten aandienen, to send up one's name
aandikken, to lay additional stress on
aandoen, to put on; to move; to affect; to call at a place
hoe kun je me dat aandoen? how can you do such a thing to me?
aandoening, emotion; affection (of the throat, etc.)
aan'doenlijk, moving
aandrang, insistence; urgency; impulse
aandringen op, to press for; to insist on
op aandringen van, at the instance of
aanduiden, to indicate
aan'een, together; consecutively
aanfluiting, mockery, byword
aangaan, to begin; to enter into (an arrangement); to concern
wat gaat U dat aan? what concern is it of yours?
aan'gaande, concerning
aangapen, to gape at
aangeboren, innate
aangedaan, moved, affected
aangelegen, adjacent
aange'legenheid, affair, concern
aangenaam, agreeable, pleasant
aangenaam! pleased to meet you!
aangenomen, adopted; assumed
aangeschoten, tipsy
aangetrouwd, connected by marriage

aangeven, to give; to hand; to indicate; to register (luggage); to notify; to inform the police

aangezicht *n,* countenance

aangezien, seeing that, since

aangifte, notification, declaration

aangorden, to gird on

aan'grenzend, adjacent

aangrijnzen, to grin at

aangrijpen, to grasp, to seize; to assail

aan'grijpend, moving, touching

aangroeien, to increase, to grow

aanhalen, to tighten; to quote; to fondle, to paw

aan'halig, physically demonstrative

aanhalingstekens *n,* inverted commas

aanhang, followers; favour

aanhangen, to adhere to

aanhanger, adherent

aan'hangig, pending, *sub judice*

aanhangmotor, outboard motor

aanhangsel *n,* appendix

aanhangwagen, trailer

aan'hankelijk, affectionate

aanhebben, to have on

aanhechten, to affix

aanhef, opening words

aanheffen, to start, to strike up

aanhitsen, to incite, to set on

aanhoren, to listen to, to hear out

aan'horig, appertaining

aanhouden, to keep on; to persist; to arrest

aanhouden op, to make for

aan'houdend, constant; persistent

aanhouding, arrest, detention

aanjagen : schrik —, to give a fright

aankijken, to look at

aanklacht, charge, accusation

aanklagen, to charge, to accuse

aanklager, plaintiff, prosecutor

aanklampen, to buttonhole, to accost

aankleden, to dress

aankleven, to adhere

aankloppen, to knock at the door; to appeal

aanknopen, to enter into

aanknopingspunt *n,* point of contact

aankomen, to arrive

daar komt het juist op aan, that is just the point

aankomst, arrival

aankondigen, to announce

aankondiging, announcement

aankoop, purchase

aankopen, to purchase

aankoppelen, to couple

aankunnen, to be a match for, to cope (with)

aankweek, cultivation

aankweken, to cultivate

aanleg, lay-out; (natural) aptitude

in aanleg, in course of construction

aanleggen, to lay out; to build; to moor; to manage

aanlegplaats, berth (at a wharf)

aanlegsteiger, landing-stage

aanleiding, occasion

naar aanleiding van, with reference to

aanlengen, to dilute

aanleren, to learn, to acquire

aanleunen, to lean against

aanliggend, adjacent

aan'lokkelijk, tempting, attractive

aanlokken, to allure

aanloop, preliminary run; preamble

veel aanloop, many callers

aanloophaven, port of call

aanlopen bij, to drop in on

aanlopen tegen, to collide with; to come across

aanmaak, manufacture

aanmaken, to manufacture; to light (a fire)

aanmanen, to urge, to exhort, to press

aanmatigen : zich —, to presume

aan'matigend, arrogant, presumptuous

aanmelden : zich —, to present oneself

aan'merkelijk, considerable

aanmerken op, to find fault with
aanmerking, critical remark
in aanmerking nemen, to take into consideration
aangemeten, made to measure
aan'minnig, charming
aanmoedigen, to encourage
aanmoediging, encouragement
aanmonsteren, to sign on
aanmunten, to coin
aan'nemelijk, acceptable, plausible
aannemen, to accept; to assume; to adopt; to contract for
aannemer, contractor
aanpakken, to take hold of; to tackle
aanpappen, to chum up
aanpassen, to try on
zich aanpassen bij, to adapt oneself to
aanpassingsvermogen *n*, adaptability
aanplakbiljet *n*, poster
aanplakbord *n*, hoarding
aanplakken, to post up
aanplakker, bill-sticker
aanplant, plantation
aanplanten, to plant
aanporren, to stir up, to prod
aanpraten, to talk (a person) into
aanprijzen, to recommend strongly
aanraden, to advise
aanraken, to touch
aanraking, contact
aanranden, to assault
aanrander, assailant
aanrecht, draining-board
aanreiken, to hand
aanrekenen, to account
iemand iets aanrekenen, to hold something against a person
aanrichten, to cause, to do
aanrijden, to run into
komen aanrijden, to drive up
aanrijding, collision, crash
aanroepen, to hail, to invoke
aanroeren, to touch (upon); to mix
aanschaffen, to procure, to purchase

aanschijn *n*, appearance; countenance
aan'schouwelijk, clear, graphic
aan'schouwen, to behold
aanschrijven, to notify officially
hij staat goed aangeschreven, he is well thought of
aanschrijving, notification
aanslaan, to strike (a note); to affix; to give tongue; to assess; to fur up; to start (up)
hoog aanslaan, to think highly of
aanslag, touch (of a piano); attempt (on one's life); (tax) assessment; moisture, fur, scale
aanslibben, to silt (up)
aansluiten, to connect, to link up
zich aansluiten bij, to join
verkeerd aangesloten! wrong number!
aansluiting, connection
aansmeren, to foist on
aansnijden, to start cutting; to broach
aanspannen, to put (the horses) to; to tighten up
aanspoelen, to drift ashore
aansporen, to urge on
aansporing, incentive
aanspraak, claim
aan'sprakelijk, answerable
aanspreken, to address
aanspreker, undertaker's man
aanstaan, to please; to be ajar
aanstaande, next; prospective
mijn aan'staande, my *fiancé(e)*
aanstalten maken, to get ready
aan'stekelijk, infectious
aansteken, to light; to infect
aansteker, (cigarette) lighter
aanstellen, to appoint
zich aanstellen, to put on airs
aan'stellerig, affected
aanstelle'rij, affectation
aanstelling, appointment
aansterken, to recuperate
aanstevenen op, to bear down upon
aanstichten, to instigate
aanstichting, instigation
aanstippen, to touch (on)
aanstonds, by and by

aanstoot, offence
aan'stotelijk, offensive
aanstrepen, to mark, to tick off
aansturen op, to head for, to aim at
aantal n, number
aantasten, to attack; to impair
aantekenen, to note; to register
aantekening, note
aantijgen, to impute
aantocht : in —, approaching
aantonen, to demonstrate
aan'toonbaar, demonstrable
aantreden, to fall in
aantreffen, to meet, to find
aan'trekkelijk, attractive
aantrekken, to attract; to put on
  trek je daar maar niets van aan! forget it!
aan'vaarden, to begin; to assume, to accept
aanval(len), (to) attack
aanvaller, assailant
aan'vallig, charming
aanvang(en), (to) start
aanvangssnelheid, initial speed
aan'vankelijk, initial
aanvaren, to collide
  aanvaren op, to make for
aanvatten, to take hold of
aan'vechtbaar, debatable
aanvechting, sudden impulse
aanvoelen, to feel; to sense
aanvoer, supply
aanvoerder, leader
aanvoeren, to supply; to adduce; to command
aanvraag, application
aanvragen, to apply for
aanvullen, to supplement
aanvuren, to spur on
aanwakkeren, to rouse; to fan
aanwas, increase
aanwenden, to apply
aanwennen: zich —, to acquire (a habit)
aanwensel n, mannerism
aanwerven, to recruit
aan'wezig, present
aanwijzen, to point out
aangewezen, obvious; dependent

aan'wijzend voornaamwoord n, demonstrative pronoun
aanwijzing, indication
aanwinst, acquisition, asset
aanwippen, to drop in
aanwrijven, to impute
aanzeggen, to notify
  men zou hem zijn leeftijd niet aanzeggen, he doesn't look his age
aanzetten, to put on; to hone; to tighten up; to egg on
aanzien, to look at: n, distinction, reputation
aanzien voor, to (mis)take for
aan'zienlijk, notable; considerable
aanzijn n, existence
aanzoek n, request, proposal
aanzuiveren, to pay off arrears
aanzwellen, to swell
aap, monkey
  de aap uit de mouw, the cat out of the bag
aar, ear (of corn)
aard, kind; nature, character
  uit de aard der zaak, naturally
  van allerlei aard, of all kinds
aardappel, potato
aardas, earth's axis
aardbei, strawberry
aardbeving, earthquake
aardbol, globe
aarde, earth; soil
aarden, to thrive
  aarden naar, to take after
aardewerk n, earthenware
aardgas n, natural gas
aardgeest, gnome
aardig, nice, pleasant
  aardig wat, a fair amount
aardigheid, joke, fun
aardkunde, geology
aardlaag, stratum
aardrijk n, earth
aardrijkskunde, geography
aardrijks'kundig, geographical
aards, earthly
aardschok, earth tremor
aard(ver)schuiving, landslide
aarts-, arch-
aarts'bisschop, archbishop

aarts'deugniet, arrant knave
aarts'lui, bone idle
aartsvader, patriarch
aarzelen, to hesitate
aarzeling, hesitation
aas *n,* ace; bait; carrion
aasvlieg, blue-bottle
ab'ces *n,* abscess
ab'dij, abbey
ab'dis, abbess
abnor'maal, abnormal
abomi'nabel, abominable
abon'nee, subscriber
abonne'ment *n,* subscription; season-ticket
abon'neren : zich — op, to subscribe to
abri'koos, apricot
ab'sent, absent(-minded)
ab'sentie, absence
absor'beren, to absorb
ab'sorptie, absorption
ab'stract, abstract(ed)
abstra'heren, to abstract
absurdi'teit, absurdity
abt, abbot
a'buis *n,* (in) error
abu'sievelijk, erroneously
aca'demie, university; academy
aca'demisch, academic
accentu'eren, to accent(uate)
accep'teren, to accept
ac'cijns, excise duty
ac'coord *n,* agreement; chord : agreed!
accor'deren, to come to an agreement
ac'countant, chartered accountant, auditor
accu, accumulator, battery
accu'raat, accurate
accura'tesse, accuracy
ach! ah!, oh!, alas
acht, eight: attention
acht slaan op, to heed
in acht nemen, to observe
achtbaar, honourable
achteloos, negligent
achten, to consider; to esteem
achtens'waardig, estimable
achter, behind, aft, behindhand
van achteren, from behind
achter'aan, last, in the rear

achter'af, on second thoughts
zich achteraf houden, to keep in the background
achteras, back-axle
achter'baks, underhand
achterblijven, to stay *or* lag behind
achterblijver, straggler
achterbuurt, back-street, slums
achterdek *n,* quarterdeck
achterdocht, suspicion
achter'dochtig, suspicious
achter'een, at a stretch
achtereen'volgend, consecutive
achtereen'volgens, successively
achtergrond, background
achter'halen, to overtake; to recover
achterhoede, rear-guard
achterhouden, to keep back
achter'in, at *or* in the back
achterklap, slander
achterkleinkind *n,* great-grand-child
achterlaten, to leave behind
achterlijf *n,* abdomen
achterlijk, backward
achter'nalopen, to run after
achternaam, surname
achterneef(-nicht), great-nephew(-niece), second cousin
achter'om, round the back
achter'op, behind(hand)
achter'over, back(wards)
achterschip *n,* aft(er end)
achterstaan bij, to be inferior to
achter'stallig, in arrear
achterstand, arrears
achterste *n,* posterior(s); hind-most
achterstellen bij, to discriminate against
achtersteven, stern(post)
achter'uit, backwards; aft
achter'uitgaan, to move backwards; to fall (off); to deteriorate
achter'uitgang, decline; deterioration
achtervoegsel *n,* suffix
achter'volgen, to pursue
achter'volging, pursuit
achterwaarts, backward(s)

achter'wege laten, to omit
achthoek, octagon
achting, esteem
achtste, eighth; quaver
achttien(de), eighteen(th)
ac'quit n, discharge
acro'baat, acrobat
acroba'tiek, acrobatics
ac'teren, to act
ac'teur, actor
actie, action, campaign
ac'tief, active
actieradius, range
ac'tiva, assets
activi'teit, activity
ac'trice, actress
actuali'teit, topic(ality)
actu'eel, topical
adder, viper
adel, nobility
adelaar, eagle
adelborst, midshipman
adeldom, nobility
adelen, to ennoble
adellijk, noble; high, gamy
adelstand, peerage
adem(loos), breath(less)
 buiten adem, out of breath
 op adem komen, to recover
 one's breath
ademen, ademhalen, to breathe
ademtocht, breath
ader, vein
aderlaten, to let blood
aderontsteking, phlebitis
aderverkalking, hardening of the
 arteries
adju'dant, adjutant; warrant-
 officer
ad'junct, assistant
administra'teur, manager; pur-
 ser
admini'stratie, bookkeeping;
 management
administra'tief, administrative
admini'streren, to keep the
 books; to manage
admi'raal, admiral
admirali'teit, admiralty
a'dres n, address; petition
 je bent aan het goede adres,
 you've come to the right place
a'dresboek n, directory

adres'sant, petitioner
adres'seren, to address
adver'tentie, advertisement
adver'teren, to advertise
ad'vies n, advice
advi'seren, to advise
advi'seur, adviser
advo'caat, barrister: egg-flip
af, off; down; finished
 af en aan, to and fro
 af en toe, now and then
afbakenen, to buoy; to stake
 out; to define
afbeelden, to depict
afbeelding, picture
afbellen, to ring off
afbestellen, to cancel
afbetalen, to pay off
afbetaling, hire purchase
afbeulen, to work to death
afbinden, to untie; to ligate
afboeken, to write off
afbraak, demolition, rubble
afbreken, to demolish; to break
 off
afbrengen, to dissuade
 het er afbrengen, to come
 through
afbreuk doen aan, to injure; to
 detract from
afbrokkelen, to crumble (away)
afdak n, penthouse
afdalen, to descend
afdammen, to dam
afdanken, to discard; to dismiss,
 to disband
afdekken, to cover (up)
afdeling, division, section, detachment, department
afdingen, to haggle
afdoen, to take off; to settle
 die theorie heeft afgedaan,
 that theory is quite exploded
afdoend, conclusive
afdragen, to hand over (money)
 vaders kleren afdragen, to
 wear father's old clothes
afdreigen, to extort
afdreiging, blackmail
afdrijven, to drift away, to float
 down; to cause abortion
afdrijving, leeway; abortion
afdrogen, to dry (up)

afdruipen, to drip off; to slink off

afdruk, copy, print; imprint

afdrukken, to print (off)

afdwalen, to stray; to digress

afdwaling, digression; aberration

afdwingen, to extort; to compel

af'fiche n, poster

af'freus, horrible

af'fuit, gun-carriage

afgaan, to go down; to go off

  van school afgaan, to leave school

  het gaat hem goed af, it comes easy to him

  op iemand afgaan, to go up to a person

  afgaande op de feiten, judging by the facts

afgelasten, to countermand

afgeleefd, decrepit

afgelegen, remote

afgemeten, measured; formal

afgescheiden van, apart from

afge'scheidene, dissenter

afgetobd, worn, jaded

afgetrokken, absent-minded

afgevaardigde, deputy

afgeven, to hand over; to hand in; to emit

  de verf geeft af, the paint comes off

afgezaagd, hackneyed

afgezant, envoy

afgezien van, apart from

afgieten, to strain off

afgietsel n, (plaster) cast

afgifte, delivery; issue

afgod, idol

afgodendienaar, idolater

afgode'rij, idolatry

afgodsbeeld n, idol

af'grijselijk, horrible

afgrijzen n, horror

afgrissen, to snatch from

afgrond, abyss

afgunst, jealousy

af'gunstig op, jealous of

afhalen, to take down; to collect; to strip; to string (beans)

afhandelen, to settle (business)

af'handig maken, to filch

afhangen, to hang down; to depend

af'hankelijk van, dependent on

afhaspelen, to reel off

afhebben, to have finished

afhechten, to cast off

afhellen, to slope down

afhelpen, to help off; to help down

afhouden, to keep off; to deduct

afkammen, to disparage

afkapen, to filch

afkappen, to chop off

afkeer, aversion

afkeren, to avert; to turn away

af'kerig van, averse to

afketsen, to glance off; to reject; to come to naught

afkeuren, to disapprove of; to reject as unfit, to condemn

afkeurens'waardig, reprehensible

afkijken, to crib; to look down

afkloppen, to beat off; to " touch wood "

afknippen, to trim, to cut off

afknotten, to truncate

afkomen, to come down

  er afkomen, to get off

  ergens van afkomen, to get rid of a thing

afkomst, origin, birth

af'komstig van, originating from

afkondigen, to proclaim

afkondiging, proclamation

afkooksel n, decoction

afkoopsom, ransom

afkopen, to buy off

afkorten, to abbreviate

afkrijgen, to get off; to get finished

afkunnen, to be able to manage

aflaat, indulgence

afleggen, to cover (a distance); to pay (a call); to take (an oath); to sit for (an examination)

afleiden, to distract; to deduce; to derive

afleiding, distraction; derivation

afleren, to unlearn; to break of a habit

afleveren, to deliver

aflevering, delivery; number, instalment

afloop, end, outcome; expiry

aflopen, to run down; to slope; to end; to expire

ik heb alle winkels afgelopen, I have been to every shop in town

af'losbaar, redeemable

aflossen, to redeem; to relieve

afluisteren, to eavesdrop

afmaken, to finish; to kill; to break off

afmatten, to tire out

af'mattend, exhausting

afmatting, exhaustion

afmeten, to measure (off)

afmeting, dimension

afmonsteren, to sign off; to pay off

afnemen, to take off; to take down; to clear away; to decrease

afnemer, customer

afpakken, to snatch out of one's hand

afpassen, to measure

afpersen, to extort

afpersing, extortion

afpingelen, to haggle

afpoeieren, to send packing

afraden, to dissuade

afranselen, to thrash

afrastering, (wire) fence

afreageren, to work off (one's emotions)

afreis, departure

het land afreizen, to travel all over the country

afrekenen, to settle accounts

afrekening, settlement

africhten, to train

afrissen, afristen, to string

afroepen, to call

afrollen, to roll down; to unroll

afronden, to round off

afrossen, to thrash

afruimen, to clear away

afrukken, to tear off

afschaffen, to abolish

afschaffing, abolition

afscheid n, parting

afscheid nemen, to take one's leave

afscheiden, to separate; to secrete

afschepen, to fob off

afschieten, to fire; to shoot off; to partition

afschieten op, to rush up to

afschilderen, to depict

afschrift n, copy

afschrijven, to copy; to write off; to cancel

afschrijving, depreciation

afschrik, horror

afschrikken, to frighten away

afschuw, loathing

af'schuwelijk, horrible, hideous

afslaan, to beat off; to decline

rechts afslaan, to turn to the right

afslachten, to butcher

afslag, Dutch auction

afslager, auctioneer

afsloven : (zich) —, to wear (oneself) out

afsluitboom, boom

afsluitdijk, dam; causeway

afsluiten, to lock; to close; to turn off; to cut off; to balance; to conclude

afsnauwen, to snap at

afsnijden, to cut off

afsnoepen, to snatch from; to forestall

afspannen, to unharness

afspelen : zich —, to be enacted

afspiegelen, to reflect

afspoelen, to rinse (off)

afspraak, appointment, date, arrangement

afspreken, to agree, to arrange

afstaan, to cede

afstammeling, descendant

afstammen, to descend

afstamming, descent

afstand, distance; cession

afstandsmars, route march

afstandsmeter, range finder

afstappen, to get down; to put up

afsteken, to push off; to let off; to deliver

afsteken bij, to contrast with

afstemmen, to negative; to reject; to attune
afstempelen, to stamp
afsterven, to die off
afstijgen, to dismount
afstoffen, to dust
afstompen, to blunt
afstormen op, to rush at
afstoten, to push off; to repel
af'stotelijk, repellent
afstraffen, to punish; to reprimand
afstraffing, dressing-down
afstropen, to skin
afstuiten op, to rebound from; to be frustrated by
afsturen, to dispatch
  afsturen op, to head for
aftakelen, to dismantle; to age badly
af'tands, long in the tooth
aftappen, to tap; to draw off
aftekenen, to sign
  zich aftekenen tegen, to stand out against
aftocht, retreat
aftrap, kick-off
aftrappen, to kick off; to kick down
aftreden, to resign
aftrek, deduction; demand
aftrekken, to deduct, to subtract; to distract
aftrekking, subtraction
aftreksel *n,* infusion
aftroeven, to trump
aftroggelen, to wheedle out of
aftuigen, to unharness; to give a hiding
afvaardigen, to delegate
afvaart, departure, sailing
afval, refuse; apostasy
afvallen, to fall down, to fall away; to lose weight
af'vallig, disloyal
af'vallige, renegade
afvaren, to (set) sail
afvegen, to wipe (off)
afvloeien, to flow down; to be discharged
afvoer, removal; discharge; waste(-pipe)
afvoeren, to carry away

afvoerkanaal *n,* drainage channel
afvragen : zich —, to wonder
afwachten, to await, to wait and see (about)
afwachting, expectation
afwasbak, washing-up bowl
afwassen, to wash up *or* off
afwateren, to drain
afwatering, drainage
afweer, defence
afweergeschut *n,* anti-aircraft guns
afwegen, to weigh out
afwenden, to avert
  zich afwenden, to turn away
afwennen, to break of a habit
afwentelen, to roll away
afweren, to ward off
afwerken, to finish off
afwerking, finish
afwerpen, to throw off; to yield
af'wezig, absent
af'wezigheid, absence
afwijken, to deviate
afwijking, deviation
afwijzen, to turn down *or* away, to reject
afwikkelen, to unroll; to wind up
afwisselen, to alternate, to vary
  elkaar afwisselen, to take turns
af'wisselend, alternating; varied
afwisseling, variation; change
afzakken, to come down
afzeggen, to cancel
afzenden, to dispatch
afzet, sale
afzetgebied *n,* market
afzetten, to take off; to depose; to amputate; to trim; to cordon off; to cheat
  een ge'voel van zich afzetten, to shake off a feeling
afzetter, cheat
afzette'rij, swindle
af'zichtelijk, hideous
afzien van, to give up
  afgezien van, apart from
  binnen af'zienbare tijd, within the not too distant future
af'zijdig, aloof
afzonderen, to isolate, to segregate

afzondering, seclusion
af'zonderlijk, separate
afzweren, to abjure
a'gaat, agate
a'genda, agenda; diary
a'gent, agent; policeman
a'gentschap *n*, agency, branch (bank)
agen'tuur *n*, agency
a'geren, to agitate
a'horn, maple
air *n*, appearance
a'jour, open-worked
akelig, nasty, unpleasant; unwell
akker, (arable) field
akkermaalshout *n*, copse
ak'koord *n*, agreement; chord: agreed!
akoes'tiek, acoustics
akte, diploma, deed; act
aktentas, brief-case
al, all: already: even though
al te, too
alar'meren, to give the alarm
al'bast *n*, alabaster
alcoholhoudend, alcoholic
alco'holica, intoxicants
al'daar, there
aldoor, all the time
al'dra, ere long
al'dus, thus
alge'meen, general, common
over het algemeen, in general
al'hier, here
alhoe'wel, although
a'linea, paragraph
al'koof, (bedroom) recess
alle'bei, both
alle'daags, commonplace, of daily occurrence
al'leen, alone; only
al'leenheerser, absolute ruler
al'leenspraak, soliloquy
alle'gaartje *n*, hotchpotch
alle'maal, all; altogether
allemaal tegelijk, all together
alle'machtig, devilish: good lor'!
allemansvriend, friend to everybody
allen, all
al'lengs, gradually

aller'liefst, most charming
aller'eerst, first of all
Aller'heiligen, All Saints' Day
allerlei, allerhande, all sorts of
aller'minst, (the) very least; not in the least
allerwegen, everywhere
allerzijds, on all sides
alles, everything
van alles, all sorts of things
alles en nog wat, anything and everything
al'licht, quite likely: I should think so!
we kunnen het allicht proberen, no harm in trying!
al'looi *n*, alloy
al'lures, airs
almacht, omnipotence
al'machtig, almighty
al'om, everywhere
alomtegen'woordig, ubiquitous
als, as; like; if; when
als'dan, then
alsem, wormwood
alsje'blieft, please; here you are; there now—what did I tell you!
als'mede, as well as
als'nog, as yet
als'nu, now
als'of, as if
alstu'blieft (*see* **alsje'blieft**)
alt, alto; contralto
altaar *n*, altar
al'thans, at least
altijd, altoos, always
altsleutel, tenor clef
altviool, viola
a'luin, alum
al'vast, meanwhile
al'vorens, before
al'waar, where
al'weer, again
al'wetend, omniscient
al'wetendheid, omniscience
al'zijdig, versatile, all-round
al'zo, thus
a'mandel, almond
a'mandelen, tonsils
amanu'ensis, laboratory assistant
ama'ril, emery
ambacht *n*, trade

ambachtsheer, lord of the manor
ambachtsman, artisan
ambas'sade, embassy
ambassa'deur, ambassador
ambi'eren, to aspire to
am'bitie, zest; ambition
ambiti'eus, ambitious
ambt n, function; office
ambtelijk, official
ambteloos burger, private citizen
ambtenaar, official, civil servant
ambtena'rij, red tape
a'mechtig, out of breath
ameuble'ment n, (suite of) furniture
amfi'bie, amphibian
am'fibisch, amphibious
ami'caal, pally
ampel, ample
amper, scarcely
amu'sant, amusing
amu'seren, to amuse
ana'loog, analogous
ana'lyse, analysis
analy'seren, to analyse
ana'lytisch, analytical
ana'nas, pine-apple
ana'toom, anatomist
anciënni'teit, seniority
ander, different; other
  des anderen daags, the next day
  om de andere dag, every other day
  onder andere (o.a.), *inter alia*
anderdeels, on the other hand; partly
anderhalf, one and a half
anders, different; else
  net als anders, just as usual
anders'denkend, andersge'zind, dissentient
anders'om, the other way round
anderzijds, on the other hand
an'dijvie, endive
ane'moon, anemone
angel, sting; fish-hook
angst, fear, terror
angstig, afraid, fearful
angst'vallig, scrupulous, timid
angst'wekkend, alarming
angstzweet n, cold sweat

a'nijszaad n, aniseed
ani'meren, to encourage
geanimeerd, animated
animo, zest
anje'lier, anjer, carnation
anker n, anchor; wall-brace; armature
ankeren, to anchor
ankergrond, anchorage
ankerhand, fluke
ankerlicht n, riding light
an'nex, annexe: enclosed; attached
an'nonce, advertisement, announcement
anno'teren, to annotate
annui'teit, annuity
ano'niem, anonymous
ansicht, picture postcard
an'sjovis, anchovy
an'tenne, aerial
anti'chambre, anteroom
anticham'breren, to wait outside
an'tiek, antique(s)
anti'monium n, antimony
antipa'thiek, antipathetic
anti'quaar, antique dealer
antiquari'aat n, secondhand bookshop, antique shop
antiqui'teiten, antiques
antwoord(en) (n), (to) answer
a'part, apart; separate
  iets zeer a'parts, something very special
a'pathisch, apathetic
apegapen: op — liggen, to be at one's last gasp
apekool, rubbish
apekuur, monkey trick
apeliefde, molly-coddling
apolo'geet, apologist
apenootje n, monkey-nut
a'postel, apostle
apo'theek, (dispensing) chemist('s)
apo'theker, pharmacist
appa'raat n, apparatus
ap'pel n, appeal; roll-call
appel, apple
appelbol, apple dumpling
appelflauwte, swoon, fit
appel'leren, to appeal

appelmoes, apple *purée*
appelsap, cydrax
appe'tijtelijk, appetizing
ap'plaus *n*, applause
applaudi'sseren, to applaud
appreci'ëren, to appreciate
approvian'deren, to provision
apro'pos, by the way
aqua'rel, water-colour
ar(reslee), horse-drawn sleigh
arbeid(en), (to) labour
arbeider, labourer
arbeidersklasse, working classes
arbeidsbeurs, arbeidsbureau *n*, labour exchange
ar'beidzaam, industrious
arbi'trair, arbitrary
ar'chief *n*, archives; record office
archi'varis, archivist; keeper of the records
are, 100 square metres
arend, eagle
arendsjong *n*, eaglet
arendsneus, aquiline nose
argeloos, unsuspecting
arglist, guile
arg'listig, crafty
argwaan, suspicion
arg'wanend, suspicious
arm, arm; branch: poor
armband, bracelet, armlet
armenzorg, poor relief
armhuis *n*, workhouse
arm'lastig, in receipt of poor-relief
armleuning, elbow-rest
armoe(de), poverty
ar'moedig, needy; shabby
armoedzaaier, poor devil
armsgat *n*, arm-hole
arm'zalig, pitiful
armslag, elbow-room
arres'tant, prisoner
arres'teren, to arrest
ar'senicum *n*, arsenic
ar'tesisch, artesian
ar'tiest, variety artist
artille'rie, artillery
artille'rist, gunner
arti'sjok, artichoke
arts, doctor
artse'nij, physic
artse'nijkunde, pharmacology

as, ash(es): axle; axis
asbakje *n*, ash-tray
as'best *n*, asbestos
as'ceet, ascetic
asem, breath
as'perge, asparagus
aspi'rant, candidate
Assepoes(ter), Cinderella
assura'deur, insurer; underwriter
assu'rantie, insurance
assu'reren, to insure
as'trant, cocky
astro'loog, astrologer
astro'noom, astronomer
a'syl, asylum; refuge
ate'lier *n*, studio, workshop
aterling, miscreant
at'leet, athlete
atle'tiek, athletics
a'toomsplitsing, nuclear fission
at'tent, attentive; considerate
at'tentie, attention; act of courtesy
at'test *n*, certificate, testimonial
attes'teren, to attest, to certify
attra'peren, to catch in the act
audi'ëntie, audience; formal interview
au'gurk, gherkin
augustus, August
aula, auditorium
au'teur, author
au'teursrecht *n*, copyright
auto, (motor-)car
autodi'dact, self-taught (person)
auto'maat, automaton; slot-machine
auto'noom, autonomous
autori'seren, to authorize
autori'tair, high-handed; authoritarian
averechts, wrong
  een recht, een averecht, knit one, purl one
ave'rij, average; damage
avond, evening
avondeten *n*, **avondmaal** *n*, supper
avondschemering, dusk
avontu'rier, adventurer
avon'tuur *n*, adventure
avon'tuurlijk, adventurous

azen op, to prey on
a'zijn, vinegar
a'zijnzuur *n,* acetic acid
a'zuur (*n*), azure

B

baai, bay
baak, beacon
baal, bale, bag
baan, way, track; orbit; (tennis) court; job
  dat is van de baan, that's shelved
baanbreker, pioneer
baar, billow: bier: ingot
baar geld, ready cash
baard, beard
  hij heeft de baard in de keel, his voice is breaking
baarmoeder, womb
baars, perch
baas, master, boss
  iets de baas worden, to get the better of a thing
baat, benefit
  ten bate van, for the benefit of
baatzucht, selfishness
babbelen, to chatter; to gossip
baby oppas, baby-sitter
bad *n,* bath
baden, to bath, to bathe
  zich in weelde baden, to wallow in luxury
badhuis *n,* public baths
ba'gage, luggage
baga'tel *n,* trifle
bagger, mud
baggeren, to dredge; to squelch
baggermolen, dredger
bak, tray; bin; pan
bakbeest *n,* huge thing
bakboord *n,* port
baken *n,* beacon
baker, maternity nurse
bakeren, to dry-nurse
bakermat, birthplace
bakerpraat, old wives' tale
bakfiets, carrier-cycle
bakkebaarden, side-whiskers
bakke'leien, to scrap
bakken, to bake, to fry
  iemand een poets bakken, to play a trick on somebody

bakker, baker
bakke'rij, bakery
bakmeel *n,* flour
baksel *n,* batch (of cakes, *etc.*)
baksteen, brick
  het regent bakstenen, it is raining cats and dogs
bakvis, teen-ager
bal, ball: *n,* dance, ball
  elkaar de bal toewerpen, to play into one another's hands
ba'lans, balance(-sheet), scales
bal'dadig, wanton, destructive
ba'lein, whalebone; rib of umbrella
balie, railing, counter
  tot de balie toelaten, to call to the bar
baliekluiver, loafer
baljuw, bailiff
balk, beam, rafter
  over de balk gooien, to squander
balken, to bray
bal'kon *n,* balcony
balling(schap), exile
bal'lon, balloon
ballo'tage, ballot
bal'orig, refractory; truculent
balsem, balm
balsemen, to embalm
ban, excommunication, ban
  in de ban doen, to excommunicate
ba'naal, banal
ba'naan, banana
band, band, tape; ligament; waveband; tyre; bond
  aan banden leggen, to put under restraint
  uit de band springen, to get out of hand
bande'lier, shoulder-belt
bandeloos, lawless
bandepech, tyre-trouble
ban'diet, bandit
banen: de weg—voor, to pave the way for
  zich een weg banen, to force one's way (through)
bang, afraid
bangmake'rij, intimidation
ba'nier, banner

bank, bench, settee; bank
bankbiljet n, bank-note
ban'ket n, banquet; fancy cakes
ban'ketbakker, pastry-cook
ban'kier, banker
bankpapier n, bank-notes
bank'roet (n), bankrupt(cy)
bankschuld, overdraught
bankstel n, sitting-room suite
bankwezen n, banking
banneling, exile
bannen, to banish
banvloek, anathema
bar, inclement: bar
　bar slecht, very bad
　hij maakt het al te bar, he is
　going too far
ba'rak, hut(ment)
bar'baar, barbarian
bar'baars, barbaric
bar'bier, barber
baren, to give birth to; to en-
　gender
barensnood, labour (pains)
ba'ret, cap, beret, biretta
bar'goens n, jargon
barm'hartig, merciful
barnsteen n, amber
barrevoets, barefoot
bars, gruff, stern
barst, crack
barsten, to burst, to crack; to
　explode
bas, bass
bas'cule, weigh-bridge, kitchen-
　scales
ba'seren, to base
basi'liek, basilica
basis, basis, base; footing
bassen, to bay
bassleutel, bass clef
bast, bark
basta! enough!
bastaard, bastard; mongrel
basterdsuiker, moist (brown)
　sugar
baten, to avail
batig saldo n, credit balance
batte'rij, battery
bavi'aan, baboon
ba'za(a)r, bazaar; sale of work
bazelen, to talk nonsense
bazig, bossy

ba'zin, mistress
ba'zuin, trumpet, trombone
be'ambte, official; employee
be'amen, to assent
be'angst, uneasy
be'angstigen, to alarm
be'antwoorden, to answer; to
　return; to correspond
be'bloed, bloody
be'boeten, to fine
be'bossen, to afforest
be'bouwen, to cultivate; to
　build on (or up)
becriti'seren, to criticize
bed n, bed
be'daard, calm, composed
be'dacht op, alive to, mindful of
be'dachtzaam, circumspect
be'danken, to thank; to decline;
　to resign
　wel bedankt! thanks very
　much!
be'dankje n, bread-and-butter
　letter
be'daren, to calm down
beddegoed n, bedding
bedding, river-bed
bede, prayer, request
be'deesd, timid; coy
bedehuis n, place of worship
be'dekken, to cover
bedeklok, angelus
bedelaar, beggar
bedela'rij, begging, mendicity
bedelen, to beg
be'delen, to endow; to distribute
　relief
be'deling, poor-relief
bedelmonnik, mendicant friar
be'delven, to bury
be'denkelijk, grave; precarious;
　questionable
be'denken, to recollect; to con-
　sider; to think up
　zich bedenken, to change one's
　mind
be'denking, objection; con-
　sideration
be'derf n, corruption; decay
be'derven, to spoil; to go bad
bedevaart, pilgrimage
bedevaartganger, pilgrim
be'diende, servant; employee

be'dienen, to serve; to (ad)minister (to)

be'diening, service

be'dilal, fault-finder

be'dillen, to find fault with

be'ding *n*: **onder geen —,** not in any circumstances

be'dingen, to stipulate

be'disselen, to see to

bed'legerig, bed-ridden

be'doelen, to mean

be'doeling, intention

be'dompt, close; stuffy

be'donderen, to bamboozle

  ben je bedonderd? are you crazy?

be'dotten, to diddle

be'drag *n*, amount

be'dragen, to amount to

be'dreigen, to threaten

be'dremmeld, shy, confused

be'dreven, proficient

be'driegen, to deceive

bedriege'rij, deception

be'drieg(e)lijk, deceptive, deceitful

be'drijf *n*, industry, business, undertaking; act

be'drijven, to commit

be'drijvigheid, bustle, activity

be'drinken: zich —, to get drunk

be'droefd, sad

  be'droefd weinig, precious little

be'droeven, to grieve

be'drog *n*, deceit, trickery

be'druipen, to baste

  zichzelf bedruipen, to pay one's (*or* its) way

be'drukt, depressed; printed

be'ducht, apprehensive

be'duiden, to signify, to indicate

be'duvelen, to fool

be'duusd, abashed, taken aback

be'dwang *n*, restraint

  zich in bedwang houden, to restrain oneself

be'dwelmen, to stun; to drug; to intoxicate

be'dwelming, stupor; narcosis

be'dwingen, to suppress, to curb

be'ëdigen, to swear in

be'ëindigen, to terminate

beek, brook

beeld *n*, image; picture, statue; beauty

  zich een beeld vormen van, to visualize

beeldenaar, effigy

beeld(er)ig, charming, very pretty

beeldhouwen, to sculpture

beeldhouwer, sculptor

beeldrijk, ornate

beeldspraak, metaphor

beeltenis, image

beemd, (lush) meadow

been *n*, leg; bone

beenbreuk, fracture

beer, bear; boar; buttress

beerput, cesspit

beest *n*, animal, beast

beestachtig, beastly

beestenboel, filthy mess, pig-sty

beestenspel *n*, menagerie

beet, bite, sting

beet hebben, to have got hold of

beetje *n*, (little) bit

beetnemen, to take in

beetpakken, to take hold of

be'faamd, famous, notorious

be'gaafd, gifted

be'gaan, to tread; to commit

  begaan met, sorry for

  een flater begaan, to drop a brick

  begane grond, ground level

be'geerlijk, desirable

be'geerte, desire

bege'leiden, to accompany

bege'nadigen, to pardon, to bless

be'geren, to desire, to covet

be'gerig, desirous, covetous

be'gerigheid, greed

be'geven, to give way; to bestow

  zich begeven, to go, to proceed

be'gieten, to water

be'giftigen, to endow

be'gin *n*, beginning

be'ginneling, beginner

be'ginnen, to start, to begin

  wat moet ik nu beginnen? whatever shall I do now?

  er is niets met hem te beginnen, there is no doing anything with him

be'ginsel *n*, principle

be'ginstadium *n*, initial stage
be'graafplaats, cemetery
be'grafenis, funeral
be'graven, to bury
be'grenzen, to bound, to limit
be'grijpelijk, understandable
be'grijpelijkerwijze, understandably
be'grijpen, to understand; include
be'grip *n*, concept(ion); notion; comprehension
 kort begrip, abstract
 vlug van begrip, quick in the uptake
be'groeid, overgrown
be'groeten, to greet, to hail
be'groten, to estimate
be'groting, estimate, budget
be'gunstigen, to favour
be'haaglijk, pleasant, comfortable
be'haagziek, coquettish
be'haard, hairy
be'hagen, to please
 behagen scheppen, to take pleasure
be'halen, to gain, to win
be'halve, except, apart from
be'handelen, to treat, to deal with
be'handeling, treatment
be'hang(sel) *n*, wall-paper
be'hangen, to paper, to drape
be'hanger, paper-hanger
be'hartigen, to have at heart, to look after
be'hartiging, care
be'heer *n*, management
be'heerder, manager, administrator
be'heersen, to rule; to control; to command (a language); to dominate
be'heksen, to bewitch
be'helpen: zich —, to make do, to rough it
be'helzen, to contain
be'hendig, dexterous
be'hept met, afflicted with
be'heren, to manage, to administer
be'hoeden voor, to protect from

be'hoedzaam, cautious
be'hoefte, need
be'hoeftig, needy
be'hoeve: ten — van, for the sake of, in aid of
be'hoeven, to need
be'hoorlijk, proper; decent
be'horen, to belong; to be fitting
 naar behoren, properly
be'houd *n*, preservation; retention
be'houden, to retain; to preserve
 behouden terugkeer, safe return
be'houdend, conservative
be'houdens, except for; subject to
be'huild, tear-stained
be'huisd: klein —, cramped for room
be'huizing, housing
be'hulp: met — van, with the aid of
be'hulpzaam, helpful
be'huwd (zuster), *etc.*, (sister-)in-law, *etc.*
beiaard, carillon
beide(n), both; two
 geen van beide(n), neither (of them)
beiderlei, of both sorts
beiderzijds, on both sides
be'ijveren : zich —, to do one's utmost
be'ïnvloeden, to influence
beitel, chisel
beits, (wood) stain
beitsen, to stain (wood)
be'jaard, aged
be'jag naar *n*, pursuit of
be'jammeren, to lament
be'jegenen, to treat
bek, mouth, beak
be'kaaid: er — afkomen, to come off badly
bekaf, dog-tired
be'keerling, convert
be'kend, (well-)known; acquainted
 ik ben hier niet bekend, I'm a stranger here
be'kende, acquaintance

be'kendheid, acquaintance; reputation, notoriety
van algemene bekendheid, generally known
be'kendmaking, announcement
be'kennen, to admit, to confess; to follow suit
be'kentenis, admission, confession
beker, cup, mug
be'keren, to convert
be'kering, conversion
be'keuren, to charge
be'keuring, charge, fine
be'kijken, to look at; to look into
be'kijk(s) hebben, to attract attention
bekken n, basin; pelvis
be'klaagde, accused
be'kladden, to besmirch
be'klag n, complaint
be'klagen, to pity
zich beklagen, to complain
beklagens'waardig, pitiable
be'kleden, to cover; to upholster
een ambt bekleden, to hold an office
be'kleding, be'kleedsel n, covering, upholstery; lagging
be'klemd, oppressed; stressed
be'klemdheid, oppression; constriction
be'klimmen, to climb
be'klinken, to rivet; to settle
be'kneld, locked, jammed
be'knibbelen, to beat down; to stint
be'knopt, concise
be'knorren, to scold
be'knotten, to curtail
be'kocht, cheated
be'koelen, to cool down
be'kogelen, to pelt
be'kokstoven, to wangle
be'komen, to recover; to agree with
be'kommeren: zich — om, to bother about
be'komst n: **zijn — eten,** to eat one's fill
ik heb er mijn bekomst van, I've had more than enough of it
be'konkelen, to scheme

be'koorlijk, charming
be'kopen (met de dood), to pay (with one's life)
be'koren, to charm, to appeal to
be'koring, charm; temptation
be'korten, to curtail
be'kostigen, to pay for
be'krachtigen, to confirm, to ratify
be'krassen, to cover with scratches
be'krimpen: zich —, to retrench
be'krompen, narrow-minded; restricted
be'kronen, to crown, to award a prize
be'kruipen, to take by surprise
het gevoel bekroop me, the feeling came over me
be'kruisen: zich —, to make the sign of the cross
bekvechten, to wrangle noisily
be'kwaam, capable
be'kwaamheid, ability
be'kwamen, to qualify, to fit
bel, bell; bubble
be'labberd, rotten
be'lachelijk, ridiculous
be'laden, to load
be'lagen, to waylay
be'landen, to land (up)
be'lang n, interest; importance
be'langeloos, disinterested
be'langrijk, important
belang'stellend, interested
be'langstelling, interest
belang'wekkend, interesting
be'lastbaar, taxable, dutiable
be'lasten, to burden; to tax; to charge; to debit
zich belasten met, to take upon oneself
be'lasteren, to slander; to libel
be'lasting, tax(ation); load
be'lazeren, to bamboozle
ben je belazerd? are you barmy?
be'ledigen, to insult
be'lediging, insult
be'leefd(heid), polite(ness)
beleefdheids'halve, out of politeness

be'leg *n*, siege
be'legen, matured
be'legeren, to besiege
be'leggen, to cover; to call (a meeting); to invest
be'legsel *n*, trimming(s); facing
be'leid *n*, administration; prudence
be'leidvol, tactful
be'lemmeren, to hamper
be'lendend, adjacent
be'lenen, to pawn, to raise a loan on
be'let *n*: — **vragen**, to ask for an appointment
be'letsel *n*, obstacle, hindrance
be'letten, to prevent
be'leven, to experience, to live through
  dat had hij moeten beleven! if only he could have lived to see this!
be'lezen, well-read
belhamel, ringleader, rascal
be'lichamen, to embody
be'lichten, to throw light upon; to expose
be'lieven, to please
  naar believen, as one pleases
be'lijden, to confess; to profess
be'lijdenis, confession, creed; confirmation
belknop, bell-pull, bell-push
bellen, to ring (the bell)
belle'trie, *belles-lettres*
be'loeren, to spy upon
be'lofte, promise
be'lonen, to reward
be'loop *n*, course
be'lopen, to amount to
  met bloed belopen ogen, bloodshot eyes
be'loven, to promise
be'luisteren, to listen to
be'lust op, eager for
be'machtigen, to secure
be'malen, to drain
be'mannen, to man
be'manning, crew; garrison
be'merken, to perceive
be'mesten, to manure
be'middelaar, intermediary
be'middeld, well-to-do

be'middelen, to mediate
be'middeling, mediation
be'minnelijk, charming, lovable
be'minnen, to love
be'moedigen, to encourage
be'moeial, busy-body
be'moeien: zich — met, to concern oneself with, to meddle with
be'moeienis, concern
be'moeilijken, to hinder
be'moeiziek, meddlesome
be'nadelen, to harm
be'naderen, to estimate; to get near
be'nadering: bij —, approximately
be'naming, name
be'nard, critical; perilous
be'nauwd, close, stuffy; constricted; afraid
  ik heb het benauwd, I can't breathe
be'nauwdheid, closeness; constriction; fear
bende, gang; mess
be'neden, below, downstairs; under, beneath
be'nedenhuis *n*, bottom flat
be'nedenverdieping, ground-floor
be'nedenwaarts, downwards
be'nemen, to take away
  de moed benemen, to discourage
be'nepen, cramped; narrow-minded; timid
be'nevelen, to befog, to fuddle
be'nevens, together with
bengel, bell-clapper; young rascal
bengelen, to dangle
be'nieuwen: het zal me —, I wonder
be'nieuwd, curious to know
benig, bony
be'nijden, to envy
benijdens'waard(ig), enviable
be'nodigd, required
be'nodigdheden, requisites
be'noemen, to appoint; to nominate
be'noorden, to the north of

be'nul *n*, notion
be'nutten, to make use of
ben'zine, petrol
be'oefenaar, student, votary
be'oefenen, to study, to practise
be'ogen, to have in view
be'oordelen, to judge, to review
be'oorlogen, to wage war against
be'oosten, to the east of
bepaald, positive; definite; appointed
in een bepaald geval, in a given case
niet bepaald beleefd, not exactly polite
be'pakken, to pack
be'palen, to determine, to define
zich bepalen tot, to confine oneself to
be'paling, definition; regulation; stipulation
be'peinzen, to muse on
be'perken, to limit, to confine
be'plakken, to plaster
be'planten, to plant
be'pleiten, to plead
be'praten, to talk over
zich laten bepraten, to be persuaded
be'proefd, well-tried
be'proeven, to try, to put to the test; to afflict
be'raad *n*, deliberation, consideration
be'raadslagen, to deliberate
be'raden: zich — (op), to consider
be'ramen, to devise
berde: te — brengen, to broach
be'rechten, to adjudicate
be'redderen, to arrange
be'reden, mounted
berede'neren, to reason out
be'reid, ready, prepared
be'reiden, to prepare
be'reids, already
bereid'vaardig, bereid'willig, ready to help
be'reik *n*, reach; range
be'reiken, to reach, to achieve
be'reikbaar, attainable
be'reisd, (much-)travelled
be'reizen, to travel (all over)

be'rekenen, to calculate; to charge
niet berekend voor het werk, not equal to the work
be'rekening, calculation
beremuts, busby
berg, mountain
de haren rezen mij te berge, it was a hair-raising experience
bergachtig, mountainous
bergen, to store; to salvage; to accommodate
hij is geborgen, he is a made man
bergengte, defile
bergingswerk *n*, salvage-operations
bergkam, bergrug, mountain-ridge
bergkloof, ravine, gorge
bergloon *n*, salvage-money
bergplaats, store, depository
bergruimte, storage space
bergzout *n*, rock-salt
be'richt *n*, news, report; notice
be'richten, to inform
be'rijden, to ride
be'rispen, to rebuke, to reprimand
berk, birch
berm, (grass) verge
be'roemd, famous
be'roemdheid, fame, celebrity
be'roemen: zich — op, to pride oneself on
be'roep *n*, profession; appeal
in hoger beroep gaan, to appeal
beroepen: zich — op, to appeal to, to plead, to refer to
be'roeps-, professional
be'roepsleger *n*, regular army
be'roerd, rotten
be'roeren, to stir, to disturb
be'roering, disturbance, turmoil
be'roerte, stroke, fit
be'rokkenen, to cause
be'rooid, penniless
be'rookt, smoky
be'rouw *n*, repentance
be'rouwen: het zal je —, you will be sorry (for it)
be'rouwvol, repentant

be'roven, to rob, to deprive

be'rucht, notorious

be'rusten bij, to be in the safe keeping of

be'rusten in, to be resigned to

be'rusten op, to rest on; to be due to

bes, berry, (red-)currant

be'schaafd, well-bred; civilized

be'schaamd, ashamed

be'schadigen, to damage

be'schamen, to shame; to dash (hope); to betray (confidence)

beschamend, humiliating

be'schaven, to civilize

be'schaving, culture, civilization

be'scheid n, reply; document

be'scheiden, modest, retiring

be'schermeling, protégé(e)

be'schermen, to protect

be'schermheer, patron

be'scherming, protection, patronage

be'schieten, to fire on

be'schijnen, to shine on

be'schikbaar, available

be'schikken over, to have at one's disposal

be'schikking: ter —, available

be'schilderde ramen, stained glass windows

be'schimmelen, to go mouldy

be'schimpen, to abuse

be'schonken, tipsy

be'schoren: hem was een ander lot —, a different fate was in store for him

be'schot n, partition

be'schouwen, to regard, to contemplate

wel beschouwd, all things considered

be'schrijven, to describe; to cover with writing

be'schroomd, timid

be'schuit, tea-rusk

be'schuldigen, to accuse

be'schutten, to shelter

be'sef n, realization; notion

be'seffen, to realize, to be aware of

besje n, old woman

be'slaan, to take up (space); to mount (with silver, etc.); to shoe; to get blurred; to tarnish

be'slag n, (metal) fitting(s), mounting(s) or ornament(s); batter; seizure

beslag leggen op, to distrain on; to take up

be'slapen, to sleep on or in

be'slissen, to decide

be'slist, decided, for certain

be'slommeringen, cares, worries

be'sloten, private; close

be'sluipen, to steal up on

be'sluit n, conclusion; decision

be'sluiteloos, irresolute

be'sluiten, to conclude; to decide

be'smettelijk, contagious, infectious

be'smetten, to infect, to contaminate

be'smeuren, to besmirch

be'sneeuwd, snow-covered

be'snijden, to circumcise

be'snoeien, to lop, to prune; to cut down

be'snuffelen, to sniff at

be'spannen, to span; to string

een met paarden bespannen wagen, a horse-drawn cart

be'sparen, to save

be'spatten, to bespatter

be'spelen, to play

be'speuren, to perceive

be'spieden, to spy on

be'spiegelend, contemplative

be'spiegeling, contemplation

be'spoedigen, to speed up

be'spottelijk, ridiculous

be'spotten, to ridicule

be'spraakt, never at a loss for a word

be'spreken, to book, to reserve; to discuss, to review

be'sprenkelen, to sprinkle

be'springen, to pounce upon

be'sproeien, to water

be'spuiten, to spray

best, best; very good; dear: very well

het is mij best, it is all right by me

ten beste geven, to contribute

be'staan *n*, existence, livelihood; to exist

bestaan uit, to consist of

bestaan van, to subsist on

be'staanbaar, possible; compatible

be'staansmiddel *n*, means of support

be'stand *n*, truce

be'stand tegen, proof against

be'standdeel *n*, ingredient, component

be'steden, to spend; to devote

be'stek *n*, compass; specification; spoon and fork

het bestek opmaken, to calculate a ship's position

be'stelen, to rob

be'stellen, to order; to deliver

be'stelwagen, (delivery) van

be'stemmen, to destine; to intend

be'stempelen, to stamp; to designate

be'stendig, constant; lasting; steady

be'stendigen, to perpetuate

be'sterven: hij bestierf het van schrik, he nearly died of fright

dat woord ligt in zijn mond bestorven, he is always using that word

be'stijgen, to mount, to ascend

be'stoken, to harass

be'stormen, to storm

be'straffen, to punish

be'stralen, to shine upon, to give X-ray treatment to

be'straten, to pave

be'strijden, to combat; to defray

be'strijken, to cover

be'strooien, to strew, to sprinkle

bestu'deren, to study

be'stuiven, to (cover with) dust; to pollinate

be'sturen, to govern; to drive; to steer

be'stuur *n*, government, administration; committee

bestwil: om uw eigen —, for your own good

een leugen om bestwil, a white lie

be'talen, to pay (for)

ik zal het hem betaald zetten, I'll get even with him

be'tamelijk, seemly

be'tamen, to behove

be'tasten, to feel

bete, morsel

be'tegelen, to tile

be'tekenen, to mean

het heeft niets te betekenen, it is of no consequence

be'tekenis, meaning; significance

beter, better

beterhand: aan de —, on the road to recovery

beterschap, recovery

be'teugelen, to curb

be'teuterd, taken aback

be'tichten, to accuse

be'timmeren, to face with wood, to panel

be'titelen, to style

be'togen, to argue

be'ton *n*, concrete

be'tonen, to accent; to show

be'tonmolen, concrete mixer

be'toog *n*, argument; exposition

be'toon *n*, demonstration

be'toveren, to bewitch, to fascinate

betovergrootmoeder, great-great-grandmother

be'traand, tear-stained

be'trachten, to do, to show

be'trappen, to catch (out)

be'treden, to tread; to set foot on

be'treffen, to concern

wat mij betreft, as far as I am concerned

be'trekkelijk, relative

be'trekken, to move into; to involve; to cloud over

be'trekking, post, job; relation(ship)

met betrekking tot, with reference to

be'treuren, to deplore

betreurens'waardig, deplorable

be'trokken, overcast

be'trokken bij, concerned in

be'trouwbaar, reliable

betten, to dab

be'tuigen, to express; to protest; to profess
betweter, know-all
be'twijfelen, to doubt
be'twistbaar, contestable
be'twisten, to dispute, to contest
beu, fed up
beuk, beech
beukehout n, beechwood
beuken, to beat, to pound
beul, executioner; brute
beunhaas, bungler
beunhazen, to dabble
beuren, to lift; to receive
beurs, purse; scholarship; exchange: over-ripe; bruised
beurt, turn
  een flinke beurt, a thorough cleaning-up
beurtelings, in turn
beurtvaart, waterway transport service
beuzelachtig, trivial
be'vallen, to please; to be confined
be'vallig, graceful
be'valling, confinement
be'vangen, to overcome
be'varen, to navigate
be'vattelijk, intelligent, intelligible
be'vatten, to contain; to comprehend
be'vechten, to fight (against)
be'veiligen, to safeguard
be'vel n, order, command
be'velen, to command
be'velhebber, be'velvoerder, commander
beven, to tremble
bever, beaver
beverig, shaky
be'vestigen, to fasten; to consolidate; to confirm; to induct
be'vinden, to find
  zich bevinden, to be (situated)
be'vlekken, to stain
be'vlieging, sudden impulse, whim
be'vloeien, to irrigate
be'vochtigen, to moisten
be'voegd, competent, qualified
be'volken, to populate

be'volking, population
be'voordelen, to benefit
bevoor'oordeeld, prejudiced
be'voorrechten, to privilege
be'vorderen, to promote
be'vorderlijk voor, conducive to
be'vrachten, to load; to charter
be'vragen: hier te —, inquire within
be'vredigen, to satisfy; to appease
be'vreemden, to surprise
be'vreesd voor, afraid of
be'vriend, on friendly terms
be'vriezen, to freeze, to get frost-bitten
be'vrijden, to liberate, to release
be'vroeden, to surmise
be'vruchten, to fertilize
be'vuilen, to soil
be'waarheiden, to confirm
be'waken, to guard
be'wandelen, to walk in or on
be'wapenen, to arm
be'waren, to keep, to preserve
be'waring, keeping, custody
  in bewaring geven, to deposit
be'weegbaar, movable
be'weeglijk, mobile; fidgety
be'weegreden, motive
be'wegen, to move; to induce
be'weging, movement, motion
  uit eigen beweging, of one's own accord
be'wenen, to weep for
be'weren, to assert, to contend
be'werkelijk, unmanageable
be'werken, to till; to work on or up; to adapt; to bring about
bewerk'stelligen, to bring about
be'westen, to the west of
be'wieroken, to incense; to praise to the skies
be'wijs n, proof; certificate; evidence
be'wijsgrond, argument
be'wijzen, to prove, to show
be'wind n, government, rule
be'wolken, to cloud over
be'wonderen, to admire
be'wonen, to inhabit
be'woner, resident, occupant, inhabitant

be'woordingen, terms
be'wust, conscious
  zich bewust zijn van, to be
  aware of
  de bewuste brief, the letter in
  question
be'wusteloos, unconscious
be'wustheid, awareness
be'wustzijn n, consciousness
  buiten bewustzijn, unconscious
be'zaaien, to sow; to litter
be'zadigd, sober-minded
be'zegelen, to seal
be'zeilen, to sail
  er· is geen land met hem te
  bezeilen, you cannot do a
  thing with him
bezem, broom
be'zending, consignment
  de hele bezending, the whole
  lot
be'zeren, to hurt
be'zet, occupied, engaged; set
be'zeten, possessed
be'zetten, to occupy; to set
be'zetting, garrison; occupation; cast (of a play)
be'zichtigen, to view
be'zielen, to inspire
  wat bezielt je? what has come
  over you?
be'zien, to look at
  dat staat nog te bezien, that
  remains to be seen
bezig, occupied, busy
  druk bezig, hard at work
bezigen, to use
bezigheid, occupation
bezighouden, to keep occupied
be'zijden, beside
be'zingen, to sing (the praises of)
be'zinken, to settle (down); to
  sink in
be'zinksel n, sediment
be'zinnen: zich —, to reflect; to
  change one's mind
be'zinning: tot — komen, to
  come to one's senses
be'zit n, possession(s), estate
be'zittelijk voornaamwoord n,
  possessive pronoun
be'zitten, to possess

be'zittingen, property, posses-
  sions
be'zoedelen, to defile
be'zoek, n, visit
  we krijgen bezoek, we are
  expecting visitors
be'zoeken, to visit; to afflict
be'zoldigen, to pay a salary
be'zoldiging, salary, pay
be'zondigen: zich — aan, to
  perpetrate
be'zonken, considered
be'zonnen, level-headed
be'zopen, tipsy; crazy
be'zorgd, anxious; provided for
be'zorgen, to procure; to give;
  to deliver
be'zuiden, to the south of
be'zuinigen, to economize
be'zuren, to suffer for
be'zwaar n, objection; drawback
be'zwaard, weighted; burdened,
  oppressed
be'zwaarlijk, scarcely
  bezwaarlijk vinden, to object
  to
be'zwaarschrift, n, petition
be'zwangeren, to impregnate
be'zwarende omstandigheden,
  aggravating circumstances
be'zweet, sweating
be'zweren, to adjure; to exorcise
be'zwijken, to succumb, to collapse
be'zwijmen, to faint
bibberen, to shiver
bibliothe'caris, librarian
biblio'theek, library
bidden, to pray, to say grace
bidstond, prayer-meeting
biecht, confession
biechten, to confess; to go to
  confession
biechtvader, confessor
bieden, to offer; to bid
biefstuk, rump-steak
bier n, ale, beer
biet, beet
  rode biet, beetroot
biezen, (made of) rushes
big, piglet
biggelen, to trickle
biggen, to farrow

bij, near, at, with, by; present; in addition: bee

bij zijn leven, during his lifetime

hij is goed bij, he is all there

er ligt me iets van bij, I seem to remember something of it

bij-, secondary, in addition

bijbedoeling, ulterior motive

Bijbel, Bible

bijblijven, to keep pace with; to stick in the memory

bijbrengen, to adduce (reasons); to bring round; to inculcate

bijde'hand, smart; "all there"

bijde'handje *n*, bright child

bijdraaien, to heave to; to come round

bijdrage, contribution

bijdragen, to contribute; to tend

bij'een, together

bij'eenkomen, to come together

bij'eenkomst, meeting, gathering

bij'eengenomen: alles —, all things considered

bijenkorf, bee-hive

bijenstal, apiary

bijgaand, enclosed

bijgebouw *n*, outhouse

bijgedachte, implication; association

bijgeloof *n*, superstition

bijge'lovig, superstitious

bijgenaamd, nicknamed

bijge'val, by any chance; in case

bijge'volg, in consequence

bijhouden, to keep (the books); to keep up with

bijkantoor *n*, branch-office

bijkeuken, scullery

bijknippen, to trim

bijkomen, to come to, to revive

er komt nog bij, what is more

bijkomend, bij'komstig, attendant; incidental

bijl, hatchet, axe

het bijltje erbij neerleggen, to down tools

bijlage, enclosure; appendix

bijleggen, to make up (a quarrel); to add (money) to

bijlichten, to give (a person) some light

bijltjesdag, day of reckoning

bijna, almost

bijna niet, hardly

bijnaam, nickname

bijoorzaak, contributory cause

bijpassen, to pay the difference

bijpassend, matching

bijschenken, to fill up

bijschrift *n*, caption

bijslaap, cohabitation; bedfellow

bijslag, additional payment

bijsmaak, trace, tang

bijspringen, to help

bijstaan, to assist

bijstand, assistance

bijstelling, apposition

bijster: het spoor—zijn, to have lost one's way

niet bijster, not particularly

bijt, hole cut in the ice.

bijten, to bite

van zich af bijten, to show fight

bijtend, caustic; cutting; corrosive

bij'tijds, in good time

bijtrekken, to pull up; to improve

bijvak *n*, subsidiary subject

bijval, approbation; applause

bijvallen, to back up

bijvoegen, to add

bij'voeglijk naamwoord *n*, adjective

bijvoegsel *n*, supplement

bij'voorbeeld, for instance

bijwerken, to touch up; **to** bring up to date; to give extra coaching

bijwijf *n*, concubine

bijwonen, to attend

bijwoord *n*, adverb

bijzaak, matter of secondary importance

bijzettafeltje *n*, occasional table

bijzetten, to inter; to add

bijzetting, interment

bij'ziend(e), short-sighted

bijzijn *n*, presence

bijzin, subordinate clause

bijzit, concubine

bijzitter, assessor

bij'zonder, special, particular; private

niets bijzonders, nothing out of the ordinary

bij'zonderheden, particulars

bil, buttock

bil'jart *n,* billiard-table, billiards

bil'jet *n,* (bank)note; ticket

billijk, fair

billijken, to justify; to approve of

binden, to bind, to tie (up); to thicken

binnen, within, inside, in

het schoot me te binnen, it (suddenly) struck me

binnen'door gaan, to take a short cut

binnengaan, to go in

binnenhuis *n,* interior

binnenkomen, to come in

binnen'kort, shortly

binnenlands, internal, home . . .

Ministerie van Binnenlandse Zaken, Home Office

binnens'huis, indoors

binnens'monds, under one's breath, indistinctly

binnenste'buiten, inside out

binnenvaart, inland navigation

binnenwaarts, inward(s)

bint, tie-beam

bio'loog, biologist

bios'coop, cinema

bisdom *n,* diocese

bisschop, bishop

bis'schoppelijk, episcopal

bisschopszetel, (episcopal) see

bis'seren, to encore

bits, snappish

bitter, bitter

bitter weinig, next to nothing

bitterkoekje *n,* macaroon

bittertje *n,* gin and bitters

bivak *n,* bivouac

blaadje *n,* petal; leaflet; tray

ik sta bij hem in een goed blaadje, I am in his good books

blaag, whipper-snapper

blaam, blame

blaar, blister

blaas, bladder; bubble

blaasbalg, pair of bellows

blaasinstrument, wind-instrument

blaaskaak, gasbag

blad *n,* (*pl.* **bladen**), leaf; sheet of paper; newspaper; tray: (*pl.* **bladeren**), leaf of a tree

hij neemt geen blad voor de mond, he does not mince his words

van het blad spelen, to play at sight

bladgroente(n), greens

bladzij(de), page

blaffen, to bark

blaken, to blaze, to glow

in blakende welstand, in the pink of health

blakeren, to scorch

blanco, blank

blank, white; pure; naked (sword); flooded

blaten, to bleat

blauw (*n*), blue

blauwe'regen, wistaria

blauwtje: een—lopen, to be turned down

blauwsel *n,* washing-blue

blauwzuur *n,* prussic acid

blazen, to blow; to spit (cat)

hoog van de toren blazen, to brag

bleek, pale

bleekheid, pallor

bleken, to bleach

bleren, to shout, to bawl

bles'seren, to wound

bles'suur, wound

bleu, bashful

blieven, (cf. *believen*): **wat blieft u?** what can I do for you? I beg your pardon?

ik blief het niet, I don't like it

blij(de), glad

blijdschap, gladness

blijk *n* **geven van,** to show signs of

blijkbaar, apparently

blijken, to appear, to transpire

't moet nog blijken, it remains to be seen

blijkens, as appears from

blij'moedig, cheerful

blijspel n, comedy
blijven, to stay, to remain
blijvend, lasting, permanent
blik, glance, look; eyes: n, tin (-plate); dustpan
blikken: zonder — of blozen, without turning a hair
bliksem, lightning; blazes
  handige bliksem! smart fellow!
blind, blind: n, shutter
  zich blind staren op, to be obsessed by
  de blinde, dummy (at bridge)
blinddoeken, to blindfold
blinde'darmontsteking, appendicitis
blindelings, blindly
blindheid, blindness
blinken, to shine, to gleam
bloed n, blood
bloedarmoede, anæmia
bloedbad n, carnage
bloedeigen, of one's own (flesh and) blood
bloeden, to bleed
bloederig, bloody
bloedig, bloody; bitter
bloedlichaampje n, blood-corpuscle
bloedneus, nose-bleed
bloedschande, incest
bloedsomloop, circulation (of the blood)
bloedwraak, vendetta
bloei, bloom, blossom(ing); prosperity
bloeien, to bloom; to flourish
bloeitijd, blossom-time; hey-day
bloem, flower; flour
  de bloemetjes buiten zetten, to paint the town red
bloemig, floury
bloe'mist, florist
bloemkool, cauliflower
bloemlezing, anthology
bloempjesdag, flag-day
bloemrijk, florid
bloemstuk n, bouquet
bloesem, blossom
blok n, block; log
blokfluit, recorder

blok'kade, blockade
blokken, to swot
blok'keren, to block; to blockade
blokwachter, signalman
blond, fair
blon'dine, blonde
bloodaard, coward
bloot, bare, naked; sheer
blootgeven: zich —, to lay one-self open (to attack)
blootleggen, to reveal
blootshoofds, bareheaded
blootstaan aan, to be exposed to
blootstellen, to expose
blos, blush; bloom
blozen, to blush
bluffen, to brag
blussen, to extinguish; to quell
blut, broke
bobbel(ig), lump(y)
bochel, hump; hunchback
bocht, bend: n, awful stuff
bochtig, winding
bod n, bid
bode, messenger; carrier
bodem, bottom; soil; territory
  de bodem inslaan, to frustrate
bodemloos, bottomless
boedel, household goods; personal estate
boef, rogue
boefje n, guttersnipe
boeg, bow(s)
  het over een andere boeg gooien, to try another tack
  veel werk voor de boeg, a lot of work on hand
boegspriet, bowsprit
boei, buoy
boeien, fetters: to fetter; to hold the attention
boeiend, fascinating
boek n, book
  te boek staan als, to have the reputation of
  je gaat buiten je boekje, you are overstepping the mark
boekdeel n, volume
boekelegger, book-mark(er)
boeken, to book
boekenkast, bookcase
boekenwijsheid, book-learning

boeke'rij, library
boekhandel, bookshop
boekhouden (*n*), book-keeping: to keep accounts
boekjaar *n*, financial year
boel: een —, a lot
  een armoedig boeltje, a shoddy outfit
  je boeltje *n*, your goods and chattels
boemelen, to be on the spree
boemeltrein, slow train
boender, scrubbing-brush
boenen, to scrub
boenwas, wax polish
boer, peasant, farmer; knave (at cards); **boor:** belch
boerde'rij, farm
boeren, to belch
boeren'jongens, brandy and raisins
boeren'kool, kale
boe'rin, peasant woman, farmer's wife
boers, boorish
boertig, slapstick
boete, penalty, fine; penance
boeten voor, to atone for
boet'seren, to model
boet'vaardig, penitent
boezelaar, apron
boezem, bosom
bof, stroke of luck: mumps
boffen, to be lucky
bogen op, to boast (of)
bok, buck; billy-goat
  een bok schieten, to make a blunder
bo'kaal, goblet
bokkesprong, caper
bokkig, churlish
bokking, bloater
boksen, to box
bol, globe, sphere; crown (of hat); bulb; head: convex, bulging
bolhoed, bowler hat
bolleboos, adept
bollen, to bulge
bolster, shell, husk
bolwerk *n*, bulwark
bolwerken: hij kon het niet—, he could not manage it

bom, bomb
bombar'deren, to shell; to bomb(ard)
bom'barie, fuss and bother
bomen, to punt; to chat
bomgat *n*, bung-hole
bon, voucher; coupon
bond, alliance, union
bondgenoot, ally
bondig, terse
bonk, chunk, lump
bonken, to thump
bonkig, bony
bons, bump, thud
  de bons geven, to sack, to throw over
bont, many-coloured; gaudy; piebald; varied; motley: *n*, fur
  je maakt het te bont, you are going too far
bonzen, to throb; to pound; to bump
boodschap, message, errand
  boodschappen doen, to go shopping
boog, arch, arc; bow
boom, tree; boom; barrier; pole
boomgaard, orchard
boomstam, tree-trunk
boon, bean
boor, drill, gimlet
boord *n*, collar; (ship)board
  aan boord, on board
boordevol, brim-full
boos, angry; evil
boos'aardig, malicious
boosheid, anger
booswicht, villain
boot, boat
bootsman, bo'sun
bootwerker, dock labourer
bord *n*, plate; board
bor'deel *n*, brothel
bor'des *n*, (flight of) steps
bor'duren, to embroider
boren, to drill, to bore
borg, surety, security, bail
borgstelling, borgtocht, security; bail
borrel, short drink
borrelen, to (have a) drink; to bubble

borst, breast, chest: lad
  tegen de borst stuiten, to go
  against the grain
borstbeeld *n,* bust
borstel, brush; bristle
borstelen, to brush
borstelig, bristly
borstkas, chest
borstplaat, fondant
borstvliesontsteking, pleurisy
borstwering, parapet
bos, bunch, bundle, tuft: *n,*
  wood
bosachtig, wooded
bosbes, bilberry
bosbouw, forestry
bosgrond, woodland
bosje *n,* spinney
boskat, wild cat
bosrijk, wooded
bos'schage *n,* grove
boswachter, (forest)-keeper
bot, blunt: flounder: *n,* bone
  bot vangen, to meet with a curt
  refusal
botvieren, to give rein to
boter, butter
boterbloem, buttercup
boterham, slice of bread and
  butter
botsen, to collide, to bump
botsing, collision
botte'lier, butler, steward
botweg, flatly
boud, bold
bou'gie, sparking plug
bouil'lon, beef-tea, stock
bout, bolt; wooden pin; leg cut
  of meat
bouw, build, construction; cultivation; structure
bouwen, to build
bouw'kundig, architectural
bouwkunst, architecture
bouw'vallig, tumble-down, dilapidated
boven, above, over
  te boven gaan, to exceed
  te boven komen, to get over
bovenaan, at the top
boven'dien, moreover
bovenhuis *n,* upstairs flat
bovenlicht *n,* skylight

bovenloop, upper reaches
boven'mate, exceedingly
boven'menselijk, superhuman
bovenna'tuurlijk, supernatural
bovenop, on (the) top of
bovenste, topmost
boventoon, overtone
  de boventoon voeren, to (pre-)
  dominate
box, play-pen
braaf, good, decent, upright
braak, fallow
braam(bes), blackberry
brabbelen, to jabber
braden, to roast
brak, brackish
braken, to vomit
brallen, to brag
bran'card, stretcher
brand, fire
  in brand vliegen, to catch
  fire
brandbaar, inflammable
branden, to burn
brander, blow-lamp
brandewijn, French brandy
brandkast, safe
brandmerken, to brand
brandnetel, stinging nettle
brandpunt *n,* focus
brandschatten, to hold to ransom
brandspuit, fire-engine
brandstapel, stake; funeral pile
brandstichter, incendiary
brandstof, fuel
brandweer, fire-brigade
branie, daring; swank(-pot)
brasem, bream
braspartij, orgy
bra'voure, bravado
breed, broad, wide
breed'sprakig, prolix
breedte, breadth, width; latitude
breed'voerig, detailed
breekbaar, breakable, fragile
breekijzer *n,* crowbar
breidel, bridle
breidelen, to curb
breien, to knit
brein *n,* brain
breiwerk *n,* knitting

bre'kage, breakage(s)
breken, to break
brem(struik), broom
brengen, to bring, to take
  er toe brengen, to induce
bres, breach
bre'tels, braces
breuk, fracture, fraction, rupture
bre'vet *n*, certificate
bre'vier *n*, breviary
brief, letter
briefkaart, postcard
briefwisseling, correspondence
bries, breeze
briesen, to snort
brievenbesteller, postman
brievenbus, letter-box
brik, brig; break, wagonette
bril, glasses
Brits, British
Brit'tanje *n*, Brit'tannië *n*, Britain
broche, brooch
broed *n*, brood
broeden, to brood
broeder, brother
broeds, broody
broeibak, cold frame
broeien, to brood; to brew; to heat
broeierig, sultry
broeikas, greenhouse
broeinest *n*, hotbed
broek, (pair of) trousers, knickers
  jong broekje *n*, whippersnapper
broekspijp, trouser-leg
broer, brother
brok, fragment; lump
bro'kaat, bro'caat *n*, brocade
brokkelen, to crumble
brommen, to growl, to grumble
bromvlieg, bluebottle
bron, spring, source
bronader, fountain-head
brood *n*, bread, loaf
  zijn brood verdienen, to earn one's living
brood'dronken(heid), wanton-(ness)
broodje *n*, (bread-)roll
broos, brittle, fragile, frail

bros, brittle; crisp
brouwen, to brew
brouwe'rij, brewery
  leven in de brouwerij brengen, to liven things up
brouwsel *n*, brew; concoction
brug, bridge
  over de brug komen, to pay up
Brugman: praten als —, to have the gift of the gab
brui: er de — aan geven, to chuck it
bruid, bride
brui(de)gom, bridegroom
bruidsjapon, wedding-dress
bruidsjonker, groomsman, best man
bruidsmeisje *n*, bridesmaid
bruidspaar *n*, bride and bridegroom
bruidsschat, dowry
bruikbaar, serviceable
bruikleen: in —, on loan
bruiloft, wedding (feast)
bruin (*n*), brown
bruisen, to effervesce; to seethe
brullen, to roar
bru'taal, impudent
bru'taalweg, calmly
brutali'teit, insolence
bruto, gross (weight)
bruusk, brusque
bruut, brute: brutish
buffel, buffalo
buf'fet *n*, sideboard; buffet
bui, shower; fit
buidel, pouch, purse
buigbaar, flexible
buigen, to bend, to bow; to submit
buiging, bow, bend; inflexion
buigtang, (pair of) pliers
buigzaam, pliable; yielding
buiig, showery
buik, belly
  twee handen op één buik, hand in glove
buikje *n*, tummy; corporation
buikpijn, stomach-ache
buikspreker, ventriloquist
buikvliesontsteking, peritonitis
buil, swelling

buis, tube, pipe; jacket

buiten, outside; beyond; without; in the country

het ging buiten mij om, it occurred without my knowledge

van buiten kennen, to know by heart

buiten(huis) *n*, country-seat

buiten'dien, moreover

buitenge'meen, buitenge'woon, uncommon, extraordinary

buite'nissig, odd

buitenkansje *n*, stroke of luck

buitenkant, outside

buitenland: in het —, abroad

buitenlander, foreigner

buitenlands, foreign

buitenlucht, open air

buitens'huis, out of doors

buiten'spel, off-side

buiten'sporig, excessive

buitenstaander, outsider

buitenste, outermost

buitenwaarts, outwards

buitenwijken, outskirts

bukken, to duck, to stoop

gebukt gaan onder, to be weighed down by

bul, bull, diploma

bulderen, to roar

bulken, to bellow

bulken van het geld, to roll in money

bullebak, bully

bullen, belongings

bult, hump, lump

bundel, bundle; collection (of poems, etc.)

bungelen, to dangle

bunkeren, to take on fuel

burcht, castle, citadel

bu'reau *n*, office; desk

burengerucht *n*, breach of the peace

burge'meester, burgomaster

burger, citizen, civilian

dat geeft de burger moed, that puts heart into a chap

burger-, civil(ian), civic

burgerlijk, bourgeois, civil

burgelijke stand, registry of births, marriages and deaths

bus, tin, canister: bus

in de bus blazen, to loosen the purse-strings

buskruit *n*, gunpowder

buste, bust

bustehouder, brassière

buur, buurman, buurvrouw, neighbour

buurt, neighbourhood

b.v., e.g.

C

For words not given under C, see also K

ca'cao, cocoa

ca'chet *n*, seal, *cachet*

ca'chot *n*, punishment cell

ca'deau *n*, present

ca'mee, cameo

camou'fleren, to camouflage

cam'pagne, campaign

cana'pé, settee

candi'daat, candidate; holder of the first university degree

canon, ground-rent; canon

cano'niek, canonical

ca'outchouc, india-rubber

capiton'neren, to pad; to stuff

capitu'leren, to capitulate

capri'ool, caper

capties maken, to make difficulties

car'bid *n*, carbide

car'bol *n*, carbolic (acid)

carbu'rator, carburettor

carga'door, ship-broker

carrosse'rie, coach-work

carrou'sel, round-about

carri'ère, career

cas'sette, cash-box; casket, canteen (of cutlery)

casta'gnetten, castanets

cas'treren, to castrate

catalogi'seren, to catalogue

ca'talogus, catalogue

catechi'satie, confirmation class, religious instruction

cate'chismus, catechism

catego'rie, category

cate'gorisch, categorical

cause'rie, talk, informal lecture

cavale'rie, cavalry

ceder, cedar

cein'tuur, belt, sash
cein'tuurbaan, circular railway
cel, cell: 'cello
celi'baat *n,* celibacy
celiba'tair, celibate
cel'list, violoncellist
cen'suur, censorship
cent, 1/100 part of **a** Dutch guilder; " brass farthing "
cen'traal, central
cen'trale, power-station; telephone exchange
centrum *n,* centre
ceremoni'eel (*n*), ceremonial
cere'moniemeester, master of ceremonies
certifi'ceren, to certify
cha'grijn *n,* chagrin
cha'grijnig, cantankerous
champi'gnon, mushroom
chan'tage, blackmail
cha'otisch, chaotic
cha'piter *n,* subject of discussion
char'geren, to exaggerate
char'mant, charming
char'meren, to charm
chas'seur, page-boy
chauf'feren, to drive (a car)
chef, head, manager, chief
chemi'caliën, chemicals
chemicus, (analytical) chemist
che'mie, chemistry
chemisch, chemical
cheru'bijn, cherub
chi'cane, chicanery
chi'rurg, surgeon
chirur'gie, surgery
chi'rurgisch, surgical
chloor, chlorine
choco'laatje *n,* chocolate(drop)
choco'la(de), chocolate
choco'la(de)melk, cocoa
Christelijk, Christian
Christen, (a) Christian
Christendom *n,* Christianity
Christenheid, Christendom
Christus, Christ
chronisch, chronic
chroom *n,* chromium
cicho'rei, chicory
cijfer *n,* figure, digit, mark
cijns, tribute money, tax
ci'linder, cylinder

ci'lindrisch, cylindrical
cim'baal, cymbal
cineac, news-theatre
ci'pier, gaoler
ci'pres, cypress
circa, approximately
circu'laire, circular (letter)
circu'leren, to circulate
cirkel(en), (to) circle
cirkel'vormig, circular
cise'leren, to chase; to emboss
ci'taat *n,* quotation
ci'teren, to quote
ci'troen, lemon
ci'troenpers, lemon-squeezer
ci'viel, civil; moderate
clau'sule, clause; proviso
cle'ment, lenient
cle'mentie, clemency
clo'set *n,* water-closet
clo'setpapier *n,* toilet-paper
club, club; armchair
coa'litie, coalition
co'con, cocoon
cognosse'ment *n,* bill of lading
coif'feren, to dress hair
cokes, coke
col'bert *n,* jacket
col'bertkostuum *n,* lounge-suit
collec'tant, person collecting money
col'lecte, collection
collec'teren, to collect money
col'lectie, collection
col'lega, colleague
col'lege *n,* board; college; university lecture
col'lege geven, to lecture
collegi'aal, friendly, harmonious
col'lier, necklace
collo *n,* (*pl.* **colli**), package
co'lonne, column (of soldiers)
colpor'teren, to hawk (printed matter)
colpor'teur, pedlar
comman'dant, commandant, commander, ship's captain
comman'deren, to command, to order about
com'mando *n,* command
com'mandobrug, navigating bridge
com'mandotoren, conning tower

commen'saal, lodger
commen'taar n, commentary
commerci'eel, commercial
com'mies, clerk
commissari'aat n, directorate; police-station
commis'saris, company director; chief inspector of police
com'missie, committee, commission
commissio'nair, commission-agent
compa'gnie, company
compa'gnon, (business) partner
comparti'ment n, compartment
compen'seren, to compensate
compi'lator, compiler
compi'leren, to compile
com'pleet, complete
comple'teren, to complete
complimen'teren met, to compliment on
complimen'teus, complimentary
compo'neren, to compose (music)
compo'nist, composer
compri'meren, to compress
compromit'tant, compromising
compromit'teren, to compromise
comptabili'teit, accountability
concen'tratievermogen n, power of concentration
concen'treren, to concentrate
con'cept n, draft (document)
con'cert n, concert, recital; concerto
con'cessie, concession
con'ciërge, caretaker, hall-porter
con'cilie n, ecclesiastical council
con'cours n, competition
  concours hippique, horse-show
concur'rent, competitor
concur'rentie, competition
concur'reren, to compete
concur'rerend, competitive
conden'sator, condenser
conden'seren, to condense
con'ditie, condition
  in conditie, fit
condo'leren, to condole with

conduc'teur, guard, tram or bus conductor
con'fectie, ready-made (clothes)
conferen'cier, compère
confi'seur, confectioner
confi'turen, candied fruit
con'frater, colleague
con'fuus, confused, abashed
con'gé n: iemand zijn — geven, to send a person packing
conse'quent, consistent
conse'quentie, consequence, consistency
conser'vator, curator
con'serven, preserves
con'siderans, preamble
con'signe n, password; instruction
consi'storiekamer, vestry
con'sorten, confederates
consta'teren, to establish
constru'eren, to construct
consu'lent, expert adviser
consul'tatiebureau n, welfare clinic
consu'ment, consumer
con'sumptie, consumption, food and/or drink(s)
con'tant, (in) cash
contrac'teren, to contract
contramine: in de —, in a contrary mood
con'trole, check, supervision
contro'leren, to check, to inspect
contro'leur, inspector
conveni'ëren, to be convenient
cor'rector, proof-reader
correspon'deren, to correspond
correspon'dentie, correspondence
corri'geren, to correct
cor'vee, fatigue-duty; tough job
cou'lant, obliging
cou'lissen, wings
cou'pé, compartment; brougham
cou'peren, to cut
cou'rant, newspaper
cour'ante maat, stock size
cou'vert n, envelope; cover (at table)
cou'veuse, incubator
cra'paud, easy chair
crea'tuur n, creature

cre'peren, to kick the bucket
cri'ant vervelend, inexpressibly boring
cri'terium n, criterion
cro'quet, croquette
cru, crude
cul'tures, plantations
cul'tuur, culture
cura'tele, guardianship
cu'rator, curator, official receiver
curiosi'teit, curio
cur'sief, italicized
cursus, school-year, course of studies
cynicus, cynic
cynisch, cynical

D

daad, deed, act (ion)
daad'werkelijk, actual
daags, see dag
daalder, one and a half guilders
daar, there: as, because
daar'achter, behind it
daarbij, near it; moreover
daardoor, through it, as a result
daaren'boven, moreover
daaren'tegen, on the other hand
daar'ginds, over there
daar'heen, thither, there
daargelaten, (quite) apart from
daar'net, just now
daarom, therefore
daarom'trent, thereabouts
daarop, on there; thereupon
daarop'volgend, subsequent, next
daarover, over it, about it
daarvandaan, from there
dadel, date
dadelijk, immediate
dader, perpetrator
dag, day (light)
  dag! hello!, goodbye
  om de drie dagen, every third day
  daagse kleren, everyday clothes
dagblad n, daily paper
dagboek n, diary
dagelijks, daily
dagen, to summon: to dawn
dageraad, dawn

dagjesmensen, trippers
dagloner, day labourer
dagtekenen, to date
dagvaarden, to summon
dak n, roof
dakgoot, gutter
daklicht n, skylight
dakloos, homeless
dakkamer, attic
dakpan, tile
dal n, valley
dalen, to go or come down
daling, descent; drop
dam, dam, causeway: king (in draughts)
da'mast n, damask
dambord n, draught-board
dame, lady
damhert n, fallow deer
dammen, to play draughts
damp, vapour
dampkring, atmosphere
dan, then: than
  dan ook, in fact
  (hoe, wat, wie) dan ook (how-, what-, who-)ever
danig, exceeding, greatly
dank, thanks
  dank zij, thanks to
dankbaar, grateful, gratifying
dankbaarheid, gratitude
danken, to thank, to say grace
dans (en), (to) dance
dapper, brave
dar, drone
darm, intestine
darmontsteking, enteritis
dartel, frisky
dartelen, to frolic, to gambol
das, (neck) tie, scarf: badger
dashond, dachshund
dat, that, which
da'teren, to date
datgene, that (one)
datum, date
dauw, dew
dauwworm, ringworm
daveren, to thunder, to resound
dazen, to talk rot
de, the
debar'keren, to disembark
de'bat n, debate
debat'teren, to debate

debet (*n*), debit : overdrawn
de'biet *n*, sale(s)
debi'teren, to debit
 een aardigheid debiteren, to crack a joke
debi'teur, debtor
de'buut *n*, début.
december, December
de'ceptie, disappointment
deci'meren, to decimate
decla'meren, to recite
decli'natie, declination ; declension
decli'neren, to decline
de'creet *n*, decree
decre'teren, to decree
deeg *n*, dough, mixture
deel *n*, part, share ; volume
deel'achtig, participating in
deelbaar, divisible
deelgenoot, participant ; partner
deelgenootschap *n*, partnership
deelnemen aan, to participate in
deelnemer, participant
deelneming, participation ; sympathy
deels, partly
deeltal *n*, dividend
deelteken *n*, diæresis
deeltje *n*, particle
deelwoord *n*, participle
deemoed, meekness
dee'moedig, meek
Deen ; Deens (*n*), Dane ; Danish
deerlijk, grievous
deern(e), wench
deernis, compassion
deernis'wekkend, pitiable
de'fect, faulty, out of order : *n*, defect, fault
de'fensie, (national) defence
defi'lé *n*, march-past ; defile
defi'leren, to march past
defini'ëren, to define
defini'tief, definite, definitive
deftig, dignified ; distinguished ; la-di-da
degelijk, sound ; substantial ; of sterling character
 hij weet het wel degelijk, he knows (it) perfectly well
degen, sword ; foil
de'gene die, the one who

degra'deren, to degrade
deinen, to heave
deining, swell ; commotion
dek *n*, cover ; bedclothes ; deck
dekbed *n*, eiderdown
deken, blanket : dean
dekhengst, stallion
dekken, to cover ; to lay (the table) ; to serve (a mare)
 zich dekken, to take cover
dekking, cover
deklast, deck cargo
dekmantel, cloak
deksel *n*, lid, cover
 deksels ! by Jove !
dekzeil *n*, tarpaulin
delen, to divide, to share, to split
deler, divisor
deling, division
delfstof, mineral
delgen, to pay off
delgingsfonds, sinking fund
delica'tesse, delicacy
de'licit *n*, offence
delven, to dig
de'mi(-sai'son), light overcoat
demo'craat, democrat
democra'tie, democracy
demon'teren, to dismantle
dempen, to fill in (with earth) ; to subdue
den(neboom), fir-tree
denderend, smashing
Denemarken *n*, Denmark
denkbaar, conceivable
denkbeeld *n*, idea
denk'beeldig, imaginary
denkelijk, probably
denken (aan), to think (of)
 doen denken aan, to remind of
 denk eens aan ! just fancy !
denkvermogen *n*, intellectual capacity
denneappel, fir-cone
dennehout *n*, pine-wood
depo'neren, to deposit, to file, to register
de'pot *n*, depot ; branch establishment
depri'meren, to depress
derail'leren, to run off the rails

deran'geren, to inconvenience
derde, third
 ten derde, thirdly
derdemachtswortel, cube root
derde'rangs, third rate
deren, to harm
dergelijk, such (like)
 iets dergelijks, something of the sort
der'halve, hence
dermate, to such a degree
dertien(de), thirteen(th)
dertig, thirty
derven, to lack
derwaarts, thither
des, of the
 des te (meer), all the (more)
desalniette'min, nevertheless
desavou'eren, to disavow
desbe'treffend, relating to this
desem n, leaven
desge'lijks, likewise
desge'wenst, if desired
desillusie, disillusionment
des'kundig(e), expert
des'noods, if need be
deson'danks, nevertheless
des'poot, despot
des'sin n, design
des'tijds, at the time
deta'cheren, to detail
de'tail n, detail; retail
deti'neren, to detain
deto'neren, to detonate; to be out of tune, to be out of keeping
deugd, virtue
 lieve deugd! good gracious!
deugdelijk, reliable
deugdzaam, virtuous
deugen: niet —, to be no good
deugniet, rascal, good-for-nothing
deuk(en), (to) dent
deuntje n, tune
deur, door
 met de deur in huis vallen, to come straight to the point
deurwaarder, bailiff
de'vies n, motto, device
de'viezen, foreign currency
de'voot, devout
de'wijl, because

deze, this, these
 deze of gene, (some)one or other
de'zelfde, the same
diaco'nes, protestant nursing sister
diaco'nie, poor relief board
di'aken, church worker; deacon
dia'loog, dialogue
dia'mant, diamond
dia'mantslijper, diamond cutter
diar'ree, diarrhœa
dicht, closed; dense
 dicht bij, near (to)
dichten, to write poetry; to stop a leak
dichter('es), poet(ess)
dichterlijk, poetic(al)
dichtkunst, (art of) poetry
dichtmaat, metre
dic'taat n, dictation; lecture-notes; note-book
dic'tee n, dictation
die, that, those; who, which; he, she, it, they
di'eet n, diet
dief, thief
diefstal, theft
diennan'gaande, as to that
dienaar, servant
diender, cop (per)
 dooie diender, dull dog
dienen, to serve
 waar dient dit voor? what is the use of this?
 daar ben ik niet van gediend, I take exception to that
dienovereen'komstig, accordingly
dienst, service, duty
dienstbode, (house)maid
dienstplicht, compulsory (military) service
dienstregeling, time-table
dienst'vaardig, obliging
dienstweigeraar, conscientious objector
dientafel, (tea-)trolley
dientenge'volge, in consequence
diep, deep; profound
diepgaand, searching
diepgang, draught
diepte, depth

diep'zinnig, profound; abstruse
dier *n,* animal
dierbaar, dearly loved
dierenriem, zodiac
diergaarde, zoo(logical gardens)
dierkunde, zoology
dierlijk, animal; bestial
die'vegge, female thief
differenti'aal-rekening, (differential) calculus
dij, thigh
dijk, dike, embankment; dam
  aan de dijk zetten, to shelve
dik, thick; fat; dense
  zich dik maken, to get het up
dikkerd, fatty
dikte, thickness
dikwijls, often
dikzak, fatty
dili'gence, stage-coach
dimmen, to dim, to dip
di'neren, to dine
ding *n,* thing
dingen, to bargain
  dingen naar, to compete for, to sue for
dinsdag, Tuesday
diplo'maat, diplomat(ist)
diploma'tie, diplomacy
direc'teur, director, manager, head(-master)
di'rectie, management
diri'gent, conductor
diri'geren, to conduct
dis, D sharp: table
discon'teren, to discount
dis'conto *n,* (rate of) discount
discu'teren, to discuss, to argue
dispo'neren over, to have at one's disposal
dispo'nibel, available
dis'puut *n,* dispute; debating society
dissel(boom), pole (of a carriage)
disser'tatie, thesis for a doctorate
distel, thistle
distilla'teur, distiller
distilleerde'rij, distillery
distri'butie, distribution, (food) allocation; radio-diffusion
dit, this, these
ditmaal, this time
dobbelaar, gambler

dobbelen, to play dice
dobbelstenen, dice
dobber, float
  een harde dobber hebben, to be hard put to it
dobberen, to bob up and down
do'cent, teacher
do'ceren, to teach
doch, but; however
dochter, daughter
docto'raal(e'xamen) *n,* examination for master's degree
docto'randus, person who has passed the *doctoraalexamen*
dode, dead (wo)man, deceased
dodelijk, mortal, deadly
doden, to kill, to mortify
doedelzak, bagpipe
doek, cloth; (*n*), canvas; screen
doel *n,* target, goal; aim
doelbe'wust, purposeful
doeleinde *n,* purpose
doelen op, to allude to
doelloos, aimless, pointless
doel'matig, appropriate; efficient
doel'treffend, effective
doemen, to doom
doen, to do, to make; to ask; to put
  ik kan er niets aan doen, I can't help it
  ik heb met je te doen, I am sorry for you
  het doet er niet(s) toe, it makes no difference
  doen in, to deal in
  doen en laten, behaviour, doings
does, poodle
doetje *n,* softy
doezelen, to drowse
dof, dull, dim
doffer, cock-pigeon
dog, mastiff
dogger, cod-fisher; dogger
dok *n,* dock
dokken, to dock
  je zult moeten dokken, you'll have to fork out
dokter, doctor
dol, mad, frantic; stripped (of a screw): rowlock
dolblij, overjoyed

dol'driftig, beside oneself (with rage)

dolen, to wander

dol'fijn, dolphin

dolgraag, only too gladly

dolheid, frenzy

dolk, dagger

dolleman, madman

dollen, to romp

dol'zinnig, frantic

dom, stupid: cathedral, dome

do'mein n, domain

domheid, stupidity

dominee, minister, clergyman

domi'neren, to dominate; to play dominoes

domkop, blockhead

dommelen, to doze

domoor, blockhead

dompelaar, diver (bird); plunger

dompelen, to plunge

dona'teur, donor, supporter

donder, thunder

  iemand op zijn donder geven, to give a person a damn' good hiding

  het kan me geen donder schelen, I don't care a damn

donderbui, thunderstorm

donderbus, blunderbuss

donderdag, Thursday

donderen, to thunder

donderslag, thunderclap

donders, deuced

donker, dark

dons n, down

donzig, downy

dood, dead: death

doodaf, dead beat

doodbloeden, to bleed to death

doodgaan, to die

doodgraver, grave-digger

doodkist, coffin

doodlopende straat, cul de sac

doodop, dead beat

doods, deathly, mortally

doodslag, homicide

doodsnood: in —, worried to death

doodstraf, capital punishment

doodsstrijd, death struggle, throes of death

doodzwijgen, to ignore

doof(heid), deaf(ness)

doofpot, copper peat-extinguisher

  in de doofpot stoppen, to hush up

doof'stom, deaf-mute

dooi(en), (to) thaw

dooier, yolk

doolhof n, labyrinth

doop, baptism

doopceel, certificate of baptism

  iemands doopceel lichten, to show a person up

doopsel n, baptism

doopsge'zind(e), Mennonite

doopvont, font

door, through; by

  door de week, on week-days

doorbladeren, to glance through

door'boren, to transfix

doorbrengen, to spend

door'dacht, carefully considered

doordat, owing to

doordraaien, to keep going; to remain unsold

  geld er doordraaien, to blue money

doordrijven, to get one's own way

doordringen, to penetrate

  door'drongen van, fully alive to

door'een, pell-mell

door'eenmengen, to mix together

dooreten, to go on eating

doorgaan, to go on

  doorgaan voor, to pass for

  er van doorgaan, to bolt

  doorgaande trein, through train

doorgaans, usually

doorgang, passage, way through

doorgangshuis n, asylum

doorgeven, to pass (on)

door'gronden, to fathom

doorhalen, to strike out (words); to pull through

door'heen, through

door'kneed in, well-versed in

doorkomen, to get through

door'kruisen, to traverse

doorlichten, to X-ray

doorlopen, to walk *or* run on; to get a move on; to run (of colours); to walk through

door'lopend, continuous, continual

door'luchtig, illustrious

doormaken, to go through

doorn, thorn

doornat, wet through

door'regen spek, streaky bacon

door'schijnend, translucent

doorslaand bewijs, convincing proof

doorslag, carbon copy
 de doorslag geven, to turn the scale

doorsnede, section
 de doorsneemens, the average person

door'spekken, to interlard

door'staan, to stand, to endure

door'tastend, thorough-going, go-ahead

door'trapt, unmitigated, out and out

door'trokken, soaked; imbued

door'voed, well fed

door'waadbare plaats, ford

door'wrocht, elaborate, thorough

doorzetten, to persevere

doorzicht n, discernment

door'zichtig, transparent

doos, box, case; quod
 uit de oude doos, antiquated

dop, shell, husk, pod; top

dopen, to baptize, to dip

doperwten, (green) peas

doppen, to shell

dor, dry, arid

dorp n, village

dorpel, threshold

dorpeling, villager

dorsen, to thresh

dorst, thirst

dorsvlegel, flail

dosis, dose

dot, tuft; pet

dotterbloem, king-cup

douairi'ère, dowager

dou'ane, Customs

dou'blé, plate(d work)

dou'bleren, to double

dou'ceur(tje n), gratuity

dove, deaf person

doven, to extinguish, to dim

dove'netel, dead nettle

do'zijn n, dozen

dra, erelong

draad, thread, wire

draadloos, wireless

draagbaar, stretcher: portable

draagkracht, carrying capacity, range

draaglijk, tolerable

draagstoel, sedan-chair

draai, turn, twist
 een draai om de oren, a box on the ears
 zijn draai vinden, to find one's niche

draaibaar, revolving

draaibank, lathe

draaiboek n, scenario

draaien, to turn, to revolve; to prevaricate

draaierig, dizzy

draaikolk, whirlpool

draaimolen, roundabout

draaiorgel n, barrel-organ

draaischijf, turn-table

draaispil, capstan

draak, dragon
 de draak steken met, to make fun of

drab, dregs

dracht, dress, wear; gestation

drachtig, with young

draderig, stringy

draf, trot: pig-swill

dragen, to bear; to wear; to carry

dra'gonder, dragoon

dralen, to tarry

drama'tiek, drama(tic art)

drang, pressure; urge

drank, drink; medicine
 aan de drank zijn, to be addicted to drink

dra'peren, to drape

drassig, marshy

drastisch, drastic

draven, to trot

dreef, avenue, lane; mead(ow)
 op dreef, in form

dreg(gen), (to) drag

dreige'ment n, threat

dreigen, to threaten

dreinen, to whine

drek, muck, ordure

drempel, threshold
drenkeling, drowning person
drenken, to water (cattle); to drench
drentelen, to saunter
drenzen, to whine
dres'seren, to train (animals)
dres'soir *n,* sideboard
dres'suur, training (of animals)
dreumes, toddler
dreun, drone, rumbling
dreunen, to drone, to rumble
dribbelen, to toddle
drie, three
drie'delig, tripartite; three-piece
drie'dubbel, triple
Drie'ëenheid, Trinity
driehoek, triangle
driehoeksmeting, trigonometry
drie'jaarlijks, triennial
Drie'koningen, Epiphany, Twelfth-Night
driekroon, tiara
drie'ledig, tripartite
drieling, triplet(s)
drieluik *n,* triptych
drie'maandelijks, quarterly
driepoot, tripod; trivet
driesprong, cross-roads
driest, audacious
drietand, trident
drievoud, treble: *n,* triplicate
driewieler, tricycle
drift, passion; drift
driftig, hot-tempered; in a temper
driftkop, hothead
drijfhout *n,* drift-wood
drijfkracht, drive
drijfnat, sopping wet
drijfveer, mainspring; incentive
drijfwerk *n,* chased work
drijfzand *n,* quicksand(s)
drijven, to float, to drift; to drive; to carry on (a business); to chase (metal work)
dril(len), (to) drill
dringen, to crowd, to jostle
de tijd **dringt,** time presses
dringend, urgent
drinkebroer, tippler
drinken, to drink
droef, sad

droefenis, sorrow
droef'geestig, mournful
droefheid, sadness
droesem, dregs
droevig, sad
drogbeeld *n,* illusion
droge *n,* dry land
drogen, to dry
dro'gist, druggist
drogiste'rij, chemist's (shop)
drogrede, sophism
drom, throng
dromen, to dream
dromerig, dreamy
drome'rij, reverie
drommel, devil
dronk, drink, draught, toast
dronkaard, drunkard
dronken, drunk(en)
dronkelap, soak(er)
droog, dry
droogleggen, to drain, to reclaim
drooglijn, clothes-line
droogrek *n,* clothes-horse
droogstoppel, old stick
droom, dream
drop, liquorice: drop
druif, grape
druilerig: het is — weer, there is rain in the air
druipen, to drip
druipsteen, stalactite, stalagmite
druisen, to roar, to churn
druk, busy; fussy; gaudy: pressure; print
maak je niet **druk,** don't fuss
druk bezochte vergadering, well-attended meeting
drukfout, misprint
drukken, to (de)press; to oppress; to print; to shake (hands)
drukkend, oppressive
drukker('ij), printer('s works)
drukletters, type
drukte, bustle; pressure of business; fuss
drukwerk *n,* printed matter
druppel, drop, drip
druppelen, to drip
dubbel, double
dubbelganger, double

dubbelpunt *n*, colon
dubbeltje *n*, ten-cent-piece
dubbel'zinnig, ambiguous
dubbel'zinnigheid, ambiguity, *double entendre*
dubi'eus, doubtful
dubio: in —, in doubt
duchten, to dread
duchtig, thorough, manful
duf, musty
duidelijk, clear, obvious
duidelijkheidshalve, for clarity's sake
duiden op, to point to
duif, dove, pigeon
duig, stave (of a barrel)
  het plan viel in duigen, the plan fell through
duikboot, submarine
duikelen, to tumble
duiken, to dive
duim, thumb; inch
duimstok, foot-rule
duin, dune
duister(nis), dark(ness)
duit, farthing
Duits(er) (*n*), German
Duitsland *n*, Germany
duivel(s), devil(ish)
duivels'toejager, factotum
duiventil, dovecot(e)
duizelen, to get dizzy *or* giddy
duizelig, dizzy, giddy
duizeling, (fit of) dizziness, giddiness
duizend, a thousand
duizendpoot, centipede
duizendschoon, sweet-william
duk'dalf, mooring-buoy
dulden, to bear, to endure
dun, thin
dunk, opinion
dunkt mij, I think
dunnen, to thin
duorijder, pillion-rider
du'peren, to hit; to let down
du'pliek, rejoinder
duplo: in —, in duplicate
dur, major
duren, to last
durf, daring
durven, to dare
dus, so

dus'danig, (in) such (a way)
dusver: tot —, thus far
dutje *n*: een — doen, to have a nap
dutten, to doze
duur, expensive: duration
  op de duur, in time
duurte, high cost(s)
duurzaam, durable
duw(en), (to) push, (to) shove
dwaalbegrip *n*, misconception, fallacy
dwaalspoor *n*, wrong track
dwaas, fool: foolish
dwaasheid, foolishness
dwalen, to wander; to err
dwaling, error
dwang, compulsion
dwangarbeid, penal servitude
dwangarbeider, convict
dwangbuis *n*, straight jacket
dwarrelen, to whirl
dwars, transverse; cross-grained
  het zit me dwars, it worries me, it annoys me
dwarsbomen, to thwart
dwars door, straight through
dwarsdoorsne(d)e, cross-section
dwarsdrijver, obstructionist
dwarskijker, furtive observer
dwarsligger, sleeper
dwarsschip *n*, transept
dwarsschot *n*, bulkhead
dweepziek, fanatic
dweil, floor-cloth; slut
dwepen met, to think the world of; to rave about
dweper, zealot; fan(atic)
dwerg, dwarf, midget
dwingeland, tyrant
dwingen, to force

E

eb, ebb(-tide)
ebbehout *n*, ebony
é'chec *n*, set-back
echt, real, genuine, thorough: matrimony
echtbreuk, adultery
echtelijk, matrimonial
echter, however
echtgenoot, husband
echtgenote, wife

echtpaar *n*, married couple
echtscheiding, divorce
econo'mie, economy; economics
eco'noom, economist
ec'zeem *n*, eczema
edel, noble
Edel'achtbare, Your Worship
edelgesteente *n*, precious stone(s)
edel'moedig, generous
edelsteen, gem
e'ditie, edition
e'doch, however
eed, oath
eega, spouse
eekhoorn, squirrel
eelt *n*, hard skin
een, a(n); one
  een en al, all; nothing but
eend, duck
eender, the same
eendracht, concord
een'drachtig, united
eenheid, unit(y)
eenhoorn, unicorn
een'jarig, yearling
een'kennig, unfriendly, shy
eenletter'grepig, monosyllabic
eenmaal, once
  het is nu eenmaal zo, but there
  it is
een'parig, unanimous
een'parigheid, unanimity
eens, once, one day; just
  het eens zijn, to agree
eensdeels, partly
eens'denkend, of one mind
eensge'zind, at one, unanimous
eensge'zindheid, harmony, unanimity
eensklaps, suddenly
eensluidend, similar, true
een'stemmig, in unison; with
one accord
eens'stemmigheid, unanimity
een'tonig, monotonous
een'voudig, simple
eenvoud, simplicity
eenzaam, lonely, solitary
eenzaamheid, solitude
een'zelvig, self-contained
een'zijdig (heid), one-sided (ness),
bias (ed)

eer, honour: before
  eer aandoen, to do credit to
eerbaar, virtuous
eerbetoon *n*, eerbewijs *n*, mark
of honour, homage
eerbied, respect
eer'biedig, respectful
eer'biedigen, to respect
eerbied'wekkend, imposing
eerder, before, sooner; rather
eer'gisteren, the day before
yesterday
eerherstel *n*, restitution
eer'lang, before long
eerlijk, honest, fair
eerloos, infamous
eerst, first, former
  de eerste de beste, the first
  (man, opportunity) that comes
  along
  ten eerste, in the first place
  voor het eerst, for the first time
eerstdaags, one of these days
eersteling, eerstge'boren, first-
born
eertijds, formerly
eervol, honourable
Eer'waarde: de — Heer, the
Reverend
eerzaam, respectable
eerzucht, ambition
eer'zuchtig, ambitious
eest, oast-house
eetbaar, edible
eetgelegenheid, eating-place
eetgerei *n*, dinner things
eetkamer, dining-room
eetlepel, table-spoon
eetlust, appetite
eetservies *n*, dinner-service
eetwaren, provisions
eetzaal, dining hall
eeuw, century, age
eeuwfeest *n*, centenary
eeuwig, eternal, everlasting
  ten eeuwigen dage, for ever
eeuwigheid, eternity
ef'fecten, stocks (and shares)
effec'tief, effective
effen, level, smooth; self-
coloured
effenen, to level, to smooth
(down)

eg, harrow
e'gaal, smooth, uniform
E'geïsche Zee, Ægean Sea
egel, hedge-hog
eggen, to harrow
ei *n,* egg
eierdooier, egg-yolk
eierdop, egg-shell
eierdopje *n,* egg-cup
eierstok, ovary
eigen, (of one's) own; private
eigenaar, owner
eigen'aardig, peculiar, strange
eigen'aardigheid, peculiarity
eigenbaat, egoism
eigenbelang *n,* self-interest
eigendom *n,* property
eigendomsbewijs *n,* title-deeds
eigendunk, self-conceit
eigenge'maakt, home-made
eigenge'rechtig(heid), self-righteous(ness)
eigenge'reid, opionated
eigenlijk, actual, proper, real
eigen'machtig(heid), high-handed(ness)
eigennaam, proper name
eigenschap, quality, property
eigenwaan, self-conceit
eigenwaarde, self-respect
eigen'wijs, self-opinionated, pig-headed
eigen'zinnig, self-willed
eik, oak
eikel, acorn
eiland *n,* island
eind *n,* end(ing); length, distance
  ten einde te, in order to
  ten einde raad, at one's wits' end
einddiploma *n,* school-leaving certificate
eindelijk, at last
eindeloos, endless
eindexamen *n,* school-leaving examination
eindig, finite
eindigen, to finish (off)
eindproduct *n,* finished article
eindpunt *n,* **eindstation** *n,* terminus
eis, demand, claim
  aan de eisen voldoen, to satisfy the requirements

eisen, to demand, to claim
eiser, plaintiff, prosecutor
eivol, chock-full
eiwit *n,* white of egg; protein
ekster, magpie
eksteroog, *n,* corn
el, ell (nearly 1 yard)
eland, elk
elas'tiek (*n*), elastic
elas'tiekje *n,* rubber band
elders, elsewhere
electrici'teit, electricity
e'lectrisch, electric
electri'seren, to electrify
elemen'tair, elementary
elf, eleven: elf
  op zijn elf-en-dertigst, at a snail's pace
elfde, eleventh
elftal *n,* eleven, team
elk, each, any
el'kaar, el'kander, each other, one another
  alles bij elkaar genomen, all things considered
  ik kan ze niet uit elkaar houden, I can't tell one from the other
  alles is voor elkaar, everything is settled
elleboog, elbow
el'lende, misery
el'lendeling, rotter
el'lendig, wretched, miserable; rotten
els, alder: awl
e'mail *n,* enamel
embal'lage, packing
em'bleem *n,* emblem
emi'greren, to emigrate
emmer, pail
e'motie, emotion
em'pirisch, empirical
emplace'ment *n,* railway yard
em'plooi *n,* employ(ment)
employ'eren, to employ
en, and
  en . . . en, both . . . and
encanail'leren: zich —, to mix with the lower classes
encyclope'die, (en)cyclopædia
end *n,* distance
endeldarm, rectum

endos'seren, to endorse
enenmale: ten —, absolutely
ener'gie, energy
ener'giek, energetic
enerlei, of the same kind
enerzijds, on the one hand
en'fin, in short
  maar enfin, but there (it is)
eng, narrow; horrible, creepy
engel, angel
engelachtig, angelic
engelenbak, (upper) gallery
Engels(man) (*n*), English(man)
  Engelse ziekte, rickets
en gros, wholesale
engte, strait(s), isthmus; narrowness
enig, only, unique; marvellous: some, any, a few
eniger'mate, to some extent
enigs'zins, somewhat, in a way
enkel, single, only; ankle
enkeling, individual
enkelvoud *n*, singular
enkel'voudig, singular, simple
e'norm, enormous
en pas'sant, in passing
en'quête, official inquiry
ensce'neren, to stage(-manage)
ensce'nering, staging
ent(en), (to) graft
enteren, to board
enthousi'ast, enthusiast(ic)
en'tree, entrance; entrée; *début*
entre'pot *n*, bonded warehouse
enz(ovoort), etc(etera), and so on
epi'loog, epilogue
e'pitheton *n*, epithet
epos *n*, epic
er, there: of it, of them
  er zijn er, die . . ., there are those who . . .
  wat is er? what's the matter?
er'barmelijk, pitiable
er'barmen: zich — over, to have mercy on
ere-, honorary, of honour
eredienst, divine worship
eren, to honour
erf *n*, (farm)yard
erfdeel *n*, portion
erfelijk, hereditary
erfelijkheid, heredity

erfenis, heritage, legacy
erfgenaam, heir
erfgename, heiress
erfgoed *n*, inheritance
erflater, testator
erflating, bequest
erfpacht, long lease
erfrecht *n*, law *or* right of succession, hereditary right
erfstuk *n*, heirloom
erfzonde, original sin
erg, bad; very (much)
  zonder erg, unintentionally
  ik had er geen erg in, I was not aware of it
ergens, somewhere, anywhere
ergeren, to annoy; to scandalize
  zich ergeren, to be vexed, to take offence
  het is om je dood te ergeren, it's infuriating
ergerlijk, annoying, offensive
ergernis, annoyance, offence
er'kennen, to acknowledge, to admit
er'kentelijk, grateful
erker, bay window
ernst, seriousness
ernstig, serious
erts *n*, ore
er'varen, to experience: experienced
er'varing, experience
erven, to inherit: heirs
erwt, pea
es, E♭: ash-tree
esdoorn, maple-tree
es'kader *n*, eska'dron *n*, squadron
esp(en), asp(en)
essenti'eel, essential
esta'fette, dispatch-rider; relay race
Estland *n*, Esthonia
e'tage, floor, storey
e'tagewoning, flat
eta'lage, shop-window
e'tappe, stage, lap
eten, to eat, to have a meal: *n*, food; meal
e'thiek, ethics
ethisch, ethical
eti'ket *n*, label

etmaal *n,* (space of) 24 hours
ets, etching
etsen, to etch
ettelijke, several
etter, pus
etteren, to fester
é'tui *n,* case
euvel *n,* evil
  euvel duiden, to take ill
evacu'eren, to evacuate
evan'gelie *n,* gospel
evan'gelisch, evangelical
even, even, equally; just
  het is mij om het even, it's all the same to me
  even . . . als, as . . . as
evenaar, equator
evenals, just as
eve'naren, to equal
evenbeeld *n,* (split) image
even'eens, likewise
evene'ment *n,* event
evengoed, (just) as well
evenknie, equal
evenmin . . . als, no more . . . than
even'redig, proportional
even'redigheid, proportion
eventjes, just, (for) a moment
eventu'eel, possible; by any chance
evenveel, as much, as many
even'wel, however
evenwicht *n,* balance
even'wichtig, (well-)balanced, level-headed
evenwichtsleer, statics
evenwichtstoestand, equilibrium
even'wijdig, parallel
even'zeer, as much
even'zo, likewise
everzwijn *n,* wild boar
e'xamen *n,* examination
  een examen afnemen, to examine
ex'amenopgaaf, examination paper
excentrici'teit, eccentricity
excer'peren, to make a *précis* of
excu'seren, to excuse
ex'cuus *n,* excuse, apology
exem'plaar *n,* specimen; copy

exer'ceren, to drill
expe'ditie, expedition; forwarding (business)
exploi'tatie, operation; exploitation
expo'sitie, exhibition
ex'pres, express
ex'tase, ecstasy
ex'tern, non-resident
extra'heren, to extract
ex'traneus, external (candidate)
ezel, ass, donkey; easel
ezelachtig, asinine
ezelsbrug, mnemonic
ezelsoren maken, to dog-ear

F

f., fl., (= *florijn*), guilder(s)
faam, fame, repute
fabel, fable, fabrication
fabelachtig, fabulous
fabri'cage, manufacture
fabri'ceren, to manufacture
fa'briek, factory
fa'brieksgeheim *n,* trade secret
fa'brieksmerk *n,* trade-mark
fabri'kaat *n,* manufacture
fabri'kant, manufacturer
face-à-'main, lorgnette
facie, mug, phiz
fac'tuur, invoice
facul'teit, faculty
fa'got, bassoon
fail'liet, bankrupt
faillisse'ment *n,* bankruptcy
fakkel, torch
falen, to fail
falie'kant, wrong
fal'saris, forger
fal'set, falsetto
fa'meus, famous, wonderful
famili'aar, familiar, informal
fa'milie, family, relation(s)
fa'naticus, fanatic
fana'tisme *n,* fanaticism
fanta'seren, to indulge in fancies
fanta'sie, fantasy, fancy, imagination
fan'toom *n,* phantom
fat, dandy
fa'taal, fatal

fat'soen *n*, decency, good manners; shape

 houd je fatsoen, behave yourself

fatsoe'neren, to shape, to remodel

fat'soenlijk, decent, respectable

fatum *n*, fate

fau'teuil, arm-chair

 fauteuils de balcon, dress-circle

fa'zant, pheasant

fee, fairy

feeë'riek, fairy-like

feeks, shrew

feest *n*, feast, festival, fête

feestelijk, festive

 dank je feestelijk! thank you for nothing!

feestje *n*, party

feestmaal *n*, banquet

feestvarken *n*, hero of the party

feestvieren, to celebrate, to go on the spree

feilbaar, fallible

feil, fault

feilloos, faultless

feit *n*, fact

feitelijk, actual

fel, fierce

felici'tatie, congratulation

felici'teren met, to congratulate on

ferm, firm; brave

fes'tijn *n*, feast

fes'toen *n*, festoon

fê'teren, to fête

feuille'ton *n*, serial story

fiche, counter

fic'tief, fictitious

fi'deel, jovial

fiedel, fiddle

fielt, knave

fier, proud, undaunted

fiets, bicycle

fietsen, to cycle

figu'rant, super(numerary)

figu'reren, to figure

fi'guur (*n*), figure, character

 een gek figuur slaan, to cut a ridiculous figure

fijn, fine; subtle

fijnge'voelig, sensitive

fijnproever, connoisseur

fijntjes, nicely, subtly

fijt, whitlow

fiks, robust, vigorous; brave

fil d'é'cosse, lisle

fi'leren, to fillet

fileverkeer *n*, single-line traffic

fili'aal *n*, branch (establishment)

filmjournaal *n*, news-reel

filter, filter; percolator

fil'treren, to filter

Fin(s) (*n*), Finn(ish)

fi'naal, final; quite

financi'eel, financial

fi'nanciën, finance(s)

finan'cieren, to finance

fi'neerhout *n*, veneer

fi'neren, to veneer; to refine

fi'nesses, niceties

fin'geren, to simulate

firma, firm

fir'mant, partner

fiscus, treasurer, treasury

fix'eren, to fix; to look intently at

fla'con, (scent-)bottle

fladderen, to flutter; to flit

flakkeren, to flicker

flam'bouw, torch

fla'nel *n*, flannel

fla'neren, to saunter

flan'keren, to flank

flappen: eruit —, to blurt out

flapuit, blabber

flarden, tatters

 aan flarden, in rags; to shreds

flater, blunder

flat'teren, to flatter, to be becoming

flat'teus, flattering

flauw, insipid, feeble, faint

flauwi'teit, feeble joke

flauwte, fainting fit

flauwtjes, faintly

flemen, to cajole

flens, flange

flensje *n*, thin pancake

fles, bottle

 op de fles gaan, to go to pot

flessentrekker, swindler

flets, lack-lustre, pale

fleurig, gay, colourful

flikflooien, to cajole

flikje *n*, chocolate drop

flikkeren, to flicker

flink, tough, capable; considerable

flits, flash

flodder, slattern
  losse flodder, blank cartridge

flodderig, shapeless, flimsy

floers *n*, veil

flonkeren, to sparkle, to twinkle

flo'reren, to flourish

flo'ret, foil

floris'sant, flourishing

fluisteren, to whisper

fluit, flute

fluiten, to whistle

fluitje *n*, whistle

fluks, promptly

flu'weel *n*, velvet

fnuiken, to break, to ruin

fnuikend, fatal

foe'draal *n*, case

foefje *n*, trick, dodge

foei! shame (on you)! fie!

foei'lelijk, as ugly as sin

foelie, mace

foe'rier, quartermaster-sergeant

foeteren, to grumble, to rage

fok, foresail; specs

fokhengst, stud-horse

fokken, to breed

foli'ant, folio (volume)

folteren, to torture

fonds *n*, fund

fonkelen, to sparkle

fon'tein, fountain

fon'teintje *n*, small hand-basin (fitted in W.C. or passage)

fooi, tip

foppen, to hoax

fopspeen, baby's dummy

for'ceren, to force; to strain

fo'rel, trout

fo'rens, season-ticket holder, commuter

for'maat *n*, size; stature

formali'teit, formality

for'meel, formal

for'mule, formula

formu'lier *n*, form

for'nuis *n*, cooker

fors, robust, strong, vigorous

fort *n*, forte; fort(ification)

for'tuin (*n*), fortune

for'tuinlijk, fortunate

fos'siel *n*, fossil

fouil'leren, to search (a person)

foura'geren, to forage

fourni'turen, haberdashery

fout, mistake, fault, error

fou'tief, wrong, erroneous

fraai, nice, handsome

fractie, fraction

fragmen'tarisch, fragmentary

fram'boos, raspberry

franco, postage paid

franje, fringe

fran'keren, to stamp

Frankrijk *n*, France

Frans (*n*), French; Francis
  een vrolijk Frans, a gay dog

frap'pant, striking

fratsen, pranks

fraude, fraud

fraudu'leus, fraudulent

fre'gat *n*, frigate

fret *n*, ferret

friemelen, to fumble

fries *n*, frieze: Frisian

frik, school-ma'am

fris, fresh, refreshing
  het is frisjes vanavond, it's chilly this evening

fri'vool, frivolous

fröbelschool, kindergarten

frommelen, to crumple

fronsen, to frown

fruiten, to fry

fuga, fugue

fuif, party

fuifnummer *n*, gay spark

fuik, eel-pot

fuiven, to feast

functie, function

functio'naris, functionary

functio'neren, to function

fun'dering, foundation

fu'nest, fatal

fun'geren, to function

fust *n*, cask

fut, spirit, go

futili'teit, futility

futloos, lifeless

G

gaaf, sound, whole

gaai, jay

gaan, to go
hoe gaat het? how are you (getting on)?
het gaat om ... it is a question of ...
gaande, afoot, going
gaandeweg, gradually
gaar, cooked, done
gaarkeuken, communal kitchen; cook-shop
gaarne, gladly
gaas *n,* gauze; wire netting
gade, spouse
gadeslaan, to watch
gading, liking
gaffel, pitchfork; gaff
gage, pay
gal, bile, gall
ga'lant, courteous: best boyfriend
galante'rieën, fancy-goods
ga'lei, galley
gale'rij, gallery
galg, gallows
galgemaal *n,* last meal
galmen, to resound, to reverberate
ga'lon *n,* braid
ga'lop, gallop
gammel, ramshackle
gang, passage; gait; way
aan de gang, going, working
op gang, in form; (in) working (order)
ga je gang, go ahead; help yourself
gangbaar, current, available
gans, entire: goose
gapen, to yawn; to gape
gaping, gap
gappen, to pinch
garan'deren, to guarantee
garde, guard(s)
garde'robe, wardrobe; cloak-room
ga'reel *n,* horse-collar, harness
garen, to gather: *n,* cotton, thread
gar'naal, shrimp
gar'neren, to trim
garni'zoen *n,* garrison
gasfabriek, gas-works
gashouder, gasometer

gaskomfoor *n,* gas-ring(s)
gaspedaal *n,* accelerator
gaspit, gas-ring, gas-jet
gasstel *n,* gas-ring(s)
gast, guest
gastheer, host
gasthuis *n,* hospital
gastvrij, hospitable
gast'vrijheid, hospitality
gastvrouw, hostess
gasvormig, gaseous
gat *n,* hole
een gat in de nacht praten, to talk deep into the night
in de gaten krijgen, to spot
in de gaten houden, to keep an eye on
gauw, quick
gauwdief, sneak-thief
gave, gift
ga'zeus, aerated
ga'zon *n,* lawn
ge'aardheid, disposition
geaffec'teerd, affected
gealli'eerd, allied
ge'armd, arm in arm
ge'baar *n,* gesture
ge'baard, bearded
ge'bak *n,* fancy cake(s)
ge'barenspel *n,* mime
ge'bed *n,* prayer
ge'beente *n,* bones
ge'belgd, offended
ge'bergte *n,* mountain range
ge'beten zijn op, to have a grudge against
ge'beuren, to happen
ge'beurtenis, event
ge'bied *n,* territory; field, realm
ge'bieden, to order
ge'bit *n,* set of teeth
ge'bladerte *n,* foliage
ge'bod *n,* command(ment)
ge'boefte *n,* riff-raff
ge'boomte *n,* trees
ge'boorte, birth
ge'boortecijfer *n,* birth-rate
ge'boorteland *n,* native country
ge'boortig uit, born at
ge'boren, born
ge'bouw *n,* building
ge'brek *n,* lack; failing; infirmity

ge'brekkig, defective, faulty; deformed
ge'broed n, brood
ge'broeders, brothers
gebrouil'leerd, not on speaking terms
ge'bruik n, use; custom
ge'bruikelijk, customary
ge'bruiken, to use; to partake of
ge'bruiksaanwijzing, directions for use
gechar'meerd op, captivated by
gecommit'teerde, delegate
gecompli'ceerd, complicated
gecostu'meerd, in fancy dress
ge'daagde, defendant
ge'daante, shape, figure, form
ge'daanteverwisseling, metamorphosis
ge'dachte, thought
ge'dachteloos, thoughtless
ge'dachtengang, train of thought
ge'deelte n, part
ge'deeltelijk, partly
gedele'geerde, delegate
ge'denkdag, anniversary
ge'denken, to commemorate
ge'denkteken n, monument
gedenk'waardig, memorable
gedepu'teerde, deputy
ge'dicht n, poem
ge'dienstig, obliging
ge'dijen, to thrive
ge'ding n, lawsuit; issue
gediplo'meerd, qualified
gedispo'neerd, inclined, disposed
gedistil'leerd, distilled : n, spirits
gedistin'geerd, distinguished-looking
ge'doe n, fuss; business
ge'dogen, to permit
ge'donder n, hell of a mess (row, etc.)
ge'drag n, behaviour
ge'dragen: zich —, to behave
ge'dragslijn, policy
ge'drang n, crowd, crush
ge'drocht n, monstrosity
ge'drongen, thick-set; impelled
ge'druis n, rumbling, roaring
ge'ducht, formidable
ge'duld n, patience
ge'duldig, patient

ge'durende, during
ge'durfd, daring; risky
ge'dwee, submissive
geel (n), yellow
geelkoper n, brass
geelzucht, jaundice
geen, not a, not any, no
geënga'geerd, engaged
geenszins, by no means
geest, spirit; mind; wit
geest'dodend, soul-destroying
geestdrift, enthusiasm
geestelijk, spiritual, mental
geestelijke, priest
geestelijkheid, clergy
geestesgaven, intellectual gifts
geestesgesteldheid, mentality
geestgrond, sandy peat (behind the dunes)
geestig, witty
geestigheid, wit, witticism
geestkracht, fortitude
geestver'heffend, sublime
geestvermogens, mental faculties
geestverschijning, apparition
geestverwant, kindred spirit
geeuw(en), (to) yawn
gefortu'neerd, wealthy
ge'gadigde, prospective buyer; applicant
ge'gevens, data
ge'goed, well-off
ge'grond, well-founded
ge'haaid, canny
ge'hakt n, minced meat
ge'halte n, content; quality
ge'hard, seasoned; inured; tempered
ge'harrewar n, bickering
ge'havend, battered
ge'heel, whole, all, quite
  in het geheel niet, not at all
ge'heelonthouder, teetotaller
ge'heim (n), secret
ge'heimenis, mystery
ge'heimhouding, secrecy
ge'heimschrift n, cipher
geheim'zinnig, mysterious
ge'hemelte n, palate
ge'heugen n, memory
ge'hoor n, hearing, ear; audience, congregation

ge'hoorzaam, obedient
ge'hoorzaamheid, obedience
ge'hoorzamen, to obey
ge'horig, far from sound-proof, noisy
ge'hucht n, hamlet
ge'huichel n, hypocrisy
gehu'meurd: goed —, good-tempered
ge'ijkt, recognized, accepted
geil, lecherous, randy; rank
gein, high jinks
geiser, geyser
geit, goat
geitebok, billy goat
ge'jaagd, agitated
gek, mad, foolish; queer: idiot
voor de gek houden, to make a fool of
gekheid, foolishness, joke
alle gekheid op een stokje, joking apart
gekkenhuis n, madhouse
ge'knipt voor, cut out for
gekscheren, to joke
ge'kunsteld, artificial
ge'laat n, countenance
ge'laatskleur, complexion
ge'laatstrek, feature
ge'lag n: het — betalen, to foot the bill
dat is een hard gelag, hard lines!
ge'lagkamer, taproom
ge'lang: naar — van, according to
ge'lasten, to order
ge'laten, resigned
geld n, money
geldelijk, financial, monetary
gelden, to apply, to count
zich doen gelden, to assert one-self
de algemeen geldende mening, the generally accepted view
geldig, valid
geldschieter, money-lender
geldstuk n, coin
geldwolf, money-grubber
geldzuivering, currency reform
ge'leden, ago
ge'leerd, learned
ge'leerde, scholar; scientist

ge'legen, situated; convenient
er is veel aan gelegen, much depends on it
ge'legenheid, occasion, opportunity; place
ge'lei, jelly
ge'leide n, escort
ge'leidelijk, gradually
ge'leiden, to conduct
ge'letterd(e), (man) of letters
ge'lid n, rank
ge'liefd, beloved, popular
ge'liefkoosd, favourite
ge'lieven, to please
ge'lijk, equal, alike; level
je hebt gelijk, you are right
iemand gelijk geven, to agree with a person
ge'lijkelijk, equally; evenly
ge'lijken, to resemble
ge'lijkenis, resemblance; parable
gelijkge'zind, like-minded
gelijk'luidend, identical
gelijk'matig, equable; even
gelijk'moedigheid, equanimity
gelijk'slachtig, homogeneous
ge'lijkstroom, direct current
gelijk'tijdig, simultaneous
gelijk'vloers, on the ground floor; on the same floor
ge'lofte, vow
ge'loof n, belief, faith
ge'loofsbrieven, credentials
geloof'waardig, credible
ge'loven, to believe, to think
ge'lovig(en), faithful
ge'lui n, ringing
ge'luid n, sound
ge'luidloos, noiseless
ge'luimd: goed —, in a good humour
ge'luk n, luck, good fortune; happiness
ge'lukken, to succeed
ge'lukkig, happy; fortunate, lucky
ge'lukshanger, charm
ge'lukskind n, spoilt child of fortune
ge'luksvogel, lucky one
ge'lukwens, congratulation
ge'lukwensen, to congratulate
geluk'zalig, blessed

ge'lukzoeker, adventurer
ge'maakt, affected, feigned; ready-made
ge'maal, spouse: *n*, pumping engine
ge'mak *n*, ease, comfort; convenience
ge'makkelijk, easy, comfortable; convenient
ge'makshalve, for the sake of convenience
gemak'zuchtig, easy-going
gema'lin, spouse
ge'matigd, temperate; moderate
gember, ginger
ge'meen, (in) common; foul
ge'meenlijk, commonly
ge'meenplaats, platitude
ge'meenschap, community; intercourse
gemeen'schappelijk, common, joint
ge'meenschapsgevoel *n*, public spirit
ge'meente, municipality; congregation; parish
ge'meentebelasting, (local) rates
ge'meentelijk, municipal
ge'meenzaam, familiar
gemelijk, peevish
gemene'best *n*, commonwealth
ge'middeld, average
ge'mis *n*, lack, want, loss
ge'moed *n*, heart, mind, feeling(s)
ge'moedelijk, kindly, informal
ge'moedsaandoening, emotion
ge'moedsrust, peace of mind
ge'moeid, involved
gems, chamois
ge'mutst: goed —, in a good mood
ge'naakbaar, accessible
ge'naamd, named
ge'nade, grace; mercy; pardon
ge'nadeloos, merciless
ge'nadeslag, finishing stroke
ge'nadig, merciful; lightly
ge'naken, to approach
gene, that; the other
deze en gene, several people
ge'neesheer, physician

genees'krachtig, curative
ge'neeskunde, medicine
ge'neesmiddel *n*, remedy; medicine
ge'negen, inclined, disposed
ge'negenheid, affection
ge'neigd, inclined, prone
gene'raal, general
generale repetitie, dress rehearsal
ge'neren, to incommode
zich generen, to feel embarrassed
ge'neugte, pleasure
ge'nezen, to cure, to heal; to recover
ge'nezing, cure; recovery
geni'aal, brilliant
geniali'teit, genius
ge'nie *n*, military, engineers; (man of) genius
ge'niepig, underhand
ge'nieten (van), to enjoy
genitief, genitive
ge'nodigden, invited guests
ge'noeg, enough
ge'noegdoening, satisfaction, reparation
ge'noegen *n*, pleasure
ge'noeglijk, pleasant
ge'noegzaam, sufficient •
ge'nootschap *n*, society
ge'not *n*, joy, delight
geo'graaf, geographer
geo'loog, geologist
ge'oorloofd, permitted
georiën'teerd (op), with leanings towards, minded
ge'paard gaan met, to be accompanied by
ge'parenteerd, related
ge'past, fitting, seemly
gepast geld, the exact amount
ge'peperd, peppered, pungent
ge'peupel *n*, mob
gepi'keerd, offended
ge'pluimd, plumed
ge'poseerd, sedate; matronly
ge'raakt, nettled
ge'raamte *n*, skeleton
ge'raden, advisable
geraffi'neerd, refined; unmitigated; artful

ge'raken, to become, to get

ge'recht *n*, dish: court of justice

ge'rechtelijk, judicial, legal

ge'rechtigd, entitled

ge'rechtigheid, justice

ge'rechtshof *n*, court of justice

ge'reed, ready

ge'reedschap *n*, tools

gerefor'meerd, strict(ly) Calvinist

ge'regeld, regular

gerenom'meerd, renowned

ge'reutel *n*, death-rattle; drivel

ge'richt: het jongste —, the Last Judgement

ge'rief *n*, convenience

ge'rief(e)lijk, convenient

ge'rieven, to oblige

ge'ring, small, slight

ge'ringschattend, disparaging

ge'ringschatting, disdain

Ger'maan, Teuton

ge'roezemoes *n*, buzz, bustle

ge'ronnen, clotted

gerouti'neerd, experienced

gerst, barley

ge'rucht *n*, rumour; noise

ge'ruchtmakend, sensational

ge'ruim, ample

ge'ruisloos, noiseless

ge'ruit, checked

ge'rust, easy

neem (het) maar gerust, you're welcome (to it)

ge'ruststellen, to reassure

gesalari'eerd: (te laag) —, (under)paid

ge'schater *n*, peals of laughter

ge'schenk *n*, present

ge'schieden, to happen, to come about

ge'schiedenis, history; story; affair

geschied'kundig, historical

ge'schiedschrijver, historian

ge'schift, dotty

ge'schikt, suitable; decent

ge'schil *n*, dispute

ge'schoeid, shod

ge'schoold, trained, skilled

ge'schrift *n*, writing

ge'schubd, scaly

ge'schut *n*, artillery

gesel, scourge

geselen, to flog, to scourge

ge'stitueerd: goed —, well-off

ge'slaagd, successful

ge'slacht *n*, stock; generation; sex; gender

ge'slachtelijk, sexual

ge'slachtsboom, family tree

ge'slachtsdelen, genitals

ge'slachtsziekte, venereal disease

ge'slepen, cunning; sharpened

geslepen glas, cut glass

ge'sloten, close(d); uncommunicative

ge'sluierd, veiled

gesp, buckle, clasp

ge'span *n*, team of horses

ge'spannen, tense, strained

gespen, to buckle

ge'spierd, muscular

ge'spikkeld, speckled, dotted

ge'spoord, spurred

ge'sprek *n*, conversation

ge'spuis *n*, rabble

ge'stadig, steady

ge'stalte, figure; stature

ge'stand: zijn woord — doen, to keep one's promise

geste, gesture

ge'steente *n*, stone(s); rock

ge'stel *n*, constitution

ge'steldheid, condition; nature, character

ge'stemd, tuned; disposed

ge'sternte *n*, constellation, star

ge'sticht *n*, institution

ge'streept, striped

ge'stroomlijnd, streamlined

getai'lleerd, tailored, close-fitting

ge'tal *n*, number

ge'tand, toothed, cogged

ge'tapt, popular; tapped

ge'tij *n*, tide

ge'tikt, dotty

ge'titeld, (en)titled

ge'touw *n*, gear; loom

ge'tralied, barred, latticed

getroe'bleerd, deranged

ge'troosten: zich veel moeite —, to take great pains

ge'trouw, faithful

ge'tuige, witness
ge'tuigen, to testify
ge'tuigenis n, testimony, evidence
ge'tuigschrift n, certificate; testimonial
geul, channel; gully
geur, scent
iets in geuren en kleuren vertellen, to go into elaborate details about something
geuren, to smell
geuren met, to flaunt
geurig, fragrant
ge'vaar n, danger
ge'vaarlijk, dangerous
ge'vaarte n, huge object
ge'val n, case
in geen geval, on no account
ge'vangene, prisoner
ge'vangenis, prison
ge'vangenschap, imprisonment
ge'vat, quick-witted
ge'vecht n, fight
gevel, façade
geveltoerist, cat burglar
geven, to give
het geeft niets, it does not matter; it is no use
gever, donor
ge'vest n, hilt
ge'vlamd, flamed
ge'vleugeld, winged
ge'vlij: bij iemand in het — komen, to worm oneself into a person's favour
ge'vleugeld, winged
ge'voeglijk, decently; just as well
ge'voel n, feeling, sense
ge'voelen n, opinion, feeling
ge'voelig, sensitive; tender
ge'voelloos, numb; unfeeling
ge'voelsmens, emotional person
ge'vogelte n, birds; poultry
ge'volg n, consequence; retinue
gevolg geven aan, to comply with
ge'volgtrekking, conclusion
ge'waad n, garment
ge'waagd, bold, risqué
aan elkaar gewaagd, well-matched

ge'waarworden, to become aware of
ge'waarwording, sensation
ge'wagen van, to make mention of
gewapender'hand, by force of arms
ge'was n, vegetation; crops
ge'weer n, gun, rifle
ge'wei n, antlers
ge'weld n, violence, force
geweld aandoen, to violate
geweld'dadig, violent
ge'weldig, terrific
ge'welf n, vault
ge'welfd, vaulted, domed
ge'wennen, to accustom
ge'west n, region
ge'westelijk, regional
ge'weten n, conscience
ge'wetenloos, unprincipled
ge'wetensbezwaar n, scruple
ge'wezen, late; ex-
ge'wicht n, weight; importance
ge'wichtig, weighty; important
gewichtig doen, to be pompous
ge'wiekst, smart
ge'wild, in demand; would-be
ge'willig, willing
ge'wis, certain
ge'woon, usual, ordinary; accustomed
ge'woonlijk, usually
ge'woonte, custom, habit
ge'woonterecht n, common law
ge'woonweg, simply
ge'wricht n, joint
ge'wrichtsband, ligament
ge'wrocht n, creation, work
ge'wrongen, laboured; twisted
ge'zag n, authority, command
ge'zaghebbend, authoritative
ge'zagvoerder, captain; pilot
ge'zamenlijk, joint; complete
ge'zang n, singing; hymn
ge'zant, ambassador, minister
ge'zantschap n, legation
ge'zegde n, (old) saying; predicate
ge'zeglijk, obedient
ge'zel, mate, companion
ge'zellig, cosy; pleasant; sociable

ge'zelschap *n*, company, party
ge'zelschapsdame, lady-companion
ge'zet, corpulent; set
ge'zeten, established; sitting
ge'zicht *n*, sight; face
ge'zichtseinder, horizon
ge'zichtsbedrog *n*, optical illusion
ge'zichtskring, ken, mental outlook
ge'zichtspunt *n*, point of view
ge'zichtsveld *n*, field of vision
ge'zien, seen; highly thought of; in view of
ge'zin *n*, family
ge'zind, disposed, minded
ge'zindte, religious denomination
ge'zocht, sought (after), far-fetched
ge'zond, healthy, sound
ge'zondheid, health
ge'zusters, sisters
ge'zwel *n*, tumor, swelling
ge'zwind, swift
ge'zwollen, swollen; bombastic
gids, guide
giechelen, to giggle
giek, gig
gier, vulture
gieren, to scream
gierig, miserly
gierigaard, miser
gierigheid, avarice
gierpont, rope-ferry
gierst, millet
gierzwaluw, swift
gietbui, downpour
gieten, to pour; to cast
gieter, watering can; founder
giete'rij, foundry
gietijzer *n*, cast iron
gietkroes, crucible
gif(t) *n*, poison
gift, gift
giftig, poisonous; venomous
giftmenger, poisoner
gij, thou, ye, you
gijlieden, you
gijpen, to gybe
gijzelaar, hostage
gijzelen, to take as a hostage

gilde *n*, guild
gil(len), (to) yell
ginder, ginds, over there
ginnegappen, to giggle
gips *n*, gypsum, plaster (of Paris)
gipsafgietsel *n*, plaster cast
gi'reren, to pay by *giro*
giro(dienst), money order (service), (system of payment by) post-office cheque
gis, guess
  op de gis, by guess-work
gispen, to censure
gissen, to guess
gissing, guess
gist, yeast
gisten, to ferment
gisteren, yesterday
gister'avond, last night
gisting, ferment(ation)
git *n*, jet
gi'taar, guitar
glaasje *n*, small glass; slide
gla'ceren, to glaze; to ice
glad, smooth, slippery; glib, cunning
  glad mis, all wrong
gladheid, slipperiness
gladjanus, slyboots
gladweg, clean
glans, gloss, sheen, lustre
glansrijk, brilliant
glanzen, to shine, to gleam
glanzig, glossy
glas *n*, glass
glashelder, crystal clear
glazen, (made of) glass
glazenmaker, glazier
glazenwasser, window-cleaner
glazenwisser, squeegee
glazig, glassy, waxy
gla'zuren, to glaze, to ice
gla'zuur(sel) *n*, glaze, enamel (of teeth), icing
gletscher, gletsjer, glacier
gleuf, groove, slit, slot
gleufhoed, trilby
glibberen, to slither
glibberig, slippery
glijbaan, slide
glijden, to slide; to glide
glimlach(en), (to) smile

glimmen, to shine, to gleam
glimp, glimpse
glimworm, glow-worm
glinsteren, to glitter, to glisten
glippen, to slip
glo'baal, rough, broad
gloed, glow; blaze; ardour
gloednieuw, brand-new
gloeidraad, filament
gloeien, to glow
  gloeiend heet, burning hot
gloeikousje *n,* gas-mantle
gloeilamp, electric light bulb
glooien, to slope
glooiing, slope
glorie, glory
glorierijk, glori'eus, glorious
gluiper(d), sneak
gluiperig, sneaking
glunderen, to beam (with joy)
gluren, to peer
gniffelen, gnuiven, to laugh in
  one's sleeve
God'dank, thank God
goddelijk, divine
goddeloos, godless
god'dorie, by gad
god'ganselijke dag, whole blessed day
godgeklaagd, crying (to heaven)
godgeleerdheid, theology
godheid, godhead
go'din, goddess
godsdienst, religion
gods'dienstig, religious
godsdienstoefening, divine service
godsdienstwaanzin, religious
  mania
godslasteraar, blasphemer
gods'lasterlijk, blasphemous
god'vruchtig, pious
god'zalig, godly
goed, good; well: *n,* good(s),
  material
goe'daardig, good-natured; benign
goeddunken, to think fit: *n,*
  discretion
goederen, goods
goeder'tieren, merciful
goed'geefs, open-handed
goedge'lovig, credulous

goedge'zind, well disposed
goed'hartig, kind-hearted
goedheid, kindness
  grote goedheid! good gracious!
goedig, sweet natured
goedje *n,* stuff
goedkeuren, to approve of
goedkeuring, approval, assent
goed'koop, cheap
goed'lachs, easily amused
goed'leers, teachable
goed'moedig, good-natured
goedpraten, to explain away
goedschiks of kwaadschiks,
  willing or unwilling
goeds'moeds, cheerful
goedvinden, to approve
goedzak, gentle soul
goeierd, kind soul
gokken, to gamble, to chance
gokker, gambler
golf, wave; bay; gulf: golf
golfbreker, breakwater
golfkarton *n,* corrugated cardboard
golflengte, wave-length
golfslag, dashing of the waves
golven, to wave, to undulate
gom, gum; rubber
gomelas'tiek *n,* india rubber
gommen, to gum
gondel, gondola
gonzen, to buzz
goochelaar, conjurer, juggler
goochela'rij, conjuring, juggling
goochelen, to conjure, to juggle
goochem, smart
gooi(en), (to), fling, (to) throw
goor, dingy; sallow
goot, gutter; drain
gootsteen, (kitchen) sink
gordel, belt; girdle
gordeldier *n,* armadillo
gordelroos, shingles
gorden, to gird
gor'dijn *n,* curtain
gorgeldrank, gargle
gorgelen, to gargle
gort, groats
gortig: het te — maken, to go
  too far
goud *n,* gold
gouden, gold(en)

gouden'regen, laburnum
goudgalon *n,* gold lace
goudhoudend, auriferous
goudklomp, nugget
goudsbloem, marigold
Goudse pijp, church-warden
gouver'nante, governess
gouverne'ment *n,* government
gouver'neur, governor, private tutor
gouw, district
gouwenaar, church-warden
graad, degree, rank, grade
graadboog, protractor
graaf, count, earl
graafschap *n,* county
graafwerk *n,* excavation(s)
graag, eager; gladly
 (ja) **graag,** yes please
 ik zou **graag** willen weten, I should (dearly) like to know
graagte, eagerness
graaien, to rummage; to grab
graan *n,* grain, corn
graanschuur, granary
graansoorten, cereals
graanzuiger, (corn) elevator
graat, fish-bone
 hij is niet zuiver op de **graat,** there's something fishy about him
 van de **graat** vallen, to be ravenous(ly hungry)
grabbel: te — gooien, to throw away
grabbelen, to scramble
grabbelton, lucky dip
gracht, (town) canal; moat
gra'deren, to graduate
gradu'eel verschil *n,* difference in degree
gradu'eren, to graduate; to confer a degree upon
graf *n,* grave, sepulchre
gra'fiek, graph; graphic art
grafkelder, (family) vault
grafschrift *n,* epitaph
grafstem, sepulchral voice
grafzerk, tomb-stone
gram *n,* gramme
gram'matica, grammar
gram(m)o'foonplaat, gramophone record

gramschap, wrath
gra'naat, shell, grenade
gra'naatappel, pomegranate
gra'naatscherf, (piece of) shrapnel
gra'niet *n,* granite
grap, joke
 uit de **grap,** for fun
grapjas, grappenmaker, wag
grappig, funny
gras *n,* grass
grasduinen, to browse
grashalm, grasspriet, blade of grass
graszode, turf, sod
gratie, grace; free pardon; favour
grati'eus, graceful
gratifi'catie, bonus
grauw (*n*), grey; rabble
grauw(en), (to) snarl, (to) growl
gra'veerder, engraver
graven, to dig
Graven'hage: 's —, the Hague
gra'veren, to engrave
gra'veur, engraver
gra'vin, countess
gra'vure, engraving
grazen, to graze
 iemand te **grazen** nemen, to lead a person up the garden path
greep, grip, grasp; hilt; fork
grein *n,* grain ($1/700$ lb)
grendel(en), (to) bolt
grenehout *n,* deal
grens, bound(ary), frontier, limit
grensgeval *n,* border-line case
grensrechter, linesman
grenzen aan, to border on
grenzeloos, boundless
greppel, field-drain; narrow ditch
gretig, eager
gribus, hovel, slum
grief, grievance
Griekenland *n,* Greece
Griek(s) (*n*), Greek
griend, osier bed
grienen, sniffle
griep, influenza
griesmeel *n,* semolina
griet, brill
grieven, to grieve
griezel, monstrosity

griezelen, to shudder
griezelig, gruesome
grif, readily
griffel, slate-pencil
griffelkoker, pencil-case
griffie, record-office, secretariate
grif'fier, clerk of the court
grijns, grin, sneer
grijnzen, to sneer, to grin
grijpen, to seize
grijs, grey
grijsaard, old man
grijzen, to (go) grey
gril, caprice; freak
grillig, capricious
gri'mas, grimace
grime, (stage) make-up
grimmig, grim
grinniken, to chuckle, to snigger
grint n, gravel
grissen, to snatch
groef, groove; furrow
groeien, to grow
groeistuipen, growing pains
groen, green
groente(n), vegetables
groenteboer, greengrocer
groentijd, freshmen's initiation period
groep, group; clump
groepsgewijze, in groups
groet, salute, greeting
  de groeten doen, to give one's kind regards
groeten, to greet, to nod good-day
groeve, grave, pit, quarry
groezelig, grubby
grof, coarse; rude; gross
  grof spelen, to play for high stakes
  grof geld verdienen, to earn big money
grollen, antics
grommen, to growl, to grumble
grommig, grumpy
grond, ground, earth, soil
  in de grond van de zaak, basically
  te gronde gaan, to go to pieces
grondbeginsel n, basic principle
grondbelasting, land-tax
grondbezitter, landowner

grondeloos, unfathomable; absymal
gronden, to base
grondgebied n, territory
grondig, thorough
grondkleur, primer; primary colour
grondlegging, foundation
grondoorzaak, root cause
grondpacht, ground rent
grondslag, foundation
grondstelling, axiom
grondstof, raw material
grondverf, undercoat
grondvesten, to found: foundations
grondwerker, navvy
grondwet, constitution
grond'wettelijk, constitutional
groot, large, big, great, tall
  in het groot, on a large scale
grootboek n, ledger
grootbrengen, to bring up
grootdoen, to swagger
groothandel, wholesale trade
grootheid, magnitude
grootheidswaanzin, megalomania
groothertog, grand duke
groothouden: zich —, to put a brave face on it
grootje n, grannie
grootmoeder, grandmother
groot'moedig, magnanimous
grootouders, grandparents
groots, grand(iose)
groot'scheeps, in grand style
grootsheid, grandeur
grootspraak, boasting
grootspreken, to boast
groot'steeds, city
grootte, size
grootvader, grandfather
groot'waardigheidsbekleder, high dignitary
gros n, gross; mass
gros'sier, wholesaler
grot, grotto, cave
grotendeels, for the greater part
gruis n, grit, slack
gruizele'menten, gruzele'-menten, smithereens
grut n: **klein —,** little ones

grutte'rij, corn-chandler's (shop)
gruwel, atrocity, horror
gruweldaad, atrocity
gruwelijk, horrible
gruwen, to shudder; to abhor
guit, little rogue
guitig, roguish
gul, open-handed
gulden, guilder (approx. 2/-): golden
gulheid, generosity
gulp, fly
gulzig, greedy
gulzigaard, glutton
gummi *n*, (india) rubber
gunnen, to grant
  het is je gegund, you're welcome to it
gunst, favour
  gunst! gracious (me)!
gunstbewijs *n*, mark of favour
gunsteling, favourite
gunstig, favourable
gut! Lor'!
gutsen, to gush
guur, bleak, raw
gym'nasium *n*, grammar school
gymnas'tiek, gymnastics
gymnas'tiekzaal, gymnasium

H

haag, hedge
  Den Haag, The Hague
haai, shark
haaibaai, shrew
haak, hook
  niet in de haak, not all that it should be
  tussen haakjes, in brackets; by the way
haakgaren *n*, **haakkatoen** *n*, crochet-cotton
haaknaald, **haakpen**, crochet-hook
haaks op, at right angles to
haal, (pen-)stroke; pull
  aan de haal gaan, to take to one's heels
haan, cock
  er zal geen haan naar kraaien, nobody will be any the wiser
  haantje de voorste, cock of the walk

haar, her: *n*, hair
  het scheelde geen haar, it was touch and go
haard, stove; centre; hotbed
  open haard, fireplace
haardkleedje *n*, hearth-rug
haardos, head of hair
haarfijn, minute
haarklove'rij, hair-splitting
haarmiddel *n*, hair restorer
haas, hare
haast, almost: haste
haasten: zich —, to hurry
haastig, hasty
haat, hatred
haat'dragend, vindictive
ha'chee, hash
hachelijk, precarious
hachje *n*: **bang voor zijn —**, afraid to risk one's life
hage'dis, lizard
hagedoorn, hawthorn
hagel, hail; shot
hagelen, to hail
hagelkorrel, hail-stone; pellet
hagelwit, white as snow
hak, (shoe-)heel
  van de hak op de tak springen, to jump from one subject to another
  iemand een hak zetten, to play a person a dirty trick
hakbijl, chopper
hakblok *n*, chopping block
haken, to crochet; to hook
  haken naar, to hanker after
hakenkruis *n*, swastika
hakhout *n*, copse
hakkelaar, stammerer
hakkelen, to stammer
hakken, to chop, to hack
hakmes *n*, cleaver
hal, hall
halen, to fetch, to get; to catch
  hij haalt het nooit, he will never manage it
  dat haalt er niet bij, there's no comparison
half, half, semi-
  half zes, half past five
halfbloed, half-breed
half'gaar, underdone; half-witted

halfgod, demigod
halfrond n, hemisphere
half'slachtig, half-hearted
half'stok, at half mast
halm, stalk, blade
hals, neck
 om hals brengen, to kill
halsband, (dog-)collar
halssnoer n, necklace
hals'starrig, stubborn
halster(en), (to) halter
halte, stop(ping-place)
halter, dumb-bell, bar-bell
hal'veren, to halve
halver'hoogte, half-way up
halverwege, half-way
hamer, hammer, mallet
hameren, to hammer
hamsteren, to hoard
hand, hand
 handen thuis! hands off!
 **de handen uit de mouw
 steken,** to give a helping hand
 er is niets aan de hand, there
 is nothing wrong
 bij de hand, up and doing;
 handy
 met de handen in het haar, at
 one's wits' ends
 op handen dragen, to worship
 van de hand doen, to dispose of
 voor de hand liggen, to go
 without saying
handboeien, handcuffs
handdoek, towel
handdruk, handshake
handel, trade
 in de handel, in business; on
 the market
handelaar, dealer
handelbaar, tractable
handelen, to act; to trade
handeling, act(ion)
handelsrecht, commercial law
handelsvloot, mercantile marine
handelswaren, merchandise
handelwijze, method(s) (of dealing), behaviour
handenarbeid, manual labour,
 arts and crafts
handgemeen worden, to come
 to blows
handgreep, grip; knack

handhaven, to maintain
handig, handy, deft
handkoffer, suitcase
handlanger, accomplice
handleiding, guide
handschoen, glove
 met de handschoen trouwen,
 to marry by proxy
handschrift n, manuscript; handwriting
hand'tastelijk, aggressive
hand'tastelijkheden, blows,
 fighting; pawing
handtekenen n, free-hand drawing
handtekening, signature
handvat n, handle
handvest n, charter
handwerk n, (handi)craft;
 needlework
handwerken, to do needlework
handwerksman, artisan
hangbrug, suspension bridge
hangen, to hang
hangend(e), drooping; pending
hanger, (coat-)hanger; pendant
hangerig, listless
hangmat, hammock
hangop, curds
hangslot n, padlock
han'sop, child's sleeping suit
hans'worst, clown
han'teren, to handle, to operate
hap, mouthful, bite
haperen, to falter
 er hapert iets, there is a hitch
 somewhere
happen, to take a mouthful
happig, keen, eager
hard, hard
 hard nodig, very necessary
 ik heb er een hard hoofd in, I
 have my doubts (about the
 result)
harden, to harden, to temper
 ik kon het niet langer harden,
 I couldn't stand it any longer
hard'horig, hard of hearing
hard'leers, dunderheaded
hard'lijvig, constipated
hardlopen, to run
hard'nekkig, stubborn
hardop, aloud

hard'vochtig, callous

harig, hairy

haring, herring; tent-peg

hark, rake; gawk

harken, to rake

harlekijn, harlequin

har'monika, concertina

harmo'nie, harmony

harmoni'ëren, to harmonize

harnas n, armour

iemand in het harnas jagen, to put a person's back up

har'poen, harpoon

harrewarren, to squabble

hars, resin, rosin

hart n, heart

heb het hart niet! don't you dare!

van harte bedankt, thank you very much

hartedief, darling

hartelijk, cordial, hearty

harteloos, heartless

hartelust: naar —, to one's heart's content

hartewens, heart's desire

hart'grondig, whole-hearted

hartig, savoury; forthright

hart'roerend, touching

hartstikke, not half

hartstocht, passion

harts'tochtelijk, passionate

hartsvriend(in), bosom friend

hartver'heffend, ennobling, sublime

hartverlamming, heart-failure

hartversterking, pick-me-up

hartzeer n, heart-break

hatelijk, spiteful

hatelijkheid, spite(ful remark)

haten, to hate

have en goed, goods and chattels

levende have, live-stock

haveloos, ragged

haven, harbour

havenarbeider, dock-worker

havenbestuur n, port authority

havengeld n, harbour dues

havenhoofd n, jetty

havenstad, port

haver, oats

van haver tot gort kennen, to know inside out

haverklap: om de —, at the slightest provocation; every other minute

havermout, porridge (oats)

havik, hawk

haviksneus, aquiline nose

hazelaar, hazel(nut tree)

hazelip, hare-lip

hazepeper, jugged hare

hazeslaap, snooze

haze'wind, greyhound

hebbelijkheid, peculiar habit

hebben, to have

hoe laat heb je het? what do you make the time?

wat heb ik eraan? what's the good of it to me?

het hebben over, to talk about

hebberig, acquisitive

hebzucht, greed

heb'zuchtig, grasping

hecht, firm, solid: n, handle, haft, hilt

hechten, to attach; to stitch (up)

ge'hecht aan, fond of, attached to

hechtenis, custody

hechtheid, solidity

hechting, stitch

hechtpleister, adhesive plaster

heden, to-day

heden ten dage, nowadays

heden'avond, this evening

hedendaags, present-day

heel, whole, entire; quite, very

heelhuids, unscathed

heelkunde, surgery

heen en weer, to and fro

waar wil je heen? where do you want to go? what are you driving at?

heengaan, to go away

heenweg: op de —, on the way there

heer, gentleman; master; lord

heerbaan, (modern) trunk-road

heerlijk, delicious; delightful

heerschaar, host

heerschap n, gent, cove

heerschap'pij, dominion, rule

heersen, to rule; to prevail

heerser, ruler

heers'zuchtig, ambitious
hees, hoarse
heester, shrub
heet, hot
heetge'bakerd, quick-tempered
hefboom, lever
hefbrug, lift-bridge
heffen, to raise
heffing, levy; stress
  heffing-in-eens, capital levy
heft *n,* handle, haft
heftig, violent; vehement
heg, hedge
heibel, din, racket
heide, moor, heath(er)
heiden, heathen, pagan
heidendom *n,* paganism, pagan
  world
heidens, pagan, heathen(ish)
heien *n,* pile-driving
heiig, hazy
heil *n,* salvation; welfare; good
Heiland, Saviour
heilbot, halibut
heildronk, toast
heilgymnastiek, physiotherapy
heilig, holy, sacred
heiligdom *n,* sanctuary, sanc-
  tum
heilige, saint
heiligen, to hallow, to keep holy
heiligheid, holiness
heiligmakend, sanctifying
heiligschennis, sacrilege
heiligverklaring, canonization
heilloos, evil; disastrous, fatal
heilzaam, salutary
heimelijk, secret, furtive
heimwee *n,* homesickness, nostal-
  gia
heinde en ver, near and far
heining, fence
heipaal, (concrete) pile
hek *n,* railings; gate
hekel, hackle
  ik heb er een hekel aan, I dislike it intensely
  over de hekel halen, to criticize
  sharply
hekeldicht *n,* satire
hekelen, to heckle, to satirize
hekkensluiter, last comer
heks, witch; hag

heksenketel, cacophony
heksentoer, insuperable task
hel, hell: bright
he'laas, alas
held, hero
heldendicht *n,* epic
heldenmoed, heroism
helder, clear, lucid; bright;
  clean
helder'ziend, clairvoyant
held'haftig, heroic
hel'din, heroine
helemaal, altogether
  hele'maal niet, not at all
helen, to receive stolen goods: to
  heal
heler, fence
helft, half
hellebaard, halberd
hellen, to slope, to slant
helling, slope, incline, slipway
helm, helmet: beach-grass
helmhoed, sun-helmet
helmstok, tiller
helpen, to help, to be effective
hels, infernal, hellish
  hels zijn, to be wild (with rage)
hem, him
hemd *n,* vest, shirt
  het hemd is nader dan de rok,
  blood is thicker than water
hemel, heaven, sky; canopy
hemelgewelf *n,* firmament
hemellichaam *n,* celestial body
hemels, heavenly
hemelsbreed verschil *n,* all the
  difference in the world
hemel'tergend, flagrant, crying
  (to heaven)
Hemelvaart, Ascension
hen, them: hen
hengel, fishing-rod
hengelaar, angler
hengelen, to angle, to fish
hengsel *n,* handle; hinge
hengst, stallion
hennep, hemp
her: van eeuwen —, from times
  immemorial
  van ouds her, of old
her-, re-, again
her'ademen, to breathe again
heral'diek, heraldry: heraldic

he'raut, herald
herberg, inn
herbergen, to accommodate; to harbour
herber'gier, inn-keeper
her'denken, to commemorate; to recall
her'denking, commemoration
herder, shepherd; herdsman
herderlijk, pastoral
herdershond, sheep-dog
herdersstaf, shepherd's crook, crosier
her'drukken, to reprint
hereboer, gentleman farmer
here'miet, hermit
her'enigen, to reunite
herfst(achtig), autumn(al)
herfstdraden, gossamer
her'haald(elijk), repeated(ly)
her'halen, to repeat; to revise
her'haling, repetition; revision
her'inneren aan, to remind of
zich herinneren, to remember
her'innering, recollection, memory
her'kauwen, to chew the cud; to ruminate
her'kenbaar, recognizable
her'kennen, to recognize
her'kiezen, to re-elect
herkomst, origin
her'krijgen, to recover
her'leiden, to convert, to reduce
her'leven, to revive; to live again
herme'lijn (n), ermine
her'nemen, to resume; to take again
her'nieuwen, to renew
her'overen, to recapture
herrie, row, hullabaloo
her'rijzenis, resurrection
her'roepen, to revoke
her'scheppen, to re-create; to transform
hersenen, brain(s)
hersenpan, cranium
hersenschim, chimera
hersenschudding, concussion
her'stel n, recovery, convalescence
her'stelbetaling, reparation

her'stellen, to mend; to restore; to recover
her'stellingsoord n, convalescent home
hert n, deer, stag
hertebout, (haunch of) venison
hertenkamp, deer-park
hertog, duke
hertogdom n, duchy
herto'gin, duchess
her'trouwen, to remarry
her'vatten, to resume
her'vormd, reformed; orthodox protestant
her'vorming, reform(ation)
herwaarts en derwaarts, hither and thither
her'winnen, to regain
her'zien, to revise; to review
het, it: the
heten, to be called
het'geen, (that) which
het'zelfde, the same
het'zij ... of (or dan wel), either or whether ... or
heugen: dat zal je —, you won't forget that in a hurry
heuglijk, joyful
heulen met, to be in league with
heup, hip
heus, real; courteous
heuvel, hill
hevel, siphon
hevig, violent
hi'aat n, hiatus
hiel, heel
hier, here
hier te lande, in this country
hierheen, this way
hier'naast, next to this; next door
hier'namaals n, (life) hereafter
hieruit, out (of) here; from this
hij, he
hijgen, to pant
hijsblok n, pulley-block
hijsen, to hoist
hik, hiccups
hinde, hind
hinderen, to hinder; to annoy
hinderlaag, ambush
hinderlijk, annoying; inconvenient

hindernis, hinderpaal, obstacle
hinken, to limp; to hop
hinniken, to neigh
his'torisch, historic(al)
hit, pony; skivvy
hitte, heat
hobbel(ig), bump(y)
hobbelen, to jolt
hobbelpaard *n*, rocking-horse
hobo, oboe
hoe, how
  hoe eerder hoe beter, the sooner the better
  hoe dan ook, however
hoed, hat
hoe'danigheid, quality
hoede, guard, care
hoeden, to guard
hoef, hoof
hoefijzer *n*, horseshoe
hoegenaamd niets, nothing whatever
hoek, angle; corner, nook
hoekig, angular
hoen *n*, (barndoor) fowl
hoenderhok *n*, hen-coop
hoenderpark *n*, poultry-farm
hoepel, hoop
hoer, whore
hoes, loose cover; dust-sheet
hoest(en), (to) cough
hoeve, farm(stead)
hoeveel, how much, how many
hoe'veelheid, quantity
hoeveelste: de — is het van- daag? what is the date to- day?
hoeven, to need
hoe'ver, how far
  in hoeverre, to what extent
hoe'zeer, how(ever) much
hof, garden: *n*, court
  het hof maken, to court
hofdame, lady-in-waiting
hoffelijk, courteous
hofhouding, royal household
hofmeester('es), steward(ess)
hoge'school, university
hok *n*, kennel, pen, sty, hutch
hokken, to huddle; to hang fire
hokvast, stay-at-home
hol, hollow, concave: *n*, den, cave
  op hol raken, to run wild

Hollands (*n*), Dutch
hollen, to dash (along)
hol'ogig, hollow-eyed
holte, cavity
hom, soft roe
hommel, bumble-bee, drone
homp, lump, chunk
hond, dog, hound
  rode hond, German measles
hondeweer *n*, foul weather
honderd, a hundred
  honderd uit praten, to talk nineteen to the dozen
honderderlei, a hundred and one
honds, churlish
honds'dolheid, rabies
honen, to scoff at
Honga'rije *n*, Hungary
honger(en), (to) hunger
hongerig, hungry
hongerloon *n*, starvation wage
hongersnood, famine
honi(n)g, honey
honi(n)graat, honeycomb
honk *n*, base, home
hono'rair, honorary
hono'rarium *n*, fee
hono'reren, to honour; to pay
hoofd *n*, head; principal, chief
hoofdartikel *n*, leading article
hoofdbreken *n*, brain-racking
hoofdgetal *n*, cardinal number
hoofdkussen *n*, pillow
hoofdkwartier *n*, headquarters
hoofdletter, capital letter
hoofdpijn, headache
hoofdstad, capital, principal town
hoofdstraat, main street
hoofdstuk *n*, chapter
hoofdzaak, main thing
hoofd'zakelijk, mainly
hoofs, courtly
hoog, high, tall
  drie hoog, on the third floor
hoogachten, to esteem
  hoogachtend Uw (dw.), yours faithfully
hoog'dravend, bombastic
hoog'hartig, haughty
Hoogheid, Highness
hooghouden, to uphold
hoog'leraar, professor

hoogmoed, pride
hoog'moedig, proud
hoogmoedswaanzin, megalomania
hoog'nodig, very necessary
hoogoven, blast-furnace
hoogst, highest; extremely
 ten hoogste, at most
hoogstaand, of high moral character
hoogstens, at most
hoogte, height, altitude
 op de hoogte, well-informed
 uit de hoogte, supercilious
hoogtepunt n, acme, zenith
hoogtezon, ultra-violet light
hoogtij vieren, to be rampant
hoogtijdag, heyday; high day
hoogvlakte, plateau
hoogvlieger: hij is geen —, he's no genius
hoog'waardigheidsbekleder, (high) dignitary
hoog'water n, high tide
hooi n, hay
 teveel hooi op zijn vork nemen, to bite off more than one can chew
 te hooi en te gras, haphazardly
hooiberg, hay-stack
hooien, to make hay
hooimijt, hay-stack
hooivork, pitchfork
hoon, scorn
hoop, hope: heap, stack
hoopvol, hopeful
hoorbaar, audible
hoorn, horn, bugle; telephone receiver
hoornblazer, bugler
hoorngeschal n, flourish of trumpets
hoornvlies n, cornea
hoorspel n, radio play
hop(pe), hop
hopeloos, hopeless
hopen, to hope
hopje n, burnt caramel
hopmeester, scoutmaster
hor, gauze screen
horde, horde: hurdle
horen, to hear: to belong (to); to be right (and proper), ought

horizon'taal, horizontal
horlepijp, hornpipe
hor'loge n, watch
horrelvoet, club-foot
hort: met horten en stoten, jerkily
horzel, horse-fly
hospes, hospita, landlord, landlady
hossen, to sing and dance arm in arm
hotsen, to jolt
houdbaar, tenable
houden, to hold; to keep
 houden van, to like, to love
 houden voor, to take for
 zich goed houden, to control oneself
houding, attitude; bearing
hout n, wood
houterig, starchy
houtje n, bit of wood
 op zijn eigen houtje, all off his own bat
houtskool, charcoal
houtsne(d)e, woodcut
houtsnijwerk n, wood-carving
houtsnip, woodcock
houtvester, forester
houvast n, hold
hou'weel, pick-axe
houwen, to hew
ho'vaardig, haughty
hoveling, courtier
hove'nier, gardener
hozen, to bale
huichelaar, hypocrite
huichela'rij, hypocrisy
huichelen, to dissemble
huid, skin, hide
huidig, present-day
huifkar, covered wagon
huig, uvula
huilebalk, cry-baby
huilen, to cry, to howl
huis n, house, home
huisarts, family doctor
huisbaas, landlord
huisbewaarder, caretaker
huisdier n, domestic animal
huiselijk, domestic(ated); homely
huisgenoot, member of the household

huis'houdelijk, domestic, household

huishouden n, household; housekeeping

huishouden, to keep house

   vreselijk huishouden, to play havoc

huishoudkunde, domestic science

huishoudster, housekeeper

huiskamer, living-room

huisraad n; household goods

huis-tuin-of-keuken, common or garden

huisvesten, to house

huiswerk n, homework

huiveren, to shudder

huiverig voor, wary of

huivering, shudder

huivering'wekkend, horrible

huizenmakelaar, house-agent

hulde(betoon n), homage

huldigen, to pay tribute to

hullen, to envelop

hulp, help

hulpe'hoevend, invalid; needy

helpeloos, helpless

hulpmiddel n, expedient

hulptroepen, auxiliaries

hulp'vaardig(heid), helpful-(ness)

hulpverlening, assistance

hulpwerkwoord n, auxiliary verb

huls, pod; (cartridge-)case

hulst, holly

humeur n, mood; temper

hu'meurig, moody

hummel, tiny tot

humor, humour

hun, their; (to) them

hunkeren naar, to hanker after

huppelen, to hop

hups, affable

huren, to hire, to rent

hurken, to squat

hut, cabin, hut

hutkoffer, trunk

hutspot, hotchpotch

huur, rent

huurder, tenant

huurling, hireling, mercenary

huurwaarde, rateable value

huwbaar, marriageable

huwelijk n, marriage

huwelijksaanzoek n, proposal (of marriage)

huwelijksinzegening, blessing of the Church (after civil marriage)

huwelijksreis, honeymoon

huwelijksvoltrekking, marriage ceremony

huwelijksvoorwaarden, marriage settlement(s)

huwen, to marry

hu'zaar, hussar

hypo'theek, mortgage

hyste'rie, hysteria

hys'terisch, hysterical

I

ide'aal (n), ideal

ideali'seren, to idealize

i'dee n, idea

ide'ëel, imaginary

idem, ditto

iden'tiek, identical

identifi'ceren, to identify

identi'teit, identity

idi'oom n, idiom

idi'oot, idiot: idiotic

ido'laat van, infatuated with

ieder, every, each, any

ieder'een, everyone, anyone

iemand, someone, anyone

iep(eboom), elm (tree)

Ier, Irishman

Iers (n), Irish

Ierland n, Ireland

iets, something, anything

ietsje, ietwat, somewhat

ijdel, vain

ijdelheid, vanity

ijdeltuit, vain person

ijl: in aller —, hastily

ijl, thin; rarefied

ijlbode, express messenger

ijlen, to be delirious; to hasten

ijlings, in hot haste

ijs n, ice

ijsbaan, skating rink

ijsbeer, polar bear

ijsberen, to pace up and down

ijsberg, iceberg

ijselijk, horrible

ijsgang, ice-drift

ijskast, refrigerator
ijskegel, icicle
ijskoud, icy (cold), iced
ijsshots, ice-floe
ijstijd, ice-age
ijsvogel, kingfisher
IJszee, Polar Sea
ijver, diligence
ijveren voor, to champion
ijverig, diligent, keen
ijverzucht, jealousy
ijzel, ice on the roads
ijzen, to shudder
ijzer *n,* iron
ijzerdraad *n,* wire
ijzerhoudend, ferreous
ijzeroer *n,* bog-ore
ijzerwaren, hardware
ijzig, icy-cold; frightful
ijzing'wekkend, ghastly
ik, I
 het ik, the ego
ille'gaal, illegal
il'lusie, illusion
illus'treren, to illustrate
imker, bee-keeper
immer, ever
immers, surely; after all
immo'reel, immoral
impo'neren, to impress
impo'sant, impressive
in'achtneming, observance
inademen, to breathe in
inbakeren, to wrap up warm
inbeelden: zich —, to imagine
inbeelding, imagination; conceit
inbegrepen, including
inbegrip: met — van, inclusive of
inbe'slagneming, seizure (of goods)
inbinden, to bind
 je moet je wat inbinden, you must climb down
inblazen, to suggest
inboedel, household effects
inboeten, to forfeit
 hij heeft er het leven bij ingeboet, the attempt cost him his life
inboezemen, to inspire
inboorling, native

inborst, disposition
inbraak, burglary
inbreken, to burgle, to break in
inbreker, burglar
inbrengen, to bring in; to put forward
 hij heeft niets in te brengen, he has no say in the matter
inbreuk, infringement
inburgeren, to become current; to settle down
incas'seren, to cash; to collect
in'cluis, included
inconse'quent, inconsistent
incou'rante maat, odd size
indampen, to moisten; to reduce by evaporation
indelen, to class(ify), to allocate
indeling, classification, grouping
indenken: zich —, to imagine, to visualize, to conceive
inder'daad, indeed
inder'haast, in haste
inder'tijd, at one time, at the time
indeuken, to dent
in'dien, if
indienen, to introduce, to submit
indijken, to surround with dikes
indivi'du *n,* individual
individu'eel, individual
indommelen, to doze off
indringen: zich —, to intrude
indroevig, very sad
indrogen, to dry up
indruisen tegen, to run counter to
indruk, impression
indruk'wekkend, impressive
indus'trie, industry
industri'eel, industrial(ist)
indutten, to doze off
in'een, together
in'eengedoken, hunched up
in'eenkrimpen, to cower, to double up
in'eens, at once
in'eenstorten, to collapse, to come crashing down
in'eenzakken, in el'kaar zakken, to collapse, to cave in
inenten, to inoculate, to vaccinate

in'faam, infamous
infante'rie, infantry
infante'rist, infantryman
inferi'eur, inferior
influisteren, to whisper in a person's ear
infor'matie, information
 informaties inwinnen, to make inquiries
infor'meren (naar), to inquire (about)
ingaan, to enter; to take effect
 niet ingaan op, to ignore
ingang, entrance
 met ingang van heden, as from today
 ingang vinden, to be well received
ingebeeld, imaginary; conceited
ingeboren, innate
ingehouden, restrained
ingekankerd, inveterate
inge'meen, vile
ingenaaid, in paper covers
ingeni'eur, (qualified) engineer
ingeni'eus, ingenious
ingenomen met, pleased with
ingespannen, strenuous; intent
ingetogen, modest, subdued
inge'val, in case
ingevallen wangen, hollow cheeks
ingeven, to prompt; to administer
ingeving, inspiration
inge'volge, in accordance with
ingewanden, intestines
ingewijde, adept; insider
inge'wikkeld, complicated
ingeworteld, deep-seated
ingezetene, inhabitant
ingezonden stuk n, letter to the editor
ingooien, to throw in(to); to smash
ingrijpen, to intervene
in'grijpend, far-reaching
inhalen, to catch up, to overtake; to take in
inha'leren, to inhale
in'halig, grasping
inham, creek
in'hechtenisneming, arrest

in'heems, indigenous
inhoud, content(s); capacity
inhouden, to contain; to restrain; to dock
inhoudsmaat, cubic measure
inhoudsopgave, table of contents
inhuldigen, to inaugurate
inkalven, to cave in
inkeer: tot — komen, to repent
inkeping, notch
inklaren, to clear (at the customs)
inkleden, to put into words
inkomen, to come in; n, income
 daar komt niets van in, nothing doing
inkomsten, income, revenue
inkoop, purchase
inkorten, to shorten, to curtail
inkrimpen, to shrink, to cut down
inkt, ink
inktpotlood n, indelible pencil
inktvis, squid
inkwartieren, to billet
inlaat, inlet
inlander, native
inlassen, to fit in, to insert
inlaten, to let in
 zich inlaten met, to have dealings with
inleggeld n, deposit, membership fee
inleiden, to introduce
inleiding, introduction
inleven: zich — in, to imagine oneself as
inleveren, to hand in
inlichten, to inform
inlichting, information
inlijsten, to frame
inlijven, to incorporate
inlossen, to redeem
inluiden, to ring in
inmaak, preserving; preserves
inmaken, to preserve
inmenging, interference
in'middels, meanwhile
innemen, to take (in, up); to capture; to please
innen, to collect
innerlijk, inner; intrinsic: n inner being

innig, heartfelt, intimate

inpakken, to pack (up), to wrap up

inpalmen, to grab; to inveigle

inpeperen, to pay (a person) out

inpikken, to grab; to tackle

inpolderen, to reclaim (land)

inpompen, to pump in; to cram

inpreten, to inculcate

inrichten, to arrange, to rig up, to furnish

inrichting, institute; institution; arrangement, furnishing

inrijden, to ride or drive into; to break or run in

inrit, entrance

inroepen, to call in, to invoke

inruilen, to trade in, to exchange

inruimen, to clear, to vacate; to put back

inrukken, to dismiss
ruk in! clear out!

inschakelen, to switch on; to put into gear

inschenken, to pour out

inschepen: zich —, to embark

inschieten: erbij —, to go by the board

in'schikkelijk, accommodating

inschikken, to move in closer

inschrijven, to register; to tender; to subscribe

insge'lijks, likewise

in'signe n, badge

inslaan, to beat or smash in; to lay in; to turn into; to catch on

inslag, woof, weft

inslapen, to fall asleep

insluiten, to enclose, to surround; to include, to comprise

inspannen, to put (horses) to; to exert, to strain

in'spannend, strenuous

inspanning, exertion

inspec'teur, inspector

inspraak, dictate(s)

inspreken: iemand moed —, to put heart into a person

inspringen, to leap into the breach
inspringende regel, indented line

inspuiten, to inject

instaan voor, to vouch for

instal'leren, to install; to induct

in'standhouden, to maintain

in'stantie, authority
in laatste instantie, in the last resort

instellen, to institute; to focus
er op ingesteld zijn, to be used to it

instelling, institution

instemmen, to agree

instemming, approval

instinc'tief, instinct'matig, instinctive

instoppen, to tuck in

instorten, to collapse

instru'eren, to instruct

instuderen, to practise; to study

instuif, informal party

in'tegendeel, on the contrary

inte'grerend, integral

intekenen op, to subscribe to

inten'dance, Army Service Corps

interen, to live on one's capital

interes'sant, interesting

interes'seren: zich — voor, to be interested in

interlo'caal gesprek n, trunk call

in'tern, internal; resident

inter'naat n, boarding school, (student) hostel

inter'neren, to intern

interrum'peren, to interrupt

in'tiem, intimate

intimi'teit, intimacy

intocht, (ceremonial) entry

intomen, to curb; to rein in

intrappen, to kick open; to tread down

intre(d)e, entry, commencement

intreden, to enter (upon), to set in

intrek: zijn — nemen in, to take up residence at

intrekken, to draw in; to move in; to withdraw, to retract

intri'gant, intriguer

in'trige, intrigue

introdu'cé, guest

in'tussen, meanwhile

inval, invasion; raid; brain-wave

inva'lide, disabled person, invalid

invalidi'teit, disablement

invallen, to fall in; to deputize; to occur to

inven'taris, inventory

inventari'satie, stock-taking

invetten, to grease

invliegen: er —, to fall for a trick

invloed, influence

invloedrijk, influential

invoegen, to insert

invoer, import(s)

invorderen, to collect (debts)

in'vrijheidstelling, release

in'wendig, internal, inward

inwerken op, to act upon

inwijden, to consecrate; to initiate

inwilligen, to comply with

inwinnen, to obtain

inwisselen, to (ex)change, to cash

inzage: ter —, for inspection, on approval

in'zake, with reference to

inzakken, to collapse

inzamelen, to collect

inzegenen, to consecrate

inzender, contributor; exhibitor

inzending, contribution; exhibit(s)

inzepen, to soap

inzet, stake(s)

inzetten, to put in; to start; to stake

inzicht n, insight, understanding

inzien, to glance through; to realize

  iets ernstig inzien, to take a grave view of something

  bij nader inzien, on second thoughts

  mijns inziens, in my opinion

inzinken, to subside; to decline

inzinking, subsidence; relapse

inzitten: erover —, to be worried about something

  hij zit er warmpjes in, he's living in clover

  de inzittenden, the occupants

in'zonderheid, in particular

iro'nie, irony

i'ronisch, ironical

irri'teren, to irritate

ischias, sciatica

iso'latie, insulation

isole'ment n, isolation

iso'leren, to isolate, to insulate

i'voor n, ivory

i'voren, (made of) ivory

J

ja, yes

jaaglijn, tow-rope

jaagpad n, tow-path

jaap, gash

jaar n, year

jaarbeurs, industries fair

jaargang, a year's issue (of a periodical), volume

jaargeld n, annuity

jaargenoot, contemporary

jaargetij(de) n, season

jaarlijks, annual

jaartal n, date

jaartelling, era

jaarwisseling, turn of the year

jacht, hunt(ing); shoot(ing); pursuit; n, yacht

jachten, to hustle

jachtgeweer n, sporting gun

jachthond, gun-dog, hound

jachtschotel, hot-pot

jachtsneeuw, driving snow

jachtvliegtuig n, fighter

jac'quet n, morning-coat

jagen, to hunt; to shoot; to race

jager, hunter, sportsman

jak n, smock

jakhals, jackal

jakkeren, to hustle

jakkes! bah!

ja'loers(heid), jealous(y)

jaloe'zie, jealousy; Venetian blind

jambe, iamb

jammer, distress

  jammer genoeg, unfortunately

  wat jammer! what a pity!

jammeren, to lament

jammerklacht, lamentation

jammerlijk, miserable

Jan en alle'man, every Tom, Dick and Harry
Jan Klaassen en Katrijn, Punch and Judy
Jan Salie, stick-in-the-mud
janboel, muddle
janken, to yelp
janmaat, jack-tar
ja'pon, dress
jarenlang, for years
jarig, one year old
  ik ben jarig, it is my birthday
jarre'tel(le), suspender
jas, coat
jas'mijn, jasmine
jaspanden, coat-tails
jassen, to peel (spuds)
jasses! bah!
ja'wel, certainly
jawoord *n,* consent
je, you; your
jegens, towards
jekker, monkey-jacket
je'never, Dutch gin
je'neverbes, juniper berry *or* tree
jengelen, to whimper
jeugd, youth
jeugdherberg, youth hostel
jeugdig, youthful, young
jeuk, itch
jeuken, to itch; to scratch
jicht, gout
jij, you
j.l., ult., last
jochie *n,* kid, lad(die)
Jodendom *n,* Judaism; Jewry
Jo'din, Jewess
jodium *n,* iodine
joelen, to cheer; to howl
jokken, to fib
jokkebrok, fibber
jol, yawl, dinghy
jolig, jolly
jo'lijt *n,* merry-making
jonassen, to swing a child by its arms and legs
jong, young
jongeling, youth
jonge'lui, young people
jongen, boy: to bring forth young
jongensachtig, boyish
jongensjaren, boyhood

jongenskop, Eton crop
jongge'huwden, newly-weds
jong'leur, juggler
jong'mens *n,* young man
jongs: van — af aan, right from childhood
jongst'leden, last
jonker, nobleman
Jood(s), Jew(ish)
jool, rag, fun
Joost: dat mag — weten, goodness only knows
jota, iota
jou, you
jour'naal *n,* log-book; journal; news-reel
journalis'tiek, journalism
jouw, your
jouwen, to hoot
jubel, rejoicing
jubelen, to shout for joy
jubi'laris, man celebrating some personal anniversary
jubi'leren, to celebrate some anniversary in one's life
jubi'leum *n,* jubilee, anniversary
juffrouw, (unmarried) woman; Miss, (Mrs), Madam
juichen, to shout for joy
juist, exact; right; just (now)
  daarom juist, for that very reason
juistheid, correctness; justness
juk *n,* yoke
jukbeen *n,* cheek-bone
juli, July
jullie, you (people)
juni, June
ju'ridisch, juridical, legal
ju'rist, lawyer
jurk, dress
jus, gravy
jus'titie, judicature; justice, law
ju'weel *n,* jewel; gem
juwe'lier, jeweller

K

ka, kaai, quay
kaak, jaw; gill; pillory
  aan de kaak stellen, to expose
kaakje *n,* biscuit
kaakkramp, lock-jaw

kaal, bald; bare; threadbare; penniless
kaap, cape
kaapstander, capstan
kaapvaarder, privateer
kaapvaart, privateering
kaars, candle
kaarsrecht, bolt upright
kaarsvet *n*, candle-grease
kaart, card; map, chart; hand (at cards)
kaarten, to play cards
kaartje *n*, (visiting) card; ticket
kaartlegster, fortune-teller
kaartsysteem *n*, card index
kaas, cheese
　ik heb er geen kaas van gegeten, I don't know the first thing about it
kaasmijt, cheese-mite
kaasschaaf, cheese slicer
kaasstolp cheese-cover
kaaswei, whey
kaatsbaan, fives-court
kaatsen, to play ball
ka'baal *n*, shindy
kabbelen, to lap, to ripple
kabel, cable, hawser
kabel'jauw, cod
kabi'net *n*, cabinet
ka'bouter, goblin, gnome
kachel, stove: tipsy
kachelhout *n*, firewood
ka'daster *n*, land-registry
kade, quay
kader *n*, cadre, framework, scope
kaf *n*, chaff
kaft, (book-)cover, book-jacket
ka'juit, cabin, ward-room
kakelbont, gaudy, motley
kakelen, to cackle, to chatter
kaken, to gut (herrings)
kake'toe, cockatoo
kakkerlak, cockroach
kale'bas, gourd
ka'lender, calendar
kalf *n*, calf
kal(e)'fat(er)en, to caulk; to patch up
kalfsvlees *n*, veal
kalium *n*, potassium
ka'liber *n*, calibre
kalk, lime; mortar

kal'koen, turkey
kalkoven, lime-kiln
kalm, calm
kal'meren, to calm
　kalmerend middel, sedative
kalmpjes, calmly
kalmte, calm(ness), composure
ka'lotje *n*, skull-cap
kalven, to calve
kalverliefde, calf-love
kam, comb; crest; bridge (of a violin)
　over één kam scheren, to treat alike
ka'meel, camel
kame'nier, lady's maid
kamer, room, chamber
kame'raad, comrade
kameraad'schappelijk, friendly
kamerdienaar, valet
kamerheer, chamberlain
kamerjas, dressing-gown
kamermeisje *n*, parlour-maid
kamerscherm *n*, screen
kamfer, camphor
kamgaren (*n*), worsted
ka'mille, camomile
kammen, to comp
kamp *n*, camp; contest
kampen, to fight; to contend
kam'peren, to camp
kamper'foelie, honeysuckle
kampi'oen(schap *n*), champion(ship)
kamrad *n*, cog-wheel
kan, jug, can
ka'naal *n*, canal; channel
ka'narie, canary
kandelaar, candle-stick
kande'laber, candelabrum
kandi'daat, candidate; holder of the first university degree
kan'dijsuiker, sugar-candy
ka'neel, cinnamon
kanjer, whopper
kanker, cancer; canker
kankeraar, grumbler
kankeren, to cancerate; to grouse
kanni'baal, cannibal
kano, canoe
ka'non *n*, gun
kano'neerboot, gunboat

ka'nonnenvlees *n*, cannon-fodder
kans, chance
kansel, pulpit
kansela'rij, chancery
kanse'lier, chancellor
kansspel *n*, game of chance
kant, side, edge; lace
  dat raakt kant nog wal, that is quite irrelevant
  iets over zijn kant laten gaan, to put up with something
  kant en klaar, all set and ready
  zich van kant maken, to do oneself in
  op 't kantje af, only just
kan'teel *n*, battlement
kantelen, to topple over; to tilt
kanten, (made of) lace
  zich kanten tegen, to oppose
kan'tine, canteen
kantklossen *n*, lace-making
kan'tongerecht *n*, district court
kan'toor *n*, office
kan'toorbediende, clerk
kan'toorbehoeften, stationery
ka'nunnik, cannon
kap, cap; hood; bonnet; lamp-shade
ka'pel, chapel; band : butterfly
kape'laan, curate
ka'pelmeester, band-master
kaper, privateer
kaphout *n*, copse
kapi'taal *n*, capital
kapitaal'krachtig, financially strong
kapitali'seren, to capitalize
kapi'teel *n*, capital
kapi'tein, captain
ka'pittel *n*, chapter
kaplaars, top-boot, wellington
kapmantel, (hooded) cloak; toilet cape
ka'pot, broken
ka'pothoed, bonnet
kappen, to cut *or* chop down; to dress hair
kapper, hairdresser
kapseizen, to capsize
kapsel *n*, coiffure
kapstok, hall-stand, hat-rack
kaptafel, dressing table
kar, cart

ka'raat *n*, carat
kara'bijn, carbine
ka'raf, carafe, decanter
ka'rakter *n*, character
karakteri'seren, to characterize
karakteris'tiek, characteristic
kara'vaan, caravan
kar'bies, shopping-basket
karbo'nade, chop
kar'bouw, buffalo
kardi'naal, cardinal
karig, parsimonious; sparing, scanty
kar'mijn (*n*), carmine
karmo'zijn (*n*), crimson
karn(ton), churn
karnemelk, buttermilk
karnen, to churn
ka'ronje *n*, shrew
ka'ros, state-coach
karper, carp
kar'pet *n*, carpet
karrepaard *n*, cart-horse
karrespoor *n*, (wheel-)rut
kartelen, to notch, to mill
kar'tets, round of grape-shot
kar'ton *n*, cardboard; carton
kar'wats, riding-whip
kar'wei *n*, job (of work)
kar'wijzaad *n*, caraway-seed
kas, socket; greenhouse; cash (-desk); (watch-)case
  goed bij kas, in funds
kassa, pay-desk, box-office; till
kas'sier, cashier
kast, cupboard; case; quod
kas'tanje, chestnut
kaste, caste
kas'teel *n*, castle
kaste'lein, publican
kas'tijden, chastise
kastje *n*, locker
  van het kastje naar de muur, from pillar to post
kastpapier *n*, lining paper
kat, cat
  de kat uit de boom kijken, to play a waiting game
  als een kat in een vreemd pakhuis, like a fish out of water
  een kat in de zak kopen, to buy a pig in a poke
kater, tom-cat; hang-over

kathe'draal, cathedral
katje *n,* kitten; catkin
ka'toen, cotton; *n,* wick
ka'toenspinnerij, cotton-mill
ka'trol, pulley
kattebak, cat's box; dickey seat
kattebelletje *n,* scribbled note
kattekwaad *n,* mischief
katterig, chippy
katzwijm, feigned swoon
kauw, jackdaw
kauwen, to chew
kauwgom *n,* chewing gum
kavalje *n,* shack; jade
kavelen, to parcel out
kaze'mat, casemate
ka'zerne, barracks
ka'zernewoning, tenement dwelling
ka'zuifel, chasuble
keel, throat
  het hangt me de keel uit, I'm sick and tired of it
keelklep, epiglottis
keelpijn, a sore throat
keer, turn; time(s)
  een doodenkele keer, once in a blue moon
  te keer gaan, to storm
keerdam, weir
keerkringen, tropics
keerpunt *n,* turning point
keerzijde, reverse side
keet, shed, hut; shindy
keffen, to yap
kegel, cone; skittle
kegelen, to play skittles
kei, boulder, cobble-stone, set; " wizard "
keilen, to fling; to play ducks and drakes
keizer, emperor
keize'rin, empress
keizerlijk, imperial
keizerrijk *n,* empire
keizersnede, cæsarian
kelder, cellar, vault
kelderen, to go to the bottom; to slump
kelen, to cut the throat of
kelk, chalice; calyx
kelner, waiter
kemelsgaren *n,* mohair

kemphaan, fighting-cock
kenau, amazon
kenbaar, distinguishable
  kenbaar maken, to make known
kenmerk *n,* characteristic
kenmerken, to characterize
kennelijk, apparent, clear
kennen, to know
  te kennen geven, to intimate
  men heeft mij er niet in gekend, I was not consulted
kenner, connoisseur
kennis, knowledge; acquaintance
  kennis geven van, to announce
  buiten kennis, unconscious
kennisgeving, notification
kenschetsen, to characterize
kenteken *n,* distinguishing mark
kenteren, to turn
keper, twill
  op de keper beschouwd, on close inspection; when all is said and done
kerel, fellow
keren, to turn, to stem
kerf, notch
kerfstok, tally-stick
  hij heeft veel op zijn kerfstok, he has a lot to answer for
kerk, church
kerkbank, pew
kerkdienst, (divine) service
kerkelijk, ecclesiastical; church (-going)
kerker, dungeon
kerkgang, church attendance
kerkhof *n,* churchyard
kerks(ge'zind), churchy
kermen, to moan
kermis, fair
kermiswagen, caravan
kern, kernel, core; crux, gist
kernachtig, pithy
kerngezond, fit as a fiddle
kerrie, curry
kers, cherry
Kerstavond, Christmas Eve
Kerstdag, Christmas Day
  tweede Kerstdag, Boxing Day
Kerstenen, to Christianize
Kerstfeest, Kerstmis, Christmas
kersvers, quite fresh

kervel: dolle —, hemlock
 wilde kervel, sheep's parsley
kerven, to carve, to notch, to cut
ketel, kettle, boiler
ketellapper, tinker
ketelsteen, scale, fur
keten(en), (to) chain
ketsen, to misfire
ketter, heretic
ketteren, to swear, to rage
kette'rij, heresy
ketting, chain; necklace
keu, (billiard) cue
keuken, kitchen; cuisine
keukenfornuis n, kitchen-range
keukengerei n, kitchen utensils
keur, choice; pick; hall-mark
keuren, to examine; to inspect;
 to sample
keurig, trim, very nice
keuring, medical examination;
 inspection
keurkorps n, picked body of men
keurs(lijf n), bodice
keurvorst(endom n), elector(ate)
keus, choice
keutels, droppings
keuterboer, crofter
keuvelen, to chat(ter)
kever, beetle
kibbelen, to squabble
kiek(je n), snapshot
kieken, to take a snap of
kiektoestel n, camera
kiel, blouse, smock; keel
kielzog n, wake
kiem, germ; seed
kiemen, to germinate
kienen, to play lotto
kier, chink
 op een kier, ajar
kies, molar: delicate
kiesbaar, eligible
kiesdistrict n, constituency
kieskauwen, to munch
kies'keurig, fastidious
kieskring, poling district
kiespijn, toothache
kiesrecht n, franchise
kietelen, to tickle
kieuw, gill
kievit, lapwing
kievitsei n, plover's egg

kiezel n, gravel, shingle; silicon
kiezelsteen, pebble
kiezen, to choose; to elect
kiezerslijst, electoral roll
kijf: buiten —, beyond dispute
kijk, view, outlook, idea; prospect
kijken, to (have a) look
kijker, telescope, binoculars;
 viewer
kijkgat n, peep-hole
kijven, to quarrel
kik: hij gaf geen —, he did not
 utter a sound
kikken: je hebt maar te —,
 you've only to say the word
kikker, frog; cleat
kikvors, frog
kil, chilly
kilo n, kilogram (2·205 lb)
kim, horizon
kin, chin
kina, quinine
kind n, child
kinderachtig, childish
kinderbed n, cot
kinderbewaarplaats, crèche
kinderjuffrouw, nurse-maid,
 nannie
kinderkamer, nursery
kinderlijk, childlike
kinderloos, childless
kindersterfte, infant mortality
kinderverlamming, infantile
 paralysis
kinderwagen, pram
kinds, infantine
kindsbeen: van — af, ever since
 childhood
ki'nine, quinine
kink, kink
 een kink in de kabel, a hitch
kinkel, lout
kinkhoest, whooping-cough
kinnebak, jaw-bone
kip, chicken, hen
kipkar, tip-cart
kiplekker, as right as rain
kippeborst, pidgeon-chest
kippegaas n, wire-netting
kippenfokkerij, poultry farm
 (-ing)
kippenhok n, hen-house

kippekuur, whim
kippevel *n*, goose-flesh
kippig, short-sighted
kirren, to coo
kist, (packing-)case, chest; coffin
kit, coal-hod
kitte'lorig, touchy
kittig, spruce; spry
klaaglied *n*, lamentation, dirge
klaaglijk, plaintive
klaar, clear; ready, finished
  klare wijn schenken, to make
  one's meaning clear
  klaar wakker, wide awake
klaar'blijkelijk, evident
klaarheid, clarity
klaarkomen, to get ready, to
  (get) finish(ed)
klaarlichte dag, broad daylight
klaarspelen: het —, to manage it
klacht, complaint
klad, blot; *n* rough draft
  **iemand bij de kladden pak-
  ken,** to grab hold of a person
kladden, to daub, to scrawl
kladpapier *n*, scribbling paper
kladschilderen, to daub
kladwerk *n*, badly written work;
  daub
klagen, to lament
  het is God geklaagd, it cries
  out to heaven
klakkeloos, groundless, off-hand,
  rash
klam, clammy
klamboe, mosquito-net
klamp(en), (to) clamp
klan'dizie, custom(ers)
klank, sound
klankleer, phonetics
klankloos, toneless
klanknabootsend, onomatopœic
klankrijk, klankvol, sonorous
klant, customer, client
klap, blow, smack, crack
klapbes, gooseberry
klapbus, pop-gun
klaplopen, to cadge
klaploper, sponger
klappen: in de handen —, to
  clap
  met een zweep klappen, to
  crack a whip

klapper, index: coco-nut
**klappertanden: hij klapper-
  tandde,** his teeth were chatter-
  ing
klaproos, poppy
klapstoel, tip-up seat, folding
  chair
klapwieken, to flap the wings
klapzoen, loud kiss
klas, klasse, class(-room), form
klassenstrijd, class-war
klas'siek, classic(al)
klateren, to splatter, to cascade
klatergoud *n*, tinsel
klauteren, to clamber
klauw, claw, talon
klauwzeer *n*, foot-rot
klave'cimbel, harpsichord
klaver, clover.
klaver'aas *n*, ace of clubs
kla'vier *n*, keyboard
kleden, to dress; to clothe
klederdracht, local costume
kle'dij, kleding, clothes, attire
kledingstuk *n*, garment
kleed *n*, carpet; cloth; gown
kleedgeld *n*, dress allowance
kleedje *n*, rug, (table-)cloth
kleedkamer, dressing-room,
  changing-room
kleefpleister *n*, adhesive plaster
kleerborstel, clothes-brush
kleermaker, tailor
klef, sticky, soggy
klei, clay
kleimasker *n*, mud-pack
klein, little, small
  klein geld, small change
  de kleine vaart, inland *or* coast-
  al navigation
klein'burgerlijk, bourgeois
kleindochter, granddaughter
klei'neren, to belittle
klei'nering, disparagement
klein'geestig, narrow-minded
kleinge'lovig, of little faith
kleinhandel, retail trade
kleinigheid, trifle
kleinkind *n*, grandchild
kleinkrijgen, to break (a person)
klei'nood *n*, trinket
klein'steeds, provincial

kleintje *n*, baby, little one
  op de kleintjes passen, to take care of the pence
klein'zerig, easily hurt, soft
klein'zielig, petty(-minded)
kleinzoon, grandson
klem, trap; clip; emphasis
klemmen, to pinch, to clench
  een klemmend betoog *n*, a convincing argument
klemtoon, stress
klep, valve; flap; peak
klepel, clapper
kleppen, to clang, to clatter
klepperen, to rattle, to bang to and fro
kleren, clothes
klerenkast, wardrobe
klerk, clerk
klets, smack; twaddle
kletsen, to chatter; to talk rubbish
kletskop, brandy-snap; scald-head
kletskous, gossip, chatter-box
kletteren, to clatter, to patter
kleur, colour; suit (cards)
  kleur bekennen, to follow suit; to show one's colours
kleurecht, fast (dyed)
kleuren, to colour; to blush
kleurenpracht, blaze of colour
kleurling, coloured person
kleurloos, colourless
kleurstof, colouring matter
kleuter, toddler
kleven, to cleave, to stick
kleverig, sticky
kliederen, to make a mess
kliek, clique
kliekjes *n*, scraps, left-overs
klier, gland; dirty rotter
klieven, to cleave
klif *n*, cliff
klikspaan, tell-tale
kli'maat *n*, climate
klimato'logisch, climatic
klimmen, to climb
  bij het klimmen der jaren, with advancing years
klimop, ivy
kling, blade (of a sword)
klingelen, to tinkle

kli'niek, clinic
klink, latch
klinkbout, rivet
klinken, to sound, to ring (out); to clink glasses: to rivet
klinker, vowel: riveter: clinker
klinkklaar, utter, pure
klinknagel, rivet
klip, rock, reef
  blinde klip, sunken rock
klis, **klit**, burr, burdock; tangle
klodder(en), (to) clot; (to) daub
kloek, brave; stout; substantial: mother hen
klok, clock; bell
  alles wat de klok slaat, all one hears about
klokhuis *n*, core
klokkenspel *n*, carillon, chimes
klokluider, bell-ringer
klokrok, flared skirt
klokslag, stroke (of the clock)
klomp, clog; lump; nugget
klompvoet, club-foot
klont(er), lump, clod, clot
klonteren, to clot
klonterig, lumpy
kloof, cleft, crevice; rift
klooster *n*, monastery, convent
klop, knock, throb
klopjacht, beat(-up)
kloppen, to knock, to tap, to beat; to tally
  dat klopt als een bus, that tallies all along the line
klos, bobbin, reel; coil
klossen, to clump
klotsen, to dash
kloven, to cleave, to split
klucht, farce
kluchtig, funny
kluif, knuckle of pork; (meaty) bone
  een hele kluif, quite a job
kluis, hermitage; strong-room
kluisters, shackles
kluisteren, to fetter
kluit, clod, lump
  flink uit de kluiten gewassen, strapping
kluiven, to gnaw a bone
kluiver, jib
kluizenaar, hermit

klungel, (piece of) trash; bungler

klungelen, to tinker; to bungle

kluts : de — kwijtraken, to lose one's head

klutsen, to whisk

kluwen *n,* ball (of wool *etc.*)

knaagdier *n,* rodent

knaap, boy; coat-hanger

knabbelen, to nibble

knagen, to gnaw

knakken, to snap, to break

knakworst, Frankfurt sausage

knal, report, bang

knallen, to bang, to ring out

knalpatroon, detonator

knalpot, silencer

knap, handsome, pretty; clever; neat

knappen, to snap; to crackle
  een uiltje knappen, to take forty winks

knarsen, to grate; to crunch

knarsetanden, to gnash one's teeth

knauwen, to gnaw, to munch; to damage *or* hurt seriously

knecht, (man-)servant

knechten, to enslave

kneden, to knead; to mould

kneedbaar, malleable

kneep, pinch; dodge

knel : in de — zitten, to be in a fix

knellen, to pinch

knetteren, to crackle

kneukel, knuckle

kneuzen, to bruise

kneuzing, bruise

knevel, big moustache

knevela'rij, extortion

knevelen, to gag, to pinion

knibbelen, to haggle

knie, knee
  onder de knie krijgen, to master

kniebroek, knickerbockers

kniebuiging, genuflexion; curtsey

knielbank, kneeler

knielen, to kneel

knieschijf, knee-cap

kniesoor, mope

kniezen, to mope

knijpen, to pinch
  ik knijp 'm, I've got the wind up

knikkebollen, to nod (with sleep)

knikken, to nod

knikker, marble

knip, snip; trap; catch, clasp

knipogen, to wink; to blink

knippen, to cut, to clip
  geknipt voor, cut out for

knipperen, to flicker

knipsel *n,* cutting

knobbel, bump

knobbelig, gnarled

knoedel, dumpling; bun (of hair); knot

knoei : in de — zitten, to be in difficulties

knoeiboel, mess; swindle

knoeien, to make a mess; to bungle

knoeie'rij, corruption; bungling

knoeiwerk *n,* shoddy work

knoest, knot (in wood)

knoet(je *n),* bun (of hair)

knoflook *n,* garlic

knok(kel), knuckle

knokken, to scrap

knol, tuber; turnip; jade
  in zijn knollentuin, as pleased as Punch

knolraap, swede

knoop, knot; button; node

knooppunt *n,* junction

knoopsgat *n,* button-hole

knop, bud; knob

knopje *n,* (push-)button, switch

knopen, to tie, to knot
  iets in zijn oor knopen, to make a mental note of something

knorren, to grunt; to grumble

knorrig, peevish

knot, skein

knots, club

knotten, to pollard

knuffelen, to cuddle

knuist, fist

knul, duffer; fellow

knuppel, cudgel

knus(jes), snug

knutselen, to make things (for a hobby)

koddig, droll

koe, cow

  oude koeien uit de sloot halen, to rake up old stories

koeio'neren, to badger

koek, gingerbread

koeke'loeren, to stare inquisitively

koekepan, frying-pan

koekje n, sweet biscuit

koekoek, cuckoo; dormer window, skylight

koel, cool

koel'bloedig, cool-headed

koelen, to cool (down)

  zijn woede koelen, to vent one's anger

koelhuis n, cold storage

koelinrichting, refrigerating plant

koelte, cool(ness)

koeltje n, cool breeze

koen, bold

koepaard n, piebald horse

koepel, dome; summer-house

koepeldak n, domed roof

koe'rier, courier

koers, course; price (of stocks); rate of exchange

koesteren, to cherish

  zich koesteren, to bask

koeter'waals n, double Dutch

koetjes en kalfjes, trifling matters

koets, coach

koet'sier, coachman

koevoet, crow-bar

koffer, suit-case

koffergrammofoon, portable gramophone

koffie, coffee

koffiedik n, coffee-grounds

koffiedrinken, to have lunch (i.e. coffee and a bread meal)

kogel, bullet; ball

kogelbaan, trajectory

kogellager n, ball-bearing

kok, cook

ko'karde, cockade

koken, to cook; to boil

koker, (long) case

kokette'rie, flirtation

kokhalzen, to retch

kokosmat, coconut mat(ting)

kokosnoot, coconut

kolbak, busby

kolder, staggers; tomfoolery

kolen, coal(s)

  op hete kolen, on tenterhooks

kolenbak, coal-scuttle

kolendamp, carbon monoxide

kolenhok n, coal-shed

kolf, (rifle-)butt; retort

koli'brie, humming-bird

ko'liek n, colic

kolk, whirlpool; (lock-)chamber

kologen, goggle-eyes

ko'lom, column

koloni'aal, colonial (soldier)

koloni'ale waren, groceries

ko'lonie, colony

kolos'saal, colossal

kom, basin, bowl; the populous part, centre

kom'aan! come along!

kom'af, descent, birth

kom'buis, galley

komedi'ant, play-actor, comedian

ko'medie, play; theatre; comedy

ko'meet, comet

komen, to come

  hoe komt dat? how did that happen?

kom'foor n, chafing dish; gas-ring, heater

ko'miek, comical: low comedian

komisch, comic(al)

kom'kommer, cucumber

komma, comma, (decimal) point

komma'punt, semi-colon

kommer, sorrow, distress

kommerlijk, **kommervol,** wretched

kom'pas n, compass

kom'pashuisje n, binnacle

kom'plot n, plot

komst, coming

  op komst, on the way

kond doen, to notify

ko'nijn n, rabbit

koning, king

koning'in, queen

koningschap n, kingship

koningsgezind, royalist

koningsmoord, regicide
koninklijk, royal, regal
koninkrijk *n,* kingdom
konkelen, to scheme
kon'vooi *n,* convoy
kooi, cage, pen ; bunk
kook, boil
kookboek *n,* cookery book
kool, cabbage: coal(s) ; carbon
  iemand een kool stoven, to
  play a trick on someone
koolhydraat *n,* carbohydrate
koolmees, titmouse
koolzaad *n,* rape-seed
koolzuur *n,* carbonic acid
koon, cheek
koop, purchase
  te koop, for sale
  te koop lopen met, to show
  off
  op de koop toe, into the bargain
koopacte, title-deed
koophandel, commerce
koopje *n,* bargain
koopkracht, purchasing power
koopman, merchant
koopvaar'dij, merchant service
koopvaar'dijschip *n,* merchant-
  ship
koopwaar, merchandise
koor *n,* choir, chorus ; chancel
koorbank, choir-stall
koord *n,* cord ; flex
koorddansen *n,* tight-rope walking
koorhemd *n,* surplice
koorts, fever
  koorts hebben, to have a temperature
koorts(acht)ig, feverish
kootje *n,* phalanx
kop, head ; large cup ; bowl (of a
  pipe)
  de kop indrukken, to nip in the
  bud
  op de kop tikken, to pick up, to
  find (a bargain)
  op de kop af, precisely
kopen, to buy
koper, purchaser: *n,* copper,
  brass
kopergroen *n,* verdigris
koperslager, coppersmith

kopervijlsel *n,* brass-filings
ko'pie, copy
kopi'ëren, to copy
ko'pijrecht *n,* copyright
kopje *n,* (tea-)cup
  kopje duikelen, to turn somer-
  saults
koplamp, head-light
koppel, belt ; leash: *n,* couple,
  brace
koppelaar, match-maker
koppela'rij, procuration
koppelen, to couple, to join
koppeling, coupling ; clutch
koppelteken *n,* hyphen
koppelwerkwoord *n,* copula
koppensnellen *n,* head-hunting
koppig, obstinate
koppigheid, obstinacy
kopstuk *n,* leading light
kopzorg, worry
ko'raal *n,* choral(e): coral
kor'daat, resolute
koren *n,* corn
korenschuur, granary
korf, basket ; hive
korfbal, basket-ball
korhoen *n,* black grouse
kor'nuit, crony
korrel, grain ; pellet ; foresight
korrelig, granular
korst, crust, rind ; scab
korstdeeg *n,* short pastry
korstmos *n,* lichen
kort, short, brief
  kort en bondig, terse
  kort maar krachtig, short and
  snappy
kor'tademig, short of breath
kor'taf, curt
kortelings, recently
korten, to deduct ; to while
  away
kortheids'halve, for the sake of
  brevity
korting, discount, deduction
kor'tom, in short
kortsluiting, short circuit
kort'stondig, short-lived
kortweg, without wasting words
kortwieken, to clip the wings of
kort'zichtig, short-sighted
korzelig, grumpy

kost, food; living; board
  kost en inwoning, board and lodging
kostbaar, expensive; precious
kostbaarheden, valuables
kostbaas, landlord
kostelijk, superb; priceless
kosteloos, (cost-)free
kosten, expense(s), cost, charges: to cost
koster, verger
kostganger, boarder
kostgeld n, board
kostschool, boarding-school
kostwinner, bread-winner
kot n, sty
kotsen, to puke
kotter, cutter
kou(de), cold
  kou vatten, to catch cold
koud, cold
koud'vuur n, gangrene
koukleum, chilly person
kous, stocking
  met de kous op de kop, with a flea in one's ear
kouseband, garter
kousje n, (incandescent) mantle
kout, chat
kouwelijk, sensitive to cold
ko'zijn n, window-sill, window-frame
kraag, collar, ruff
kraai(en), (to) crow
kraakbeen n, cartilage
kraakstem, grating voice
kraakzindelijk, spotlessly clean
kraal, bead
kraam, booth, stall
kraambed n, childbed
kraamheer, father of the (new-born) child
kraaminrichting, maternity home
kraamvrouw, woman in childbed
kraan, tap; crane, derrick: dab(-hand)
kraanwagen, break-down truck
krab, crab
krabbel(en), (to) scratch, (to) scrawl
krabben, to scratch

kracht, force, strength, power
  volle kracht vooruit, full speed ahead
  op krachten komen, to regain strength
kracht'dadig, vigorous
krachteloos, powerless
krachtens, by virtue of
krachtig, powerful
krachtprestatie, feat (of strength); (power) output
krachtsinspanning, exertion
kra'kelen, to quarrel
kraken, to crack; to creak; to crunch
kram, staple
kramer, pedlar
krammen, to cramp, to rivet
kramp, cramp; spasm
kram'pachtig, desperate; taut
kranig, smart; brave; brilliant
krank, sick, ill
krank'zinnig, insane
krank'zinnigengesticht n, lunatic asylum
krans, wreath
krant, newspaper
krap, tight; short of money
kras, scratch; strong (for one's age)
  dat is kras! that's a bit thick!
krassen, to scratch; to screech
krat, crate
krater, crater
krauwen, to scratch
kreeft, lobster
kreek, creek
kreet, cry, scream
kregel, peevish
kreng n, carrion; rotter, bitch
krenken, to offend
krent, currant; skinflint
krenterig, niggardly
kreuk(el)(en), (to) crease
kreunen, to groan
kreupel, lame
kreupelhout n, thicket
krib(be), manger, crib
kribbebijter, cross-patch
kribbig, testy
kriebelen, to itch, to tickle; to write a niggling hand
kriebelig, nettled

kriek, black cherry
krieken : bij het — van de dag, at the crack of dawn
krielkip, bantam
krijg, war
krijgen, to get
te pakken krijgen, to get hold of
krijger, warrior
krijgertje n, tig
krijgsgevangene, prisoner of war
krijgs'haftig, warlike
krijgs'haftigheid, valour
krijgslist, stratagem
krijgsman, warrior
krijgsraad, council of war; court-martial
krijgstocht, campaign
krijgsvolk n, soldiers
krijgs'zuchtig, bellicose
krijsen, to screech
krijt n, chalk: lists
krijten, to cry
krijtrots, chalk cliff
krimp geven, to yield
krimpen, to shrink; to back
krimpvrij, unshrinkable
kring, circle
kringloop, cycle
kri'oelen, to swarm
krip n, crape
kris'tal n, crystal
kri'tiek, criticism; review: critical
kritisch, critical
kriti'seren, to criticize
kroeg, pub
kroegbaas, publican
kroep, croup
kroes, mug, crucible: frizzy
krols, on heat
krom, crooked, bent, curved
je lacht je krom, it's a perfect scream
kromliggen, to pinch and scrape
kromming, bend, curve
kromtrekken, to warp
kronen, to crown
kro'niek, chronicle
kroning, coronation, crowning
kronkel, twist, kink
kronkelen, to twist, to wind

kronkelig, winding
kronkeling, convolution
kroon, crown; corolla, chandelier
dat spant de kroon, that crowns everything
kroonlijst, cornice
kroos n, duckweed
kroost n, progeny
kroot, beetroot
krop, gizzard
kropgezwel n, goitre
kropsla, cabbage lettuce
krot n, hovel
kruid n, herb
kruiden, to season
kruide'nier, grocer
kruide'rijen, spices
kruidnagel, clove
kruien, to wheel (in a barrow); to break up, to drift (of ice)
kruier, (luggage-)porter
kruik, stone bottle; hot-water bottle
kruim(el) n, crumb
kruimelig, crumbly
kruin, crown, top
kruipen, to creep; to crawl; to cringe
kruiperig, cringing
kruis n, cross; sharp (in music); croup, crupper, crutch; seat
kruis of munt, heads or tails
kruisbeeld n, crucifix
kruisbes, gooseberry
kruiselings, crosswise
kruisen, to cross; to cruise
kruiser, cruiser
kruisgang, cloister
kruisigen, to crucify
kruiskoppeling, universal joint
kruispunt n, point of intersection, cross-roads
kruistocht, kruisvaart, crusade
kruit n, (gun-)powder
kruiwagen, (wheel)barrow; influential friend
kruk, crutch; door-handle; crank; stool
krul, curl; scroll
krullebol, curly-head
krullenjongen, carpenter's apprentice
kubiek, cubic

kubus, cube
kuch, dry cough
kuchen, to give a slight cough
kudde, herd, flock
kuieren, to stroll
kuif, quif, crest
kuiken n, chicken
kuil, pit, (pot-)hole
kuiltje n, dimple
kuip, tub
kuipen, to cooper; to intrigue
kuipe'rij, machinations
kuis, chaste
kuisheid, chastity
kuit, calf (of the leg); spawn; roe
kuitschieten, to spawn
kuitbroek, knee-breeches
kul : flauwe —, poppycock
kundig, able; knowledgeable
   ter zake kundig, expert
kundigheden, accomplishments
kunne, sex
kunnen, to be able to, may
   dat kan (wel), that is (quite) possible, maybe
kunst, art; trick
   daar is geen kunst aan, there's nothing to it
kunst-, artificial; art
kunsteloos, artless
kunstenaar, artist
kunstig, ingenious
kunstkenner, connoisseur
kunst'matig, artificial
kunst'nijverheid, applied art
kunstrijden n, figure-skating
kunststuk n, masterpiece
kunst'vaardig, skilful
kunst'zinnig, artistic
ku'ras n, cuirass
kurk(en), (to) cork
kurketrekker, corkscrew
kus, kiss
kushandjes geven, to blow kisses
kussen, to kiss: n, pillow, cushion
kussensloop n, pillow-case
kust, coast, shore
   te kust en te keur, in plenty
kustvaart, coastwise trade
kuur, whim; cure

kwaad, bad; angry
   kwaad geweten, guilty conscience
   het te kwaad krijgen, to break down
kwaad n, evil; harm
kwaa'daardig, malicious
kwaad'denkend, suspicious
kwaadschiks, with an ill grace
kwaadspreke'rij, scandal
kwaad'willig, malevolent
kwaal, complaint, ailment
kwabbig, flabby
kwa'draat n, square
kwa'jongen, (young) rascal
kwa'jongensachtig, mischievous
kwak, thud; blob
kwaken, to quack; to croak
kwakkelen, to have poor health
kwakkelwinter, mild winter
kwakzalver, quack
kwal, jelly-fish; rotter
kwalifi'ceren, to describe
kwalijk nemen, to take ill
   neem me niet kwalijk, I am sorry
kwanselen, to swop
kwan'suis, for form's sake
kwant, young fellow
kwanti'teit, quantity
kwart, fourth: n quarter
kwar'taal n, quarter, term
kwar'taalsgewijze, quarterly
kwartel, quail
kwar'tier n, quarter of an hour; quarter(s)
kwar'tiermuts, forage-cap
kwartje n, 25 cent-piece
kwartjesvinder, confidence trickster
kwartnoot, crotchet
kwarts n, quartz
kwast, brush, tassel: knot (in wood): coxcomb: lemon-squash
kwasterig, foppish
kwebbel, chatterbox
kwebbelen, to chatter
kweek(school), training-college
kwee(peer), quince
kwekeling, student teacher
kweken, to grow; to foster
kweker, nurseryman

kweke'rij, nursery
kwekken, to yap; to chatter
kwelen, to warble
kwellen, to torment
kwelling, torment
kwestie, question
kwets, purple plum
kwetsbaar, vulnerable
kwetsen, to wound, to injure
kwet'suur, wound
kwetteren, to twitter
kwezel, pietist
kwibus: een rare —, a queer cove
kwiek, spry
kwijlen, to dribble
kwijnen, to languish
kwijt zijn, to have lost
kwijtraken, to lose
kwijten: zich — van, to discharge
kwijtschelden, to remit, to forgive
kwik n, mercury
kwinke'leren, to warble
kwinkslag, witticism
kwispedoor, spittoon
kwispel(staart)en, to wag the tail
kwistig, lavish
kwi'tantie, receipt
kwi'teren, to receipt

L

la(de), drawer, till
laadboom, derrick
laadvermogen n, loading capacity
laag, layer, stratum: low (-pitched)
 hij gaf me de volle laag, he let me have it
 lager onderwijs, primary education
laag-bij-de-'gronds, crude
laag'hartig, base
laagte, low level, dip
laag'veen n, peat-bog
laagvlakte, plain
laag'water n, low tide
laaie: in lichte —, ablaze
laaien, to blaze
laakbaar, blameworthy

laan, avenue
laantje n, path, lane
laars, boot
 dat lap ik aan mijn laars, I couldn't care less
laat, late
laat'dunkend, arrogant
laatst, last, latest; recently
laatstgenoemde, latter
la'biel, unstable
labora'torium n, laboratory
lach(en), (to) laugh
lachlust: de — opwekken, to raise a laugh
lachspiegel, distorting mirror
lach'wekkend, laughable
la'cune, gap
ladder, ladder
laden, to load, to charge
ladenkast, chest of drawers
lading, load, cargo; charge
laf, cowardly
lafaard, lafbek, coward
lafenis, refreshment
laf'hartig, cowardly
lafheid, cowardice
lager, bearing(s)
Lagerhuis, Lower House, House of Commons
la'gune, lagoon
lak n, sealing-wax; lacquer
 ik heb er lak aan, a fat lot I care
la'kei, footman
laken, to blame: n, cloth, sheet
 de lakens uitdelen, to rule the roost
 hij kreeg van hetzelfde laken een pak, he was treated in just the same way
lakken, to lacquer; to seal
lakmoes n, litmus
laks(heid), lax(ity)
lakschoen, patent leather shoe
lam, paralysed; nasty: n, lamb
lambri'zering, wainscot(ting)
lam'lendig, wretched; indolent
lammeling, wretch
lamp, lamp, bulb, valve
 tegen de lamp lopen, to get into trouble
lam'petkan, ewer
lampi'on, Chinese lantern

lamstraal, wretch
lan'ceren, to launch
land *n*, land, country, field
 ik heb er het land aan, I hate it
 aan land gaan, to go ashore
landarbeider, agricultural labourer
landbouw(kunde), agriculture
landbouw'kundige, agricultural-
 ist
landelijk, rural; nation-wide
landen, to land
landengte, isthmus
landerig, in the dumps
lande'rijen, landed property
landgenoot, compatriot
landgoed *n*, estate
landheer, landowner
landingsgestel *n*, undercarriage
landkaart, map
landleger *n*, land forces
landloper, tramp
landmeter, surveyor
landschap *n*, landscape
**landsman: wat is hij voor een
 — ?** What nationality is he?
landstaal, vernacular
landstreek, region
landsvrouwe, sovereign lady
landverhuizer, emigrant
landverraad *n*, high treason
landvoogd, governor
lang, long, tall
 lang van stof, long-winded
 lang niet, not nearly
lang'dradig, long-winded
lang'durig, lengthy
langge'rekt, protracted
langs, along, past
 langs elkaar heen praten, to
 talk at cross purposes
lang'uit, at full length
lang'werpig, oblong, elongated
langzaam, slow
langzamerhand, gradually
lank'moedig(heid), long-suffering
lans, lance
lan'taarn, lan'taren, lantern;
 skylight; lamp
lan'taarnpaal, lamp-post
lan'taarnplaatje *n*, lantern-slide
lanterfanten, to loaf

lap, piece (of cloth), rag; patch;
 steak
lapmiddel *n*, makeshift
lappen, to patch; to wipe; to
 manage
lappendeken, patchwork quilt
lappenmand, work basket
 in de lappenmand, under the
 weather
lapwerk *n*, patchwork
larie, stuff and nonsense
larve, larva
las, joint, weld
lassen, to weld
last, load, burden; instruction(s);
 trouble
lastbrief, mandate
laster(en), (to) slander
lasterlijk, slanderous
lastgever, principal
lastig, difficult, tiresome
 lastig vallen, to trouble
lastpost, nuisance
lat, lath, slat
laten, to let; to leave (off)
 ik kan het niet laten, I can't
 help it
 iets laten doen, to have something done
later, afterwards, later
La'tijn(s) (*n*), Latin
latwerk *n*, trellis
lau'rier, laurel
lauw, tepid
lauweren, laurels
lave'ment *n*, enema
laven, to refresh
la'vendel, lavender
la'veren, to tack
la'waai *n*, din
la'wine, avalanche
la'xeermiddel *n*, laxative
la'xeren, to purge
lebberen, to lap, to sip
lector, university lecturer
lec'tuur, reading (matter)
ledematen, limbs
leden, limbs; members
ledepop, dummy
leder *n*, leather
ledig, empty
ledi'kant *n*, bed(stead)
leed *n*, sorrow

leedvermaak n, pleasure at other people's misfortune
leedwezen n, regret
leefregel, regimen
leeftijd, age
op leeftijd, elderly
leeftijdsgrens, age-limit
leeftocht, provisions
leefwijze, manner of living
leeg(gieten), (to) empty
leegloper, idler
leegte, emptiness
leek, layman
leem n, loam
leemte, gap, hiatus
leen n, fief, loan
leenheer, liege lord
leenman, vassal
leenstelsel n, feudal system
leep, cunning
leer, doctrine: ladder: n, leather
in de leer bij, apprenticed to
leerboek n, text book
leergang, course of study
leergeld n: ik heb — betaald, I have learnt my lesson
leer'gierig, studious
leerjaar n, year's school-work
leerjongen, apprentice
leerkracht, teacher
leerling, pupil
leerlooien, to tan
leerlooie'rij, tannery
leermeester, teacher
leerplan n, curriculum
leerrijk, instructive
leerstelling, tenet
leerstoel, chair
leerzaam, instructive; teachable
leesbaar, readable, legible
leeskabinet n, reading-room
leest, last
leesteken n, punctuation mark
leeuw('in), lion(ess)
leeuwerik, (sky)lark
lef n, pluck; swank
le'gaat n, legacy
le'gatie, legation
le'gende, legend
leger n, army
Leger des Heils, Salvation Army

legeren, to encamp
le'gering, alloy
legerstede, couch
leges, legal dues
leggen, to lay, to put
legio, legion
legi'oen n, legion, army
legiti'matiebewijs n, identification paper
legkaart, jig-saw puzzle
lei, slate
leiband, apron strings
leiboom, espalier
leiden, to lead
leider, leader
leiding, guidance, direction, lead; pipe(-line)
leidsel(s) n, reins
leidsman, mentor, guide
leien: alles ging van een — dakje, everything went smoothly
lek (n), leak(y)
een lekke band, a puncture
lekken, to leak
lekker, nice
ik ben niet lekker, I am not very well
iemand lekker maken, to rouse a person's expectations
dank je lekker! thanks for nothing!
lekkerbek, gourmet
lekker'nij, delicacy
lel, lobe: slut
lelie, lily
lelijk, ugly; badly
dat treft lelijk, that's awkward
lemmer n, **lemmet** n, blade
lende, small of the back, loin
lendenen, loins
lenen, to lend; to borrow
lengte, length, height; longitude
lenig, supple, lithe
lenigen, to alleviate
lening, loan
lenspomp, bilge pump
lente, spring
lepel, spoon, ladle
leperd, shrewd fellow
leraar, school-master
lera'res, school-mistress

leren, (made of) leather: to teach; to learn
de tijd zal het leren, time will tell
lering, instruction
les, lesson
lesgeld *n,* tuition fee
lesrooster *n,* time-table
lessen, to quench, to slake
lessenaar, desk
leste: ten lange —, at long last
lesvliegtuig *n,* trainer
letsel *n,* injury
letten op, to pay attention to; to look after
let wel ! mark you!
letter, letter, type
letteren, literature
lettergreep, syllable
letterkunde, literature
letterlijk, literal
letterteken *n,* character
letterzetter, compositor
leugen, lie
leugenaar, liar
leugenachtig, mendacious
leuk, nice, cute, amusing
leukerd, fine one
leukweg, coolly
leunen, to lean
leuning, (hand-)rail; parapet; back, arm(-rest)
leunstoel, armchair
leuren met, to hawk
leus, leuze, slogan, device
voor de leus, for appearance's sake
leut, fun
leuteren, to talk drivel; to loiter
leven, tó live, to be alive
levend, (a)live, living
leven *n,* life; noise
levendig, lively
levenloos, lifeless
levensbehoeften, necessities of life
levensbericht *n,* obituary (notice)
levensbeschouwing, philosophy of life
levensbeschrijving, biography
levensge'vaarlijk, deadly dangerous

levensgroot, life-size(d)
levens'krachtig, vigorous
levenskwestie, matter of life and death
levenslang, lifelong
levenslust, *joie de vivre*
levensmiddelen *n,* provisions
levensmoe(de), weary of life
levensonderhoud *n,* subsistence
levensopvatting, outlook (on life)
levens'vatbaar, viable
levensverzekering, life-insurance
levenswandel, conduct
lever, liver
leveran'cier, purveyor, retailer
leve'rantie, delivery, supply
leveren, to supply, to deliver
levertraan, cod-liver oil
leverworst, liver-sausage
lezen, to read; to gather
lezer('es), reader
lezenaar, lectern
lezing, lecture; version
li'as, file
li'bel, dragon-fly
libe'raal, liberal
lichaam *n,* body
lichaamsbeweging, exercise
lichaamsbouw, physique
li'chamelijk, bodily, physical
licht, light, mild, slight; easily: *n,* light
zijn licht bij iemand opsteken, to ask someone for information
lichtbundel, beam of light
lichtekooi, prostitute
lichtelijk, slightly
lichten, to weigh, to lift
de bus lichten, to collect the mail
lichter, lighter
lichtge'lovig, credulous
lichtge'raakt, touchy
lichtgevend, luminous
lichtgranaat, star-shell
lichting, draft, class, levy; collection (of mail)
lichtkogel, Very light
lichtma'troos, ordinary seaman
lichtmis, libertine: Candlemas

lichtpunt *n*, point of light; lighting point; ray of hope
licht'vaardig, rash, lightly
licht'zinnig, frivolous, flighty
lid *n*, limb, finger-joint; member; sub-section; term
uit het lid, dislocated
lidmaat, member of the Protestant Church
lidmaatschap *n*, membership
lidwoord *n*, article
lied(eren) *n*, song(s)
lieden, people
liederlijk, debauched
zich liederlijk vervelen, to be bored to tears
liedertafel, glee-club; sing-song
liedje *n*, ditty
het is het oude liedje, it's the same old story
lief, dear, sweet, nice
meer dan me lief is, more than I care for
voor lief nemen, to put up with
lief *n* **en leed** *n*, joys and sorrows
lief'dadig, charitable
lief'dadigheid, charity
liefde, love
liefdeloos, loveless
liefderijk, loving
liefdesgechiedenis, romance
liefdesverklaring, proposal
liefdezuster, sister of mercy
liefelijk, charming, sweet
liefhebben, to love
liefhebber, lover, votary
liefhebbe'rij, hobby
liefje *n*, sweetheart
liefkozen, to fondle
liefst, dearest; preferably
lief'tallig, sweet, winsome
liegen, to tell lies
lier, lyre; winch
lies, groin
lieve'heersbeestje, lady-bird
lieveling, darling
liever, rather, sooner
lieverd, darling
lieverlede: van —, gradually
liften, to hitch-hike
lift(koker), lift(-shaft)
liga, league

liggeld *n*, harbour dues
liggen, to lie
waar ligt het aan ? what is the cause of it?
ligging, situation
ligplaats, berth
li'guster, privet
lij(boord), lee(-side)
lijdelijk, passive
lijden, to suffer: *n*, suffering, passion
ik mag hem wel lijden, I rather like him
lijdend voorwerp, direct object
Lijdensweek, Holy Week
lijdzaam, submissive
lijf *n*, body; bodice
het heeft weinig om het lijf, it is of little importance
lijfarts, personal physician
lijfblad *n*, favourite newspaper
lijfeigene, serf
lijfrente, annuity
lijfsbehoud *n*, self-preservation
lijfspreuk, motto
lijk *n*, corpse
lijken (op), to resemble; to seem
lijkenhuis(je) *n*, mortuary
lijkkist, coffin
lijkkleed *n*, pall
lijkkoets, hearse
lijkschouwer, coroner
lijkschouwing, post-mortem
lijkverbranding, cremation
lijm, glue; bird-lime
lijmen, to glue
zich ervoor laten lijmen, to let oneself be talked into it
lijn, line; route
lijnolie, linseed oil
lijnrecht, straight; diametrically
lijntekenen, geometrical drawing
lijntrekken, to slack
lijnwaad *n*, linen
lijnzaad *n*, linseed
lijs, slowcoach
lijst, list; frame
lijster, thrush
lijsterbes, mountain ash
lijvig, corpulent, bulky
lijzig, drawling
lik, lick; swipe
likdoorn, corn

li'keur, liqueur
likkebaarden, to lick one's lips
likken, to lick; to curry favour
lila, lilac(-coloured)
li'miet, limit
limo'nade, (fruit) cordial
linde, lime-tree
lini'aal, ruler
linie, line
  over de hele linie, all round
lini'ëren, to rule
linker-, left
links, (to the) left; left-handed; gauche
  links laten liggen, to cold-shoulder
linksaf, linksom, to the left
linnen n, linen
lint n, ribbon
lintworm, tapeworm
linzen, lentils
lip, lip
lippenstift, lipstick
liqui'deren, to wind up (a business)
lis, flag, iris; loop
lispelen, to lisp
list, ruse
listig, cunning
lite'rair, literary
lite'rator, man of letters
lits ju'meaux, twin beds
litteken n, scar
li'vrei, livery
lob, lobe
lobbes, big good-natured person or animal
locomo'tief, (railway-)engine
lodderig, drowsy
loden, lead(en): to plumb
loeder, swine, bitch
loef, luff
  de loef afsteken, to gain the weather-gage (of); to get the better of
loeien, to low; to roar
loens, cross-eyed
loensen, to squint
loep, magnifying glass
loer: op de — liggen, to lie in wait
  iemand een loer draaien, to play a dirty trick on a person

loeren, to peer; to spy
loeven, to luff
lof, praise: n, Benediction
lofdicht n, panegyric
loffelijk, laudable
lofrede, eulogy
log, unwieldy: log
loge, lodge; (theatre) box
lo'gé(e), guest
lo'geerkamer, spare-room
loge'ment n, inn
logenstraffen, to give the lie to
lo'geren, to stay
logger, drifter, lugger
logica, logic
lo'gies n, accommodation
  logies met ontbijt, bed and breakfast
logisch, logical
lok, lock (of hair)
lo'kaal n, room
lo'kaaltrein, local train
lokaas n, bait
lokduif, stool-pigeon
lo'ket n, counter, booking-office
lokken, to (al)lure
lokmiddel n, lure, bait
lokvogel, decoy
lol, lark, fun
lollig, funny
lommer n, shade; foliage
lommerd, pawn-broker's shop
lommerrijk, shady
lomp, boorish, clumsy
lompen, rags
lomperd, lout
lonen, to (re)pay
long, lung
longontsteking, pneumonia
lonk(en), (to) ogle
lont, fuse
  lont ruiken, to smell a rat
loochenen, to deny
lood n, lead
  lood om oud ijzer, six of one and half a dozen of the other
  uit het lood geslagen, bewildered
  het loodje leggen, to get the worst of it
loodgieter, plumber
loodlijn, perpendicular (line)

lood'recht, perpendicular, ver-
.tical
loods, shed: pilot
loodsen, to pilot
loodswezen n, pilotage
loodwit n, white-lead
loof n, foliage
loog, lye
looien, to tan
looistof, tannin
loom, languid
loon n, wages
loop, gait; course; (gun-)barrel
op de loop gaan, to take to one's
heels
loopbaan, career
loopgraaf, trench
loopjongen, errand-boy
looppas: in de —, at the double
loopplank, gangway
loops, on heat
loopvlak n, (tire-)tread
loor: te — gaan, to be lost
loos, cunning; false
loot, shoot, cutting
lopen, to walk, to go, to run
lopend, running; current
loper, runner; roundsman;
skeleton-key
lor, rag; straw; dud
lor'gnet n, pince-nez
lorrenboel, trash
los, loose, detachable: lynx
er op los, recklessly
losse arbeider, casual labourer
los'bandig, dissolute
losbarsten, to burst out
losbinden, to untie
los'bladig, loose-leaf
losbol, rake
losgeld n, ransom
losjes, loosely
loskopen, to ransom
loslaten, to let go
los'lippig, indiscreet
loslopen, to run free
het zal wel loslopen, it won't be
all that bad
losplaats, discharging-berth
losprijs, ransom
lossen, to discharge, to unload
losstormen op, to rush upon
loszinnig, frivolous

lot n, fate; lottery-ticket
loten, to draw lots
lote'rij, lottery
lotgenoot, partner in adversity
lotgevallen, adventures
loupe, magnifying-glass
louter, pure, sheer
louteren, to purify
loven, to praise
loven en bieden, to haggle
lover n, foliage
lozen, to get rid of; to drain
lucht, air; sky; smell
lucht geven aan, to vent
luchtaanval, air-raid
luchtafweer, anti-aircraft defence
luchtalarm n, air-raid alarm
luchtband, pneumatic tire
luchtdruk, atmospheric pressure
luchten, to air, to vent(ilate)
ik kan hem niet luchten, I
can't abide him
luchter, candelabrum, chandelier
lucht'hartig, light-hearted
luchthaven, air-port
luchtig, airy
luchtkasteel n, castle in the air
luchtkoker, ventilating-shaft
lucht'ledig n, vacuum
luchtmacht, air-force
luchtpijp, windpipe
luchtpost, airmail
luchtstreek, zone, climate
luchtvaart, aviation
luchtverversing, ventilation
lucifer, match
lu'guber, lugubrious
lui, people: lazy
luiaard, sloth
luid, loud
luiden, to ring
de brief luidt als volgt, the
letter reads as follows
luidkeels, at the top of one's
voice
luid'ruchtig, noisy
luidspreker, loud-speaker
luier, nappie
luieren, to laze
luiermand, layette; baby basket
luifel, penthouse, canopy
luiheid, laziness

luik *n*, hatch; trap-door; shutter
luilak, lazy-bones
luilakken, to (be) idle
luim, mood, whim, humour
luipaard, leopard
luis, louse
luister, splendour
luisteraar(ster), listener
luisteren, to listen
luisterrijk, splendid, glorious
luistervink, eavesdropper
luit, lute
luitenant, lieutenant
luiwagen, scrubbing broom
luiwammes, lazy-bones
lukken, to succeed
  het lukt me nooit, I shall never manage it
lukraak, haphazard
lumi'neus, luminous
  een lumineus idee, a brain-wave
lummel, lout
lummelen, to loiter
lunapark *n*, amusement park
lurven: bij de — pakken, to take by the scruff of the neck
lus, loop; noose
lust, inclination, liking
  een lust voor het oog, a sight for sore eyes
lusteloos, listless
lusten, to like, to fancy
lusthof, pleasure garden
lustig, lusty
lustprieel *n*, bower
luttel, little
luwen, to abate, to flag
luxe, luxury
luxu'eus, luxurious
ly'riek, lyric poetry
lyrisch, lyrical

M

maag, stomach: kinsman
maagd, virgin, maid(en)
maagdelijk(heid), virgin(ity)
maagpijn, stomach-ache
maagsap *n*, gastric juice
maagzuur *n*, gastric acid; heartburn
maagzweer, gastric ulcer

maaien, to mow
maaksel *n*, make, manufacture
maakwerk *n*, hackwork
maal *n*, time: meal
  tienmaal, ten times
maalstroom, whirlpool
maaltijd, meal
maan, moon
  loop naar de maan, go to blazes
maand, month
maandag, Monday
maandblad *n*, monthly periodical
maandelijks, monthly
maandenlang, for months on end
maandgeld *n*, monthly allowance
maandverband *n*, sanitary towel
maangestalte, phase of the moon
maanjaar *n*, lunar year
maansverduistering, eclipse of the moon
maanziek, moonstruck
maar, but: only; just
maarschalk, marshal
maarschalksstaf, marshal's baton
maart, March
maas, mesh; loop-hole
maasbal, darning ball
maat, measure, size; time, bar: mate, partner
  blinde maat, dummy (at bridge)
maatgevoel *n*, sense of rhythm
maatje *n*, decilitre: pal
maatregel, measure
maat'schappelijk, social
maatschap'pij, society; company
maatstaf, criterion
maatwerk *n*, clothing made to measure
machi'naal, mechanical
ma'chine, engine, machine
ma'chinefabriek, engineering works
ma'chinegeweer *n*, machine-gun
machine'rieën, machinery
ma'chineschrijven *n*, type-writing
machi'nist, ship's engineer; engine-driver

macht, power, might
  macht der ge'woonte, force of habit
  niet bij machte, unable
machteloos, powerless
machtig, mighty, terrific; rich (food)
  een taal machtig zijn, to have command of a language
machtigen, to authorize
machtiging, authorization
machtspositie, position of authority
machtsverheffing, involution
made, maggot, cheese-mite
made'liefje *n*, daisy
maffen, to snooze
maga'zijn *n*, store(s); magazine
maga'zijnmeester, store-keeper
mager, thin, lean, meagre
ma'gie, magic
magiër, magician
magisch, magic(al)
magi'straal, imposing
magi'straat, magistrate
mag'naat, magnate
mag'neet, magnet; magneto
mag'netisch, magnetic
magneti'seren, to magnetize; to mesmerize
magni'fiek, magnificent
ma'honiehout(en) (*n*), mahogany
mailboot, mail-boat
mailzak, mail-bag
maïs, maize
maïskolf, cob of corn
maï'zena, cornflour
majesteit, majesty
majesteitsschennis, *lèse-majesté*
majestu'eus, majestic
majeur, major (key)
ma'joor, major
mak, tame, gentle
makelaar, broker
maken, to make; to mend
  dat heeft er niets mee te maken, that has nothing to do with it
  hoe maakt U het? how do you do?
makkelijk, easy
makker, comrade

ma'kreel, mackerel
mal, mould, template; stencil: foolish
ma'laise, trade depression
Ma'leier, Malay
melen, to grind
maliënkolder, coat of mail
maling hebben aan, to care not a rap for
  in de maling nemen, to make a fool of
malle'jan, lumber wagon
malle'molen, roundabout
mallepraat, silly nonsense
mal'loot, silly creature
mals, tender; lush; gentle (rain)
man, man; husband
  aan de man brengen, to sell
  op de man af, point blank
manche, game (at cards)
man'chet(knopen), cuff (-links)
mand, basket
  door de mand vallen, to make a clean breast of it
man'daat *n*, mandate
manda'rijn, mandarin; tangerine
ma'nege, riding-school
manen, mane: to dun; to exhort
maneschijn, moonlight
man'gaan *n*, manganese
mangat *n*, man-hole
mangel, wringer: *n*, lack
mangelen, to mangle
man'haftig, manly
ma'nie, mania
ma'nier, manner, way
mani'fest *n*, manifesto, manifest
manifes'tatie, manifestation, demonstration
manipu'leren, to manipulate
mank, lame, crippled
manke'ment *n*, defect
man'keren, to be lacking or absent; to fail
  wat mankeert je? what's come over you?
man'moedig, manful
man(ne)lijk, male, masculine, manly
mannengek, man-mad woman
mannetje *n*, little man; male (animal)

mannetjesputter, he-man
manoeu'vreren, to manœuvre
mans: niet veel —, not very
  strong
manschappen, ratings, men
manslag, manslaughter
manspersoon, male (person)
mantel, coat, cloak
 iemand de mantel uitvegen,
  to haul someone over the
  coals
mantelpak n, costume
manu'aal n, gesture; manual
manufac'turen, piece-goods
manufactu'rier, draper
manusje n van alles, odd job
  man
manwijf n, virago
manziek, man-mad
map, folder, file
ma'quette, model
marchan'deren, to bargain
mar'cheren, to march
marco'nist, wireless operator
mare, tidings
marechaus'see, military con-
  stabulary
maretak, mistletoe
marge, margin
ma'rine, navy
ma'rineluchtmacht, fleet air
  arm
mari'neren, to pickle, to souse
mari'nier, marine
mar'kant, striking
mar'keren, to mark
mar'kies, marquis: sun-blind
marke'zin, marchioness
markt(plein n), market(-place)
marktkraam, stall
marmer n, marble
mar'mot, marmot; guinea-pig
mars, march: pedlar's pack;
  (fighting) top
 hij heeft heel wat in zijn mars,
  he knows a great deal
marse'pein n, marzipan
marskramer, pedlar
marsoefening, route-march
marssteng, topmast
mars'vaardig, ready to march
marszeil n, topsail
martelaar, martela'res, martyr

martelaarschap n, martyrdom
martelen, to torture, to torment
marteling, torture
marter, marten
masker n, mask
mas'keren, to camouflage
massa, mass, crowd
mas'saal, massive
mas'seren, to massage
mas'sief, solid
mast, mast
mastbos n, fir-wood; forest of
  masts
mat, weary; matt; dim: checkmate: mat
mateloos, boundless
materi'aal n, material(s)
ma'terie, matter
materi'eel, material; plant
 rollend materieel n, rolling
  stock
matglas n, frosted glass
mathe'maticus, mathematician
matig, moderate; abstemious
matigen, to moderate
matigheid, moderation; frugal-
  ity; temperance
mati'neus, up early
matje n, (table-)mat
 op het matje roepen, to carpet
ma'tras, mattress
ma'trijs, matrix
ma'troos, sailor
mattenklopper, carpet-beater
mazelen, measles
mazen, to darn
mecani'cien, mechanic
me'chanica, mechanics
mecha'niek n, mechanism
me'chanisch, mechanical
me'daille, medal
medaill'on n, medallion; locket
mede, with, also: fellow-
mede'deelzaam, communicative
mededelen, to inform
mededeling, communication; information
mededingen, to compete
mededinger, rival
mededogen n, compassion
mede'klinker, consonant
me(d)eleven, to sympathize
me(d)elij(den) n, pity

mede'plichtig, accessary
me(d)evoelen met, to feel for
me(d)ewerken, to co-operate
medewerker, contributor, collaborator
medewerking, active support
medeweten *n.* knowledge
medezeggenschap *n,* say (in the matter)
medi'cijn(en), medicine
medicus, doctor; medical student
medisch, medical
mee, with
meebrengen: met zich —, to bring with one; to entail
meedoen, to take part
mee'dogenloos, merciless
meegaan, to go, to come (along)
mee'gaand, accommodating
meekomen, to come (along); to keep pace
meekrap, madder
meel *n,* meal, flour
meeloper, fellow-traveller
meemaken, to experience
meenemen, to take (along)
meent, common
meepraten, to join in the conversation
meer, more: *n,* lake
meerdere, superior; several
meerderheid, majority
meerder'jarig, of age
meerekenen, to include
meerijden, to drive with, to be given a lift
meermalen, more than once
meermin, mermaid
meervoud *n,* plural
mees, titmouse
meeslepen, to drag along; to carry away
meesmuilen, to smirk
meest(al), most(ly)
meester, master
meeste'res, mistress
meester'knecht, foreman
meesterschap *n,* mastery, command
meesterstuk *n,* masterpiece
meet: van — af aan, from the start
meetkunde, geometry

meet'kundige reeks, geometrical progression
meetronen, to inveigle
meeuw, gull
meevallen, to be better than one expected
dat valt niet mee, that is not easy
meevaller, bit of luck
mee'warig, compassionate
mei, May
meiboom, may-pole
meid, maid(-servant), girl
meidoorn, hawthorn
meineed, perjury
meisje *n,* girl, girl-friend
meisjesachtig, girlish
meisjesgek, philanderer
meisjesnaam, maiden name; girl's name
me'juffrouw, Madam, Miss
mekk(er)en, to bleat
me'laats, leprous
me'laatse, leper
me'laatsheid, leprosy
me'lange, blend
me'lasse, molasses
melden, to report; to announce
meldens'waard(ig), worth mentioning
melding maken van, to mention
mê'leren, to blend
melig, mealy; floury
melk, milk
melkboer, milkman
melken, to milk
melke'rij, dairy-farm
melkinrichting, dairy (shop)
melkkan, milk-jug
melkweg, Milky Way
me'loen, melon
me'morie, memory; memorandum
men, one, people, they, you
me'neer, Sir; (gentle)man
menen, to think, to mean; to fancy
't wordt menens, it's getting serious
mengelmoes *n,* jumble
mengelwerk *n,* miscellany
mengen, to mix, to mingle, to blend
zich mengen in, to meddle with

mengsel *n*, mixture, blend
menie, red-lead
menig, many a
menigeen, many a person
menigmaal, many a time
menigte, crowd
menig'vuldig, manifold
mening, opinion
mennen, to drive (a carriage)
mens, man; human being
  het is een goed mens *n*, she is
  a good soul
mensdom *n*, mankind
menselijk, human
menselijkerwijs gesproken,
  humanly speaking
menselijkheid, humanity
menseneter, cannibal
mensenhater, misanthrope
mensenkenner, judge of character
mensenleeftijd, lifetime
mensheid, mankind
mens'lievend, humane
mens'waardig, worthy of a
  human being
menswording, incarnation
mep(pen), (to) smack
meren, to moor
merendeel *n*, greater part
merendeels, mostly
merg *n*, marrow; pith
mergpijp, marrow-bone
merk *n*, mark, brand
merkbaar, noticeable
merrie, mare
mes *n*, knife
messenlegger, knife-rest
Mes'sias, Messiah
messing *n*, brass
mest, dung, manure
mesten, to fatten; to manure
mesthoop, mestvaalt, dunghill
met, with
  met dat al, for all that
  met Pasen, at Easter
me'taal *n*, metal
me'taalzaag, hacksaw
meta'foor, metaphor
met'een, straight away; presently
meten, to measure
meter, metre; meter

metgezel('lin), companion
me'thodisch, methodical
me'triek, metric: prosody
metrum *n*, metre
metselaar, bricklayer
metselen, to build (using mortar)
metselkalk, mortar
metselwerk *n*, masonry
metten: korte — maken met,
  to make short work of
metter'daad, in fact
metter'tijd, in due course
meubel *n*, piece of furniture
  een raar meubel, a queer
  body
meubelen, to furnish: furniture
meubelmaker, cabinet-maker
meubi'lair *n*, furniture
meubi'leren, to furnish
me'vrouw, Mrs; Madam; lady
middag, midday; afternoon
middageten *n*, **middagmaal** *n*,
  midday meal
middel(s) *n*, waist(s)
middel(en) *n*, means, remedy
  (-ies)
middelaar, mediator
middelbaar, average, medium
  middelbaar onderwijs *n*, secondary education
middeleeuwen, Middle Ages
middeleeuws, mediæval
Middellandse Zee, Mediterranean
middellijn, diameter
middel'matig, mediocre, average
middelmoot, middle cut
middelpunt *n*, centre, pivot
middelpunt'vliedend, centrifu-
gal
middelste, middlemost, centre
midden *n*, middle, midst
midden'door delen, to bisect
midden'in, in the middle (of)
middenrif *n*, diaphragm
middenstand, middle-classes
middenweg, (happy) mean
midder'nacht, midnight
mid'scheeps, amidships
mier, ant
mierenhoop, ant-hill
miezerig, drizzly; puny
mijden, to shun

mijl, mile; kilometre
mijlpaal, milestone
mijmeren, to muse
mijn, my; mine: pit
mijnbouw(kunde), mining
mijnenveger, mine-sweeper
mijnentwille: om —, for my sake
mijnerzijds, on my part
mijngas *n*, fire-damp
mijn'heer, Sir; Mr; (gentle-)man
mijnwerker, miner
mijnwezen *n*, mining
mijt, mite
mijter, mitre
mikken (op), to aim (at)
mikpunt *n*, aim, target, butt
mild, liberal; mild
mild'dadig, generous
mili'cien, conscript
mili'tair, soldier; military
mi'litie, militia
mil'joen *n*, million
mille, (one) thousand (guilders)
millimeteren, to crop (hair) close
milt, spleen
miltvuur *n*, anthrax
mi'mitafeltjes, nest of tables
min, wet nurse: love: less; mean, bad
minachten, to regard with disdain
minachting, contempt
minder, less(er), fewer
minderen, inferiors: to decrease
minderheid, minority
minder'jarig, under age
minder'waardig, inferior
minder'waardigheidscomplex *n*, inferiority complex
mineur, minor (key)
mi'niem, minute
mini'maal, minimum
mi'nister, minister, secretary (of State)
Minister President, Prime Minister
mini'sterie *n*, ministry, Office
minnaar, lover
minna'res, mistress

minne, love
  in der minne schikken, to settle amicably
minnekozen, to bill and coo
minnelijke schikking, amicable arrangement
minnen, to love
minnetjes, poorly
minst, least
minstens, at least
minuti'eus, meticulous
mi'nuut, minute
minver'mogend, poor
minzaam, affable
mirre, myrrh
mirt(eboom), myrtle(-tree)
mis, wrong: Mass
  het is mis, it is no good
  niet mis, pretty good
mis'baar *n*, clamour
misbaksel *n*, monstrosity
misbruik *n*, abuse
  misbruik maken van, to abuse
mis'bruiken, to abuse, to misuse
misdaad, crime
mis'dadig, criminal
misdadiger, criminal
mis'deeld, poor; handicapped
misdienaar, server
mis'doen, to do wrong
mis'dragen: zich —, to misbehave
misdrijf *n*, offence
misgreep, blunder
mis'gunnen, to begrudge
mis'handelen, to maltreat
miskelk, chalice
mis'kennen, to fail to appreciate
miskraam, miscarriage
mis'leiden, to mislead
mislopen, to go wrong
mis'lukken, to miscarry
mis'lukking, failure
mis'maakt, deformed
mis'moedig, disheartened
mis'noegen *n*, displeasure
mispel, medlar
mis'plaatst, misplaced, out of place
mis'prijzen, to disapprove of
mispunt *n*, beast, bounder
mis'rekening, miscalculation
mis'schien, perhaps

misselijk, sick; disgusting
missen, to miss; to lack
missie, mission
missio'naris, (R.C.) missionary
mis'staan, to be unbecoming
misstand, abuse
misstap, false step, slip
mist, fog
misten, to be foggy
mis'troostig, disconsolate
misvatting, misunderstanding
misverstaan, to misunderstand
misverstand n, misunderstanding
mis'vormd, misshapen
mi'taine, mitt(en)
mitrail'leur, machine-gun
mits, provided (that)
mits'dien, consequently
modder(ig), mud(dy)
modderpoel, quagmire
mode, fashion
mo'del n, model, pattern
modemagazijn n, fashion-house, gentlemen's outfitters
modeshow, fashion-parade
modi'eus, fashionable
mo'diste, milliner
moe(de), tired
moed, courage
moedeloos, dejected
moeder, mother; dam; matron
moederliefde, motherly love
moederlijk, motherly
moederloos, motherless
moedermoord, matricide
moedernaakt, stark naked
moeder-'overste, mother superior
moederschap n, motherhood
moederschapsuitkering, maternity benefit
moederschip n, depot ship
moedertaal, mother tongue
moedervlek, birth-mark, mole
moederziel alleen, quite alone
moedig, courageous
moedwil, wantonness
moed'willig, wilful
moeheid, fatigue
moeien: de politie in een zaak —, to call in the police
er is een week mee ge'moeid, it will take a week

moeilijk, difficult, with difficulty
moeilijkheid, difficulty
moeite, trouble; difficulty
de moeite waard, worth while
moeizaam, laborious
moer, nut: dam
moe'ras n, marsh
moe'rassig, marshy
moerbei, mulberry
moeren, to pinch, to steal; to tamper with
moes n, mash, pulp
moesgroente, greens
moesson, monsoon
moestuin, kitchen-garden
moet, stain; mark
moeten, must, to have to
wat moet dat? what's going on (there)?
je moest je schamen, you ought to be ashamed of yourself
moezen, to mash, to pulp
mof, muff: Hun
moffelen, to enamel: to smuggle away
mogelijk, possible
mogelijker'wijs, possibly
mogelijkheid, possibility
mogen, to be allowed, may; to like
mogendheid, power
moker, sledge-hammer
mokka, mocha
mokkelen, to cuddle
mokken, to sulk
mol, mole: flat, minor (key)
molen, mill
molenaar, miller
molenbeek, mill-race
molenwiek, sail of a windmill
mo'lestverzekering, war-damage insurance
mollen, to do (a person) in
mollevel n, moleskin
mollig, chubby
molm, mould
molshoop, mole-hill
molton n, swan-skin
mom n, mask, cloak
mombakkes n, carnival mask
momen'teel, momentary; at present
mo'mentopname, instantaneous photograph

mompelen, to mutter
mond, mouth; muzzle
  met de mond vol tanden, tongue-tied
  iemand naar de mond praten, to play up to a person
mon'dain, fashionable
mondeling, oral
mond-en-'klauwzeer *n,* foot-and-mouth disease
mondig, of age
mondje dicht! mum's the word!
  zij is niet op haar mondje ge'vallen, she has a ready tongue
mondjes'maat, bare minimum
mondkost, provisions
mondspoeling, mouth-wash
mondvoorraad, provisions
monnik, monk
monnikenwerk *n,* labour to no purpose
monnikenwezen *n,* monasticism
monnikskap, cowl
monnikspij, monk's habit
mono'toon, monotonous
monster *n,* monster: (free) sample
monsterachtig, monstrous
monsteren, to muster; to sign on
monstru'eus, monstrous
monstrum *n,* **monstruosi'teit,** monstrosity
mon'tage, assembly, mounting
monter, lively
mon'teren, to assemble, to set (up)
mon'teur, fitter, mechanic
mon'tuur *n,* (spectacle-)frame, mount, setting
mooi, beautiful, fine
mooidoene'rij, airs and graces
moord, murder
moordaanslag, murderous attempt
moord'dadig, murderous
moordenaar, murderer
moordpartij, massacre
Moors, Moorish
moot, fillet (of fish)
mop, joke
  moppen tappen, to crack jokes
mopje *n,* popular tune

mop(s)neus, snub-nose
mopperen, to grumble
mopshond, pug-dog
mo'raal, moral(s)
morali'seren, to moralize
mo'reel, moral: *n,* morale
mores, manners, customs
morgen, morning; tomorrow
  's morgens, in the morning, every morning
morgenland *n,* Orient
morgen'ochtend, tomorrow morning
morgenstond, early morning
mormel *n,* freak
mor'fine, morphia
morrelen, to fumble
morren, to grumble
morsdood, stone-dead
morsen, to spill, to make a mess
mor'tier, mortar
mos *n,* moss
mos'kee, mosque
Moskou, Moscow
mos'kovisch gebak *n,* sponge-cake
mossel, mussel
most, must, new wine
mosterd, mustard
  (als) mosterd na de maaltijd, a bit late in the day
mot, moth: bust-up
motie, motion, vote
mo'tief *n,* motive; motif
moti'veren, to justify, to defend
motor, motor, engine
motorordonnance, despatch rider
motorpech, engine trouble
motregen(en), (to) drizzle
mousse'line, muslin
mous'seren, to effervesce
mout, malt
mouw, sleeve
  ergens een mouw aanpassen, to manage somehow
  ze achter de mouw hebben, to be a sly-boots
  iemand iets op de mouw spelden, to fool a person
mouwschort *n,* overall
moza'iek *n,* mosaic
mud, hectolitre

muf, musty

mug, gnat

muggenzifte'rij, hair-splitting

muil, muzzle: slipper

muilband(en), (to) muzzle

muildier, muilezel, mule

muilkorf, muzzle

muis, mouse; ball of the thumb

muisjes, sugared caraway seeds

dit muisje zal een staartje hebben, we've not heard the last of this

muiteling, mutineer

muiten, to mutiny

muite'rij, mutiny

muitziek, mutinous

muizenissen, nagging thoughts

muizeval, mouse-trap

mul, loose, sandy

multiplex n, plywood

mummelen, to mumble

mummie, mummy

mu'nitie, ammunition, munitions

munt, coin(age); currency; mint

kruis of munt, heads or tails

munteenheid, monetary unit

munten, to mint

dat was op mij gemunt, that (remark) was aimed at me

muntkunde, numismatics

muntmeter, slot-meter

muntstuk n, coin

muntwezen n, coinage

murmelen, to babble

murmu'reren, to grumble

murw, soft, tender; at a low ebb

mus, sparrow

muscus, muskus, musk

musi'ceren, to make music

musicus, musician

mus'kaat(noot), nutmeg

mus'kaatwijn, muscatel

muska'del, muscadine

mus'kiet, mosquito

muskusrat, musquash

muts, cap, bonnet

muur, wall

muuranker, wall-tie

muurschildering, mural

muurvast, firm as a rock

muze, muse

mu'ziek, music

mu'ziekkorps n, band

mu'ziektent, band-stand

muzi'kaal, musical

muzi'kant, street-musician; bandsman

mys'terie n, mystery

mysteri'eus, mysterious

mys'tiek, mystic(ism)

mythe, myth

N

na, after; close

op één na, all but one

naad, seam, suture

het naadje van de kous willen weten, to want to know every detail

naaf, hub

naaidoos, work-box

naaien, to sew

naaister, needle-woman

naaiwerk n, sewing, needlework

naakt, naked, nude

naaktloper, nudist

naald, needle

naaldbos n, pine-wood

naaldenkoker, needle-case

naam, name

naambord n, name-plate

naamgenoot, namesake

naamloze vennootschap, limited company

naamval(suitgang), case(-ending)

naäpen, to ape

naäpe'rij, (slavish) imitation, parody

naar, to; according to: unpleasant, nasty

naar men zegt, according to reports

hij is er naar aan toe, he is in a bad way

naar'geestig, gloomy

naarling, nasty specimen

naar'mate, (according) as

naarstig, diligent

naast, next to; nearest

ten naaste bij, approximately

naast'bijzijnd, nearest

naaste, fellow-man

naasten, to expropriate

naastenliefde, love of one's fellow-man

nabestaanden, relatives
nabestellen, to put in a further
order
na'bij, near at hand
na'bijgelegen, neighbouring
na'bijheid, neighbourhood; near-
ness
nablijven, to stay behind
nabootsen, to imitate
nabootsing, imitation
na'burig, neighbouring
nacht, night
  bij nacht en ontij, at all hours of
the day and night
nachtbraken, to revel all night
nachtegaal, nightingale
nachtelijk, nocturnal
nachtevening, equinox
nachtgoed n, nightwear
nachtkaars, night-light
nachtkastje n, bedside cupboard
nachtlogies n, a bed for the night
nachtmerrie, nightmare
nachtploeg, night-shift
nachtpon, nightdress
nachtspiegel, chamber(-pot)
nachtuil, screech-owl
nachtverblijf n, lodging for the
night
nadat, after
nadeel n, disadvantage, detriment
na'delig, disadvantageous, detri-
mental
nadenken, to reflect
na'denkend, thoughtful
nader, nearer; further
  bij nader inzien, on second
thoughts
nader'bij, nearer
  van naderbij, more closely
naderen, to approach
nader'hand, afterwards
na'dien, since (then)
nadoen, to imitate
nadruk, emphasis; reprint
na'drukkelijk, emphatic
nagaan, to examine, to trace
nagalmen, to reverberate
nagedachtenis, memory
nagel(en), (to) nail: clove(s)
nagellak, nail-varnish
nagelriem, cuticle

nagemaakt, imitation, spurious
nagenoeg, almost
nagerecht n, dessert
nageslacht n, posterity
nageven: dat moet ik hem —,
I'll say that for him
nahouden: er op —, to maintain
na'ïef, naïve
naijver, jealousy
najaar n, autumn
najagen, to pursue
naken, to approach
nakijken, to gaze after; to check
na'komeling, descendant
na'komelingschap, offspring
nakomen, to carry out
nalaten, to leave (behind); to
omit
  **ik kon niet nalaten u te ver-
tellen,** I could not help telling
you
na'latenschap, inheritance
na'latig, negligent, remiss
na'latigheid, negligence
naleven, to observe, to live up to
nalezen, to read over or again
nalopen, to run after; to be slow
namaak, imitation
namaken, to imitate, to forge
namelijk, namely, i.e.; because
nameloos, unutterable
namens, on behalf of
namiddag, afternoon
nanacht, the early hours
na-oorlogs, post-war
nap, bowl
napluizen, to examine in detail
napraten, to parrot; to stay behind talking
napret, fun after the event
nar, jester
nar'cis, daffodil
nar'cose, narcosis
nar'coticum n, narcotic
narcoti'seur, anæsthetist
narekenen, to check
narigheid, unpleasantness
narijden, to ride or drive after;
to drive
narrig, peevish
na'saal, nasal
naschrift n, postscript
naslaan, to look up

nasleep, aftermath
nasmaak, after-taste
naspel *n*, (organ) voluntary; sequel
nasporing, investigation
nastaren, to (turn round and) stare
nastreven, to strive after
nat, wet
natafelen, to linger at the dinner table
natellen, to check
natie, nation
nationali'seren, to nationalize
nattigheid, moisture
 nattigheid voelen, to smell a rat
na'tura: in —, in kind
natu'rel, natural
na'tuur, nature; scenery
 van nature, by nature
na'tuurgetrouw, true to nature
na'tuurkunde, physics
natuur'kundige, physicist
na'tuurlijk, natural, of course
na'tuurschoon *n*, beautiful scenery
na'tuurverschijnsel *n*, natural phenomenon
na'tuurvolk *n*, primitive race
nauw, narrow, tight, close: *n*, straights
 hij neemt het niet te nauw, he is not very particular
nauwelijks, scarcely
nauwge'zet, conscientious
nauw'keurig, accurate
nauw'sluitend, close-fitting
nauwte, defile; straights
navel, navel
navelstreng, umbilical cord
navertellen, to repeat
naver'want, closely related
navolgen, to follow, to imitate
navorsen, to investigate
navraag, enquiries
naweeën, after affects
nawerken, to make its effect felt
nawerking, after-effect
nazaat, descendant
nazien, to check
nazitten, to pursue
nazomer, late summer

neder, down
Nederduits *n*, Low German
nederig, humble
nederlaag, defeat
Nederlander, Dutchman
Nederlands(e) (*n*), Dutch (woman)
nederzetting, settlement
neef, cousin, nephew
nee(n), no
neer, down
neer'buigend, condescending
neerhalen, to haul down; to run down
neerkomen, to come down
 het komt hierop neer, it boils down to this
neerleggen, to put down; to resign
neerslaan, to strike down; to precipitate
 de ogen neerslaan, to cast down one's eyes
neer'slachtig, dejected
neerslag, precipitation, sediment
neet, nit
negen, nine
negende, ninth
negenoog, carbuncle
negentien(de), nineteen(th)
negentig, ninety
neger, negro
negeren, to bully
ne'geren, to ignore
nege'rin, negress
nego'rij, hole, back of beyond
neigen, to incline
neiging, inclination, tendency
nek, (nape of the) neck
 met de nek aankijken, to cold-shoulder
nekken, to break, to ruin
nekvel *n*, scruff of the neck
nemen, to take
 we zullen het er eens van nemen, let's enjoy ourselves
nerf, grain, vein
nergens, nowhere
 ik weet nergens van, I know nothing about it
nering, trade, custom
ner'veus, nervous
nest *n*, nest; minx

nestelen, to nest

  zich nestelen, to ensconce oneself; to nestle

net (*n*), net (work); system: tidy
neat, decent; just

  achter het net vissen, to miss
the boat

  in het net schrijven, to make a
fair copy

netel, nettle

neteldoek *n*, muslin

netelroos, nettle-rash

netjes, tidily, neat, nice, decent

nettenboet(st)er, net-mender

netto, nett

netvlies *n*, retina

neuriën, to hum

neu'rose, neurosis

neus, nose, nozzle

  het is maar een wassen neus,
there is nothing to it

  **met de neus in de boter
vallen,** to come at the right
moment

neusgat *n*, nostril

neusholte, nasal cavity

neushoorn, rhinoceros

neusje van de zalm *n*, acme of
perfection

neusvleugel, nostril

neuswijs, cocky

neu'traal, neutral

neuzen in, to pry into

nevel, mist, haze

nevelachtig, misty, hazy

nevelvlek, nebula

nicht, cousin, niece

niemand, nobody

nieman'dal, nothing at all

nier, kidney

niet, not

niet(en), (to) staple

nietig, null and void; diminutive; trivial

nietigheid, futility

nietigverklaring, nullification

niets, nothing

**nietsbe'duidend, nietsbe'te-
kenend,** insignificant

nietsnut, good-for-nothing

niets'zeggend, meaningless

niettegen'staande, notwithstanding

niette'min, nevertheless

nieuw, new

nieuw'bakken, new-fangled

nieuweling, novice

nieuwer'wets, new-fangled

nieuwigheid, novelty

nieuw'lichter, modernist

nieuws *n*, news

nieuwsblad *n*, newspaper

nieuws'gierig(heid), inquisitive-
(ness)

nieuwtje *n*, piece of news

niezen, to sneeze

nihil, nil

nijd, envy

nijdas, cross-patch

nijdig, angry

nijgen, to curtsey, to bow

nijlpaard *n*, hippopotamus

nijpen, to nip

  het begint te nijpen, (we)
are beginning to feel the
pinch

nijptang, (pair of) pincers

nijver, industrious

nijverheid, industry

nikkel *n*, nickel

nikker, nigger

niks, nothing

nimf, nymph

nimmer, never

nippertje: op het —, in the nick
of time

nis, niche, alcove

ni'veau *n*, level

nivel'leren, to level

n.l., i.e.; you see

nobel, noble-minded

noch . . . noch, neither . . . nor

nochtans, nevertheless

node, reluctantly

nodeloos, needless

nodig, necessary

  nodig hebben, to need

nodigen, to invite

noemen, to name, to call; to
mention

noemens'waard(ig), worth mentioning

noemer, denominator

noenmaal *n*, luncheon

noest, diligent

nog, still, yet

vandaag nog, this very day
nog vele jaren! many happy returns!
noga, nougat
nogal, rather, fairly
nogmaals, once again
nok, ridge of the roof
no'made, nomad
non, nun
nonac'tief, half-pay
nonnenklooster *n,* convent
nonsens, nonsense
nood, need, emergency; distress
noodanker *n,* sheet-anchor
noodbrug, temporary bridge
nooddruft, destitution
noodgedwongen, perforce
noodgeval *n,* emergency
noodlanding, forced landing
nood'lijdend, destitute
noodlot *n,* fate
nood'lottig, fatal
noodmast, jury-mast
noodrem, safety-brake; communication cord
noodtoestand, state of emergency; untenable situation
noodweer *n,* deluge
noodgebouw *n,* temporary building
noodzaak, necessity
nood'zakelijk, necessary
noodzaken, to oblige
nooit, never
Noor, Norwegian
noord, north
noordelijk, northern, northerly
noorden *n,* North
noorder'breedte, North latitude
noorderlicht *n,* northern lights
noorderzon: met de — vertrekken, to cut and run
noordpool, north pole
noordpool'cirkel, arctic circle
noordwaarts, northward(s)
Noors (*n*), Norwegian
Noorwegen *n,* Norway
noot, note: nut
hele, halve noot, kwartnoot
etc., breve, minim, crotchet *etc.*
hij heeft veel noten op zijn zang, he is hard to please
nootmus'kaat, nutmeg

nop(pen), (to) nap
in zijn nopjes, greatly pleased
nopen, to induce
nopens, concerning
nor, clink, quod
nor'maal, normal
nor'maalschool, teacher training college
nor'maliter, normally
nors, gruff
nota, note; bill, account
no'tabelen, leading citizens
no'taris, notary
noteboom, (wal)nut-tree
notedop, nut-shell
notehout *n,* walnut
notekraker, nut-crackers
notenbalken, staves
no'teren, to note (down)
notie, notion
no'titie, note; notice
notulen, minutes
nou, now: you bet!
nouveau'tés, novelties, fancy goods
no'velle, short story
no'viet, freshman
novum *n,* novelty
nu, now (that)
van nu af aan, from now on
nuchter, sober, level-headed
op de nuchtere maag, on an empty stomach
nuf, stand-offish little miss
nukkig, wayward
nul, nought, nil, zero; nonentity
nul op het re'kwest krijgen, to meet with a refusal
nulpunt *n,* zero
nummer *n,* number; issue
iemand op zijn nummer zetten, to put a person in his place
nummeren, to number
nurks, grumpy
nut *n,* use, benefit
nutteloos, useless
nuttig, useful
nuttigen, to partake of
N.V., Ltd. (Company)

O

o.a., *inter alia*; including
o'ase, oasis

o-benen, bandy legs
ober(kelner), (head-)waiter
ob'ject n, object(ive)
obli'gaat n, obligato
obli'gatie, bond
obliga'toir, obligatory
ob'sceen, obscene
obser'vator, observer
oce'aan, ocean
och, ah!, oh
ochtend, morning
  's ochtends, in the morning(s)
ochtendgloren n, day-break
oc'taaf, octave
oc'trooi n, patent; charter
oc'trooiraad, patent-office
o'deur, perfume
oefenen, to train, to practise
oefening, exercise, practice
oer n, bog-ore
Oeral, Urals
oerdier n, protozoon
oergermaans n, primitive ger-
  manic
oermens, prehistoric man
oerwoud n, virgin forest, jungle
oester, oyster
oever, bank, shore
of, or; whether, if
  of . . . of,   either . . . or;
  whether . . . or
offer n, sacrifice, victim
offerande, oblation
offeren, to sacrifice; to offer up
offergave, offering
of'ferte, offer
offer'vaardig, willing to make
  sacrifices
offici'eel, official
offi'cier, officer
  officier van Justicie, public
  prosecutor
offi'ciersaanstelling,   commission
offici'eus, semi-official
of'freren, to offer
of'schoon, although
ogen, to eye; to be attractive
ogenblik n, moment
ogen'blikkelijk, immediate
ogen'schijnlijk, seemingly
ogenschouw: in — nemen, to
  look over

o.i., in our opinion
oker n, ochre
okkernoot, walnut
oksel, armpit
okshoofd n, hogshead
olie, oil
oliebol, doughnut
olie'dom, fat-headed
oliejas, oilskin (coat)
oliën, to oil
olienoot, monkey-nut
oliesel n, extreme unction
olieslage'rij, oil-mill
olifant, elephant
o'lijf, olive
olijk, roguish
olijkerd, rogue
olm, elm
om, round, about; at
  om de andere dag, every other
  day
  om te, in order to
  de tijd is om, time is up
oma, grandma
om'armen, to embrace
ombrengen, to kill
omdat, because
omdoen, to put on, to wrap
  round
omdraaien, to turn (round), to
  twist
omduwen, to knock over
om'floersen, to muffle; to
  shroud
omgaan, to go round
  het hoekje omgaan, to peg out
omgaande: per —, by return (of
  post)
omgang, social intercourse, dealings; procession; gallery
omgangstaal, everyday speech
omgangsvormen, manners
omgekeerd, upside-down; re-
  verse(d)
om'geven, to surround
om'geving, surroundings
omgooien, to overturn
omhaal, fuss; verbiage
omhakken, to cut down
om'heen, round (about)
om'heinen, to fence in
om'heining, fence, enclosure
om'helzen, to embrace

om'hoog, up(wards)
om'hullen, to envelope
om'hulsel *n*, cover, wrapping, casing
omkantelen, to topple over
omkeren, to turn (round)
omkijken, to look round
om'kleden, to clothe
omkomen, to perish
om'koopbaar, venal
omkopen, to bribe
omkope'rij, bribery
om'laag, down (below)
om'lijnen, to outline
om'lijsten, to frame
omloop, circulation, course; gallery
omlopen, to walk round
't hooft loopt me om, my head reels
ommekeer, change; turn
ommezien: in een —, in a trice
ommezijde, other side, back
omploegen, to plough up
ompraten, to talk round
om'rasteren, to enclose in wire-netting *or* railings
omrekenen, to convert, to work out
om'ringen, to surround
omroep, broadcasting service
omroepen, to broadcast
omroeper, announcer
omroeren, to stir
omruilen, to exchange
omschakelen, to switch over
om'schrijven, to define; to circumscribe
om'schrijving, definition; paraphrase
om'singelen, to encircle
omslaan, to turn (over); to apportion
om'slachtig, cumbrous; prolix
omslag, wrapper; ado; compress
omslagdoek, wrap
om'sluiten, to enclose
omsmelten, to melt down
om'spannen, to span
omspitten, to dig (over)
omspoelen, to rinse
omspringen met, to handle, to manage

omstander, bystander
om'standig, circumstantial
om'standigheid, circumstance, condition
om'streden, contested
omstreken, environs
omstreeks, about
omtoveren, to transform as if by magic
omtrek, outline, contour; neighbourhood; circumference
om'trent, about
omvallen, to fall over
omvang, extent; girth
om'vangrijk, extensive
om'vatten, to comprise; to encompass
om'ver, down; over
om'verwerpen, to overthrow
omvouwen, to fold down
omwaaien, to (be) blow(n) down
omwassen, to wash up
omweg, detour, roundabout way
omwenteling, revolution, rotation
omwerken, to remodel, to rewrite
omwisselen, to (ex)change
omwoners, neighbours
om'zeilen, to get round
omzet, turnover
omzetbelasting, purchase-tax
omzetten, to transpose; to convert; to sell
om'zichtig(heid), circumspect(ion)
omzien, to look round
onaan'doenlijk, impassive
on'aangenaam(heid), unpleasant(ness)
onaan'nemelijk, unacceptable, improbable
onaan'tastbaar, unassailable
onaan'zienlijk, insignificant
on'aardig: niet —, not at all bad
on'achtzaam(heid), inattentive(ness)
on'afgebroken, continuous
onaf'hankelijk, independent, irrespective
onaf'scheidelijk, inseparable
onbaat'zuchtig, disinterested

onbe'daarlijk, uncontrollable
onbe'dorven, unspoilt
onbe'duidend, trivial
onbegonnen werk, hopeless task
onbeheerd, ownerless, un-
  attended
onbeholpen, awkward
onbe'hoorlijk, unseemly
onbehouwen, unwieldy; un-
  gainly; uncouth
onbe'kend, unfamiliar
onbekommerd, carefree
onbe'kookt, rash, wild
onbe'kwaam, (drunk and) incapable
onbe'lemmerd, unrestricted
onbe'middeld, without means
onbe'nullig, inane
onbe'paalbaar, indeterminable
onbepaald, indefinite
onbeperkt, unrestricted
  onbeperkt vertrouwen, implicit faith
onbe'raden, thoughtless
onbe'rekenbaar, incalculable
onbe'rispelijk, irreproachable
onbeschaafd, ill-mannered; un-
  civilized
onbeschaamd, shameless; brazen
onbe'scheiden, indiscreet
onbe'schoft, impertinent
onbe'schrijfelijk, indescribable
onbe'schroomd, fearless
onbeslecht, onbeslist, undecided
onbesproken, not discussed; un-
  reserved; beyond reproach
onbe'staanbaar, impossible; incompatible
onbestelbare brief, dead letter
onbestemd, indeterminate
onbe'stendig, unstable
onbestorven weduwe, grass
  widow
onbestreden, uncontested
onbesuisd, reckless
onbe'taalbaar, priceless
onbetekenend, insignificant
onbeteugeld, unbridled
onbe'tuigd: ik liet me niet —,
  I did justice (to the meal)
onbetwist, undisputed
onbe'twistbaar, indisputable

onbevangen, unbiased
onbe'vattelijk, dull-witted; incomprehensible
onbevlekt, immaculate
onbe'voegd, not qualified; unauthorized
onbe'vredigend, unsatisfactory
onbewaakt, unguarded
onbeweeglijk, motionless, immovable
onbewerkt, untreated
onbewogen, unmoved
onbe'woonbaar, uninhabitable
onbewoond, uninhabited
onbe'wust, unconscious
onbe'zield, inanimate, lifeless;
  uninspired
onbezoldigd, unpaid; honorary
onbe'zorgd, carefree
on'billijk, unfair
on'breekbaar, unbreakable
onbruik n, disuse
on'bruikbaar, useless
ondank, ingratitude
on'dankbaar, ungrateful, thankless
ondanks, despite
on'denkbaar, unthinkable
onder, under(neath); among;
  during
onder'aan, at the foot of
onder'in, at the bottom (of)
onder'aards, subterranean
onderafdeling, subdivision
onderbewust, subconscious
onderbe'wustzijn n, subconscious
onder'breken, to interrupt
onderbrengen, to accommodate,
  to place
onderbroek, pants
onderbuik, abdomen
onderdaan, subject
onderdak n, shelter, accommodation
onder'danig, submissive
onderdeel n, part
onderdoen: niet — voor, to be
  in no way inferior to
onderdompelen, to immerse
onder'door, under, through
onder'drukken, to oppress, to
  suppress

onderduiken, to dive; to go into hiding

ondergaan, to go down; to perish

onder'gaan, to undergo

ondergang, downfall, ruin

onderge'schikt, subordinate; secondary

onderge'tekende, (the) undersigned

ondergoed *n*, underwear

onder'graven, to undermine

ondergrond, sub-soil; foundation

onder'handelen, to negotiate

onder'handelingen, negotiations

onder'hands, private; underhand

onder'havige geval, (the) case in question

onder'hevig aan, subject to

onder'horig, subordinate

onderhoud *n*, maintenance; interview

onder'houden, to maintain, to support

zich onderhouden met, to converse with

onder'houdend, entertaining

onderhuids, subcutaneous, hyperdermic

onderjurk, slip

onderkant, underside

onder'kennen, to discern

onderkin, double chin

onderkomen *n*, shelter

onderkoning, viceroy

onderkruiper, blackleg

onder'legd: goed —, well-grounded

onderlegger, blotting pad; under-blanket

onderlijf *n*, abdomen

onderling, mutual

onderlopen, to get flooded

onder'maanse: het —, here below

onder'mijnen, to undermine

onder'nemen, to undertake

onder'nemend, enterprising

onder'nemer, employer, contractor

onder'neming, enterprise; plantation

onderofficier, N.C.O., petty-officer

onder'onsje *n*, friendly get-together

onderpand *n*, pledge, security

onderricht *n*, instruction

onder'schatten, to underestimate

onderscheid *n*, difference, distinction

jaren des onderscheids, years of discretion

onder'scheiden, to distinguish

onder'scheiding, distinction, honour

onder'scheidingsvermogen *n*, discrimination

onder'scheidingsteken *n*, badge, distinguishing mark

onder'scheppen, to intercept

onderschrift *n*, caption

onder'schrijven, to subscribe to

onders'hands, privately

onderspit: het — delven, to get the worst of it

onderstaand, (mentioned) below

onderstand, support, relief

onderste, bottom(most)

onderste'boven, upside-down

ondersteek, bed-pan

onderstel *n*, under-carriage

onder'steld, hypothetical; supposing

onder'stellen, to (pre)suppose

onder'stelling, hypothesis

onder'steunen, to support

onder'steuning, support, relief

onder'stoppen, to tuck in

onder'strepen, to underline

onderstuurman, second mate

onder'tekenaar, signatory

onder'tekenen, to sign

onder'tekening, signature

ondertrouw, registration of intended marriage

onder'tussen, meanwhile

onder'vangen, to obviate

onderverhuren, to sub-let

onder'vinden, to experience

onder'vinding, experience

onder'voed, under-nourished

onder'vragen, to interrogate

onder'weg, on the way

onderwerp n, subject
onder'werpen, to subject; to subdue; to submit
onder'wijl, meanwhile
onderwijs n, education
onder'wijzen, to teach
onder'wijzer, school-teacher
onder'worpen, submissive
onder'zeeboot, submarine
onderzoek n, enquiry, investigation, examination, research
onder'zoeken, to investigate, to examine
onder'zoekend, searching
onder'zoekingstocht, exploratory expedition
ondeugd, vice; scamp
on'deugend, naughty
ondienst, disservice
ondienst'vaardig, disobliging
on'diep, shallow
ondiepte, shallow (patch)
ondier n, monster
onding n, useless or ugly thing; absurdity
ondoel'matig, inadequate
on'doenlijk, not feasible
ondoor'dacht, thoughtless
ondoor'dringbaar, impenetrable
ondoor'grondelijk, inscrutable
ondoor'schijnend, opaque
ondoor'zichtig, not transparent
on'draaglijk, unbearable
ondubbel'zinnig, unequivocal
on'duidelijk, indistinct
on'duldbaar, insufferable
ondu'leren, to wave (hair)
onecht, spurious; illegitimate
onedel, ignoble, base
on'eens: het — zijn, to disagree
on'eerbaar, indecent
oneer'biedig, disrespectful
on'effen(heid), uneven(ness)
on'eindig, infinite
on'eindigheid, infinity
on'enigheid, discord
oner'varen, inexperienced
oneven, odd
oneven'redig, disproportionate
onfat'soenlijk, improper
on'feilbaar, infallible
on'fris, stale; sallow
on'gaarne, reluctantly

ongeacht, irrespective of
ongebaand, trackless
onge'bonden, unbound; dissolute
ongebreideld, unbridled
ongebuild meel, wholemeal
ongecompli'ceerd, unsophisticated
onge'daan maken, to undo
ongedacht, unexpected
onge'deerd, unhurt
ongedierte n, vermin
ongeduld n, impatience
onge'duldig, impatient
onge'durig, restless
onge'dwongen, unconstrained
ongeëvenaard, unequalled
ongefrankeerd, unstamped, carriage forward
ongegeneerd, unceremonious
onge'grond, groundless
onge'hinderd, unimpeded
ongehoord, unheard-of
onge'huwd, unmarried
ongekend, unprecedented
onge'kleed, not (properly) dressed
ongekunsteld, artless
on'geldig, invalid
on'geldigverklaring, nullification
onge'legen, inopportune
onge'legenheid: in — brengen, to inconvenience
onge'lijk, uneven, unequal
ongelijk n (**hebben**), (to be) wrong
ongelijk'slachtig, heterogeneous
ongelikte beer, rough customer
ongelimiteerd, unlimited
ongelinieerd, ongelijnd, unruled
onge'lofelijk, incredible
ongelogen, really and truly
ongeloof'waardig, improbable
onge'lovig, incredulous
onge'lovige, unbeliever
ongeluk n, accident, misfortune
onge'lukkig, unhappy, unfortunate, unlucky
onge'lukkige, poor wretch; cripple
onge'lukkigerwijs, unfortunately

ongemak *n*, inconvenience, discomfort

onge'makkelijk, uncomfortable; hard to please; awkward

ongemanierd, ill-mannered

ongemeen, rare, uncommon

ongemeubileerd, unfurnished

onge'moeid laten, to leave in peace

ongemotiveerd, uncalled-for

onge'naakbaar, unapproachable

ongenade, disgrace, disfavour

onge'nadig, merciless

onge'neeslijk, incurable

onge'nietbaar, unpalatable; unbearable

ongenoegen *n*, displeasure, variance

ongeoorloofd, impermissible

onge'past, improper

ongeraden, ill-advised

ongeregeld, irregular

onge'regeldheden, disturbances

ongerekend, exclusive of

ongerept, inviolate, untouched

ongerief *n*, inconvenience

onge'riefelijk, incommodious

onge'rijmd(heid), absurd(ity)

onge'rust, anxious, uneasy

onge'schikt, unfit, unsuitable

ongeschonden, undamaged; unimpaired

ongeschoold, untrained

onge'steld, unwell

ongestoord, undisturbed

onge'straft, unpunished; with impunity

ongetrouwd, single, unmarried

ongetwijfeld, undoubtedly

ongeval *n*, accident

ongeveer, approximately

ongeveinsd, sincere

onge'voelig, unfeeling

ongewapend, unarmed

ongewenst, undesirable

ongewijzigd, unaltered

ongewild, unintentional

ongewillig, refractory

ongewis, uncertain

onge'woon, unusual

onge'zeglijk, disobedient

onge'zellig, unsociable; cheerless

ongezouten, unsalted; plain

on'gunstig, unfavourable

onguur, sinister, unsavoury

on'handelbaar, intractable

on'handig, clumsy; awkward

on'hebbelijk, rude, objectionable

onheil *n*, calamity

onheil'spellend, ominous

onher'bergzaam, inhospitable

onher'roepelijk, irrevocable

onher'stelbaar, irreparable

on'heuglijk, immemorial

onheus, onhoffelijk, discourteous

on'houdbaar, untenable

onjuist, inaccurate

onkies, indelicate

onklaar, out of order; fouled

onkosten, expenses

on'kreukbaar, unimpeachable

onkruid *n*, weed(s)

onkunde, ignorance

on'kundig van, unaware of

onlangs, recently

on'ledig, occupied

onleesbaar, illegible

on'lekker, out of sorts

on'loochenbaar, undeniable

onlusten, disturbances

onmacht, impotence; swoon

on'machtig, powerless

onmens, brute

on'menselijk, inhuman

on'merkbaar, imperceptible

on'metelijk, vast

on'middellijk, immediate

onmin, discord

on'misbaar, indispensable

onmis'kenbaar, unmistakable

on'mogelijk, impossible, not possible

on'mondig, under age, incapable

onna'denkend, thoughtless

onna'volgbaar, inimitable

on'neembaar, impregnable

onnodig, unnecessary

on'noembaar, on'noemelijk, immeasurable

on'nozel, silly; innocent

onom'stotelijk, incontestable

onomwonden, frank

ononderbroken, uninterrupted

onont'beerlijk, indispensable

onont'koombaar, inescapable
on'ooglijk, unsightly
onoordeelkundig, injudicious
onopgevoed, ill-bred
onop'houdelijk, incessant
onoplettend, inattentive
on'ordelijk, disorderly
onovergankelijk, intransitive
onover'komelijk, insuperable
onover'troffen, unsurpassed
onover'winnelijk, invincible
onpartijdig, impartial
on'passelijk, sick
on'peilbaar, unfathomable
onper'soonlijk, impersonal
onraad *n,* danger
onrecht *n,* injustice
  ten onrechte, wrongly
onrecht'matig, unlawful
on'redelijk, unreasonable
onroerende goederen, immovables
onrust, unrest
onrust'barend, alarming
on'rustig, restless
onruststoker, onrustzaaier, trouble-maker
ons, us: *n,* 100 grammes
onsamen'hangend, incoherent
on'schadelijk, harmless
on'schatbaar, priceless; invaluable
on'schendbaar, inviolable
onschuld, innocence
on'schuldig, innocent
on'smakelijk, unsavoury
onsolide, flimsy; unsound
on'sterfelijk, immortal
on'stuimig, impetuous; tempestuous
onsympathiek, uncongenial
ont'aard(en), (to) degenerate
ont'aarding, degeneration
on'tactisch, tactless
on'tastbaar, intangible
ont'beren, to lack
ont'bering, hardship
ont'bieden, to summon
ont'bijt(en) *(n),* (to have) breakfast
ont'binden, to undo; to decompose, to disintegrate, to dissolve; to disband; to factorize

ont'binding, decomposition, disintegration, dissolution
ont'bloot, bare; devoid
ont'bloten, to bare, to uncover, to strip
ont'boezeming, effusion
ont'brandbaar, inflammable
ont'branden, to catch fire; to flare up
ont'breken, to be missing
  het ontbrak me aan moed, I lacked the courage
ont'cijferen, to decipher
ont'daan, cut up, shaken
ont'dekken, to discover
ont'dekking, discovery
ont'dekkingsreiziger, explorer
ont'doen, to divest
ont'dooien, to thaw (out)
ont'duiken, to elude, to evade
ontegen'zeglijk, undeniable
ont'eigenen, to expropriate
on'telbaar, innumerable
on'tembaar, indomitable
ont'eren, to dishonour
ont'erend, degrading
ont'erven, to disinherit
onte'vreden, discontented, dissatisfied
ont'fermen: zich — over, to take pity on
ont'futselen, to filch
ont'gaan, to elude
ont'gelden, to suffer for
ont'ginnen, to reclaim
ont'glippen, to slip (out); to escape
ont'goocheling, disillusionment
ont'groeien, to outgrow; to become estranged to
ont'groenen, to initiate
ont'haal *n,* reception
ont'halen, to regale
ont'haren, to depilate
ont'heemde, displaced person
ont'heffen, to relieve; to exempt
ont'heiligen, to desecrate
ont'hoofden, to behead
ont'houden, to remember; to withhold
  zich onthouden van, to abstain from
ont'hullen, to unveil; to reveal

ont'hutst, disconcerted
on'tijdig, untimely
ont'kennen, to deny
ont'kenning, denial, negation
ont'ketenen, to unchain; to unleash
ont'kiemen, to germinate
ont'kleden, to undress
ont'knoping, denouement
ont'komen, to escape
ont'kurken, to uncork
ont'laden, to unload, to discharge
ont'lasten, to unburden, to relieve, to discharge
ont'leden, to analyse; to dissect
ont'lenen, to borrow, to derive
ont'loken, full-blown
ont'lokken, to elicit
ont'lopen, to evade
ont'luiken, to open, to blossom (out)
ont'luizen, to delouse
ont'mantelen, to dismantle
ont'maskeren, to unmask, to expose
ont'moedigen, to discourage
ont'moeten, to meet
ont'moeting, encounter, meeting
ont'nemen, to deprive of
ont'nuchteren, to disillusion
ontoe'gankelijk, inaccessible
ontoe'geeflijk, unaccommodating
ontoe'laatbaar, inadmissible
ontoe'passelijk, inapplicable
ontoe'reikend, inadequate
ontoe'rekenbaar, not responsible for one's actions
ontoe'schietelijk, unresponsive
on'toombaar, uncontrollable
on'toonbaar, not fit to be seen
ont'plofbare stof, explosive
ont'ploffen, to explode
ont'plooien, to unfurl; to deploy; to unfold, to open out
ont'poppen: zich — als, to turn out to be
ont'raden, to advise against
ont'rafelen, to unravel
ont'redderd, battered
ont'reddering, disorder
ont'rieven, to inconvenience
ont'roeren, to move, to touch
ont'roering, emotion

on'troostbaar, inconsolable
ontrouw, disloyal(ty)
ont'roven, to rob of
ont'ruimen, to vacate, to evacuate
ont'rukken, to snatch away from
ont'schepen, to disembark
ont'schieten, to escape (one's memory)
ont'sieren, to disfigure, to mar
ont'slaan, to discharge
ont'slag n, discharge
ontslag nemen, to resign
ont'slapen, to pass away
ont'sluieren, to unveil
ont'sluiten, to unlock
ont'smetten, to disinfect
ont'smettingsmiddel n, disinfectant
ont'snappen, to escape
ont'spannen, to relax
ont'spanning, relaxation, recreation
ont'sporen, to be derailed
ont'springen, to have its source
de dans ontspringen, to have a narrow escape
ont'spruiten, to sprout; to arise from
ont'staan, to originate, to come into being: n, origin
doen ontstaan, to bring about
ont'steken, to kindle, to ignite; to inflame
ont'steking, inflammation; ignition
ont'steld, alarmed
ont'stellend, alarming, appalling
ont'steltenis, consternation
ont'stemd, upset, put out
ont'stemming, annoyance
ont'stentenis: bij — van, in the absence of
ont'stichten, to give offence
ont'takelen, to dismantle
ont'trekken, to withdraw
zich onttrekken aan, to shirk
ont'tronen, to dethrone
ontucht, immorality
ontuig n, riff-raff
ont'vallen, to slip out
zijn vrouw ontviel hem, he lost his wife

ont'vangbewijs *n*, receipt
ont'vangdag, at-home
ont'vangen, to receive
ont'vangenis, conception
ont'vanger, recipient
ont'vangst, reception, receipt
ont'vankelijk, susceptible
ont'veinzen: zich —, to deceive oneself
ont'vellen, to skin; to graze
ont'vlambaar, inflammable; excitable
ont'vlammen, to inflame
ont'vlekken, to dry-clean
ont'vlieden, to flee from
ont'vluchten, to escape from
ont'voeren, to abduct
ont'volken, to depopulate
ont'vouwen, to unfold
ont'vreemden, to steal
ont'waken, to wake up
ont'wapenen, to disarm
ont'waren, to perceive
ont'warren, to disentangle
ont'wennen, to lose the habit of
ont'werp *n*, project; design
ont'werpen, to devise, to design, to plan
ont'wijden, to desecrate
on'twijfelbaar, unquestionable
ont'wijken, to evade, to avoid
ont'wijkend, evasive
ont'wikkeld, educated, developed
ont'wikkelen, to develop, to generate
ont'wikkeling, development, education
ont'winden, to unwind
ont'woekeren aan, ont'worstelen aan, to wrest from
ont'wortelen, to uproot
ont'wrichten, to dislocate
ont'zag *n*, awe
ont'zaglijk, tremendous
ontzag'wekkend, awe-inspiring
ont'zeggen, to deny, to refuse
ont'zenuwen, to unnerve; to disprove
ont'zet, appalled: *n*, relief
ont'zetten, to relieve; to deprive; to put out
ont'zettend, terrible, appalling

ont'zetting, horror; relief; dismissal
ont'zield, inanimate
ont'zien, to spare, to save
ont'zinken, to fail
on'uitgesproken, unspoken
onuit'puttelijk, inexhaustible
onuit'spreekbaar, unpronounceable
onuit'sprekelijk, unspeakable
onuit'staanbaar, intolerable
onuit'voerbaar, impracticable
onuit'wisbaar, indelible
onvast, unstable, unsteady
onveranderd, unaltered
onveranderlijk, invariable
onverantwoord, unwarranted; unaccounted for
onverant'woordelijk, irresponsible, inexcusable
onver'beterlijk, incorrigible
onver'biddelijk, inexorable
onverbloemd, plain
onverbrekelijk, indissoluble
onverdeeld, undivided, unqualified
onverdiend, undeserved
onver'dienstelijk, undeserving
onver'draagzaam, intolerant
onverdroten, indefatigable
onverenigbaar, incompatible
onverflauwd, unabated
onvergankelijk, imperishable
onver'geeflijk, unpardonable
onverge'lijkelijk, incomparable
onver'getelijk, unforgettable
onverhinderd, unimpeded
onverhoeds, unexpected
onverholen, undisguised
onverhoopt, contrary to expectations
onverkiesbaar, ineligible
onverkieslijk, undesirable
onver'klaarbaar, inexplicable
onver'kort, unabridged
onver'krijgbaar, unobtainable
onver'kwikkelijk, unsavoury
onverlaat, miscreant
onvermengd, unmixed
onver'mijdelijk, unavoidable
onverminderd, undiminished
onvermoed, unsuspected
onvermoeibaar, indefatigable

onvermoeid, untiring

onvermogen *n*, inability; indigence

onver'mogend, impecunious; powerless

onvermurwbaar, inexorable

onverpoosd, unceasing

onverrichter zake, with nothing accomplished

onversaagd, undaunted

onver'schillig, indifferent, unconcerned

onver'schoonbaar, inexcusable

onver'schrokken, intrepid

onverslapt, unflagging

onver'slijtbaar, indestructible, very hard-wearing

onver'staanbaar, unintelligible

onverstand *n*, folly

onver'standig, unwise

onver'stoorbaar, imperturbable

onver'taalbaar, untranslatable

onver'teerbaar, indigestible

onver'togen, unseemly

onvervaard, undismayed

onver'valst, unadulterated

onverwacht(s), unexpected

onverwijld, immediate

onver'woestbaar, inextinguishable

onver'zadelijk, insatiable

onver'zettelijk, stubborn

onver'zoenlijk, irreconcilable

onverzorgd, unprovided for, uncared for

on'voegzaam, indecent

onvoldaan, unsatisfied; unpaid

onvoldoende, insufficient, unsatisfactory

onvol'prezen, beyond praise

onvoltooid, unfinished; imperfect (tense)

onvol'waardig, debile

on'voorbereid, unprepared, extempore, unseen

onvoor'delig, unprofitable, uneconomical

onvoor'waardelijk, unconditional

onvoor'zichtig, incautious

onvoorzien, unforeseen

on'vriendelijk, unkind

onvriend'schappelijk, unfriendly

onvrij, not free, without any privacy

on'vruchtbaar, infertile, fruitless

onwaarde: van —, null and void

on'waardig, unworthy, undignified

onwaar'schijnlijk, improbable

on'wankelbaar, unwavering

onweer *n*, thunder-storm

onweer'legbaar, irrefutable

onweersbui, thunder-shower

onweer'staanbaar, irresistible

on'wel, unwell

onwel'levend, discourteous

onwel'luidend, inharmonious

onwelge'voeglijk, indecorous

onwel'riekend, malodorous

on'wennig, ill at ease

onweren, to thunder

on'wetend, ignorant

on'wettig, unlawful, illegal, illegitimate

on'wezenlijk, unreal

onwijs, foolish

onwil, unwillingness

onwille'keurig, involuntary

on'willig, unwilling, obstinate

onwrikbaar, unshakable

onzacht, rough, none too gentle

on'zalig uur, unholy hour

onze, our(s)

on'zedelijk, immoral

on'zeker, uncertain

on'zekerheid, insecurity, uncertainty

onzelf'standig, dependent on others

onze-lieve-'heersbeestje *n*, lady-bird

onzentwille: om —, for our sake

onzerzijds, for our part

on'zichtbaar, invisible

on'zijdig, neutral, neuter

onzin, nonsense

on'zinnig, senseless

on'zuiver, impure, inaccurate, out of tune

ooft *n*, fruit

oog *n*, eye

oogappel, eyeball

oogarts, occulist, ophthalmic surgeon

ooggetuige, eye-witness

oogharen, eye-lashes
oogholte, oogkas, eye-socket
oogkleppen, blinkers
ooglid *n,* eyelid
oogluikend toelaten, to connive
oogmerk *n,* object, aim
oogopslag, glance, look
oogpunt *n,* point of view
oogst, harvest, crop
oogvlies *n,* cornea
oogwenk, twinkling of an eye
ooi, ewe
ooievaar, stork
ooit, ever
ook, also, too; either
wat (dan) ook, whatever
waar (dan) ook, wherever
oom, uncle
oomzegger, nephew
oor *n,* ear; handle
oorbaar, seemly
oorbel, ear-ring
oord *n,* place, region, resort
oordeel *n,* opinion, judgement
oordeel'kundig, judicious
oordelen, to judge
oorijzer *n,* (gold *or* silver) head-
brooch
oorkonde, charter, (ancient)
document
oorkussen *n,* pillow
oorlel, ear-lobe
oorlog, war (fare)
oorlogsbodem, warship
oorlogshaven, naval port
oorlogsvloot, navy, fleet
oorlogs'zuchtig, bellicose
oorlogvoerend, belligerent
oorpijn, ear-ache
oorschelp, auricle
oorsprong, origin, source
oor'spronkelijk, original
oorveeg, oorvijg, box on the
ear
oorver'dovend, deafening
oorworm, earwig
oorzaak, cause
oost, east, Orient
oostelijk, easterly, east (of)
oosten *n,* East
Oostenrijk *n,* Austria
oosterling, Oriental
oosters, eastern, oriental

oostindische'kers, nasturtium
oostwaarts, eastward (s)
Oost'zee, Baltic
ootmoed, meekness
oot'moedig, meek
op, on; at; in; up
het bier is op, the beer is
finished
ik heb veel met hem op, I like
him a lot
op en top, every inch
opa, grandad
o'paal, opal
opbaren, to place on a bier
opbellen, to ring up
opbergen, to put away
opbeuren, to lift up; to cheer up
opbiechten, to own up
opblazen, to inflate
opbloei, revival
opbod, auction
opbouwen, to build up
opbreken, to break up
opbrengen, to yield; to run in
opbrengst, yield, proceeds
opcenten, surtax
opdagen, to turn up
op'dat, in order that
opdienen, to dish up, to serve
opdiepen, to dig up
opdirken, to titivate
opdissen, to dish up
opdoeken, to close down, to clear
out
opdoemen, to loom (up)
opdoen, to obtain; to lay in; to
contract; to dish up
opdonder, biff
opdonderen: donder op! get
the hell out of here!
opdraaien, to turn up; to take
the can back
opdracht, instruction (s), commission; dedication
opdragen, to instruct, to order;
to dedicate
opdrijven, to force up; to drive
opdringen, to thrust upon (a
person)
op'dringerig, obtrusive
opdruk, surcharge
opduikelen, to rake up
opduiken, to bob up, to crop up

op'een, together, on top of one another

op'eenhoping, accumulation, congestion

op'eens, all at once

opeen'volgend, successive

opeisen, to claim, to demand

open, open

open'baar, public

open'baarheid, publicity

open'baren, to reveal

open'baring, revelation

opendoen, to open; to answer the door

openen, opengaan, to open

open'hartig, frank

open('hartig)heid, frankness

opening, opening

openlijk, public, open

openmaken, to open, to undo

openrijten, to rip open

openslaan, to open

openslaande deur, folding door(s), French window

openslaand raam, casement window

opensperren, to distend

openstaande rekening, unsettled account

openstellen, to (throw) open (to the public)

openvouwen, to open out

ope'ratie, operation

ope'ratiekamer, operating theatre

ope'reren, to operate (on)

ope'rette, operetta

opeten, to eat (up), to finish (up)

opflikkeren, to flare up

opfrissen, to refresh

opgaaf, opgave, statement, return; task, problem, (examination-)paper

opgaan, to rise, to go up; to be absorbed; to come off

dat gaat niet altijd op, that does not always hold good

opgeblazen, puffed-up, bumptious

opgeld doen, to be at a premium

opgelucht, relieved

opgeruimd, cheerful

opgeschoten jongen, stripling

opgeschroefd, affected, forced

opgesloten, locked up; implied

opgetogen, enraptured

opgeven, to give (up); to cough up; to state

hoog opgeven van, to speak highly of

opgevreten, eaten away, consumed

opgewassen tegen, a match for

opgewekt, cheerful

opgewonden, excited

opgezet, swollen; stuffed

groot(s) opgezet, ambitious

opgooien, to toss (up)

opgraven, to dig up

opgravingen, excavations

ophaalbrug, draw-bridge

ophaaldienst, carrier service

ophalen, to draw up; to pick up; to shrug; to sniff (up)

op'handen, at hand

ophef, fuss

opheffen, to lift up; to abolish, to close (down)

ophelderen, to elucidate; to clear

ophemelen, to extol

ophitsen, to incite, to set on

ophoepelen, to buzz off

ophopen, to pile up; to accumulate

ophouden, to hold up; to uphold; to cease; to delay

zich ophouden met, to have dealings with

o'pinie, opinion

opiumkit, opium-den

opkikkeren, to perk up

op'klapbaar, folding

opklapbed *n,* tip-up bed

opklaren, to clear up

opknappen, to smarten up; to cope with; to get well

opkomen, to come up, to (a)rise; to come on; to stick up (for)

het kwam bij me op, it occurred to me

daar kom ik tegen op, I object to that

opkomst, rise; attendance

opkrassen, to clear out

opkroppen, to bottle up

oplaag, oplage, number of copies printed

oplaaien, to flare up

oplappen, to patch up

oplaten, to fly

oplawaai, wallop

opleggen, to impose; to lay on; to store

opleiden, to train

opleiding, training, education

opletten, to pay attention

op'lettend, attentive

opleven, to revive

opleveren, to produce, to present

oplichten, to lift (up); to swindle

oplichter, swindler

oploop, tumult

oplopen, to run up; to rise; to mount up; to incur

op'lopend, short-tempered

op'losbaar, soluble

oplossen, to (dis)solve

oplossing, solution

opluchting, relief

opluisteren, to add lustre to

opmaak, lay-out

opmaken, to make (up); to gather

op'merkelijk, remarkable

opmerken, to observe

opmerking, remark

op'merkzaam maken op, to call attention to

opmonteren, to cheer up

opname, recording, photograph; admission

opnemen, to take (up); to take in; to record

op'nieuw, anew

opnoemen, to enumerate

opoe, granny

opofferen, to sacrifice

oponthoud n, delay

oppas, sitter-in

oppassen, to take care (of); to beware; to try on

oppasser, caretaker, attendant, batman

opperbest, excellent

opperbevel n, supreme command

opperbevelhebber, commander-in-chief

opperen, to propose

opperhoofd n, chief (tain)

oppersen, to press

oppervlak n, (outer) surface

opper'vlakkig, superficial

oppervlakte, surface, area

Opperwezen n, Supreme Being

oppeuzelen, to relish at one's leisure

oppikken, to pick up, to peck up

oppo'neren, to raise objections

opportuni'teit, expediency

oppotten, to hoard

opprikken, to pin up

opraken, to give out

oprakelen, to poke (up); to rake up

oprapen, to pick up

op'recht, sincere

opredderen, to tidy up

oprichten, to erect; to establish zich oprichten, to raise oneself up

oprichter, founder

oprichting, foundation, establishment

oprijlaan, drive

oprijzen bij, to occur to

oprispen, to belch

oprit, drive

oproep, summons, call

oproepen, to call (up)

oproer n, revolt

op'roerig, rebellious

oproerkraaier, agitator

oproerling, rebel

opruien, to incite to rebellion

opruimen, to clear (away)

opruiming, clearance sale; tidy-up

oprukken, to press onward

opscharrelen, to dig up

opschepen met, to saddle with

opscheppen, to serve; to brag

opschepper, braggart

opschieten, to get (a move) on met elkaar opschieten, to get on (well) together

opschik, finery

opschikken, to move up

opschommelen, to dig up

opschorten, to suspend

opschrift n, inscription, caption

opschrijfboekje n, note-book

opschrijven, to note down
opschrikken, to start, to be startled
opschrokken, to gobble up
opschudding, commotion
opschuiven, to push up, to move up
opslaan, to raise; to turn up; to lay in; to rise (in price)
opslag, rise; storage
opslobberen, to lap up
opslokken, to gulp down
opslorpen, opslurpen, to drink noisily; to absorb
opsluiten, to lock (up)
opsmuk, finery
opsnijden, to cut up; to brag
opsnij(d)er, braggart
opsnorren, opsnuffelen, to dig up
opsommen, to enumerate
opsou'peren, to blue
opspelen, to kick up a row
opsporen, to track (down)
opspraak, disrepute
opstaan, to rise
opstand, rising; elevation
  in opstand komen, to rebel
opstandeling, rebel
op'standig, rebellious
opstanding, resurrection
opstap, step
opstapelen: zich —, to accumulate
opstappen, to get on, to get along
opsteken, to put up; to light; to get up
  opsteken van, to profit by
opstel n, essay
opstellen, to draft; to place
opstijgen, to rise; to climb up, to mount
opstoken, to stir up (animosity)
opstootje n, disturbance
opstopper, punch
opstrijken, to run an iron over; to rake in
opstropen, to roll up
opstuiven, to fly up
optekenen, to note down
optellen, to add up
optocht, procession

optornen tegen, to make headway against
optreden, to appear; to act
optrekken, to pull up; to raise
  optrekken tegen, to march against
  optrekken met, to go about with
optrommelen, to round up
optuigen, to rig; to harness
opvallen, to be conspicuous, to strike
op'vallend, conspicuous
opvangen, to catch; to overhear
opvarenden: de —, those on board
opvatten, to take (up), to interpret, to conceive
  weer opvatten, to resume
opvatting, conception
opvliegen, to fly up, to flare up
op'vliegend, irascible
opvoeden, to educate
opvoeding, upbringing
  lichamelijke opvoeding, physical training
opvoedingsgesticht n, reformatory school
opvoeren, to raise; to perform
opvoering, performance
opvolgen, to succeed; to carry out
opvolger, successor
opvouwbaar, collapsible
opvreten, to devour
opvrolijken, to cheer up
opwaarts, upward(s)
opwachten, to wait for
opwachting maken, to pay (one's) respects
opwegen tegen, to offset
opwekken, to arouse, to stimulate, to generate
op'wekkend, encouraging
opwellen, to well up
opwelling, surge, impulse
opwerken: zich —, to work one's way up
opwerpen, to throw up; to raise
opwinden, to wind (up), to excite
opwinding, excitement

opzeggen, to recite; to terminate, to cancel
 zijn betrekking opzeggen, to give notice
opzet, plan, intent(ion)
op'zettelijk, met opzet, deliberate
opzetten, to set up; to put on; to turn (against); to swell
 een grote mond opzetten, to harangue
opzicht n, respect
opzichter, superintendent
op'zichtig, flashy
opzien tegen, to look up to; to dread
opzien'barend, sensational
opzoeken, to look up
o'ranje (n), orange
ora'torium n, oratorio; oratory
orchi'dee, orchid
orde, order
 aan de orde, up for discussion
orde'lievend, or'delijk, orderly
ordeloos, disorderly
ordenen, to (put in) order
or'dentelijk, decent
order, order, command
ordi'nair, vulgar
ordner, file
ordon'nans, orderly
o'reren, to hold forth
or'gaan n, organ
organi'seren, to organize
orgel n, organ
orgeldraaier, organ-grinder
oriën'teren zich —, to find one's bearings
origi'neel, original
or'kaan, hurricane
or'kest n, orchestra
or'naat n, robes of office
os, ox, bullock
oscil'leren, to oscillate
ossenhaas, fillet of beef
ostenta'tief, ostentatious
oud, old, ancient
 bij het oude laten, to leave (things) as they were
oud'bakken, stale
oude van dagen, aged
oudejaars'avond, New Year's Eve

ouder, older, elder; parent
ouderdom, (old) age
ouderlijk, parental
ouderling, elder
ouder'wets, old-fashioned
oudge'diende, veteran
oudheid, antiquity
oudheidkunde, archaeology
oudje n, old (wo)man
oudoom, great uncle
oud'roest n, old iron
oudsher: van —, (from) of old
oudst, oldest, elder; senior
oud'strijder, veteran
oudtante, great-aunt
outil'leren, to equip
ouv'reuse, usherette
ouwel, wafer
ouwelijk, elderly
o'vaal, oval
oven, oven, furnace, kiln
over, over, across; via; past; about; left (over)
 over en weer, mutually
 tijd te over, time to spare
 ik heb veel voor hem over, I would do anything for him
 over een paar dagen, in a few days' time
overal, everywhere
overbekend, widely known
overbelasten, to overburden; **to** overload
overbelicht, over-exposed
overblijfsel n, remains, relic
overblijven, to be left; to stay (at school for lunch)
over'bluffen, to abash
over'bodig, superfluous
over'boord, overboard
overbrengen, to convey
overbrieven, to let on about
over'bruggen, to bridge
overbuur, neighbour across the road
overdaad, excess
over'dadig, excessive
over'dag, during the day
over'dekt, covered in
over'denken, to consider
overdoen, to do again; to pass on
over'donderen, to knock all of **a** heap

overdracht, transfer
over'drachtelijk, metaphorical
overdragen, to transfer, to convey
over'dreven, exaggerated
overdrijven, to blow over
over'drijven, to exaggerate
overdruk, reprint; overprint
overdrukplaatje *n*, transfer
over'duidelijk, obvious
over'dwars, across, athwart
over'eenbrengen, to reconcile
over'eenkomen, to agree
over'eenkomst, agreement, similarity
overeen'komstig, corresponding (to)
over'eenstemmen, to agree
over'eind, upright, on end
over'erfelijk, hereditary
overgaan, to cross over; to pass (on); to go up (to a higher form)
overgang, transition, change; crossing
overgangsmaatregel, temporary measure
over'gankelijk, transitive
overgave, surrender
overgelukkig, over-joyed
overgeven, to hand over, to surrender; to vomit
overge'voelig, hypersensitive
overgieten, to transfer, to decant
overgooier, tunic
overgordijn *n*, (running) curtain
overgoten met, bathed in
overgrootmoeder, great-grandmother
overgrootvader, great-grandfather
over'haast, precipitate
overhalen, to pull over; to persuade
overhand, upper hand
over'handigen, to hand (over)
over'heen, across, over
   er gaan jaren overheen, it takes years
overheerlijk, exquisite
over'heersen, to (pre)dominate

over'heersing, domination
overheid, authorities
overhellen, to incline, to lean over
overhemd *n*, shirt
overhevelen, to siphon
over'hoop, in confusion; at loggerheads
over'horen: iemand —, to hear a person's lesson
overhouden, to have left
overig, remaining
overigens, for the rest
over'ijld, precipitate
overjas, overcoat
overkalken, to crib
overkant, opposite side
over'kapping, roof(ing)
over'koepelend, co-ordinating
over'komen, to happen to
over'kropt gemoed, pent-up feelings
overladen, to transfer
over'laden, to overload
over'langs, lengthwise
overlast, inconvenience
overlaten, to leave
over'leden, deceased
over'leg *n*, deliberation
overleggen, to produce; to put by
over'leggen, to deliberate
over'leven, to survive
over'levende, survivor
overleveren, to hand down: to deliver up
overlevering, tradition
overlezen, to read through, to read again
over'lijden, to die
overloop, landing
overlopen, to run over; to go over
overloper, deserter, traitor
overmaat, excess
   tot overmaat van ramp, to crown it all
overmacht, superior force; force majeure
overmaken, to do again; to transfer
over'mannen, to overpower; to overcome

over'matig, excessive
over'meesteren, to overpower
overmoed, presumption
over'moedig, presumptuous
over'morgen, the day after tomorrow
overnaads, clinker-built; overcast (seam)
over'nachten, to stay the night
overnemen, to take over; to adopt
over'peinzen, to muse on
over'peinzing, reflection
overplaatsen, to transfer
overplanten, to transplant
over'reden, to persuade
overreiken, to hand
overrijden, to run over
over'rompelen, to take by surprise
overschenken, to decant
overschepen, to tranship
overschieten, to be left
overschoenen, galoshes
overschot n, remainder, surplus
over'schreeuwen, to shout down
over'schrijden, to exceed; to step across
overschrijven, to copy (out); to transfer
overslaan, to skip; to estimate; to crack
overslag, overlap; estimate
over'spannen, to span: overwrought
overspel n, adultery
overstaan: ten — van, in the presence of
over'stag gaan, to go about
overstapje n, transfer ticket
overstappen, to change
overste, lieutenant-colonel; prior
oversteekplaats, (pedestrian) crossing
oversteken, to cross
over'stelpen, to overwhelm
over'stemmen, to drown, to shout down
over'stromen, to flood, to inundate
over'stuur, upset

over'tallig, surplus
over'tekenen, to over-subscribe
overtocht, crossing, passage
over'tollig, superfluous
over'treden, to transgress; to infringe
over'treffen, to surpass
   overtreffende trap, superlative
overtrek, (loose) cover
over'trekken, to (re)cover
overtrekken, to cross; to trace; to blow over
over'troeven, to over-trump; to score on
over'tuigen, to convince
over'tuiging, conviction
overuren, overtime
overval, surprise attack
over'vallen, to surprise
oververtellen, to repeat
over'vleugelen, to surpass; to outflank
overvloed, abundance
over'vloedig, abundant
over'voeren, to glut
over'vragen, to over-charge
overwaarde, additional value
overweg, level crossing
over'weg kunnen, to get on
over'wegen, to consider
over'wegend, preponderant
over'weging, consideration
over'weldigen, to overpower
over'weldigend, overwhelming
over'weldiger, despotist
overwerken, to work overtime
over'werken, to overwork
overwicht n, preponderance, authority
over'winnaar, victor
over'winnen, to conquer
over'winning, victory
overwinstbelasting, excess profits tax
over'winteren, to winter
overzetveer n, ferry
overzicht n, summary
over'zichtelijk, conveniently arranged
over'zien, to survey
overzijde, opposite side
oxi'deren, to oxidize

P

paadje *n*, (foot-)path
paaien, to pacify
paal, pole, pile, post
  als een paal boven water, as clear as daylight
paaps, popish
paar *n*, pair, couple; few
paard *n*, horse
paardebloem, dandelion
paardeknecht, groom
paardekracht, horse-power
paardemiddel *n*, drastic remedy
paardenstoeterij, stud (-farm)
paardenvilder, knacker
paardenvolk *n*, cavalry
paardetoom, bridle
paardevijgen, horse-droppings
paarle'moer *n*, mother of pearl
paars (*n*), violet, purple
paarsgewijs, in pairs
paartijd, mating season
Paasvest, Sunday best
Paasdag: de eerste —, Easter Day
  de tweede Paasdag, Easter Monday
Paasfeest *n*, Easter
pacht, lease, rent
pachten, to rent (a farm)
pachter, tenant farmer
pad, toad: *n*, path
paddestoel, toad-stool, mushroom
padvinder, boy-scout
padvindster, girl-guide
paf staan, to be dumbfounded
pafferig, puffy
pa'gaai(en), (to) paddle
pagina, page
pais en vree, peace and quiet
pak *n*, pack(age); suit
  pak slaag, thrashing
pakhuis *n*, warehouse
pakje *n*, parcel, packet
pakijs, ice-pack
pakken, to pack; to seize; to hug
  iemand te pakken krijgen, to get hold of a person
  ik heb het erg te pakken, I've got it badly
pakkend, fascinating; catchy

pakkerd, hug
pak'ketpost, parcel post
pakpapier *n*, brown paper
pal, pawl, ratchet
  pal staan, to stand firm
  pal oost, due east
pa'leis *n*, palace
pa'let *n*, palette
palfre'nier, footman
paling, eel
palis'sanderhout(en) (*n*), rosewood
pal'jas, clown; palliasse
palm, palm
Palmpasen, Palm Sunday
pam'flet *n*, pamphlet, lampoon
pan, pan; tile; shindy
  in de pan hakken, to kill to a man
pand *n*, forfeit; premises: (coat-)tail
pandjeshuis *n*, pawn-shop
pandjesjas, tail-coat
pa'neel *n*, panel
pa'neermeel *n*, bread-crumbs
pa'niek, panic
panne, break-down
pannekoek, pancake
pannelap, kettle-holder
pannenbakke'rij, tile-works
panta'lon, trousers; knickers
panter, panther
pan'toffel, slipper
pan'toffelheld, henpecked husband
pantser *n*, armour
pantserdier *n*, armadillo
pantseren, to armour; to brace
pap, milk pudding
pa'paver, poppy
pape'gaai, parrot
pape'rassen, papers, litter
pa'pier *n*, paper
  pa'pieren, papers; stocks and shares; credentials
pa'piermand, waste-paper basket
papil'lotten, curl-papers
papje *n*, paste
papkind *n*, molly-coddle
Pappenheimers: ik ken mijn —, I know the people I'm dealing with
pappie, daddy

pa'raaf, initials
pa'raat, ready
pa'rade, review
para'dijs *n*, paradise
para'feren, to initial
para'nymf, usher
paranoot, Brazil nut
para'plu, umbrella
para'siet, parasite
par'cours *n*, course
par'does, slap(-bang)
par'don, pardon; mercy
parel, pearl
parel'moer *n*, mother of pearl
paren, to mate
  zich paren aan, to be coupled
  with
pa'reren, to parry
par'fum *n*, scent
parfu'meren, to scent
pari: à —, at par
pari'teit, parity
park *n*, park
par'keerterein *n*, car-park
par'keren, to park
par'ket (*n*), front stalls; public
  prosecutor's office: parquet
  in een lastig parket, in a predicament
par'kiet, parakeet
parle'ment *n*, parliament
parlemen'tair, parliamentary:
  bearer of flag of truce
parle'vinken, to jabber
parle'vinker, bum-boat
par'mantig, perky
parochi'aan, parishioner
pa'rochie, parish
paro'die, parody
parodi'ëren, to parody
pa'rool *n*, parole; password
part *n*, portion
  parten spelen, to play false
par'terre, pit; ground -floor
particu'lier, private: (private)
  individual
par'tij, part(y); game; consignment
  een goede partij doen, to make
  a good match
  partij kiezen, to take sides
  partij trekken van, to take
  advantage of

par'tijdig, biased
par'tijdigheid, partiality
par'tijganger, partisan
par'tijschap *n*, faction
pas, only (just): pace, step:
  pass
  te pas en te onpas, at random
  te pas, van pas, (be)fitting
Pascha *n*, Passover
Pasen, Easter
pasgeboren, new-born.
pasgeld *n*, small change
pasge'trouwden, newly-weds
paskamer, fitting-room
pasklaar, ready for fitting
pas'kwil *n*, absurdity
paslood *n*, plumb-line
paspoort *n*, passport
pas'saat, trade-wind
pas'sage, passage; arcade
pas'sagebiljet *n*, travel-voucher
passa'gier, passenger
passa'gieren, to be on shore-
  leave
passa'giersgoed *n*, accompanied
  luggage
pas'sant, traveller breaking his
  journey; passer-by
passen, to fit; to try on; to
  match; to be fitting; to pass
  ik pas ervoor, I won't do it
  passen op, to take care (of)
passend, fitting, appropriate
passer, pair of compasses
pas'seren, to pass (over); to
  happen
passie, passion
pas'sief, passive
passiva, liabilities
pasta, paste
pas'tei, patty; paste
pas'toor, parish priest
pasto'rie, parsonage
pa'tates frites, potato chips
pa'tent (*n*), licence; patent:
  capital
pater, father
pa'triciër, patrician
pa'trijs, partridge
pa'trijshond, spaniel
pa'trijspoort, port-hole
pa'troon, employer: cartridge:
  n, pattern

pa'trouille, patrol
pats, smack; bang!
pauk, kettledrum
paus, pope
pauselijk, papal
pauw, peacock
pauze, interval, pause
pavil'joen *n*, pavilion; marquee
pavoi'seren, to dress overall
pech, bad luck
pe'daal *n*, pedal
pe'dant, pedant(ic)
peddelen, to pedal; to paddle
pe'del, beadle
pedi'cure, chiropodist
pee: ik heb er de — in, I'm fed
    to the teeth
 ik heb de pee aan hem, he gets
    my goat
peel, marshy land
peen, carrot
peer, pear; light bulb
 met de gebakken peren zitten,
    to be left holding the baby
pees, tendon; gristle
peet, godparent
peetoom, godfather
peil *n*, gauge, level
 er is op hem geen peil te trek-
    ken, he is quite unpredictable
peilen, to gauge, to sound
peilloos, unfathomable
peinzen, to muse
peinzend, thoughtful
pek *n*, pitch
pekel, brine; pickle
pekelvlees *n*, salted meat
pelgrim, pilgrim
pelgrimstocht, pilgrimage
peli'kaan, pelican
pellen, to peel, to shell
pelo'ton *n*, platoon
pels, pelt; fur-coat
pelte'rij, peltry
peluw, bolster
pen, pen, nib, quill; peg, pin
pe'nant *n*, pier
pe'narie: in de —, in a fix
pen'dule, pendulum clock
pe'nibel, grim
peni'tentie, penitence; ordeal
pennen, to pen
pennelikker, pen-pusher

penning, medal; official badge
 op de penning, cheese-paring
penningmeester, treasurer
pens, paunch; tripe
pen'seel *n*, (artist's) brush
pen'sioen *n*, pension
 met pensioen gaan, to retire
    (on a pension)
pen'sion *n*, guest-house; board
pensio'naat *n*, boarding-school
pension'neren, to pension (off)
pentekening, pen-and-ink draw-
    ing
peper, pepper
peperduur, ruinous(ly expensive)
peperkoek, gingerbread
peper'munt, peppermint
pepernoot, ginger-nut
per'ceel *n*, plot; premises
per'centsgewijze, proportional
pereboom, pear-tree
perfection'neren, to perfect
per'fide, perfidious
pe'rikel *n*, peril
peri'ode, period
perio'diek, periodical
perk *n*, flower-bed; limit
perka'ment *n*, parchment
permit'teren, to permit
per omgaand, by return (of post)
per'plex, perplexed
per'ron *n*, platform
pers, press: Persian (rug)
persbureau *n*, press-agency
per se, emphatically
persen, to press, to squeeze
perso'neel *n*, staff, personnel
 personele belasting, household
    tax
per'soon(lijk), person(al)
per'soonlijkheid, personality
per'soonsbewijs *n*, identity
    card
perspec'tief *n*, perspective
perstribune, press gallery
perti'nent, emphatic, positive
per'vers, perverse
Perzië *n*, Persia
perzik, peach
Perzisch, Persian
pest, plague, pest(ilence)
pesten, to bait, to tease the life
    out of

pestkop, bully
pet, cap
  't gaat boven mijn pet, it beats me
petekind *n,* godchild
peter'selie, parsley
pe'tieterig, puny, minute
pe'troleum, paraffin
pe'troleumbron, oil-well
pe'troleumleiding, pipe-line
peukje *n,* cigar(ette)-butt
peultjes, young pea-pods
peulvruchten, legumes
peuter, tiny tot
peuteren, to fiddle, to tinker
peuterwerk(je) *n,* finicky job
peuzelen, to eat daintily with relish
ph- : *see under* f-
pianokruk, music stool
pi'as, clown
piccolo, piccolo: page-boy
picknick(en), (to) picnic
piek, pike; peak
piekeren, to puzzle, to brood
piekfijn, posh
pienter, bright, smart
piepen, to squeak, to cheep
piepjong, very young
piepkuiken *n,* (young) pullet
piepzak: in de —, in a blue funk
pier, pier, jetty: (earth)worm
  ik ben altijd de kwaaie pier, I get the blame for everything
piere'ment *n,* hurdy-gurdy
pierewaaien, to be on the spree
Piet(er), Peter
  Piet de Smeerpoe(t)s, Struwelpeter
  een hele Piet, quite a lad
piëteit, piety
pieter'selie, parsley
piet'luttig, pettifogging
pietsje *n,* wee bit
pij, (monk's) habit
pijjekker, pea-jacket
pijl, arrow
pijler, pillar
pijlkoker, quiver
pijn, pain, ache
  pijn doen, to hurt
pijnappel, fir-cone
pijnbank, rack

pijnigen, to torture, to rack
pijnlijk, painful
pijn'stillend, sedative, soothing
pijp, pipe; tube; funnel; trouser-leg
pijpkaneel, whole cinnamon
pik, pitch: pickaxe: peck
  de pik hebben op, to have a down on
pi'kant, piquant, spicy
pi'keur, riding-master
pikhouweel *n,* pickaxe
pikken, to peck; to pick: to pitch
pil, pill; chunk
pi'laar, pillar
pilo *n,* corduroy
pi'loot, pilot
pimpelaar, tippler
pimpelpaars, purple
pin, peg, pin
pin'cet *n,* tweezers
pinda(kaas), peanut (butter)
pingelen, to haggle
pinguin, penguin
pink, little finger: fishing boat
  bij de pinken, all there
Pinksteren, Whitsun(tide)
pi'oenroos, peony
pi'on, pawn
pio'nieren, to pioneer
pi'pet, pipette
pips, off colour
pi'raat, pirate
pi'raatje *n,* gasper
pisang, banana
pis'ton, cornet
pis'tool *n,* pistol
pit, kernel, stone, pip; burner; pith
pittig, pithy, racy; spry
plaag, nuisance, plague
plaaggeest, tease
plaat, plate; slab; (gramophone-)record; picture
plaatijzer *n,* sheet-iron
plaats, place; room; yard; seat
  in plaats van, instead of
  ter plaatse, on the spot
plaatsbewijs *n,* ticket
plaatselijk, local
plaatsen, to place

plaatsruimte, space
plaatsvervanger, deputy
pla'fond n, ceiling
plagen, to tease, to worry
plage'rij, teasing
plag(ge), sod of turf
plagi'aat n, plagiarism
plak, slice; slab
 onder de plak zitten, to be under a person's thumb
plakband, adhesive tape
pla'ket, plaque
plak'kaat n, placard
plakken, to stick
plakzegel, adhesive stamp
pla'muren, to fill (the grain), to stop
plan n, plan, project
 van plan zijn, to intend
pla'neet, planet
pla'neren, to hover
plank, plank, board; shelf
plankenkoorts, stage-fright
plan'kier n, platform
plant, plant
plant'aardig, vegetable
plan'tage, plantation
planten, to plant
plantengroei, vegetation
plantkunde, botany
plant'soen n, gardens, flower-bed
plas, pool, puddle; lake
plasregen, downpour
plassen, to splash; to piddle
plas'tiek n, plastisch, plastic
plat, flat; vulgar
pla'taan, plane-tree
platboomd, flat-bottomed
pla'teel n, pottery
platheid, flatness; vulgarity
platina n, platinum
platte'grond, (ground-)plan
platte'land n, country(side)
platte'lands, country, rural
plattrappen, to trample down
platweg, flatly
platzak, penniless, empty-handed
pla'veien, to pave
pla'veisel n, paving
pla'vuis, flag-stone
ple'bejer, plebeian
plebs n, hoi polloi
plecht('stat)ig, solemn

plechtigheid, ceremony, solemnity
pleeg-, foster-
pleegzuster, sick-nurse; foster-sister
plegen, to commit
 hij placht te zeggen, he used to say
 overleg plegen, to consult together
plei'dooi n, plea, (address for the) defence
plein n, square, open space
pleister(en) n, (to) plaster
pleisterplaats, road-house
pleit, n, dispute
pleiten, to plead
 dat pleit voor hem, that's a point in his favour
plek, spot
ple'nair, plenary
plengen, to shed
pletten, to roll out, to crush
pletter: te — slaan, to smash to smithereens
pleur('it)is, pleurisy
ple'zier n, pleasure
ple'zierig, pleasant
plicht, duty
plicht(s)getrouw, plicht'-matig, dutiful
plichtpleging, ceremony
plint, plinth; skirting-board
plis'sé, pleat(ing)
ploeg, plough: gang, shift, team
ploegen, to plough
ploegschaar, ploughshare
ploert, cad
ploertendoder, cosh
ploerte'rij, owners of digs
ploeteren, to splash; to plod; to drudge
plof(fen), (to) thud, (to) plop
plom'beren, to fill
plombière, sundae
plomp, unwieldy: thud: water-lily
plons, (s)plash
plonzen, to (s)plash
plooi, fold, pleat, crease
 uit de plooi komen, to unbend
plooibaar, pliable

plooien, to fold, to pleat
plotseling, sudden
pluche, plush
pluim, plume, feather; tuft
pluimpje *n,* compliment
plui'mage, plumage
pluimstrijker, toady
pluimvee *n,* poultry
pluis: niet —, fishy
pluisje *n,* piece of fluff
pluizen, to (give off) fluff
pluk, pick
  een hele pluk, quite a job
plukken, to pick, to pluck
plu'meau, feather duster
plunderen, to plunder
plunje, togs
plunjezak, kit-bag
plus'minus, approximately
p.o., by return (of post)
pochen, to boast
po'cheren, to poach
po'chette, breast-pocket handkerchief
podium *n,* dais
poedel, poodle
poedelnaakt, stark naked
poeder, powder
poederdons, powder-puff
poedersuiker, icing sugar
poe'ha, fuss, la-di-da
poeieren, to powder
poel, pool, puddle
poe'lier, poulterer
poen, spiv
poes, puss
  niet voor de poes, no chickenfeed
poeslief, honey-lipped
poespas, fuss about nothing
poets: een — bakken, to play a trick on
poetsen, to polish, to brush
poetskatoen *n,* cotton waste
poezelig, chubby
poë'zie, poetry
pof: op de —, on tick
pofbroek, plus-fours
poffen, to puff: to pop
poffertjes, small fritters
pofmouw, leg-of-mutton sleeve
pogen, to endeavour
poging, attempt

pok('dalig), pock(-marked)
pokken, smallpox
pol, tussock
po'lair, polar
Polen *n,* Poland
po'lijsten, to polish
polikli'niek, out-patients' department
polis, insurance policy
po'liticus, politician
po'litie, police
po'litieagent, policeman
po'litiebureau *n,* police-station
poli'tiek, policy; politics: political
poli'toer(en), (to) French polish
pollepel, wooden spoon
pols, pulse, wrist
polsen, to sound
polsslag, pulse, pulsation
polsspringen *n,* pole-vaulting
pom'made, pomade
pomp(en), (to) pump
pom'peus, pompous
pom'poen, pumpkin
pond *n,* pound, 500 grammes
ponsma'chine, punching-machine
pont, ferry-boat
pontifex, pontiff
pon'ton, pontoon
pony, pony; fringe
pooier, ponce
pook, poker
pool, pole
poolcirkel, polar circle
poolreiziger, arctic explorer
Pools, Polish
  Poolse landdag, bear-garden
poolshoogte nemen, to see how the land lies
poolster, pole-star
poolzee, (ant)arctic sea
poort, gate(way)
poorter, burgher
poos(je *n),* (little) while
poot, paw, leg
  poot aan spelen, to buckle to
pootaardappel, seed-potato
pootjebaden, to paddle
pop, doll; puppet; dummy; court-card; pupa
  nu heb je de poppen aan het dansen! that's torn it!

popelen, to quiver, to itch
pope'line, poplin
poppenkast, puppet-show, Punch and Judy show
popperig, diminutive
popu'lair, popular
popu'lier, poplar
por, prod
po'reus, porous
porie, pore
porren, to poke, to prod
porse'lein n, china(-ware)
port, postage: port(-wine)
por'taal n, porch; hall, landing
porte-bri'sée, sliding doors
por'tée, purport
porte'feuille, portfolio; wallet
porte-man'teau, hall-stand
portemon'naie, purse
portie, share, helping
por'tiek n, portico, porch
por'tier, (hall-)porter; door
porto, postage
por'tret n, portrait
po'seren, to pose, to sit
po'sitie, position, situation
in positie, expecting
posi'tief, positive
po'sitiejapon, maternity-gown
posi'tieven, wits
post, post; mail; item; picket
op post, on duty
postbode, postman
postbus, post-office box
postdirecteur, postmaster
postduif, carrier-pigeon
poste'lein, purslane
posten, to post; to picket
pos'teren, to post, to station
poste'rijen, postal service
pos't(h)uum, posthumous
postpapier n, note-paper
poststempel n, postmark
pos'tuur n, figure; posture
postwissel, money order
postzegel, postage stamp
pot, pot, jar; kitty
potas, potash
potdicht, shut tight
potdoof, stone-deaf
poteling, seedling; hefty fellow
poten, to plant, to dibble
poten'tieel, potential

potig, hefty
potlood n, pencil; black-lead
pot'nat: één —, six of one and half a dozen of the other
pot'sierlijk, grotesque
potten, to pot; to hoard
pottenbakker, potter
potver'dikkie! Great Scott!
potvis, sperm-whale
pover, poor, meagre
pozen, to pause
praal, pomp, splendour
praalziek, ostentatious
praat(je n), talk, chat, gossip
veel praats hebben, to talk big
praatgraag, praatziek, garrulous
pracht, splendour
prachtband, de luxe binding
prachtig, splendid, magnificent
practicum n, practical (work)
practisch, practical
pr(a)eses, chairman
prak, hash
prakken, to mash (up)
prakke'zeren, to have a think
prak'tijk, practice
prakti'zeren, to practice
pralen, to shine; to flaunt
prangen, to pinch
prat gaan op, to pride oneself on
praten, to talk
pre'cair, precarious
pre'cies, precise, exact
predi'kant, minister
predi'katie, sermon
prediken, to preach
preek, sermon
preekstoel, pulpit
prefe'reren, to prefer
prei, leek
preken, to preach
pre'laat, prelate
premie, premium
prent, print, picture
prenten, to imprint
prepa'raat n, preparation
presen'teerblad n, salver, tray
presen'teren, to offer; to present
pre'sent-exemplaar n, complimentary copy

pre'sentielijst, attendance list
presi'dentschap n, presidency
presi'deren, to preside (at)
pre'sidium n, chairmanship
pressen, to press
presse-pa'pier, paper-weight
pressie uitoefenen, to bring pressure to bear
pres'tatie, achievement
pres'teren, to achieve
pret, fun
preten'dent, pretender
pre'tentie, pretension
 zonder pretenties, unassuming
pre'tentieloos, unpretentious
preten'tieus, presumptuous
prettig, pleasant, nice
 prettig vinden, to like
preuts, prudish, squeamish
preva'leren, to prevail
prevelen, to mutter
pri'ëel n, arbour
priem, awl
priester, priest
priesterschap n, priesthood
prijken, to (be) display(ed)
prijs, price; prize
 op prijs stellen, to appreciate
prijscourant, price-list
prijsgeven, to abandon
prijsnotering, quotation (of prices)
prijsuitdeling, prize-giving
prijsvraag, competition
prijzen, to praise; to price, to mark
prijzens'waardig, praiseworthy
prijzig, expensive
prik, prick, stab
prikkebeen, spindle-shanks
prikkel, sting, goad; spur
prikkelbaar, irritable
prikkeldraad n, barbed wire
prikkelen, to prickle; to irritate, to provoke; to stimulate
prikken, to prick; to tingle
pril, tender, vernal
prima, first-rate
pri'mair, primary
pri'meur, scoop
primi'tief, primitive, crude
prin'cipe n, principle

principi'eel, fundamental, of or on principle
prins, prince
 van de prins geen kwaad weten, to be as innocent as an unborn babe
prinselijk, princely
prin'ses, princess
prin'sesseboon, dwarf bean
priori'teit, priority
prisma n, prism
pri'vaat, private: n, rears
pri'vaatdocent, external (university) lecturer
pri'vaatles, private tuition
privé, private
pro'baat, proven
pro'beren, to try (out)
pro'bleem n, problem
procé'dé n, process
proce'deren, to take it to court
pro'cent n, percent
pro'ces n, lawsuit; process
 iemand een proces aandoen, to bring an action against a person
pro'ces-ver'baal n, official report
procla'meren, to proclaim
procu'ratie, power of attorney
procu'reur, attorney
pro Deo, voluntary, for love
produ'cent, producer
produ'ceren, to produce
pro'duct n, product(ion)
proef, test; proof
proefkonijn n, laboratory rabbit; guinea-pig
proefneming, experiment
proefonder'vindelijk, experimental
proefschrift n, thesis
proefstation n, research station
proeftijd, noviciate; apprenticeship; probation
proefwerk n, test (paper)
proesten, to splutter
proeven, to taste
pro'faan, profane
profa'neren, to profane
pro'feet, prophet
professo'raal, professorial
professo'raat n, professorship

profe'teren, to prophesy
profe'tie, prophecy
pro'fiel n, profile; cross-section
pro'fijt n, profit, advantage
profi'teren van, to profit by, to take advantage of
pro'gramma n, programme
progres'sief, progressive
projec'teren, to project, to plan
pro'jectie, projection
pro'leet, pariah
prole'tariër, proletarian
prolon'geren, to continue
pro'loog, prologue
pro'motie, promotion, graduation (ceremony)
pro'motor, company-promoter; director of research (studies)
promo'veren, to obtain a doctor's degree
pronk: te — staan, to be on show
pronken, to show off
pronkjuweel n, gem
pronkstuk n, show-piece
pronon'ceren, to pronounce
prooi, prey
proost ! cheers!
prop, plug, wad
  met een voorstel op de proppen komen, to come out with a suggestion
propae'deutisch, preliminary
propa'geren, to propagate
propje n, pellet; tubby little person
proper, clean and tidy
propvol, chock-full
prostitu'ée, prostitute
prote'geren, to patronize, to befriend
protes'teren, to protest
pro'these, artificial teeth (or limb etc.)
protserig, ostentatious
provi'and, provisions
provian'deren, to provision
provinci'aal, provincial
pro'vincie, province
pro'visie, provision; commission
pro'visiekast, store-cupboard
provi'sorisch, provisional

provo'ceren, to provoke
pro'voost, punishment-cell
proza n, prose
pruik, wig
pruikentijd, the time of 18th century dandyism
pruilen, to pout
pruim, plum; quid
pruime'dant, prune
pruimemondje n: een — trekken, to purse the lips
pruimen, to chew tobacco
Pruisen n, Prussia
prul n, trash; wastrel
prullenmand, waste-paper basket
prut, curds, mire, grounds
prutsen, to mess about, to botch
pruttelen, to simmer; to grumble
psychi'ater, psychiatrist
psycho'loog, psychologist
puber'teit, adolescence
publi'ceren, to publish
pu'bliek (n), public, audience
puffen, to puff
puik, choice
puimsteen, pumice-stone
puin n, rubble
puinhoop, ruins, debris
puistje n, **pukkel**, pimple
pul, ewer, large vase, tankard
pulken, to pick
pulver n, powder
pummel, yokel
pu'naise, drawing-pin
punctu'eel, punctual
punt (n), point, tip; full-stop
  dubbel(e) punt, colon
  punt komma, semi-colon
  als puntje bij paaltje komt, when it comes to the point
puntdicht n, epigram
punter, punt
puntig, pointed, jagged
pu'pil, ward; pupil
pur'geermiddel n, purgative
Puri'tein(s), Puritan(ical)
purper(en) (n), purple
put, pit, well
  in de put zitten, to be depressed
putten, to draw, to derive
puur, sheer, neat

Q

quaran'taine, quarantine
quartre-'mains, duet
quitte, quits

R

ra, yard(-arm)
raad, advice; council, board
raadgevend, advisory
raadgeving, (piece of) advice
raadhuis *n*, council offices
raadplegen, to consult
raadsel *n*, riddle, puzzle;
  enigma
raadselachtig, mystifying
raadsheer, justice
raadslid *n*, councillor
raadsman, adviser
raadzaam, advisable
raaf, raven
raak, well-aimed, to the point
  maar raak, at random
raaklijn, tangent
raam *n*, window; frame
raamkozijn *n*, window-frame,
  window-sill
raapstelen, turnip-tops
raar, queer; silly
raaskallen, to blather
ra'barber, rhubarb
rab'bijn, rabbi
rad, voluble: *n* wheel
  een rad voor de ogen draaien,
  to throw dust in (a person's)
  eyes
radbraken, to wreck, to mangle
radeloos, at a loss, distraught
raden, to guess; to advise
raderboot, paddle-steamer
ra'deren, to erase
radi'caal, radical, fundamental
ra'dijs, radish
radiolamp, (wireless) valve
radio-omroep, broadcasting-
  service
rafelen, to fray
raffinade'rij, refinery
rage, craze
ragebol, mop (of hair)
ragfijn, gossamer(y)
rakelings langs gaan, to skim
  past

raken, to hit, to touch; to concern; to get
ra'ket, racquet; rocket
rakker, rascal
ram, ram
ramen (op), to estimate (at)
ramen'as, black radish
ram'meien, to batter, to ram
rammelaar, rattle
rammelen, to rattle, to clank
  door elkaar rammelen, to
  give a thorough shaking to
rammelkast, tin-can
rammen, to ram
ramp, disaster
rampo'neren, to wreck
rampspoed, adversity
ramp'zalig, disastrous, wretched
ran'cune, rancour
rand, edge, (b)rim
rang, rank, grade
ran'geren, to shunt
rangschikken, to arrange
rangtelwoord *n*, ordinal number
rank, slender, sleek-lined; tendril
ransel, knapsack, satchel; hiding
ranselen, to thrash
rans(ig), rancid
rant'soen *n*, ration
rantsoe'nering, rationing
rap, nimble
ra'paille, ra'palje *n*, rabble
rapen, to gather
rappe'leren, to recall
rap'port *n*, report
rappor'teren, to report
rari'teit, curio(sity)
ras, quick, soon: thoroughbred:
  n, race; breed;
rasecht, true-born
rasp, grater, rasp
raspen, to grate, to rasp
raster, lath
rat, rat
rata'plan, caboodle
ratel, rattle; tongue
ratelen, to rattle, to roll
rationali'seren, to rationalize
ratio'neel, rational
ratje'toe, hotchpotch
rats, blue funk
ratsen, to whip, to pinch

rattekruid *n*, arsenic
rauw, raw; raucous
 dat valt me rauw op het lijf, that's an unexpected blow
rauwkost, uncooked vegetables *or* fruit
ravezwart, jet-black
ra'vijn *n*, ravine
ravitai'lleren, to victual
ra'votten, to romp
razen, to roar, to rage
 het water raast, the kettle sings
razend, furious, wild, frantic
razer'nij, frenzy
re'actie, reaction
rea'geerbuis, test-tube
rea'geren, to react, to respond
reali'seren : zich —, to realize
reali'teit, reality
re'bel('leren), (to) rebel
recen'sent, reviewer
re'censie, review
re'cept *n*, recipe; prescription
re'ceptie, reception
re'cherche, criminal investigation department
recher'cheur, detective
recht, straight; right: *n*, right; law
rechtbank, (law-)court(s)
rechtens, by right(s)
rechter, judge
rechter-, right
rechterhand, right hand (side)
rechterlijk, judicial
rechtge'aard, right-minded; honest
rechthoek, rectangle
recht'hoekig, rectangular, right-angled
recht'matig, lawful, legitimate
recht'op, upright, erect
rechts, (on) the right; right-handed; Right(-winged)
rechts'af, to the right
recht'schapen, honest
rechtsgeding *n*, lawsuit
rechts'geldig, legal
rechtsgeleerde, lawyer
rechtsgeleerdheid, jurisprudence
rechtsom'keert! about turn!

rechtspositie, legal status
rechtspraak, administration of justice
rechtspreken, to administer justice
recht'standig, perpendicular
rechtstreeks, direct
rechtsvervolging, prosecution
rechtzaak, lawsuit
rechtzaal, court-room
rechtzekerheid, legal security
recht'uit, straight (on)
recht'vaardig, just
recht'vaardigen, to justify
recht'zinnig, orthodox
recipi'ëren, to receive
reci'teren, to recite
re'clame, advertisement; claim
 re'clame maken voor, to advertise
recla'meren, to (put in a) claim
reclas'sering, (prisoner) rehabilitation
recomman'deren, to recommend
reconstru'eren, to reconstruct
recru'teren, to recruit
rector principal, master
 rector mag'nificus, Vice-Chancellor
re'çu *n*, receipt, ticket
redac'teur, editor
re'dactie, editorial staff
reddeloos, irretrievable
redden, to save, to rescue
 ik kan me wel redden, I can manage (all right)
reddingsboot, life-boat
reddingsgordel, life-belt
rede, reason; speech: roads(tead)
 in de rede vallen, to interrupt
redekavelen, to bandy arguments, to dispute
redekunde, redekunst, (art of) rhetoric
redelijk, reasonable; rational
redeloos, senseless, irrational
reden, reason
redenaar, orator
rede'natie, rede'nering, reasoning
rede'neren, to reason; to hold forth
reder('ij), ship-owner(s)

rederijker, rhetorician
redetwisten, to dispute
redevoering, speech, oration
redeziften, to split hairs
redi'geren, to edit
redmiddel *n,* expedient
re'ductie, reduction
ree(bok), roe(-buck)
reebout, haunch of venison
reebruin (*n*), fawn
reeds, already
re'ëel, real(istic)
reeks, series, row, string
reep, strip, bar; rope
reet, chink
refe'raat *n,* paper, lecture
refe'renties, references
refe'reren, to refer
re'ferte : onder — aan, with
  reference to
reflec'tant, interested party
reflec'teren op, to answer; to
  entertain
refor'matie, reformation
re'frein *n,* refrain
regel, rule; line
regelen, to arrange; to regulate
  zich regelen naar, to conform to
regeling, arrangement
regelmaat, regularity
regel'matig, regular
regelrecht, straight
regen, rain
  van de regen in de drop, from
  the frying-pan into the fire
regenachtig, rainy
regenen, to rain
regenjas, rain-coat
re'gent, regent, governor
re'gentenregering, oligarchy
regenton, water-butt
re'gentschap *n,* regency, govern-
  orship
re'geren, to govern, to rule
re'gering, government, reign
re'gie, production
regis'seur, producer
re'gister *n,* register; index;
  organ-stop
regis'treren, to register
regle'ment *n,* regulation(s)
reglemen'tair, regular
regu'leren, to regulate

rei, chorus (of dancers)
reiger, heron
reiken, to reach, to stretch
reikhalzend, longingly
reilen : zoals het reilt en zeilt,
  lock, stock and barrel
rein, clean; chaste
  je reinste, utter
  in het reine brengen, to
  straighten out
reine-claude, greengage
reinigen, to clean(se)
reinigingsmiddel *n,* detergent
reis, journey, voyage
reisbureau *n,* travel-agency
reisgelegenheden, travelling
  facilities
reisgoed *n,* luggage
reis-necessaire, dressing-case,
  toilet-case
reis'vaardig, ready to leave
reisvereniging, travel association
reizen, to travel
reiziger, traveller, passenger
rek, elasticity: *n,* rack
  dat is een hele rek, it's a tidy
  stretch
rekbaar(heid), elastic(ity)
rekel, rascal
rekenen, to reckon, to count; to
  charge
  reken maar ! you bet!
rekenfout, (mathmatical) error
rekening, bill, account
  rekening houden met, to take
  into consideration
rekening-cou'rant, current account
rekenkunde, arithmetic
rekenliniaal, slide-rule
rekenmachine, calculating-
  machine
rekenschap, account
  zich rekenschap geven van,
  to realize (to the full)
rekken, to stretch; to protract
rekstok, horizontal bar
re'k(w)est *n,* petition
rekwi'reren, to requisition
rel, riot
re'laas *n,* account
re'latie, (business) relation, connection

rela'tief, relative
reli'ëfdruk, die-stamping
re'ligie, religion
reli'kwi, reli'qui, relic
reling, (ship's) rail(s)
relletje *n*, disturbance
rem, brake
rem'bours *n*, cash on delivery
re'mise, remittance; tram depot; draw(n game)
remmen, to brake; to restrain, to retard
rempla'cant, substitute
rempla'ceren, to replace
renbaan, race-course; speedway
ren'dabel, profitable, paying
ren'deren, to pay (its way)
rendier *n*, reindeer
rennen, to run
renom'mee, fame
renpaard *n*, race-horse
rente, interest
rentekaart, insurance card
renteloos, free of interest
rente'nieren, to live on private means
rentestandaard, rate of interest
rentmeester, agent
rep en roer, an uproar
repa'ratie, repair(s)
repa'reren, to repair, to mend
repatri'ëren, to return home, to repatriate
repe'teren, to repeat; to rehearse; to coach (for an examination)
repe'titie, (revision-)test; rehearsal
repe'titor, coach, tutor
re'pliek, rejoinder
repor'tage, commentary
reppen van, to make any mention of
zich reppen, to hurry (up)
repre'saillemaatregel, reprisal
re'prise, repeat(-performance)
rep'tiel *n*, reptile
repu'bliek, republic
republi'kein(s), republican
repu'tatie, reputation
requi'reren, to requisition
reser'vaat *n*, reserve
re'serve, reserve(s)

re'servewiel *n*, spare wheel
resi'dentie, royal residence; residency
reso'luut, resolute
reso'neren, to resound
respec'tievelijk, respectively
res'pijt *n*, respite
res'sort *n*, jurisdiction
ressor'teren onder, to come under the jurisdiction of
rest, rest, remainder
res'tant *n*, remnant
restau'ratie, restoration, renovation; refreshment-room, dining-car
resten, to remain
res'terend, remaining
restitu'eren, to pay back
resul'taat *n*, result
resu'meren, to summarize
reti'rade, toilet
retou'cheren, to touch up
re'tour, return
re'traite, retreat
reu, male dog
reuk, smell, scent, odour
reukwater *n*, scent
reü'nie, reunion
reü'nisten, past members
reus, giant
reus'achtig, tremendous
reutel(en), (to) rattle
reuze, enormous, wizard
reuzel, lard
reuzenarbeid, gigantic task
re'vanche, revenge
reven, to reef (down)
revé'rence, curtsey
re'vers, lapel
re'visie, revision
revolution'nair, revolutionary
re'vue, review; revue
r(h)e'torisch, rhetorical
r(h)euma'tiek, rheumatism
riant, delightful
rib, rib
ribbel(ig), rib(bed)
ribbenkast, body
richel, ledge, ridge
richten, to direct, to aim; to address
zich richten naar, to conform to

richting, direction, trend
  iets in die richting, something of the sort
richtlijn, guiding principal
richtsnoer, guidance
ridder, knight
ridderlijk, chivalrous
ridderorde, order of knighthood
ridderroman, romance of chivalry
ridderslag, accolade
ridderstand, knighthood, knightage
rieken, to smell
riem, strap, belt: oar: ream
riet n, reed; cane
rieten dak n, thatched roof
rietje n, (drinking-)straw
rietsuiker, cane-sugar
rif n, reef
rij, row
  op de rij af, consecutively
rijbaan, riding track; carriageway
rijbewijs n, driving-licence
rijbroek, riding breeches
rijden, to ride, to drive, to run
rijdier n, mount
rijgen, to tack; to thread
rijgnaald, rijgpen, bodkin
rijk, rich, wealthy, sumptuous: n, state, realm
  het Britse Rijk, the British Empire
  het rijk alleen hebben, to have it all to oneself
rijkdom, riches, wealth
rijkelijk, richly, amply
rijknecht, groom
rijksambtenaar, civil servant
rijksbureau n, government department
rijks'daalder, 2½ guilders
rijkskosten: op —, at the public expense
rijksweg, trunk road
rijkswege: van —, on government authority
rijm n, rhyme
rijmelaar, versifier
rijmela'rij, doggerel
rijmen, to rhyme; to tally, to reconcile

Rijn, Rhine
Rijnvaart, Rhine trade
rijp, ripe, mature: hoar-frost
rijpelijk, seriously
rijpen, to ripen, to mature
  het heeft gerijpt, there has been a hoar-frost
rijs(hout) n, osier(s)
rijschool, riding-school
rijst, rice
rijste'brij, rijstepap, rice-pudding
rijsttafel, meal of savoury dishes with rice
rijtuig n, carriage
rijweg, carriage-way
rijwiel n, (bi)cycle
rijwielstalling, cycle store-(house)
rijzen, to (a)rise
rijzig, tall
riksja, rickshaw
rillen, to shiver, to shudder
rimboe, jungle
rimpel(en) (to) wrinkle (up); (to) ripple; (to) gather
ring, ring
ringbaard, dundreary whiskers
ringeloren, to browbeat
ringsteken, to tilt at the ring
ringwerpen n, quoits
rinkelen, to jingle, to tinkle
rins, acidulous
rio'lering, sewerage
ri'ool n, sewer, drain
ris, bunch
ri'see, laughing stock
risico n, risk
ris'kant, risky
ris'keren, to risk
rist, string
risten, to strip, to string
rit, (tram-, bus-)ride, drive, rally
ritme n, rhythm
ritmisch, rhythmic(al)
ritselen, to rustle
ritssluiting, zip-fastener
ritu'eel n, ritual
ritus, rite
rivali'teit, rivalry
ri'vier, river
rob, seal
robbedoes, tomboy

robber, rubber
ro'bijn, ruby
ro'buust, robust
rochelen, to rattle, to ruckle
roddelen, to gossip
rode'hond, German measles
roebel, rouble
roe(de), rod, birch; rood
roef, deck-house: whiz!
roeiboot, rowing-boat
roeien, to row
roeipen, rowlock
roeispaan, oar
roek, rook
roekeloos, reckless
roem, glory, renown
roemen, to praise; to boast
Roe'menië n, Roumania
roemer, goblet
roemrijk, roemvol, glorious
roep, call, cry; fame
roepen, to call (out)
roeping, calling, vocation
roepstem, call (of duty)
roer n, rudder, helm
roerdomp, bittern
roerei n, scrambled egg
roeren, to stir; to move
roerend, moving, pathetic
roerende goederen, movables
roerganger, helmsman
roerig, restless
roerloos, motionless: rudderless
roerpen, tiller
roersteven, sternpost
roes, intoxication, fever of excitement
roest, perch, roost: n, rust, blight
oud roest, scrap iron
roesten, to rust
roestig, rusty
roestvrij, rustproof, stainless
roet n, soot
roet in het eten gooien, to throw a spanner in the works
roezemoezig, rowdy
roffel, (drum-)roll
rogge, rye
rok, skirt; tails
rokbeschermer, dress-guard
rokkostuum n, dress-suit
roken, to smoke

rol, roll; part, role
aan de rol zijn, to be on the spree
rolgordijn n, blind
rol'lade, collared beef
rollen, to roll
rolletje n, roll, packet; castor
rolluik n, roller shutter
rolmops, Bismarck herring
rolpens, spiced mince pudding done up in tripe
rolschaats(en), (to) roller-skate
rolstoel, wheel-chair
roltrap, escalator
rolvast, word-perfect
rolveger, carpet-sweeper
rolverdeling, cast
roman, novel
roman'tiek, romantic(ism)
romantisch, romantic
Ro'mein(s), Roman
rommel, mess, rubbish, junk
rommelen, to rummage; to rumble
rommelig, untidy
rommelkamer, lumber-room
romp, trunk; hull; fuselage
rompslomp, fuss and bother
rond, round; forthright
in het rond, round (about)
rondas, buckler
rondbazuinen, to blaze abroad
rond'borstig, forthright
ronde, round(s), lap, heat
ron'deel n, rondeau
rondhout n, spa
ronding, rounding, curve, camber
rondje n, round (of drinks or cards)
rondkomen, to make ends meet
rondom, all round
rondreis, tour
rondreizend, itinerant, touring
rondrit, (coach-)tour
rondschrijven n, circular letter
rondtasten, to grope about
rondte: in de —, in a circle, round about
ronduit, outright
rondvaart, boat-trip
rondvertellen, to spread
rondvlucht, (joy-)flight

rondvraag, question time
rondwaren, to haunt
ronken, to snore; to roar
ronselen, to recruit
röntgenen, to (give) X-ray (treatment)
rood (n), red
 rood koper, copper
roodborstje n, robin
roodgloeiend, red-hot
roodvonk, scarlet fever
roof, plunder, robbery, prey
roofdier n, beast of prey
roofoverval, hold-up
rooftocht, foray
roof'zuchtig, rapacious
rooien, to dig (up); to manage
rook, smoke
 onder de rook van, within a stone's throw of
rookgordijn n, smoke-screen
rooktabak, pipe-tobacco
rookvlees n, smoked beef
room, cream
roomboter, butter
roomijs n, ice-cream
Rooms(-Katholiek), Roman (Catholic)
roomsoes, cream-puff
roos, rose; dandruff; bull's eye
roos'kleurig, rosy
rooster, grating, grate, grill, ventilator; rota, time-table
roost(er)en, to roast, to grill, to toast
ros n, steed
ro'sarium n, rose-garden
rosbief n, roast beef
rose (n), pink
roskammen, to curry; to slate
rossen, to tear (along)
rot, rotten
 zich rot lachen, to laugh oneself stupid
ro'teren, to rotate
rots, rock, cliff
rotsachtig, rocky
rotsblok n, boulder
rotspartij, rockery
rotsvast, firm as a rock
rotten, to rot, to decay
rotting, cane
rotzooi, ruddy mess(-up)

rou'leren, to be in circulation
rouw, mourning
rouwbeklag n, condolence
rouwdienst, memorial service
rouwen, to rue
rouwig, sorry
rouwkoets, funeral coach
rouwrandjes n, dirty nails
roven, to pillage, to steal, to kidnap
rover, robber
ro'yaal, generous, sporting, lavish, ample
royal'istisch, royalist
royali'teit, open-handedness
ro'yeren, to strike off the register
rozebottel, rose-hip
rozelaar, rose-bush
rozenkrans, rosary; garland of roses
ro'zet, rosette
ro'zijn, raisin
rubber, rubber
ru'briek, heading, rubric, column
ruchtbaar maken, to make known
ruchtbaarheid, publicity
rug, back, ridge
 achter de rug, over and done with
ruggegraat, backbone
ruggelings, backward(s), back to back
ruggespraak, consultation
rugleuning, back of the chair
rugzak, rucksack
rui(en), (to) moult
ruif, manger
ruig, shaggy, hairy; rough
ruiken, to smell, to scent
ruiker, posy
ruil, exchange
ruilen, to (ex)change, to swop
ruim, ample, spacious, wide: n, hold
ruimen, to clear (away)
 het veld ruimen, to give way to
ruimschoots, amply
ruimte, room, space
ruin, gelding
ru'ïne, ruin(s), wreck
ruï'neren, to ruin
ruisen, to rustle, to rush, to swish

ruit, (glass) pane(l); check; diamond

ruiten'boer, knave of diamonds

ruiter, horseman, trooper

ruiteraanval, cavalry charge

ruite'rij, calvalry

ruiterlijk, frank

ruiterpad n, bridle-path

ruitewisser, squeegee, wind-screen wiper

ruitijd, moulting season

ruk(ken), (to) tug, (to) jerk

rukwind, squall

rul, loose, running

ru'moer n, clamour

ru'moerig, noisy

run, tanning

rund n, ox

runderen, cattle

runderhaas, fillet of beef

runderlap, beefsteak

rundvee n, (horned) cattle

rundvet n, suet

rundvlees n, beef

runenschrift n, runic script

rups, caterpillar

Rus(sisch), Russian

rust, rest, quiet, peace; half-time

op de plaats rust! stand easy!

rustbank, rustbed n, couch

rusteloos, restless, untiring

rusten, to rest

wel te rusten! good night!

rustend, retired

rus'tiek, rustic, rural

rustig, quiet, tranquil

rustoord n, retreat

rustpoos, breathing-space

rutschbaan, switch-back, chute

ruw, rough, coarse, raw

ruzie, quarrel, row

S

saai, dull, drab

saam'horigheid, solidarity

saam'horigheidsgevoel n, team-spirit

sabbat, sabbath

sabbelen, to suck

sabel, sabre

sabelbont n, sable

sabo'teren, to sabotage

sacramen'teel, sacramental

sa'disme n, sadism

saf'fiaan n, morocco

saf'fier, sapphire

saf'fraan, saffron

sage, saga, legend

sa'jet(ten), wool(len)

sakker'loot! by Jove!

Saksisch (n), Saxon

Saksisch porcelein, Dresden china

sa'lade, salad

sa'laris n, salary

saldo n, balance

per saldo, after all

salie, sage

salmi'ak, sal-ammoniac

sa'lon, drawing-room; saloon

sa'lonmuziek, light music

sal'peterzuur n, nitric acid

salto mor'tale, somersault

salu'eren, to salute

sa'luut n, salute; cheerio!

salvo n, salvo, volley; round

samen, together

samendoen, to put together; to go shares

samenflansen, to concoct, to slap together

samengesteld, compound(ed), complex, composite

samenhangen, to be connected

samenhokken, to herd together

samenkomen, to (for)gather

samenloop van omstandig-heden, coincidence

samenscholing, gathering

samensmelten, to fuse, to amal-gamate

samenspannen, to conspire (to-gether)

samenspanning, plot, conspir-acy

samenspel n, *ensemble*, team-work

samenspraak, dialogue, con-fabulation

samenstellen, to compose

samenstelling, composition, compound

samenstroming, concourse; confluence

samentrekken, to contract, to concentrate

samenvallen, to coincide

samenvatten, to summarize

samenvloeien, to unite; to merge, to blend

samenvoegen, to join

samenweefsel n, texture, web

samenzweerder, conspirator

samenzwering, conspiracy

sanctie, sanction

san'daal, sandal

sani'tair, sanitary

sans-a'tout, no trumps

santenkraam, (the whole) bang shoot

sap n, sap, juice

sapperde'kriek, sapper'loot! by Jove!

sappig, juicy, luscious

sar'castisch, sarcastic

sarren, to bait

sas: in zijn —, pleased as Punch

sa'tanisch, fiendish

sater, satyr

sa'tijn, n, satin

sa'tiricus, satirist

sau'cijzebroodje n, sausage-roll

saus, sauce

sausen, to flavour; to pelt (with rain)

sauskom, sauce-boat

sau'teren, to quick-fry

savou'reren, to relish

sawa(h), paddy-field

scal'peren, to scalp

scan'deren, to scan

schaaf, plane, slicer

schaafwond, graze, abrasion

schaakmat, checkmate; stale-mate

schaakspel n, game of chess; chess-set

schaal, scale; shell; dish

schaldier n, crustacean

schaalverdeling, graduation

schaambeen n, pubis

schaamdelen, private parts

schaamrood n, blush of shame

schaamte(loos), shame(less)

schaap n, sheep; ninny

zwaart schaap, scapegoat

schaar, (pair of) scissors, shears; host

schaars, scarce, sparse

schaarste, scarcity, shortage

schaats(en) (rijden), (to) skate

schab'loon, stencil-plate, tem-plate

schacht, shaft

schade, damage, harm, detriment

de schade inhalen, to make up arrears

schadelijk, harmful, noxious

schadeloos stellen, to indemnify

schaden, to harm, to do damage to

schadepost, financial set-back

schadevergoeding, compensa-tion

schaduw(en), (to) shadow, (to) shade

schaduwrijk, shady

schaduwzijde, shaded side; drawback

schaffen, to provide

schaften, to knock off for lunch

schakel, link

schakelaar, switch

schaken, to play chess: to ab-duct

scha'kering, shade

schalk, rogue

schalks, roguish

schallen, to (re)sound, to ring out

schal'mei, shawm

schamel, meagre, wretched

schamen: zich —, to be ashamed

schampen, to graze; to mock

schamper, scornful

schan'daal n, scandal, shame

schan'dalig, disgraceful, shame-ful

schanddaad, outrage

schande, disgrace, shame

schandelijk, disgraceful

schandpaal, pillory

schandvlek, stain, disgrace

schapebout, leg of mutton

schapewolkjes, fleecy clouds

schappelijk, fair, decent

schar, dab

scharen, to range, to rally

scharensliep, scharenslijper, knife-grinder

schar'laken n, scarlet

schar'minkel, spindle-shanks

schar'nier n, hinge

scharrelen, to rummage; to get along somehow

schat, treasure, wealth; darling

schatbewaarder, treasurer

schateren, to scream (with laughter)

schatkist, treasury

schatrijk, fabulously rich

schattebout, poppet

schatten, to value; to estimate

schattig, sweet

schatting, estimate, valuation; tribute

schaven, to plane; to graze; to polish

scha'vot n, scaffold

scha'vuit, rascal

schede, sheath; vagina

schedel, skull

scheef, crooked, lop-sided, raked

scheve voorstelling, misrepresentation

scheve verhouding, wry relationship

scheel, cross-eyed

scheelkijken, scheelzien, to squint

scheenbeen n, shin(-bone)

scheepgaan, to embark

scheepsbeschuit, ship's biscuit

scheepsbouw, ship-building

scheepsjournaal n, log(-book)

scheepsrecht n, maritime law

scheepsroeper, loud hailer

scheepsruimte, tonnage; cargo space

scheepsterm, nautical term

scheepsvolk n, (ship's) crew

scheepvaart, shipping

scheepvaartkunde, navigation

scheerapparaat n, (safety) razor

scheerlijn, guy(-rope)

scheermes n, cut-throat razor

scheermesje n, razor-blade

scheerriem, strop

scheerzeep, shaving-soap

schegbeeld n, figure-head

scheidbaar, separable

scheiden, to separate, to part; to divorce

scheiding, separation; parting; divorce

scheiding van tafel en bed, legal separation

schei(ds)lijn, dividing-line

scheidsmuur, partition-wall; barrier

scheidsrechter, umpire, referee; arbitrator

scheikunde, chemistry

schei'kundig, chemical

schei'kundige, (analytical) chemist

schel, shrill, glaring; bell

schelden (op), to swear (at)

scheldnaam, (rude) name

scheldpartij, slanging-match

scheldwoord n, term of abuse

schelen, to matter; to make a difference

het kan me niet schelen, I don't mind

we schelen maar twee jaar, there is only two years between us

schellak, shellac

schellen, to ring (the bell)

schellinkje n, gallery

schelm, rascal

schelmenroman, picaresque novel

schelms, roguish

schelp, shell, scallop

schelpdier n, shell-fish

schelvis, haddock

schema n, sketch diagram, rough draft

sche'matisch, schematic

schemer(ing), twilight, dusk

schemer(acht)ig, dim, vague

schemerdonker (n), twili(gh)t, half-dark(ness)

schemeren, to dawn, to grow dusk; to be dimly visible

zitten schemeren, to sit in the twilight

schemerlamp, shaded lamp

schenden, to violate; to damage, to disfigure; to desecrate

schenkel, shank; femur

schenken, to pour (out); to present with, to grant

schenking, gift

schep, shovel, scoop

  een schep geld, heaps of money

schepel, bushel

schepeling, member of the crew

schepen, to ship: sheriff

schepje *n*, spoonful

  er een schepje opdoen, to go one better

scheppen, to scoop, to shovel, to ladle: to create

  een luchtje scheppen, to take a breather

  vreugde scheppen, to derive great pleasure

scheppend, creative

schepper, creator

schepping, creation

scheprad *n*, paddle wheel, water-wheel

schepsel *n*, creature

scheren, to shave, to shear, to skin

  scheer je weg ! be off with you !

scherf, fragment, splinter

schering en inslag, warp and woof; everyday occurrence

scherm *n*, screen, curtain

  achter de schermen, behind the scenes

schermdegen, foil

schermen, to fence

scher'mutseling, skirmish

scherp, sharp, keen; trenchant

  scherpe hoek, acute angle; sharp corner

scherp *n*, edge; live cartridge

scherpen, to sharpen; to whet

scherp'hoekig, acute-angled

scherprechter, executioner

scherpschutter, marksman

scherpte, sharpness, definition

scherpziend, keen-sighted; penetrating

scherp'zinnig, acute, astute

scherp'zinnigheid, acumen

scherts, joking, jest; joke

schertsen, to jest

schets(en), (to) sketch

schetteren, to blare; to rant, to gas

scheur, tear, crack

scheurbuik, scurvy

scheuren, to tear; to plough up; to crack

scheuring, split, cleavage

scheut, dash; shooting pain

scheutig, open-handed

schichtig, shy, skittish

schielijk, quick, swift

schier, nearly

schiereiland *n*, peninsula

schietbaan, rifle-range

schieten, to shoot, to fire

  een plan laten schieten, to drop a plan

  te binnen schieten, to dawn on

schietgat *n*, loop-hole

schietkatoen *n*, gun-cotton

schietlood *n*, plummet

schietschijf, target

schiften, to sift, to screen; to curdle

schijf, disk; slice; target, dial

schijn, light; appearance, semblance

schijnaanval, sham-attack

schijnbaar, seemingly

schijnbeeld *n*, phantom

schijnbeweging, apparent movement; feint

schijnen, to shine; to seem

schijngestalte, phase

schijn'heilig, hypocritical

schijnsel *n*, light, glimmer

schijntje *n*, scrap

schijnwerper, spot-light, search-light, flood-light

schijt(en), (to) shit

schik: in zijn — zijn, to be pleased (with life)

schikgodinnen, Fates

schikken, to arrange, to settle to be convenient (to)

  zich schikken, in, to resign one-self to

schikking, arrangement, agreement

schil, peel, skin

schild *n*, shield

  iets in het schild voeren, to be up to something

schilder, painter; decorator

schilderachtig, picturesque

schilderen, to paint; to depict; to hang about

schilde'rij, painting, picture
schilderkunst, painting, art
schilderstuk *n*, painting, picture
schildklier, thyroid gland
schildknaap, shield-bearer, varlet
schildpad, tortoise(-shell), turtle
schildwacht, sentry
schilferen, to peel, to flake off
schillen, to peel
schillenboer, kitchen-waste collector
schim, shadow, ghost
schimmel, mildew; grey (horse)
schimmelen, to go mouldy
schimmel(plant), fungus
schimpen (op), to scoff (at)
schinkel, shank, femur
schip *n*, ship; nave
　schoon schip maken, to clear
　out (*or* up)
schipbreuk lijden, to be shipwrecked; to miscarry
schipbrug, pontoon-bridge
schipper, skipper, bargee
schipperen, to manage somehow
schisma *n*, schism
schitteren, to glitter, to be brilliant; to be conspicuous
schitterend, brilliant, splendid
schlager, (song-)hit
schmink(en), (to) make up
schobbejak, blackguard
schoeisel *n*, foot-wear
schoelje *n*, bad lot
schoen, shoe
　de stoute schoenen aantrekken, to pluck up courage
　iemand iets in de schoenen
　schuiven, to lay something at
　a person's door
schoener, schooner
schoenlapper, cobbler
schoenmaker, shoe-repairer
schoensmeer, shoe-polish
schoep, paddle, blade
schoffel(en) (to) hoe; (to) shuffle
schoft, cad: withers
schoftje *n*, gutter-snipe
schok, shock, jolt
schokbreker, shock-absorber
schokken, to shake, to jerk, to jolt

schol, plaice: (ice-)floe
scholen, to shoal, to flock together; to school
scho'lier, pupil
schommel, swing; lumbersome woman
schommelen, to swing, to rock, to roll; to fluctuate
schone, beauty
schonk(ig), big bone(d)
schoof, sheaf
schooier, beggar, tramp; wretch
school, school; shoal
schoolblijven: moeten —, to be kept in
schoolbord *n*, black-board
schoolgeld(en) *n*, school-fees
schoolgeleerdheid, book-learning
schooljuffrouw, school-mistress
schoolmeester, school-master; pedant
schoolplicht, compulsory school-attendance
schoolreisje *n*, school outing
schools, scholastic
schoolslag, breast stroke
schoolverzuim *n*, absence(s)
schoolwet, education act
schoolziek, shamming (illness)
schoon, clean; beautiful, fine
schoonheid, beauty
schoonheidsmiddel *n*, beauty preparation
schoonhouden, to keep clean
schoonmaak, (spring-)cleaning; clear-out
schoonmaken, to clean
schoonouders, schoonvader en schoonmoeder, father- and mother-in-law
schoonrijden *n*, figure-skating
schoonschrift *n*, calligraphy; copy-book
schoonzoon, son-in-law
schoonzuster, sister-in-law
schoor, shore, prop
schoorsteen, chimney(-pot); funnel
schoorsteenmantel, mantelpiece
schoorsteenplaat, hearth-plate
schoorsteenveger, sweep

schoorvoetend, reluctantly
schoot, lap; womb, bosom; sheet
schootkindje *n*, pampered child, baby
schootsvel *n*, leather apron
schop, spade; shovel: kick
schopje *n*, trowel, child's spade
schoppen to kick (up)
schoppen'heer *etc*, king *etc* of spades
schopstoel: hij zit op de —, he may be turned out at any moment
schor, hoarse: mud-flat
schoren, to shore up
schorpi'oen, scorpion
schorr(i)emorrie *n*, riff-raff
schors, bark
schorsen, to suspend; to adjourn
schorse'neer, salsify
schort, apron, pinafore
schort: wat — eraan? what is the matter?
schot *n*, shot; partition, bulkhead
Schot, Scot(sman)
shotel, dish, saucer
schots, (ice-)floe
schots en scheef door elkaar, here, there and everywhere
Schotse ruit, tartan
shouder, shoulder
schouderblad *n*, shoulder-blade
schout, sheriff
schout-bij-'nacht, rear-admiral
schouw, fireplace; scow
schouwburg, theatre
schouwing, autopsy
schouwspel *n*, spectacle
schraag, trestle
schraal, meagre, lean, bleak
schraalhans is daar keukenmeester, you'll get nothing but short commons there
schraapijzer *n*, scraper
schraapzucht, rapacity
schragen, to shore up; to sustain
schram(men), (to) scratch
schrander, shrewd, intelligent
schransen, to gorge

schrap, scratch
zich schrap zetten, to take a firm stand, to brace oneself
schrapen, to scrape; to clear
schrappen, to scrap(e), to cross out
schrede, stride, step
schreeuw(en), (to) yell, (to) cry (out)
schreeuwend, crying; garish; blatant
schreeuwlelijk, bawler
schreien, to cry (out), to weep
schriel, frail; meagre; mingy
schrift *n*, (hand)writing; exercise-book
de Heilige Schrift, (the) Holy Scripture(s)
schriftelijk, written, in writing
schriftgeleerde, scribe
schriftvervalsing, forgery
schrijden, to stride
schrijfbehoeften, stationary
schrijfbureau *n*, desk
schrijffout, slip of the pen
schrijfletters, script
schrijfmachine, typewriter
schrijfmap, writing-case
schrijftaal, formal language
schrijftrant, style (of writing)
schrijlings, astride
schrijnen, to smart; to gall
schrijnwerker, cabinet-maker
schrijven, to write; *n*, communication
schrik, fright, terror
schrikaanjagend, terrifying
schrikachtig, nervy
schrik'barend, appalling
schrikbeeld *n*, nightmarish vision
schrikbewind *n*, reign of terror
schrikkeljaar *n*, leap-year
schrikken, to have a (nasty) fright, to be taken aback
wakker schrikken, to wake with a start
schrik'wekkend, terrifying
schril, shrill, glaring
schrobben, to scrub
schrob'bering, wigging
schroef, screw, propeller
op losse schroeven staan, to be uncertain

schroeien, to scorch, to singe
schroevedraaier, screw-driver
schroeven, to screw
schrokken, to gorge
schromelijk, gross
schromen, to have qualms
schroom, diffidence
schroom'vallig, diffident
schroot *n*, canister-shot
schub(ben), (to) scale
schuchter, bashful
schuddebollen, to nod (with sleep)
schudden, to shake; to shuffle
schuieren, to brush
schuif, slide, damper
schuifdak *n*, sunshine roof
schuifdeur, sliding door
schuifelen, to shuffle, to slither
schuifladder, extending ladder
schuifraam *n*, sash-window
schuiftrompet, trombone
schuilen, to (take) shelter, to lurk
schuilgaan, to go in, to hide
schuilhouden, to lie low
schuilkelder, air-raid shelter
schuilkerk, clandestine church
schuilnaam, pen-name
schuilplaats, hiding-place
schuim *n*, foam, froth, lather; scum; meringue
schuimbekken, to foam at the mouth
schuimen, to foam, to froth, to lather; to skim
schuimkoppen, white horses
schuin, slanting, oblique; smutty
schuit, boat, barge
schuiven, to push
   laat hem maar schuiven, he can fend for himself
   met de eer gaan schuiven, to take the credit
schuld, debt; fault, blame, guilt
schuldbekentenis, IOU; confession of guilt
schuldbe'wust, guilty
schuldeiser, creditor
schuldenaar, debtor
schuldig, guilty
   schuldig zijn, to be guilty; to owe

schuldige, culprit, guilty party
schulp, shell
schulpen, to scallop
schunnig, shabby; bawdy
schuren, to scour, to sandpaper; to graze
schurft, scabies, mange
schurk, scoundrel
schurken, to writhe, to rub
schurkenstreek, caddish trick
schutblad *n*, fly-leaf, bract
schutkleur, camouflage
schutsengel, guardian angel
schutsluis, lock
schutspatroon, patron saint
schutten, to pass through a lock; to dam up
schutter, marksman
schutterig, clumsy, awkward
schutte'rij, civic guard
schutting, fence
schuur, barn
schuurkatoen *n*, schuurlinnen *n*, emery cloth
schuurmiddel *n*, abrasive
schuurpapier *n*, sand-paper
schuw, timid, shy
schuwen, to shun, to fight shy of
schuwlelijk, dreadfully ugly
scorbutt, scurvy
scriptie, essay
scru'pule, scruple
sec, neat, dry, bare
secon'dair, secondary
secon'dant, second
se'conde(wijzer), second (s-hand)
secreta'resse, (female) secretary
secretari'aat *n*, secretaryship; secretariate
secreta'rie, town clerk's office
secre'taris, secretary
secre'taris-gene'raal, permanent under-secretary
sectie, section; incision, autopsy
secu'lair, secular
se'cuur, safe; accurate; certain
sedert, since, for
sein *n*, signal
seinen, to signal, to wire
seinhuisje *n*, signal-box
seinpaal, semaphore

seinsleutel, transmitting key
seinwachter, signalman
sei'zoen *n*, season
sei'zoenopruiming, (clearance) sale(s)
sekse, sex
sekte, sect
selderij, celery
sema'foor, semaphore
semi-arts, first part of the qualifying examination in medicine; student who has passed this examination
se'naat, senate
se'niel, senile
sen'satie, sensation
sensu'eel, sensual
sentimen'teel, sentimental
sepa'reren, to separate
sep'time, seventh
septisch, septic
sera'fijn(en), seraph(im)
serge, serge
serie, series
seri'eus, serious
sérieux: au — nemen, to take seriously
se'ring, lilac
ser'pent *n*, serpent; shrew
serpen'tine, streamer
serre, conservatory, sun-parlour
ser'veerboy, dumb waiter
ser'veren, to serve
ser'vet *n*, napkin
ser'viel, servile
ser'vies *n*, dinner-service, tea-set
sext, sixth
sexu'eel, sexual
sfeer, (atmo)sphere
sferisch, spherical
shag, cigarette tobacco
sibbekunde, geneaology
sidderen (voor), to quake (at the thought of)
siddering, shudder
sieraad *n*, ornament, (piece of) jewellery
sieren, to adorn, to enhance
sierlijk, elegant
sierplant, ornamental plant
si'gaar, cigar
si'garenwinkel, tobacconist's (shop)

siga'ret, cigarette
si'gnaal *n*, signal
signale'ment *n*, (police) description
signa'leren, to see, to signalize
  overal signaleren, to circulate a description
sijpelen, to seep
sijs: een rare —, a queer bird
sik, goatee
sikkel, sickle, crescent: shekel
sikke'neurig, querulous
sikkepit: geen —, not a thing
simpel, simple, silly
simu'lant, humbug
simu'leren, to simulate
sinaasappel, orange
sinds('dien), (ever) since (then)
singel, girdle; (street on either side of a) town canal
sint, saint
sintel, cinder
Sinter'klaas, Santa Claus
Sinterklaas'avond, St Nicholas' Eve (Dec. 5)
Sint Juttemis: met —, on the Greek calends
sip kijken, to look glum
Sire, your Majesty
si'rene, siren
si'roop, syrup
sissen, to hiss, to sizzle
sisser: met een — aflopen, to fizzle out
sjaal, shawl
sjab'loon, stencil-plate, template
sjacheren, to run a shady business; to haggle
sjees, gig
sjerp, sash
sjezen, to be ploughed
sjoelbak, shovelboard
sjofel, shabby
sjokken, to trudge
sjorren, to lash (up); to haul
sjouwen, to lug; to drudge
sjouwer, dock-hand; porter
ske'let *n*, skeleton
skiën, to ski
sla, salad; lettuce
slaaf, slave
slaafs, slavish, servile
slaags raken, to come to blows

slaan, to hit, to strike, to beat, to smack;
  dat slaat op mij, that applies to me
slaap, sleep: temple
  slaap hebben, to feel sleepy
  slaap vatten, to get to sleep
slaapdrank, sleeping draught
slaapdronken, not fully awake
slaapje *n,* nap; bed-mate
slaapkop, sleepy-head
slaapliedje *n,* lullaby
slaapmiddel *n,* opiate
slaapmuts, night-cap
slaapplaats, (sleeping-)berth
slaapwagen, sleeping-car
slaap'wekkend, soporific
slaapzaal, dormitory
slaapziekte, sleeping sickness
slaatje *n,* salad
slab(be), bib
sla'bakken, to slack(en), to dawdle
slaboon, French bean
slachten, to slaughter
slachting, slaughter
slachtoffer *n,* victim
sla'dood: lange —, lofty (fellow)
slag, blow, stroke, beat, crash; battle; knack; turn; kind
  men moet een slag maken om aan de slag te komen, one has to make a trick in order to get the lead
  een slag om de arm houden, not to commit oneself
  zijn slag slaan, to strike while the iron is hot
slagader, artery
slagbal *n,* rounders
slagboom, boom, barrier
slagen, to succeed, to pass
slager('ij), butcher('s shop)
slaghamer, mallet
slaghout *n,* bat
slaglinie, slagorde, line of battle
slagregen, down-pour
slagroom, (whipped) cream
slagtand, fang, tusk
slag'vaardig, ready for battle
slagwerk *n,* striking mechanism; percussion (section)

slagwoord *n,* **slagzin,** slogan
slagzij(de) (maken), (to) list, (to) bank
slagzwaard *n,* broadsword
slak, snail, slug: slag
slaken, to utter, to heave
slakkegang, snail's pace
slakkehuis *n,* snail-shell; cochlea
slam'pamper, gadabout, lout
slang, snake, serpent; hose (-pipe)
slangemens, contortionist
slangenbezweerder, snake-charmer
slank, slim, slender
slaolie, salad oil
slap, slack, soft, flabby, weak; spineless
slape'loosheid, insomnia
slapen, to (be a)sleep
slaperig, sleepy
slapjes, slack, weak
slappe'koord *n,* slack-rope
slappeling, weakling, jelly-fish
slavenarbeid, slavery
slavendrijver, slave-driver
slaver'nij, slavery, servitude
Slavisch, Slav(onic)
slecht, bad, poor
slechten, to level (out); to demolish; to settle
slechts, only
sle(d)e, sled(ge); (ship's) cradle
  een slee van een wagen, a sleek limousine
sleef, ladle
sleep, train, trail, tow
sleepboot, tug
sleepnet *n,* drag-net
sleeptouw *n,* tow-rope
sleets zijn, to be hard on one's clothes
slenteren, to saunter
slepen, to drag; to tow
sleper, haulier
sleperspaard *n,* dray-horse
slet, slut
sleuf, groove; slot
sleur, rut, humdrum routine
sleuren, to drag (on)
sleutel, key; clef
sleutelbeen *n,* collar bone

sleutelbloem, primrose, primula
Sleutelstad, Leyden
slib *n,* silt, mire
slier(t), stream(er); winding trail
slijk *n,* mire, slime
  aardse slijk, filthy lucre
slijm *n,* slime; phelgm, mucus
slijmvlies *n,* mucous membrane
slijpen, to sharpen, to grind; to
  cut and polish
slij'tage, wear (and tear)
slijten, to wear out, to wear off;
  to spend, to retail
slijte'rij, off-license shop
slikken, to swallow
sliknat, sopping wet
slim, clever, crafty; bad
slinger, festoon;   pendulum;
  sling; (crank-)handle
slingeren, to swing; to lurch;
  to wind; to lie about; to fling
slingerplant, creeper
slinken, to shrink (to nothing),
  to subside
slinks, sly, underhand
slip, tail(-end)
  slip vangen, to draw (a) blank
slipgevaar ! beware of skidding!
slipover, pull-over
slippedrager, pall-bearer
slippen, to slip, to skid
slippertje maken, to take French
  leave
slobberen, to suck in, to guzzle
  noisily
slobkous, gaiter, spat
slodderig, slovenly
sloddervos, slattern
sloep, (ship's) boat, (naval) barge
sloerie, slut
slof, slipper; briquette; carton
  het op zijn sloffen doen, to take
  things easy,
sloffen, to shuffle
slok, gulp, draught
slokdarm, gullet
slokje *n,* sip, drop
slokken, to guzzle
slons, slattern, frump
sloof, apron: drudge
sloom, languid
  slome duikelaar, slowcoach
sloop, pillow-case; dismantling

sloot, ditch
slop *n,* back street
slopen, to demolish, to break up
slordig, untidy, slipshod
  een slordig sommetje, a tidy
  sum
slorpen, to sip noisily, to gulp
slot *n,* lock; castle; conclusion
  ten slotte, finally
  per slot van rekening, when
  all is said and done
slotakkoord *n,* final chord
slotrede, peroration
slotsom, conclusion; upshot
slotzin, closing sentence
sloven, to drudge (and toil)
sluier(en), (to) veil
sluif, slit; sheath
sluik, lank
sluikhandel, trafficking, smuggling
sluimer(en), (to) slumber
sluipen, to steal, to creep
sluipmoordenaar, assassin
sluis, lock; floodgate
sluisdeur, lock-gate
sluiskolk, lock-chamber
sluitboom, (drop-)boom
sluiten, to shut (up), to close
  (down), to lock (up); to conclude; to fit
sluiting, closing(-down); fastening
sluitring, washer
sluitsteen, key-stone
slungel, stripling
slurf, trunk, proboscis
slurpen, to sip noisily, to gulp
sluw, sly, wily
smaad, libel, contumely
smaak, taste, flavour; relish;
  palate
  in de smaak vallen, to be
  popular, to be to (a person's)
  liking
smaakvol, in good taste
smachten, to pine (away)
smachtend, love-lorn
smadelijk, ignominious
smak, thud
smakelijk, toothsome
  smakelijk eten ! I hope you'll
  enjoy your meal

smakeloos, tasteless; in bad taste

smaken (naar), to taste (of)

smakken, to fall with a thud; to fling; to smack (one's lips)

smal, narrow

smaldeel *n*, squadron

smalen op, to jeer at

smalfilm, 16 mm. film

smaragd(en), emerald

smart, grief, anguish

smartelijk, grievous

smeden, to forge; to plan

smede'rij, smithy, forge

smeedijzer *n*, wrought iron

smeekbede, supplication

smeer, grease

smeerkaas, cheese spread

smeerkees, smeerlap, muck-rake(r); blackguard

smeermiddel, *n*, lubricant

smeerolie, lubricating oil

smeerpoets, dirty tyke

smekeling, suppliant

smeken, to implore, to beseech

smelten, to (s)melt, to fuse

smeltende tonen, mellow tone(s)

smeltkroes, crucible

smeren, to spread; to grease, to lubricate

'm smeren, to beat it

smerig, filthy, shabby

smeris, cop(per)

smet, stain, blemish

smetteloos, spotless, blameless

smeuig, smooth; colourful

smeulen, to smoulder

smid, blacksmith

smidse, forge, smithy

smiezen: ik heb het in de —, I've got it taped

smijten (met), to chuck; to throw (about)

smoel, mug, phiz

smoesje *n*, bit of eye-wash, excuse

smoezelig, soiled

smoezen, to whisper together

smoking, dinner-jacket

smokkela'rij, smuggling

smokkelen, to smuggle; to cheat

smokkelwaar, contraband

smokken, to smock

smoor: de — hebben, to be utterly fed up

smoordronken, dead drunk

smoorheet, sweltering

smoorverliefd, madly in love

smoren, to strangle, to stifle

smullen, to tuck in

smulpaap, gourmand(izer)

snaak(s), wag(gish)

snaar, string, chord

snakken naar, to yearn for, to gasp for

snappen, to get, to twig; to nab

snars, the slightest bit

snater: hou je —! hold your tongue!

snateren, to quack, to cackle

snauw(en), (to) snarl

snavel, beak, bill

sne(d)e, cut; slice

goud *or* **verguld op snee**, with gilt edges

snedig, witty

sneeuw(en), (to) snow

sneeuwjacht, blizzard, driving snow

sneeuwklokje *n*, snowdrop

sneeuwpop, snow-man

snel, quick, fast

snelbuffet *n*, snack-bar

snelduik(en), (to) crash-dive

snelheid, speed

snellen, to hurry

snelschrijven *n*, shorthand

snerpend, biting, bitter

snert, pea-soup; trash(y)

snertvent, rotter

sneu, rotten (luck)

sneuvelen, to be killed (in action)

snibbig, snappily, snappish

snijbiet, beet spinach

snijbloemen, cut flowers

snijboon, runner bean

rare snijboon, queer cove

snijden, to cut (in), to carve; to intersect; to finesse

snijtand, incisor

snijzaal, dissecting-room

snik, sob, gasp

niet goed snik, not all there

snikheet, sweltering

snikken, to sob
snip(penjacht), snipe(-shooting)
snipper, snippet, scrap; candied peel
snipperuur *n*, spare hour
snit, cut
snoeien, to prune, to lop, to clip
snoek, pike
  een snoek vangen, to fall in the water; to catch a crab
snoep(e'rij), sweets
snoepen, to eat sweets, to tuck in
snoepreisje *n*, joy-ride
snoer *n*, flex; string; line
snoeren: iemand de mond —, to shut a person up
snoes, duck(y)
snoeshaan, chap, specimen
snoet, snout; face
snoeven, to boast
snoezig, sweet, dinky
snood, vile
snor, moustache
snorken, to snore
snorren, to roar, to drone, to hum
snotaap, snotjongen, urchin
snotneus, snotty nose; urchin
snuffelen, to sniff; to ferret (about)
snufje *n*, knick-knack
snugger, bright, brainy
snuif(je) *n*, (pinch of) snuff
snuiste'rij, trinket
snuit, snout, trunk; (little) face
snuiten, to blow (one's nose); to snuff
snuiter, chap, fellow
snuiven, to (give a) sniff, to snort
snurken, to snore
soci'ale ver'zorging, welfare work
socië'teit, club(-house)
soebatten, to beg
soep, soup; balderdash
soepballetje *n*, (force-)meat ball
soepel, supple
soepkip, boiling fowl
soes, puff
soezen, to doze
sok, sock
sokophouder, suspender

sol'daat, soldier
  sol'daat maken, to finish up
sol'deerbout, soldering-iron
sol'deren, to solder
sol'dij, army pay
soli'dair, loyal
so'lide, sound, substantial
so'list, soloist
sollen, to romp; to push around
sollici'tant, applicant
sollici'teren, to apply
solospel *n*, solo (performance)
som, sum
somber, gloomy, sombre
somma, (total) amount
som'meren, to summon
sommige(n), some
som(tijd)s, sometimes; perhaps
sonate, sonata
so'noor, sonorous
soort, brand, species; *n*, kind
soortelijk ge'wicht *n*, specific gravity
soortgelijk, similar
soos, club
sop *n*, broth; (soap-)suds
  het ruime sop, the sea
soppen, to sop, to steep
so'praan, soprano, treble
sor'teren, to (as)sort, to grade
sor'tering, assortment
souff'leren, to prompt
souff'leur(shokje *n*), prompter('s box)
sou'peren, to sup
sou'tane, cassock
souterrain *n*, basement
souvereini'teit, sovereignty
spaak, spoke, rung
  spaak lopen, to come to grief
spaander, sliver, chip
Spaans (*n*), Spanish
spaarbank, savings bank
spaarkas, thrift club
spaarpot, money-box
spaarzaam, sparing, thrifty
spade, spade
spalk(en), (to) splint
span *n*, span; team, yoke
spanbroek, (pair of) tights
span'deren, to spend
spandoek, banner
Spanje *n*, Spain

spankracht, tensile strength
spannen, to stretch, to strain
  de haan spannen, to cock (a rifle)
  het zal er om spannen, it will be touch and go
spannend, tense, thrilling
spanning, tension; span
spanwijdte, span
spar, rafter; spruce(-tree)
sparappel, fir-cone
sparen, to save (up); to spare
spartelen, to sport, to splash, to kick
spatader, varicose vein
spatbord *n*, mud-guard
spatie, space
spatten, to splash, to spatter
spece'rij, spice
specht, woodpecker
speci'aal, special
specie, mortar
specifi'ceren, to specify
speci'fiek, specific
specu'laas, spice cake *or* biscuit
specu'lant, speculator
specu'leren, to speculate
speeksel *n*, saliva
speelbal, cue ball; plaything
speelbank, gaming-room
speelgoed *n*, toy(s)
speelkwartier *n*, break, recreation
speelplaats, playground
speelpop, puppet
speels(heid), playful(ness)
speeltuin, playground
speen, teat, dummy
speenvarken *n*, sucking-pig
speer, spear, javelin
spek *n*, bacon, fat pork; blubber
spekken: zijn beurs —, to line one's purse
spektakel *n*, racket; spectacle
spekzool, crepe sole
spel *n*, game; pack, hand (of cards), play(ing), acting
  op het spel staan, to be at stake
spelbreker, spoil-sport
spel(den), (to) pin
  ik kon er geen speld tussen krijgen, I couldn't get a word in edgewise; he had a watertight argument

spelen, to play, to act; to chime
spelenderwijs, frivolously
speler, player, musician, actor
spelevaren *n*, boating
spelfout, spelling mistake
speling, (free) play; scope; freak
spelleider, games master
spellen, to spell
spelletje *n*, game
spe'lonk, cave, grotto
spelregel, rule (of the game): spelling-rule
spenen, to wean
sperballon, barrage balloon
speruur *n*, curfew
spervuur *n*, barrage
sperzieboon, French bean
spett(er)en, to spatter
speuren, to search
speurhond, sleuth-hound, gun-dog
speurzin, keen nose
spichtig, spiky, spidery
spie, cent, bean, dough
spiegel, mirror
spiegelbeeld *n*, reflection; phantom
spiegelei *n*, fried egg
spiegelen: zich — aan, to learn from
spiegelgevecht *n*, mock battle
spiegelglas *n*, plate glass
spiegeling, reflection
spiegelkast, (mirror-fronted) wardrobe
spiegelruit, plate-glass window
spieken, to crib
spier, muscle
spiernaakt, stark naked
spierwit, white as a sheet
spies, spear
spijbelen, to play truant
spijker, nail
  spijkers met koppen slaan, to get down to business
  spijkers op laag water zoeken, to make a song and dance about nothing; to quibble
spijl, bar, spike
spijs, fare
spijskaart, menu
spijsvertering, digestion
spijt, regret; spite

spijten, to upset
het spijt me, I am sorry
spijtig: het is —, it is a pity
spijzen, food
spikkel, speck
spiksplinternieuw, gleaming new
spil, pivot, axis; capstan
spillebeen, spindle-shank(s)
spilziek, spendthrift
spin(nekop), spider
spi'nazie, spinach
spinnen, to spin; to purr
spinne'rij, spinning-mill
spinneweb, n, cobweb
spinnewiel n, spinning-wheel
spinnijdig, as cross as two sticks
spinrag n, cobweb
spi'on, spy; window mirror
spio'neren, to spy
spi'raal, spiral; woven bed-spring
spiri'tisme n, spiritualism
spiritus, methylated spirit(s)
spit, n, spit: lumbago
spits, point(ed), sharp: peak
spitse toren, steeple, pinnacle
op de spits drijven, to bring to a head
spitsboef, scoundrel
spitsboog, pointed arch
spitsen, to sharpen; to prick up
spitsuur n, rush hour, peak hour
spits'vondig(heid), (over)-subtle(ty)
spitten, to dig
spleet, slit, split
splijten, to split, to cleave
splinter(en), (to) splinter
splinternieuw, brand-new
split, slit, placket
splitsen, to split (up), to fork
splitsing, split(ting up), fork, fission
spoed(en), (to) haste(n)
spoedgeval n, emergency case
spoedig, soon, speedy
spoel, spool, coil, reel
spoelen, to rinse, to wash
spoelkom, slop-basin
spoken, to haunt; to be astir
sponde, bed(side)
spons, sponge

spon'taan, spontaneous
spook n, ghost; freak, bogey
spookhuis n, haunted house
spookverschijning, apparition
spoor n, spur: foot-mark, track, scent, trace; rail(way)
spoorbaan, railway
spoorboekje n, (railway) time-table
spoordijk, railway embankment
spoorlijn, railway(-line)
spoorloos, without a trace
spoorslags, hell for leather
spoorstudent, student travelling from a distance
spoorverbinding, railway com-munication; connection
spoorweg, railway
spoorwegovergang, level cross-ing
spo'radisch, sporadic
sporen, (to go) by rail
sport, sport; rung
sportbroek, slacks, flannels
sportbroekje n, shorts
spor'tief, sporting; informal
sportjasje n, sports-coat
sportkousen, knee-length stock-ings
spot, mockery
spotgoedkoop, dirt-cheap
spotprent, caricature, cartoon
spotten (met), to mock; to defy
spraak(gebrek n), (impediment of) speech
spraakgebruik n, usage
spraakkunst, grammar
spraakleraar, teacher of elocu-tion
spraakzaam, talkative
sprake, talk, question
ter sprake, up for discussion
sprakeloos, speechless
sprank(elen), (to) spark(le)
spreekbeurt, lecturing engage-ment
spreekbuis, voice-tube; mouth-piece
spreekgestoelte n, rostrum, pul-pit
spreekkamer, consulting-room
spreektaal, conversation(al lan-guage)

spreekuur *n*, consulting-hour
spreekwoord *n*, proverb
spreek'woordelijk, proverbial
spreeuw, starling
sprei, bed-spread
spreken, to speak (to), to mention
het spreekt vanzelf, it stands to reason
sprekend, striking, telling
spreker, speaker
sprenkelen, to sprinkle
spreuk, motto, maxim
spriet, blade (of grass); antenna
sprietig, spindly
springen, to jump; to snap, to burst; to become insolvent
ik zit erom te springen, I just can't wait for it
spring-in-'t-veld, tomboy
springlevend, very much alive
springpaard *n*, vaulting-horse
springstof, explosive
springtij, *n*, springvloed, spring tide
springtouw *n*, skipping-rope
sprinkhaan, locust, grass-hopper
sprint(en), (to) sprint
sprits, butter-biscuit
sproeien, to sprinkle, to spray
sproet, freckle
sprokkelen, to gather (wood)
sprong, jump, leap, bound
sprookje *n*, fairy-tale
sprookjesachtig, make-believe, dream-like
sprot, sprat
spruit, sprout; offspring
spruiten, to sprout; to spring
spruitjes, Brussel sprouts
spugen, to spit
spuien, to sluice; to vent(ilate)
spuigaten: dat loopt de — uit, that crowns everything
spuit, syringe; gamp; shooting-iron
spuiten, to gush(out), to spray
spuitfles, (soda-water) siphon
spuitgast, fireman
spuitwater *n*, soda-water
spul *n*, stuff; trouble
spullen, bits and pieces; togs
spullebaas, showman, booth attendant

sputteren, to sputter
spuug *n*, spit
spuwen, to spit, to vomit
staaf, bar, rod
staak, stake, bean-stick
staal *n*, steel: sample, piece
staal(draad)kabel, steel-wire rope
staan, to stand, to be; to suit
laat staan, leave alone; let alone
erop staan, to insist on it
hoe staat hij ervoor? how is he doing?
staande houden, to stop; to maintain
zich staande houden, to keep on one's feet; to hold one's own
op staande voet, then and there
staanplaats(en), standing-room
staar, cataract
staart, tail; pigtail
staat, state; rank; list
in staat zijn, to be able
staat maken op, to depend on
staat'huishoudkunde, economics
staatkunde, politics
staatsambtenaar, civil servant
staatsexamen *n*, matriculation
staatsgreep, *coup d'état*
statie, state; procession
staatsman, statesman
staatsrecht *n*, constitutional law
staatsschuld, national debt
sta'biel, stable
stad, town, city
stad'huis *n*, town hall, city hall
stadion *n*, stadium
stadium *n*, stage, phase
stadslichten, side-lights
stadsschouwburg, municipal theatre
stads'timmerhuis *n*, corporation department of works
staf, staff; mace, crosier
stafkaart, ordnance-map
stafrijm *n*, alliteration
stag'neren, to stagnate
sta-in-de-weg, obstacle
staken, to stop, to strike
staking, stoppage, suspension, strike; tie

stakker(d), poor devil, poor thing
stal, stable, cow-shed, stall
stalen, (to) steel, iron
stalknecht, groom
stallen, to stable, to put away
stalles, stalls
stalmeester, equery
stalvoe(de)r *n*, fodder
stam, stem, trunk; tribe, race
stamboek *n*, herd-book, stud-book
stamboekvee *n*, pedigree cattle
stamboom, family tree
stamelen, to stammer
stamgast, *habitué*
stamhouder, son and heir
stamhuis *n*, dynasty
stamkaart, national registration card
stammen, to hail, to date
stamouders, ancestors
stampen, to pound, to mash; to stamp, to drum; to pitch
stamper, pestle, (potato-)masher, rammer; pistil
stamppot, mashed vegetables
stampvoeten, to stamp (one's foot)
stampvol, packed out
stamroos, standard rose
stamvader, ancestor
stand, position, attitude; score class, order, state
  tot stand komen, to come into being
standaard, standard; stand
standbeeld *n*, statue
stander, (hall-)stand
standhouden, to hold (one's own)
standje *n*, ticking-off; cross-patch; shindy
standplaats, stand, pitch, (taxi-)rank; post, living
standpunt *n*, point of view
stand'vastig, steadfast
stang, bar, rod, stancheon
  op stang jagen, to bait
stank, stench
stap, step, pace; move
  op stap, on (our) way
stapel, pile, heap
  van stapel lopen, to glide off the stocks; to go (off) smoothly

stapelen, to stack, to heap
stapel(gek), quite daft
stappen, to step, to get
stapvoets, at a walking-pace
star, fixed, rigid
staren, to stare, to gaze
startbaan, runway
starten, to start
Statenbijbel, Authorized Version (of the Dutch Bible)
Staten-Gene'raal, States General, the Upper and Lower Chambers
statie, Station of the Cross
sta'tief *n*, tripod, stand
statiegeld *n*, deposit
statig, stately, majestic
sta'tion *n*, station
sta'tionschef, station-master
statis'tiek, statistics
sta'tuut *n*, statute, regulation
sta'vast, (high) resolve
staven, to substantiate
stedeljik, urban, municipal
stedeling, townsman
steeds, ever, still: town(ish)
steeg, alley, lane
steek, stitch, sting, stab, dig; cocked hat
  in de steek laten, to leave in the lurch
  geen steek, not a thing
steek'houdend, sound, valid
steekproef, sample taken at random
steekvlam, torch flame
steel, stem, stalk; handle
steelpan, saucepan
steels, stealthy
steen, stone
steenbakke'rij, brick-works
steenbok, ibex; Capricorn
steendruk, lithograph(y)
steengroeve, quarry
steenhouwer, stone-mason
steenkool, (bituminous) coal
steenoven, brick-kiln
steenpuist, boil
steentijdperk *n*, stone-age
steentje *n*, stone, pebble
  een steentje bijdragen, to do one's (little) bit
steevast, regularly

steiger, landing-stage; scaffolding

steigeren, to rear

steil, steep, sheer

stek, cutting

stekeblind, blind as a bat

stekel, prickle, spine

stekelbaars, stickleback

stekelig, prickly; caustic

stekelvarken *n*, porcupine

steken, to sting, to stab, to smart; to stick

  blijven steken, to get stuck

  van wal steken, to push off

stekker, plug(-top)

stel *n*, set, couple; stove

stelen, to steal

stelkunde, algebra

stel'lage, scaffolding

stellen, to put; to adjust; to suppose; to manage

stellig, definite

stelling, proposition, thesis, theorem; position, line of fortifications; scaffolding

stelpen, to sta(u)nch

stelregel, maxim

stelsel *n*, system

stelsel'matig, systematic

stelten, stilts

  op stelten staan, to be at sixes and sevens

stem, voice, part; vote

stembanden, vocal chords

stembiljet *n*, voting-paper

stembuiging, modulation

stembureau *n*, polling-station

stembus, ballet-box

stemgeluid *n*, voice

stemge'rechtigd, entitled to vote

stemhamer, tuning-key

stemhebbend, voiced; entitled to vote

stemloos, voiceless

stemmen, to vote; to tune (up)

  iemand gunstig stemmen, to put a person in a good mood

stemmer, tuner; voter

stemmig, demure

stemming, mood, atmosphere: vote

stempel *n*, stamp, (post)mark; stigma

stempelen, to stamp, to (post-, hall-)mark

stempelkussen *n*, ink-pad

stemplicht, compulsory voting

stemrecht *n*, franchise

stemspleet, glottis

stemvork, tuning-fork

stengel, stalk, stem

stenigen, to stone (to death)

steno(gra'fie), shorthand

step, step; scooter

steppehond, prairie-dog

ster, star

stereo'tiep, stereotype(d)

sterfbed *n*, death-bed

sterfelijk(heid), mortal(ity)

sterfgeval *n*, death

sterftecijfer, mortality-rate

ste'riel, sterile

sterk, strong; extraordinary; greatly

  sterk verhaal, tall story

sterken, to strengthen; to comfort

sterkgekleurd, highly coloured

sterkte, strength; all the best !

sterk'water *n*, spirits

sterrekijker, telescope

sterrenbeeld *n*, constellation

sterrenkunde, astronomy

sterrenwacht, observatory

sterrenwichelarij, astrology

sterretje *n*, star, asterisk

sterveling, mortal

sterven (aan), to die (from)

steun, support

steunbeer, buttress

steunen, to support, to lean : to groan

steunfonds *n*, relief-fund

steunpilaar, pillar, mainstay

steuntrekkend, on the dole

steunzool, arch support

steven, prow

stevig, firm, substantial, sturdy

stichtelijk, edifying

  dank je stichtelijk ! thank you for nothing !

stichten, to found, to establish; to edify

stichting, foundation, institution; edification

stief(moeder), step(mother)

stiekem, on the quiet
stier, bull
stierlijk: zich — vervelen, to be bored stiff
stift, stylo, pin, pencil(-lead)
stifttand, crowned tooth
stijf, stiff, starchy
stijfkop, pig-headed person
stijfsel, starch, paste
stijgbeugel, stirrup
stijgen, to rise; to (dis)mount
stijl, style: stanchion
stijlfiguur, figure of speech
stijven, to starch; to encourage
stikdonker n, pitch-dark(ness)
stikken, to stifle, to suffocate: to stitch
stikstof, nitrogen
stikvol, chock-full
stil, silent, quiet; still
de stille week, Holy Week
stilhouden, to stop; to keep quiet
stilleggen, to stop
stillen, to quiet(en), to alleviate
stilletje n, commode
stilletjes, quietly, stealthily
stilliggen, to lie still, to lie idle
stilstaan, to stand still; to pull up
stilstaan bij, to give (some) thought to
stilstaand, stationary, stagnant
stilstand, standstill
stilte, silence
in stilte, quietly, privately
stilzwijgen n, silence
stil'zwijgend, tacit
stimu'lans, stimulant, stimulus
stimu'leren, to stimulate
stinkdier n, skunk
stinken, to stink
stip(pel), dot, speck
stipt, punctual, prompt; strict
stoeien, to romp
stoel, chair
stoelendans, musical chairs
stoelgang, motion(s)
stoep, front-door step(s); pavement, kerb
stoer, stalwart
stoet, procession
stoete'rij, stud(-farm)

stoethaspel, duffer
stof, material, (subject-)matter: n, dust
lang van stof, long-winded
stofbril, goggles
stofdoek, duster
stof'feerder, upholsterer
stoffelijk, material, mortal
stoffen, to dust
stoffer, brush
stof'feren, to upholster
stoffig, dusty
stofgoud n, gold-dust
stofje n, speck of dust: bit of material
stoflaken n, dust-sheet
stofnest n, dust-trap
stofregen, drizzle
stofwisseling, metabolism
stofzuiger, vacuum-cleaner
stoï'cijn(s), stoic(al)
stok, stick; perch, roost; truncheon; stock(s)
het aan de stok krijgen, to fall out
stokboon, runner-bean
stokdoof, stone deaf
stoken, to burn, to keep a fire going; to distil; to stir up
stoker, fireman, stoker; distiller; firebrand
stokje n, stick, baton
er een stokje voor steken, to scotch
stokken, to falter, to break down: to stake
stokoud, ancient
stokpaard n, hobby(-horse)
stokroos, hollyhock
stokstijf, rigid
stokvis, stockfish
stola, stole
stollen, to congeal
stolp, glass cover
stolpplooi, box-pleat
stom, dumb, mute, speechless; stupid
stomen, to steam, to smoke; to dry-clean; to cram
stome'rij, dry-cleaners
stommelen, to clump (about)
stommeling, stommerik, fathead

stommi'teit, stupidity, blunder
stomp, blunt, obtuse : stump : punch, dig
stompen, to punch, to jab
stomp'zinnig, obtuse
stomverbaasd, stupefied
stomvervelend, deadly dull
stoof, foot-warmer
stoofpeer, stewing pear
stookgat *n*, stoke-hole
stookolie, fuel-oil
stoom, steam
stoomgemaal *n*, steam pump
stoomketel, boiler
stoomwals, steam-roller
stoornis, disturbance
stoot, bump, jab, dig
stootblok *n*, buffer
stoottroepen, shock troops
stop, plug, stopper ; darn
stopcontact *n*, (wall-)socket
stoplap, stop-gap
stopnaald, darning-needle
stoppel, stubble
stoppen, to stop (up) ; to put ; to fill ; to darn ; to constipate
stoptrein, slow train
stopverf, putty
stopwoord *n*, expletive
stopzetten, to stop, to shut down
storen, to disturb, to interrupt
 zich storen aan, to bother about
storing, interference, failure, dislocation
storm, gale, storm
stormen, to storm, to blow a gale
stormenderhand, by storm
stormklok, gale tocsin
stormladder, rope-ladder
stormlamp, hurricane-lamp
stormloop, rush, stampede
stormram, battering-ram
stormsein *n*, storm-cone
stormtroep, assault party
stormvloed, gale-swept high water
stortbui, heavy shower
storten, to plunge, to dump, to shed ; to pay in
stortregenen, to pour with rain

stortvloed, torrent
stortzee, (green) sea
stoten, to bump, to knock, to butt
 zich stoten aan, to take offence at
stotend, offensive
stotteren, to stammer
stout, naughty ; bold
stout'moedig, undaunted
stoven, to stew
straal, ray ; radius ; jet
straalaandrijving, jet propulsion
straalbreking, refraction
straalvliegtuig *n*, jet-plane
straat, street, road ; straits
straatarm, poor as Job
straatdeun, street-song
straatjongen, street-arab
straatlantaarn, street-lamp
straatmaker, road-mender
straatschende'rij, hooliganism
straatstenen, paving-stones
straatweg, high-road
straf, punishment, penalty : severe, strong
strafbaar, punishable
straffeloos, with impunity
straffen, to punish
strafkolonie, convict settlement
strafport, postage due
strafrecht *n*, criminal law
strafschop, penalty kick
straftijd, term of imprisonment
strafwerk *n*, imposition
strafwet, criminal law
strafwetboek *n*, penal code
strak, tight, hard
strak(je)s, in a moment, soon
stralen, to shine, to beam
stralend, radiant
stralenkrans, halo
stram, stiff, rigid
stra'mien *n*, canvas
strand *n*, beach
stranden, to (be) strand(ed)
strandjutter, beach-comber
stra'teeg, strategist
streek, district, region : trick ; stroke
 van streek, upset
streekroman, regional novel

streep, stripe, stroke, line
  er een streep onder zetten, to call it a day
streepje *n*, dash, hyphen
strekken, to stretch
  iemand tot eer strekken, to do a person credit
strekking, purport
strelen, to stroke; to tickle
stremen, to curdle; to hold up
streng, severe, strict, strand, skein
strengelen, to twine
streven naar, to strive for
striem, weal
striemen, to lash
strijd, fight, struggle, conflict
strijdbaar, fit for service
strijden met, to fight (against), to go against
strijdig, contrary
strijdkrachten, military forces
strijd'lustig, bellicose, pugnacious
strijdperk *n*, lists
strijd'vaardig, fighting-fit
strijkbout, flat-iron
strijken, to iron : to haul down; to stroke, to brush
strijkgoed *n*, ironing
strijkijzer *n*, iron
strijkinstrument *n*, stringed instrument
strijkkwartet *n*, string quartet
strijkplank, ironing-board
strijkstok, bow
strik, bow(-tie); snare
strikken, to tie; to (en)snare
strikt, strict
strikvraag, catch question
stro *n*, straw
stroef, stiff, harsh
stroken met, to tally with
stromen, to flow
stroming, current; trend
strompelen, to hobble
stronk, stump, stalk
strontje *n*, sty
strooibiljet *n*, handbill
strooien, to strew, to sprinkle: straw
strooisel *n*, litter

strook, strip; frill; counterfoil
stroom, stream, flood, current
stroom'af(waarts), downstream
stroomgebied *n*, (river-)basin
stroom'op(waarts), upstream
stroomsterkte, amperage
stroomversnelling, rapid(s)
stroop, syrup, treacle
strooplikken, to curry favour
strooptocht, marauding expedition
strootje *n*, gasper
strop, noose; tough luck
stropdas, stock, tie
stropen, to skin, to strip; to poach, to pillage
stroper, poacher
strot, throat
strottehoofd *n*, larynx
strozak, palliasse
strubbelingen, friction, snags
struc'tuur, structure
struif, omelet
struik, bush, shrub
struikelblok *n*, stumbling-block
struikelen, to stumble, to trip (up)
struikgewas *n*, brushwood
struikrover, highwayman
struis, robust
struisveer, ostrich-feather
struisvogel, ostrich
struisvogelpolitiek, escapism
stu'deerkamer, study
stu'dentencorps *n*, students' union
stu'dentenhaver, almonds and raisins
studenti'koos, undergraduate, varsity
stu'deren, to study, to read; to practice; to be at the university
studie, study
studiebeurs, scholarship
studieboek *n*, text-book
stuf *n*, (india-)rubber
stug, dour, gruff; tough
stuifmeel, *n*, pollen
stuip, convulsion; daft notion
stuiptrekking, convulsion
stuit(been *n*), tail-bone
stuiten, to check; to bounce

stuiten op, to encounter
  tegen de borst stuiten, to go against the grain
stuitend, offensive
stuiven, to blow dust about; to dash
stuiver, 5-cent piece
stuivertje wisselen, general post
stuk (*n*), piece; play; document; lot: broken, to pieces
  een stuk of vier, three or four
  aan één stuk door, without a break
  op geen stukken na, not by a long chalk
  klein van stuk, small
  iemand van zijn stuk brengen, to upset a person
stuka'door, plasterer
stukgoed (eren) *n*, general cargo; piece-goods
stukhakken, to chop up
stukloon *n*, piece-rates
stukslaan, to smash (to pieces)
stumper(d), duffer; wretch
stuntelig, clumsy
sturen, to send; to steer
stutten, to prop (up)
stuur *n*, handle-bar(s), (steering-) wheel, helm
stuurboord *n*, starboard
stuurknuppel, control-column
stuurman, mate; cox(swain)
stuurs, surly
stuurstang, control-column
stuw, weir
stuwa'door, stevedore
stuwen, to drive; to stow; to dam up
stuwkracht, driving force
su'biet, sudden, at once
su'bliem, sublime
sub'sidie, subsidy
sub'stantie, substance
substitu'eren, to substitute
sub'tiel, subtle
suc'ces *n*, success
suc'cessie, succession
suc'cessierechten, death-duties
succes'sievelijk, successively
suc'cesvol, successful
suf, muzzy; nitwitted
suffen, to day-dream

suffer(d), noodle
sugge'reren, to suggest, to prompt
suiker, sugar
suikergoed *n*, candy
suikeroom, rich uncle
suikerpot, sugar-bowl
suikerriet *n*, sugar-cane
suikerstrooier, sugar-caster
suikerziekte, diabetes
suizebollen, to have a reeling head
suizen, to whisper, to murmur
su'kade, candied peel
sukkel, muggins
  aan de sukkel zijn, to be an invalid
sukkelaar, weakling; booby
sukkeldraf, jog-trot
sukkelen, to be in poor health; to plod
sul, nincompoop
summum *n*, acme
supple'toir, supplementary
sup'poost, custodian
surro'gaat *n*, substitute
surveil'leren, to supervise, to invigilate
sussen, to soothe; to salve
symboliek, symbolism
sym'bool *n*, symbol
sympa'thiek, congenial, engaging
symp'toom *n*, symptom
syno'niem (*n*), synonym(ous)
syn'thetisch, synthetic
sys'teem *n*, system

T

taai, tough, dogged, tedious
taai-'taai *n*, tough kind of gingerbread
taak, task
taal, language
taalboek *n*, grammar
taaleigen *n*, idiom
taalfout, solecism
taalgeleerde, taal'kundige, linguist
taart, tart, *gâteau*
ta'bak, tobacco
  ergens tabak van hebben, to be fed up with something

TAB 188 TEG

ta'bakszak, tobacco-pouch
tabbard, tabberd, tabard
ta'bel, table, index
tabel'larisch, tabulated
ta'blet, tablet
tachtig, eighty
tachtiger, octogenarian; writer of the movement of 1880
tac'tiek, tactic(s)
tactloos, tactless
tafel, table
tafelblad *n*, table-top, table-leaf
tafeldame, partner (at table)
tafeldekken, to lay the table
tafelen : lang —, to linger over a meal
tafelgebed *n*, grace
tafelgoed *n*, table-linen
tafelheer, partner (at table)
tafelkleed *n*, table-cover
tafellaken *n*, table-cloth
tafelschuier, crumb-brush
tafelstoel, high chair
tafe'reel *n*, scene
tafzij(de), taffeta
taille, waist(-line), bodice
tak, branch
takel, tackle, rigging
takelen, to rig (out) ; to hoist
takelwagen, break-down lorry
takkenbos, faggot
tal *n*, number
  een viertal, twaalftal, twintigtal *etc*, (about) four, a dozen, a score *etc*.
talen, to be interested in
talg, talk, tallow, talc(um powder)
talloos, countless
talmen, to linger
talrijk, numerous
talstelsel *n*, (numerical) system
tam, tame(d), domestic(ated)
tamboe'rijn, tambourine
tamelijk, fair(ly), rather
tand, tooth, prong
  iemand aan de tand voelen, to put a person through his paces
tandarts, dentist
tandestoker, tooth-pick
tandheelkunde, dental surgery
tandrad *n*, cog-wheel
tandradbaan, rack-railway

tandvlees *n*, gum(s)
tanen, to tan; to wane
tang, (pair of) tongs, forceps: witch
  dat slaat als een tang op een varken, that is neither here nor there
tanig, tawny
tanken, to (re)fuel
tankschip *n*, tanker
tantali'seren, to tantalize
tante, aunt; woman
tantième *n*, bonus
ta'pijt *n*, carpet
tapisse'rie, tapestry
tapkast, bar
tappen, to tap; to crack
taps, tapering
taptemelk, skimmed milk
taptoe, tattoo
tapverbod *n*, prohibition
tapzaag, tenon saw
tarbot, turbot
ta'rief *n*, tariff, terms, fare
tarten, to defy
tarwe, wheat
tas, (hand)bag, brief-case
tast: op de —, by feeling
tastbaar, tangible
tasten, to feel, to grope
tateren, to jabber
tatoe'ëren, to tattoo
taxa'teur, valuer
tax'eren, to value, to assess
te, at, in; too; to
tech'niek, technique; technics
technisch, technical
te(d)er, tender, delicate
teef, bitch, vixen
teelaarde, humus
teelbal, testicle
teelt, cultivation, culture, breeding
teen, toe : osier
teenhout *n*, osier(s)
teer, tar : (*see* **teder**)
teerling, die
tegel, tile
tege'lijk(ertijd), at the same time
tege'moet-, to ... to meet
tege'moetgaan, to go to meet; to head for

tege'moetkomen, to (come to) meet (halfway)

tege'moetkomend, accommodating

tege'moetzien, to await

tegen, against; towards; at
ik kan er niet tegen, I cannot stand it

tegen-, counter-

tagen'aan, against, into

tegenbeeld *n,* counterpart

tegenbericht *n,* word to the contrary

tegenbenzoek *n,* return visit

tegenbezwaar *n,* (counter-)objection

tegencandidaat, opposing candidate

tegendeel *n,* contrary

tegengaan, to counter(act)

tegengesteld, opposite

tegengif *n,* antidote

tegenhanger, counterpart

tegenhouden, to check, to hold

tegenkanting, opposition

tegenkomen, to come across

tegenligger, oncoming vehicle *or* vessel

tegenlopen: het liep me tegen, I had bad luck

tegen'over, opposite (to), (as) against, towards

tegen'overgesteld(e *n*), contrary

tegenpartij, opponent

tegenpool, antipole

tegenprestatie: als —, in return

tegenslag, set-back

tegenspartelen, to struggle; to protest

tegenspeler, opponent; opposite number

tegenspoed, adversity

tegenspraak, contradiction

tegenspreken, to contradict

tegenstaan, to be repugnant to

tegenstand, resistance

tegenstander, adversary

tegenstelling, contrast

tegenstemmen, to vote against

tegenstribbelen, to struggle; to protest

tegen'strijdig, conflicting

tegenvallen, to be disappointing
het viel tegen, it was worse than (*or* not what) I'd expected

tegenvaller, blow

tegenvoeter, antipode

tegenwaarde, equivalent

tegenweer, resistance

tegenwerken, to oppose

tegenwerking, obstruction(ism)

tegenwerping, objection

tegenwicht *n,* counterpoise

tegen'woordig, present(-day), nowadays

tegen'woordigheid, presence

tegenzin, aversion
met tegenzin, reluctantly

tegenzitten: alles zit me tegen, I'm up against it

te'goed *n,* credit: owing

te'huis *n,* home

teil, (zinc, enamel) bowl *or* bath

teisteren, to ravage

teken *n,* sign, token
in het teken staan van, to be overshadowed by

tekenen, to draw; to sign

tekenfilm, cartoon

tekenhaak, T-square

tekening, drawing, plan; marking(s)

te'kort (*n*), shortage, deficit: short

te'kort doen, to stint; to wrong

te'kortkoming, shortcoming

tekst, text, script, words

tekstuitlegger, exegete

tekstwoord *n,* text

tel, count; second
in tel zijn, to be highly thought of

tele'foon(tje *n*), telephone(-call)

tele'fooncel, call-box

tele'fooncentrale, telephone-exchange

tele'foongids, telephone-directory

telegra'feren, to wire, to cable

te'leurstellen, to disappoint

te'leurstelling, disappointment

telex, teleprinter

telg, offspring

telkenmale, telkens (weer), again and again, every time

tellen, to count, to total

te'loorgaan, to get lost
telwoord *n,* numeral
temen, to drawl, to moan
temmen, to tame
tempel, temple
tempera'mentvol, tempera- mental
tempera'tuur, temperature
temperen, to temper, to moderate
tempo *n,* tempo, pace
ten'dens, tendency
tenger, slight, delicate
tenge'volge van, as a result of
te'nietdoen, to nullify, to vitiate
ten'lastelegging, charge
ten'minste, at least
tennissen, to play tennis
tent, tent, booth, "dive"
ten'tamen *n,* preliminary ex- amination
tentdoek *n,* canvas
ten'toonspreiden, to display
ten'toonstelling, exhibition, show
te'nue *n* : (groot) —, (full) dress
ten'zij, unless
tepel, nipple, teat
ter'aardebestelling, interment
ter'dege, thoroughly
te'recht, rightly
te'rechtbrengen, to make a job of
te'rechtkomen, to turn out all right ; to turn up ; to end up
te'rechtstaan, to stand one's trial
te'rechtstelling, execution
te'rechtwijzing, reprimand
teren op, to live on
tergen, to provoke
ter'handstelling, presentation
tering, consumption
ter'loops, incidental
term, term
ter'mijn, term ; instalment
  op korte termijn, at short notice ; short-term
ter'nauwernood, scarcely
ter'neerdrukken, to depress
ter'neergeslagen, disheartened
terpen'tijn, turpentine
ter'ras *n,* terrace

ter'rein *n,* terrain, ground, field
ter'reinknecht, groundsman
ter'reur, reign of terror
ter'rine, tureen
ter'sluiks, stealthily
ter'stond, at once
terts : (grote) —, (major) third
te'rug, back
te'rugblik, retrospect(ion)
te'rugdeinzen, to shrink (back)
te'rugdenken aan, to recall (to mind)
te'ruggetrokken, retiring
te'ruggeven, to give back, to re- turn
terug'houdend, reserved
te'rugkaatsen, to strike back, to rebound, to (be) reflect(ed), to (re-)echo
te'rugkeer, return
te'rugkeren, to return, to turn back
te'rugkomen, to come back, to return
te'rugkrabbelen, to back out
te'ruglopen, to walk back ; to de- cline
te'rugnemen, to take back, to withdraw
te'rugreis, return-journey, way back
te'rugroepen, to call back, to re- call
te'rugschrikken, to recoil
te'rugslaan, to hit back, to re- pulse ; to back-fire
te-rugslag, reaction
te'rugtraprem, back-pedal brake
te'rugtrekken, to draw back, to retract ; to retreat
  zich terugtrekken, to retire
te'rugwerkende kracht heb- ben, to be retrospective
ter'wijl, while ; whereas
ter'wille van, for the sake of
ter'zijde, aside
testa'ment *n,* will, Testament
testen, to test
teug, gulp
teugel, rein
teugelloos, unbridled
teugje *n,* sip

teuten, to dawdle
te'veel n, surplus
tevens, as well
tever'geefs, to no purpose
te'vreden, content(ed), satisfied
te'vredenheid, satisfaction, contentment
te'waterlating, launching
te'weegbrengen, to bring about
tex'tiel, textile
te'zamen, together
thans, at present
thea'traal, theatrical
thé com'plet, afternoon tea
thee, tea
theelichtje n, (heated) tea-pot stand
theeleut, inveterate tea-drinker
Theems, Thames
theemuts, tea-cosy
theeservies n, tea-set
theestoof, tea brazier
theezeefje n, tea-strainer
thema n, theme; exercise
theo'loog, theologian, theological student
theo'reticus, theorist
theo'retisch, theoretical
theo'rie, theory
thera'pie, therapy, therapeutics
thermosfies, thermos (flask)
thesau'rier, treasurer
thuis, (at) home
thuisbrengen, to take home; to place
thuishoren, to belong
thuiskrijgen: zijn trekken —, to find one's pranks coming home to roost
tien, ten
tiend(e), tithe
tien'delig, ten-piece, in ten parts; decimal
tien'tallig, decimal
tientje n, ten-guilder note; tenth share (in a lottery ticket)
tier(e)lan'tijntje n, frill, furbelow
tieren, to thrive: to rage
tij n, tide
tijd, time; tense
tijdelijk, temporary; temporal
tijdens, during
tijdgenoot, contemporary

tijdig, timely, in good time
tijding(en), tidings, news
tijdlang: een —, for some time
tijdopname, time-exposure; timing
tijdpassering, pastime
tijdperk n, period
tijd'rovend, protractive
tijdsbestek n, space of time
tijdschrift n, periodical
tijdstip n, epoch, moment
tijdstroom, trend of the times
tijdsverloop n, lapse
tijdvak n, period
tijdverdrijf n, pastime
tijdverspilling, waste of time
tijgen, to set (out)
tijger, tiger
tijk, tick(ing)
tik, tap, rap
tikje n, gentle tap; touch, shade
tikken, to tap; to tick; to type
tik-tak-tol, noughts and crosses
til, dove-cot
  iets op til, something brewing
tillen, to raise, to lift
timmeren, to carpenter, to hammer
timmerman, carpenter
tingelen, to tinkle
tinne, pinnacle, battlement
tinnen, pewter
tint, tint, shade
tintelen, to sparkle, to twinkle; to tingle
tip, tip, corner
tippel(en), (to) tramp
tippen, to tap, to dab: to tiptoe
ti'ran, tyrant
tiranni'seren, to bully
titel, title, heading
titelplaat, frontispiece
titula'tuur, style, titles
tjilpen, to chirp
tjokvol, chock-full
tobbe, tub
tobben, to brood; to slave; to have a tough time
toch, still, for all that; surely, after all
  zeg het toch! do tell me!
  waarom toch? whatever for?
tocht, draught; trip, drive

tochtdeur, hall-door
tochten, to be draughty
tochtig, draughty
toe, to
 toe maar !, toe nou ! go on!
 er slecht aan toe zijn, to be in a bad way
 het is tot dear aan toe, it is bad enough
toebedelen, ['tubədelə], to allot
toebehoren, to belong to: n, accessories
toebereidselen, preparations
toebrengen, to inflict on
toedekken, to cover up; to mulch
toedienen, to administer to
toedoen, to close; to matter: n, influence
toedracht, (case-)history
toedragen, to think of (a person) with
 zich toedragen, to come about
toeëigenen: zich —, to appropriate
toegaan: het gaat er raar toe, there are strange goings-on there
toegang, admission, entry
toegangsbewijs n, ticket of admission
toe'gankelijk, accessible, open
toegedaan, (kindly) disposed to(wards)
toe'geeflijk, lenient
toegenegen, affectionate
toegeven, to admit; to give way (to)
toegewijd, devoted
toegift, encore
toehoorders, audience, observers
toejuichen, to applaud; to welcome
toekennen, to confer upon, to attach to
toekeren, to turn to(wards)
toekijken, to look on
toekomen, to come to(wards); to make ends meet; to be due to
 doen toekomen, to send
toe'komend, future; due
toekomst(ig), future

toekrijgen: ik kreeg . . . toe, that was thrown in (for nothing); I had . . . for pudding
toelage, allowance
toelaten, to admit, to permit
toelatingsexamen n, entrance examination
toeleggen op, to contribute towards
 zich toeleggen op, to apply oneself to
toelichten, to elucidate
toeloop, concourse, rush
toelopen, to run (up) to; to taper
toen, then; when
toenaam: met naam en —, in detail
toenadering, rapprochement
toename, increase
toenemen, to increase
toenmaals, at that time
toen'malig, then, of the day
toenter'tijd, at the time
toe'passelijk, applicable, appropriate
toepassen, to apply
toepassing: van —, applicable
 in toepassing brengen, to put into practice
toer, tour; feat; rev(olution); row (of knitting)
 een hele toer, quite a job
toereiken, to hand (to)
toe'reikend, sufficient
toe'rekenbaar, responsible
toeren: gaan —, to go for a drive
toe'rist(enverkeer n), tourist (traffic)
toer'nooi n, tournament
toe'schietelijk, responsive, obliging
toeschijnen, to seem to
toeschouwer, spectator, onlooker
toeschrijven, to attribute
toeslaan, to slam
toeslag, excess (fare); bonus
toespeling, allusion
toespijs, dessert
toespraak, address
toespreken, to speak to, to address

toestaan, to allow, to grant

toestand, state of affairs, situation, position, condition

toestel *n,* apparatus, machine

toestemmen (in), to consent (to)

toestemming, permission

toestoppen, to stop up; to slip into (a person's) hand; to tuck in

toestromen, to pour (in)

toet, face: bun

toetakelen, to doll up; to knock about

toetasten, to help oneself

toeten: hij weet van — noch blazen, he doesn't know a thing (about it)

toeter(en), (to sound the) horn

toetje *n,* pudding, second course

toetreden tot, to join

toets, key; test

toetsen, to test

toetssteen, touchstone

toeval *n,* accident; epileptic fit

toe'vallig, (by) chance
  wat toevallig! what a coincidence!

toeverlaat, refuge

toevertrouwen, to (en)trust with
  dat is hem wel toevertrouwd, you can leave that to him

toevloed, influx

toevlucht, recourse

toevluchtsoord *n,* asylum

toevoegen, to add

toevoer, supply

toewenden, to turn to(wards)

toewensen, to wish

toewijding, devotion

toewijzen, to allocate

toezeggen, to promise

toezicht *n,* supervision

toezien, to look on; to take care (of)

tof, ripping

toga, gown, cassock

toi'lettafel, dressing-table

toilet'teren: zich —, to dress

tokkelen, to pluck, to strum

tol, toll: top

tolboom, turnpike

tole'reren, to tolerate

tolk, interpreter; spokesman

tollen, to play with a top, to spin round

tollenaar, publican

to'maat, tomato

tomeloos, unbridled

tom'poes, cream slice: chubby umbrella

ton, barrel; buoy; ton; 100,000 guilders

tondeldoos, tinder-box

ton'deuse, hair-clippers

to'neel *n,* stage; scene, theatre

to'neelgezelschap *n,* repertory company

to'neelkijker, (pair of) opera glasses

to'neelknecht, stage-hand

to'neelrecensent, dramatic critic

to'neelschool, school of dramatic art

to'neelschrijver, playwright

to'neelspel *n,* play; acting

to'neelspeler, actor

to'neelstuk *n,* play

to'neelvereniging, dramatic club

to'neelvoorstelling, theatrical performance

to'neelzolder, fly

tonen, to show

tong, tongue: sole

tongval, accent

tonicum *n,* tonic

toog, arch: cassock

tooi, attire; finery

tooien, to adorn

toom, bridle
  in toom houden, to keep in check

toon, tone; pitch

toonaangevend, leading

toonaard, key

toonbaar, presentable

toonbank, counter

toonbeeld *n,* model

toonder, bearer

toonhoogte, pitch

toonkamer, show-room

toonkunst, music

toonladder, scale; gamut

toonloos, toneless; unaccented

toonsoort, key

toontje lager zingen, to come down (a) peg or two

toonval, cadence
toonvast, in tune, note-perfect
toonzaal, show-room
toonzetting, (musical) setting
toorn, rage
toorts, torch
toost, toast
top, top, tip: agreed!
topo'grafisch, topographical, ordnance
topprestatie, record
toppunt n, summit, height; limit
tor, beetle
toren, tower
torenhoog, towering
torenspits, spire
torentje n, turret
torentrans, gallery
tornen, to unpick; to meddle
torpe'deren, to torpedo; to scotch
tor'pedojager, destroyer
torsen, to labour under (the weight of)
tossen, to toss
tot, till, (up) to; as
  tot aan, as far as
  tot op, to within; up till
to'taal, total, utter
totdat, until
tou'cheren, to touch (up)
tour'nee, tour
touw n, rope, string
  op touw zetten, to set on foot
  ik kon er geen touw aan vast-knopen, I couldn't make head or tail of it
touwtje n, piece of string
  touwtje springen, to skip
touwtrekken n, tug-of-war
tovenaar, magician
tovena'res, enchantress
toverachtig, magic, enchanting
toverdrank, magic potion
toveren, to work charms, to conjure (up)
toverkol, witch
toverlantaarn, magic lantern
tovermiddel n, charm
toverstaf, magic wand
traag, slow, sluggish
traan, tear: oil
trachten, to attempt, to try

tra'ditie, tradition
tra'gedie, tra'giek, tragedy
tragisch, tragic
trainen, to train, to coach
trai'neren, to hold up
tra'ject n, stretch, stage, line
trak'taat n, treatise, tract; treaty
trak'tatie, treat
trakte'ment n, salary
trak'teren (op), to treat (to)
tralies, bars, grating
traliewerk n, trellis
tram(halte), tram(-stop)
tranen, to water
trans, gallery, battlement
transfor'mator, transformer
tran'sito(haven), transit(-port)
transpi'reren, to perspire
transpor'teren, to transport; to bring forward
trant, style, manner
trap, kick; stairs; degree
  een hele trap, quite a way (by bike)
trapgevel, step-gable
trapje n, step, stair
trapleer, step-ladder
trapleuning, banisters
traploper, stair-carpet
trapnaaimachine, treadle sewing-machine
trappelen, to stamp
trappen, to kick; to tread; to pedal
trappenhuis n, staircase well
trappers, pedals: brogues
trapsgewijs, step by step
tra'want, satellite
trechter, funnel, hopper
trechtermonding, estuary
tred, step, pace; gait
trede, step, stair
treden, to tread; to go, to come
treeft(je n**),** trivet
treeplank, footboard
tref, bit of luck
treffen, to hit, to strike; to meet
  het (goed) treffen, to be lucky
treffend, striking, touching
treffer, good shot, hit
trein, train
treiteren, to bait, to nag

trek, pull, draught; stroke; feature, trait; inclination, appetite; migration

in trek, in demand

trekharmonica, accordian

trekken, to draw, to drag; to migrate, to trek

trekker, trigger; hiker

trekking, (lottery) draw

trekpaard *n*, draught-horse

trekpen, drawing-pen

trekpleister, vesicant plaster; (fatal) attraction

trektocht, hiking-tour

tres, braid

treurdicht *n*, elegy

treuren, to grieve

treurig, sad

treurmars, funeral march

treurspel *n*, tragedy

treurwilg, weeping-willow

treurzang, dirge

treuzelen, to dawdle

tri'bune, platform, gallery, stand

tricot *n*, stockinette; tights

tries(ig), gloomy

trijp *n*, velveteen

trillen, to vibrate, to quiver

tri'omf, triumph

triom'fantelijk, triumphant

triom'feren, to triumph

triplex, three-ply

trippelen, to trip

trip'tiek, triptych; triptyque

troebel, turbid

troef, trump(s)

troel, slut

troep, crowd, troop, pack, company; rowdy lot, mess

troepenmacht, military forces

troetelkind *n*, spoiled child

troeven, to trump

trog, trough

trom, drum

trommel, tin, (bread-)bin; drum

trommelen, to drum; to strum

trommelvlies *n*, ear-drum

trom'pet, trumpet

trom'petgeschal *n*, blare of trumpets

tronen, to sit enthroned; to lure

tronie, mug, dial

troon, throne

troonsbestijging, accession

troost, consolation

troosteloos, disconsolate

troosten, to comfort

tropen, tropics

tros, cluster, bunch; hawser

trots, proud : pride : despite

trot'seren, to brave, to face

trot'toir *n*, pavement

trot'toirband, kerb

trouw, faith(ful), loyal(ty)

trouw-, marriage-, wedding-

trouwakte, marriage-certificate

trouweloos, disloyal

trouwen (met), to marry, to be married (to)

zo zijn we niet getrouwd, that's not playing fair

trouwens, for that matter

trouw'hartig, candid

truc, trick, stunt

trui, jersey, sweater

Tsjech(isch *n*), Czech

tsjirpen, to chirp

tucht, discipline

tuchtigen, to chastise

tuchtschool, Borstal (institution)

tuig *n*, rigging, harness; scum

tui'gage, rigging

tuiltje *n*, posy

tuimelen, to tumble, to topple over

tuimel, spill, fall

tuin, garden

tuinboon, broad bean

tuinbouw, horticulture

tuinder, market-gardener

tuinhuisje *n*, summer-house

tui'nieren, to garden

tuinman, gardener

tuit, spout

tuiten, to tingle

tuk op, keen on

tukje *n*, snooze

tulband, turban; ring(-cake)

tule(n), tulle

tulp, tulip

tunnel, tunnel, subway

ture'luurs, dotty

turen, to peer, to pore over

turf, peat

turfmolm, turfstrooisel *n*, moss-litter

turnen, to do gymnastics
tussen, between, among
  iemand er tussen nemen, to pull a person's leg
tussen'beide komen, to intervene
tussen'door, through
tussenhandel, middleman's trade
tussen'in: er —, in between
tussenkamer, middle room
tussenkomst, intervention
tussenmuur, partition-wall
tussenpersoon, middleman; go-between
tussenpoos, interval
tussenschot *n,* partition
tussentijd, interim
  tussentijdse verkiezing, by-election
tussenuur *n,* free period
tussenvoegen, to insert
tussenvoegsel *n,* interpolation
tussenwerpsel *n,* interjection
tussenzetsel *n,* insertion
tutoy'eren, to drop the formalities
twaalf, twelve
twaalftallig, duodecimal
twaalfuurtje *n,* midday meal
twaalfvingerige darm, duodenum
twee, two
tweede, second
tweede'hands, second-hand
tweedekker, double-decker; biplane
tweede'rangs, second-rate
tweedraads, two-ply
tweedracht, discord
tweegevecht *n,* dual
twee'hoevig, cloven-hoofed
tweeklank, diphthong
twee'ledig, twofold, dual
tweeling, (pair of) twin(s)
tweeloopsgeweer *n,* double-barrelled gun
tweemaal, twice
tweepersoons, double
twee'slachtig, bisexual; amphibious; ambiguous
tweespalt, discord
tweespan *n,* pair (of horses)

tweespraak, duologue
tweesprong, fork; cross-roads
twee'stemmig, two-part
tweestrijd, inner conflict
twee'talig, bilingual
twee'zijdig, bilateral
twijfel(achtig), doubt(ful)
twijfelen (aan), to doubt
twijg, twig
twintig, twenty
twist(en), (to) quarrel
twistappel, bone of contention
twistgesprek *n,* dispute
twistpunt *n,* vexed question
twistziek, quarrelsome
ty'peren, to typify
ty'perend voor, typical of
tyfus, typhus, typhoid
typisch, typical; quaint

U

u, you
überhaupt, at all; anyway
ui, onion; joke
uier, udder
uil, owl
uilskuiken *n,* numbskull
uit, out (of), from; finished
  ergens op uit, out for (bent on) something
uitbeelden, to depict, to render
uitbesteden, to put out to contract; to board out
uitblijven, to stay away; to fail to materialize
uitblinken, to excel
uitbotten, to bud
uitbouw, extension
uitbraak, escape (from prison)
uitbraken, to vomit; to belch out
uitbrander, dressing-down
uitbreiden, to extend
uitbuiten, to exploit
uit'bundig, exuberant
uitdagen, to challenge
uitdelen, to distribute
uitdenken, to think up
uitdeinen, to serve; to have its day
uitdiepen, to deepen
uitdijen, to expand

uitdoen, to take off; to put out
uitdoven, to extinguish
uitdraaien, to turn out
 zich er uitdraaien, to wriggle out of it
 op (ruzie) uitdraaien, to end in (a quarrel)
uitdrage'rij, junk-shop
uitdrinken, to drink up, to finish
uit'drukkelijk, express
uitdrukken, to express; to stub out
uitdrukking, expression
uitduiden, to point out
uit'eengaan, to separate
uit'eenlopend, divergent
uit'eenzetten, to state, to explain
uiteinde n, extremity
uit'eindelijk, ultimate
uiten, to utter, to express
uiten'treuren, on and on (and on)
uiter'aard, naturally
uiterlijk, outward; at the latest: n, appearance
uitermate, exceedingly
uiterst, ut(ter)most, extreme
uiterste n, extreme
uiterwaarden, water-meadows,
uitflappen, to blurt out
uitfluiten, to cat-call
uitfoeteren, to blow up
uitgaan, to go out
 uitgaan op, to end in; to go out (to look) for
uitgang, exit; ending
uitgangspunt n, point of departure
uitgave, expense; publication, edition
uitgebreid, extensive
 uitgebreid lager onderwijs n, "secondary modern" education
uitgehongerd, famished
uitgelaten, elated
uitgeleide doen, to see off
uitgelezen, select
uitgemergeld, emaciated, exhausted
uitgestreken: met een — gezicht, without batting an eyelid

uitgeteerd, emaciated
uitgeven, to spend; to issue; to publish
 zich uitgeven voor, to pose as
uitgever, publisher
uitgewekene, refugee
uitgezonderd, except (for)
uitgieren: het — van het lachen, to scream with laughter
uitgifte, issue
uitglijden, to slip
uitgommen, to rub out
uitgroeien, to (out)grow
uithaal, whoop; swerve
uithalen, to turn out; to unpick; to be up to (tricks)
 de kosten er uithalen, to cover the costs
uithangbord n, sign(board)
uithangen, to hang out; to act
uit'heems, foreign; outlandish
uithoek, out-of-the-way place
uithollen, to hollow out
uithoren, to wheedle information from
uithouden: het —, to stand (it)
uithoudingsvermogen n, stamina
uit'huizig, gadabout
uithuw(elijk)en, to give in marriage
uiting, expression
uitje n, jaunt: small onion
uitjouwen, to barrack (at)
uitkeren, to pay
uitkering, pay(ment), benefit
uitkienen, to figure (out)
uitkiezen, to select
uitkijk, view; look-out
uitkijken, to look out, to look forward
 je raakt er nooit uitgekeken, there's no end to be seen there
uitklaring(skosten), clearance (dues)
uitkleden, to undress, to strip
uitknijpen, to squeeze out; to do a bunk; to peg out
uitknipsel n, cutting
uitkno(b)belen, to figure out
uitkoken, to boil (out), to scald, to render

uitkomen, to come out, to work out

ervoor uitkomen, to state openly

uitkomst, result; remedy

uitkramen, to spout, to parade

uitlaat, exhaust

uitlachen, to laugh at, to have a good laugh

uitlaten, to let out; to leave off (wearing)

zich uitlaten, to express an opinion

uitleenbibliotheek, lending-library

uitleg, explanation, construction

uitleggen, to lay out; to explain; to let out

uitlenen, to lend

uitleven: zich —, to live one's (own) life (to the full)

uitgeleefd, decrepit

uitleveren, to deliver up

uitlezen, to finish (reading)

uitlokken, to invite

uitlopen, to run out; to sprout

uitlopen op, to lead to

uitloper, runner; spur

uitloven, to offer

uitmaken, to break off; to constitute; to decide; to matter; to put out

iemand uitmaken voor al wat lelijk is, to call a person all the names under the sun

uitmesten, to clear out

uitmonden in, to discharge into

uitmoorden, to massacre

uitmunten, to excel

uit'muntend, excellent

uit'nemendheid: bij —, par excellence

uitnodigen, to invite

uitnodiging, invitation

uitoefenen, to exercise; to carry on, to hold

uitpakken, to unpack

uitpluizen, to go through with a fine tooth-comb

uitpraten, to finish talking; to talk over

zich ergens uitpraten, to talk one's way out of something

uitpuilen, to bulge

uitputten, to exhaust

uitreiken, to distribute, to issue

uitrekenen, to calculate

uitroeien, to root out, to exterminate: to row out

uitroepen, to call (out), to exclaim; to proclaim

uitroep(steken n), exclamation(-mark)

uitrusten, to rest; to equip

uitrusting, outfit, equipment

uitschakelen, to cut out (of the circuit); to count out

uitscheiden (met), to stop

uitschelden, to slang

uitschot n, trash, rejects

uitschuiftafel, extending table

uitslaan, to knock (shake, fling) out; to break out; to sweat

uitslag, result; rash; condensation

uitslapen, to sleep long enough, to lie in; to sleep off

uitsloven, to slave

uitsluiten, to exclude

uitgesloten! out of the question!

uit'sluitend, exclusively

uitsluitsel n, decisive answer

uitsmijter, fried egg on bread and ham

uitspanning, tea-garden(s)

uitspansel n, firmament

uitsparen, to save

uitspatting, extravagance, excess

uitspelen, to finish (a game); to play (off)

uitspoken, to be up to (mischief)

uitspraak, pronunciation; verdict

uitspreiden, to spread (out)

uitspreken, to pronounce, to express; to finish speaking

uitspringen, to jut out; to jump out

uitstaan, to stick (out); to bear interest

uitstallen, to display

uitstapje n, outing

uitstappen, to alight, to get out

uit'stedig, out of town

uitsteeksel *n*, protuberance
uitstek: bij —, pre-eminently
uitsteken, to put out, to stick out
uitstekend, protruding
uit'stekend, excellent
uitstel *n*, postponement
uitstellen, to postpone
uitstippelen, to work out (in detail
uitstorten, to pour out
uitstralen, to radiate
uitstrekken, to stretch (out)
uitstulping, bulge
uittocht, exodus
uittreden, to resign
uittrekken, to pull out; to take off; to march out
uittreksel *n*, extract, *précis*
uitvaagsel *n*, scum
uitvaardigen, to issue
uitval, sally, break-through; outburst
uitvallen, to fall out; to turn out; to flare up; to make a sortie
uitvaren, to sail (out); to storm
uitverkiezing, predestination
uitverkocht, sold out
uitverkoop, (clearance-)sale
uitverkoren, chosen
uitvinden, to invent
uitvissen, to fish out; to ferret out
uitvlucht, pretext
uitvoer, export(s)
  ten uitvoer brengen, to put into effect
uit'voerbaar, practicable
uitvoeren, to export; to carry out, to perform
uit'voerig, detailed, fully
uitvorsen, to unearth
uitvragen, to ask out; to pump
uitwasemen, to exhale; to emanate
uitwedstrijd, away match
uitweg, way out, escape, outlet
uitweiden, to digress
uit'wendig, external
uitwerken, to work out, to elaborate; to mature, to wear off
uitwerking, effect; elaboration

uitwerpselen, excrements
uitwijken, to move to one side; to flee the country
uitwijzen, to show; to decide; to expel
uitwippen, to nip out(side)
uitwisselen, to exchange
  uitwonen, to dilapidate
uitwonend, non-resident
uitzenden, to send out; to broadcast
uitzet, outfit, trousseau
uitzetten, to expand; to turn out; to set (out); to lower (boats)
uitzicht *n*, view, prospect
uitzieken, to get over an illness
uitzien, to look out
uitzingen: het —, to hold out
uitzitten: zijn straf —, to serve one's sentence
uitzoeken, to pick out
uitzondering, exception
uitzuigen, to suck out; to bleed white
uk(je *n*), nipper
una'niem, unanimous
unicum *n*, unique specimen
unie, union
u'niek, unique
univer'seel, universal; sole
universi'tair, universi'teit, university
urenlang, for hours
urmen, to worry, to fumble
uur *n*, hour; o'clock
uurwerk *n*, timepiece
uw, your
uwentwil(le): om —, for your sake
uwerzijds, for your part

V

vaag, vague
vaak, often
vaal, faded, sallow
vaandel *n*, colour(s)
vaandeldrager, standard-bearer
vaandrig, ensign; standard-bearer
vaarboom, punting-pole
vaardig, skilful; ready

vaargeul, fairway, channel
vaars, heifer
vaart, speed; waterway
 (grote) vaart, (ocean-going)
 trade
vaartuig n, vessel
vaarwater n, fairway
 iemand in het vaarwater
 zitten, to thwart a person
vaar'wel, farewell
vaas, vase
vaatdoek, dish-cloth
va'cantie, holiday(s), vacation
vaca'ture, vacancy
vacci'neren, to vaccinate
vacht, pelt, coat
vadem, fathom
vader, father
vanderlander, patriot
vanderlands'lievend, patriotic
vaderlands, native, national
vaderliefde, paternal love
vaderlijk, paternal
vadermoorder, parricide: stick-
 up collar
vaderschap n, paternity, father-
 hood
vadsig, slothful, flaccid
vagevuur n, purgatory
vak n, compartment, panel; subject, trade
vakje n, pigeon-hole
vakman, expert
vakterm, technical term
vakvereniging, trade-union
val, (down)fall; trap; valance
valbijl, guillotine
valbrug, draw-bridge
valdeur, trapdoor
va'lies n, portmanteau
valk(e'nier), falcon(er)
valkuil, pitfall
val'lei, valley
vallen, to fall
 er valt niets aan te doen,
 nothing can be done about it
valluik n, trapdoor
valpoort, portcullis
valreep: één op de —, one for
 the road
vals, false, vicious
 vals spelen, to cheat; to play
 out of tune

valscherm n, parachute
valsheid in geschrifte, forgery
valstrik, trap
va'luta, currency
valwind, squall
van, of; from
 van de week, this week
van'af, (as) from
van'avond, this evening
van'daag, today
van'daan, from
van'daar, hence
 vandaar dat, that is why
van'door: er — (gaan), to be off
vangarm, tentacle
vangen, to catch
vangnet n, safety net
vangst, haul, catch
va'nille, vanilla
van-, this (afternoon, morning)
van'nacht, last night, tonight
van'ouds (her), of old
van'waar, whence
van'wege, on account of
vanzelf'sprekend, self-evident,
 quite obvious
varen, to sail, to fare: fern
 laten varen, to give up, to drop
varensgezel, sailor
varia, miscellaneous (items)
vari'ëren, to vary
varken n, pig
varkensdraf, hogwash
varkenshoeder, swineherd
varkenskot n, pigsty
varkensvlees n, pork
vast, fixed, permanent, firm,
 regular, stock; solid; certainly
 maar vast, in the meantime
vastbe'raden, resolute
vastbinden, to tie up (tight)
vastdoen, to fix
vaste'land n, continent, mainland
vastenavond, Shrove Tuesday
vastentijd, Lent
vastgrijpen, to catch hold of
vastheid, firmness, consistency,
 stability
vasthouden, to hold (on to), to
 clutch; to detain
vast'houdend, tenacious; conservative

vastklampen: zich — aan, to cling to

vastleggen, to fix, to tie up; to record

vastlopen, to run aground; to jam; to bog down

vastmaken, to fasten

vastpakken, to seize

vastraken, to run aground; to get jammed

vastroesten, to rust (solid); to root (deeply)

vaststaan, to stand firm; to be definite(ly) established

vaststellen, to fix, to establish

vastzetten, to fix (in position); to corner

vastzitten, to be stuck
  er aan vastzitten, to be entailed

vat *n,* cask, vat, vessel; hold

vatbaar, susceptible, capable

vatenkwast, washing-up mop

vatten, to catch; to understand; to set

vechten, to fight

vecht'lustig, pugnacious

vechtpartij, scrap

vee *n,* cattle

veearts, veterinary surgeon

veeg, streak: ominous
  een veeg uit de pan, a piece of one's mind

veel, much, a good deal, many

veelal, often

veelbe'lovend, promising

veelbe'tekend, significant, suggestive

veelbe'wogen, eventful

veeleer, rather

veel'eisend, exacting

veelhoek, polygon

veelom'vattend, comprehensive

veel'soortig, manifold

veelvoud *n,* multiple

veelvraat, glutton

veel'vuldig, frequent; manifold

veel'zeggend, significant

veel'zijdig, many-sided, catholic, versatile

veem *n,* warehouse(-company)

veen *n,* peat(-moor)

veenkolonie, fen-colony

veer, feather; spring: *n,* ferry(-boat)

veerkracht, resilience

veer'krachtig, buoyant, resilient

veertien, fourteen

veertig, forty

veestapel, live-stock

veeteelt, stock-breeding

vegen, to sweep, to brush, to wipe

vege'tariër, vegetarian

vege'teren, to vegetate

veil: zijn leven — hebben, to hold one's life cheap

veilen, to auction

veilig(heid), safe(ty)

veiligheidshalve, for safety's sake

veiligheidsraad, Security Council

veiligheidsstop, fuse

veiligheidsverdrag *n,* security pact

veiling, auction

veine, (run of) luck

veinzen, to feign, to sham

vel *n,* skin, hide; sheet
  om uit je vel te springen, enough to make you wild

veld *n,* field
  het veld ruimen, to retire from the field; to make way
  uit het veld geslagen, taken aback

veldbed *n,* camp-bed

veldfles, water-bottle, flask

veldheer, general

veldloop, cross-country run

veldpost, army post-office

veldprediker, army-chaplain

veldslag, battle

veldtocht, campaign

veldwachter, village policeman

velen, to stand: many (people)

velerlei, all kinds of

velg, rim

vellen, to fell: to pass

ven *n,* fen

ven'duhuis *n,* auction room(s)

ve'nijn *n,* venom

ve'nijnig, venomous

ven'noot, partner

ven'nootschap,   partnership, company

venster *n*, window

vensterbank, window-sill

vensterglas *n*, window-pane

vent, chap, cove

venten, to peddle, to hawk

venter, hawker, costermonger

ven'tiel *n*, valve

venti'leren, to ventilate

ver, far, distant

ver'aangenamen,   to   make pleasant

ver'achtelijk, contemptible, contemptuous

ver'achten, to despise

ver'ademen, to breathe again

veraf, far (away)

ver'afgoden, to idolize

ver'afschuwen, to detest

ver'anderen, to change, to alter

ver'andering,   change,   transformation

ver'anderlijk, changeable, variable, inconstant

verant'woordelijk, responsible

verant'woordelijkheid(sgevoel *n*), (sense of) responsibility

ver'antwoorden, to answer for; to justify

ver'antwoording, account; justification

var'armen, to impoverish; to become poor

ver'assen, to cremate

ver'band *n*, connection; context; bandage, dressing; bond

ver'bandkist, first-aid box

ver'bannen, to exile

ver'basteren, to degenerate, to corrupt

ver'bazen, to astonish, to amaze

ver'beelden, to represent

   zich verbeelden, to imagine, to fancy

ver'beelding,   imagination, (self-)conceit

ver'beiden, to await; to (a)bide

ver'bergen, to hide

ver'beten,   obdurate,   pent-up, grim

ver'beteren, to improve; to correct

ver'beteringsgesticht *n*, approved school

ver'beurdverklaren,   to   confiscate

ver'beuren, to forfeit

ver'beuzelen, to fritter away

ver'bidden, to mollify

ver'bieden, to forbid, to prohibit

ver'bijsteren, to bewilder

ver'bijten: zich —, to clench one's teeth

ver'binden, to join, to connect

   zich verbinden tot, to commit oneself to

ver'binding,   connection,   communication

ver'bindingsofficer,   liaison officer

ver'bintenis, contract

ver'bitterd, embittered

ver'bleken, to grow pale; to fade

ver'blijden, to cheer (up)

ver'blijf *n*, stay; residence

ver'blijfkosten, hotel expenses

ver'blijven, to stay, to remain

ver'blinden, to blind, to dazzle

ver'bloemen, to disguise

ver'bluffend, staggering

ver'bod *n*, prohibition, ban

ver'boemelen, to squander

ver'bolgen, incensed

ver'bond *n*, alliance; covenant

ver'bouwen, to rebuild; to grow

verbouwe'reerd, flabbergasted

ver'branden, to burn (down); to be burnt (down, out, up), to tan

ver'brandingsproces *n*, process of combustion; cremation

ver'brassen, to dissipate

ver'breden, to widen

ver'breiden, to spread

verbreken, to break (off), to cut (off)

ver'brijzelen, to shatter

ver'broedering, fraternization

ver'brokkelen, to crumble

ver'bruien: het bij iemand —, to get into a person's bad books

ver'bruik *n*, consumption

ver'bruiken, to consume, to use up

ver'buigen, to bend, to buckle; to decline
ver'buiging, declension
ver'chroomd, chromium-plated
ver'dacht, suspect(ed); suspicious; prepared
ver'dagen, to adjourn
ver'dampen, to evaporate
ver'dedigen, to defend
ver'dediger, defender, council for the defence
ver'dediging, defence
ver'deeldheid, disagreement
ver'dekt, under cover
ver'delen, to divide (up)
ver'delgen, to destroy
ver'denken, to suspect
verder, further(more)
ver'derf n, ruin
ver'derfelijk, pernicious
ver'dichten, to invent
ver'dienen, to earn; to deserve
ver'dienste, wages, profit; merit
ver'dienstelijk, useful
ver'diepen: zich — in, to become engrossed in
ver'dieping, floor, storey
ver'dikke(me), ver'dikkie ! drat it! by Jove!
ver'dobbelen, to gamble away
ver'doemen, to damn
ver'doemenis, damnation
ver'doen, to waste
ver'domd, damn(ed)
ver'dommen: ik verdom het ! I'm damned if I do!
ver'donkeremanen, to spirit away
ver'doolde, pervert
ver'dorie ! darn (it) !
ver'dorren, to wither, to parch
ver'dorven, depraved
ver'doven, to deaden, to benumb, to stun, to give an anæsthetic; to deafen
ver'dovingsmiddel n, anæsthetic, narcotic
ver'draagzaam, tolerant
ver'draaid, distorted: deuced: dash it all!
ver'draaien, to distort, to twist
ver'drag n, treaty
ver'dragen, to bear

ver'driet n, grief; regrets
ver'drieten, to grieve
ver'drietig, pained, sad, sullen
ver'drijven, to drive off; to dispel; to while away
ver'dringen, to oust
  zich verdringen om, to crowd round
ver'drinken, to be drowned; to drown; to squander on drink; to inundate
ver'drogen, to dry up
ver'dromen, to waste (time) in dreaming
ver'drukking : in de — komen, to suffer
ver'drukte, underdog, oppressed
ver'dubbelen, to (re)double
ver'duidelijken, to elucidate
ver'duisteren, to eclipse, to black out; to embezzle
ver'duiveld, devilish; darned
ver'dunnen, to thin, to dilute
ver'duren, to put up with
ver'dwaasd, vacant
ver'dwijnen, to disappear
ver'edelen, to enhance the quality of
vereen'voudigen, to simplify
vereen'zelvigen, to identify
ver'eeuwigen, to immortalize
ver'effenen, to settle
ver'eisen, to require
ver'eiste n, requirement
veren, to (be) spring(y)
veren(bed n), feather(-bed)
ver'en(ig)en, to unite, to join; to reconcile
ver'eniging, association, union
ver'eren, to honour
ver'ergeren, to deteriorate, to aggravate
verf, paint; dye
ver'fijnen, to refine
ver'filmen, to film
ver'flauwen, to flag, to fade
ver'foeien, to detest
ver'fomfaaien, to dishevel
ver'fraaien, to beautify
ver'frissen, to refresh
ver'frommelen, to crumple up
verg., cf.

ver'gaan, to perish, to decay, to go down
hoe zal het ons vergaan ? what is in store for us?
een lawaai, dat horen en zien me verging, a noise fit to wake the dead
ver'gaarbak, reservoir
ver'gaderen, to assemble
ver'gadering, meeting
ver'gallen, to embitter, to spoil
vergalop'peren zich —, to let oneself in for something
ver'gankelijk, transitory
vergapen: zich —, to become infatuated
ver'garen, to collect
ver'gassen, to vaporize; to gas
ver'gasten, to treat, to feast
ver'geeflijk, pardonable
ver'geefs, (in) vain
ver'geetachtig, forgetful
ver'geetboek n: in het — raken, to be forgotten
ver'gelden, to repay, to pay for
ver'geldingsmaatregel, retaliatory measure
ver'gelen, to turn yellow
verge'lijk n, agreement; comparison
verge'lijken, to compare
verge'lijkend, comparative; competitive
verge'lijking, comparison, simile; equation
verge'makkelijken, to facilitate
vergen, to make demands on, to require
verge'noegd, contented
ver'getelheid, oblivion
ver'geten, to forget
ver'geven, to forgive
ver'gevensgezind, forgiving
ver'geving, pardon, forgiveness
vergevorderd, (far-)advanced
verge'wissen: zich —, to make sure
verge'zellen, to accompany
vergezicht n, prospect
verge'zocht, far-fetched
ver'giet, colander
ver'gieten, to shed; to refound
ver'gif(t) n, poison

ver'giffenis, forgiveness
ver'giftig, poisonous
ver'giftigen, to poison
ver'gissen: zich —, to be mistaken, to make a mistake
ver'gissing, mistake, slip
ver'goddelijking, deification
ver'goeden, to compensate (for), to reimburse
ver'goelijken, to palliate
ver'gooien, to throw away
zich vergooien, to throw oneself away; to play the wrong card
ver'grijp n, offence, breach
ver'grijpen: zich — aan, to lay hold on
ver'grooien, to disappear in time; to grow out of shape
ver'grootglas n, magnifying-glass
ver'groten, to enlarge, to increase, to magnify
ver'gruizen, to crush
ver'guizen, to vilify
ver'guld, gilt; delighted
ver'gulden, to gild
ver'gunnen, to permit
ver'gunning, permission, licence
ver'haal n, story: redress
op zijn verhaal komen, to take it easy (for a bit)
ver'haasten, to quicken, to expedite, to precipitate
ver'halen, to relate; to vent
het verhalen op, to take it out of
ver'handelen, to deal in; to discuss
ver'handeling, treatise
ver'harden, to harden
verharde weg, metalled road
ver'haren, to moult
ver'haspelen, to make a hash of
ver'heerlijken, to glorify, to elate
ver'heffen, to lift (up), to raise, to exalt
ver'heimelijken, to secrete
ver'helderen, to clarify
ver'helen, to conceal
ver'helpen, to remedy
ver'hemelte n, palate; canopy

ver'heugen, to delight
zich verheugen, to rejoice
zich verheugen op, to look forward to
ver'heven, exalted, lofty
ver'hinderen, to prevent, to hinder
ver'hip! dash!
ver'hitten, to heat
ver'hoeden, to forefend
ver'hogen, to raise, to heighten
ver'hoging, increase; platform; temperature
ver'holen, secret
ver'hongeren, to starve (to death)
ver'hoor n, interrogation, hearing
ver'horen, to hear, to grant; to interrogate
ver'houden: zich — als, to be in the ratio of
ver'houding, relation(ship), proportion
ver'huiswagen, removal-van
ver'huizen, to move (house)
ver'huizing, move
ver'hullen, to conceal
ver'huren, to let (out on hire)
ver'huur, hire, hiring out
ver'huurder, landlord, lessor
verifi'ëren, to verify
ver'ijdelen, to frustrate
vering, springiness, springs
ver'jaard, fallen by default, out of date
ver'jaardag, birthday
ver'jagen, to drive away
ver'jaren, to have one's birthday
ver'kalken, to harden, to calcerate
ver'kapt, disguised, veiled
ver'kavelen, to parcel out
ver'keer n, traffic; intercourse
ver'keerd, wrong, mis-(understood etc)
ver'keersheuvel, traffic-island
ver'keerstoren, control-tower
ver'keersweg, thoroughfare
ver'kennen, to reconnoitre
ver'kenner, scout
ver'kenning(svlucht), reconnaissance (flight)
ver'keren, to be, to move

ver'kering hebben, to be courting
ver'kerven: het bij iemand —, to incur a person's displeasure
ver'kiesbaar, eligible
ver'kies(e)lijk, preferable; desirable
ver'kiezen, to prefer; to elect, to chose
ver'kiezing, election; preference
ver'kiezingsdag, polling-day
ver'kijken: zich —, to make a mistake
je kans is verkeken, you've missed your chance
ver'kikkerd, dead keen
ver'killen, to chill
ver'klappen, to let on (about)
ver'klaren, to explain; to declare, to certify
ver'klaring, explanation; declaration; certificate
ver'kleden: (zich) —, to change
ver'kleinen, to reduce, to cut down; to belittle
ver'kleinwoord n, diminutive
ver'kleumen, to get numb with cold
ver'kleuren, to fade
ver'klikken, to split (on)
ver'klikker, tell-tale
ver'klungelen, to fritter away
ver'kneukelen, ver'kneuteren: zich —, to gloat
ver'knippen, to cut up; to spoil by cutting wrongly
ver'knocht, devoted
ver'knoeien, to bungle; to waste
ver'koelen, to cool (off)
ver'koken, to boil away; to overcook
ver'kolen, to char, to carbonize
ver'kondigen, to proclaim
verkoop, sale
ver'kooplokaal n, auction-room
ver'koopster, shop-assistant
ver'kopen, to sell: to crack (jokes)
ver'koping, (auction-)sale
ver'korten, to shorten; to beguile
ver'kouden worden, to catch cold
je bent verkouden, you've got a cold; you've walked right into it

ver'koudheid, cold
ver'krachten, to violate, to rape
ver'kreuk(el)en, to crumple (up)
ver'krijgbaar, obtainable
ver'krijgen, to obtain
ver'kroppen, to swallow
ver'kropt, pent-up
ver'kruimelen, to crumble (away)
ver'kwanselen, to barter away, to squander
ver'kwikken, to refresh
ver'kwisten, to waste, to dissipate
ver'laden, to ship
ver'lagen, to lower
ver'lakken, to diddle
ver'lammen, to paralyse
ver'lamming, paralysis
ver'langen, to desire, to long; to require
ver'laten, to leave, to desert: lonely, deserted
zich verlaten op, to rely on
ver'leden, last: n, past
ver'legen, shy, embarrassed: perished
ver'legenheid, shyness, embarrassment, quandary
ver'leggen, to shift
ver'leidelijk, tempting
ver'leiden, to tempt, to seduce
ver'lenen, to grant, to give
ver'lengen, to lengthen, to extend
ver'lengstuk n, extension piece
ver'leppen, to wilt; to jade
ver'leren, to lose the art
ver'licht, lit (up); enlightened; relieved
ver'lichten, to light (up), to illuminate; to lighten; to alleviate
ver'liefd, in love, amorous
ver'lies n, loss
ver'liezen, to lose
ver'lof n, leave, permission; licence
ver'lokken, to entice
ver'loochenen, to deny, to belie
ver'loofde, fiancé(e)

ver'loop n, course, (re)lapse
ver'lopen, to elapse; to go down(hill); to go (off): expired: down-and-out
ver'loren gaan, to get lost; to be wasted
ver'loskunde, obstetrics
ver'lossen, to deliver
ver'lossing, redemption; deliverance
ver'loten, to raffle
ver'loven, to get engaged
ver'loving, engagement
ver'luchten, to illuminate
ver'luiden, to murmur
ver'lummelen, to laze away
ver'lustigen: zich — in, to revel in
ver'maak n, pleasure, amusement
ver'maard, celebrated
ver'mageren, to reduce or lose weight
ver'mageringskuur, slimming course
ver'makelijk, amusing
ver'maken, to amuse; to alter; to bequeath
vermale'dijd, accursed
ver'manen, to admonish
ver'mannen: zich —, to brace oneself
ver'meend, supposed
ver'meerderen, to increase
ver'meien: zich —, to enjoy oneself
ver'melden, to mention, to record
vermeldens'waard, worth mentioning
ver'menen, to opine
ver'mengen, to mix, to mingle
vermenig'vuldigen, to multiply
ver'metel, audacious
ver'mijden, to avoid, to evade
vermil'joen (n), vermilion
ver'minderen, to reduce, to diminish
ver'minken, to maim, to mutilate
ver'mist, missing
ver'moedelijk, presumably, probable

ver'moeden, to presume; to suspect: *n,* conjecture; suspicion

ver'moeid(heid), tired(ness), fatigue(d)

ver'moeiend, tiring

ver'mogen *n,* fortune; ability, capacity

niets vermogen, to be powerless

ver'mogend, wealthy

ver'mogensbelasting, property-tax

ver'molmd, mouldered

ver'mommen, to disguise

ver'moorden, to murder

ver'morzelen, to crush

ver'murwen, to mollify

ver'nachelen, to fox

ver'nauwen, to take in, to narrow

ver'nederen, to humble, to humiliate

ver'nemen, to learn, to hear

ver'nielen, to destroy, to wreck

ver'nielziek, verniel'zuchtig, destructive

ver'nietigen, to destroy; to annul, to reverse

ver'nieuwen, to renew

ver'nikkelen, to nickle(-plate); to diddle

ver'nis *n,* varnish; veneer

ver'noemen naar, to name after

vernuft *n,* ingenuity, wit

veron'aangenamen, to make unpleasant

veron'achtzamen, to neglect

veronder'stellen, to suppose, to assume

ver'ongelijkt, hurt, injured

ver'ongelukken, to be wrecked, to crash, to be killed

veront'heiligen, to desecrate

veront'reinigen, to pollute

veront'rusten, to alarm

veront'schuldigen, to excuse

zich verontschuldigen, to apologize, to excuse oneself

veront'waardigd, indignant

veront'waardiging, indignation

ver'oordelen, to condemn, to convict

ver'oorloofd, allowed, permissible

ver'oorloven: zich —, to permit oneself, to take the liberty of; to afford

ver'oorzaken, to cause

ver'orberen, to consume

ver'ordening, regulation(s), by-law

ver'ouderd, obsolete, aged

ver'overen, to conquer, to capture

ver'pachten, to let (out) on lease

ver'pakken, to pack

ver'panden, to pawn; to pledge

ver'patsen, to trade

verper'soonlijken, to personify

ver'pesten, to contaminate; to wreck

ver'pieterd, scrubby (little)

ver'plaatsen, to move, to transfer

zich verplaatsen, to imagine oneself

ver'planten, to transplant

ver'pleegster, nurse

ver'plegen, to nurse

ver'pletteren, to shatter

ver'plicht, obliged, indebted; compulsory

ver'plichten, to oblige; to compel

ver'plichting, obligation, commitment

ver'pozen: zich —, to relax

ver'praten: tijd —, to spend time talking

zich verpraten, to let on

ver'prutsen, to muck up

ver'raad *n,* treason

ver'raden, to betray

ver'rader, traitor

ver'raderlijk, treacherous, insidious

ver'rassen, to surprise

ver'rassing, surprise

verre'gaand, gross, outrageous

ver'regend, washed out (by the rain)

verreikend, far-reaching

ver'reisd, travel-weary

ver'rekenen, to settle
　zich verrekenen, to miscal-
　culate
verrekijker, telescope
ver'rekken, to sprain, to strain:
　to go to hell
verre'weg, by far
ver'richten, to carry out, to do
ver'rijken, to enrich
ver'rijzen, to (a)rise, to spring
　up
ver'roeren, to stir
ver'roest, rusty: darn(ed)
ver'rotten, to rot
ver'ruilen, to exchange
ver'ruimen, to broaden
ver'rukkelijk, delicious; gor-
　geous
ver'rukking, rapture
ver'rukt, delighted
vers, fresh, new(-laid): n, verse,
　poetry, poem
ver'sagen, to quaver
ver'schaffen, to provide
ver'schalken, to beguile
ver'schansen, to entrench, to
　ensconce
ver'scheiden, various, several:
　n, decease
ver'scheidenheid, diversity
ver'schepen, to (tran)ship
ver'scherpen, to intensify
ver'scheuren, to tear (to pieces),
　to rend
ver'schiet n, distance; prospect
ver'schieten, to use up; to turn
　pale, to fade
ver'schijnen, to appear
ver'schijning, appearance;
　figure
ver'schijnsel n, phenomenon;
　symptom
ver'schil n, difference
ver'schillen, to differ
ver'schillend, different
ver'schonen, to put on clean
　sheets or clothes; to excuse;
　to spare
ver'schoppeling, outcast
ver'schrikkelijk, terrible
ver'schrikking, fright, horror
ver'schroeien, to scorch
ver'schrompelen, to shrivel (up)

ver'schuilen, to hide, to shelter
ver'schuiven, to shift
ver'schuldigd, indebted, due
versie, version
ver'sieren, to adorn
ver'siering, decoration
ver'siersel n, ornament
ver'sjacheren, to barter away, to
　squander
ver'sjouwen, to shift
ver'slaafd, addicted
ver'slaan, to beat, to defeat; to
　cover
ver'slag n, report
ver'slagen, defeated; put out
ver'slaggever, reporter, com-
　mentator
ver'slapen: zich —, to over-
　sleep
ver'slappen, to weaken, to flag
ver'slepen, to tow away, to shift
ver'slijten, to wear out; to
　while away
　waar verslijt je me voor?
　what do you take me for?
ver'slikken: zich —, to choke
ver'slinden, to devour
ver'slingeren: zich —, to throw
　oneself away
ver'sloffen, ver'slonzen, to neg-
　lect
versmaat, metre
ver'smachten, to pine away
ver'smaden, to despise
ver'smelten, to melt, to blend
ver'snapering, titbit, refresh-
　ment
ver'snellen, to accelerate
ver'snelling, acceleration; gear
ver'snipperen, to cut up; to
　fritter away
ver'snoepen, to spend on sweets
ver'soberen, to live more simply
ver'spelen, to throw away
ver'sperren, to block (up)
ver'spieden, to spy out
ver'spillen, to waste
ver'splinteren, to (break into)
　splinter(s)
ver'spreiden: (zich) —, to
　spread, to scatter
ver'spreken: zich —, to make a
　slip (of the tongue)

verspringen n, long-jump
ver'staan, to understand, to hear
ver'staanbaar, audible, intelligible
ver'stand n, sense(s), mind; knowledge
 met dien verstande, on the understanding
 daar staat mijn verstand bij stil, it is beyond me
ver'standelijk, intellectual, rational
ver'standhouding, understanding, terms
ver'standig, sensible
ver'standshuwelijk n, marriage of convenience
ver'standskies, wisdom tooth
ver'standsmens, man of thought
ver'standsverbijstering, mental derangement
ver'stard, rigid
ver'steend, petrified; fossilized
ver'stek, n, default
ver'stekeling, stowaway
ver'stelbaar, adjustable
ver'steld, dumbfounded
ver'stellen, to adjust; to mend
ver'sterken, to fortify, to reinforce, to intensify; to amplify
ver'sterker, amplifier
ver'stevigen, to consolidate
ver'stijven, to stiffen; to grow numb
ver'stikken, to stifle
ver'stoken, to consume, to burn
ver'stoken van, without
ver'stokt, hardened, confirmed
ver'stolen, furtive
ver'stommen, to fall silent, to be struck dumb
ver'stoord, disturbed; vexed
ver'stoppen, to block (up); to hide
ver'stoppertje n, hide-and-seek
ver'storen, to disturb, to upset
ver'stoten, to cast off
ver'stouten: zich —, to make bold
ver'stouwen, to stow (away)
ver'strekken, to furnish, to issue
verstrekkend, far-reaching, sweeping

ver'strijken, to expire, to elapse
ver'strikken, to ensnare
ver'strooid, scattered; absent-minded
ver'strooien: zich —, to disperse; to find amusement
ver'stuiken, to sprain
ver'stuiven, to (be) blow(n) about
ver'suft, stupefied; doting
ver'takken: zich —, to branch
ver'talen, to translate
ver'taling, translation
verte, distance
ver'tederen, to mollify; to mellow
ver'teerbaar, digestible
ver'tegenwoordigen, to represent
ver'tellen, to tell, to say
 zich vertellen, to miscount
ver'telling, ver'telsel n, story
ver'teren, to consume, to spend; to digest: to perish
ver'tering, food and/or drink(s)
ver'tier n, (signs of) life, gaiety
ver'tikken, to jib, to refuse flatly
ver'tillen, to lift
 zich vertillen, to strain oneself (lifting something)
ver'timmeren, to make alterations to
ver'toeven, to sojourn
ver'tolken, to interpret
ver'tonen, to show, to produce
ver'toon n, show, presentation
ver'tragen, to retard
ver'traging, delay
ver'trappen, to trample under foot
ver'trek n, room: departure
ver'trekken, to leave; to distort
ver'troebelen, to confuse
ver'troetelen, to molly-coddle
ver'trouwd, trusty, safe; conversant
ver'trouwelijk, confidential; intimate
ver'trouweling, confidant(e)
ver'trouwen, to (en)trust; to rely: n, trust, confidence
ver'twijfeld, desperate

ver'twijfeling, desperation
veruit, by far
veruitziend, far-sighted
ver'vaard, alarmed
ver'vaardigen, to manufacture
ver'vaarlijk, frightful, terrific
ver'vagen, to fade
ver'val n, decline; disrepair; fall
ver'vallen, to lapse, to be cancelled, to expire, to fall (due); to go to ruin
ver'valsen, to fake
ver'vangen, to replace
ver'vat, couched; included
ver'velen: (zich) —, to (be) bore(d)
  tot vervelens toe, ad nauseam
ver'velend, boring; annoying
ver'veling, boredom
ver'vellen, to peel; to slough
verveloos, in need of a coat of paint
verven, to paint; to dye
ver'versen, to refresh; to renew
ver'vlakken, to become colourless
ver'vliegen, to evaporate, to vanish
ver'vloeken, to curse
ver'voegen, to conjugate
  zich vervoegen bij, to apply to
ver'voer n, transport
ver'voeren, to transport
ver'voering, rapture
ver'voermiddel n, (means of) conveyance
ver'volg n, continuation; future
ver'volgen, to continue; to pursue; to persecute, to prosecute
ver'volgens, after that
ver'volgverhaal n, serial story
ver'vreemden, to alienate, to grow estranged
ver'vroegen, to put forward
ver'vuilen, to get filthy
ver'vullen, to fill, to fulfil
ver'vulling, fulfilment
ver'waaid, dishevelled
ver'waand, conceited
ver'waardigen: (zich) —, to vouchsafe
ver'waarlozen, to neglect

ver'wachten, to expect
ver'wachting, expectation
ver'want, related
  verwanten, relatives
ver'wantschap, relationship affinity
ver'warmen, to heat
ver'warren, to confuse, to (en)tangle
ver'warring, confusion, disorder
ver'waterd, watered (down)
ver'wedden, to bet
ver'weer n, resistance; defence
ver'weerd, weather-beaten
ver'weking, softening
ver'wekken, to arouse, to raise; to beget
ver'welken, to wither, to wilt
ver'welkomen, to welcome
ver'wennen, to spoil
ver'wensen, to curse
ver'weren, to weather: to defend
ver'werken, to cope with; to work up
ver'werpen, to reject
ver'werven, to acquire
ver'wezen, dazed
ver'wezenlijken, to realize
  zich ver'wezenlijken, to materialize
ver'wijden, to widen
ver'wijderen, to remove, to turn out
  zich verwijderen, to withdraw
ver'wijdering, removal, expulsion; estrangement
ver'wijfd, effeminate
ver'wijlen, to linger
ver'wijt(en) (n), (to) reproach
ver'wijzen, to refer
ver'wikkelen, to implicate, to complicate
ver'wikkeling, complication, plot
ver'wilderen, to run wild, to degenerate
ver'wisselen, to (ex)change
ver'wittigen, to notify
ver'woed, furious
ver'woesten, to devastate
ver'wonden, to injure, to wound

ver'wonderen, to surprise
  zich verwonderen, to be surprised
ver'wonen, to pay in rent
ver'wording, degeneration
ver'wringen, to twist, to distort
ver'zachten, to alleviate
ver'zadigen, to saturate; to satisfy
ver'zaken, to forsake
ver'zakken, to sag, to subside
ver'zamelen, to collect, to muster (up)
ver'zamelnaam, collective
ver'zanden, to silt up
ver'zegelen, to seal (up)
ver'zeilen, to land (up)
ver'zekeren, to assure, to insure; to secure
  zich verzekeren, to make sure
ver'zekering, assurance, insurance
ver'zenden, to send (off)
ver'zet n, resistance
ver'zetje n, break
ver'zetten, to move; to get through; to get over
  zich verzetten, to oppose, to resist
ver'zien : het — hebben op, to be out to get
verziend, long-sighted
ver'zilveren, to silver(-plate); to convert into cash
ver'zinken, to become immersed; to countersink
ver'zinnen, to think (up)
ver'zinsel n, fabrication
ver'zitten, to move to another chair; to shift one's position
ver'zoek n, request
ver'zoeken, to request; to tempt
ver'zoeking, temptation
ver'zoekschrift n, petition
ver'zoenen, to reconcile
ver'zolen, to re-sole
ver'zorgen, to take care of
ver'zot op, mad on
ver'zuchten, to sigh
ver'zuchting, sigh, moan
ver'zuim n, omission; non-attendance
  zonder verzuim, without fail

ver'zuimen, to fail (in); to miss
ver'zuipen, to drown; to blue on drink
ver'zuren, to (turn) sour
ver'zwakken, to weaken
ver'zwaren, to increase (the standard of)
  ver'zwarende omstandigheden, aggravating circumstances
ver'zwelgen, to swallow up
ver'zwijgen voor, to keep from
ver'zwikken, to sprain
vest n, waistcoat
vesti'aire, cloak-room
vesti'bule, hall
vestigen, to establish; to fix
  zich vestigen, to settle
vesting, fortress
vet, fat; greasy; rich: n, fat
  vet gedrukt, in heavy type
vete, feud
veter, (shoe-)lace
vete'raan, veteran
vetgehalte n, fat content
vetmesten, to fatten (up)
vetplant, succulent plant
vettigheid, richness, greasiness
vetvrij, grease-proof
vetzak, fatty
vetzucht, obesity
veulen n, foal
vezel, fibre
vgl., cf.
via'duct n, (railway-)bridge, viaduct
vib'reren, to vibrate
vici'eus, vicious
vief, lively
vier, four
  onder vier ogen, in private
vieren, to celebrate: to ease off
vierendelen, to quarter
vierhoek, quadrilateral
vierkant (n), square
vierkantsvergelijking, quadratic equation
vierkantswortel, square root
vierling, (set of) quadruplets
viersprong, cross-road(s)
viervoeter, quadruped
vies, dirty, filthy; wry
  ik ben er vies van, it turns my stomach

viezerik, muck-pot, filthy specimen
vijand, enemy
vij'andelijk, enemy('s)
vij'andig, hostile
vijandschap, enmity
vijf, five
vijfling, (set of) quintuplets
vijftien, fifteen
vijftig, fifty
vijg, fig
vijl(en), (to) file
vijver, pond
vijzel, mortar
villen, to skin, to fleece
vilt n, felt
vin, fin
vinden, to find; to think; to get on
vindingrijk, inventive
vinger, finger
  door de vingers zien, to overlook
vingerafdruk, finger-print
vingerdoekje, n, small napkin
vingerhoed, thimble
vingervlug, nimble-fingered
vingerwijzing, hint, pointer
vink, finch
vinnig, cutting, sharp
vio'list, violinist
violon'cel, violoncello
vi'ool, violin: violet, pansy
vi'oolsleutel, treble clef
virtu'oos, virtuoso
vis, fish
visboer, fishmonger
viscouvert n, fish-knife and fork
visie, visi'oen n, vision
vi'site, visit(or)(s)
vislijm, isinglass
vissen, to fish
visser, fisherman
visse'rij, fishing(-industry)
vissnoer n, fishing-line
visspaan, fish-slice
visvangst, fishing
vi'taal, vital
vi'trage, (curtain-)net
vi'trine, show-case
vitten op, to find fault with
vi'zier n, visor
  in het vizier krijgen, to catch sight of

vla, (dessert) cream
vlaag, gust; fit
Vlaams, Flemish
vlag, flag
vlaggen, to put out the flag(s)
vlak, flat, smooth; right, close: n (sur)face
vlakgom n, india-rubber
vlakte, plane; stretch
vlam, flame
vlammen, to blaze, to be ardent
vlas n, flax
vlasblond, flaxen
vlassen op, to be all agog for
vlecht, plait
vlechten, to plait, to weave
vleermuis, bat
vlees n, meat, flesh
vleesboom, fleshy growth
vleeshouwer, butcher
vleesmes n, carving-knife
vleesmolen, mincing-machine
vleeswording, incarnation
vleet : geld bij de —, pots of money
vlegel, flail; (insolent) youth
vleien, to flatter, to coax
vlek, blot, spot, stain
vlekkeloos, spotless
vlekkenwater n, dry cleaner
vlerk, wing, arm; lout
vlet(schuit), flat-bottomed boat
vleug, nap; glimmer; whiff
vleugel, wing; grand piano
vlezig, fleshy, plump
vlieg, fly
vliegdekschip n, aircraft-carrier
vliegdienst, air-service
vliegen, to fly
  in brand vliegen, to burst into flames
vliege'nier, airman
vliegenkast, meat-safe
vliegenklap, fly-swatter
vliegensvlug, as quick as lightning
vlieger, kite; airman
vlieghaven, airport
vliegkunst, aviation
vliegmachine, aeroplane
vliegtuig n, aircraft, plane
vliegveld n, airfield

vliegwerk *n*, stage machinery
vliegwiel *n*, fly-wheel
vlier(bes), elder(berry)
vliering, loft
vlies *n*, fleece; film, membrane
vlijen, to nestle
vlijmscherp, sharp as a razor
vlijt, diligence
vlijtig, industrious
vlinder, butterfly
vlo, flea
vloed, flood (tide), flow
vloedgolf, tidal wave
vloeibaar, liquid
vloeiblok *n*, blotting-pad
vloeien, to flow; to blot
vloeiend, flowing; fluent
vloeipapier *n*, blotting-paper;
tissue-paper
vloeistof, liquid
vloeitje *n*, cigarette-paper
vloek, curse, oath
vloeken, to swear, to curse; to
clash
vloer, floor(ing)
vloeren, to floor
vloerkleed *n*, carpet
vlok, flake, tuft
vlonder, plank (thrown across a
ditch); wooden platform
vloot, fleet
vlootbasis, naval base
vlootvoogd, admiral of the fleet
vlos(sig), floss(y)
vlot, fluent, smooth, slick, sprightly; afloat: *n*, raft
vlotgaand, shallow-draught
vlotten, to float; to proceed
smoothly
vlucht, flight; wing-span
vluchteling, fugitive
vluchten, to fly, to flee
vluchtheuvel, traffic island;
mound
vluchtig, cursory, fleeting, volatile
vlug, quick
vlugschrift *n*, pamphlet
vlugzout *n*, sal volatile
vocabu'laire *n*, vocabulary
vocht *n*, fluid, moisture
vochtig, damp, moist
vod *n*, rag, tatter

voddenkoopman, rag-and-bone
man
voeden, to feed, to nourish
voeder(en) (*n*), (to) fodder
voederzak, nose-bag
voeding, feed; nourishment
voedingsbodem, breeding-
ground
voedingsleer, dietetics
voedsel *n*, food
voedster, wet-nurse
voedsterkind *n*, foster-child
voedzaam, nourishing
voeg, joint
voegen, to join, to add; to point;
to behove
zich voegen, to join; to comply
voegwoord *n*, conjunction
voelbaar, perceptible
voelen, to feel
voelhoren, voelspriet, feeler
voer, *n*, fodder; load
voeren, to take, to carry (on), to
wield, to conduct: to feed: to
line
voering, lining
voerloon *n*, carriage
voerman, carter
voertaal, official language
voertuig *n*, vehicle
voet, foot; footing
voet bij stuk houden, to stick
to one's guns
voetangel, mantrap
voetbal(schoen), football(boot)
voet(en)bank, foot-stool
voet(en)einde *n*, foot (of the
bed)
voetganger, pedestrian
voetkussen *n*, hassock
voetreis, walking tour
voetspoor *n*, foot-mark
voetstuk *n*, pedestal
voetvolk *n*, foot(-soldiers)
voetzoeker, (jumping) cracker
vogel, bird
vogelbekdier *n*, platypus
vogelverschrikker, scarecrow
vogelvlucht, bird's-eye view
vogelvrij, outlawed
vol, full
vo'lant, flounce
volbloed, thorough(bred)

vol'brengen, to accomplish

vol'daan, satisfied; paid

vol'doen, to satisfy, to give satisfaction, to pay

  voldoen aan, to fulfil

vol'doend, satisfactory; sufficient

vol'doening, satisfaction; settlement

vol'dongen, accomplished

vol'dragen, fully developed

vol'eind(ig)en, to complete

vol'gaarne, right gladly

volgauto, car in procession

volgeboekt, booked up

volgeling, follower

volgen, to follow

volgend, following, next

volgens, according to

volgieten, to fill

volgnummer n, serial number

volgorde, order, sequence

volgzaam, docile

vol'harden, to persevere

volhouden, to keep up, to maintain, to insist

voli'ère, aviary

vol'ijverig, sedulous

volk n, nation, people

Volkenbend, League of Nations

volkenkunde, ethnology

volkenrecht n, international law

vol'komen, complete

vol'korenbrood n, whole-meal bread

volksaard, national character

volksbuurt, working-class quarter

volksconcert n, popular concert

volksdans, folk-dance

volksdracht, national costume

volksgebruik n, national custom

volkshogeschool, village college

volkskunde, folk-lore

volkslied n, national anthem; folk-song

volksmond : in de — heten, to be popularly called

volksstam, tribe

volksstemming, plebiscite

volkstelling, census

volkstuin, allotment

volksuitgave, popular edition

volksuniversiteit, people's college

volksverhaal n, folk-tale

volksverhuizing, mass-migration

vol'ledig, complete, full

vol'leerd, consummate

vollopen, to fill up

vol'maakt, perfect

volmacht, power of attorney, proxy

vol'mondig, whole-hearted

volon'tair, student apprentice

volop, plenty (of)

volproppen, to stuff, to clutter up

vol'slagen, utter, total

vol'staan : laat ik — met te zeggen, suffice it to say

vol'strekt, absolute, at all

vol'tallig, complete, plenary

volte, crowd

vol'tooien, to complete

voltreffer, direct hit

vol'trekken, to solemnize, to execute

vol'uit, in full

volvette kaas, full-cream cheese

vol'voeren, to carry out

vol'waardig, sound (in body and mind)

vol'wassen(e), grown-up, full-grown, adult

volzee, high sea

volzin, sentence

vondeling, foundling

vondst, find

vonk(en), (to) spark

vonnis n, sentence, verdict

voogd('es), guardian

voog'dij, guardianship

voor, for; before; in front of: furrow

  voor . . . uit, ahead

voor'aan, in front, at this end

voor'aanstaand, prominent

vooraanzicht n, front view

voor'af, beforehand

voor'afgaand, foregoing, preliminary

voor'al, especially, by all means, on any account

voorals'nog, as yet

vooravond, early evening; eve

voorbaat : bij —, in anticipation

voor'barig, premature

voorbedachte : met — rade, with malice aforethought

voorbede, intercession

voorbeeld *n,* example, model

voor'beeldig, exemplary

voorbehoedmiddel *n,* prophylactic

voorbehoud *n,* reservation

voorbehouden, to reserve

voorbereiden, to prepare

voorbereiding, voorbereidsel *n,* preparation

voorbericht *n,* preface

voorbeschikken, voorbestemmen, to predestine

voorbidden, to lead in prayer

voor'bij, past

voor'bijgaan, to pass (by)

voor'bijgaand, passing, temporary

voor'bijganger, passer-by

voor'bijpraten : zijn mond —, to let one's tongue run away with one

voor'bijstreven, to outstrip, to overshoot

voorbode, herald; prelude

voordat, before

voordeel *n,* advantage, profit

voor'delig, economical, advantageous

voordeur, front door

voor'dien, until then

voordoen, to give a demonstration; to put on

 zich voordoen, to arise; to (re)present oneself

voordracht, recitation, lecture; delivery, rendering; nomination

voordragen, to recite; to propose

voor'eerst, in the first place; for the present

voorgaan, to lead (the way); to come first

voorgaand, preceding

voorganger, predecessor; minister

voorgerecht *n,* entrée

voorgeslacht *n,* ancestors

voorgevel, façade

voorgevoel *n,* presentiment

voor'goed, for good

voorgrond, foreground, fore-(front)

voorhamer, sledge-hammer

voor'handen, available

voorhebben, to intend; to have the advantage

voor'heen, formerly

voorhistorisch, prehistoric

voorhoede, advanced guard; forwards

voorhoofd *n,* forehead

voor'in, in (the) front

voor'ingenomen, prejudiced

voorjaar *n,* spring

voorkamer, front room

voorkauwen, to repeat over and over again

voorkennis, (fore)knowledge

voorkeur, preference

voorkomen, to occur; to seem; to drive up; to get ahead; to appear : *n,* appearance; incidence

voor'komen, to prevent; to anticipate

voor'komend, charming, considerate

voorlaatst, penultimate, last but one

voorland *n,* foreland; future

voorleggen, to submit to

voorletter, initial

voorlezen, to read (out) to

voorlichten, to light the way; to enlighten

voorlichting, information

voorliefde, predilection

voorliegen, to tell lies about

voorlijk, forward

voorlopen, to go in front; to gain, to be fast

voorloper, precursor

voor'lopig, interim, provisional, for the time being

voor'malig, one-time

voor'meld, above-mentioned

voormiddag, morning

voornaam, Christian name

voor'naam, distinguished, prominent

het voornaamste is, the main point is

voornaamwoord *n,* pronoun

voor'namelijk, principally

voornemen: zich —, to resolve, to propose

voornemen *n,* intention

voor'noemd, afore-mentioned

voor'onder *n,* forecastle

voor'oordeel *n,* prejudice

voor'oorlogs, pre-war

voor'op, in front

voor'opgezet, preconceived

voor'opstellen, to take for granted; to put first and foremost

voorouders, ancestors

voor'over, forward

voorplecht, forecastle

voorpost, outpost

voorpraten, to prompt

voorproefje *n,* foretaste

voorraad, stock, store

vorraadschuur, granary

voor'radig, in stock

voorrang, precedence; right of way

voorrangsweg, major road

voorrecht *n,* privilege

voorrede, preface

voorrijder, postilion; outrider

voorruit, wind-screen

voorschieten, to advance

voorschijn: te — brengen, to produce

te — halen, to take out

te — komen, to appear

te — roepen, to evoke

voorschoot, apron

voorschot *n,* advance

voorschrift *n,* regulation, order

voorschrijven, to prescribe, to lay down

voorsnijmes *n,* carving knife

voorspel *n,* voluntary, prologue; prelude

voorspelen, to play for

voor'spellen, to predict; to presage

voorspiegelen, to hold out prospects of

voorspoed, prosperity

voor'spoedig, prosperous, successful

voorspraak, intercession; advocate

voorsprong, start, lead

voorstaan, to stand in front; to come to mind

zich laten voorstaan op, to pride oneself on

voorstad, suburb

voorstander, advocate

voorste, foremost, front

voorstel *n,* proposal, suggestion

voorstellen, to (re)present, to introduce; to propose

zich voorstellen, to introduce oneself; to imagine; to intend

voorstelling, performance; representation

zich een voorstelling maken van, to visualize

voorstemmen, to vote in favour (of)

voorsteven, stem

voort-, on, forward

voortaan, in future

voortbestaan *n,* future life

voortbrengen, to produce, to beget

voortbrengsel *n,* product

voort'durend, continual, continuous

voorteken *n,* sign, omen

voortgang, progress; haste

voortkomen uit, to emanate from

voortmaken, to make haste

voortplanten, to propagate

voor'treffelijk, excellent

voortrein, relief train

voortrekken, to favour

voortrekker, pioneer

voorts, further (more)

voortslepen, to drag along

voortspruiten uit, to arise from

voort'varend, go-ahead

voort'varendheid, enterprise, drive

voortvloeien uit, to result from

voort'vluchtig, at large, fugitive

voortwoekeren, to spread

voortzetten, to continue

voor'uit, forward, ahead; before (hand)

voor'uitbetalen, to pay in advance

voor'uitgaan, to go on ahead; to make progress

voor'uitgang, progress, improvement

voor'uitkomen, to get on

voor'uitlopen op, to anticipate

vooruit'strevend, progressive

voor'uitzicht *n,* prospect

voorvader, ancestor

voorval *n,* incident

voorvechter, champion

voorvoegsel *n,* prefix

voor'waar, verily

voorwaarde, condition

voorwaarts, forward(s)

voorwenden, to feign

voorwendsel *n,* pretext, pretence

voor'wereldlijk, prehistoric

voorwerp *n,* object

voorwoord *n,* foreword

voorzeggen, to prompt

voorzet, centre

voorzetsel *n,* preposition

voor'zichtig, careful, cautious

voor'zichtigheid, caution

voor'zien, to foresee; to provide (for)

  het op iemand voorzien hebben, to have one's eye on a person

  het niet op iemand voorzien hebben, to have no time for a person

voor'zienigheid, providence

voorzitter, chairman

voorzorg(smaatregel), precaution(ary measure)

voos, spongy, rotten

vorderen, to (make) progress; to requisition, to demand

vordering, progress: claim

voren: naar —, to the front

te voren, before(hand)

van voren, (from) in front

van voren af aan, from the beginning

vorig, last, previous

vork, fork

vorm, form, shape, mould

vormelijk, formal

vormen, to form, to constitute

vorming, formation; education

vormleer, accidence

vorm(e)loos, shapeless

vormsel *n,* confirmation

vorsen, to search

vorst, frost: prince, monarch

vorstelijk, royal, regal

vorstendom *n,* principality

vorstenhuis *n,* dynasty

vors'tin, queen

vos, fox; bay (horse)

vossen, to swot

vouw, fold, crease

vouwbeen *n,* paper-knife

vouwen, to fold

vraag, question, request, demand

vraagbaak, fund of information

vraaggesprek *n,* interview

vraagstuk *n,* problem

vraagteken *n,* question-mark

vraat'zuchtig, voracious(ly)

vracht, freight, load, cargo

vrachtauto, lorry

vrachtboot, cargo-boat

vrachtbrief, bill of lading

vrachtgoed *n,* goods, cargo

vrachtrijder, carrier (service)

vrachtwagen, lorry

vragen, to ask; to charge; to require

vrede, peace

vredesnaam: in —, for goodness' sake

vredestichter, peacemaker

vredig, peaceful

veedzaam, peaceable

vreemd, strange; foreign, alien

vreemde: in den —, abroad

vreemdeling, stranger; foreigner

vreemdelingeverkeer *n,* tourist traffic

vreemd'soortig, unusual

vrees, fear

vreesaanjagend, terrifying

vreetzak, greedy-guts

vrek(kig), miser(ly)

vreselijk, frightful

vreten, to devour, to eat, to stuff

vreugde, joy

vreugdebetoon *n,* rejoicing(s)

vreugdeschot *n,* salute

vreugdevol, joyful
vreugdevuur *n,* bonfire
vrezen, to fear
vriend, friend
vriendelijk, kind, friendly
vriendendienst, kind turn
vrien'din, (lady, girl) friend
vriendschap, friendship
vriend'schappelijk, friendly, amicably
vriespunt *n,* freezing-point
vriezen, to freeze
vrij, free: rather, quite
  vrije etage, self-contained flat
  vrij beroep, profession
  het vrij veld, the open
  zo vrij zijn om te, to take the liberty of
vrijaf, time off
vrijbiljet *n,* free pass
vrijblijvend, subject to alteration in price; without obligation
vrijbrief, free pass; passport
vrijbuiter, privateer
vrijdag, Friday
vrijen, to make love
vrijer, suitor, sweetheart
vrijgeleide *n,* safe-conduct
vrijgeven, to decontrol; to give (time) off
vrij'gevig, liberal
vrijgevochten, undisciplined
vrijge'zel, bachelor
vrijheid, liberty, freedom
vrijkomen, to get off; to fall vacant; to be decontrolled; to be liberated
vrijkopen, to ransom
vrijlaten, to release, to emancipate; to leave free
vrijloop, free wheel
vrij'metselaar, freemason
vrij'moedig, frank, outspoken
vrijpleiten, to exonerate
vrij'postig, forward, impertinent
vrijspreken, to acquit
vrijstaan, to be detached
  het staat je vrij om te, you are at liberty to
vrijstellen, to exempt, to excuse
vrijster, sweetheart; (old) maid
vrijuit, freely

vrijwaren voor, to safeguard against
vrijwel, practically
vrij'willig, voluntary
vrij'williger, volunteer
vrij'zinnig, liberal
vroedschap, City Fathers
vroedvrouw, midwife
vroeg, early
  vroeg of laat, sooner or later
vroeger, earlier, former, previous
  ik woonde daar vroeger, I used to live there
vroegte, early morning
vroeg'tijdig, early
vrolijk, cheerful
vrome, pious person
vroom, pious
vroomheid, piety
vrouw, woman; wife
vrouwelijk, female, feminine
vrouwenarts, gynæcologist
vrouwen'kiesrecht *n,* women's suffrage
vrucht, fruit, fœtus
vruchtbaar, fertile; fruitful, prolific
vruchtbeginsel *n,* ovary
vruchtdragend, fruit-bearing; fruitful
vruchteloos, fruitless, in vain
vruchtenbowl, fruit-cup
vruchtvlees *n,* pulp
vuig, sordid
vuil, dirty: *n,* dirt, muck
vuilak, filthy blighter
vuilbek, foul-mouthed fellow
vuil(ig)heid, filth; obscenity
vuilmaken, to (make) dirty; to waste
vuilnis, refuse
vuilnisbak, dustbin
vuilnisbelt, rubbish-dump
vuilnisman, dustman
vuist, fist
  voor de vuist (weg), extempore
vul'gair, vulgar
vul'kaan, volcano
vulkachel, slow-combustion stove
vullen, to fill, to stuff
vulpen, fountain-pen
vulpotlood *n,* propelling pencil

vulsel *n*, filling; stuffing
vuns, vunzig, musty, fusty
vuren, to fire
vurehout(en) (*n*), deal
vurig, fiery; fervent, ardent
vuur *n*, fire
 vuur geven, to fire; to give (a person) a light
vuurbaak, beacon(-light)
vuurmond, gun
vuurpeloton *n*, firing-squad
vuurpijl, rocket
 de klap op de vuurpijl, the crowning sensation
vuurproef, ordeal by fire; crucial test
vuurrood, flaming red
vuurspuwende berg, volcano
vuursteen, flint
vuurtoren, lighthouse
vuurvast, fire-proof
 vuurvaste steen, fire-brick
vuurwapen *n*, fire-arm
vuurwerk *n*, firework(s) (display)
vuurzee, blaze

W

waag, weigh-house
waaghals, dare-devil
**waagschaal : zijn leven in de —
 stellen,** to risk one's life
waagstuk *n*, risky enterprise
waaien, to blow, to fan
 ik laat de boel maar waaien,
 I couldn't care less (about it)
waaier, fan
waakhond, watch-dog
waaks, waakzaam, watchful
waakzaamheid, vigilance
Waals(e), Walloon
waan, delusion
waanwijs, (self-)conceited
waanzin, madness
waan'zinnig, mad, crazy
waar, where: true: ware(s), commodity, stuff
 niet waar ? isn't that so ?
waar-(aan *etc*), (to *etc*) what, which, whom
waar'achtig, true, real(ly and truly), actually
waarborg(en), (to) guarantee

waard, landlord : worth
 waarde vriend, dear friend
waarde, value
waardeloos, worthless
waar'deren, to appreciate, to value
waardevol, valuable
waardig, dignified, worthy
waardigheid, dignity
waar'din, landlady
waarheen, waar . . . heen, whither, where
waarheid, truth
waarlijk, truly
waarmaken, to verify
waarmerk(en) (*n*), (to) stamp (to) hall-mark
waar'neembaar, perceptible
waarnemen, to observe; to avail oneself of; to deputize; to discharge
waarom, why
waar'schijnlijk, probable
waar'schijnlijkheid, probability
waarschuwen, to warn
waarschuwing, warning; de-mand-note, reminder
waartoe, for which, for what, where, to which
waarzegster, fortune-teller
waas *n*, film, haze, bloom; air
wacht, watch(man), guard(-duty)
 in de wacht slepen, to scrounge, to rake in
wachten (op), to wait (for)
 zich wachten voor, to beware of
wachter, watchman
wachtgeld *n*, reduced salary, re-tainer
wachtkamer, waiting-room
wachtlijst, waiting-list
wachtmeester, sergeant
wachtrol, watch-bill
wachtwoord *n*, password
wad *n*, mud-flat
waden, to wade
wafel, waffle, wafer; trap
wagen, car, cart: to risk, to venture
wagenrennen, chariot races
wagenspoor *n*, (cart-)rut
wagenziek, train-sick, car-sick

wagenwijd, wide

waggelen, to totter, to waddle, to wobble

wa'gon, (railway-)carriage, van, truck(-load)

wak *n*, hole (in the ice)

waken, to (keep) watch; to wake

wakend, watchful

waker, watchman

wakker, awake

  wakker schrikken, to wake with a start

wal, rampart; bank

  aan wal, ashore

  langs de wal, alongside

  aan lager wal, on one's beam ends

  van wal steken, to push off; to fire away

  van twee wallen eten, to have it both ways

walg(e)lijk, disgusting

walgen, to be nauseated

walging, loathing

walm(en), (to) smoke

walnoot, walnut

wals, waltz; (motor-)roller

walvis(vaarder), whale(r)

wambuis *n*, jacket, doublet

wanbedrijf *n*, crime

wanbegrip *n*, fallacy

wanbeheer *n*, **wanbeleid** *n*, mismanagement

wanbetaling, non-payment

wanbof(fen), (to have) bad luck

wand, wall

wandaad, outrage

wandelaar, walker, stroller

wandelen, to walk, to wander

  gaan wandelen, to go for a walk

wandeling, walk, stroll

wandelkaart, large-scale map

wandelpad *n*, footpath

wandelstok, walking-stick

wandluis, bed-bug

wandschildering, mural

wandtapijt *n*, hanging carpet, tapestry

wanen, to fancy

wang, cheek

wangedrag *n*, misconduct

wangedrocht *n*, monster

wanhoop, despair

wanhopen, to despair

wan'hopig, desperate, despairing, hopeless

wankel, unsteady, rickety

wankelbaar, unstable

wankelen, to stagger, to sway from side to side; to waver

wankel'moedig, irresolute

wanklank, jarring note

wanneer, when(ever)

wanorde, disorder

wan'staltig, deformed

want, for: **mitten**: *n*, rigging

wantoestand, chaotic situation

wantrouw(en), (to) distrust

wan'trouwend, wan'trouwig, suspicious

wanverhouding, disparity

wapen *n*, weapon, arm; coat of arms

wapendrager, armour-bearer

wapenen, to arm, to reinforce

wapenfeit *n*, feat of arms

wapenrusting, (suit of) armour

wapenschild *n*, escutcheon

wapenschouwing, inspection, review

wapenspreuk, heraldic device

wapenstilstand, armistice, truce

wapperen, to flutter

war: **in de —,** in a muddle, upset

warboel, muddle, clutter

ware, right person (*or* thing) (for the job)

  je ware, the real thing

wa'rempel, truly, actually

waren, to wander

warenhuis *n*, departmental store

warm, warm, hot

warmen, to warm

warmoeze'nier, market-gardener

warmpjes, warmly

warmte, warmth, heat, temperature

warnet *n*, tangle, labyrinth

warrelen, to whirl

wars van, averse to

wartaal, gibberish

warwinkel, muddle, clutter

was, wax: wash(ing)

  goed in de slappe was zitten, to be in velvet

wasbaar, washable
wasbak, wash-basin
wasbenzine, benzine
wasbleek, waxen
wascommode, wash-stand
wasecht, washable, fast
wasem(en), (to) steam
was(-en-strijk)inrichting, laundry
wasgoed n, washing
washandje n, washing-glove
wasketel, (wash-)boiler
wasknijper, clothes-peg
waskom, wash-bowl
waslijn, clothes-line
waslijst, laundry list ; catalogue
wasmerk n, laundry-mark
wasmiddel n, detergent
waspit, taper
wassen, to wash; to shuffle : to swell, to wax: wax(en)
wassenbeeld n, waxwork (model)
wasse'rij, laundry
wastafel, wash-basin, wash-stand
wasvrouw, washer-woman
wat, what, which; how; some-(thing), any(thing); somewhat
wat voor, what (sort of)
wat (dan) ook, wat maar, whatever
wàt blij, only too pleased
water n, water
waterbouwkunde, hydraulic engineering
waterdamp, vapour
waterdicht, waterproof, water-tight
wateren, to (make) water
waterglas n, tumbler; water-glass
waterhoen n, moor-hen
waterig, watery
waterkamp n, boating camp
waterkant, water's edge, water-front
waterkering, weir
waterklerk, ship-broker's clerk
waterkoud, raw
waterkruik, pitcher
waterlaarzen, waders
waterlanders, tears
waterleiding, waterworks
waterlinie, flooding defence line

waterpas n, spirit-level
waterplaats, urinal; watering-place
waterpokken, chicken-pox
waterrjik, abounding in water
waterschap n, district controlled by polder-board
waterscheiding, watershed
watersnood, floods
waterspiegel, water-level
waterstaat, Ministry of Works
waterstand, water(-level)
waterstof, hydrogen
watertanden: doen —, to make the mouth water
waterverf, water-colour, dis-temper
watervlak n, expanse of water
watervliegtuig n, sea-plane
watervrees, hydrophobia
waterzoeker, water-diviner
waterzucht, dropsy
watje n, piece of cotton wool
watjekou, clout
watten, cotton-wool, wadding
wat'teren, to pad, to quilt
wauwelen, to blather
wazig, hazy, filmy
web(be) n, web
wecken, to bottle
wedden, to bet
weddenschap, wager
we(d)er, again, re-
wederantwoord n, rejoinder
wederdienst, service in return
wederhelft, better half
weder'kerend, reflexive
weder'kerig, mutual
weder'om, (once) again
weder'opbouw, rebuilding, re-construction
weder'opstanding, resurrection
weder'rechtelijk, unlawful
weder'waardigheden, vicissi-tudes
wederwoord n, repartee
wederzijds, mutual
wedijveren, to compete
wedijver(ing), rivalry
wedloop, (running-)race
wedren, race(-meeting)
westrijd, match, competition
weduwe, widow

weduwnaar, widower

wee, sickly, faint : *n*, woe, labour pain

weefgetouw *n*, loom

weefsel *n*, tissue, fabric, texture

weegschaal, (pair of) scales, weighing-machine

week, week : soft

 was in de week zetten, to put washing in to soak

weekblad *n*, weekly (paper)

weekdier *n*, mollusc

week'hartig, soft-hearted

weeklacht, lamentation

weeklagen, to (be)wail

weelde, luxury, profusion

weelderig, luxurious, luxuriant

weemoed, melancholy

wee'moedig(heid), melancholy

weer, again, re- : *n*, weather

 in de weer zijn, to be on the move; to be busy

weerbaar, defensible; able-bodied

weer'barstig, unruly

weerbericht *n*, weather-forecast

weerga, equal

weer'galmen, to reverberate

weergeven, to render, to reflect

weerglas *n*, barometer

weerhaak, barb(ed hook)

weerhaan, weathercock

weer'houden, to restrain, to suppress

weer'kaatsen, to reflect, to (re)echo

weerklank, echo

weer'klinken, to resound

weerkunde, meteorology

weer'leggen, to refute

weerlicht *n*, summer lightning

weerloos, defenceless

weermacht, (fighting) services

weer'omstuit : van de —, in sympathy

weerschijn, reflection

weersgesteldheid, weather conditions

weerskanten, both sides

weer'spannig, recalcitrant

weer'spiegelen, to reflect

weer'staan, to resist

weerstand, resistance

weer'streven, to oppose

weersverwachting, weather-forecast

weerwil : in — van, in spite of

weerzien *n*, meeting, reunion

weerzin, aversion

weerzin'wekkend, repugnant

wees(huis *n*), orphan(age)

weetal, know-all

weet'gierig, studious

weg, way, road : away, gone

 veel van iemand weg hebben, to be very like a person

wegbergen, to put away

wegbrengen, to take away; to see off

wegcijferen, to efface, to set aside

wegdek *n*, road surface

wegen, to weigh

wegennet *n*, road-system

wegens, on account of

weggaan, to leave, to go away

wegkomen, to get away

weglaten, to omit, to leave out

wegleggen, to put aside

 weggelegd zijn voor, to be in store for

wegmaken, to get rid of, to lose; to put under an anæsthetic

wegnemen, to take away, to allay

 dat neemt niet weg dat, that does not alter the fact that

wegomlegging, diversion

wegpinken, to brush away

wegpraten, to explain away

wegraken, to get lost

wegscheren : zich —, to make oneself scarce

wegtrekken, to pull away; to march away; to disappear

wegvagen, to sweep away

wegvallen tegen, to cancel (out)

wegwerken, to get rid of

wegwijs maken, to show the ropes

wegwijzer, sign-post

wei, whey; serum : meadow

weide, meadow, pasture

weiden, to graze; to travel

weids, grandiose

weifelen, to waver

weigeren, to refuse, to misfire, to jib

weiland *n*, pasture

weinig, little, few

weitas, game-bag

wekelijks, weekly

weken, to soak, to soften

wekken, to wake, to arouse, to create

wekker, alarm-clock

wel, well; very much; certainly, probably, quite

  wel neen, oh no

  ik geloof het (*or* van) wel, I think so

  ik zie het wél! I do see it!

  hij is niet ziek, wel? he isn't ill is he?

welbehagen *n*, well-being

welbeschouwd: alles —, after all

welbespraakt, fluent, eloquent

welbezocht, (much) frequented

weldaad, good deed

wel'dadig, beneficial, pleasant

wel'dadigheid, charity

weldoen, to do good

weldoener, benefactor

weldoordacht, well thought-out

weldra, soon

Weledelgeboren heer, Esquire

wel'eer, of old

Weleerwaard(e heer), Reverend

welgeaard, good-natured

welgedaan, plump

welgemutst, good-humoured

welgesteld, well-to-do

welgevallen *n*, pleasure, discretion

  zich laten welgevallen, to put up with

welge'vallig, agreeable

welgezind, kindly disposed

welhaast, soon

welig, lush

weliswaar, it is true

welk, which, what

welkom, welcome

welkomstgroet, (word of) welcome

wellen, to weld: to cook without boiling

welletjes, enough

wel'levendheid, good manners

wellicht, perhaps

wel'luidend, melodious

wellust, lust; delight

welnaad, weld

welnemen: met Uw —, by your leave

wel'nu, well (now)

weloverwogen, (well-)considered

welp, cub

wel'riekend, fragrant

welslagen *n*, success

wel'sprekend, eloquent

welstand, well-being, prosperity

welste: van je —, like nobody's business

welvaart, prosperity

welvaren, to thrive

welven, to vault, to arch

welving, vault(ing), camber

wel'voeglijk, seemly

wel'willend, obliging, sympathetic

welzijn *n*, welfare, health

wemelen van, to swarm with

wenden: (zich) —, to turn; to apply

wending, turn

wenen, to weep

wenk: een — geven, to beckon; to drop a hint, to give the tip

wenkbrauw, eyebrow

wenken, to beckon

wennen, to get used to

wens, wish

wenselijk, desirable

wensen, to wish, to desire

wentelen, to roll (over)

wenteling, revolution

wentelteefje *n*, sop in the pan

wenteltrap, winding staircase

wereld, world

  uit de wereld helpen, to dispose of

werelddeel *n*, continent

wereldlijk, wordly, secular

wereldreiziger, globe-trotter

werelds, wordly(-minded)

wereldstad, metropolis

wereldtaal, universal language

wereldtentoonstelling, world fair

weren, to avert; to (de)bar

  zich weren, to exert oneself

werf, shipyard, dockyard; wharf
werfdepot *n*, recruiting-office
werk *n*, work, job
  er werk van maken, to do
  something about it
werkborstel, scrubbing brush
werkelijk, real
werkelijkheid, reality
werkeloos, unemployed, idle
werke'loosheid, unemployment
werken, to work, to be active; to
  warp
  naar binnen werken, to get
  down (one's throat)
werkezel, (hard) worker
werkgever, employer
werking, action, operation
werkkamer, work-room, study
werkkrachten, energies; labour
werkkring, occupation
werkloon *n*, wage(s)
werkloos, unemployed, idle
werkman, workman, working-
  man
werknemer, employee
werkplaats, workshop
werkster, charwoman
werktuig *n*, tool
werktuigkunde, mechanics
werk'tuiglijk, mechanical
werkvolk *n*, workers
werkvrouw, charwoman
werkwoord *n*, verb
werkzaam, active, (hard-)work-
  ing
werkzaamheden,   activities,
  duties, tasks
werpen, to throw
werpspeer, javelin
wervel, vertebra
wervelkolom, spinal column
werven, to rope in, to enlist
werwaarts, whither
wesp, wasp
westelijk, westerly, western
westen *n*, west
  buiten westen, unconscious
westerlingen, western world
westers, western
wet, law, act
  de wet voorschrijven, to lay
  down the law
wetboek *n*, code

weten, to know; to manage: *n*,
  knowledge
  er iets op weten, to know the
  answer
  te weten, to wit
wetenschap, science; learning,
  knowledge
wetenschappelijk werk *n*, research; scientific work
wetgevend, legislative
wethouder, alderman
wetsontwerp *n*, bill
wettelijk, wettig, legal, lawful
wettigen, to legalize; to justify
weven, to weave
wezel, weasel
wezen, to be: *n*, being, essence
  — hij mag er wezen, he's got
  what it takes
wezenlijk, real, essential
wezenloos, vacant
wichelroede, divining-rod
wicht *n*, creature
wie, who(m), anyone who
  wie ook, whoever
wiebelen, to wobble
wieden, to weed
wieg, cradle
  in de wieg gelegd voor, cut
  out for
wiegelied *n*, lullaby
wiegen, to rock
wiek, wing, sail
wiel *n*, wheel
wielrennen *n*, cycle-racing
wielrijder, cyclist
wiemelen, to fidget
wier *n*, sea-weed
wierook, incense
wig, wedge
wij, we
wijd, wide, spacious
wijd en zijd, far and wide
wijdbeens, with legs apart
wijden, to consecrate, to dedicate,
  to devote, to ordain
wijdte, width
wijduitstaande, distended, bulging, prominent
wijdvertakt, widespread
wijf *n*, hag, woman
wijfje *n*, wifey; female (animal)
wijfjesvos, vixen

wijk, district; refuge
wijken, to yield; to pass (off)
wijkgebouw n, parish-hall
wijkverpleegster, wijkzuster, district-nurse
wijlen, (the) late
wijn, wine
wijnberg, hill vineyard
wijngaard, vineyard
wijnlezen n, vintage
wijnsteen(zuur n), tartar(ic acid)
wijs, manner, way; tune; mood: wise
van de wijs, at sea
wijs maken, to convince; to dupe
wijsbegeerte, philosophy
wijselijk, wisely
wijsgeer, philosopher
wijsheid, wisdom
wijsje n, tune, air
wijsneus, know-all
wijsvinger, forefinger
wijten, to impute
het is aan het weer te wijten, it is due to the weather
wijwater n, holy water
wijze, manner, way
wijzen, to point (out), show
wijzer, pointer, hand
wijzerplaat, (clock-)face
wijzigen, to modify
wikkelen, to wrap (up); to involve
wikken en wegen, to weigh (up)
wil, will, wish
tegen wil en dank, against one's will
ter wille van, for the sake of
ter wille zijn, to oblige
wils, wild
wild n, game
in het wild(e weg), wildly, at random
wildbraad n, venison
wilde, savage
wildebras, young tough, tomboy
wildernis, wilderness
wildvreemd, utterly strange
wilg, willow
willekeur: naar — handelen, to do as one pleases
willekeurig, arbitrary

willen, to want, to like, to be willing
dat wil zeggen, that is to say
willens, on purpose
willig, willing
willoos, will-less
wilsbeschikking, will
wilskracht, will-power
wimpel, pennant
wimper, eyelash
wind, wind
ik heb er de wind onder, I've got them under my thumb
windas n, windlass
windbuks, air-gun
winden, to wind
winderig, windy
windhond(rennen), greyhound (racing)
windhoos, whirlwind
windpokken, chicken-pox
windsel n, bandage
windstil(te), calm
windstoot, gust of wind
windstreek, point of the compass
windvaan, windwijzer, weather vane
wingerd, vine(yard); (Virginia) creeper
wingewest n, (conquered) province
winkel(en), (to) shop
winkelhaak, set-square; three-cornered tear
winkelhuis n, shop with residence over
winkelier, shopkeeper, retailer
winkeljuffrouw, shop-assistant
winkelstand, tradespeople
winkelweek, shopping-week
winnaar, winner
winnen, to win, to gain
winst, profit, gain
winstgevend, profitable
winter, winter; chilblain(s)
wintergezicht n, wintry scene
wintergoed n, winter clothes
wintergroen n, evergreen
winterhanden, chilblained hands
winters, wintry
winterslaap, hibernation
wip, seesaw; jiffy
wipneus, snub nose

wippen, to rock (to and fro), to nip; to kick out
wipplank, seesaw
wipstoel, rocking-chair
wirwar, tangle
wis, certain
wiskunde, mathematics
wispel'turig, fickle
wissel, points; bill of exchange
wisselbeker, challenge-cup
wisselen, to (ex)change; to shed milk-teeth
wisselgeld *n,* (small) change
wisseling, (ex)change
wisselspoor *n,* siding
wisselstroom, alternating current
wissel'vallig, precarious
wisselvalligheid, vicissitude
wisselwerking, interaction
wissen, to wipe
wissewasje *n,* slightest little thing, trifle
wit, white
  Witte Donderdag, Maundy Thursday
witgloeiend, white-hot
witkalk, whitewash
witkiel, porter
witlof *n,* chicory
wittebroodsweken, honeymoon
witten, to whitewash
woede(n), (to) rage
woedend, furious
woekeraar, usurer
woekeren, to be rife
woekeren met, to make the most of
woekerplant, parasite
woelen, to toss and turn
woelig, turbulent, restless
woelwater, fidget
woensdag, Wednesday
woerd, drake
woest, wild, waste, desolate
woesteling, ruffian
woeste'nij, wilderness
woes'tijn, desert
wol, wool
  hij is in de wol geverfd, he has been through the mill; he's a double-dyed rogue
wolf, wolf

wolfram *n,* tungsten
wolk, cloud
wolkenkrabber, sky-scraper
wolkje *n,* little cloud; puff, drop
wollen, woollen
wollig, woolly
wond(en), (to) wound
wonder *n,* wonder, miracle
wonder'baarlijk, miraculous, stupendous
wonderkind *n,* infant prodigy
wonderlijk, strange, surprising
wondermiddel *n,* panacea
wonderolie, castor-oil
wondroos, erysipelas
wonen, to live
woning, house, flat
woningbureau *n,* estate-agent's office
woningnood, housing shortage
woningtoestanden, housing conditions
woon'achtig, resident
woonhuis *n,* private house
woonkamer, living-room
woonplaats, (place of) residence
woonschip *n,* **woonschuit,** house-boat
woonwagen, caravan
woonwijk, residential district
woord *n,* word
  het hoogste woord hebben, to monopolize the conversation
  het woord voeren, to speak, to be spokesman
  onder woorden brengen, to put into words
  iemand te woord staan, to see a person
woordelijk, literal, word for word, verbatim
woordenboek *n,* dictionary
woordenschat, vocabulary
woordentwist, dispute
woordenwisseling, altercation
woordsoort, part of speech
woordspeling, play on words, pun
woordvoerder, spokesman
worden, to be(come), to get, to grow, to go
worgen, to strangle
worm, worm, grub
wormstekig, maggoty

worp, throw; litter

worst, sausage

worstelen, to struggle, to wrestle

wortel, root; carrot

wortelen, to be rooted

woud *n,* forest

wraak, revenge

wraak'gierig, wraak'zuchtig, vindictive

wrak, rickety, dilapidated : *n,* wreck

wrakhout *n,* wreckage

wrang, sour, tart; bitter

wrat, wart

wreed, cruel

wreedaard, (cruel) brute

wreef, instep

wreken, to revenge, to avenge

wrevel, resentment

wrevelig, resentful

wriemelen, to crawl, to tickle

wrijfwas, furniture-polish

wrijven, to rub; to polish

wrijving, friction

wrikken, to jerk

wringen, to wring, to wrench
  zich wringen, to wriggle

wrochten, to work, to do

wroeging, remorse

wroeten, to root, to rummage

wrok, rancour

wrokken, to fret

wrong, knot (of hair)

wrongel, curds

wuft, frivolous, flighty

wuit, projecting jaw

wuiven, to wave

wulps, lewd

wurgen, to strangle

wurmen, to wriggle

Z

zaad *n,* seed, semen
  op zwart zaad zitten, to be on the rocks

zaag, saw; interminable grumbler

zaagmeel *n,* **zaagsel** *n,* sawdust

zaaien, to sow

zaak, business, affair; case; cause
  het is zaak, the great thing is
  ter zake, to the point
  niet veel zaaks, no great shakes

zaakgelastigde, agent

zaakwaarnemer, solicitor

zaal, hall, ward, auditorium

zacht, soft, mild, gentle

zacht'aardig, gentle

zachtjes, gently, quietly

zachtjes aan, gradually

zacht'moedig, gentle

zacht'zinnig, good-natured

zadel *n,* saddle

zadeldek *n,* saddle-cloth

zadelen, to saddle

zagen, to saw; to harp (on a subject)

zak, pocket; sack, bag

zakboekje *n,* note-book, diary

zakdoek, handkerchief

zakelijk, business-like, to the point

zakenbrief, business letter

zakformaat *n,* pocket-size

zakken, to sink, to fall; to fail

zakkenroller, pickpocket

zaklantaarn, torch

zaklopen *n,* sack-race

zalf, ointment

zalig, blessed; heavenly

zaliger, late

zaligheid, bliss

Zaligmaker, Saviour

zaligsprekingen, beatitudes

zaligverklaring, beatification

zalm, salmon

zalven, to anoint

zalvend, unctuous

zamen: te —, together

zand *n,* sand

zandbak, sand-pit

zanderig, sandy

zandgebak *n,* shortbread

zandgroeve, sand-pit

zandloper, hour-glass

zandplaat, sand-bank

zandruiter, thrown rider

zandtaart, shortbread

zandverstuiving, drift-sands

zandweg, sandy lane

zang, song, canto

zanger('es), singer

zangerig, melodious, sing-song

zanggezelschap *n,* choral society

zangles, singing lesson

zangstem, singing voice; voice part

zanguitvoering, choral concert

zangvogel, singing-bird
zaniken, to natter
zanikkous, cantankerous grumbler
zat, more than enough, tight
  zich zat eten, to eat one's fill
Zaterdag, Saturday
zatlap, soak(er)
ze, they, them; she
zede, custom
  zeden, morals; manners
zedelijk, moral
zedeloos, immoral
zedenkunde, ethics
zedenpreek, homily
zedenspreuk, maxim
zedig, modest, demure
zee, sea
  recht door zee, straight
zeeboot, ocean steamer
zeeëngte, straits
zeef, sieve, strainer
zeegat n, entrance to channel
zeegezicht n, seascape
zeehond, seal
zeekasteel n, leviathan
zeem n, wash-leather
zeemacht, naval forces
zeeman, seaman
zeemanskunst, seamanship
zeemeermin, mermaid
zeemeeuw, sea-gull
zeemlap, (wash-)leather
zeemleer n, chamois leather
zeemogendheid, sea-power
zeen, sinew
zeeofficier, naval officer
zeep, soap
zeepbel, soap-bubble
zeepsop n, soap-suds
zeer, very (much): sore
  zeer doen, to hurt
zeeramp, shipping disaster
zeerecht n, maritime law
zeerob, seal; seadog
zeerover, private
zeerste: ten —, highly, greatly
zeeschildpad, turtle
zeeslang, sea-serpent
zeesleepboot, deep-sea tug
zeesoldaat, marine
zeespiegel, sea-level
zeester, star-fish

zeestraat, straights
Zeeuw(se), inhabitant of Zealand
zeevaart, navigation
zeevaartschool, nautical college
zeevarend, seafaring
zeeverkenners, sea-scouts
zee'waardig, seaworthy
zeeweg, sea-route
zeewering, sea-wall
zeewier n, seaweed
zeeziek, seasick
zege, victory, triumph
zegel, seal; stamp
zegelen, to seal
zegellak, sealing-wax
zegelrecht n, stamp-duty
zegelring, signet-ring
zegen(ing), blessing
zegenen, to bless
zegenrijk, full of blessings
zegepoort, triumphal arch
zegepraal, victory
zegeteken n, trophy
zegetocht, triumphal march
zegevieren, to triumph
zegevuur n, bonfire
zeggen, to say, to tell
  liever gezegd, rather
  wat zegt U? (I beg your) pardon?
  er valt niets op te zeggen, there is nothing to be said against it
  dat zegt niets, that doesn't mean a thing
  je hebt niets te zeggen, your opinion is not asked for
zeggenschap, say, part-interest
zegsman, informant
zegswijze, expression
zeil n, sail, tarpaulin, American cloth, lino(leum)
zeildoek n, canvas, oil-cloth
zeilen, to sail
zeilwagen, land-yacht
zeilwedstrijd, sailing regatta
zeis, scythe
zeker, certain, (for) sure
  dat weet je zeker wel, I expect you know that
zekerheid, certainty; security
  voor alle zekerheid, to be on the safe side

zekerheidshalve, for safety('s sake)
zekering, fuse
zelden, seldom, rarely
zeldzaam, rare, scarce; exceptionally
zelf, (one)self
 ik (*etc*) **zelf,** I (*etc*) myself
 de eenvoud zelf, simplicity itself
zelfbeheersing, self-control
zelfbehoud *n,* self-preservation
zelfbe'wust, self-assured
zelfge'noegzaam, self-sufficient
zelfkant, selvage
zelfmoord, suicide
zelfs, even
zelf'standig, independent
 zelfstanding naamwoord *n,* noun
zelfverloochening, self-denial, self-sacrifice
zelfvertrouwen *n,* self-confidence
zelfverzekerd, self-confident
zelfvoldaan, self-satisfied
zelfzucht, egoism
zelf'zuchtig, selfish
zemelaar, cantankerous grumbler
zemelen, bran
zemen, to clean
zendeling, missionary
zenden, to send
zender, sender; transmitter
zending, mission; consignment
zendstation *n,* transmitting station
zenuw, nerve; tendon
zenuwachtig, nervous, nervy; flustered
zenuwarts, nerve-specialist
zenuwgestel *n,* nervous system
zenuwontsteking, neuritis
zenuwpees, bundle of nerves
zenuwpijn, neuralgia
zenuw'slopend, nerve-racking
zenuwtrekking, nervous spasm
zenuwziek, neurotic
zes(de), six(th)
zeshoek, hexagon
zestien(de), sixteen(th)
zestig, sixty
zet, move, coup; push
 een hele zet, a tough job

zetbaas, manager
zetel, seat ; see
zetmeel *n,* starch
zetsel *n,* forme; brew
zetten, to set, to put; to make; to stake
 ik kan het niet zetten, I can't stomach it
zetting, arrangement
zeug, sow
zeulen, to lug
zeuren, to whine, to nag
zeurkous, zeurpiet, grouser
zeven, seven: to sieve, to strain
zeventien(de), seventeen(th)
zeventig, seventy
zich, one (him, her, it, your)self, themselves
zicht *n,* sight; visibility
 op zicht, on approval; at sight
zichtbaar, visible
zich'zelf, one (him, her, it)self, themselves
 uit zichzelf, of his own accord
zieden, to seethe
ziek, ill, sick; diseased
zieke, patient
ziekelijk, sickly, in bad health
ziekenauto, ambulance
ziekenfonds *n,* national health insurance
ziekte, illness, disease
ziekteuitkering, sickness benefit
ziel, soul; heart, lifeblood
zieleheil *n,* salvation
zielig, pitiful, pathetic
zielkunde, psychology
zielsbedroefd, heart-broken
zielsverwant, congenial
zielverheffend, exalting
zien, to see, to look
 er uit zien, to look (like)
 iemand niet kunnen zien, to hate the sight of a person
 iets zien te doen, to try and do something
 laten zien, to show
 hij ziet niet op geld, he is not worried about money
zienderogen, visibly
ziener, seer
ziens: tot —, good-bye for now

zienswijze, way of thinking, attitude

zier, scrap

ziezo, there we are

ziften, to sift

zi'geuner, gipsy

zij, she; they

zijbeuk, aisle

zij(de), side : silk
  op zij, ter zijde, aside
  ter zijde staan, to help

zijdelings, sidelong, indirect, oblique

zijden, silk(en)

zijderups, silk-worm

zijgen, to sink down

zijkant, side

zijn, to be : his, its, one's
  zij zijn weg(gegaan), they have gone
  dat mag er zijn, that takes a lot of beating

zijnerzijds, for his part

zijrivier, tributary

zijspan n, side-car

zijspoor n, siding

zijwaarts, sideways, sideward

zilt, salt(y)

zilver(en) n, silver

zin, sense; mind, way; sentence
  er zin in hebben, to feel like it
  naar mijn zin, to my liking

zindelijk, clean

zingen, to sing

zink n, zinc

zinken, to sink: zinc

zinloos, senseless

zinnebeeld n, emblem, symbol

zinne'beeldig, symbolic

zinnelijk, sensual, sensory

zinnen, to brood

zinsbedrog n, illusion

zinsnede, passage, clause

zinsontleding, analysis

zinspelen op, to hint at

zinspreuk, motto

zinsverband n, context

zinswending, turn of speech

zintuig n, sense

zin'tuiglijk, sensory

zinvol, pregnant

zit: een hele —, a long time sitting down

zitbad n, hip-bath

zitbank, settee

zitdag, session

zitje n, (cosy) nook

zitkamer, sitting-room

zitplaats, seat

zitten, to sit; to be; to fit
  gaan zitten, to sit down
  iemand laten zitten, to walk out on a person
  er zit niets anders op, there's no alternative
  daar zit ik met de gebakken peren, I'm left holding the baby

zittend, sitting, sedentary

zitting, session; seat

zitvlak n, bottom

zo, so, like that; in a minute; just now: straight: if
  de zaak zit zo, it's like this
  zó gaat het niet, that won't do
  zo iets, such a thing
  zo maar, just like that; for no reason in particular

zoals, (such) as, like

zo'danig, such, in such a way

zodat, so that

zode, sod

zo'doende, in that way

zo'dra, as soon as

zoek, missing
  op zoek naar, in search of

zoekbrengen: de tijd —, to pass the time

zoeken, to look (for), to seek: n, search

zoeklicht n, searchlight

zoekmaken, to mislay

zoekraken, to get lost

zoel, mild

zoemen, to buzz, to drone

zoen(en), (to) kiss

zoenoffer n, (expiatory) sacrifice

zoet, sweet; good

zoetekauw: een — zijn, to have a sweet tooth

zoetemelkse kaas, cream cheese

zoethoudertje, n, sop

zoethout n, liquorice(-root)

zoetig, slightly sweet

zoetigheid, sweet things

zoetjes aan, gradually

zoetluidend, melodious
zoet'sappig, mealy-mouthed
zoet'vloeiend, mellifluous
zoetwater *n*, fresh water
zoet'zuur, partially sweet(ened); sweet pickle
zoëven, just now
zog *n*, (mother's) milk; wake
zogen, to suckle
zoge'naamd, so-called; ostensibly
zolang, as long as; meanwhile
zolder, loft, attic
zoldering, ceiling
zolderkamer, garret
zolderverdieping, attic, top storey
zolen, to re-sole
zomen, to hem
zomer(s), summer(-like)
zomersproeten, freckles
zo'n, such (a), a sort of
zon, sun
zondaar, sinner
zondag, Sunday
zondagsruiter, would-be horseman
zondagsviering, Sunday observance
zonde, sin; shame; waste
zondebok, scape-goat
zonder, without
zonderling, queer; eccentric
zondeval, Fall
zondig, sinful
zondigen, to sin, to offend
zondvloed, Flood
Zon-en-feestdagen, Sundays and bank-holidays; high-days and holidays
zonnebaden *n*, sun-bathing
zonnebrand, sun-burn
zonnebril, sun-glasses
zonneklaar, clear as daylight
zonnen, to bask (in the sun)
zonnescherm *n*, sun-shade, sun-blind
zonneschijn, sunshine
zonnestand, sun's altitude, position of the sun
zonnesteek, sun-stroke
zonnestelsel *n*, solar system
zonnestilstand, solstice

zonnestraal, sunbeam; ray of sunshine
zonnetent, awning
zonnetijd, solar time
zonnewijzer, sun-dial
zonnig, sunny
zons'ondergang, sunset
zons'opgang, sunrise
zonsverduistering, eclipse of the sun
zoogdier *n*, mammal
zooi, mob, bang shoot
zool, sole
zoölo'gie, zoology
zoom, seam, hem; edge; outskirts
zoon, son
zootje *n*, mess; lot
zorg, care, concern, worry
het zal mijn zorg zijn ! fat lot I care!
zorg baren, to cause anxiety
zorgeloos, care-free
zorgen voor, to look after; to provide (for)
zorg, dat je op tijd bent, mind you're not late
zorg'vuldig, careful
zorg'wekkend, worrying, alarming
zorgzaam, careful, conscientious
zot, fool(ish)
zotteklap, zottepraat, silly nonsense
zout (*n*), salt(ed)
zouteloos, saltless; insipid, pointless
zouten, to salt (down)
zoutje *n*, cocktail biscuit
zoutvaatje *n*, salt-cellar
zoutzak, sack of potatoes
zoutzuur *n*, hydrochloric acid
zoveel, so much, so many
honderd zoveel, a hundred and something
zover, so far, thus far
in zover(re), to the extent, in so far as
voor zover, as far as
zo'waar, believe it or not
zo'wel, as well
zo'zeer, so much
zucht, sigh; craving

zuchten, to sigh

zuid, south

zuidelijk, southern, south(erly), southward(s)

zuiden n, south

zuiderhalfrond n, southern hemisphere

zuiderling, southerner

Zuid'poolzee, Antarctic (Ocean)

zuidvruchten, subtropical fruit

zuid'wester, sou(th)wester

Zuidzee: Stille —, Pacific (Ocean)

zuigeling, infant (in arms)

zuigen, to suck

zuiger, piston

zuigfles, feeding-bottle

zuil, pillar, column

zuilengalerij, colonnade

zuinig, economical.

zuinigheid, economy, thrift

zuipen, to booze, to swill

zuiplap, sot

zuivel, dairy produce

zuiver, pure, sheer; clear

zuiveren, to purify, to clean(se), to refine; to clear

zuivering, purge

zuiveringszout n, epsom salts

zulk, such

zullen, shall, will

dat zal wel, I quite believe it

wat zou dat? so what!

zus en zo, so-and-so, this and that

zus(je n), sister

zuster, sister; nurse

zusterovertse, Mother Superior

zuur, sour: n, acid; pickles

zuurdeeg n, zuurdesem, leaven

zuurkool, sauerkraut

zuurpruim, grouch

zuurstof, oxygen

zuurtje n, acid-drop

zwaai, swing, sweep

zwaaien, to wave, to wield, to swing

zwaan, swan

zwaar, heavy; hard; severe; full-bodied, stodgy

zwaard n, sword; lee-board

zwaardvechter, gladiator

zwaar'lijvig, corpulent

zwaar'moedig(heid), melancholy

zwaarte, weight

zwaartekracht, gravitation

zwaartepunt n, centre of gravity; crux

zwaar'tillend, pessimistic

zwaar'wichtig, weighty

zwabber, swab, mop

aan de zwabber, on the razzle

zwabberen, to swab, to mop

zwachtel, bandage

zwachtelen, to swathe

zwager, brother-in-law

zwak, weak, delicate, feeble: n, weakness

zwakkeling, weakling

zwakte, weakness

zwak'zinnig, mentally deficient

zwalken, to drift about

zwaluw, swallow

zwaluwstaart, swallow-tail; dovetail

zwam, fungus

zwammen, to gas

zwamneus, gas-bag

zwang, vogue

zwanger, pregnant

zwangerschap, pregnancy

zwarigheid, difficulty, objection

zwart (n), black

zwart maken, to blacken; to denigrate

zwarte kunst, black magic

zwaat'gallig, melancholy, pessimistic

zwartje n, darky

zwavel, sulphur

zwavelstok, safety-match

zwavelzuur n, sulphuric acid

Zweeds, Swedish

zweefvliegen, to glide

zweefvliegtuig n, glider

zweem, trace

zweep, whip, hunting-crop

zweepslag, lash (with the whip)

zweer, ulcer

zweet n, sweat

zwelgen, to guzzle; to revel

zwellen, to swell

zwembad n, zwembassin n, swimming-bath

zwembroek, bathing-trunks

zwemen naar, to be somewhat like
zwemgordel, life-jacket
zweminrichting, public baths
zwemmen, to swim
zwempak *n*, bathing-costume
zwemvest *n*, life-jacket
zwemvlies *n*, web
zwendel(a'rij), swindle, racket
zwengel, pump-handle, crank
zwenken, to swing round, to swerve
zweren, to swear : to fester
zwerftocht, peregrination, ramble
zwerk *n*, firmament
zwerm(en), (to) swarm
zwerven, to roam, to wander
zwerver, wanderer, vagabond
zweten, to sweat
zwetsen, to gas ; to brag
zweven, to float, to glide, to hover
zwezerik, sweetbread

zwichten voor, to yield to
zwiepen, to swish
zwier, flourish, dash
  aan de zwier zijn, to be on the spree
zwieren, to glide to and fro, to reel
zwierig, stylish, flamboyant
zwijgen, to be silent, to keep quiet
  tot zwijgen brengen, to silence
zwijgend, silent, tacit
zwijgzaam, taciturn
zwijm, swoon
zwijmelen, to feel dizzy
zwijn *n*, hog, swine
zwijnenboel, pigsty
zwijntje *n*, fluke
zwik, caboodle
zwikken, to sprain
Zwitser(s), Swiss
zwoegen, to toil
zwoel, sultry
zwoerd *n*, bacon-rind, pork-rind

AN ENGLISH–DUTCH DICTIONARY

For notes on the use of this Dictionary see the Introduction

A

a(n), een
abandon, opgeven, ver'laten: overgave
abashed, ver'legen
abate, ver'flauwen
abbey, ab'dij
abbot, abt
abbess, ab'dis
abbreviate, afkorten, ver'korten
abbreviation, afkorting
abdicate, afstand doen van
abdomen, onderlijf *n*
abduct, ont'voeren
aberration, dwaling
abeyance: in —, tijdelijk in on-bruik
abhor, ver'afschuwen
abhorrent, weerzin'wekkend
abide, toeven; uitstaan
to abide by, zich houden aan
ability, ver'mogen *n*, be'kwaam-heid
abject, ver'slagen; laag'hartig
abjure, afzweren
ablaze, in lichte laaie
able, in staat; be'kwaam
to be able to, kunnen
able seaman, vol matroos
abnegation, ver'loochening
abnormal, abnor'maal
aboard, aan boord
abode, woonstede
abolish, afschaffen
abolition, afschaffing
abominable, af'schuwelijk
abomination, afschuw, gruwel
aborigines, inboorlingen
abortion, ab'ortus

abortive, voor'barig
abound, in overvloed zijn
abounding in, rijk aan
about, om(streeks), onge'veer; over; in de buurt
about to go, op het punt te gaan
above, boven
the above, het bovenstaande
abrasion, schaafwond
abrasive, schuurmiddel *n*: afschurend
abreast, naast el'kaar; ter (*or* op de) hoogte (van)
abridge, ver'korten
abroad, in (*or* naar) het buiten-land; naar alle kanten verspreid
abrogate, afschaffen
abrupt, ab'rupt, kort'af
abscess, ab'ces *n*
abscond, er van'door gaan
absence, af'wezigheid, ge'brek *n*
absent, af'wezig
to absent oneself, ver'stek laten gaan
absentee, af'wezige
absenteeism, absente'isme *n*
absent-minded(ness), ver'-strooid(heid)
absolute, vol'slagen, vol'strekt; defini'tief; abso'luut
absolution, abso'lutie
absolve, ver'geven, vrijspreken
absorb, (in zich) opnemen
absorbed, ver'diept
absorbent, absor'berend
absorbing, boeiend
abstain, zich ont'houden
abstemious, matig
abstinence, ont'houding
abstract, ab'stract: uittreksel *n*

abstruse, duister

absurd, onge'rijmd; be'lachelijk, gek

abundance, overvloed

abundant, meer dan vol'doende

abundantly, in overvloed, rijkelijk

abuse, misbruik *n*; scheldwoorden: mis'bruiken; uitschelden

abusive, be'ledigend

abut on, grenzen aan

abysmal, bodemloos, grenzeloos

abyss, afgrond

academic(al), aca'demisch

academy, aca'demie

accede to, be'stijgen, aan'vaarden; toestemmen in

accelerate, ver'snellen, gas geven; in snelheid toenemen

acceleration, ver'snelling

accelerator, gaspedaal *n*

accent, ac'cent *n*, klemtoon

accent(uate), accentu'eren

accept, aannemen

acceptable, be'vredigend; welkom

acceptance, gunstige ont'vangst

access, toegang

accessary, mede'plichtige

accessible, (gemakkelijk) be'reikbaar; ge'naakbaar

accession, (troons)bestijging: toetreding; aanwinst

accessories, toebehoren *n*

accessory, mede'plichtige

accident, ongeluk *n*; toeval *n*

accidental, toe'vallig; per ongeluk: kruis *n* of mol

acclaim, toejuiching; accla'matie: toejuichen

acclimatize, acclimati'seren

accolade, ridderslag; acco'lade

accommodate, onderdak ver'lenen, (her)bergen; aanpassen

accommodating, in'schikkelijk

accommodation, accommo'datie

accompaniment, bege'leiding

accompany, verge'zellen, ge'paard gaan met; bege'leiden

accomplice, mede'plichtige

accomplish, vol'brengen

accomplished, ta'lentvol; vol'dongen (fact)

accomplishment, gave, pres'tatie

accord, over'eenstemming: ver'lenen; over'eenstemmen

of my own accord, uit eigen be'weging

according to, volgens

accordingly, dienovereen'komstig

accordion, accorde'on

accost, aanklampen

account, ver'slag *n*; rekening; rekenschap; be'lang *n*

to account for, ver'klaren

to take into account, in aanmerking nemen

on account of, van'wege

on no account, in geen ge'val

accountancy, boekhouding

accountant, (hoofd)boekhouder

accoutrements, uitrusting

accredit, toeschrijven aan

accredited, er'kend

accretion, aanwas

accrue, toenemen

accumulate, (zich) ophopen

accumulator, accu(mu'lator)

accuracy, nauw'keurigheid

accurate, nauw'keurig; pre'cies

accursed, ver'vloekt

accusation, be'schuldiging

accuse, be'schuldigen

accused, ver'dachte

accustom, wennen aan

accustomed, ge'wend; ge'woon

ace, aas; kraan

acerbity, scherpheid

ache, pijn (doen); hunkeren (naar)

achieve, be'reiken

achievement, pres'tatie; bereiken *n*

acid, zuur (*n*)

acknowledge, er'kennen; be'antwoorden

acknowledgement, er'kenning; be'antwoording; be'richt van ont'vangst *n*

acme, toppunt *n*

acolyte, misdienaar

acorn, eikel

acoustic, ge'luids-

acoustics, a'custica, acus'tiek

acquaint, in kennis stellen
acquaintance, kennis
acquainted, be'kend, op de hoogte
acquiesce in, instemmen met; be'rusten in
acquire, ver'werven, aanschaffen
acquirements, kundigheden
acquisition, aanwinst
acquisitive, heb'zuchtig
acquit, vrijspreken; kwijten
acquittal, vrijspraak
acre, 4047 vierkante meter (m²)
acrid, scherp
acrimonious, bits
acrobat, acro'baat
across, aan (or naar) de overkant (van); (dwars) over or door
act, daad; be'drijf n, nummer n; wet: handelen, werken; (to'-neel)spelen
acting, waarnemend: to'neelspel n
action, handeling, werking; actie
activate, aanzetten (tot)
active, ac'tief
activity, be'drijvigheid
actor, to'neelspeler
actress, to'neelspeelster
actual, werkelijk
actually, eigenlijk, feitelijk
actuate, (aan)drijven
acumen, scherp'zinnigheid
acute, scherp; a'cuut
adamant(ine), onver'murwbaar
adapt, aanpassen, be'werken
adaptability, aanpassingsver-mogen n
adaptable, aan te passen; plooi-baar
adaptation, be'werking; aanpas-sing
add (to), toevogen aan, voegen bij
add to, ver'meerderen
add up, optellen; oplopen
addict, ver'slaafde
addicted, ver'slaafd
addition, optelling; toevoeging
in addition, boven'dien
additional, extra
addled, be'dorven; ver'dwaasd
address, a'dres n; toespraak: adres'seren; aanspreken, toe-spreken

adenoids, neusamandelen
adept, be'dreven(e) (in)
adequate, vol'doende, ge'schikt
adhere, (aan)kleven; aanhangen, blijven bij
adherent, aanhanger
adhesion, ad'hesie
adhesive, plak-: plakmiddel n
adjacent, aan'grenzend
adjective, bij'voeglijk naam-woord n
adjoin, grenzen aan
adjourn, ver'dagen; (uit'een)-gaan
adjudicate, uitspraak doen
adjunct, aanhangsel n; be'paling
adjure, be'zweren
adjust, regu'leren, (ver')stellen
adjustable, ver'stelbaar
administer, be'heren; toedienen
administration, be'heer n, re'gering
administrative, administra'tief
admirable, loffelijk; uit'stekend
admiral, admi'raal
admiralty, admirali'teit
admiration, be'wondering
admire, be'wonderen
admissible, ver'oorloofd; aan'ne-melijk
admission, toegang(sprijs), toe-lating; er'kenning
admit, toelaten tot, opnemen in; toegeven
admittance, toegang
admittedly, weliswaar
admonish, ver'manen
ad nauseam, tot ver'velens toe
ado, drukte
adolescence, puber'teit
adolescent, opgroeiend: jonge man, jong meisje n
adopt, aannemen
adorable, allerliefst
adoration, aan'bidding
adore, aan'bidden; dol zijn op
adorn, (ver')sieren
adornment, ver'siering, sieraad n
adrift, drijvend, los
adroit(ness), handig(heid)
adulation, kruipe'rij
adult, vol'wassen(e)
adulterate, ver'valsen

adultery, overspel *n*
advance, voor'uitgang; opmars;
voorschot *n* : naar voren komen
oprukken; voorschieten
in advance, van te voren
advanced, (ver)ge'vorderd
advancement, voor'uitgang, be'-
vordering
advantage, voordeel *n*
to take advantage of, ge'bruik
maken van
advantageous, gunstig
advent, (aan)komst; Ad'vent
adventure, avon'tuur *n*, (ge'waag-
de) onder'neming
adventurer, avontu'rier; specu'-
lant
adventurous, avon'tuurlijk;
ge'waagd
adverb, bijwoord *n*
adversary, tegenstander
adverse, on'gunstig; na'delig
adversity, tegenspoed
advertise, adver'teren, re'clame
maken (voor); be'kend maken
advertisement, adver'tentie, re'-
clame
advice, raad
advisable, raadzaam
advise, aanraden
advisedly, met over'leg
adviser, raadsman
advisory, raadgevend
advocate, voorspraak; voorstander : be'pleiten
aerial, an'tenne
aerodrome, vliegveld *n*
aeronautics, luchtvaartkunde
aeroplane, vliegtuig *n*
aesthetic, aes'thetisch
afar, verre
affable, minzaam
affair, zaak; ver'houding
affect, (be')treffen; voorwenden
affectation, ge'maaktheid; voorwendsel *n*
affected, ge'maakt
affection, ge'negenheid
affectionate, aan'hankelijk,harte-
lijk; toegenegen
affidavit, be'ëdigde ver'klaring
affiliated to, aangesloten bij
affinity, ver'wantschap

affirm, plechtig ver'klaren
affirmation, be'vestiging
affirmative, be'vestigend
afflict, kwellen, teisteren
affliction, kwelling, ramp
affluent, (schat)rijk
afford, zich ver'oorloven; ver'-
schaffen
afforestation, aanplant(ing)
affront, be'lediging
afield : far —, ver weg
afloat, drijvend
afoot, aan de gang
aforementioned,   aforesaid,
voor'noemd
afraid, bang
afresh, op'nieuw
aft, (naar) achter
after, (daar')na: na'dat
after-effect(s), nawerking
aftermath, nasleep
afternoon, (na)middag
afterthought, latere over'weging
afterwards, later, nader'hand
again, weer (eens); te'rug
again and again, telkens weer
against, tegen
agate, a'gaat
age, leeftijd, ouderdom; eeuw:
ouder worden
of age, meerder'jaarig
aged, be'jaard; oud
agency, a'gentschap *n*
agenda, a'genda
agent, tussenpersoon, a'gent
agglomeration, op'eenhoping
aggrandize, ver'heffen
aggravate, (ver')ergeren
aggravating, ver'velend; ver'-
zwarend
aggregate, (ge'zamenlijk) to'taal
n
aggression, ag'gressie
aggressive, aggres'sief
aggressor, aanvaller
aghast at, ont'zet over
agile, be'hendig
agitate, a'geren; schudden
agitation, actie; be'roering; ge'-
jaagdheid
agitator, opruier
aglow, gloeiend
agnostic, ag'nosticus

ago, ge'leden

agog: to be —, zitten te springen

agonizing, (vreselijk) pijnlijk

agony, folterende pijn

agrarian, a'grarisch

agree, het eens zijn; over'een-komen; toestemmen

  fish doesn't agree with me, ik kan niet tegen vis

agreeable, aangenaam; be'reid

agreement, over'eenkomst

agricultural, landbouw('kundig)

agriculture, landbouw

aground, aan de grond

ahead, voor'op, voor'uit; in het voor'uitzicht

aid, hulp

ail, man'keren; sukkelen

ailment, kwaal

aim, doel(einde) *n*: mikken op; munten op; streven naar

aimless, doelloos

air, lucht; schijn; wijs: luchten

  airs (and graces), airs

aircraft, vliegtuig(en) *n*

aircraft-carrier, vliegdekschip *n*

airfield, vliegveld *n*

airforce, luchtmacht

airgun, windbuks

airily, lucht'hartig

air-lift, luchtbrug

air-line, luchtvaartlijn

air-liner, lijnvliegtuig *n*

airman, vlieger

airport, vlieghaven

air-raid, luchtaanval

airtight, luchtdicht

airways, luchtvaartmaatschappij

airy, luchtig

aisle, zijbeuk, gangpad *n*

ajar, op een kier; ge'prikkeld

akimbo: arms —, met de handen in de zij

akin, ver'want

alacrity, levendigheid

  with alacrity, vol'gaarne

alarm, a'larm *n*; ont'steltenis: ont'stellen

alarm-clock, wekker

alarmist, alar'mist(isch)

alas, he'laas

alb, albe

albeit, (al)hoe'wel

albumen, eiwit *n*

alcohol, alcohol

alcoholic, alco'holisch: alco-ho'list

alcove, nis; al'koof

alderman, wethouder

ale, bier *n*

alert, waakzaam

algebra, algebra

alien, vreemd(eling)

alienate, ver'vreemden

alight, aan(gestoken): af (*or* uit)stappen; neerstrijken

align, op één lijn plaatsen

alike, evenzeer

  to be alike, op el'kaar lijken

alive, levend, in leven; zich be'wust van

alkali(ne), al'kali(sch) (*n*)

all, al(le); alles, allen; ge'heel, alle'maal

  all along, steeds

  all but, bijna

  all in, bek'af: alles inbegrepen

  all right, in orde

  all the more, des te meer

  after all, ten'slotte

  all in all, al met al

  at all, über'haupt

  not at all, hele'maal niet

  for all that, desondanks

  for all I know, voor zo'ver ik weet

allay, stillen

allegation, be'wering

allege, be'weren

alleged(ly), zoge'naamd

allegiance, trouw

allegory, allego'rie

allergic, al'lergisch

alleviate, ver'lichten

alley(way), steeg

alliance, ver'bond *n*

allied, ver'bonden; ver'want

alliteration, allite'ratie

allocate, toewijzen

allot, toebedelen

allotment, volkstuintje *n*

allow, toestaan; rekenen

allowance, toelage

  to (make) allow(ance) for, rekening houden met

alloy, le'gering

all-round, veel'zijdig
allude to, zinspelen op
alluring, aan'lokkelijk
allusion, toespeling
ally, bondgenoot: ver'binden
almighty, al'machtig
almond, a'mandel
almoner, administra'teur
almost, bijna
alms, aalmoes
aloft, in 't want, in de hoogte
alone, al'leen
  let alone, laat staan
along, langs; mee; voort
  along with, met . . . mee,
  samen met
alongside, langs'zij
aloof, op een afstand
aloud, hardop
alphabet, alfabet *n*
alphabetical, alfa'betisch
already, al, reeds
also, ook; boven'dien
altar, altaar *n*
alter, ver'anderen, (zich) wijzigen
alteration, ver'andering
altercation, twistgesprek *n*
alternate, afwisselen
  on alternate days, om de andere
  dag
alternately, om de beurt
alternating current, wisselstroom
alternative, alterna'tief (*n*)
alternatively, aan de andere
  kant
although, hoe'wel
altitude, hoogte
alto, alt
altogether, hele'maal; alles bij
  el'kaar
altruism, altru'isme *n*
aluminium, alu'minium *n*
always, al'tijd
amalgamate, samensmelten
amass, op'eenhopen
amateur, ama'teur
amaze, ver'bazen
amazement, ver'bazing
ambassador, (af)gezant
amber, barnsteen *n*
ambiguity, dubbel'zinnigheid
ambiguous, dubbel'zinnig

ambition, eerzucht; aspi'ratie,
  ide'aal *n*
ambitious, eer'zuchtig; groots
  opgezet
amble, kuieren
ambulance, ziekenauto
ambush, hinderlaag
amenable, ont'vankelijk (voor)
amend, ver'beteren, wijzigen
amendment, amende'ment *n*
amends: to make —, het weer
  goedmaken
amenity, ge'mak *n*
amiable, be'minnelijk
amicable, vriend'schappelijk
amidships, mid'scheeps
amid(st), te midden van
amiss, ver'keerd
amity, pais en vree
ammonia, ammoni'ak
ammunition, (am)mu'nitie
amnesty, amnes'tie
among(st), onder, tussen
amorous, ver'liefd; liefdes-
amount, be'drag, hoe'veelheid
  to amount to, be'dragen; be'-
  tekenen
amphibian, amfi'bie; twee'slachtig
ample, ruim (vol'doende)
amplify, aanvullen; ver'sterken
amply, ruimschoots
amputate, ampu'teren
amuse, ver'maken; pret hebben
amused: to be —, grappig vinden
amusement, ver'maak *n*, tijdverdrijf *n*
amusing, amu'sant, onder'houdend
anaemia, bloedarmoede
anaesthetic, ver'dovend: ver'-
  dovingsmiddel *n*
analogous, ana'loog
analogy, analo'gie
analyse, anali'seren
analysis, ana'lyse
anarchy, anar'chie
anathema, banvloek; pesti'lentie
anatomy, anato'mie
ancestor, voorvader
ancestral, voorvaderlijk

ancestry, voorgeslacht *n*; afstamming

anchor, anker *n*: (ver)'ankeren

anchorage, ankergrond; steun

anchovy, an'sjovis

ancient, (zeer) oud

and, en

anecdote, anek'dote

anew, op'nieuw

angel, engel

angelic(al), engelachtig, engelen-

anger, boosheid: ver'toornen

angle, hoek; ge'zichtspunt *n*: hengelen

Anglican, Angli'caan(s)

angry, boos

anguish, zielssmart; folterende pijn

angular, hoekig

animal, dier *n*: dierlijk, dieren-

animate, levend: be'zielen

animated, geani'meerd

animation, enthousi'asme

animosity, vij'andigheid

ankle, enkel

annals, an'nalen

annex, anne'xeren; toevoegen

annexe, uitbouw, depen'dance; bijlage

annihilate, ver'nietigen

anniversary, jaarfeest *n*, ge'denkdag

announce, aankondigen

announcement, aankondiging

announcer, omroeper

annoy, ergeren

annoyance, ergenis

annoying, ver'velend

annual, jaarlijks: éénjarige plant; jaarboek *n*

annuity, jaargeld *n*, lijfrente

annul, te niet doen

anoint, zalven

anomaly, afwijking

anon, straks

anonymous, ano'niem

another, een ander(e), nog een

answer, antwoord *n*, oplossing: (be')antwoorden

answerable, aan'sprakelijk; te be'antwoorden

ant, mier

antagonism, vijandschap

antagonist, tegenstander

antagonize, ophitsen

antarctic, Zuidpool(gebied *n*)

antecedent, voor'afgaand: ante-ce'dent *n*

anteroom, voorvertrek *n*

anthem, mo'tet *n*

ant-hill, mierenhoop

anthology, bloemlezing

anthracite, antra'ciet

anti-aircraft, luchtafweer-

antics, dolle streken

anticipate, ver'wachten; voor'uit-lopen op, vóór zijn

anticipation, ver'wachting

anticlimax, anti'climax

antidote, tegengif *n*

antipathy, antipa'thie

antiquarian, oudheid'kundig(e), anti'quair

antiquated, ouder'wets

antique, an'tiek; antiqui'teit

antiquity, oudheid; ouderdom

antiseptic, anti'septisch (middel *n*)

antithesis, tegenstelling, tegen-ge'stelde *n*

antlers, ge'wei *n*

anvil, aanbeeld *n*

anxiety, be'zorgdheid; vurig ver'-langen *n*

anxious, be'zorgd

to be anxious to, heel graag willen

any, ieder, iemand; wat (ook), enig

not any, geen; niets

have you any bread (*etc*) ? hebt U (ook) brood (*etc*)?

anybody, anyone, iemand, iedereen; wie ook

anyhow, hoe dan ook; zo maar

anything, iets; alles

anyway, in ieder ge'val

anywhere, ergens; over'al

apace, vlug

apart, uit el'kaar; afgezien; afgezonderd

apartment, ver'trek *n*

apathetic, a'patisch

apathy, onver'schilligheid

ape, aap (zonder staart): naäpen

aperture, opening
apex, top(punt *n*)
apiary, bijenstal
apiece, per stuk, elk
apologetic, veront'schuldigend
apologize, zich veront'schuldigen
apology, veront'schuldiging
apoplectic fit, be'roerte
apostate, af'vallig(e)
apostle, a'postel
apostrophe, apos'trof
appal, ont'zetten
appalling, schrik'barend
apparatus, appa'raten, appa'raat *n*, toestel(len) *n*
apparel, kle'dij
apparent, duidelijk; ogen'schijnlijk
apparently, blijkbaar
apparition, ('geest)ver'schijning
appeal, be'roep *n*, smeekbede; aantrekkingskracht: een be'roep doen (op), smeken; in be'roep gaan (bij); aantrekken
appear, (ver')schijnen, blijken
appearance, ver'schijning, optreden *n*; voorkomen *n*
appease, sussen, stillen
appeasement, ver'zoening
append, (bij) voegen
appendage, aanhangsel *n*
appendicitis, blinde'darmontsteking
appendix, ap'pendix; aanhangsel *n*
appertain to, be'trekking hebben op; be'horen aan
appetite, (eet)lust
appetizing, smakelijk
applaud, toejuichen, applaudis'seren
applause, ap'plaus *n*, toejuiching(en)
apple, appel
appliance, appa'raat *n*; toepassing
applicable, toe'passelijk
applicant, sollici'tant
application, aanbrengen *n*; (ma'nier van) toepassing, ge'bruik *n*; sollici'tatie; ijver
applied, toegepast

apply, aanbrengen; toepassen, van toepassing zijn; zich wenden; sollici'teren; toeleggen (op)
appoint, be'noemen, aanwijzen
appointed time, vastgesteld uur
appointment, afspraak; be'noeming, ambt *n*
apportion, ver'delen
apposite, toe'passelijk
appraisal, schatting
appreciable, aan'merkelijk
appreciate, waar'deren, ge'voelig zijn voor; stijgen
appreciation, waar'dering, ge'voel *n*; stijging
appreciative, dankbaar
apprehend, ge'vangen nemen; vatten; vrezen
apprehension, in'hechtenisneming; be'grip *n*; angst
apprehensive, angstig
apprentice, leerling: in de leer doen
approach, nader'bij komen (*n*); toegang(sweg); aanpak: naderen; zich wenden tot
approachable, toe'gankelijk
approbation, goedkeuring
appropriate, ge'schikt: zich toeëigenen, be'stemmen
approval, goedkeuring, bijval
on approval, op zicht
approve, goedkeuren, er'kennen
approximate, be'naderen
  the (approximate) length is (approximately), de lengte is onge'veer
approximation, schatting
apricot, abri'koos
April, a'pril
apron, schort, voorschoot
apse, apsis
apt, ge'neigd; passend; vlug
aptitude, aanleg
aquarium, a'quarium *n*
aquatic, water-
aqueduct, waterleiding
aquiline, arends-
Arab, Ara'bier
Arabian, Arabic, A'rabisch
arable, bouw-
arbitrary, wille'keurig

arbitration, arbi'trage

arc, boog

arcade, gale'rij

arch, boog, ge'welf n; aarts-, schalks

archaeology, oudheidkunde

archaic, ver'ouderd

arched, ge'bogen

archer, boogschutter

archery, boogschieten n

architect, archi'tect

architectural, bouw'kundig

architecture, bouwkunde, bouw-stijl

archives, ar'chief n, ar'chieven

archway, poort

arctic, Noordpool(gebied n)

ardent, vurig

arduous, zwaar

area, oppervlak n, ge'bied n

arena, a'rena

argue, debat'teren; tegen-spreken; be'togen

argument, argu'ment n, de'bat n; ge'dachtengang

argumentative, twistziek

arid, dor

aright, juist

arise, ont'staan, zich voordoen; ver'rijzen

aristocracy, aristocra'tie

aristocrat, aristo'craat

arithmetic, rekenkunde

ark, ark

arm, arm, leuning: wapen n: be'wapenen

  arm in arm, ge'armd

armament, be'wapening

armchair, fau'teuil

armful, vracht

armistice, wapenstilstand

armour, harnas n; wapenrus-ting

armoured, pantser-

armoury, wapenzaal

armpit, oksel

army, leger n

aroma, a'roma n

aromatic, geurig

around, rond('om); over'al; in de buurt (van)

arouse, opwekken; wakker ma-ken

arraign, aanklagen; be'schul-digen

arrange, (rang)schikken; rege-len, afspreken; arran'geren

arrangement, schikking; af-spraak; arrange'ment n

arrant, door'trapt

array, (slag)orde; uitstalling; dos: opstellen; uitdossen

arrears, achterstand

arrest, ar'rest n, arres'tatie: arres'teren; tegenhouden

arrival, (aan)komst; aange-komene

arrive, (aan)komen

arrogance, aanmatiging

arrogant, arro'gant

arrow, pijl

arsenal, arse'naal n

arsenic, ar'senicum n

arson, brandstichting

art, kunst(greep)

arterial road, hoofdverkeersweg

artery, (slag)ader

artful, ge'slepen

arthritis, ge'wrichtsontsteking

artichoke, arti'sjok

article, ar'tikel n; voorwerp n; lidwoord n

  article of clothing, kledingstuk n

articulate, duidelijk: articu'-leren; koppelen

artifice, kunst(greep)

artificer, handwerksman

artificial, kunst'matig, ge'kunst-eld, kunst-

artillery, artille'rie

artisan, handwerksman

artist, kunstenaar, schilder

artistic, kunst'zinnig, artis'tiek

artistry, kunstenaarstalent n

artless, argeloos; ruw

as, (zo)als: ter'wijl; daar
  (just) as . . . (as), even . . . (als)

as to, wat betreft

asbestos, as'best n

ascend, (be')stijgen

ascendancy, overwicht n

Ascension, Hemelvaart

ascent, stijgen n, be'stijging; helling

ascertain, te weten komen
ascetic, as'ceet: as'cetisch
ascribe, toeschrijven
ash, as: es(seboom)
Ash Wednesday, As'woensdag
ashamed, be'schaamd
  to be ashamed, zich schamen
ashen, lijkbleek
ashore, aan wal, aan land
ash-tray, asbak
aside, op'zij, ter'zijde
asinine, ezelachtig
ask, vragen
  to ask a question, een vraag
  doen
askance, wan'trouwend
askew, scheef
aslant, schuin
asleep, in slaap
  to be asleep, slapen
asparagus, as'perge
aspect, as'pect *n*, kant; aanblik;
  ligging
aspersion, laster
asphalt, asfalt *n*
asphyxiate, (ver')stikken
aspirant, aspi'rant; postu'lant
aspiration, aspi'ratie
aspire, streven (naar)
ass, ezel
assail, be'stormen, aanvallen
assailant, aanvaller
assassin, sluipmoordenaar
assassinate, ver'moorden
assault, be'storming, aanval(len),
  be'stormen
assay, proef(neming): toetsen
assemble, (zich) ver'zamelen;
  mon'teren
assembly, bij'eenkomst; mon'-
  tering
assent, instemming: instemmen
assert, be'weren; doen gelden,
  opkomen voor
assertion, be'wering
assess, ta'xeren; aanslaan
asset, creditpost; voordeel *n*
assiduous, naarstig
assign, toewijzen; vaststellen
assignment, opdracht
assimilate, ver'werken, opnemen
assimilation, assimi'latie

assist, helpen
assistance, hulp
assistant, assis'tent, be'diende:
  hulp-
assizes, rechtzitting(en)
associate, partner; ver'want:
  ver'binden, associ'eren, omgaan
association, associ'atie; ge'nootschap *n*
assorted, ge'mengd
assortment, sor'tering; ver'-
  zameling
assuage, stillen, lessen
assume, aannemen; voorwenden;
  op zich nemen
assumption, veronder'stelling;
  aanvaarding
assurance, ver'zekering
assure, ver'zekeren
assuredly, stellig; zelfbe'wust
astern, achter('uit)
astir, op de been
astonish, ver'bazen
astonishment, ver'bazing
astound, (ten hoogste) ver'bazen
astray, op een dwaalspoor
astride, schrijlings (op)
astrology, sterrenwichelarij
astronomical, astro'nomisch
astronomy, sterrenkunde
astute, slim
asunder, uit el'kaar
asylum, ge'sticht *n*; a'siel *n*
asymmetric(al), asym'metrisch
at, aan (*position*); in, op, te
  (*place*); om (*time*); naar (*direction*); voor (*price*)
  at (my) leisure, op mijn ge'mak
  at that moment, op dat ogenblik
  at the time, toen
atheism, athe'isme *n*
athlete, at'leet
athletic, at'letisch
athletics, atle'tiek
Atlantic, At'lantische Oce'aan
atlas, atlas
atmosphere, dampkring;
  (atmo')sfeer
atmospheric, atmos'ferisch
atom, a'toom *n*; greintje *n*
atomic, a'tomisch, a'toom-
atone, boeten

atonement, boete(doening), ver'zoening

atrocious, af'schuwelijk

atrocity, gruwel(daad)

atrophy, atro'fie; (doen) uitteren

attach, vastmaken, ver'binden; hechten

attachment, onderdeel *n,* ver'binding; ge'hechtheid

attack, aanval(len)

attain, be'reiken, be'halen

attainable, be'reikbaar

attainment, be'reiken *n;* ta'lent *n*

attempt, poging, aanslag: trachten

attend, bijwonen; verge'zellen

attend to, opletten; ver'zorgen

attendance, opkomst; aan'wezigheid

in **attendance,** aan'wezig; in het ge'volg

attendant, be'diende; be'zoeker: bege'leidend; dienstdoend

attention, aandacht; at'tentie; houding

attentive, op'lettend; at'tent

attenuate, ver'dunnen; ver'zachten

attest, ge'tuigen van, attes'teren

attic, zolder(kamer)

attire, tooi(en)

attitude, houding

attorney, gevol'machtigde, procu'reur

attract, (aan)trekken

attraction, aantrekking(skracht)

attractive, aan'trekkelijk

attribute, eigenschap, kenmerk *n;* attri'buut *n:* toeschrijven

attune, (over'een)stemmen met

auburn, kas'tanjebruin

auction, veiling: veilen

auctioneer, afslager

audacious, ver'metel

audacity, ver'metelheid, bruta'li'teit

audible, hoorbaar

audience, ge'hoor *n,* toehoorders; audi'ëntie

audit, ac'countantsverslag *n:* verifi'ëren

audition, to'neel-(*or* mu'ziek-)proef

auditor, ac'countant; toehoorder

auditorium, zaal

augment, ver'meerderen, uitbreiden

augur, voor'spellen

august, ver'heven: au'gustus

aunt, tante

aura, geur; lichtkrans

auspices, au'spiciën

auspicious, gunstig

austere, streng, sober

austerity, ver'sobering

Austria, Oostenrijk *n*

authentic, authen'tiek

authenticate, verifi'ëren

authenticity, echtheid

author, schrijver; schepper, oorsprong

authoritarian, autori'tair (per'soon)

authoritative, autori'tair, ge'zaghebbend

authority, autori'teit; bron; machtiging

authorize, machtigen; be'krachtigen

autobiography, autobiogra'fie

autocracy, onbeperkte heerschap'pij

autocrat, auto'kraat

autograph, handtekening: (eigen'handig) tekenen

automatic, auto'matisch (pis'tool *n*)

automaton, auto'maat

automobile, automo'biel

autonomous, auto'noom

autopsy, lijkschouwing

auto-suggestion, autosug'gestie

autumn(al), herfst(-)

auxiliary, hulp (troep)

avail, baten

of no **avail,** vruchteloos

to **avail oneself of,** be'nutten

available, be'schikbaar

avalanche, la'wine

avarice, gierigheid

avaricious, gierig; be'gerig

avenge, wreken

avenue, laan; weg

aver, (plechtig) ver'klaren

average, ge'middeld (doen): ge'middelde *n*

averse to, af'kerig van
aversion, afkeer, tegenzin
avert, afwenden
aviary, voli'ère
aviation, luchtvaart, vliegwezen *n*
aviator, vlieger
avid, gretig, be'gerig
avoid, (ver')mijden
avoidance, ver'mijding
avow, be'lijden, be'kennen
avowal, be'kentenis, be'lijdenis
await, afwachten; wachten op
awake, wakker; zich be'wust (worden) van; ont'waken; wekken
awaken, wekken
awakening: rude —, ont'nuchtering
award, be'kroning, prijs: toekennen, toewijzen
aware, zich be'wust
awareness, be'sef *n*
awash, over'spoeld
away, weg; er op los
do away with, opruimen
awe, ont'zag *n*
awe-inspiring, ontzag'wekkend
awful, ver'schrikkelijk, vreselijk
awfully, (heel) erg
awhile, een tijdje *n*
awkward, on'handig; lastig
awning, dekzeil *n*, zonnescherm *n*
awry, scheef
axe, bijl: drastisch be'perken
axiom, axi'oma *n*
axis, as(lijn); spil
axle, as
aye, ja, stem vóór; immer
azure, hemelsblauw

B

babble, babbelen, kabbelen
babel, spraakverwarring
baboon, bavi'aan
baby, kindje *n*, baby; benjamin: jong, klein
babyish, kinderachtig
bacchanal, baccha'naal *n*: bac'chantisch
bachelor, vrijge'zel
bacillus, ba'cil

back, rug, achterkant, rugleuning: te'rug, achter-: achter'uitgaan; wedden op; bijvallen
back to front, achterste voren
at the back, achter'aan (*or* 'in)
on the back, achter'op
to back down, zich te'rugtrekken
to back out, te'rugkrabbelen
to back up, steunen
back-biting, kwaadspreke'rij
backbone, ruggegraat
backfire, te'rugslaan
background, achtergrond
backing, steun; achterkant (bekleding)
back-stage, achter de schermen
backward(s), achter'uit, te'rug-; achterlijk, traag
backwards and forwards, heen en weer
backwater, kreek, uithoek; boegwater *n*
bacon, (ge'rookt) spek *n*
bacteria, bac'teriën
bad, slecht, naar; vals; be'dorven
to go bad, be'derven
bad luck, pech
badge, in'signe *n*
badger, das: lastig vallen
badly, erg; dolgraag
bad-tempered, slecht-gehu'meurd
baffle, smoorplaat: ver'bijsteren
bag, zak, tas; vangst: gappen
baggage, ba'gage
baggy, uitgezakt, hang-
bagpipe, doedelzak
bail, borg(tocht): borgstaan: hozen
bailiff, rentmeester; deurwaarder
bait, lokaas *n*: van aas voor'zien; aanhitsen
baize, baai
bake, bakken
baker, bakker
bakery, bakke'rij
balance, evenwicht *n*; saldo *n*, rest('ant *n*); weegschaal: in evenwicht brengen, opwegen tegen; sluitend maken (*or* zijn)

balanced, even'wichtig
balance-sheet, ba'lans
balcony, bal'kon *n*
bald, kaal; naakt
bale, baal: in balen ver'pakken
baleful, onheil'spellend, ge'pij-
nigd
balk, balk: ver'ijdelen, tegenstribbelen
ball, bal(len); bal *n (dance)*
ballad, bal'lade
ballast, ballast
ball-bearing, kogellager *n*
ballet, bal'let *n*
balloon, bal'lon: bol staan
ballot, (ge'heime) stemming; lot
n
balm, balsem, geur
balmy, zacht, geurig; ge'tikt
balsam, balsem
Baltic, Oost'zee
balustrade, balu'strade
bamboo, bamboe
bamboozle, beetnemen; in de
war brengen
ban, ver'bod *n,* ban(vloek):
ver'bieden; ver'bannen
banal, ba'naal
banana, ba'naan
band, band, rand; troep; ka'pel:
ver'enigen
bandage, ver'band *n*
bandit, ban'diet
bandstand, mu'ziektent
bandy, telkens *(or* over en) weer
lan'ceren
bandy-legged, met o-benen
bane, vloek
bang, klap, knal: (dicht)slaan
banish, ver'bannen
banishment, ver'banning
banisters, trapleuning
banjo, banjo
bank, oever, berm; bank: ophopen; depo'neren; overhellen;
afdekken
  to bank on, specu'leren op
banker, ban'kier
bank-holiday, offici'ele va'cantie-
dag
bank-note, bankbiljet *n*
bankrupt, fai'lliet
bankruptcy, faillisse'ment *n*

banner, ba'nier, vaandel *n*
banns, (kerkelijke) huwelijks-
afkondiging
banquet, gastmaal *n:* banket'-
teren
banter, gekscheren *(n)*
baptism, doop
Baptist, doopsge'zinde
baptize, dopen
bar, stang, reep, staaf; barri'ère;
  bar; balie; maat: uitgezonderd: afsluiten, ver'sperren;
  uitsluiten
barb, weerhaak
barbarian, bar'baar(s)
barbarity, bar'baarsheid
barbarous, bar'baars
barbed, met weerhaken; heke-
lend
  barbed wire, prikkeldraad *n*
barber, kapper
bard, zanger-dichter
bare, (ont')bloot, kaal; mini'-
maal: ont'bloten
barefaced, onbe'schaamd
bare-foot(ed), bloots'voets
bare-headed, bloots'hoofds
barely, nauwelijks
bargain, over'eenkomst; koopje
n: dingen
  into the bargain, op de koop
  toe
  to bargain for, rekenen op
barge, schuit, sloep: botsen, zich
werken
baritone, bariton
bark, schors; ge'blaf *n:* bark:
schaven: blaffen
barley, gerst
barmaid, buf'fetjuffrouw
barn, schuur
barometer, barometer
baron, ba'ron; mag'naat
baroque, ba'rok(stijl)
barracks, ka'zerne(woning)
barrage, gor'dijnvuur *n*
barrel, vat *n,* ton; loop
barren, on'vruchtbaar, dor
barricade, barri'cade: barri-
ca'deren
barrier, barri'ère, con'trole
barrister, advo'kaat
barrow, handkar: grafheuvel

barter, ruilhandel drijven; ver'kwanselen

base, basis, voetstuk *n*: ge'meen, on'edel: ba'seren

baseball, honkbal *n*

basement, souter'rain *n*

bash, opstopper: (in) slaan

bashful, schuchter

basic, fundamen'teel, grond-

basin, kom, bak; dok *n*; stroom-gebied *n*

basis, basis

bask, zich koesteren

basket, mand

basket-ball, korfbal *n*

bass, bas: baars

bassoon, fa'got

bastard, bastaard: on'echt

baste, met vet over'gieten: rijgen: ranselen

bastion, basti'on *n*

bat, slaghout *n*: vleermuis: bat-ten

  off one's own bat, op eigen houtje

batch, par'tij, baksel *n*; groep

bath, bad *n*: in bad doen (*or* gaan)

  (public) baths, badinrichting

bathe, (zich) baden: betten

  bathed (in light), badend (in licht)

bathing-costume, badpak *n*

bathing-trunks, zwembroek

bath-robe, badjas

bathroom, badkamer

batman, oppasser

baton, stok (je *n*)

battalion, batal'jon *n*

batten, (schalm)lat

batter, be'slag *n*: beuken

battery, batte'rij, accu; **aan-**randing

battle, (veld)slag; strijd(en)

battle-axe, strijdbijl

battle-dress, veldte'nue *n*

battle-field, slagveld *n*

battlement, kan'teel

battleship, slagschip *n*

bawdy, vuil

bawl, schreeuwen, brullen

bay, baai; erker, hoek: vos: blaffen

  at bay, in het nauw

bayonet, bajo'net

bazaar, ba'zaar

be, zijn; zitten, worden

  to be hungry, sleepy, thirsty, cold, honger, slaap, dorst, het koud hebben

  how are you? hoe maakt U het?

  how is it that, hoe komt het dat

beach, strand *n*

beacon, baken *n*

bead, kraal; parel (tje *n*)

beak, snavel

beaker, beker (glas *n*)

beam, balk; stralenbundel: stralen (van)

  on the beam, op zij

bean, boon

bear, beer: (ver)dragen; baren

  to bear down, neerdrukken; afkomen op

  to bear out, staven

  to bear witness, ge'tuigen

beard, baard: trot'seren

bearer, drager, brenger; toonder

bearing, houding; be'trekking; richting; kogellager *n*

beast, beest *n*

beastly, beestachtig; akelig

beat, (maat)slag: ronde: (ver)slaan, kloppen; la'veren

beating, afranseling; klappen *n*

beautiful, mooi

beautify, ver'fraaien

beauty, schoonheid; pracht-exemplaar *n*

beaver, bever

becalmed: to be —, door wind-stilte over'vallen worden

because, omdat

  because of, van'wege

beckon, wenken

become, worden

  to become of, ge'beuren met

becoming, be'tamelijk, flat'teus

bed, bed (ding) (*n*)

bedaub, be'kladden; opdirken

bed-clothes, dek *n*, beddegoed *n*

bedding, beddegoed *n*; onderlaag

bedlam, gekkenhuis *n*

bed-pan, ondersteek

bedraggled, nat en ver'wilderd

bedridden, bed'legerig

bedroom, slaapkamer

bedspread, sprei
bedstead, ledi'kant *n*
bee, bij
beech, beuk(e'hout *n*)
beef, rundvlees *n*
beefsteak, runderlap
beehive, bijenkorf
beer, bier *n*
beet, biet
beetle, kever
beetroot, rode biet
befall, over'komen
befit, be'tamen
befog, be'nevelen
before, voor('af, 'op *or* 'uit), te
  voren; voordat
  before long, weldra
beforehand, voor'af, van te voren
befriend, vriendschap be'wijzen
befuddle, be'nevelen
beg, bedelen; smeken, ver'zoeken; zo vrij zijn
beget, voortbrengen
beggar, bedelaar; stakker: tarten
beggarly, ar'moedig
begin, be'ginnen
beginning, be'gin *n*
begrudge, mis'gunnen
beguile, be'driegen; ver'drijven
behalf: on — of, ten be'hoeve
  van, uit naam van
behave (oneself), zich (netjes)
  ge'dragen
behaviour, ge'drag *n*
behead, ont'hoofden
behind, achter(ste *n*)
behold, aan'schouwen
beige, beige
being, wezen *n*
  to come into being, ont'staan
  for the time being, voor'lopig
belated, (ver')laat
belch, boeren; uitbraken
belfry, klokketoren
Belgium, België
belie, logenstraffen
belief, ge'loof *n*
believe, ge'loven
believer, ge'lovige; voorstander
  (van)
belittle, klei'neren
bell, bel, klok

bellicose, oorlogs'zuchtig
belligerent, oorlogvoerend;
  strijd'lustig
bellow, ge'brul *n*: brullen
bellows, blaasbalg
belly, buik: uitbollen
belong, (be')horen
  to belong to, (toebe)horen aan
belongings, spullen
beloved, ge'liefd(e)
below, onder, be'neden
belt, gordel, riem; zone: afranselen
bemoan, be'jammeren
bench, (recht)bank
bend, bocht: (zich) buigen,
  ver'buigen
beneath, be'neden, onder
benediction, zegen; Lof *n*
benefactor, weldoener
benefice, bene'ficie
beneficial, heilzaam
benefit, voordeel *n*; uitkering:
  goed doen, voordeel trekken
benevolent, wel'willend
benign, goed('aard)ig, wel'dadig
bent, ge'bogen: be'sloten, uit op:
  aanleg
benumb, ver'kleumen
bequeath, ver'maken
bequest, le'gaat *n*
bereave, be'roven
bereaved, diep be'droefd
bereavement, zwaar ver'lies *n*
beret, ba'ret
berry, bes
berth, ligplaats; kooi: meren
beseech, smeken
beset, vol: om'ringen
beside, naast
  beside oneself with, buiten
  zichzelf van
besides, boven'dien: be'halve
besiege, be'legeren; be'stormen
besmirch, be'vuilen; be'zoedelen
best, (het) best
  best man, bruidsjonker
  best part of, bijna
  at best, in het gunstigste ge'val
  to make the best of, zich schikken in
bestial, beestachtig

bestow, ver'lenen, schenken
bet, wedden(schap)
betoken, be'duiden
betray, ver'raden
betrayal, ver'raad *n*
betroth, ver'loven
better, beter : ver'beteren
  better off, er beter aan toe
  had better, moet(en) maar
between, tussen
bevel, afschuinen
beverage, drank
bewail, be'jammeren
beware of, oppassen voor
bewilder, ver'bijsteren
bewitch, be'heksen
beyond, voor'bij ; boven ; meer
  dan
  it is beyond me, het gaat mij te
  hoog
bias, neiging : bevoor'oordelen
bib, slabbetje *n*
Bible, Bijbel
bibliography, bibliogra'fie
bicker, kibbelen
bicycle, fiets
bid, bod *n* : bieden ; ge'lasten
bide, beiden
bier, (lijk)baar
biff, mep
big, groot
bigamy, biga'mie
bigot(ed), kwezel(achtig)
bilge, vulling, ruimwater *n* ;
  kletskoek
bilious attack, maagstoring
bill, rekening : wetsontwerp *n* ;
  aanplakbiljet *n* : snavel
billet, kwar'tier *n* : inkwartieren
billiards, bil'jart *n*
billion, bil'joen *n*
billow, baar : bollen ; in wolken
  opstijgen
bin, bak
bind, (in-, vast- *or* ver')binden ;
  ver'plichten
binder, (boek)binder ; omslag
binding, band *n* : bindend
binoculars, kijker
biography, levensbeschrijving
biology, biolo'gie
birch, berk(ehout *n*)
bird, vogel

birth, ge'boorte
  to give birth to, het leven
  schenken aan
birthday, ver'jaardag
birth-rate, ge'boortecijfer *n*
biscuit, koekje *n*, biskwietje *n*
bishop, bisschop
bishopric, bisdom *n*
bit, beetje *n*, stukje : bit *n*
  wait a bit, even wachten
bitch, teef
bite, beet, hap : bijten
bitter, bitter
blab, ver'klikken
black, zwart, blauw (*eye*)
blackberry, braam
blackbird, merel
blackboard, schoolbord *n*
blackguard, schobbejak
blackmail, chan'tage : geld afpersen
blackout, ver'duistering ; tijde-
  lijke bewuste'loosheid
blacksmith, smid
bladder, blaas
blade, kling, lemmet *n*, mesje *n*;
  spriet
blame, (de) schuld (geven)
blameless, onbe'rispelijk
blanch, (ver')bleken, pellen
bland, (poes)lief
blank, blanco ; wezenloos ; rijm-
  loos ; los (*cartridge*)
  to draw blank, botvangen
blanket, deken
blare, schallen
blasphemy, godslastering
blast, rukwind, luchtdruk :
  ver'rek l: laten springen
blast-furnace, hoogoven
blatant, over'duidelijk
blaze, laaiend vuur *n*, (vlammen)-
  zee: opvlammen, in lichte laaie
  staan
bleach, (doen ver')bleken
bleak, troosteloos
bleat, blaten
bleed, bloeden ; uitzuigen
blemish, smet, ont'siering : be'-
  kladden
blend, mengsel *n*: (zich) ver'mengen, harmoni'ëren
bless, zegenen

blessing, zegen(ing)
blight, plantenziekte; be'derf *n*
blind, blind; doodlopend: rolgordijn *n*; foefje *n*: ver'blinden
blindfold, ge'blinddoekt: blinddoeken
blindness, blindheid
blink, knipperen
bliss, geluk'zaligheid
blister, blaar
blizzard, sneeuwjacht
block, blok *n*: (ver')stoppen
blockade, blok'kade: blok'keren
blockhead, domkop
blond(e), blond('ine)
blood, bloed *n*
bloodshed, bloedvergieten *n*
bloodshot, met bloed be'lopen
bloody, bloed(er)ig; ver'domd
bloom, bloem; waas *n*; bloei(en)
blossom, bloesem: bloeien
blot, vlek, smet: afvloeien; be'-
kladden
  to blot out, ver'nietigen
blotting-paper, vloeipapier *n*
blouse, blouse
blow, slag: waaien, blazen;
snuiten
  to blow up, opblazen; opvliegen, uitschelden; opsteken
blow-lamp, brander
blue, blauw (*n*)
blueprint, blauwdruk; plan *n*
bluff, bluf(fen); steil(e oever):
rond'borstig
bluish, blauwachtig
blunder, blunder; struikelen
blunt, stomp, bot (maken);
ab'rupt
blur, ver'vagen
blurt out, er'uit flappen
blush, blos: blozen, zich schamen
bluster, bulderen
boar, zwijn *n*
board, plank, bord *n*; kost(geld
n); be'stuur *n*
  to (go on) board, aan boord
gaan
  above board, bona fide
boarding-house, pen'sion *n*
boarding-school, kostschool
boast, pochen; bogen (op)
boat, boot

boatswain, bootsman
bob, korte buiging: dobberen:
kort knippen
bobbin, spoel
bode ill (well), wat slechts
(goeds) be'loven
bodice, (onder)lijfje *n*
bodily, li'chamelijk; in zijn
ge'heel
body, lichaam *n*, lijf *n*; sub'stantie; carrosse'rie; groep
bodyguard, lijfwacht
bog, moe'ras *n*
  to be bogged (down), vastzitten
bogey, boeman, schrikbeeld *n*
bogus, vals
boil, kook: steenpuist: koken
  to boil down, inkoken; neerkomen (op)
boiler, ketel, boiler
boisterous, on'stuimig
bold, stout('moedig); scherp
bolster, peluw: sterken
bolt, bout; grendel(en); ervan
doorgaan
  bolt upright, kaarsrecht
bomb(ard), bom(bar'deren)
bombastic, bom'bastisch
bomber, bommenwerper
bond, band; obli'gatie; entre'pot
n: ver'binden
bondage, slaver'nij
bone, been *n*, graat; ba'lein
bone-dry, kurkdroog
bonfire, (vreugde)vuur *n*
bonnet, kap
bonny, leuk, fris, knap
bonus, premie, tan'tième *n*
bony, knokig, vol benen (*or* graten)
boob(y), uilskuiken *n*
book, boek(je) *n*: be'spreken,
boeken
bookcase, boekenkast
booking-office, lo'ket *n*, plaats-
kaartenbureau *n*
book-keeping, boekhouden *n*
book-seller, boekhandelaar
boom, (haven)boom: hausse:
ge'dreun *n*: dreunen
boon, weldaad
boost, aanjagen, opdrijven; een
zetje geven

boot, laars; bak: trappen
 to boot, op de koop toe
booth, kraam
booty, buit
booze, zuippartij: zuipen
border, grens; rand; bloembed *n*:
 om'zomen
 to border on, grenzen aan
bore, boren; ver'velen
 to be bored, zich ver'velen
boredom, ver'veling
born, ge'boren
borough, (stads)ge'meente
borrow, lenen (van), ont'lenen
 (aan)
bosom, boezem; schoot
boss, baas: bult: comman'deren
botany, plantkunde
both, beide, allebei
 both . . . and, zo'wel . . . als
bother, last, drukte: bah! lastig
 vallen
bottle, fles: inmaken, bottelen
 to bottle up, opkroppen
bottom, bodem; zitvlak *n*:
 onder'aan, onderste
 he is at the bottom of it, hij zit
 er achter
bough, (grote) tak
boulder, grote kei
bounce, stuiten; springen
bound, ver'bonden; ver'plicht:
 sprong: springen; be'grenzen
 to be bound, moeten; op weg zijn
boundary, grens(lijn)
boundless, onbe'grensd
bounteous, bountiful, mild, over-
 vloedig
bout, par'tij; peri'ode, vlaag
bow, buiging: boeg: boog;
 strik; strijkstok: buigen
bowels, ingewanden; schoot
bower, pri'eel *n*
bowl, schaal, bak: bowlen
 to bowl over, om'vergooien;
 van (zijn) stuk brengen
box, doos(je *n*), kist(je *n*); loge:
 buks(boom): oorvijg: boksen
Boxing Day, tweede Kerstdag
box-office, plaatsbu'reau *n*
boy, jongen
boycott, boycot(ten)
boyhood, jongens(jaren)

boyish, jongens(achtig)
brace, klamp; boor; paar *n*:
 (zich) scherp zetten
bracelet, armband
braces, bre'tels
bracing, op'wekkend
bracken, varens
bracket, kar'beel, arm; haakje
 n: samenkoppelen
brag, pochen
braid, vlecht(en); ga'lon
braille, brailleschrift *n*
brain, hersenen
brains, hersens, ver'stand *n*
brain-wave, lumi'neus idee *n*
brainy, knap
braise, smoren
brake, rem(men)
bramble, braam(struik)
bran, zemelen
branch, tak; bijkantoor *n*; fili'-
 aal *n*; afdeling: zich ver'-
 takken
brand, merk *n*; brandmerk(en)
 (*n*)
brandish, (dreigend) zwaaien
brand-new, splinternieuw
brandy, cog'nac
brass, (geel)koper(en) (*n*)
 brass band, fan'farekorps *n*
brassiere, bustehouder
brat, aap, wicht *n*
bravado, bra'voure
brave, moedig: trot'seren
bravery, moed
brawl, vechtpartij
brawn, spieren; hoofdkaas
bray, balken
brazen, bru'taal
breach, (in)breuk, schending;
 bres: door'breken
bread, brood *n*
 slice of bread and butter,
 boterham
breadth, breedte; ruimte
break, breuk, onder'breking,
 pauze: (ver)breken
 to break down, afbreken;
 weigeren; vastlopen; over'stuur
 raken
 to break up, stukbreken; zich
 (*or* doen) ver'spreiden; eindigen

break-down, de'fect *n*; mis'lukking; instorting

breakers, branding

breakfast, ont'bijt(en) *(n)*

breakwater, golfbreker

breast, borst

breath, adem; zuchtje *n*
  out of breath, buiten adem

breathe, ademen, ademhalen

breathless, ademloos, buiten adem

breeches, (knie)broek

breed, ras *n*: voortbrengen, fokken

breeding, fokken *n*; (innerlijke) be'schaving

breeze, bries

breezy, winderig; vrolijk

brevity, kortheid

brew, brouwsel *n*: brouwen; broeien

brewery, brouwe'rij

bribe, omkoopgeld *n*: omkopen

bribery, omkope'rij

brick, baksteen, blok
  you're a brick, het is ge'weldig van je
  to drop a brick, een flater be'gaan

bricklayer, metselaar

brickwork, metselwerk *n*

bridal, bruids-

bride(groom), bruid(egom)

bridesmaid, bruidsmeisje *n*

bridge, brug: bridge *n*: over'bruggen

bridle, teugel, toom: tomen

brief, kort: instru'eren

brief-case, aktentas

brig, brik

brigade, bri'gade

brigand, ban'diet

bright, hel(der); pienter; hoopvol

brighten, oplichten; opvrolijken

brilliance, schittering; geniali'teit

brilliant, schitterend; bril'jant

brim, rand

brimful, boordevol

brine, pekel; zilte nat *n*

bring, (mee)brengen
  to bring about, te'weegbrengen

to bring back, te'rugbrengen; oproepen

to bring on, ver'oorzaken

to bring out, doen uitkomen

to bring round, bijbrengen; overhalen

to bring up, bovenbrengen; grootbrengen; te berde brengen

brink, rand

brisk, kwiek

bristle, borstel(haar *n*): gaan over'eind staan; wemelen van

Britain, Brit'tanje *n*

British, Brits

Briton, Brit

brittle, broos, bros

broach, aansteken; ter sprake brengen

broad, breed; ruim

broadcast, uitzending: uitzenden; ver'spreiden

broaden, (zich) ver'breden; ver'ruimen

broad-minded, ruim van opvatting

broadside, breedzij(vuur *n*)

brocade, bro'kaat *n*

brogue, (Iers) ac'cent *n*; stevige schoen

broil, roosteren

broke, blut

broken-hearted, diep onge'lukkig

broker, makelaar

bronchitis, bron'chitis

bronze, brons *n*: bronzen

brooch, broche

brood, broedsel *n*: broeden

brook, beek: dulden

broom, bezem; brem

broth, boui'llon

brothel, bor'deel *n*

brother, broer, broeder

brotherhood, broederschap

brother-in-law, zwager

brow, voorhoofd *n*; rand

browbeat, intimi'deren

brown, bruin *(n)*
  brown paper, pakpapier *n*

browse, grasduinen

bruise, (blauwe) plek: kneuzen

brunette, bru'nette

brunt, volle kracht

brush, borstel, kwast, pen'seel *n*; staart; scher'mutseling: (af)borstelen, (af)vegen
  to brush past, rakelings gaan langs
brush(wood), kreupelhout *n*
brusque, bruusk
Brussels sprouts, spruitjes
brutal, beestachtig
brutality, wreedheid
brute, bruut
bubble, (lucht)bel: borrelen
buccaneer, boeka'nier
buck, mannetjes(damhert *n*): bokken
  to buck up, opfleuren; opschieten; aanpakken
bucket, emmer
buckle, gesp: vastgespen; krommen
bud, knop: uitbotten
budding, in de dop
budge, (zich) ver'roeren
budget, be'groting
buff, okergeel (*n*): po'lijsten
buffalo, buffel
buffer (-state), buffer(staat)
buffet, buf'fet *n*: stomp(en)
buffoon, pi'as
bug, beestje *n*
bugle, si'gnaalhoorn
build, bouw(en)
  to build up, opbouwen; be'bouwen
builder, aannemer
building, ge'bouw *n*
bulb, (bloem)bol; gloeilamp
bulge, uitpuiling: uitpuilen
bulk, massa: grootste deel *n*
bulkhead, schot *n*
bulky, lijvig, groot
bull, stier: bul
bullet, kogel
bulletin, bulle'tin *n*
bullion, (goud)staven
bullock, os
bully, bullebak: donderen
bulwark, bolwerk *n*
bumble-bee, hommel
bump, knobbel: stoot(en); hotsen
  to bump into, aanbotsen tegen
bumptious, aan'matigend

bumpy, hobbelig
bun, luxe broodje *n*; knoet
bunch, bos(je *n*), tros: op'eenhopen
bundle, pak *n*, bos: samenbinden
bung, spon
  to bung up, (ver')stoppen
bungalow, bungalow
bungle, (ver')knoeien
bunk, kooi: kletspraat: er vandoor gaan
bunting, vlaggen
buoy, boei
buoyant: to be —, drijven; veerkracht hebben
burden, last: laden; drukken
bureau, bu'reau *n*
burglar, inbreker
burglary, inbraak
burial, be'grafenis
burlesque, (parodi'erende) klucht: koddig
burly, stoer
burn, brandwond: (ver')branden; aanbranden
burnish, po'lijsten
burrow, hol *n*: wroeten
burst, barst(en); vlaag: springen
bury, be'graven; ver'bergen
bus, bus
bush, struik; rimboe
business, zaak, zaken
businesslike, zakelijk
bust, borstbeeld *n*, buste
bustle, drukte: queue: druk in de weer zijn
busy, (druk)bezig
  to be busy, het druk hebben
busybody, be'moeial
but, maar: be'halve
butcher, slager; beul: afslachten
butler, hoofdbediende
butt, ton: kolf; peukje *n*: schietbaan: stoten
butter, boter: smeren
buttercup, boterbloem
butterfly, vlinder
buttocks, billen
button, knoop: knopen
buttonhole, knoopsgat *n*: aanklampen
buttress, beer: steunen
buxom, mollig

buy, koop : kopen
buyer, (in)koper
buzz, ge'gons *n* ; gonzen
by, door ; bij ; langs ; per ; volgens
  by train, met de trein
  by night and by day, 's nachts en over'dag
  by and large, over het alge'meen
bye-election, tussentijdse ver'kiezing
bye-law, plaatselijke ver'ordening
by-product, nevenprodukt *n*
bystander, toeschouwer

C

cab, taxi ; ca'bine
cabbage, kool
cabin, hut ; ca'bine
cabinet, kabi'net *n*, kastje *n* ; mi'nisterraad
cable, kabel : telegra'feren
caboodle, rata'plan
cackle, kakelen
cacophony, tegen'strijdig ge'schetter *n*
cactus, cactus
cad, ploert
caddie, golfjongen
caddy, (thee)busje *n*
cadence, ca'dans
cadet, ca'det
cadge, schooieren
café, ca'fé(-restau'rant) *n*
cage, kooi ; opsluiten
cajole, aftroggelen
cake, cake, ge'bak(je) *n* ; taart ; koek(en)
calamity, ramp
calculate, (be')rekenen
calendar, ka'lender
calf, kalf *n* : kuit
calibre, ka'liber *n*
call, tele'foontje *n* : roepen (*n*) ; noemen
  to give a call, roepen
  to pay a call, een be'zoek afleggen
  to be called, heten
  to call off, aflasten

  to call on, be'zoeken ; een be'roep doen op
calling, roeping
callous, onge'voelig
calm, kalm(te) : be'daren
calumny, laster
camel, ka'meel
camera, fototoestel *n*
camouflage, camou'flage : camou'fleren
camp, kamp('eren) (*n*)
campaign, veldtocht ; cam'pagne
can, kan, blik *n* ; kunnen
canal, ka'naal *n*, gracht
canary, ka'narie
cancel, schrappen, afzeggen
cancer, kanker
candid, open('hartig)
candidate, kandi'daat
candle, kaars
candlestick, kandelaar
candour, op'rechtheid
candy, kan'dij ; kon'fijten
  candied peel, su'kade
cane, rotting : riet(en) : afranselen
cannibal, kanni'baal
cannon, ka'non *n* ; ge'schut *n*
canny, slim
canoe, kano
canon, canon ; ka'nunnik
canopy, balda'kijn
cant, ge'kwezel *n* : kantelen
cantankerous, cha'grijnig
canteen, kan'tine
canter, (in) korte ga'lop (draven)
canvas, (zeil)doek *n*
canvass, stemmen werven ; col por'teren
canyon, diep ra'vijn *n*
cap, pet ; dop : over'treffen
  capped, ge'huld (in)
capable, be'kwaam, flink
  capable of, in staat tot ; vat baar voor
capacious, ruim
capacity, inhoud ; ver'mogen *n* ; hoe'danigheid
cape, kaap : cape
caper, capri'olen maken
capital, hoofdstad ; kapi'taal *n* ; hoofdletter : kapi'teel *n* : prima
capitalist, kapita'list

capitulate, capitu'leren
caprice, gril
capsize, omslaan
capstan, kaapstander
captain, kapi'tein, ge'zagvoerder, aanvoerder
caption, onderschrift *n*
captivate, be'toveren
captive, ge'vangen(e)
captivity, ge'vangenschap
capture, ver'overing: ver'overen, ge'vangennemen
car, auto
caravan, woonwagen, kam'peerwagen; kara'vaan
carbolic, car'bol(zuur *n*)
carbon, koolstof; doorslag- (papier *n*)
card, kaart(je *n*)
cardboard, kar'ton *n*
cardigan, vest *n*
cardinal, kardi'naal: hoofd-
cards, kaartspel *n*
  to play cards, kaarten
care, zorg; lust hebben
  to take care of, zorgen voor; passen op
  I don't care, het kan me niets schelen
  to care about, geven om
  to care for, (iets) voelen voor
career, loopbaan, carri'ère
carefree, onbe'zorgd
careful, voor'zichtig; zorg'vuldig
careless, slordig
caress, liefkozing: liefkozen
caretaker, conci'ërge
cargo, lading, vracht
cargo-boat, vrachtschip *n*
caricature, karika'tuur
carillon, klokkenspel *n*
carnage, slachting
carnal, vleselijk
carnation, anjer
carnival, carna'val *n*
carol, (Kerst)lied *n*: kwelen
carouse, zwelgen
carp, karper: vitten
carpenter, timmerman: timmeren
carpet, ta'pijt *n*
carriage, rijtuig *n*, wa'gon; ver'voer *n*; houding

carrier, voerman; ba'gagedrager
carrion, aas
carrot, wortel
carry, dragen, houden
  to carry away, meeslepen
  to carry off, in de wacht slepen; klaarspelen
  to carry on, doorgaan; uitoefenen; zich (slecht) ge'dragen
  to carry out, uitvoeren
cart, kar: ver'voeren
cartilage, kraakbeen *n*
carton, kar'ton *n*
cartoon, (spot)prent; tekenfilm
cartridge, pa'troon
carve, snijden; beeldhouwen
carving, snijwerk *n*: voorsnij
cascade, kleine waterval; stortvloed: neerstorten
case, koker, koffer, kist: ge'val *n*, zaak
  in case, voor het ge'val dat
casement window, openslaand raam *n*
cash, (ge'reed) geld *n*, con'tant(en): wisselen
cashier, kas'sier: cas'seren
cask, vat *n*
cassock, sou'tane
cast, worp; afgietsel *n*; rolverdeling: werpen; gieten
cast iron, ge'goten ijzer *n*
castle, kas'teel *n*
castor, rolletje *n*
casual, noncha'lant; toe'vallig: vluchtig
casualty, ongeval *n*
  casualties, doden en ge'wonden
cat, kat
catalogue, ca'talogus
catapult, katapult
cataract, waterval: staar
catastrophe, cata'strofe, ramp
catch, vangst; valstrik; haak: (op)vangen; halen; be'trappen; vatten; (blijven) haken; treffen
  to catch on, ingang vinden
  to catch up, inhalen
categorical, cate'gorisch
category, catego'rie
cater, maaltijden ver'zorgen; rekening houden (met)

caterpillar, rups
cathedral, kathe'draal
catholic, katho'liek; veel'zijdig
cattle, vee n
cauliflower, bloemkool
cause, oorzaak, (be'weeg)reden; zaak: ver'oorzaken
causeway, dam
caustic, brandend; bijtend
caution, voor'zichtigheid: waarschuwen
cautious, voor'zichtig
cavalry, cavale'rie
cave(rn), grot
   to cave in, inzakken
cavity, holte
caw, krassen
cease, ophouden (met)
ceaseless, voort'durend
cedar, ceder(hout n)
cede, afstaan
ceiling, pla'fond n; maximum n
celebrate, vieren
celebrated, ver'maard
celebration, viering, feest n
celebrity, be'roemdheid
celery, selderij
celestial, hemels, hemel-
celibacy, celi'baat n
cell, cel
cellar, kelder
cello, cel
cellophane, cello'faan n
cellulose, cellu'lose
cement, ce'ment
cemetry, be'graafplaats
censor, censor: censu'reren
censure, be'risping: bekriti'seren
census, volkstelling
centenary, eeuwfeest n
centigrade, Celsius
central, cen'traal, midden-, hoofd-
centralize, centrali'seren
centre, middelpunt n, centrum n
   in the centre of, midden in
century, eeuw
cereal, graan(pro'duct) n
ceremonial, ceremoni'eel (n)
ceremony, cere'monie, formali'teit(en)
certain(ty), zeker(heid)

certificate, di'ploma n, akte, at'test n
certify, (plechtig) ver'klaren
cessation, staken n
chafe, schuren
chaff, kaf n: voor de gek houden
chagrin, ergernis
chain, ketting; keten(en); reeks
chair, stoel
chairman(ship), voorzitter-(schap n)
chalice, kelk
chalk, krijt n
challenge, uitdaging: uitdagen, aanroepen, be'twisten
chamber, kamer
chamois, gems; zeemleer n
champ, kauwen
champion, kampi'oen; voorstander: voorstaan
chance, kans; toeval n: toe'vallig: wagen
chancel, koor n
chancellor, kanse'lier
chandelier, kroon(luchter)
change, ver'andering, overgang; kleingeld n: ver'anderen; (ver)wisselen, (ver')ruilen; (zich) ver'kleden; overstappen
   to change one's mind, zich be'denken
changeable, ver'anderlijk
change-over, overgang
channel, Ka'naal n; vaargeul, goot; weg
chant, (be')zingen; dreunen
chaos, chaos
chap, kerel: barsten
chapel, ka'pel
chaperon, chape'ron('neren)
chaplain (to the forces), (leger)-predi'kant
chapter, hoofdstuk n; ka'pittel n
char, schroeien, ver'kolen
character, ka'rakter n; type n
characteristic, kenmerk(end (voor)) (n)
characterize, kenmerken
charcoal, houtskool
charge, aanval(len); (be')last-(en); lading; be'schuldiging: laden; be'schuldigen

to be in charge of, de leiding hebben van; be'last zijn met
to (make a) charge, rekenen
charitable, mens'lievend
charity, lief'dadigheid(s-), naastenliefde
charm, charme; tovermiddel *n*; ge'lukshanger: be'koren; be'toveren
charming, char'mant; aller'aardigst
chart, kaart; grafische voorstelling: in kaart brengen
charter, charter(en) (*n*)
charwoman, werkster
chary, huiverig
chase, jacht(stoet): (na)jagen; drijven
chasm, kloof
chassis, chassis *n*
chaste, kuis
chasten, chastise, kas'tijden
chat, babbeltje *n*: babbelen
chatter, kletsen, ratelen
chatterbox, kletskous
cheap, goed'koop, waardeloos
cheat, valse speler: be'driegen, vals spelen
check, rem; ruit: stuiten; contro'leren
check(mate), schaak(mat) (zetten)
in check, in toom
to check up, nagaan
cheek, wang; brutali'teit
cheek-bone, jukbeen
cheer, juichkreet: (toe)juichen; opmonteren
three cheers, een hoe'raatje *n*; lang leve . . .
cheerful, vrolijk
cheerless, troosteloos
cheese, kaas
chemical, chemisch(e stof), schei'kundig
chemist, schei'kundige; dro'gist
chemistry, scheikunde
cheque, cheque
chequered, af'wisselend
cherish, koesteren
cherry, kers(eboom)
cherub, cheru'bijn
chess: to play —, schaken

chess(-set), schaakspel *n*
chest, borst(kas); kist
chestnut, kas'tanje(boom)
chew, kauwen
chick, kuiken *n*
chicken, kip
chicken-pox, waterpokken
chicory, cicho'rei; witlof
chide, be'rispen
chief, hoofd(-) (*n*); voor'naamste
chiefly, voor'namelijk
chieftain, opperhoofd
chilblain(ed feet), winter(voeten)
child(ren), kind(eren) *n*
childbirth, be'valling
childhood, kinderjaren
childish, kinderachtig, kinderlijk
childlike, kinderlijk
chill, kou: afkoelen
chill(y), kil; koel
chime, klokkenspel *n*, klokslag: luiden
chimney, schoorsteen
chin, kin
china, porse'lein(en) (*n*)
chink, spleet: rinkelen
chip, scherf; fiche: stoten, bikken
chiropodist, pedi'cure
chirp, tjilpen
chisel, beitel(en)
chit, jong ding *n*: briefje *n*
chivalrous, ridderlijk
chivalry, ridderlijkheid
chlorine, chloor *n*
chock, klos
chock-full, propvol
chocolate, choco'la(de), choco'laatje *n*
choice, keus: prima
choir, koor *n*
choke, (doen) stikken, zich ver'slikken; ver'stoppen
choose, (uit)kiezen, ver'kiezen
chop, karbo'nade; kaak: (fijn)hakken
chopper, hakbijl
choppy, woelig
choral, koor-
chord, ak'koord *n*; snaar
chortle, hardop grinniken van pret

chorus, koor *n*; re'frein *n*
christen, dopen
Christendom, Christenheid
christening, doop(dienst)
Christian, Christen: Christelijk
 Christian name, voornaam
Christianity, Christendom *n*;
 Christelijkheid
Christmas, Kerstmis: Kerst-
 Christmas Day, Eerste Kerstdag
chromium(-plated), (ver')-
 chroom(d) (*n*)
chronic, chronisch
chronicle, kro'niek: boekstaven
chronological, chrono'logisch
chubby, mollig
chuck, aai: smijten
chuckle, ge'grinnik *n*: grinniken
 (om)
chug, puffen
chum, maat
chunk, klomp, homp.
church, kerk
 Church of England, Angli'-
 kaanse Kerk
churchyard, kerkhof *n*
churlish, lomp
churn, karn, melkbus: karnen;
 woelen
chute, glijbaan, glijkoker
cider, cider
cigar, si'gaar
cigarette, siga'ret
cinder, sintel
cinema, bios'coop
cinnamon, ka'neel
cipher, cijferschrift *n*; nul
circle, cirkel(en); kring
circuit, kring(loop); (stroom)-
 baan
circuitous, om'slachtig
circular, cirkel'vormig, rond-
 (gaand): circu'laire
circulate, (laten) circu'leren
circulation, circu'latie; bloedsomloop; oplaag
circumference, omtrek
circumscribe, om'schrijven
circumspect, om'zichtig
circumstance, om'standigheid,
 bij'zonderheid
circus, circus *n*

cistern, waterreservoir *n*
cite, ci'teren; noemen
citizen, (staats)burger
city, stad(s-)
civic, burger-, stads-
civil, burgerlijk, burger-; be'leefd
 civil servant, ambtenaar
civilian, burger
civilization, be'schaving
civilize, be'schaven
clad, ge'kleed
claim, aanspraak (maken op);
 vordering: (op)eisen; be'weren
clamber, klauteren
clammy, klam
clamorous, luid('ruchtig)
clamour, ge'tier *n*: schreeuwen
clamp, klamp(en)
clan, stam
clang, galm: kletteren
clap, slag; klap(pen (met)),
 applaudis'seren; slaan
clarify, klaren; ophelderen
clarity, duidelijkheid
clash, botsing: botsen; vloeken
clasp, gesp(en); (vast)grijpen
class, klas(se); stand: lesuur *n*:
 plaatsen
classic, klas'siek (werk *n*)
classical, klas'siek
classify, klassifi'ceren
classroom, klaslokaal *n*
clatter, ge'kletter *n*: kletteren
clause, clau'sule, bijzin
claw, klauw(en), poot
clay, klei
clean, schoon(maken), rein(igen);
 zindelijk
cleanliness, zindelijkheid
cleanse, zuiveren
clear, helder, duidelijk; vrij-
 (maken): ophelderen; vrijspreken; ont'ruimen
 to clear off, maken dat men
 wegkomt
 to clear up, ver'duidelijken;
 opruimen; ophelderen
clear-cut, scherp om'lijnd
clearing, open plek
cleavage, scheuring
cleave, kloven; kleven
cleft, kloof: ge'spleten
clemency, mildheid

clench, ballen ; vastklemmen
  clenched teeth, tanden op
  el'kaar
clergy, geestelijken
clergyman, dominee
clerical, administra'tief ; geestelijk
clerk, klerk, grif'fier
clever, knap
click, klik(ken)
client, klant
cliff, klif
climate, kli'maat *n*
climax, climax
climb, (be')klim(men)
  to climb down, afklimmen ;
  inbinden
clinch, vastklinken ; be'klinken,
  be'slechten
cling, zich vastklemmen, plakken
clinic, kli'niek
clink, klink(en)
clip, klem(metje *n*) ; mep : klemmen ; knippen
clippers, schaar, ton'deuse ; klip-
  pers
clipping, (uit)knipsel *n*
cloak, (dek)mantel : hullen
cloak-room, garde'robe
clock, klok
clockwise, met de klok mee
clockwork, (met) mecha'niek *n*
clod, (aard)kluit
clog, klomp : ver'stoppen
cloister, klooster(gang)
close, dicht'bij ; scherp ; nauw ;
  in'tiem : ingesloten ruimte ;
  einde *n* : (af)sluiten
  to close down (*or* **up**), sluiten
close-fisted, gierig
closet, kabi'net *n* ; opsluiten.
clot, kluit : klonteren, stollen
cloth, stof ; kleed *n*, doek
clothe, kleden
clothes, kleren
clothes-line, drooglijn
clothes-peg, knijper
clothing, kleding
cloud, wolk : ver'troebelen
  to cloud over, be'trekken
cloudy, be'wolkt ; troebel
clout, mep (geven)
clove, kruidnagel

clover, klaver
clown, clown
club, knots ; club, socië'tiet ;
  klaver : knuppelen
cluck, klokken
clue, aanwijzing, sleutel
clump, groep, brok : klossen
clumsy, on'handig
cluster, tros, bos, groep : zich
  scharen
clutch, klauw ; koppeling : (vast)-
  pakken
clutter, warboel : volproppen
coach, koets, dili'gence, touring-
  car, spoorrijtuig *n* ; trainer,
  repe'titor : trainen, repe'teren
coagulate, stremmen
coal, kolen(-) ; steenkool
coalesce, samensmelten
coalition, coa'litie
coarse, grof
coast, kust : glijden, freewheelen
coat, jas, mantel ; vel *n* ; (verf)-
  laag : be'dekken
  coat of arms, wapen *n*
coat-hanger, kleerhanger
coax, vleiend be'praten
cobble(-stone), keisteen
cobbler, schoenlapper
cobweb, spinneweb *n*
cock, haan : de haan spannen
  van ; scheefhouden
cock-eyed, scheef
cockpit, cockpit
cocktail, cocktail
cocky, bru'taal
cocoa, ca'cao
coconut, kokosnoot
cod, kabel'jauw
code, code(stelsel *n*) ; wet
coercion, dwang
coffee, koffie
coffin, doodkist
cog, tandrad *n*
cogent, effec'tief
cogitate, nadenken
coherent, samenhangend, logisch
coil, tros, spi'raal : oprollen
coin, munt(stuk *n*) : smeden
coincide, samenvallen
coincidence, samenloop van omstandigheden
coke, cokes

colander, ver'giet

cold, koud; koel: ver'koudheid

  to have a cold, ver'kouden zijn

collaborate, samenwerken

collapse, instorting: in el'kaar zakken

collapsible, op'vouwbaar

collar, kraag, boord, halsband

colleague, col'lega

collect, (zich) ver'zamelen

collection, ver'zameling, col'lecte; buslichting

collector, ver'zamelaar

college, college n, (hoge')school

collide, botsen

colliery, kolenmijn

collision, botsing, aanvaring

colon, dubbel punt

colonel, kolo'nel

colonial, koloni'aal

colonize, koloni'seren

colonnade, zuilengang

colony, ko'lonie

colossal, reus'achtig

colour, kleur(en), verf

colourful, kleurrijk

colt, (hengst)veulen

column, zuil; ko'lom

coma, coma n

comb, kam(men); afzoeken

combat, strijd: be'strijden

combination, combi'natie

combine, syndi'caat n; com'bine: combi'neren

combustion, ver'branding

come, komen, meegaan

  to come about, ge'beuren

  to come across, overkomen; tegenkomen

  to come round, aanlopen; (bij)draaien; bijkomen

  to come in, binnenkomen; mode worden

  to come off, afkomen; doorgaan, lukken

comedian, ko'miek, komedi'ant

comedy, blijspel n

comely, be'vallig

comet, ko'meet

comfort, troost(en); ge'mak n, welstand

comfortable, be'hagelijk

  to be comfortable, ge'makkelijk zitten (or liggen)

comfortably off, in goede doen

comic, komisch; (kinder)krantje n

coming, (op)komend; komst

comma, komma

command, be'vel(en) (n); com'mando n (voeren); be'schikking: be'schikken over; be'strijken

  commanding officer, comman'dant

commandeer, (op)vorderen

commander, be'velhebber; kapi'tein-luitenant

commandment, ge'bod n

commemorate, her'denken

commence, be'ginnen

commend, prijzen; aanbevelen

commendable, prijzens'waardig

comment, opmerking(en maken)

commentary, commen'taar n

commentator, ver'slaggever

commerce, handel(sverkeer n)

commercial, handels-

commiserate, sympathi'seren

commission, opdracht (geven); (offi'ciers) aanstelling; pro'visie: machtigen; aanstellen; in dienst stellen

commissioner, ge'volmachtigde, (hoofd)commis'saris

commit, plegen, be'gaan; toevertrouwen

  to commit oneself, zich ver'binden

commitment, ver'plichting

committee, comi'té n, be'stuur n, com'missie

commodious, ruim

commodity, ge'bruiksartikel n

common, ge'meen('schappelijk), ge'woon, algemeen: meent

  common sense, ge'zond ver'stand n

  in common, ge'meen

commonplace, alle'daags: ge'meenplaats

commonwealth, gemene'best n

commotion, opschudding

communal, gemeen'schappelijk

communicate, ver'binding heb-

ben, zich in ver'binding stellen;
mededelen

communication, mededeling,
schrijven *n*; ver'binding (sweg)

communicative, mede'deelzaam

communion, ge'meenschap;
Com'munie

communism, commu'nisme *n*

community, ge'meenschap;
broederschap

compact, com'pact: over'eenkomst

companion, metgezel; ge'zelschapsdame

companionable, ge'zellig

companionship, ge'zelschap *n*,
vriendschap

company, ge'zelschap *n*; ven'-
nootschap; compag'nie; be'-
zoek *n*

comparable, te verge'lijken

comparative, be'trekkelijk,
verge'lijkend

compare, (te) verge'lijken (zijn)

comparison, verge'lijking

compartment, afdeling; cou'pé

compass, kom'pas *n*; passer;
omtrek, be'stek *n*; vatten

compassion, er'barmen *n*

compassionate, mee'warig

compatriot, landgenoot

compel, (af)dwingen

compensate for, schadeloos stellen voor, ver'goeden; opwegen
tegen

compensation, ver'goeding,
compen'satie

compete, wedijveren, mededingen (naar)

competence, be'voegdheid, be'-
kwaamheid

competent, be'kwaam, be'voegd

competition, wedstrijd; concur'rentie

competitive, verge'lijkend

competitor, deelnemer, concur'rent

compile, samenstellen

complacent, gauw te'vreden

complain, klagen

complaint, (aan)klacht; kwaal

complement, aanvuling; be'-
manning

complete, vol'ledig, vol'tallig,
vol'slagen; vol'tooien; be'-
sluiten, aanvullen

complex, com'plex (*n*)

complexion, ge'laatskleur

compliance, inwilliging

complicate, compli'ceren

complicated, inge'wikkeld

complication, compli'catie

complicity, mede'plichtigheid

compliment, compli'ment ('eren)
(*n*)

complimentary, complimen'-
teus; pre'sent-, vrij-

comply with, vol'doen aan

component, be'standdeel *n*:
samenstellend

compose, samenstellen, compo'neren

to be composed of, be'staan uit

to compose oneself, be'daren

composer, compo'nist

composite, samengesteld

composition, samenstelling; compo'sitie; opstel *n*

composure, zelfbeheersing

compound, samengesteld:
samenstelling, ver'binding: erf
n: (ver')mengen

comprehend, (om')vatten

comprehension, be'grip *n*

comprehensive, veelom'vattend

compress, kom'pres *n*: samen-
persen, compri'meren

comprise, be'vatten

compromise, compro'mis *n*: tot
een schikking komen; com-
promit'teren

compulsion, dwang

compulsory, ver'plicht

compunction, scru'pules

compute, be'rekenen

comrade, kame'raad

concave, hol

conceal, ver'bergen

concede, toegeven, toestaan

conceit, ver'waandheid; spits'-
vondigheid

conceited, ver'waand

conceivable, denkbaar

conceive, zich een voorstelling
maken van; be'vrucht worden

concentrate, (zich) concen'treren

concentric, con'centrisch

concept, be'grip n

conception, voorstelling, opvatting; be'vruchting

concern, zaak, be'lang n; be'zorgdheid; onder'neming: aangaan

to be concerned, be'lang hebben bij; be'trokken zijn bij; zich bezighouden met; be'zorgd zijn over

as far as I'm concerned, wat mij be'treft

concerning, be'treffende

concert(o), con'cert n

concerted, ge'zamenlijk

concession, con'cessie

conciliate, gunstig stemmen

concise, be'knopt

conclude, (be')sluiten; opmaken

conclusion, be'sluit n, slot n; ge'volgtrekking

conclusive, afdoend

concoct, brouwen; ver'zinnen

concord, eendracht

concrete, be'ton(nen) (n); con'creet

concubine, bijzit

concur, het eens zijn; bijdragen

concurrence, instemming; samenwerking

concurrent, gelijk'tijdig

concussion, (hersen)schudding

condemn, ver'oordelen, afkeuren

condensation, conden'satie

condense, conden'seren; samenvatten

condescend, zich ver'waardigen

condescending, neer'buigend

condition, voorwaarde; con'ditie, staat, toestand

(weather) conditions, (weers)-om'standigheden

condolence, deelneming

condone, ver'goelijken

conducive, be'vorderlijk

conduct, ge'drag(en) (n); be'handeling: (ge')leiden; diri'-geren

conductor, (ge')leider; diri'gent; conduc'teur

cone, kegel; (denne)appel

confectionery, suikergoed n

confederate, mede'plichtige: ver'bonden

confederation, ver'bond n

confer, ver'lenen (aan); be'raadslagen

conference, confe'rentie

confess, be'kennen; be'lijden; biechten

confession, be'kentenis; biecht

confidant(e), ver'trouweling(e)

confide in, in ver'trouwen nemen

confide to, toevertrouwen

confidence, ver'trouwen n

confident, vol ('zelf)ver'trouwen; over'tuigd

confidential, ver'trouwelijk

confine, grens: be'perken

to be confined to one's bed or barracks, het bed moeten houden; kwar'tier-arrest hebben

confinement, be'valling; ge'vangenschap

confirm, be'vestigen; be'krachtigen; vormen

confirmed, vaststaand; chronisch, ver'stokt

confiscate, ver'beurd ver'klaren

conflagration, vlammenzee

conflict, con'flict n: in strijd zijn

conflicting, (tegen')strijdig

conform, zich schikken (naar); over'eenkomen

confound, in de war brengen; ver'vloeken

confront, confron'teren

to be confronted by, komen te staan tegen'over; zich ge'plaatst zien in

confuse, ver'warren

confusion, ver'warring

confute, weer'leggen

congeal, stollen

congenial, prettig, sympa'thiek

congenital, (aan)ge'boren

congest, (zich) ophopen

conglomeration, conglome'raat n

congratulate, ge'lukwensen

congratulation, ge'lukwens

congregate, (zich) ver'zamelen

congregation, ge'meente; ver'zameling

congress, con'gres *n*
conical, kegelvormig
coniferous, kegeldragend
conjecture, gissing
conjugate, ver'voegen
conjunction, voegwoord *n*
  in conjunction with, samen met
conjure, goochelen : be'zweren
  to conjure up, oproepen
conjurer, goochelaar
connect, (aan el'kaar) ver'binden; in ver'band brengen; aansluiten (op)
connexion, ver'binding; ver'band *n*; re'latie
connive at, door de vingers zien; — **(with),** in ge'heime ver'standhouding staan (met)
connoisseur, fijnproever, kenner
connote, (tege'lijk) be'tekenen
conquer, ver'overen, over'winnen; meester worden
conscience, ge'weten *n*
conscience-smitten ge'kweld
conscientious, plichtsgetrouw
conscious, (zich) be'wust; bij kennis
consciousness, be'wustzijn *n*
conscript, dienst'plichtig(e) : oproepen, vorderen
conscription, con'scriptie
consecrate, (in)wijden
consecutive, op'eenvolgend, samenhangend
consent, toestemming, instemming; toe(*or* in)stemmen
consequence, ge'volg *n*
  in consequence, dientenge'volge
  of consequence, be'langrijk
consequent, daaruit voortvloeiend
consequently, dientenge'volge
conservation, in'standhouding, be'houd *n*
conservative, conserva'tief
conservatory, serre
conserve, op peil houden; conser'veren
consider, over'wegen; be'schouwen als, in aanmerking nemen, rekening houden met; menen

all things considered, alles welbe'schouwd
considerable, aan'zienlijk
considerate, at'tent
consideration, over'weging; factor; conside'ratie; ver'goeding
considered, welover'wogen; ge'acht
considering, ge'zien; (alles) welbe'schouwd
consign, depo'neren; over-leveren, toevertrouwen
consignment, zending
consist of, be'staan uit
consistency, consis'tentie
consistent, conse'quent; op één lijn met
consolation, troost
consolidate, ver'sterken; con-soli'deren
consonant, medeklinker
consort, ge'maal : omgaan
conspicuous, in het oog lopend; treffend
conspiracy, samenzwering
conspirator, samenzweerder
conspire, samenzweren; samen-werken
constable, po'litieagent; slot-voogd
constancy, stand'vastigheid; trouw
constant, vast; voort'durend; trouw : con'stante
constellation, sterrenbeeld *n*
consternation, ont'steltenis
constipation, consti'patie
constituency, kiesdistrict *n*
constituent, be'standdeel *n*; kiezer
constitute, vormen; aanstellen
constitution, ge'stel *n*; samenstelling; grondwet
constitutional, aangeboren, voor het ge'stel; constitutio'neel
constrain, be'dwingen
constraint, (be')dwang; ge'-dwongenheid
constrict, be'klemmen; binden; samentrekken
construct, (op)bouwen
construction, (aan)bouw, con'-structie; uitleg

constructive, opbouwend

construe, ver'klaren; con-stru'eren

consul(ate), consul('aat n)

consult, raadplegen

consultation, raadpleging, con'sult n; be'raadslaging

consume, ver'bruiken, ver'orber-en; ver'teren, ver'nietigen

consummate, vol'maakt: in-ver'vulling doen gaan

consumption, ver'bruik n, con'sumptie; tering

contact, con'tact n; zich in ver'binding stellen met

contagious, be'smettelijk; aan'stekelijk

contain, be'vatten; inhouden

container, blik n, doos

contaminate, veront'reinigen

contemplate, (over')peinzen; be'schouwen; van plan zijn

contemplation, ge'peins n, over'weging; be'spiegeling

contemporary, van de'zelfde tijd, hedendaags: tijdgenoot

contempt, ver'achting

contemptible, ver'achtelijk

contemptuous, minachtend

contend, be'togen

   to contend with, kampen met, aankunnen

content(s), inhoud; ge'halte n

content(ed), te'vreden

contention, twist; be'wering

contentment, te'vredenheid

contest, (wed)strijd: be'twisten

contestant, mededinger, deel-nemer

context, ver'band n

continent, vaste'land n, wereld-deel n

continental, continen'taal

contingency, eventuali'teit

contingent, af'hankelijk, even-tu'eel: contin'gent n; situ'atie

continual(ly), voort'durend, her'haald(elijk)

continuance, voortzetting

continuation, voortzetting, ver'volg n

continue, voortgaan (met); voortzetten

continuity, samenhang; con-tinuï'teit

continuous, on'afgebroken, door'lopend

contort, (ver')draaien

contour, con'tour

contraband, contrabande

contract, con'tract n (aangaan); (zich) samentrekken; aannemen, oplopen

contraction, inkrimping, samen-trekking

contractor, aannemer

contradict, tegenspreken, ont'kennen

contradiction, tegenspraak, tegen'strijdigheid

contradictory, (tegen')strijdig, weer'spannig

contralto, alt

contraption, uitvindsel n, meka'niek(je n)

contrary, tegengesteld(e n), tegen-; ba'lorig

   contrary to, tegen . . . in

   on the contrary, in'tegendeel

contrast, tegenstelling: tegen-over al'kaar stellen, een con'trast n vormen

contravene, in strijd zijn met

contribute, bijdragen

contribution, bijdrage

contributory, secun'dair, zij-

contrition, diep be'rouw n

contrivance, uitvinding

contrive, be'ramen; ervoor zor-gen

control, be'heer(sing) (n); con'trole; stuurinrichting: in be'dwang houden, be'heersen, be'heren, regelen

controversial, be'twistbaar, strijd-

controversy, ge'schil n

convalescence, her'stel n

convene, bij'eenroepen, bij'een-komen

convenience, ge'rief(elijkheid) (n), ge'mak n

convenient, ge'schikt, ge'rie-felijk

convent, nonnenklooster n; zusterschool

convention, con'ventie; samenkomst; over'eenkomst
conventional, conventio'neel
converge, conver'geren; zich
concen'treren
conversant, ver'trouwd
conversation, ge'sprek *n*
converse, omgekeerd (e *n*):
conver'seren
conversion, omzetting; be'-
kering
convert, be'keerling: omzetten,
ver'anderen; be'keren
convex, bol
convey, ver'voeren, overdragen;
betekenen, overbrengen
conveyance, ver'voer (middel) *n*;
overdracht; overbrengen *n*
convict, dwangarbeider:
schuldig ver'klaren
conviction, over'tuiging:
schuldigverklaring
convince, over'tuigen
convivial, feestelijk
convoy, kon'vooi ('eren) (*n*)
convulse, (doen) schudden;
samentrekken; stuiptrekken
coo, kirren (*n*)
cook, kok ('kin): koken; knoeien
met
cooker, for'nuis *n*
cookery, koken *n*; kook-
cooking, koken *n*, keuken:
moes (appel), stoof (peer)
cool, koel (te); kalm; bru'taal:
ver'koelen, afkoelen
coop, hok: opsluiten
co-operate, samenwerken
co-operative, be'hulpzaam;
coöpera'tief
co-ordinate, coördi'neren
cope, koorkap: klaarspelen
to cope (with it), het aankunnen
copious, ruim
copper, (rood) koper (en) (*n*);
kopergeld *n*; wasketel:
smeris
copse, kreupelbosje *n*
copy, ko'pie; exem'plaar *n*:
namaken, nadoen
to copy out, overschrijven
copyright, ko'pijrecht *n*
coquetry, kokette'rie

coral, ko'raal: ko'ralen
cord, koord *n*
cordial, hartelijk: sap *n*, drank
corduroy, ribfluweel *n*
core, klokhuis *n*; kern
cork, kurk (en)
corkscrew, kurketrekker
corn, koren *n*: likdoorn
corner, hoek: in het nauw
drijven
cornflour, mai'zena
coronation, kroning
coroner, magi'straat bij een
lijkschouwing
coronet, kroontje *n*
corporal, korpo'raal: lijf-
corporate, met rechtspersoon-
lijkheid; ge'zamenlijk
corporation, rechtspersoon, cor-
po'ratie; buikje *n*
corps, korps *n*
corpse, lijk *n*
corpulent, zwaar'lijvig
correct, juist, goed, cor'rect:
corri'geren
correction, cor'rectie
corrective, ver'beterend; cor-
rec'tief *n*
correspond, over'eenkomen;
correspon'deren
correspondence, correspon'dentie; over'eenkomst
correspondent, correspon'dent
corresponding, overeen'komstig
corridor, gang
corroborate, be'vestigen
corrode, aantasten, ver'roesten
corrosion, cor'rosie
corrugated, golf-
corrupt, cor'rupt, ver'dorven:
be'derven
corruption, cor'ruptie, ver'derf *n*
corset(s), kor'set *n*
cosh, ploertendoder
cosmetic, kos'metisch: schoonheidsmiddel *n*
cosmopolitan, kosmopo'litisch
cost, prijs, kosten
costermonger, venter
costly, duur, kostbaar
costume, kos'tuum *n*, klederdracht
cosy, knus: muts

cot, kinderbedje *n*
cottage, huisje *n*
cotton, ka'toen(en) (*n*), garen *n*:
snappen
cotton-wool, watten
couch, rustbank: stellen
cough, hoest(en)
council, raad
counsel, raad(geven), be'raadslaging; advo'caat
count, tel(ling): graaf: (mee)-
tellen; rekenen
to count out, uittellen; uitschakelen
countenance, ge'laat(suitdruk-
king) (*n*): sanctio'neren
counter, toonbank, balie, lo'ket
n; fiche, teller: tegen ... in:
be'antwoorden
counter-, tegen-
counteract, neutrali'seren,
tegenwerken
counterbalance, tegenwicht;
opwegen tegen
counterfeit, nagemaakt: namaken
counterfoil, strook
countermand, annu'leren
counterpart, tegenhanger
countersign, medeondertekenen
countess, gra'vin
countless, talloos
country, (platte')land *n*, streek:
landelijk
in the country, buiten
countryman, landgenoot;
buitenman
countryside, landschap *n*
county, graafschap *n*
couple, paar *n*, stel *n*: koppelen;
combi'neren
coupon, bon, cou'pon
courage(ous), moed(ig)
courier, koe'rier
course, (be')loop (*n*), koers,
richting; gang; renbaan;
cursus; ge'dragslijn
in due course, te zijner tijd
in the course of, in de loop van
of course, na'tuurlijk
court, hof(houding) (*n*), (binnen)-
plaats; rechtbank, rechtszaal;
baan: het hof maken; zoeken

courteous, hoffelijk
courtesy, hoffelijkheid; gunst
courtier, hoveling
court-martial, (voor de) krijgsraad (brengen)
courtyard, binnenplaats
cousin, neef, nicht
cove, inham: vent
covenant, ver'bond *n*; con'tract
n
cover, deksel *n*; (buiten)band;
dekking: (be')dekken; ver'bergen; afleggen; onder vuur
hebben; ver'slaan
covert, heimelijk: schuilplaats
covet, be'geren
cow, koe: intimi'deren
coward, lafaard
cowardice, lafheid
cower, in'eenkrimpen
cowhide, rundleer *n*
cowl, monnikskap; schoor-
steenkap
cowslip, sleutelbloem
coxswain, stuurman
coy, schuchter
crab, krab
crack, barst(en), kier; klap(pen);
krieken *n*: prima: kraken;
tappen (*jokes*); overslaan
to crack up, be'zwijken; ophemelen
cracker, knalbonbon, voetzoeker; cracker
crackle, knappen, kraken
cradle, wieg; bakermat
craft, ambacht *n*, kunst'vaardigheid; sluwheid; vaartuig(en) *n*
craftsman(ship), vakman(schap
n)
crafty, listig, sluw
crag, steile rots(punt *n*)
cram, (vol)proppen, schrokken;
(in)pompen
cramp, kram(p): opsluiten,
be'krimpen; be'lemmeren
crane, kraan(vogel): uitrekken
crank, slinger; zonderling:
aanslingeren
crash, klap, slag; botsing, neer-
storting: in('een)storten, neerstorten; over de kop gaan
crass, grof

crate, krat
crater, krater
cravat, cra'vate
crave, hunkeren; smeken
craving, be'geerte
crawl, slakkengang: kruipen; wemelen
crayon, kleurpotlood n; kleuren
craze, rage
crazy, gek; fanta'sie-
creak, kraken
cream, (slag)room, crème; puik n: afromen
creamy, roomachtig
crease, vouw(en); kreuken
create, scheppen; te'weegbrengen
creation, schepping; cre'atie
creative, scheppend
creature, schepsel n
credentials, ge'loofs(or in-tro'ductie)brieven
credible, geloof'waardig
credit, kre'diet n, te'goed n, batig saldo n; ge'loof n, eer: credi'teren; ge'loven; toe-schrijven
creditor, schuldeiser
credulous, lichtge'lovig
creed, ge'loofsbelijdenis
creek, kreek
creep, kruipen, sluipen
creeper, klimplant
cremate, ver'assen
creosote, creo'soot
crepe, crêpe
crescent, wassende maan; ge'bogen straat
cress, sterre'kers
crest, kuif, pluim; helmteken n; top
crestfallen, ter'neergeslagen
crevasse, gletscherspleet
crevice, scheur
crew, be'manning, ploeg; troep
crib, kribbe; spiekbriefje n: spieken
crick, kramp
cricket, cricket n: krekel
crime, misdaad, misdrijf n
criminal, mis'dadig, straf-: misdadiger
crimson, karmo'zijn(rood) (n)
cringe, in'eenkrimpen; kruipen

crinkle, kronkel(en)
crinoline, crino'line
cripple, ge'brekkige: ver'minken; ont'wrichten, ver'lammen
crisis, crisis
crisp, bros; scherp
criss-cross, kriskras
criterion, maatstaf
critic, criticus
critical, kritisch; kri'tiek
criticism, kri'tiek
criticize, (be)kriti'seren
croak, ge'kwaak n: kwaken, krassen
crochet, haken
crock, aarden pot; wrak n
crockery, ser'viesgoed n
crocodile, kroko'dil
crocus, krokus
crony, boezemvriend(in)
crook, staf; oplichter: krommen
crooked, scheef, krom; vals
croon, neuriën; croonen
crop, oogst, ge'was n; krop; zweep: afvreten; kortknippen
croquet, croquet n
croquette, cro'quet
cross, kruis(ing) (n): dwars-; boos: (el'kaar) kruisen; tegen-werken
to cross oneself, een kruis slaan
to cross out, doorhalen
to cross (over), oversteken
it crossed my mind, het schoot me door het hoofd
cross-country, dwars door het land
cross-examination, kruisver-hoor n
cross-eyed, scheel
crossing, kruispunt n; over-tocht; oversteekplaats
cross-purposes: at —, langs el'kaar heen
cross-roads, kruispunt n; tweesprong
cross-section, (dwars)doorsnee
crosswise, kruiselings
crochet, kwartnoot
crouch, in el'kaar duiken
croup, kroep
crow, kraai(en)
crowbar, koevoet

crowd, menigte, stel n: (zich)
(ver')dringen

crowded, vol, druk

crown, kroon, krans; kruin, bol:
kronen (tot); be'kronen

crucial, kri'tiek

crucible, smeltkroes

crucifix, kruisbeeld n

crucifixion, kruisiging

crucify, kruisigen

crude, ruw; grof

cruel(ty), wreed(heid)

cruet, peper-en-'zoutstel n

cruise, (zee)reis: kruisen

cruiser, kruiser

crumb, kruimel(en)

crumble, (ver')kruimelen; afbrokkelen

crumple, ver'frommelen

crunch, (fijn)kauwen, knarsen

crusade, kruistocht; cam'pagne

crush, ge'drang n: (samen)-
persen, ver'brijzelen; ver'pletteren

crust, (met een) korst (be'dekken)

crutch, kruk; kruis n; vork

crux, kern

cry, kreet; leus: huilen;
schreeuwen, roepen

crying, ge'huil n: schreeuwend

crypt, crypt

cryptic, ge'heim('zinnig)

crystal, kris'tal(len) (n)

crystallize, kristalli'seren

cub, welp, jong n; vlegel

cube, kubus, blokje n; derde'macht

cubic, kubusvormig; ku'biek,
inhouds-; derde'machts-

cuckoo, koekoek; sul: stapel

cucumber, kom'kommer

cud: to chew the —, her'kauwen

cuddle, pakkerd; knuffelen

cudgel, knuppel(en)

cue, vingerwijzing, wachtwoord
n: keu

cuff, man'chet: oorveeg (geven)

cuff-link, man'chetknoop

cul-de-sac, doodlopende weg

culinary, keuken-, kook-

cull, plukken; uitzoeken

culminate, culmi'neren

culpable, be'rispelijk

culprit, schuldige

cult, cultus

cultivate, be(or ver)'bouwen;
aankweken, ont'wikkelen

cultural, cultu'reel

culture, cul'tuur, be'schaving;
aankweking; teelt

cultured, be'schaafd; ge'kweekt

cumbersome, on'handelbaar

cumulative, cumula'tief

cunning, listig(heid)

cup, kopje n; kelk : hol maken

cupboard, kast

cupid, cupido(otje n)

cur, (straat)hond

curate, hulppredikant

curb, trot'toirband, rand: be'-
teugelen

curds, wrongel

curdle, schiften

cure, ge'nezing, ge'neesmiddel n,
kuur: ge'nezen; zouten en
roken

curfew, avondklok; spertijd

curio, curiosi'teit

curiosity, nieuws'gierigheid;
curiosi'teit

curious, nieuws'gierig; vreemd,
curi'eus

curl, krul(len)

currant, krent, bes

currency, be'taalmiddel n;
ruchtbaarheid

current, stroom; stroming:
cou'rant, actu'eel; in omloop,
heersend

curriculum, leerplan n

curry, kerrie(schotel) : met kerrie
kruiden

curse, ver'vloeking, vloek(en),
ver'vloeken

cursory, vluchtig

curt, bruusk, kort'af

curtail, ver'korten; be'knotten

curtain, gor'dijn n, doek n

curtsy, révé'rence (maken)

curve, bocht, kromming, ronding: (zich) buigen

cushion, kussen; bil'jartband

custard, custard

custody, zorg, be'waring; hechtenis

custom, ge'woonte, (oud) ge'bruik *n*; klan'dizie
customs, dou'ane(rechten)
customary, ge'bruikelijk
customer, klant
cut, snee, knip; ver'mindering; snit: (door)snijden, (af)-knippen; slijpen; graven; banen; (door')klieven; ver'minderen; cou'peren; ne'geren; ver'zuimen; maaien
to take a short cut, afsnijden
to cut across, oversteken
to cut down, vellen; ver'minderen
to cut in, snijden; in de rede vallen
to cut off, afsnijden; afsluiten; iso'leren; ver'breken
to cut out, (uit)knippen, ver'wijderen; afslaan; schrappen, uitscheiden met
to cut up, kleinsnijden, ver'snipperen; erg aangrijpen; opspelen
cuticle, nagelriem
cutlery, be'stek *n*, zilver *n*
cutlet, kote'let
cutting, scherp; holle weg; uitknipsel *n*; stek
cycle, kringloop, cyclus: fietsen
cyclist, fietser
cyclone, cy'cloon
cygnet, jonge zwaan
cylinder, ci'linder
cymbal, cim'baal
cynic, cynicus
cynical, cynisch
cypress, ci'pres
cyst, cyste
Czech, Tsjech(isch (*n*))

D

dab, tik, likje *n*; schar: kei: betten, aantippen
dabble, ploeteren; liefhebberen
dachshund, taks
dad(dy), pappie, vader
daffodil, gele nar'cis
daft, dwaas
dagger, dolk

daily, dagelijks, dag-
dainty, sierlijk, fijn, tenger; kies'keurig: lekker'nij
dairy, melkinrichting, melke'-rij: melk-, zuivel-
daisy, made'liefje *n*, mar'griet
dale, dal *n*
dally, talmen; spelen
dam, dam; moer: afdammen
damage, schade(n); be'schadigen
damages, schadevergoeding
damask, da'mast(en) *n*
dame, vrouwe, moedertje *n*
damn, donder: ver'domme! (ver')doemen
damnable, ver'vloekt
damp, vochtig(heid); gas *n*: be'vochtigen; doen dempen be'koelen
damsel, jonge dame
damson, da'mastpruim
dance, dans(partij), bal *n*: dansen
dandelion, paardebloem
dandle, spelen met
dandruff, roos
dandy, fat: reuze
danger(ous), ge'vaar(lijk) (*n*)
dangle, bengelen
Danish, Deens (*n*)
dank, muf en vochtig
dapper, kwiek
dappled, ge'vlekt
dare, (aan)durven; tarten
daring, durf: ge'durfd
dark, donker (*n*); duister (*n*)
darken, donker maken (*or* worden) -
darkness, donker *n*
darling, lieveling; liefste
darn, stop(pen): ver'dikkeme!
dart, pijl(tje *n*): schieten
dash, streepje *n*; scheutje *n*, snuifje *n*; run; zwier: jakkes! slaan; hollen; ver'nietigen
dastardly, laf'hartig
data, ge'gevens
date, datum, jaartal *n*; afspraak: dadel(palm): da'teren, ver'-ouderen
out of date, uit de tijd; ver'lopen
to date, tot op heden

up to date, tot dusver; op de hoogte: mo'dern

daub, (be')smeren; kladschilderen

daughter, dochter

daughter-in-law, schoondochter

daunt, afschrikken

dauntless, onver'vaard

davit, davit

dawdle, treuzelen

dawn, dageraad: aanbreken; doordringen tot

day, dag; tijd

all day, de hele dag

daybreak, het aanbreken van de dag

daydream, mijmeren, dromen

daylight, daglicht n

daytime: in the —, over'dag

daze, ver'bijstering: ver'doven, ver'bijsteren

dazzle, ver'blinden

deacon, kape'laan, hulppredikant

deaconess, diaco'nes

dead, dood(s), levenloos, ge'voelloos; abso'luut; pal: dode(n); holst n

dead beat, doodop

deaden, dempen, ver'doven

dead-lock, im'passe

deadly, dodelijk; dood(s)-, ver'schrikkelijk

deaf (and dumb), doof('stom)

deafen, ver'doven

deafening, oorver'dovend

deal, trans'actie, be'handeling: vurehout n: handelen; geven; toebrengen

a good (or great) deal, nogal (or heel) veel

to deal out, uitdelen

to deal with, te doen hebben met, be'handelen, helpen; afrekenen met

dealer, handelaar; gever

dealings, zaken, omgang

dean, deken

dear, lief, dierbaar; duur; ach!

Dear Sir, Mijne Heren, Zeer geachte Heer

Dear Mr X, Geachte Heer X

Dear John, Beste Jan

dearly, dolgraag, innig; duur

dearth, schaarste, ge'brek n

death, dood; sterfgeval n

to (bleed) to death, dood(bloeden)

death-duties, suc'cessierechten

debar, uitsluiten, be'letten

debase, ver'lagen; ver'nederen

debatable, be'twistbaar

debate, de'bat('teren (over)) (n); be'twisten

debauched, liederlijk

debauchery, los'bandigheid

debility, ge'brek n

debit, debet(saldo) n: debi'teren

débris, puin n, rommel

debt(or), schuld(enaar)

to be in debt, schuld(en) hebben

début, de'buut n

decade, de'cennium n

decadence, deca'dentie

decamp, opbreken; zijn biezen pakken

decant, overgieten

decanter, ka'raf

decapitate, ont'hoofden

decay, ver'rotting: (in) ver'val (raken) (n); (doen) ver'rotten

decease, over'lijden (n)

deceased, over'leden(e)

deceit, be'drog n

deceitful, vals

deceive, be'driegen

decency, fat'soen n

decennial, tienjaarlijks

decent, net(jes), aardig; be'hoorlijk

deception, be'drog n

deceptive, be'drieglijk

decide, (doen) be'sluiten; be'slissen

decided, be'slist; vastbesloten

deciduous tree, loofboom

decimal, tien'tallig, tien'delig

decipher, ont'cijferen

decision, be'slissing, be'sluit n; be'slistheid

decisive, be'slissend; be'slist

deck, dek n: tooien

deck-chair, ligstoel

declaim, decla'meren

declaration, ver'klaring; aangifte

declare, ver'klaren, be'kendmaken; aangeven

decline, daling, achter'uitgang: be'danken (voor); afdalen, achter'uitgaan; ver'buigen

decompose, ont'binden

decorate, ver'sieren; schilderen (en be'hangen); deco'reren

decoration, ver'siering; deco'-ratie

decorative, decora'tief

decorous, wel'voeglijk

decorum, de'corum *n*

decoy, lok(aas *n*): in de val lokken

decrease, afname: ver'minderen

decree, de'creet *n*: decre'teren

decrepit, af'tands

decry, afkeuren, in diskrediet brengen

dedicate, wijden; opdragen

dedication, (toe)wijding; op-dracht

deduce, afleiden

deduct, aftrekken

deduction, aftrek, korting; ge'volgtrekking

deed, daad, akte

deem, achten

deep, diep

deepen, dieper worden (*or* maken)

deer, hert(en) *n*

deface, ont'sieren

defamatory, lasterlijk

defame, be'lasteren

default, ver'zuim *n*; in ge'breke blijven

defeat, nederlaag: ver'slaan; ver'ijdelen

defeatist, defai'tist

defect, ge'brek *n*

defection, af'valligheid

defective, ge'brekkig, de'fect

defence, ver'dediging

defenceless, weerloos

defend, ver'dedigen

defendant, ge'daagde

defensive, ver'dedigend

defer, uitstellen; zich onder-werpen aan

deference, eerbied

defiance, tarting

  in defiance of . . ., . . . ten spijt

defiant, uit'dagend

deficiency, te'kort *n*

deficient, ontoe'reikend

deficit, te'kort *n*

defile, bergengte: defi'leren; be'vuilen, be'zoedelen

define, defini'eren

definite, be'paald, defini'tief, vast

definition, om'schrijving; scherpte

deflate, laten leeglopen; de'flatie tot stand brengen van

deflect, ombuigen

deform, mis'vormen

deformed, mis'maakt

defraud, valselijk be'roven

defray, be'strijden

deft, vaardig

defunct, over'leden; ver'ouderd

defy, trot'seren

degenerate, ont'aard (en)

degradation, degra'datie

degrade, degra'deren; ver'-nederen

degree, graad, mate, rang

dehydrate, drogen

deify, ver'goddelijken

deign, zich ver'waardigen

deity, godheid

dejected, neer'slachtig

delay, ver'traging, uitstel (len) (*n*); ver'tragen

delectable, ge'notvol

delegate, afgevaardigde: afvaardigen, overdragen

delegation, dele'gatie

delete, doorhalen

deliberate, op'zettelijk, wel-overwogen, be'dachtzaam: over'wegen, be'raadslagen

delicacy, fijnheid; hachelijkheid; zwak ge'stel *n*; delica'tesse

delicate, fijn (ge'voelig); teer

delicious, heerlijk

delight, ge'not *n*, ver'rukking: ver'rukken, ge'noegen be'zorgen

delightful, ver'rukkelijk, enig

delineation, tekening, omtrek

delinquent, schuldig (e)

delirious, aan het ijlen; waan'zinnig

deliver, be'zorgen, overleveren; geven; ver'lossen

delivery, be'zorging, over'handig-
ing; voordracht; ver'lossing
dell, (nauw) dichtbegroeid dal *n*
delude, mis'leiden, be'goochelen
deluge, wolkbreuk, (stort)vloed:
over'stromen, over'stelpen
delusion, be'drog *n*, waan
de luxe, luxe
delve, delven; vorsen
demagogue, dema'goog
demand, vraag, aanspraak : eisen,
vragen
demarcation, afbakening
demeanour, optreden *n*
demented, waan'zinnig
demigod, halfgod
demise, over'lijden *n*; overdracht
demobilize, demobili'seren
democracy, democra'tie
democratic, demo'cratisch
demolish, afbreken
demolition, afbraak
demon, boze geest, duivel
demonic, de'monisch
demonstrate, demon'streren,
aantonen
demonstration, demon'stratie,
be'wijs *n*, ver'toon *n*
demonstrative, demonstra'tief;
aan'wijzend
demoralize, demorali'seren
demur, pro'test('eren) (*n*)
demure, zedig; preuts
den, hol *n*; hok *n*
denial, ont'kenning, ver'loochening
Denmark, Denemarken *n*
denomination, be'naming;
ge'loofsrichting
denote, duiden op, aanduiden
denouement, ont'knoping
denounce, openlijk ver'oordelen,
aanbrengen
dense, dicht; dom
density, dichtheid; domheid
dent, (in)deuk(en)
dental, tand ...
dentist, tandarts
dentures, kunstgebit *n*
denude, ont'doen van
deny, ont'kennen, ver'loochenen;
ont'houden

depart, ver'trekken
departed, over'ledene (*n*)
department, afdeling
departure, ver'trek *n*; afwijking
depend on, af'hankelijk zijn van,
ver'trouwen op, afhangen van
dependable, be'trouwbaar
dependant, af'hankelijk persoon
dependent, af'hankelijk
depict, afbeelden
deplete, ver'minderen, uitputten
deplorable, betreurens'waardig
deplore, be'treuren
deploy, ont'plooien
depopulate, ont'volken
deport, depor'teren; ge'dragen
deportment, optreden *n*
depose, afzetten
deposit, be'zinksel *n*, laag; storting, waarborgsom : achterlaten;
depo'neren
depot, de'pot *n*
depraved, ont'aard
depravity, ver'dorvenheid
deprecate, (ernstig) afkeuren
depreciate, in waarde (doen)
dalen; onder'schatten
depreciation, waardeverminder-
ing; ge'ringschatting
depredation, plundering
depress, neerdrukken; de-
pri'meren
depression, daling, uitholling;
ma'laise; neer'slachtigheid
deprive of, ont'nemen
depth, diepte, hoogte
deputation, afvaardiging
deputize, waarnemen
deputy, afgevaardigde; plaatsvervanger : plaatsvervangend
derail, (doen) derai'lleren
derange, in de war brengen
derelict, ver'laten (schip *n*);
ver'vallen
deride, honend uitlachen
derision, be'spotting
derisive, spottend
derive, afleiden; ont'lenen;
ver'krijgen
derogatory, ge'ringschattend
derrick, laadboom; boortoren

descant, dis'cant

descend, afdalen; overgaan (op)

descendant, afstammeling

descent, (af)daling; afstamming

describe, be'schrijven

description, be'schrijving, signale'ment *n*; soort

descriptive, be'schrijvend

descry, be'speuren

desecrate, ont'wijden

desert, woes'tijn: ver'diende loon *n*: ver'laten; deser'teren

deserter, deser'teur, af'vallige

deserve, ver'dienen

deservedly, te'recht

deserving, waardevol, ver'dienstelijk

design, ont'werp(en) (*n*), des'-sin *n*; oogmerk *n*, opzet

designate, be'noemd: aan-duiden; (be')noemen

designer, ont'werper

desirable, wenselijk

desire, ver'langen (*n*), be'geerte: be'geren

desist, ophouden (met)

desk, bu'reau *n*, lessenaar; kas

desolate, ver'laten, triest: ver'woesten

desolation, woeste'nij; troosteloosheid; ver'woesting

despair, wanhoop: wanhopen

desperado, woesteling

desperate, tot het uiterste ge'dre-ven, wanhopig, schreeuwend

desperation, de moed der wan-hoop, ver'twijfeling

despicable, ver'achtelijk

despise, ver'achten, ver'smaden

despite, on'danks

despoil, plunderen

despondent, moedeloos

despot, des'poot

despotism, despo'tisme *n*

dessert, des'sert *n*

destination, (plaats van) be'-stemming

destine, be'stemmen

he was destined never to re-turn, het lot wilde, dat hij nooit te'rug zou komen

destiny, (nood)lot *n*; be'stem-ming

destitute, be'hoeftig, be'rooid

destroy, ver'nietigen, ver'nielen

destroyer, tor'pedojager

destruction ver'nietiging, ver'-woesting; ver'derf *n*

destructive, ver'nielziek, schade-lijk; afbrekend

desultory, te hooi en te gras

detach, scheiden, losmaken; de-ta'cheren

detached, los(geraakt), vrij-staand; onbe'vangen

detachment, detache'ment *n*; losmaken *n*; onbe'vangenheid

detail, de'tail *n*; deta'chering: deta'cheren

detailed, uit'voerig

detain, ophouden, vasthouden

detect, be'speuren, be'trappen

detective, detec'tive, recher'cheur

detention, oponthoud *n*; ge'vang-enhouden *n*, schoolblijven *n*

deter, afschrikken

detergent, wasmiddel *n*

deteriorate, achter'uitgaan

deterioration, achter'uitgang

determination, vastbe'raden-heid; vaststellen *n*; be'slissing

determine, be'sluiten; vàststel-len, be'palen

determined, vastbe'sloten, vast-be'raden

deterrent, afschrikkend middel *n*

detest, ver'afschuwen

detestable, ver'foeilijk

dethrone, ont'tronen

detonate, (doen) ont'ploffen

detour, omweg

detract from, afbreuk doen aan

detriment(al), schade(lijk)

deuce, twee, veertig ge'lijk: drommel

devastate, ver'woesten

develop, (zich) ont'wikkelen, uit-werken

development, ont'wikkeling

deviate, afwijken

device, toestel *n*; list; sym'bool *n*, de'vies *n*

devil, duivel

devilish, duivels; ver'duiveld

devious, om'slachtig

devise, ver'zinnen

devoid of, zonder

devolve, overdragen (aan), overgaan (op)

devote, (toe)wijden

devoted, (toe)gewijd, ver'knocht

devotee, enthousi'ast

devotion, toewijding, ver'knocht-heid; de'votie; ge'bed *n*

devour, ver'slinden

devout, vroom

dew(drop), dauw(droppel)

dexterous, be'hendig

diabetes, suikerziekte

diabolic(al), duivels

diadem, dia'deem

diaeresis, deelteken *n*

diagnose, diag'nose opmaken

diagnosis, diag'nose

diagonal, diago'naal

diagram, dia'gram *n*

dial, wijzer(plaat), schijf; facie: draaien

dialect, dia'lect *n*

dialogue, dia'loog

diameter, middellijn

diametrically, diame'traal; lijnrecht

diamond, dia'mant(en); ruit (-'vormig)

diaphragm, middenrif *n*; dia'fragma *n*

diarrhoea, dia'rree

diary, dagboek *n*, a'genda

diatribe, schimprede

dice, dobbelstenen: dobbelen

dickens, drommel

dictate, voorschrift *n*; stem: dic'teren; voorschrijven

dictation, dic'teren *n*; dic'tee *n*; voorschrift *n*

dictator, dic'tator

dictatorial, dictatori'aal

dictatorship, dicta'tuur

diction, dictie

dictionary, woordenboek *n*

dictum, uitspraak; ge'zegde *n*

didactic, di'dactisch

diddle, be'dotten

die, sterven, doodgaan; snakken naar

  to die out, uitsterven

die-hard, onver'zettelijk

diesel, diesel

diet, di'eet(houden) (*n*)

differ, ver'schillen; het niet eens zijn

difference, ver'schil *n*

different, ver'schillend, anders

differentiate, onder'scheiden; onderscheid maken

difficult, moeilijk

difficulty, moeilijkheid, be'zwaar *n*

diffident, be'schroomd

diffuse, dif'fuus: (zich) ver'spreiden

dig, por; steek: graven, omspitten, rooien (potatoes); porren; vorsen

digest, overzicht *n*: ver'teren; ver'werken

digestion, (spijs)ver'tering

dig(ging)s, kamers

digit, vinger; cijfer *n*

dignified, waardig

dignify, opluisteren

dignitary, waardigheidsbekleder

dignity, waardigheid

digress, afdwalen, uitweiden

dilapidated, bouw'vallig

dilate, (zich) uitzetten

dilatory, traag

dilemma, di'lemma *n*

dilettante, dilet'tant

diligence, vlijt; dili'gence

diligent, vlijtig

dilute, ver'dund: ver'dunnen

dim, flauw, vaag, schemerig; dom: dof worden, ver'flauwen, ver'zwakken

dimension, afmeting, di'mensie

diminish, ver'minderen

diminutive, klein: ver'klein-woord *n*

dimple, kuiltje *n*

din, la'waai *n*

dine, di'neren

diner, eter

dinghy, jol

dingy, vuil, goor

dining-car, restau'ratiewagen

dining-room, eetkamer, eetzaal

dinky, snoezig

dinner, warme maaltijd, di'ner *n*

dinner-service, eetservies *n*

dint: by — of, door middel van

diocese, bisdom *n*

dip, duik(en); inzinking: dompelen; dalen; salu'eren (met)

diphtheria, difte'ritis

diphthong, tweeklank

diploma, di'ploma *n*

diplomacy, diploma'tie

diplomat, diplo'maat

diplomatic, diploma'tiek

dire, ver'schrikkelijk

direct, rechtstreeks, di'rect; on'middellijk; open'hartig: leiden; ge'lasten; de weg wijzen; richten; adres'seren

direction, richting; aanwijzing; leiding

directly, on'middellijk; pre'cies

director, direc'teur; raadsman

directory, ad'resboek *n*, gids

dirge, klaagzang

dirt, vuil *n*; aarde

dirt-cheap, spotgoedkoop

dirty, vuil(maken); ge'meen

disability, onvermogen *n*

disabled, inva'lide

disablement, invalidi'teit

disadvantage, nadeel *n*

  at a disadvantage, in een na'delige po'sitie

disadvantageous, na'delig

disagree with, het on'eens zijn met; slecht be'komen

disagreeable, on'aangenaam

disagreement, (menings)verschil *n*

disallow, van de hand wijzen

disappear(ance), ver'dwijnen (*n*)

disappoint, te'leurstellen

  to be disappointing, tegenvallen

disappointment, te'leurstelling, tegenvaller

disapproval, afkeuring; misnoegen *n*

disapprove, afkeuren; erop tegen zijn

disarm, ont'wapenen

disarmament, ont'wapening

disaster, ramp

disastrous, ramp'spoedig

disavow, loochenen

disband, ont'binden

disbelief, ongeloof *n*

disbelieve, onge'lovig zijn, in twijfel trekken

disburse, uitbetalen

disc, schijf

discard, op'zij ge'legde kaart: ver'werpen, afdanken; uittrekken; wegleggen

discern, onder'scheiden

discernible, waar'neembaar

discernment, onder'scheidingsvermogen *n*, inzicht *n*

discharge, ont'lading; ont'ploffing; ont'slag *n*; afvoer; etteren (*n*); zich kwijten van (*n*): lossen; afschieten; ont'laden; ont'slaan; uitmonden; afdoen

disciple, dis'cipel

disciplinary, discipli'nair, tuchtdiscipline

discipline, disci'pline: discipli'neren

disclaim, van de hand wijzen, ont'kennen

disclose, ont'hullen, blootleggen; loslaten

discolour, (doen) ver'kleuren

discomfort, onbe'haaglijkheid

disconcert, van de wijs brengen

disconcerting, storend

disconnect, uitschakelen, afkoppelen

disconnected, on'samenhangend

disconsolate, troosteloos

discontent(ment), onte'vredenheid

discontented, onte'vreden

discontinue, opheffen, ophouden met, staken; opzeggen

discord, tweedracht; disso'nant

discordance, wangeluid *n*

discordant, dishar'monisch; tegen'strijdig

discount, korting: discon'teren; buiten be'schouwing laten

discourage, ont'moedigen; afraden; weer'houden

discouragement, ont'moediging; tegenwerping; afschrikking

discourse, ver'handeling (houden)

discourteous, on'hoffelijk

discover, ont'dekken

discovery, ont'dekking

discredit, schande, oneer: in diskrediet brengen (*n*); geen ge'loof hechten aan (*n*)

discreet, dis'creet

discrepancy, onregel'matigheid, ver'schil *n*

discretion, goedvinden *n*; tact; onderscheid *n*

discriminate, onder'scheiden, onderscheid maken (*n*)

discrimination, onderscheid-(ingsvermogen) *n*

discursive, on'samenhangend

discuss, be'spreken

discussion, be'spreking, dis'cussie

disdain, ver'achting: ver'smaden

disdainful, ver'achtelijk

disease, ziekte; kwaal

diseased, ziek, be'smet

disembark, (zich) ont'schepen

disengage, losmaken

disengaged, onbe'zet

disentangle, ont'warren

disfavour, tegenzin; ongenade

disfigure, ont'sieren, mis'vormen

disgorge, uitbraken; uitstorten

disgrace, schande; ongenade: te schande maken; laken

disgraceful, schandelijk

disgruntled, ver'zuurd

disguise, (ver') mom (ming): ver'mommen, ver'bloemen

disgust, afkeer, walging: doen walgen

  to be disgusted at, walgen van

  to be disgusted with, meer dan ge'noeg hebben van

disgusting, walgelijk, af'schuwelijk

dish, schaal; ge'recht *n*

  to dish up, opdoen

disharmony, disharmo'nie

dish-cloth, vaatdoek

dishearten, ont'moedigen

dishevelled, ver'fomfaaid

dishonest(y), on'eerlijk (heid)

dishonour, oneer, schande: ont'eren

dishonourable, ont'erend; on'-eervol

disillusion, ont'goochelen

disillusionment, ont'goocheling

disinclination, tegenzin

disinclined, onge'negen

disinfect, ont'smetten

disinfectant, ont'smettingsmiddel *n*

disinherit, ont'erven

disintegrate, uitel'kaar vallen, (zich) ont'binden

disinterested, be'langeloos

disjointed, on'samenhangend

dislike, afkeer: on'prettig vinden

dislocate, ont'wrichten

dislodge, losmaken; ver'drijven

disloyal(ty), ontrouw

dismal, triest

dismantle, ont'mantelen

dismay, ont'zetting: ont'stellen

dismiss, ont'slaan, wegsturen; afwijzen

dismissal, ont'slag *n*

dismount, afstijgen; demon'-teren

disobedience, onge'hoorzaam-heid

disobedient, onge'hoorzaam

disobey, geen ge'hoor geven (aan), onge'hoorzaam zijn

disorder, wanorde; onge'regeld-heid; onge'steldheid

disorderly, wan'orderlijk; op'-roerig

disorganize, in de war sturen

disown, ver'loochenen

disparage, klei'neren

disparity, onge'lijkheid

dispassionate, onpar'tijdig, ob-jec'tief

dispatch, ver'zending; (offici'eel) be'richt *n*; spoed: ver'zenden; afmaken; ver'orberen

dispel, ver'drijven

dispensary, apo'theek

dispensation, uitdeling; dis-pen'satie; be'schikking

dispense, uitdelen; klaarmaken

  to dispense with, het stellen zonder

dispersal, ver'spreiding

disperse, ver'strooien

dispirit, ont'moedigen

displace, ver'plaatsen, ver'vang-en

displacement, (water)ver'plaatsing

display, ver'toon *n*, demon'stratie: (ver')tonen, ten'toonspreiden; ont'plooien

displease, mis'hagen

displeased, ont'stemd

displeasing, on'aangenaam

displeasure, mis'noegen *n*

disport, ver'maken

disposal, opruimen *n*; (be')-schikking

dispose, (rang)schikken: be'wegen

 to dispose of, van de hand doen, ver'maken

disposed, ge'neigd, ge'stemd

disposition, rangschikking; aard, neiging

dispossess, uit het be'zit stoten

disproportionate, oneven'redig

disprove, weer'leggen

dispute, woordentwist, dis'puut *n*: (be')twisten, dispu'teren; be'strijden

disqualification, diskwalifi'catie; be'lemmering

disqualify, diskwalifi'ceren; onge'schikt maken

disquiet, onrust: veront'rusten

disregard, veron'achtzaming: veron'achtzamen

disrepair, ver'val *n*

disreputable, be'rucht; haveloos

disrespect, oneer'biedigheid

disrupt, uit'eenrukken

disruption, scheuring

dissatisfaction, onte'vredenheid

dissatisfied, onte'vreden

dissect, ont'leden

dissemble, (zich) ont'veinzen, veinzen

disseminate, ver'spreiden

dissension, tweedracht

dissent, van mening ver'schillen

dissenter, afgescheidene

dissertation, ver'handeling

disservice, ondienst

dissimilar(ity), onge'lijk(heid)

dissipate, ver'strooien; ver'doen

dissipated, ver'lopen, los'bandig

dissociate, (af)scheiden, niet stellen achter

dissolute, liederlijk

dissolution, opheffing

dissolve, (zich) oplossen; ont'binden; wegsmelten

dissonant, wan'luidend

dissuade, afraden, afbrengen (van)

distance, afstand; verte

distant, ver; weg; koel

distaste, afkeer

distasteful, on'smakelijk

distemper, (honde)ziekte; tempera; vloebaren

distend, opzwellen, opensperren

distil, distil'leren; puren

distillery, distilleerde'rij

distinct, duidelijk; ver'schillend; be'slist

distinction, onderscheid *n*, onder'scheiding; aanzien *n*

distinctive, kenmerkend

distinguish, onder'scheiden, onderscheid maken

distinguished, aan'zienlijk

distort, ver'wringen; ver'draaien

distract, afleiden; krank'zinnig maken

distraction, afleiding; rade'loosheid

distraught, radeloos

distress, ellende, smart: be'droeven

distribute, uitdelen, ver'spreiden

distribution, uitreiking, ver'deling

district, streek, wijk

distrust, wantrouwen (*n*)

disturb, storen; komen aan; veront'rusten

disturbance, storing; ver'warring; stoornis

disuse, onbruik *n*

disused, oud, in onbruik ge'raakt

ditch, sloot: lozen

ditty, deuntje *n*

divan, divan(bed *n*)

dive, duik(en); tent: tasten

diver, duiker; duikvogel

diverge, uit'eenlopen

divergence, ver'schil *n*

divers(e), ver'scheiden

diversion, ver'legging, weg-omlegging; ont'spanning

diversity, ver'scheidenheid

divert, ver'leggen; afleiden

divest, ont'doen

divide, (zich) ver'delen; stemmen

dividend, divi'dend *n*; deeltal *n*

dividers, (steek)passer

divine, goddelijk, gods-; aan'bid-delijk: godgeleerde: peilen, gissen

divinity, god(delijk)heid; god-geleerdheid

divisible, deelbaar

division, (ver')deling, afdeling; di'visie; ver'deeldheid; stem-ming

divorce, (echt)scheiding: (zich laten) scheiden (van)

divulge, be'kend maken

dizzy, duizelig, duizeling'wekkend

do, doen

  how do you do? hoe maakt u het?

  that will do, dat is ge'noeg

  did you say that you did want it or that you didn't? zei je, dat je het wel wilde of dat je het niet wilde?

  to do away with, afschaffen

  to do out of, afzetten; pro-fi'teren van

  to do up, vastmaken, inpakken; opknappen

  to do well, het goed maken; er goed aan doen

  to do with, ge'bruiken; maken met

  to do without, het stellen zonder

docile, volgzaam

dock, dok(ken) (*n*); be'klaagden-bank: korten

dockyard, ma'rinewerf

doctor, dokter; doctor: be'han-delen

doctrine, leer(stuk *n*)

document, docu'ment('eren) (*n*)

documentary, documen'tair(e film)

dodder, wankelen

dodge, foefje *n*: op'zijspringen; ont'wijken

doe, hinde; wijfje *n*

doff, afzetten, uittrekken

dog, hond: (achter)volgen

dog-ear, ezelsoren maken

dogged, hard'nekkig

doggerel, rijmela'rij

doggo: to lie —, zich koest houden

dogma, dogma *n*

dogmatic, dog'matisch

dog-tired, hondsmoe

doily, kleedje *n*

doings, ge'doe *n*; spul(len) *n*

doldrums, streek der windstil-ten; put

dole, steun

  to dole out, ronddelen

doleful, somber

doll, pop

  to doll up, opdirken

dollar, dollar

dolphin, dol'fijn

dolt, domkop

domain, do'mein *n*, landgoed *n*; ge'bied *n*

dome, koepel

domestic, huis('houd)elijk, huis-(houd)-; binnenlands

domesticated, huiselijk; ge'temd

domicile, domi'cilie *n*

dominant, (over')heersend; do-mi'nerend; domi'nant

dominate, (over')heersen, be'-heersen; be'strijken

domination, over'heersing

domineer, de baas spelen over

domineering, bazig

dominion, heerschap'pij; ge'bied (met zelf bestuur) *n*

dominoes, dominospel *n*

don, ge'leerde: aandoen

donate, schenken

donation, do'natie

done, klaar, af; gaar

  done for, op; er ge'weest

donkey, ezel

donor, schenker, donor

doom, noodlot *n*, ondergang; laatste oordeel *n*: doemen

door, deur, ingang

  out of doors, buiten

doorstep, stoep; pil

door-way, deuropening

dope, spanlak; be'dwelmend mid-del *n*; inlichtingen; stomkop: be'dwelmen

dormant, slapend
dormer window, koekóek
dormitory, slaapzaal
dorsal, rug(ge)-
dose, dosis : do'seren
dot, stip(pelen), punt
dotage, kindsheid
dote, kinds zijn; ver'zot zijn op
dotty, niet goed snik
double, dubbel, tweepersoons-:
   dubbele n, dubbelganger:
   (zich)ver'dubbelen, dubbelvou-
   wen; zich omwenden; dou'bleren
  to double up, in'eenkrimpen;
   opschieten
double-barrelled, dubbel(loops)
double-cross, dubbel spel spelen (n)
doublet, wambuis n
doubt, twijfel(en), be'twijfelen
doubtful, twijfelachtig
doubtless, onge'twijfeld
douche, douche
dough, deeg n; duiten
doughnut, oliebol
doughty, koen
dour, stug
douse, drijfnat maken
dove, duif(je n)
dovecot, duiventil
dowager, douai'rière
dowdy, lijzig ge'kleed, sjofel
down, naar be'neden, neder; af:
   down: dons n
  down and out, door en door;
   aan lager wal
  a down on, iets tegen
  down payment, bedrag n in'eens
  down with, weg met
downcast, (ter')neergeslagen
downfall, val; zware bui
down-hearted, neer'slachtig
downhill, de heuvel af; berg'afwaarts
downpour, plasregen
downright, uitgesproken
downstairs, (naar) be'neden
downstream, stroom'afwaarts
down-trodden, platgetrapt;
   ver'trapt
downward(s), naar be'neden
downy, donzig

dowry, bruidschat
doze, dutje n; dutten
dozen, do'zijn n
drab, saai; vaal(bruin)
draft, schets, klad n; detache'ment n; wissel: inlijven,
   deta'cheren
draftsman, ont'werper
drag, rem: slepen; dreggen;
   kruipen
  to drag on, zich voortslepen
dragon, draak
dragon-fly, waterjuffer
dragoon, dra'gonder: ringeloren
drain, afvoer(buis), ri'ool n; afvoeren, lopen; droogleggen;
   ont'trekken
  to be a drain on, veel vergen
   van
drainage, afwatering; afvoer
draining-board, aanrecht n
drainpipe, afvoerbuis
drake, woerd
dram, drachme; boompje n
drama, drama('tiek) (n)
dramatic, dra'matisch
dramatics, to'neelkunst
dramatist, drama'turg
dramatize, (zich laten) dramati'-
   seren
drape, drape'rie: dra'peren
drapery, drape'rie; manufac'-
   turen
drastic, drastisch
drat, drommels
draught, tocht, trek; vangst;
   diepgang; teug: trek-; ge'tapt
draughts, damspel n
draughty, tochtig
draw, ge'lijk spel(en) (n);
   at'tractie; ver'loting: trekken:
   tekenen
  to draw near, naderen
  to draw up, stilhouden; opstellen; bijschuiven
drawback, be'zwaar n, nadeel n
drawbridge, ophaalbrug
drawer, la(de): tekenaar
drawers, panta'lon
drawing, tekening, tekenen n
drawing-pin, pu'naise
drawing-room, sa'lon
drawl, ge'teem n: temen

drawn, afgetobd; onbe'slist

dread, (met) angst (en beven tege'moetzien)

dreadful, vreselijk

dream, droom: dromen

dreamy, dromerig; vaag

dreary, somber

dredge, baggermolen; (uit)baggeren

dregs, be'zinksel n; grondsop n

drench, door'weken

dress, ja'pon; kleding, te'nue n: gala-: (zich) (aan)kleden; tooien; ver'binden

to dress up, (zich) opdirken

dresser, (keuken)buf'fet n

dressing, ver'band n; saus

dressing-gown, kamerjapon

dressmaker, naaister

dressmaking, naaien n

dress-rehearsal, gene'rale repe'titie

dress-suit, rokkos'tuum n

dressy, pronkziek; ge'kleed

dribble, druppelen, kwijlen; dribbelen

drier, droogtoestel n

drift, drijven (n); jachtsneeuw; neiging, strekking: zich laten meeslepen, dwalen

driftwood, drijfhout n

drill, dril(boor); oefening, exer'citie; kleine voor: (door)-boren; drillen

drink, (iets te) drinken, borreltje n

to drink to, drinken op

drip, druppel(en), druipen

dripping, braadvet n

drive, rit; oprijlaan; drijf-kracht; cam'pagne; slag: (voort)drijven; rijden; slaan

to drive at, doelen op

drivel, ge'wauwel n: wauwelen

driver, be'stuurder

driving licence, rijbewijs n

drizzle, motregen(en)

droll, grappig, zot

drone, dar, luilak; ge'gons: gonzen, dreunen

droop, hangen; omvallen

drop, druppel; glaasje n; dal-ing; hoogte: (laten) vallen;

(laten) dalen; weglaten; afzet-ten

to drop in, (even) langskomen

to drop off, in slaap vallen

dropsy, waterzucht

dross, afval

drought, droogte

drown, ver'drinken; over'stem-men

to be drowned, ver'drinken

drowse, dommelen

drowsy, slaperig; slaap'wekkend

drudge, werkezel: sloven

drudgery, ge'zwoeg n

drug, be'dwelmend middel n: be'dwelmen

drum, trom(mel), ton: trommelen

drummer, trommelslager

drunk, dronken: dronkeman

drunkard, dronkaard

dry, droog: (af)drogen

dry-clean(ing), chemisch reinigen (n)

dual, twee'ledig, dubbel

dub, tot ridder slaan

dubious, twijfelachtig, dubi'eus

ducal, her'togelijk

duchess, herto'gin

duchy, hertogdom n

duck, eend; snoes; nul: duiking: (onder)duiken

duct, ka'naal n, buis

dud, sukkel, blindganger: snert

due, ver'schuldigd, ver'diend, ge'past; ver'wacht; zuiver: wat iemand toekomt

due to, dank zij, ten ge'volge van

duel, du'el n; duel'leren

duet, du'et n, quatre'mains

duffer, sufferd

dug-out, uitgegraven schuilplaats

duke, hertog

dull, dof; saai; traag; somber: afstompen

duly, dan ook; dus, naar be'horen

dumb, stom, sprakeloos

dumb-bell, halter

dumbfound, ver'stomd doen staan

dummy, pop; blinde: na-maak-

dump, belt, stortplaats; opslag-plaats: storten, neerzetten

dumpling, knoedel
dumpy person, propje *n*
dunce, domkop
dune, duin *n*
dung, (be)mest(en)
dungarees, over'all
dungeon, kerker
dupe, dupe: be'driegen
duplicate, dupli'caat (*n*): ver'dubbelen
 in duplicate, in duplo
duplicity, dubbel'hartigheid
durable, duurzaam
duration, duur
duress, dwang
during, tijdens
dusk, schemering
dusky, donker, schemerig
dust, stof *n*: afstoffen; be'stuiven
dustbin, vuilnisbak
dustman, vuilnisman
dustpan (and brush), (veger en) blik *n*
dusty, stoffig; poeierig
Dutch, Nederlands (*n*): Nederlanders
dutiful, plichtgetrouw
duty, plicht; functie; (invoer)-rechten
dwarf, dwerg; minia'tuur: over'schaduwen
dwell, wonen
 to dwell (up)on, lang stilstaan bij
dweller, be'woner
dwelling, woning
dwelling-place, woonplaats
dwindle (away), wegteren; uitsterven, ver'dwijnen
dye, verf(stof); verven, kleuren
dynamic, dy'namisch
dynamite, dyna'miet *n*
dynamo, dy'namo
dynasty, dynas'tie
dysentery, dysente'rie

E

each, elk, ieder; per stuk
 each other, el'kaar
eager, enthousi'ast, gretig, ver'langend

 to be eager, dolgraag (zouden) willen
eagerness, enthousi'asme *n*, ver'langen *n*
eagle, arend
ear, oor *n*; ge'hoor *n*: aar
ear-drum, trommelvlies *n*
earl, graaf
early, (te) vroeg, vroeger, vroeg'tijdig
ear-mark, be'stemmen
earn, ver'dienen; ver'werven, be'zorgen
earnest, ernstig, vurig
 in earnest, in (alle) ernst
earnings, verdiensten
ear-ring, oorbel
ear-splitting, oorver'dovend
earth, aarde, grond; hol *n*; aardverbinding
 what (*or* how) on earth ... wat (*or* hoe) in vredesnaam ...
earthenware, aardewerk *n*
earthly, aards, stoffelijk
earthquake, aardbeving
earthworm, aardworm
earthy, grond-; laag bij de gronds
ease, ge'mak *n*: ver'lichten; losser maken; voor'zichtig schuiven; ver'minderen
easel, ezel
easily, (ge')makkelijk; verreweg
east, Oosten (*n*); oost(waarts)
Easter, Pasen
 Easter Day, eerste Paasdag
easterly, oostelijk, ooster-
eastern, oosters, oostelijk
easy, (ge')makkelijk; kalm
easy-going, gemak'zuchtig; flegma'tiek
eat, (op)eten; vreten
eaves, overhangende dakrand
eavesdrop, afluisteren
ebb, eb(ben); ver'val *n*: afnemen
ebony, ebbenhout(en) (*n*)
eccentric, ex'centrisch; excen'triek: zonderling
ecclesiastical, geestelijk, kerkelijk
echo, echo; weerklank: weer'klinken; weergeven, her'halen

eclipse, ver'duistering: ver'duisteren; in de schaduw stellen
economic, eco'nomisch
economical, zuinig, voor'delig; eco'nomisch
economics, econo'mie
economist, eco'noom
economize, be'zuinigen
economy, zuinigheid; be'heer *n*
ecstasy, ex'tase
ecstatic, geest'driftig
eddy, draaikolk: dwarrelen
edge, rand; scherpe kant
  on edge, zenuwachtig
edible, eetbaar
edict, e'dict *n*
edifice, ge'bouw *n*
edify, stichten
edit, uitgeven; redi'geren
edition, uitgave, e'ditie
editor, redac'teur, be'werker
editorial, hoofdartikel *n*
  editorial board (staff), re'dactie
educate, onder'wijzen, opvoeden
education, onderwijs *n*, ont'wikkeling
educational, opvoedings-, onderwijs-
eel, paling
eerie, griezelig
efface, uitwissen; wegcijferen
effect, ge'volg *n*, uitwerking, resul'taat *n*; ef 'fect *n*: be'werkstelligen
  in effect, in feite: van kracht
effective, ge'slaagd, treffend; af 'doend; van kracht
effeminate, ver'wijfd
effervesce, mous'seren; bruisen
efficacy, doel'treffendheid
efficiency, vaardigheid; nuttig ef 'fect *n*
effigy, beeltenis, beeldenaar
effort, krachtsinspanning, poging; pres'tatie
effrontery, brutali'teit
effusive, uit'bundig
egg, ei *n*
  to egg on, aanzetten
egoist, ego'ist
egotism, eigenwaan
eiderdown, donzen deken

eight(h), acht(ste)
eighteen(th), achttien(de)
eighty, tachtig
Eire, Ierland *n*
either, één (van beide); beide; elk: ook
  either . . . or, of . . . of
ejaculate, uitroepen
eject, uitwerpen, uitzetten
eke out, rekken
elaborate, inge'wikkeld, door'-wrocht, uitgebreid: be'werken, bijwerken; uitweiden
elapse, ver'strijken, ver'lopen
elastic, e'lastisch; rekbaar: elas'tiek *n*
elasticity, elastici'teit; rekbaarheid
elated, opgetogen
elbow, elleboog: door'heenwerken
elder, ouder(e), oudst(e); ouderling
elderly, op leeftijd
elect, ge'kozen(e), uitver-koren(e): (ver')kiezen (als), uitkiezen
election, (uit)ver'kiezing
elector(ate), kiezer(s)
electric(al), e'lektrisch
electrician, elektri'cien
electricity, elektrici'teit
electrify, elektrifi'ceren; elektri'seren
elegant, ele'gant
elegy, ele'gie
element, ele'ment *n*; be'standdeel *n*
elemental, na'tuur-, essen'tieel
elementary, elemen'tair; een'-voudig
  elementary school, lagere school
elephant, olifant
elevate, ver'heffen
elevation, ver'hoging, hoogte; ver'heffing; opstand
eleven, elf (tal *n*)
elf, ka'bouter, elf
elicit, ont'lokken
eligible, ver'kiesbaar; be'voegd; ge'schikt
eliminate, uitschakelen

ellipse, el'lips

elm, iep(enhout *n*)

elocution, voordracht

elongate, (zich) ver'lengen, uitrekken

elope, weglopen

eloquence, wel'sprekendheid

else, anders; verder

elsewhere, ergens anders

elucidate, toelichten

elude, ont'wijken, ont'duiken, ont'gaan

elusive, moeilijk te vinden (*or* vatten)

emaciate, uitmergelen

emanate from, voortkomen uit, uitstralen van

emancipation, emanci'patie

embalm, balsemen

embankment, kade

embargo, be'slag *n*, ver'bod *n*

embark, (zich) inschepen

to **embark on,** aanvangen

embarrass, ver'legen maken, in ver'legenheid brengen; be'moeilijken

embarrassing, pijnlijk

embarrassment, ver'legenheid

embassy, ambas'sade, ge'zantschap *n*

embedded, ge'nesteld, vastge'raakt

embellish, ver'fraaien

ember, gloeiend kooltje (*or* stuk hout) *n*

embezzle, ver'duisteren

embitter, ver'bitteren, ver'gallen

emblem, zinnebeeld *n*

embody, be'lichamen; be'vatten

embossed, gebosse'leerd, in re'liëf

embrace, om'helzing: (el'kaar) om'helzen; om'sluiten; zich eigen maken

embroider, bor'duren

embroidery, bor'duurwerk *n*

embroil, ver'wikkelen

embryo(nic), embryo('naal) (*n*)

in **embryo,** in wording

emendation, ver'betering

emerald, sma'ragd(en)

emerge, te voorschijn komen

emergency, nood(geval *n*), noodtoestand

emigrant, emi'grant: emi'grerend

emigrate, emi'greren

eminence, emi'nentie, ver'maardheid

eminent, uit'zonderlijk (ver'maard)

emissary, ge'zant

emit, uitstralen, afgeven; uiten

emolument, ver'dienste

emotion, (ge'moeds)aandoening, e'motie

emotional, emotio'neel, ge'voelsemperor,** keizer

emphasis, nadruk

emphasize, de nadruk leggen op, duidelijk doen uitkomen

emphatic, na'drukkelijk

empire, (keizer)rijk *n*

emplacement, stelling

employ, (in)dienst(hebben); ge'bruiken, bezighouden

employee, werknemer

employer, werkgever

employment, werk *n*; ge'bruik *n*

employmentexchange, arbeidsbeurs

empower, machtigen

empress, keizer'in

empty, leeg (maken *or* worden); niets'zeggend: lozen

emulate, nastreven

emulsion, e'mulsie

enable, in staat stellen

enact, tot wet ver'heffen; opvoeren

enamel, e'mail('leren) (*n*), brandverf, gla'zuur *n*: lakken

enamour, be'koren; ver'zotten

encamp, een kamp opslaan; legeren

encase, om'sluiten, opsluiten

enchant, be'toveren; ver'rukken

enchanting, sprookjesachtig, char'mant; be'toverend

encircle, om'ringen, om'singelen

enclose, insluiten

enclosure, om'sloten ruimte; bijlage

encompass, om'sluiten; be'vatten

encore, bis('seren): toegift

encounter, ont'moeting; treffen
n: tegenkomen; onder'vinden

encourage, aanmoedigen

encouragement, aanmoediging

encroach on, doordringen tot;
inbreuk maken op

encrust, be'slaan; be'zetten

encumber, be'lasten

encumbrance, be'letsel *n*

encyclopaedia, encyclope'die

end, eind(igen) (*n*); doel *n*
no end of, vreselijk veel
in the end, ten'slotte
make both ends meet, rondkomen

endanger, in ge'vaar brengen

endear, ge'liefd maken, innemen

endeavour, poging: trachten

ending, eind *n*; uitgang

endless, eindeloos, zonder einde

endorse, endos'seren; onder'schrijven

endow, be'giftigen

endowment, schenking

endue, be'giftigen

endurance, uithoudingsvermogen *n*; ver'dragen *n*

endure, ver'dragen; ver'duren

enemy, vijand(elijk)

energetic, ener'giek; krachtig

energy, ener'gie

enfold, om'wikkelen; om'helzen,
om'strengelen

enforce, (krachtig) uitvoeren;
dwingen tot

enforcement, handhaving

enfranchise, vrijmaken; kiesrecht ver'lenen

engage, in dienst nemen; in
be'slag nemen; slaags raken
met; in el'kaar grijpen

engaged, ver'loofd; in ge'sprek,
be'zet, bezig
to get engaged, zich ver'loven
met

engagement, afspraak; ver'loving; in'dienstneming; ge'vecht
n

engaging, in'nemend

engender, ver'wekken; ver'oorzaken

engine, ma'chine, motor, locomo'tief

engineer, inge'nieur, technicus,
machi'nist, lid van de ge'nietroepen: klaarspelen

engineering, tech'niek

England, Engeland *n*

English(man), Engels(man) (*n*)

engrave, gra'veren; inprenten

engraving, gra'vure, gra'veren *n*

engross, ver'diepen; fasci'neren

engulf, ver'zwelgen

enhance, ver'hogen

enigma(tic)(al), raadsel(achtig)
(*n*)

enjoin, be'velen

enjoy, ge'nieten (van)

enjoyable, prettig

enjoyment, ple'zier *n*, ge'nieten *n*

enlarge, (zich) ver'groten
to enlarge on, uitweiden over

enlighten, opheldering geven
aan; ver'lichten

enlist, (in) dienst nemen; een
be'roep doen op

enliven, opvrolijken

enmity, vijandschap

ennoble, adelen

enormous, kolos'saal

enormously, e'norm

enough, ge'noeg; heel
kind enough, zo vriendelijk

enrage, woedend maken

enrapture, in ver'voering
brengen

enrich, ver'rijken

enrol, (zich laten) inschrijven;
lid worden

ensconce, ver'schansen; nestelen

ensign, vlag; vaandrig

enslave, knechten

ensue, het ge'volg zijn, volgen

ensure, ver'zekeren

entail, met zich meebrengen

entangle, vastraken; ver'strikken

enter, binnengaan, binnenkomen;
gaan in; opgeven; boeken

enterprise, onder'neming(sgeest)

enterprising, onder'nemend

entertain, ver'maken, onder'houden; ont'halen, ont'vangen;
over'wegen; koesteren

entertaining, amu'sant: so'ciale plichten
entertainment, amuse'ment *n*
enthrall, boeien
enthrone, op de troon plaatsen, wijden
enthusiasm, enthousi'asme *n*
enthusiast(ic), enthousi'ast
entice, (ver')lokken
entire, (ge')heel
entirely, helemaal
entirety, ge'heel *n*
entitle, (be')titelen; het recht geven
entity, eenheid, ge'heel *n*, (aan)-zijn *n*
entomb, be'graven
entrails, ingewanden
entrance, ingang; opkomen *n*: in ver'voering brengen
entreat, smeken
entreaty, smeekbede
entrust, toevertrouwen
entry, intocht, ingang; boeking; inschrijving
enumerate, opnoemen
envelop, hullen
envelope, enve'loppe
enviable, benijdens'waardig
envious, af'gunstig
environment, om'geving
environs, omstreken
envisage, voor'zien
envoy, ('af)ge'zant
envy, afgunst: be'nijden
epaulet, epau'let
ephemeral, kort'stondig
epic, epos *n*, heldendaden: episch
epicure, gastro'noom
epidemic, epide'mie; rage
epigram, epi'gram *n*
epilepsy, epilep'sie
epilogue, epi'loog
Epiphany, Drie'koningen
episcopal, episco'paal
episode, epi'sode
epistle, (zend)brief
epitaph, grafschrift *n*
epithet, e'pitheton *n*
epitome, kwintessens
epoch, tijdperk *n*
equal, ge'lijk (zijn aan); eve'naren
  equal to, opgewassen tegen

equality, ge'lijkheid
equalize, ge'lijk maken
equally, even ('zeer)
equanimity, gelijk'moedigheid
equation, verge'lijking
equator, evenaar
equatorial, equatori'aal
equilateral, gelijk'zijdig
equilibrium, evenwicht *n*
equinox, dag-en-'nachtevening
equip, uitrusten, toerusten
equitable, billijk
equity, billijkheid
equivalent, ekwiva'lent (*n*)
equivocal, dubbel'zinnig, twijfel-achtig
era, tijdperk *n*, jaartelling
eradicate, uitroeien
erase, schrappen; uitwissen
erect, over'eind (zetten); oprich-ten
ermine, herme'lijn (*n*)
erode, uitschuren
erosion, e'rosie
erotic, e'rotisch
err, dwalen
errand, boodschap
erratic, inconse'quent, onregel'-matig
erroneous, on'juist
error, fout, a'buis *n*
erudite, ge'leerd
erupt, uitbarsten, uitspuwen
escalator, roltrap
escapade, esca'pade
escape, ont'vluchting: ont'snap-pen, ont'komen aan; ont'gaan
escarpment, steile wand
escort, ge'leide *n*, es'corte *n*: bege'leiden, escor'teren
especial, bij'zonder
especially, bijzonder, voor'al
espionage, spion'nage
espouse, huwen; om'helzen
espy, be'speuren
Esq(uire): A. Man —, de Wel-edelgeboren Heer A. Man
essay, opstel *n*: pogen
essence, wezen *n*, es'sentie; es'sence
essential, essen'tieel: hoofd-zaak
essentially, in wezen

establish, oprichten; (vast)-stellen; vestigen; instellen

establishment, (handels)huis *n*, instelling; oprichten *n*

estate, landgoed *n*, vast goed *n*

estate agent, makelaar

esteem, achting: achten

estimable, achtens'waardig; te be'rekenen

estimate, schatting: schatten

estimation, mening; schatting, achting

estrange, ver'vreemden

estuary, ri'viermond

etc(etera), enz(ovoorts)

etch, etsen

etching, ets

eternal, eeuwig

eternity, eeuwigheid

ether, ether

ethereal, e'therisch

ethical, ethisch

ethics, ethica

ethnology, volkenkunde

etiquette, eti'quette

etymology, etymolo'gie

eulogy, lofrede

Europe, Eu'ropa *n*

European, Euro'pees: Euro-pe'aan

evacuate, evacu'eren

evade, ont'wijken

evaluate, ta'xeren, schatten

evangelic(al), evan'gelisch

evangelist, evange'list

evaporate, ver'dampen; ver'-dwijnen

evasion, ont'wijking, ont'duiking

evasive, ont'wijkend

eve, (voor)avond, dag voor

even, ge'lijk('matig); effen; even; quitte; gelijk'moedig: zelfs; pre'cies; nog: ge'lijkmaken

even so, maar toch

evening, avond

evening-dress, avondtoilet *n*

event, ge'beurtenis, ge'val *n*; nummer *n*

at all events, in ieder ge'val

eventful, veelbe'wogen

eventual, uit'eindelijk; even-tu'eel

eventually, ten'slotte

ever, ooit, ten allen tijde

evergreen, altijd groen(e plant)

everlasting, eeuwig('durend)

evermore, altijd

every, ieder; alle

every other week, om de twee weken

every now and then, telkens

everybody, everyone, ieder'een

everyday, alle'daags, dagelijks

everything, alles

everywhere, overal (waar)

evict, uitzetten

evidence, be'wijs(materi'aal *or* stuk) *n*, ge'tuigenis; blijk *n*

to give evidence, ge'tuigenis afleggen

evident, duidelijk, klaar'blijke-lijk

evil, kwaad (*n*); onheil *n*, euvel *n*

evildoer, boosdoener

evince, (aan)tonen

evoke, oproepen

evolution, evo'lutie

evolve, (zich) ont'plooien

ewe, ooi

ewer, lam'petkan

exact, pre'cies: eisen

exacting, veel'eisend

exactitude, nauw'keurigheid

exaggerate, over'drijven

exalt, ver'heffen; ver'heerlijken

exaltation, ver'heerlijking; (geest)ver'voering

examination, e'xamen *n*; onder-zoek *n*; ver'hoor *n*

examine, exami'neren; onder'-zoeken, onder'vragen; goed be'kijken

example, voorbeeld *n*, mo'del *n*

to set an example, een voor-beeld geven

exasperate, gruwelijk ergeren

excavate, uitgraven, opgraven

excavation, opgraving

exceed, te boven gaan, over'schrijden

exceedingly, bij'zonder

excel, uitmunten; over'treffen

excellence, voor'treffelijkheid

excellency, excel'lentie

excellent, uit'stekend

except, be'halve: uitzonderen

exception, uitzondering
to take exception to, min denken over
exceptional, onge'woon, exceptio'neel
excerpt, (aangehaalde) passage
excess, overmaat; surplus *n*; uitspatting: extra
excessive, over'dadig, buiten'sporig
exchange, ruil(en); beurs; cen'trale; (uit)wisseling: (in)wisselen
exchequer, schatkist
excise, ac'cijns: uitsnijden
excitable, gauw opgewonden
excite, opwinden, prikkelen; opwekken
excitement, opwinding
exclaim, uitroepen
exclamation, uitroep
exclude, uitsluiten, buitensluiten
exclusive, uit'sluitend; exclu'sief
excommunicate, in de ban doen
excrements, uitwerpselen
excrescence, uitwas; over'tolligheid
excretion, afscheiding
excruciating, folterend, pijnlijk
excursion, ex'cursie, uitstapje *n*; uitweiding
excusable, be'grijpelijk
excuse, ex'cuus *n*: excu'seren, niet kwalijk nemen; ve-ront'schuldigen; vrijstellen
excuse me, par'don; neem me niet kwalijk
execute, uitvoeren; ter dood brengen
execution, uitvoering; te'rechtstelling
executioner, beul
executive, uitvoerend(e macht); be'drijfsleider
executor, execu'teur
exemplary, voor'beeldig
exemplify, als voorbeeld dienen van, be'lichamen
exempt, vrij(gesteld): vrijstellen
exercise, oefening: (uit)oefenen; in acht nemen
exert, aanwenden, inspannen
exertion, inspanning; ge'bruik *n*

exhale, uitademen
exhaust, uitlaat: uitputten
exhaustion, uitputting
exhibit, inzending, be'wijsstuk *n*: ten'toonstellen; (ver')tonen
exhibition, ten'toonstelling; ver'toon *n*, ver'toning
exhibitor, expo'sant
exhilarate, stimu'leren, opvrolijken
exhort, aansporen, ver'manen
exhume, opgraven
exigency, dringende aange'legenheid; noodgeval *n*
exile, balling(schap)
exist, be'staan
existence, be'staan *n*
exit, uitgang; aftreden *n*
exonerate, zuiveren
exorbitant, buiten'sporig
exorcize, be'vrijden; uitdrijven
exotic, uit'heems
expand, (doen) uitzetten, (zich) uitbreiden, (zich) uitspreiden; uitwerken
expanse, uitge'strektheid
expansion, uitzetting, uitbreiding
expatiate, uitweiden
expatriate, ver'bannen
expect, ver'wachten; denken
expectant, vol verwachting
expectant mother, aanstaande moeder
expectation, ver'wachting
expediency, opportuni'teit; eigenbelang *n*
expedient, be'vorderlijk, raadzaam, redmiddel *n*
expedite, be'spoedigen
expedition, expe'ditie
expel, uitdrijven; wegsturen, roy'eren
expend, uitgeven; be'steden
expenditure, uitgeven *n*, be'steden *n*; uitgaven
expense, (on)kosten, uitgave
expensive, duur
experience, er'varing: onder'vinden
experienced, er'varen
experiment, proef: experimen'teren

experimental, proef (onder'vindelijk)

expert, des'kundig(e), be'dreven

expiate, boeten voor

expire, aflopen; de laatste adem uitblazen; uitademen

expiry, afloop

explain, uitleggen

explanation, ver'klaring

explanatory, ver'klarend

explicit, uit'drukkelijk

explode, (doen) ont'ploffen; losbarsten; ont'zenuwen

exploit, (helden)daad; exploi'teren

exploration, onder'zoeking-(stocht)

explore, ver'kennen, onder'zoeken

explorer, ont'dekkingsreiziger

explosion, ont'ploffing; uitbarsting

explosive, springstof: ont'plofbaar; op'vliegend

exponent, expo'nent

export, uitvoer(artikel *n*): uitvoeren

expose, blootstellen; uitstallen; ont'hullen, aan de dag brengen; be'lichten

exposed, onbe'schut

exposition, uit'eenzetting; ten'toonstelling

exposure, ont'maskering; blootstellen *n*; be'lichting

expound, uit'eenzetten

express, uit'drukkelijk, speci'aal, op'zettelijk; ex'presse: ex'pres-(trein): uitdrukken; uitpersen

expression, uitdrukking

expressive, expres'sief; veel'zeggend

expropriate, ont'eigenen

expulsion, uitdrijving; wegsturen *n*, roye'ment *n*

expunge, uitwissen

exquisite, buitengewoon fijn; zeer ver'fijnd

extant, nog be'staand

extemporaneous, extempore, geïmprovi'seerd, on'voorbereid

extemporize, improvi'seren

extend, (zich) uitstrekken,

ver'lengen; uitbreiden; ver'lenen

extension, bijgebouw *n*; ver'lenging; lijn

extensive, uitgebreid, uitgestrekt

extent, uitge'strektheid; omvang **to what** (*or* **this**) **extent,** in hoe(*or* zo)'verre

extenuate, ver'zachten, ver'goelijken

exterior, buiten(kant), uit'wendig

exterminate, uitroeien

external, uit'wendig, buiten-(lands); uiterlijk(heid)

extinct, uitgestorven

extinguish, blussen, doven; een eind maken aan

extort, afpersen

extortionate, buiten'sporig

extra, extra

extract, passage; ex'tract *n*; (uit)trekken, uithalen; afpersen

extraction, ex'tractie; afkomst

extraneous, vreemd, niet ter zake dienend

extraordinary, buitenge'woon zeldzaam

extravagance, buiten'sporigheid, ver'kwisting; uitspatting

extravagant, ver'kwistend; buiten'sporig, over'dreven

extreme, uiterst(e *n*)

extremist, extre'mist(isch)

extremity, uiterste (nood) (*n*), uiteinde *n*

extricate, loswerken, losmaken, ont'warren

exuberant, uit'bundig

exude, afscheiden; ver'spreiden

exult, jubelen

exultant, triom'fantelijk, opgetogen

exultation, tri'omf, opge'togenheid

eye, oog *n*: aankijken
to catch a person's eye, de aandacht van iemand trekken
to see eye to eye, het ge'heel eens zijn
to set eyes on, onder ogen krijgen

eyebrow, wenkbrauw
eyelash, wimper
eyelid, ooglid *n*
eye-opener, open'baring
eyesight, ge'zicht *n*
eyesore, gruwel (voor het oog)
eyrie, arendsnest *n*

F

fable, fabel
fabric, stof, weefsel *n*; struc'tuur
fabricate, fabri'ceren; ver'zinnen
fabulous, legen'darisch; fabelachtig
façade, gevel; voorwendsel *n*
face, ge'zicht *n*; wijzerplaat; oppervlakte; pres'tige *n*: no-minaal: liggen op; het ge'zicht keren naar; onder de ogen zien; be'dekken
face to face, van aangezicht tot aangezicht
in the face of, ondanks; in aanmerking ge'nomen
on the face of it, ogen'schijnlijk
faced with, ge'plaatst voor (*or* in)
at its face value, zonder meer
facet, fa'cet *n*
facetious, gek(scherend), schertsend
facial, ge'zichts-
facile, (licht')vaardig, opper'vlakkig
facilitate, verge'makkelijken
facility, ge'mak(kelijkheid) (*n*)
facing, tegen'over, met het ge'zicht naar (*or* op): be'leg *n*
fact, feit *n*
in (point of) fact, in feite, eigenlijk, zelfs, immers
faction, par'tij(strijd)
factor, factor
factory, fa'briek
factual, feitelijk
faculty, ver'mogen *n*, aanleg; facul'teit; ver'gunning
fad, be'vlieging
fade, (doen)ver'schieten; ver'weken; wegsterven

fag, cor'vee(ër); strootje: (zich) afsloven
faggot, bos hout
fail, mis'lukken, (laten) zakken; nalaten; in de steek laten; opraken
without fail, zonder man'keren
failing, ge'brek *n*: bij ge'brek aan
failure, mis'lukk(el)ing
fain, gaarne
faint, flauw(te), vaag, zwak: flauwvallen
faint-hearted, blo'hartig
fair, billijk, eerlijk; be'hoorlijk; blond; mooi, net: kermis, markt
fairly, tamelijk; eerlijk
fairway, vaarwater *n*; baan
fairy, fee
fairyland, sprookjesland *n*
fairy-tale, sprookje *n*
faith, ge'loof *n*; ver'trouwen *n*; trouw
faithful, trouw; ge'lovig(en)
yours faithfully, Uw dw. (*i.e.* dienstwillige)
faithless, onge'lovig; trouweloos
fake, be'drog *n*; namaak: knoeien met; namaken; fin'geren
falcon, valk
fall, val(len), daling; overgave, ondergang; ver'val *n*: be'zwijken; dalen
to fall back on, zijn toevlucht nemen tot; te'rugtrekken op
to fall out, ruzie krijgen; uit het ge'lid treden
to fall short, te'kortschieten
to fall through, in duigen vallen
to fall to, aanpakken, toetasten; dichtvallen; ten deel vallen
fallacy, dwaalbegrip *n*, drogrede
fallow, braak: geelbruin
false, on'juist; vals; on'trouw; scheef; loos
false teeth, kunstgebit *n*
falsehood, on'waarheid
falsify, ver'valsen
falter, wankelen, weifelen; stamelen
fame, roem, ver'maardheid
famed, be'roemd

familiar, be'kend, ver'trouwd; famili'aar

familiarity, familiari'teit

family, ge'zin n, fa'milie; ge'slacht n; kinderen

famine, hongersnood; schaarste

famish, uithongeren, ver'hongeren

famous, be'roemd; prachtig

fan, waaier, venti'lator: enthousi'ast: waaieren; aanwakkeren

fanatic, dweper; fana'tiek(eling)

fanaticism, fana'tisme n

fancier, liefhebber

fanciful, fan'tastisch; grillig

fancy, ver'beelding(skracht); be'vlieging: fanta'sie-, luxe: zich in(or ver')beelden; een i'dee hebben; zin hebben in

fancy-dress, gecostu'meerd

fanfare, fan'fare

fang, giftand, slagtand

fanlight, raam boven een deur

fantastic, fan'tastisch, grillig

fantasy, fanta'sie

far, ver; veel

far off, ver weg

the far side, de overkant

as far as, voor zo'ver; tot aan

by far, far and away, verreweg

far and wide, heinde en ver

farce, klucht, pas'kwil n

farcical, kluchtig, be'spottelijk

fare, ta'rief n, vracht(je n); ver'voerskosten; kost: gaan

farewell, afscheid(s-) (n): a'dieu!

far-fetched, verge'zocht

farm, boerde'rij, fokke'rij, kweke'rij: een boerde'rij hebben (van)

farmer, boer

farmhand, boeren'arbeider

farmhouse, boeren'huis n, boerde'rij

farming, boerenbe'drijf n

farmstead, boerde'rij

farmyard, (boeren')erf n

far-off, ver

far-reaching, verstrekkend

farrier, hoefsmid

farrow, worp: biggen

far-sighted, verziend; voor'uitziend

farther, verder

farthest, verst

farthing, kwart penny; duit

fascinate, boeien, fasci'neren

fascination, iets boeiends, be'koring; ge'boeide be'langstelling

fashion, mode; ma'nier: scheppen, vormen

fashionable, modi'eus, deftig, (in de) mode

fast, snel, hard; vóór; ge'raffi'neerd: vast; wasecht; trouw: vasten

to be fast asleep, als een roos slapen

fasten, vastmaken; gooien

fastening, sluiting, knip

fastidious, kies'keurig

fat, dik, vet (n)

fatal, dodelijk; nood'lottig; be'slissend

fatalist(ic), fata'list(isch)

fate, lot n; dood

fated: he seems —, het schijnt zijn voorbestemming te zijn; hij schijnt ten ondergang ge'doemd

fateful, ge'wichtig

father, vader; pater

fathom, vadem: peilen

fathomless, peilloos

fatigue, ver'moeidheid, ver'moeienis; cor'vee: afmatten

fatten, aanzetten; vetmesten

fatty, vet(tig): dikkerd

fatuous, stom, dwars

fault, fout, de'fect n; schuld

to find fault with, vitten op; aanmerkingen maken op

faultless, onbe'rispelijk, feilloos

faulty, ge'brekkig, de'fect

favour, (be')gunst(igen); ingang: voorliefde; in'signe n: de voorkeur geven aan

in favour of, vóór; ten gunste van

to do someone a favour, iemand een ge'noegen doen

favourable, gunstig

favourite, gunsteling, favo'riet: lievelings-

favouritism, be'voorrechting

fawn, beige: jong hert n: flikflooien

fealty, (leenmans)trouw

fear, angst, vrees: vrezen, bang zijn

fearful, vreselijk

fearless, onbe'vreesd

feasible, uit'voerbaar; aan'nemelijk

feast, feest(maal) *n*: zich ver'gasten aan, ont'halen

feat, pres'tatie

feather, veer, pluim: veren

feature, (ge'laats)trek; onderdeel *n*, (op'vallende) eigenschap: gaan over

February, febru'ari

fecund(ity), vruchtbaar(heid)

federal, fede'raal

federation, fede'ratie

fee, hono'rarium *n*, be'drag *n*, (school)geld *n*

feeble, zwak, flauw

feed, voer(en) (*n*); voeding: eten
  fed up: to be —, er ta'bak van hebben

feeder, slab

feel, ge'voel *n*: (zich) voelen; (be')tasten; aanvoelen; ge'loven; (meelij) hebben
  to feel like, aanvoelen als; zich voelen (als); zin hebben in

feeling, ge'voel(en) *n*

feign, veinzen

felicitous, ge'lukkig

felicity, ge'luk('zaligheid) (*n*)

feline, katachtig

fell, hevig: (neer)vellen

fellow, kerel: mede-

fellowship, ge'meenschap

felonious, mis'dadig; snood

felony, zware misdaad

felt, vilt(en) (*n*)

female, vrouwelijk (per'soon), vrouwspersoon; wijfje *n*

feminine, vrouwelijk

fen, moe'rasland *n*, polder

fence, om'heining, schutting; heler: om'heinen; schermen

fend for oneself, voor zich'zelf zorgen
  to fend off, afweren

fender, haardrand; stootmat

ferment, gist(ing); be'roering: (doen) gisten

fern, varen

ferocious, woest

ferret, fret: opsporen; snuffelen

ferro-concrete, ge'wapend be'ton *n*

ferry, veer(pont) (*n*): overzetten

fertile, vruchtbaar; rijk

fertilize, vruchtbaar maken; be'vruchten

fertilizer, (kunst)mest

fervent, vurig, innig

fervid, heftig

fervour, vuur *n*

festal, feestelijk, feest-

fester, zweren; woekeren

festival, feest *n*

festive, feestelijk, feest-

festivity, festivi'teit

festoon, slinger: met slingers tooien

fetch, (af)halen; opbrengen

fête, lief'dadigheidsfeest (in de open lucht) *n*

fetish, fetisj

fetter, keten(en)

feud, vete

feudal, feo'daal

fever, koorts(achtige opwinding)

feverish, koorts(acht)ig

few, weinig(en)
  a few, een paar, enkele

fiancé(e), ver'loofde

fiasco, fi'asco *n*

fib, leugentje *n*; jokken

fibre, vezel; stoerheid, aard

fickle, wispel'turig

fiction, ro'mans en korte ver'halen; fictie, ver'dichtsel *n*

fictitious, fic'tief, gefin'geerd

fiddle, vi'ool (spelen); peuteren; scharrelen

fiddlesticks! nonsens!

fidelity, trouw, ge'trouwheid

fidget, draaitol: wiebelen

fie on you! schaam je!

field, veld *n*, akker; ge'bied *n*: fielden

field-marshal, veldmaarschalk

fiend, duivel; mani'ak

fiendish, duivels

fierce, woest, fel

fiery, vuur(rood); vurig

fife, fluit: pijpen

fifteen(th), vijftien(de)
fifth, vijfde : kwint
fifty, vijftig
fig, vijg ; zier
fight, ge'vecht *n*, strijd ; vecht-
lust : (be')vechten
figment, ver'zinsel *n*
figurative, fi'guurlijk
figure, cijfer *n*; prijs ; ge'daante,
fi'guur *n* : voorkomen
figure of speech, zegswijze
to figure out, uitkienen
figurehead, boegbeeld *n*; leider
in naam
filament, (gloei)draad
filch, kapen
file, dos'sier *n*, map ; file ; vijl-
(en) ; opbergen ; (een voor een)
trekken
filigree, fili'graan *n*
filings, vijlsel *n*
fill, (op)vullen ; stoppen
fillet, fi'let : fi'leren
filling, vulling
fillip, prikkel
filly, jonge merrie
film, film, vlies(je) *n*, waas *n*;
(ver')filmen
filmy, vliezig, wazig
filter, filter : fil'treren ; sijpelen
filter through, uitlekken
filth, vuiligheid ; vuile taal
filthy, vuil, vies
fin, vin
final, laatste, eind-, slot-; defini'tief : eindwedstrijd
finally, ten'slotte
finance, fi'nanciën : finan'cieren
financial, finan'cieel
financier, finan'cier
find, vondst : (be')vinden ; ont'-
dekken ; merken ; (op)zoeken
finding, be'vinding
fine, mooi ; (haar)fijn ; best :
geldboete
finery, opschik
finesse, fi'nesse, listigheid : snijden
finger, vinger : be'tasten
finger-nail, nagel
finger-print, vingerafdruk
finicky, kies'keurig, piete'peute-
rig

finish, eind(igen) (*n*) ; afwerking : af (*or* op)maken ; afwerken
finite, eindig
Finn(ish), Fin(s) (*n*)
fiord, fjord
fir, den(ne boom)
fire, vuur *n*, brand ; haard : (af)-
vuren, (af)schieten, lossen ;
bakken ; aanwakkeren ; op
straat zetten
to catch fire, vlam vatten
on fire, in brand ; brandend (van
ver'langen)
to set fire to, to set on fire, in
brand steken
fire-arm, vuurwapen *n*
fire-brand, brandende spaander ;
stokebrand
fire-engine, brandspuit
fire-escape, brandtrap
fire-extinguisher, blusappa-
raat *n*
fire-fly, glimworm
fire-guard, haardhekje *n*
fire-light, vuurgloed
fireman, brandweerman ; stoker
fire-place, open haard
fire-proof, brandvrij, vuurvast
fireside, (open) haard
firewood, brandhout *n*
fireworks, vuurwerk *n*
firm, vast(be'raden), stevig,
hecht ; stand'vastig : firma
firmament, uitspansel *n*
first, (voor het) eerst ; ten eerste
at first, in het be'gin
first of all, eerst, om te be'ginnen
first aid, eerste hulp
first-hand, uit de eerste hand
first-rate, eersteklas, prima
fiscal, fis'caal, be'lasting-
fish, vis(sen) ; opdiepen
fisher(man), visser, hengelaar
fishery, visse'rij
fishing, vissen *n*; visge'legenheid
fishing-rod, hengel
fishmonger, visboer, viswinkel
fishy, visachtig, vis-; ver'dacht
fissure, kloof, spleet
fist, vuist
fit, ge'zond ; ge'schikt ; klaar :
aanval ; bui, toeval *n*: passen ;

kloppen met; voor'zien, uitrusten

to fit in, plaats (or tijd) vinden voor; zich aanpassen, passen bij

fitful, on'rustig, grillig, hokkend

fitting, ge'past; pas: fitting

fittings, toebehoren n, be'nodigdheden

five, vijf

fix, knel: vastmaken; vaststellen; vestigen; opknappen; fi'xeren

fixed, vast

fixture, vaste fitting; (datumven een) wedstrijd

fizz, sissen

fizzle, sissen, sputteren

to fizzle out, met een sisser aflopen

flabbergast, stomverbaasd doen staan

flabby, pafferig

flag, vlag; pla'vuis; lis: ver'slappen

flagon, (1½ liter)fles; schenkkan

flagpole, flagstaff, vlaggestok

flagrant, schandelijk

flagship, vlaggeschip n

flake, vlok: (af)schilferen

flamboyant, zwierig, op'zichtig

flame, vlam(men); vuurrood zijn

flange, flens

flank, flank('eren)

flannel, fla'nel(len) (n); waslapje n

flannels, sportbroek

flap, klep, (tafel)blad n, pand: klapperen; (op en neer) slaan met

flare, opflikkering; fakkel, si'gnaalvlam

to flare up, opvlammen; opstuiven

flash, flits(en); flikkeren; schieten

flashlight, zaklantaren

flashy, op'zichtig

flask, fla'con

flat, plat, vlak; vierkant (refusal); standaard (rate); ver'schaald; mat; te laag: flat, é'tage; mol

flat-bottomed, platboomd

flatten, plat maken

flatter, vleien, flat'teren

flattery, vleie'rij

flatulence, opgeblazen ge'voel n

flaunt, geuren met

flavour, smaak; tintje n: kruiden, toebereiden

flavouring, a'roma n

flaw, fout; leemte

flawless, gaaf; onbe'rispelijk

flax, vlas n

flaxen, vlassig

flay, villen

flea, vlo

fleck, (be')spikkel(en)

flee, vlieden

fleece, vacht: villen

fleecy, wollig; schapen-

fleet, vloot; leger n: snel

fleeting, bliksemsnel, voor'bijflitsend

Flemish, Vlaams

flesh, vlees n

fleshy, vlezig

flex, snoer n: buigen

flexible, buigzaam; soepel

flick, tik(ken), knip(pen)

flicker, flikkeren

flight, vlucht; groep, zwerm; trap

flighty, wuft

flimsy, dun, teer, flodderig

flinch, te'rugdeinzen; (in'een)-krimpen

fling, smijten (met); stormen

flint, vuursteen(tje n)

flip, (weg)slaan

flippant, onge'past spottend

flirt, flirt(en); spelen

flit, fladderen, dartelen

float, dobber, drijver: (laten) drijven, vlot maken

floating, vlottend

flock, kudde, schare: (samen)-stromen

flog, (af)ranselen

flood, over'stroming; (zond)-vloed, zee: (doen) over'stromen; stromen

floodlight, floodlight n: ver'lichten

floor, vloer, ver'dieping: over'donderen

flop, fi'asco *n*; (in el'kaar) ploffen

floral, bloemen-

florid, bloemrijk

florin, tweeshillingstuk *n*, gulden

florist, bloe'mist

flotilla, flot'tielje

flounce, stuiven

flounder, ploeteren, spartelen; worstelen

flour, bloem, meel *n*

flourish, zwierig ge'baar *n*, krul, ge'schal : ge'dijen; zwaaien; geuren met

flout, in de wind slaan

flow, stroom; vloed : stromen

flower, bloem, bloei(en)

fluctuate, schommelen, op en neer gaan

flue, rookkanaal *n*

fluent, vloeiend

fluff, pluisjes : pluizen

fluffy, donzig

fluid, vloeibaar; on'vast: vloei-stof

fluke, ankerhand : bof

fluorescent, fluore'scerend

flurry, vlaag; trilling : zenuw-achtig maken

flush, blos; opwelling, roes : ge'lijk : blozen: (schoon)spoe-len

fluster, ner'veus maken

flute, fluit; groef : groeven

flutter, ge'klapwiek *n*: fladderen, klapwieken; flikkeren

flux, voort'durende ver'andering

fly, vlieg(en); gulp : vluchten (uit); oplaten; voeren

flying-boat, vliegboot

foal, veulen *n*

foam, schuim(en) (*n*)

foamy, schuimend

focus, brandpunt *n*; haard : stellen, zijn blik fi'xeren

fodder, (vee)voer *n*

foe, vijand

fog, mist : be'nevelen

foggy, mistig; vaag

foible, zwak(ke punt) *n*

foil, schermdegen : ver'ijdelen, over'treffen

foist off on, aansmeren

fold, vouw(en), plooi; kooi, kudde : slaan

folder, map; folder

folding, op'vouwbaar, vouw-

foliage, ge'baderte *n*

folio, folio *n*

folk, mensen : volks-

follow, volgen (op), opvolgen; be'grijpen

follower, volgeling

following, aanhang

folly, dwaasheid

foment, (aan)kweken

fomentation, (warme) omslag

fond, innig

  to be fond of, houden van

fondle, liefkozen

font, doopvont

food, voedsel *n*, eten *n*; stof

foodstuffs, voedingsmiddelen

fool, dwaas; nar : dwaars doen; voor de gek houden

foolhardy, roekeloos

foolish, dwaas

foot, voet, poot; voeteneinde *n*; voetvolk *n*: lopen; be'talen

  on foot, te voet; aan de gang

  to put one's foot in it, zich vergalop'peren

football(er), voetbal(ler)

footfall, voetstap

foothold, vaste voet

footing, houvast; (vaste) voet

footlights, voetlicht *n*

footman, li'vreiknecht, la'kei

footmark, voetafdruk

footpath, voetpad *n*

footprint, voetindruk

footstep, voetstap

footwear, schoeisel *n*

fop(pery), fat(terigheid)

for, voor; naar; ge'durende; wegens; ondanks: want; (om)dat

  O! for . . . had ik maar . . .

forage, fou'rage: foura'geren

foray, rooftocht : plunderen

forbear, voorzaat: nalaten

forbid, ver'bieden; ver'hoeden

forbidding, afschrik'wekkend

force, (strijd)kracht, ge'weld *n*; dwingen, for'ceren

  in force, van kracht

forceful, krachtig
forceps, tang
forcible, geweld'dadig; krachtig
ford, voord; door'waden
fore, voor('aan): voorgrond
forearm, voorarm
forebode, voor'spellen
foreboding, voorgevoel *n*; voor'-
spelling
forecast, voor'spelling: voor'-
spellen
forecastle, bak
forefather, voorvader
forefinger, wijsvinger
foregoing, voor'afgaand(e *n*)
foregone conclusion, uitge-
maakte zaak
foreground, voorgrond
forehead, voorhoofd *n*
foreign, buitenlands; vreemd
foreigner, vreemdeling, buitenlander
foreman, (ploeg)baas
foremost, voorste, eerste
forenoon, voormiddag
foresee, voor'zien
foreshadow, de voorbode zijn
van
foreshorten, ver'korten
foresight, voorzorg
forest, woud *n*
forestall, voor'komen, voorzijn
forester, houtvester
forestry, boswezen *n*, bosbouw
foretaste, voorsmaak
foretell, voor'spellen
forethought, be'leid *n*
forever, (voor) altijd
forfeit, boete, pand *n*; ver'spelen
forfeiture, ver'beurdverklaring
forgather, samenkomen
forge, smidsvuur *n*, smidse:
smeden; ver'valsen
  to forge ahead, ge'stadig voor'-
uitkomen
forgery, ver'valsing
forget, ver'geten
  I forget your name, ik ben Uw
naam ver'geten
forgetful, ver'geetachtig
forgive, ver'geven
forgiveness, ver'giffenis
forgiving, vergevensge'zind

forgo, opgeven
fork, vork; tweesprong, ver'tak-
king: zich splitsen
  to fork out, dokken
forked, ge'vorkt; zigzag
forlorn, troosteloos, zielig
form, vorm, ge'daante, lichaam
n; klas; bank; formu'lier *n*;
stijl; formali'teit; con'ditie:
(zich) vormen, (zich) opstellen
formal, for'meel
formality, formali'teit
formation, vorming, for'matie
former, eerst(genoemd); vroeger
formidable, ge'ducht, ontzag'-
wekkend
formula, for'mule; vorm
formulate, formu'leren
fornication, ontucht
forsake, ver'laten
fort, fort *n*
forth, voort; uit; te voorschijn
  and so forth, enzovoorts
forthcoming, (tege'moet)komend
forthright, open'hartig
forthwith, ter'stond
fortification, ver'sterking
fortify, ver'sterken
fortitude, geestkracht
fortnight, veertien dagen
fortress, vesting
fortuitous, toe'vallig
fortunate, ge'lukkig
fortune, for'tuin *n*; For'tuna
  good fortune, ge'luk *n*
  to tell fortunes, waarzeggen
forty, veertig
forward, voor'uit, voorwaarts;
naar voren; voorst; voorlijk;
vrij'postig: voor(speler): door-
sturen, ver'zenden; voor'uit-
helpen
fossil, fos'siel *n*
fossilize, ver'stenen
foster, kweken; koesteren
foster(-mother), pleeg(moeder)
foul, vies; laag; vals, ge'meen:
be'vuilen; on'klaar raken (*or*
maken)
found, stichten, oprichten; ba'seren
foundation, funda'ment *n*; oprichting; stichting; grond(slag)

founder, stichter, oprichter; grondlegger: ver'gaan; mis'lukken

foundling, vondeling

foundry, (me'taal)gieter'ij

fount, bron: lettertype *n*

fountain, fon'tein; bron

fountain-pen, vulpen

four, vier(tal *n*)

  on all fours, op handen en voeten

fourteen(th), veertien(de)

fourth, vierde (man); kwart (*n*)

fowl, ge'vogelte *n*; hoender

fox, vos: be'dotten

foxglove, vingerhoedskruid *n*

fraction, breuk; mi'niem ge'deelte *n*, onderdeel *n*

fractious, twistziek

fracture, breuk: breken

fragile, broos, breekbaar

fragment, frag'ment *n*, brokstuk *n*

fragrance, geur

fragrant, geurig

frail, teer

frailty, zwakheid

frame, lijst, mon'tuur *n*, ko'zijn *n*; lichaamsbouw: inlijsten; (op)stellen

  frame of mind, ge'moedstoestand

framework, ge'raamte *n*

franc, frank

franchise, kiesrecht *n*; (burger)-recht *n*

frank, open'hartig

frantic, dol, razend, wild, radeloos

fraternal, broederlijk

fraud, be'drog *n*, fraude; oplichter

fraudulent, fraudu'leus

fraught with, zwanger van

fray, strijd: (uit)rafelen, ver'stlijten

freak, gril, ge'drocht *n*

freckle(d), (vol) sproet(en)

free, vrij; gratis; los(lippig); open(lijk); over'vloedig: be'vrijden, vrijlaten

  free from (*or* **of**), zonder, be'vrijd van

  to set free, be'vrijden

freedom, vrijheid

free-hand, met de hand

freehold, vrij (grondbezit *n*)

freeze, (doen) (be')vriezen

freight, vracht(prijs)

freighter, vrachtboot, vrachtschip *n*

French, Frans(en) (*n*)

  French bean, sperzieboon

  French polish, poli'toeren

  French windows, openslaande deuren

Frenchman, Fransman

frenzied, razend

frenzy, razer'nij

frequency, veel-vuldigheid, fre'quentie

frequent, veel'voorkomend, ge'-regeld: dikwijls be'zoeken

frequently, her'haaldelijk

fresco, fresco *n*

fresh, vers, fris; nieuw; zoet

freshman, eerste'jaars (stu'dent)

fret, kniezen, pruilen; wegvreten

fret-work, uitgezaagd werk *n*

friar, monnik

friction, wrijving

Friday, vrijdag

friend, vriend('in), kennis

  to make friends with, be'vriend raken met

friendly, vriend('schapp)elijk

friendship, vriendschap

frieze, rand, fries

frigate, fre'gat *n*

fright, schrik; vogelverschrikker

frighten, doen schrikken

frightful, ver'schrikkelijk

frigid, ijzig; kil

frill, ge'rimpelde strook; tierlan'-tijntje *n*

fringe, franje; pony; buitenkant: om'zomen; grenzen (aan)

frippery, prullen

frisk, dartelen; vluchtig fouill'-eren

frisky, dartel

fritter, bei'gnet: ver'kwisten

frivolous, licht'zinnig; beuzelachtig

frizzle, sissen; fri'seren; bakken

fro: to and —, heen en weer, op en neer

frock, jurk(je *n*)

frog, kikvors

frolic, jo'lijt: dartelen

from, van('daan), van'af; uit: wegens

front, voorkant, voorste deel (*n*); front *n*: voor-, voorste
  at the front (of), voor'aan (in)
  in front of, voor
  in the front (of), voor'in (in)

frontier, grens

frost, vorst; rijp

frostbite, be'vriezing

froth, schuim *n*

frown, frons: het voorhoofd fronsen
  to frown upon, niet graag zien

frugal, sober, karig

fruit, vrucht(en), fruit *n*

fruitful, vruchtbaar

fruition, ver'vulling

fruitless, vruchteloos

frustrate, ver'ijdelen; tegenwerken

frustrated, te'leurgesteld en onbe'vredigd

frustration, wan'hopig ge'voel van onbe'vredigdheid

fry, bakken, braden

fuddle, be'nevelen

fuel, brand(stof): tanken

fugitive, vluchteling: (voort')vluchtig

fulfil, ver'vullen; waarmaken; be'antwoorden aan

full, vol('ledig)
  full of, vol
  in full, ten volle; vol'uit
fully, vol'komen, ten volle

fumble, tasten; frommelen

fume, damp(en): koken

fumigate, met dampen ont'smetten

fun, pret
  for (*or* in) fun, voor de grap
  to make fun of, de gek steken met

function, functie: functio'neren

functional, functio'neel; praktisch

fund, fonds *n*: voorraad

funds, geld *n*

fundamental, fundamen'teel, grond(beginsel *n*)

funeral, be'grafenis(-); lijk-, graf-

fungus, zwam

funk, rats: niet aandurven

funnel, trechter; pijp

funny, grappig; raar

fur, bont *n*; be'slag *n*, ketelsteen

furious, woedend

furl, oprollen

furnace, (smelt)oven, kachel

furnish, meubi'leren; voor'zien van, ver'schaffen

furnishings, stof'fering (en meubi'lering)

furniture, meubelen

furrow, voor; groef

further, verder, nader: be'vorderen

furtive, steels, heimelijk

fury, woede, razer'nij

fuse, (doorgeslagen) stop; lont: samensmelten

fuselage, romp

fusion, samensmelting; fusie

fuss, drukte: zich druk maken; zenuwachtig maken

fussy, lastig; druk

fusty, muf

futile, ver'geefs, zinloos, onbe'nullig

future, toekomst: toe'komstig
  in future, voortaan

G

gabble, snateren

gaberdine, gabar'dine

gable, gevelspits

gadget, snufje *n*, ge'val *n*

gag, prop: mop: knevelen

gaiety, vrolijkheid

gain, winst: be'halen; toenemen; ver'werven; be'reiken; voorlopen

gainsay, tegenspreken

gait, gang

gaiter, slobkous

gala, feest *n*: gala-

galaxy, schitterende ver'zameling

gale, storm

gall, gal: gruwelijk ergeren

gallant, fier, hoffelijk

gallantry, dapperheid; hoffelijkheid

galleon, gal'joen n

gallery, gale'rij; mu'seum n

galley, ga'lei; kom'buis

gallon, 4½ liter

gallop, ga'lop('peren)

gallows, galg

galore, in overvloed

galosh, overschoen

galvanize, galvani'seren

gamble, gokje n; gokken

gambler, gokker

gambol, dartelen

game, spel(letje) n; par'tij(tje n); wild n: flink; be'reid: lam: gokken

gamekeeper, jachtopziener

gamut, toonladder; re'gister n

gander, gent

gang, troep, bende

gangrene, gan'green n

gangster, gangster

gangway, pad n; loopplank

gaol, ge'vangenis

gaoler, ci'pier

gap, gat n, opening, hi'aat n

gape, gapen

garage, ga'rage: stallen

garb, kle'dij

garbage, vuilnis

garden, tuin('ieren)

gardener, tuinman, tui'nier

gargle, gorgelen

garish, schel, op'zichtig

garland, guir'lande: om'kransen

garlic, knoflook

garment, kledingstuk n, ge'waad n

garner, graanschuur: binnenhalen

garnish, gar'neren

garret, zolderkamer

garrison, garni'zoen n: legeren

garrulous, praatziek

garter, kouseband

gas, gas n: ver'gassen

gash, snee; snijden, scheuren

gasp, snak(ken)

gastric, maag-

gate, hek n, poort; ingang

gate-crash, binnenvallen

gateway, poort, hek n

gather, (zich) ver'zamelen; binnenhalen; krijgen (speed); samentrekken; opmaken(uit)

gathering, bij'eenkomst

gauche, links

gaudy, op'zichtig

gauge, (standaard)maat; meetinstrument n, manometer: meten, ijken; schatten

gaunt, (brood)mager

gauntlet, (kap)handschoen, pantserhandschoen; spitsroede

gauze, gaas n

gawky, slungelig

gay, vrolijk

gaze, starre blik: staren

gazette, staatscourant

gear, ver'snelling; inrichting; tuig: instellen

to change gear, overschakelen

out of gear, uitgeschakeld; in de war

gelatine, gela'tine

gem, edelsteen; ju'weel n

gender, ge'slacht n

general, algemeen: gene'raal

in general, over het algemeen

generalize, generali'seren

generally, ge'woonlijk; (over het) algemeen

generate, opwekken

generation, gene'ratie; opwekking

generator, gene'rator

generosity, edel'moedigheid

generous, edel'moedig; ro'yaal

genetics, ge'netica

genial, vriendelijk; groeizaam

genitive, genitief

genius, ge'nie n; ta'lent n

genteel, deftig(doend)

gentle, licht, zacht('aardig); matig

gentleman, gentleman, heer

genuine, echt, op'recht

geographic(al), aardrijks'kundig

geography, aardrijkskunde

geology, geolo'gie

geometry, meetkunde

Georgian, achttiende-'eeuws

geranium, ge'ranium

germ, kiem, ba'cil
German, Duits(er) (*n*)
 German measles, rode hond
Germany, Duitsland *n*
gesticulate, gesticu'leren
gesture, ge'baar *n*
get, krijgen; komen; worden
 I have got, ik heb
 I have got to, ik moet
 to get something done, iets
 (laten) doen; iets ge'daan
 krijgen
 to get about, buitenkomen,
 rondlopen
 to get along, (weg)gaan; opschieten; het maken
 to get around, overal komen;
 be'kend worden; om'zeilen
 to get at, be'reiken; achter
 komen; be'doelen
 to get away, wegkomen;
 ont'snappen
 to get back, te'rugkomen;
 te'rugkrijgen
 to get in, binnenkomen, in-
 stappen
 to get off, (er) afkomen (van),
 afstappen van; afkrijgen
 to get on, opstappen; aan-
 krijgen; opschieten; het stellen; het maken
 to get out, (onder')uitkomen,
 uitstappen; voor de dag halen;
 to get over, te boven komen
 to get through, doorkomen;
 antwoord krijgen
 to get to, komen in (*or* aan)
 to get up, opstaan; opsteken;
 op touw zetten
geyser, geiser
ghastly, af'grijselijk, doodsbleek
ghost, spook *n*; zweem
giant, reus('achtig)
gibber, brabbelen
gibberish, koeter'waals *n*
gibbet, galg
giblets, afval van ge'vogelte
giddy, duizelig; duizelig'wekkend; mal
gift, ge'schenk *n*; gave
gifted, be'gaafd
gig, sjees
gigantic, mas'saal, ge'weldig

giggle, giechelen
gild, ver'gulden
gill, kieuw: 0.14 liter
gilt, ver'guld(sel *n*)
gin, jonge jenever
ginger, gember
gingerly, be'hoedzaam
gipsy, zi'geuner('in)
giraffe, gi'raffe
gird, om'gorden
girder, (stalen) balk
girdle, gordel
girl, meisje *n*
girl-friend, vrien'din
girlish, meisjesachtig
girth, omvang; buikriem
gist, kern
give, geven; doorzakken, buigen
 to give away, weggeven; ver'-
 klappen
 to give in, zich ge'wonnen
 geven
 to give out, uitdelen; aankondigen; be'zwijken
 to give up, overgeven; (het)
 opgeven
given, be'paald; ge'neigd (tot)
gizzard, spiermaag; strot
glacier, gletsjer
glad, blij(de)
gladden, ver'blijden
glade, open plek
gladly, graag
glamorous, be'toverend
glamour, be'tovering
glance, (vluchtige) blik: een
 blik werpen; afschampen
gland, klier
glare, ver'blindend licht **n**;
 woeste blik : woest kijken
glaring, schel; vlammend; in
 het oog springend
glass, glas(werk) *n* : glazen
 glasses, bril
glaze, gla'zuur *n* : van glas
 voor'zien; gla'zuren
gleam, schijnsel *n*, straaltje *n*,
 glans: glimmen
glean, lezen; ver'garen
glee, vreugde, schelms ge'not *n*
glen, bergdal *n*
glib, glad, rad
glide, zweven, glijden

glider, zweefvliegtuig *n*

glimmer, flikkering; glimp: flikkeren

glimpse, glimp

glint, glinstering

glisten, glinsteren

glitter, ge'schitter *n* : schitteren

gloat, zich ver'lustigen, leedvermaak hebben

globe, (aard)bol

globule, pareltje *n*

gloom, duister *n*; droef'geestigheid

gloomy, duister, somber; droef'geestig

glorify, ver'heerlijken

glorious, roemrijk; heerlijk

glory, glorie, heerlijkheid

gloss, glans

  to gloss over, ver'doezelen

glossy, glanzend

glove, handschoen

glow, gloed; blos: gloeien; stralen

glower, dreigend kijken

glow-worm, glimworm

glue, (hout)lijm: lijmen

glum, sip

glut, (over)ver'zadiging: over'voeren

glutton, gulzigaard; werkezel

gnarled, knoestig, knokig

gnash one's teeth, knarsetanden

gnat, mug

gnaw, (af)knagen

gnome, aardmannetje *n*

go, (weg)gaan; lopen; worden; horen

  as things go, verge'leken bij anderen

  to go by, gaan per (*or* over); voor'bijgaan; zich laten leiden door; be'kend staan onder

  to go down, afgaan; naar be'neden gaan, ondergaan, zinken; er'in gaan

  to go into, binnengaan; ingaan (op); treden in (details); zich ver'diepen in

  to go off, af(*or* weg)gaan; aflopen

  to go on, gaan op; voor'uitgaan, voortgaan

  to go up, stijgen

  to go with, meegaan met; passen bij, horen bij

  to go without, het stellen zonder

  to let go, loslaten

goad, prikkel(en); aanzetten

go-ahead, vooruit'strevend

goal, doel(punt) *n*

goat, geit

gobble, schrokken; klokken

goblet, bo'kaal

goblin, ka'bouter

god, god

goddess, go'din

godly, god'vruchtig

god(mother), peet(tante)

godsend, zegen

goggle, kijken met grote ogen

going: to get (*or* **to keep)** —, aan de gang brengen, (*or* houden); lopen

gold, goud(en) (*n*)

golden, gouden; gulden

goldfish, goudvis

gold-leaf, bladgoud (*n*)

golf, golf *n*

golf-course, golf-links, golfbaan

gondola, gondel

gone, weg; op; zoek; dood

gong, gong

good, goed; zoet: bestwil

  a good deal, vrij veel

  for good, voor'goed; ten goede

good-bye, dag

good-looking, knap

good-natured, ge'moedelijk, goed'aardig

goodness, goedheid; voeding: goeie ge'nade!

good-night, wel te rusten

goods, goederen, spullen

goodwill, wel'willendheid; klan'dizie

goose, gans

gooseberry, kruisbes(sen)

gore, ge'ronnen bloed *n*; spietsen

gorge, bergengte: (zich) volstoppen

gorgeous, magni'fiek

gospel, evan'gelie *n*

gossamer, herfstdraad

gossip, ge'roddel *n*; rodde-
laar(ster); roddelen, kletsen
gothic, gotisch
gout, jicht
govern, re'geren; leiden
governess, gouver'nante
government, re'gering; be'leid *n*
governor, gouver'neur; cu'rator
gown, ja'pon; toga
grab, greep: grijpen naar
grace, gratie; ge'nade; tafelgebed *n*; res'pijt *n*: ver'eren
graceful, graci'eus
gracious, minzaam, hoffelijk:
(grote) goedheid!
grade, graad, kwali'teit: sor'teren
gradient, hellingshoek
gradual, ge'leidelijk
graft, (poli'tieke) knoeie'rij:
enten, transplan'teren
grain, graan *n*, korrel; greintje
n; nerf
grammar, gram'matica
grammar-school, gym'nasium
n
gramophone, grammo'foon
granary, graanschuur
grand, groot(s), prachtig
grandchild, kleinkind *n*
grandeur, grootsheid
grandiose, grandi'oos
grandmother, grootmoeder
granite, gra'niet(en) (*n*)
granny, grootje *n*, oma
grant, toelage: (toe)geven;
ver'lenen; inwilligen
grape, druif
grapefruit, grapefruit
graph, gra'fiek
graphic, grafisch; aan'schouwelijk
graphite, gra'fiet *n*
grapple, worstelen
grasp, greep; i'dee *n*; be'reik *n*:
vastpakken
grasping, in'halig
grass, gras *n*
grasshopper, sprinkhaan
grassy, gras(rijk)
grate, rooster: raspen; knarsen;
tegen de borst stuiten
grateful, dankbaar

gratification, vol'doening
gratify, strelen; be'vredigen
gratifying, be'vredigend, dankbaar
grating, traliewerk *n*; knarsen *n*
gratitude, dankbaarheid
gratuitous, gratis; spon'taan;
mis'plaatst
gratuity, fooi
grave, graf *n*: ernstig
gravel, grint(-) (*n*)
graveyard, kerkhof *n*
gravitation, aantrek-
king(skracht)
gravity, zwaartekracht; ernst
centre of gravity, zwaartepunt *n*
gravy, jus
graze, schaafwond: even aanraken; schaven: grazen, weiden
grazing, weiland *n*
grease, smeer, vet *n*: (in)smeren,
invetten
greasy, vet(tig), vuil
great, groot; voor'naamste;
nobel; enthousi'aste
a great deal (of), heel veel
great-grandchild, achterkleinkind *n*
great-grandmother, overgrootmoeder
greatly, zeer
greed, gulzigheid, hebzucht
greedy, gulzig; hebberig
Greek, Griek(s) (*n*)
green, groen: brink; baan
greens, bladgroenten
greengrocer, groenteboer
greenhouse, broeikas
greet, (be)groeten
greeting, groet
grey, grijs (worden), grauw
greyhound, haze'wind: wind-
honden-
grid, (braad)rooster; hoogspan-
ningsnet *n*
grief, ver'driet *n*
grievance, grief
grieve, treuren; be'droeven
grievous, hevig; schreeuwend
grill, rooster(en)
grim, onver'biddelijk; onaan'-
lokkelijk; akelig

grimace, gri'mas
grime, vuil *n* : be'vuilen
grin, grijns : grijnzen
grind, ge'zwoeg *n* : malen; slijpen; knarsen (op)
grindstone, slijpsteen
grip, (hand)greep, vat *n*, houvast *n* ; tas; be'grip *n* : (vast)pakken
gristle, kraakbeen *n*
grit, gruis *n* ; durf
grizzle, grienen
grizzly, grijs(achtig)
groan, ge'kreun *n* : kreunen
grocer, kruide'nier
groceries, kruide'nierswaren
groggy, wankel
groin, lies
groom, stalknecht : ver'zorgen
groove, groef; sleur : groeven
grope, (rond)tasten
gross, bruto; grof : gros *n*
grotesque, gro'tesk
grotto, grot
ground, grond(-); ter'rein *n*: aan de grond lopen; grondig onder'leggen
  to cover ground, ter'rein be'strijken
  to give ground, wijken
  to stand one's ground, standhouden; voet bij stuk houden
grounds, ter'rein *n*, park *n*; (koffie)dik *n*; reden(en)
ground-floor, (op de) be'nedenver'dieping
groundless, onge'grond
group, groep('eren)
grouse, korhoen(ders) *n*: kankeren
grove, bos(je *n*)
grovel, kruipen
grow, (aan)groeien; ver'bouwen, kweken; worden
  to grow up, opgroeien, ouder worden; ont'staan
growing, toenemend
growl, grom(men)
grown-up, vol'wassen(e)
growth, groei; aanwas; ge'zwel *n*
grub, larve; kost : wroeten
grudge, wrok : mis'gunnen

grudgingly, met tegenzin
gruel, gruwel
gruelling, af'mattend
gruesome, griezelig
gruff, bars
grumble, mopperen
grunt, ge'knor *n*; ge'brom *n*; knorren; brommen
guarantee, (waar)borg, ga'rantie : waarborgen, garan'deren
guard, wacht ; scherm *n*, be'scherming; hoede; conduc'teur : (be')waken; be'schermen
guarded, voor'zichtig
guardian, voogd, be'waarder: be'scherm-
guess, gis(sing) : raden
guest, gast, lo'gé(e)
guidance, leiding, ad'vies *n*
guide, gids; padvindster : leiden
guild, gilde *n*
guilder, gulden
guile, list
guileless, argeloos
guillotine, guillo'tine
guilt, schuld
guiltless, on'schuldig
guilty, schuldig, schuldbe'wust
guise, voorkomen *n*, vorm; mom *n*
guitar, gi'taar
gulf, golf; kloof
gull, meeuw : beetnemen
gullet, slokdarm, keel
gullible, lichtge'lovig
gully, geul
gulp, slok, teug : opslokken; inslikken
gum, gom(men) ; tandvlees *n*
gun, ka'non *n*, ge'weer *n*, pis'tool *n*
gunner, artille'rist, kon'stabel
gunpowder, buskruit *n*
gunwale, dolboord *n*
gurgle, kabbelen, klokken, kirren
gush, stroom : gutsen, stromen
gushing, dwepend
gust, vlaag
gusto, animo
gusty, stormachtig
gut, darm : schoonmaken; uitbranden

gutter, goot
guttersnipe, straatkind *n*
guy, stormlijn: vent: voor de gek houden
guzzle, opschrokken
gymnasium, gymnas'tiekzaal
gymnastics, gymnas'tiek

H

haberdashery, garen en band *n*
habit, ge'woonte; pij; rijkleed *n*
habitable, be'woonbaar
habitation, woonplaats
habitual, ge'woon(lijk), ge'woonte-, regel'matig
hack, rijpaard *n*: hakken
hackneyed, afgezaagd
haddock, schelvis
haemorrhage, bloeding
hag, heks
haggard, uitgeteerd
haggle, knibbelen
hail, hagel(en): toejuichen, (luidkeels) toe'groeten; aanroepen; af'komstig zijn
hair, haar *n*: haren
  to split hairs, muggeziften
hairdresser, kapper
hairy, harig, be'haard
half, half: (de) helft
  half past one, half twee
half-way, halver'wege
hall, hal, zaal
hallmark, keur; stempel(en) (*n*)
hallow, heiligen
hallucination, halluci'natie
halo, aure'ool, halo
halt, halt (houden); hokken
halter, halster
halve, hal'veren
ham, ham
hamlet, ge'hucht *n*
hammer, hamer(en)
hammock, hangmat
hamper, mand: be'lemmeren
hand, hand; wijzer; arbeider; spel *n*: over'handigen, aangeven
  at hand, bij de hand; op handen
  in hand, in be'dwang; onder handen; over

on the other hand, aan de andere kant
to hand down, overleveren
to hand in, inleveren
to hand out, uitdelen
to hand over, overdragen, over'handigen
to hand round, ronddienen, ronddelen
handbag, handtas
handbill, strooibiljet *n*
handcuff, handboei
handful, hand(je)vol
handicap, handicap(pen)
handicraft, handwerk *n*, handen-arbeid
handiwork, (hand)werk *n*
handkerchief, zakdoek
handle, handvat *n*, knop, oor *n*: be'dienen, han'teren; aanpakken; be'handelen; handelen in
handle-bars, stuur *n*
handmade, handwerk
handshake, handdruk
handsome, knap; flink, ro'yaal
handwriting, (hand)schrift *n*
handy, handig; bij de hand; van pas
hang, slag: (op)hangen; laten hangen; be'hangen
  to hang about, rondlummelen
  to hang on, (zich) vasthouden; wachten
hangar, han'gar
hanging, drape'rie
hang-over, kater
hank, streng
hanker, hunkeren
haphazard, luk'raak
happen, (toe'vallig) ge'beuren
  I happen to . . . ik . . . toe'vallig; ik . . . nu eenmaal
happenings, ge'beurtenissen
happiness, ge'luk *n*
happy, ge'lukkig
harangue, heftige toespraak (houden)
harass, be'stoken; kwellen
harbour, haven: (ver')bergen, koesteren
hard, hard('vochtig); moeilijk; vast
  to try hard, zijn best doen

harden,harder worden (*or* maken)
hard-hearted, hard'vochtig
hardly, nauwelijks: hard
hardship, ont'bering, last
hardware, ijzerwaren
hardwood, hardhout(en) (*n*)
hardy, ge'hard, sterk
hare, haas
harlequin, harle'kijn
harm, schade, letsel *n*: kwaad
doen
harmful, na'delig, schadelijk
harmless, on'schadelijk; argeloos
harmonic, har'monisch
harmonica, mondharmonika
harmonious, har'monisch, harmoni'eus
harmonize, (doen) harmoni'-
eren; harmoni'seren
harmony, harmo'nie
harness, (paarden)tuig *n*; ga'-
reel *n*: optuigen
harp, harp: hameren
harpoon, har'poen('eren)
harpsichord, klave'cimbel
harrow, eg(gen); aangrijpen
harry, plunderen; kwellen
harsh, ruw, wrang; hard
hart, mannetjeshert *n*
harvest, oogst(tijd): oogsten
hash, ha'chee; knoeieboel
haste, haast
hasten, zich haasten, ver'haasten
hasty, haastig; driftig
hat, hoed
hatch, luik *n*: uitbroeden, uitkomen
hatchet, bijl
hate, haat: haten, een hekel
hebben aan
hateful, akelig
hatred, haat
haughty, hoog'hartig
haul, vangst: slepen, halen
haunch, lende, hurk
haunt, oord *n*, speelplaats; hol
n: veel'vuldig be'zoeken;
achter'volgen
haunted, spook-, door geesten
be'zocht
have, hebben; laten; moeten;
nemen; krijgen

haven, (veilige) haven
haversack, broodzak
havoc, ver'woesting
hawk, havik: venten
hawser, tros
hawthorn, hagedoorn
hay, hooi *n*
hayrick, haystack, hooiberg
hazard, risico *n*: wagen
hazardous, ris'kant
haze, waas *n*, nevel
hazel, hazelaar: lichtbruin
hazy, wazig; vaag
he, hij
head, hoofd(-) (*n*), kop; spits:
tegen-: leiden; sturen
to keep one's head, zijn
ver'stand bij el'kaar houden
to lose one's head, in de war
raken
headache, hoofdpijn
head-dress, headgear, hoofd-
tooi
heading, ru'briek, opschrift *n*
headland, voorgebergte *n*
headlight, koplamp
headline, kop
headlong, hals over kop
headmaster, direc'teur,
(school)hoofd *n*
headquarters, hoofdkwartier *n*
headstrong, koppig
headway, voortgang
heal, ge'nezen
health, ge'zondheid
healthy, ge'zond
heap, hoop, massa: ophopen
hear, horen; luisteren
hearing, ge'hoor *n*: ver'hoor *n*
hearken, luisteren
hearsay, praatjes
hearse, lijkwagen
heart, hart *n*; moed; kern, binnenste *n*
by heart, uit het hoofd
to take heart, moed scheppen
heart-breaking, hartver'scheur-
end
heart-broken, ge'broken
hearten, opbeuren
heart-felt, innig
hearth, haard
heartless, harteloos

hearty, hartelijk; ge'zond; stevig; hart'grondig

heat, hitte; vuur *n*; loop: ver'warmen; opwinden

heater, ver'warmingsapparaat *n*

heath, heide

heathen, heiden(s)

heather, heide

heave, hijsen, lichten; trekken; slaken; deinen

to heave to, bijdraaien

heaven, hemel

heavenly, hemels, hemel-

heavy, zwaar, klef

Hebrew, He'breeuws *n*; He'breeër

heckle, jouwen, scherp onder'vragen

hectic, koortsachtig

hedge, heg: om'heinen; er omheen draaien

hedgehog, egel

hedgerow, haag

heed, aandacht: letten op

heedless, achteloos

heel, hiel,hak: overhellen

hefty, stoer

heifer, vaars

height, hoogte; top(punt *n*)

heighten, ver'hogen; ver'sterken

heinous, snood

heir, erfgenaam

heiress, erfgename

heirloom, erfstuk *n*

helicopter, helikopter

hell, hel

hello, hal'lo

helm, roer *n*

helmet, helm

helmsman, roerganger

help, hulp; steun, helper(s): helpen; nalaten

I can't help it, ik kan er niets aan doen

help yourself gaat Uw gang!

helpful, hulp'vaardig; be'vorderlijk, ge'makkelijk

helping, portie

helpless, hulpeloos

helter-skelter, hals over kop

hem, zoom: zomen

hemisphere, halfrond *n*

hemp, hennep

hen, kip: wijfjes-

hence, van'daar (dat); hier van'daan, van nu af aan

henceforth, van nu af aan

henchman, handlanger

henpeck, op de kop zitten

her, haar

herald, he'raut, voorbode: aankondigen

heraldry, heral'diek

herb, kruid *n*

herd, kudde: hokken, (samen-) drijven

herdsman, veehoeder

here, hier

hereabout(s), hier in de buurt

hereafter, hier'na(maals *n*)

hereby, hierbij, hierdoor

hereditary, erfelijk, erf-

heredity, erfelijkheid, overerving

heresy, kette'rij

heretic(al), ketter(s)

hereupon, hierop

herewith, hierbij

heritage, erfdeel *n*, erfgoed *n*

hermetic(al), her'metisch

hermit, kluizenaar

hero, held

heroic, held'haftig, helden-

heroics, bombast

heroine, hel'din

heron, reiger

herring, haring

hesitant, aarzelend

hesitate, aarzelen

hesitation, aarzeling

heterogeneous, hetero'geen

hew, houwen

heyday, bloeitijd

hiatus, hi'aat *n*

hibernate, winterslaap doen

hiccup(s), hik(ken)

to have hiccups, de hik hebben

hide, huid: afrossen: (zich) ver'bergen

hide-and-seek, ver'stoppertje *n*

hidebound, be'krompen

hideous, af'zichtelijk, af'schuwelijk

hierarchy, hiërar'chie

high, hoog; adellijk

highland, hoogland(s) (*n*)

highly, hoog-, zeer

high-pitched, hoog, schel

highway, grote weg

highwayman, struikrover

hike, trektocht : trekken

hilarious, uitgelaten

hill, heuvel, berg

hillock, heuveltje *n*

hilly, heuvelachtig

hilt, ge'vest *n*

him, hem

hind, achter(ste) : hinde

hinder, (ver)hinderen

hindrance, be'lemmering

hinge, schar'nier *n* ; spil : draaien

hint, wenk ; zweem : laten door-schemeren

to hint at, zinspelen op

hip, heup : rozebottel

hippopotamus, nijlpaard *n*

hire, huur : (ver')huren

hire-purchase, huurkoop : op afbetaling kopen

his, zijn, van hem

hiss, sissen ; (uit)fluiten

historian, ge'schiedschrijver

historic, his'torisch ; ge'wichtig

historical, his'torisch

history, ge'schiedenis

hit, slag : treffer ; suc'ces *n* : slaan ; raken, treffen

to hit upon, treffen, vinden

hitch, ruk ; kink in de kabel : (op)trekken ; vastmaken

hitch-hike, liften

hither, hier(heen)

hitherto, tot nu toe

hive, korf ; mierennest *n*

hoard, voorraad : opsparen, hamsteren

hoarding, re'clamebord *n*

hoar-frost, rijp

hoarse, hees, schor

hoax, beetneme'rij : beetnemen

hobble, strompelen

hobby, liefhebbe'rij, stokpaardje *n*

hobnob, keuvelen

hockey, hockey *n*

hod, (kalk)bak

hoe, schoffel(en)

hog, varken *n* ; zwijn *n*

hoist, hijstoestel *n* : (op)hijsen

hold, houvast *n*, vat *n* ; invloed ;

ruim *n* ; (vast)houden ; be'vatten ; (in zijn be'zit) hebben ; opgaan

to hold out, geven ; volhouden ; in leven blijven

to hold up, ophouden ; aanhouden

to hold with, goedkeuren, het eens zijn met

to get hold of, te pakken krijgen ; vastpakken

hole, gat *n*, hol *n*

holiday, va'cantie(dag), feestdag

holiness, heiligheid

Holland, Nederland *n*

hollow, hol(te) ; leeg

to hollow out, uithollen

holly, hulst

holster, holster

holy, heilig

homage, hulde(betuiging)

home, (t)huis *n*, tehuis *n* : binnenlands : naar huis ; raak

at home, thuis

homeland, ge'boorteland *n*

homeless, dakloos

homely, huiselijk ; ge'moedelijk

home-made, eigengemaakt

homesick: to be —, heimwee hebben

homestead, hofstede

homeward, huiswaarts

homicide, doodslag

homogeneous, homo'geen

honest(y), eerlijk(heid)

honey, honing

honeycomb, honingraat

honeymoon, huwelijksreis

honeysuckle, kamper'foelie

honk, toeteren ; snateren

honorary, ere-

honour, eer(gevoel *n*) ; eerbewijs *n* : (ver')eren

honourable, eervol

hood, kap

hoodwink, zand in de ogen strooien

hoof, hoef

hook, haak : aan de haak slaan

hooligan, straatvlegel

hoop, hoepel

hoot, krassen ; toeteren ; uitjouwen

hop, sprong: hop(plant): hinken, springen
hope, hoop(volle ver'wachting):
hopen
hopeful, hoopvol
hopeless, hopeloos, wan'hopig
horde, horde
horizon, horizon
horizontal, horizon'taal
horn, horen
hornet, horzel
horoscope, horos'coop
horrible, horrid, af'grijselijk,
af'schuwelijk
horrify, ont'zetten
horror, afgrijzen *n*; gruwel(daad)
horse, paard *n*; cavale'rie
horseback: on —, te paard
horseman, ruiter
horse-power, paardekracht
horse-shoe, hoefijzer *n*
horticulture, tuinbouw
hose, (tuin)slang; kousen
hosiery, trico'tages
hospitable, gastvrij
hospital, ziekenhuis *n*
hospitality, gast'vrijheid
host, gastheer, waard; (leger-)
schaar; Hostie
hostage, gijzelaar
hostel, te'huis *n*
hostess, gastvrouw
hostile, vij'andelijk, vij'andig
hostility, vij'andelijkheid, vij'-
andigheid
hot, heet, warm
hotel, ho'tel *n*
hothouse, broeikas
hound, (jacht)hond
hour, uur *n*
house, huis *n*: huisvesten
to keep house, de huishouding
doen
household, huisgezin *n*:
huis('houd)elijk
householder, ge'zinshoofd *n*
housekeeper, huishoudster
housekeeping, huishouden *n*;
huishoud(geld *n*)
housetop, dak(rand) (*n*)
housewife, huisvrouw
housework,   huishoudelijk
werk *n*

housing, woning-, woon-: huis-
vesting
hovel, krot *n*
hover, zweven, hangen
how, hoe
however, hoe . . . dan ook, hoe
. . . toch: echter
howl, huilen, janken; gillen,
joelen
howler, bok
hub, naaf; middelpunt *n*
hubbub, herrie
huddle, (bij *or* in el'kaar) kruipen
hue, tint: ge'gil *n*
hug, pakken; tegen zich aan-
drukken; koesteren
huge, reus'achtig
hulk, romp
hulking, log
hull, romp
hum, ge'gons *n*: gonzen, snorren;
neuriën
human, menselijk, mens(en-)
  human being, menselijk wezen
  n
humane, mens'lievend
humanitarian, humani'tair
humanity, het mensdom *n*
humanly, menselijkerwijs
humble, nederig: ver'nederen
humbug, bedrieger('ij)
humdrum, saai(e sleur)
humid(ity), vochtig(heid)
humiliate, ver'nederen
humility, ootmoed
humorist, humo'rist
humorous, grappig, humo'ristisch
humour, humor; hu'meur *n*;
luim: toegeven aan
hump, bult
hunch, zo'n idee *n*: samentrekken, krommen
hunchback, ge'bochelde
hundred(th), honderd(ste)
hunger, honger
hungry, hongerig
  to be hungry, trek (*or* honger)
  hebben
hunk, homp
hunt, jacht(stoet): jagen (op);
(af)zoeken
to hunt down, in het nauw
drijven; opsporen

hunter, jager; jachtpaard *n*
hurdle, horde; hindernis
hurl, slingeren
hurrah, hoe'ra
hurricane, or'kaan
hurried, haastig, ge'haast
hurry, (zich) haasten
 to be in a hurry, haast hebben
hurt, pijn doen; deren, kwetsen
hurtle, ratelen, schieten
husband, man, echtgenoot; zuinig be'heren
husbandry, (zuinig) be'heer *n*
hush, stilte: stil!: tot zwijgen brengen
husk, schede, schil
husky, schor; potig
hussy, meid
hustle, ge'jacht *n*: jachten, drijven; dringen
hut, hut, ba'rak
hybrid, hy'bride: bastaard-
hydraulic, hy'draulisch
hydrogen, waterstof
hygiene, ge'zondheidsleer
hygienic, hygi'ënisch
hymn, ge'zang *n*
hyphen(ate), (door een) streepje *n* (ver'binden)
hypnotize, hypnoti'seren
hypocrisy, huichela'rij
hypocrite, huichelaar
hypocritical, huichelachtig
hypothesis, hypo'these
hysterical, hys'terisch
hysterics, zenuwaanval

I

I, ik
ice, ijs(je) *n*: (doen) be'vriezen; gla'ceren
iceberg, ijsberg
ice-cream, roomijs *n*
iced, ijskoud; gegla'ceerd
icicle, ijskegel
icing sugar, poedersuiker
icy, ijskoud, glad; ijs-, ijzig
idea, i'dee *n*
ideal, ide'aal (*n*)
idealism, idea'lisme *n*
idealist(ic), idea'list(isch)

idealize, ideali'seren
identical, iden'tiek
identification, identifi'catie
identify, identifi'ceren, vereen'zelvigen
identity, identi'teit
idiom, idi'oom *n*
idiosyncracy, eigen'aardigheid
idiot(ic), idi'oot
idle, nietsdoend; lui; leeg: niets doen
 to be idle, niets doen; stilliggen
idler, leegloper
idol, a'god(sbeeld *n*)
idolatry, afgodendienst
idolize, ver'afgoden
idyll, i'dylle
if, als, in'dien, of
ignite, in brand steken (*or* raken)
ignoble, laag
ignominious, smadelijk
ignorance, on'wetendheid
ignorant, on'wetend, on'kundig
ignore, ne'geren
ill, ziek; slecht, kwaad (*n*); kwalijk
 to cause ill feeling, kwaad bloed zetten
ill-advised, onver'standig
ill-bred, on'opgevoed
illegal, on'wettig, onrecht'matig
illegible, on'leesbaar
illegitimate, on'wettig; onge-oorloofd
ill-fated, ramp'spoedig
illicit, onge'oorloofd
illiterate, onge'letterd: analfa'beet
illness, ziekte
illogical, on'logisch
ill-treat, slecht be'handelen
illuminate, ver (*or* be)'lichten, toelichten; ver'luchten
illumination, ver'lichting; ver'luchting
illusion, il'lusie
illustrate, illus'treren; toelichten
illustration, illus'tratie, toelichting
illustrious, door'luchtig
image, (even)beeld *n*, beeltenis
imaginable, denkbaar
imaginary, denk'beeldig

imagination, ver'beelding-(skracht)

imaginative, vindingrijk, rijk aan ver'beelding; fan'tastisch

imagine, zich voorstellen

imbecile, imbe'ciel

imbibe, drinken; (in zich) opnemen

imbue, door'drenken

imitate, nabootsen

imitation, nabootsing: namaak-

immaculate, onbe'rispelijk

immaterial, on'stoffelijk; onver'schillig, onbe'langrijk

immature, on'rijp

immeasurable, on'meetbaar; niet te over'zien, on'noemelijk

immediate, on'middellijk, naast

immense, on'metelijk

immerse, onderdompelen, indompelen

immersed, onder'water; ver'diept

immigrant, immi'grant: immi'grerend

immigration, immi'gratie

imminent, op handen, dreigend

immobile, onbe'weeglijk

immoderate, on'matig

immodest, onbe'scheiden; on'zedig

immoral, immo'reel

immortal(ity), on'sterfelijk-(heid)

immovable, on'wrikbaar

immune, im'muun voor; vrijgesteld

immutable, onver'anderlijk

imp, duiveltje *n*

impact, botsing, samentreffen *n*; ef'fect *n*

impair, na'delig be'ïnvloeden, schaden

impart, ver'lenen; mededelen

impartial(ity), onpar'tijdig(heid)

impassable, onbe'gaanbaar

impassioned, harts'tochtelijk

impassive, onver'stoorbaar; ge'voelloos

impatient, onge'duldig

impeach, in twijfel trekken; aanklagen

impeccable, onbe'rispelijk, feilloos

impede, be'lemmeren

impediment, be'letsel *n*, ge'brek *n*

impel, voortdrijven, aanzetten

impend, dreigen

impenetrable, ondoor'dringbaar

impenitent, onboet'vaardig, ver'stokt

imperative, hoogstnood'zakelijk; ge'biedend

imperceptible, on'merkbaar

imperfect, imper'fect(um *n*); afwijkend, on'gaaf

imperial, keizerlijk, keizer(s)-, rijks-

imperialism, imperia'lisme *n*

imperil, in ge'vaar brengen

imperious, aan'matigend

impermeable, ondoor'dringbaar

impersonal, onper'soonlijk

impersonate, voorstellen

impertinent, onbe'schaamd

imperturbable, onver'stoorbaar

impervious, ondoor'dringbaar; doof (voor)

impetuous, on'stuimig

impetus, drijfkracht; stuwkracht

impinge on, raken

impious, goddeloos

impish, schelms

implacable, onver'zoenlijk

implant, inplanten

implement, werktuig *n*: uitvoeren

implicate, ver'wikkelen, be'trekken (bij)

implication, bijgedachte

implicit, onvoor'waardelijk; stilzwijgend, er in be'grepen

implore, (af)smeken

imply, impli'ceren, inhouden, te ver'staan geven

impolite, onbe'leefd

import, invoer(en)

importance, be'tekenis, be'lang *n*

important, be'langrijk, ge'wichtig(doend)

importunity, op'dringerigheid

impose on, opleggen; misbruik maken van

imposing, indruk'wekkend

impossible, on'mogelijk

impostor, be'drieger

impotent, impo'tent, machteloos

impoverish, ver'armen, uitputten

impracticable, onuit'voerbaar

impregnable, on'neembaar; onaan'tastbaar

impregnate, impreg'neren; be'vruchten

impress, stempel(en) (n); indruk maken op, op het hart drukken; rekwi'reren

impression, indruk, i'dee n; afdruk; oplage

impressionable, ont'vankelijk

impressive, indruk'wekkend

imprint, afdruk; stempel(en) (n): inprenten

imprison, ge'vangen zetten (or houden)

imprisonment, ge'vangenschap

improbable, onwaar'schijnlijk

impromptu, voor de vuist

improper, incor'rect, onfat'soenlijk

improve, ver'beteren; voor'uitgaan

improvement, ver'betering; voor'uitgang

improvident, onbe'zonnen

improvise, improvi'seren

imprudent, onvoor'zichtig

impudence, brutali'teit

impudent, bru'taal

impulse, stoot; opwelling, aandrift

impulsive, stuw-; impul'sief

impunity: with —, onge'straft

impure, on'zuiver; on'kuis

impute, toeschrijven

in, in, (naar) binnen

inability, onvermogen n

inaccessible, onbe'reikbaar; onge'naakbaar

inaccurate, onnauw'keurig

inactive, nietsdoend

inactivity, nietsdoen n

inadequate, ontoe'reikend

inadvertent, onop'zettelijk

inadvisable, onver'standig

inalienable, onver'vreemdbaar

inane, zinloos

inanimate, levenloos

inappropriate, onge'schikt

inarticulate, ongearticu'leerd; sprakeloos

inasmuch as, voorzo'ver; aange'zien

inattentive, onop'lettend; onat'tent

inaudible, on'hoorbaar

inaugural, inaugu'reel

inaugurate, inhuldigen; inluiden

incalculable, onbe'rekenbaar

incandescent, gloei-

incantation, toverformule

incapable, onbe'kwaam; niet in staat

incapacitate, onge'schikt maken; ver'hinderen

incendiary, brand-; opruiend: brandstichter

incense, wierook: ver'toornen

incentive, prikkel

inception, ont'staan n

incessant, onop'houdelijk

incest, bloedschande

inch, duim

incident, voorval n; epi'sode

incidental, toe'vallig; bij'komstig

incidentally, ter'loops, tussen twee haakjes

incision, insnijding

incite, aanzetten

inclement, guur; onmee'dogend

inclination, buiging, helling; neiging

incline, helling: overhellen (tot) **to be inclined,** ge'neigd zijn, de neiging hebben

include, be(or om)'vatten; meerekenen **to be included,** (er'bij) inbegrepen zijn

including, met inbegrip van, waar'onder

inclusive, allesom'vattend, inclu'sief; tot en met

incoherent, onsamen'hangend

income, inkomen n, inkomsten

income-tax, inkomstenbelasting

incomparable, niet te verge'lijken; weergaloos

incompatible, onver'enigbaar

incompetent, onbe'voegd; in-effici'ent

incomplete, onvol'ledig

incomprehensible, onbe'grijpe-lijk

inconceivable, on'denkbaar

inconclusive, niet be'slissend, niet over'tuigend

incongruous, niet passend, on-ge'rijmd

inconsiderate, onat'tent

inconsistent, inconse'quent, tegen'strijdig

inconspicuous, onop'vallend

incontestable, onbe'twistbaar

inconvenience, last (aandoen)

inconvenient, lastig, onge'legen; onge'riefelijk

incorporate, opnemen; ver'enig-en

incorrect, on'juist

incorrigible, onver'beterlijk

increase, toename, ver'hoging: toenemen, ver'hogen

increasingly, steeds meer

incredible, onge'lofelijk

incredulous, onge'lovig

incriminate, be'schuldigen; in een ten'lastelegging be'trekken

incubator, broedmachine

inculcate, inprenten

incur, zich op de hals halen; lopen

incurable, onge'neeslijk(e zieke)

indebted, schuldig, ver'plicht

indecent, on'zedelijk; onwel'-voeglijk

indecision, be'sluiteloosheid

indecisive, onbe'slist; be'sluite-loos

indeed, inder'daad; werkelijk, (ja) zelfs

indefatigable, onver'moeibaar, onver'moeid

indefinite, onbe'paald

indelible, onuit'wisbaar; inkt-

indemnity, schadeloosstelling

independence, onaf'hankelijk-heid

independent, onaf'hankelijk

indescribable, onbe'schrijfelijk

index, re'gister *n*; aanwijzing: wijs-

Indian, Indisch: Indiër

india-rubber, gummi

indicate, aanwijzen; wijzen op

indication, aanwijzing

indicator, wijzer

indictment, aanklacht

indifferent, onver'schillig; (mid-del')matig

indigenous, in'heems

indigestible, onver'teerbaar

indigestion, indi'gestie

indignant, veront'waardigd

indignation, veront'waardiging

indignity, smaad

indirect, indi'rect

indiscreet, indis'creet

indiscretion, onbe'scheidenheid

indiscriminate, lukraak, zonder onderscheid; ver'ward

indispensable, on'misbaar

indisposed, onge'steld; onge'ne-gen

indisputable, onbe'twistbaar

indistinct, on'duidelijk

individual, individu'eel: indi-vi'du *n*

individuality, individuali'teit

indivisible, on'deelbaar

indolent, vadsig

indomitable, onover'winnelijk, on'tembaar

indoor(s), binnen(s'huis)

induce, ertoe brengen; te'weeg-brengen; afleiden

inducement, stimu'lans, lokmid-del *n*

induction, in'ductie; aanvoering; instal'latie

indulge, toegeven aan

to **indulge in**, zich permit'teren

indulgence, toe'geeflijkheid; uit-spatting; aflaat

industrial, industri'eel, be'drijfs-

industrialist, industri'eel

industrious, vlijtig

industry, indus'trie, be'drijf-(sleven) *n* ; vlijt

inebriated, dronken

inedible, on'eetbaar

ineffective, **ineffectual**, ondoel'-treffend, vruchteloos

inefficient, ondoel'matig, on-be'kwaam

inept, onge'rijmd, dwaas

inequality, onge'lijkheid
inert(ia), in'ert(ie); stil(stand)
inestimable, on'schatbaar
inevitable, onver'mijdelijk
inexcusable, onver'geeflijk
inexhaustible, onuit'puttelijk
inexorable, onver'biddelijk
inexpensive, voor'delig
inexperienced, oner'varen
inexplicable, onver'klaarbaar
inexpressible, onuit'sprekelijk
infallible, on'feilbaar
infamous, schandelijk, be'rucht
infancy, kindsheid
infant, zuigeling, kind(er-)
infantry, infante'rie
infatuated, ver'zot (op)
infect, be'smetten; aansteken
infection, in'fectie
infectious, be'smettelijk;
  aan'stekelijk
infer, afleiden; laten doorsche-
  meren
inference, ge'volgtrekking; bijgedachte
inferior, inferi'eur; onderge'schikt(e)
 to be inferior to, lager zijn dan;
  onderdoen voor
inferiority, minder'waardig-
  heid(s-)
infernal, hels, duivels
inferno, hel
infest, teisteren
infidel, onge'lovig(e)
infidelity, ontrouw
infinite, on'eindig (veel)
infinitesimal, on'eindig klein
infinity, on'eindigheid
infirmary, ziekenafdeling, ziekenhuis n
infirmity, ge'brek n
inflame, (in geestdrift doen)
  ont'steken
inflammable, ont'vlambaar
inflammation, ont'steking
inflate, opblazen, oppompen;
  opdrijven
inflation, in'flatie
inflexible onver'zettelijk, rotsvast, star
inflict, toebrengen, opleggen,
  ver'oorzaken; lastig vallen met

influence, invloed; be'ïnvloeden
influential, invloedrijk
influenza, griep
influx, toevloed
inform, mededelen, be'richten;
  aanbrengen
informal, infor'meel
informant, zegsman; aanbrenger
information, inlichting(en), be'-
  richt(en) n
infrequent, zeldzaam
infringe, inbreuk maken;
  over'treden
infuriate, woedend maken
infuse, laten trekken; be'zielen
ingenious, ver'nuftig
ingenuity, ver'nuft n
ingenuous, onge'kunsteld
ingot, baar, staaf
ingrained, inge'worteld
ingratiate, zich in de gunst
  dringen
ingratitude, on'dankbaarheid
ingredient, be'standdeel n
inhabit, wonen in
inhabitant, in(or be')woner
inhale, inha'leren
inherent, inhe'rent
inherit, erven
inheritance, erfenis
inhibition, remming
inhospitable, ongast'vrij, onher'bergzaam
inhuman, on'menselijk
inimical, vij'andig
inimitable, onna'volgbaar
iniquitous, hoogst onrecht'vaardig
iniquity, onrecht'vaardigheid,
  ver'derf n
initial, be'gin-, eerst: voorletter:
  para'feren
initially, in het be'gin
initiate, inwijden
initiative, initia'tief n
inject, inspuiten
injudicious, onoordeel'kundig
injunction, be'vel n
injure, wonden; schade doen,
  kwetsen
injurious, schadelijk
injury, ver'wonding; schade;
  be'lediging

injustice, onrecht('vaardigheid) (*n*)

ink, inkt

inkling, flauw i'dee *n*

inlaid, ingelegd

inland, binnen(land)(s); het land in

in-laws, schoonfamilie

father-(mother- or sister-)in-law, schoonvader(moeder *or* zuster)

inlet, inham, zeegat *n*

inmate, (tijdelijk) ('mede) be'woner

inn, herberg

innate, aangeboren

inner, binnen-; innerlijk

innermost, binnenste

innkeeper, waard

innocence, onschuld

innocent, on'schuldig

innocuous, on'schadelijk

innovation, nieuwigheid

innuendo, (hatelijke) toespeling

innumerable, on'telbaar

inoculate, inenten

inoffensive, on'schuldig

inopportune, onge'legen

inordinate, buiten'sporig

inquest, ge'rechtelijk onderzoek naar de doodsoorzaak *n*

inquire, infor'meren (naar), vragen (naar)

inquiry, vraag, poging (om inlichtingen in te winnen); onderzoek *n*

inquisitive, nieuws'gierig

inroad, inval, ver'overing; gat *n*

insane, krank'zinnig

insatiable, onver'zadelijk

inscribe, schrijven op, gra'veren; inschrijven

inscription, opschrift *n*; opdracht

inscrutable, ondoor'grondelijk

insect, in'sekt *n*

insensible, onge'voelig voor; onbe'wust

inseparable, onaf'scheidelijk

insert, inlas(sen), insteken, plaatsen

inside, binnen(kant); naar binnen; in

insidious, arg'listig; ver'raderlijk

insight, inzicht *n*

insignia, onder'scheidingstekens

insignificant, zonder be'tekenis, onbe'tekenend, onbe'duidend

insincere, onop'recht

insinuate, indringen; insinu'eren

insipid, flauw

insist, er op staan; (blijven) volhouden; (er op) aandringen

insistent, vol'hardend; dringend

insolent, onbe'schoft

insoluble, onop'losbaar

insomnia, slape'loosheid

inspect, onder'zoeken; inspec'teren

inspection, in'spectie; onderzoek *n*

inspector, inspec'teur

inspiration, inspi'ratie; be'zielend voorbeeld *n*; ingeving

inspire, inspi'reren; inblazen; inboezemen

install, instal'leren

instalment, ter'mijn; ge'deelte *n*, aflevering

instance, voorbeeld *n*; plaats; ver'zoek *n*: aanhalen

instant, ogenblik *n*: ogen'blikkelijk

instantaneous, on'middellijk

instead of, in plaats van

instep, wreef

instigate, aanstichten

instil, bijbrengen

instinct(ive), in'stinct('ief) (*n*)

institute, insti'tuut *n*: instellen

institution, instelling; tra'ditie

instruct, onder'richten; ge'lasten; mededelen

instruction, onderricht *n*; in'structie

instructive, leerzaam

instrument, instru'ment *n*

instrumental, instrumen'taal; be'vorderlijk (voor)

insubordinate, weer'spannig

insufferable, onuit'staanbaar

insufficient, onvol'doende

insular, eiland-; geïso'leerd, be'krompen

insulate, iso'leren

insult, be'lediging: be'ledigen
insuperable, onover'komelijk
insurance, ver'zekering
insure, ver'zekeren
insurgent, oproerling; op'roerig
insurrection, opstand
intact, in'tact, gaaf
intake, inlaat; aanvoer
intangible, on'tastbaar
integral, inte'grerend; inte'graal
integrate, (tot één ge'heel) ver'-enigen
integrity, on'kreukbaarheid
intellect(ual), intel'lect(u'eel) (*n*)
intelligence, intelli'gentie; in-lichtingen
intelligent, intelli'gent, be'vat-telijk
intelligible, be'grijpelijk
intemperate, on'matig
intend, van plan zijn; be'doelen
intense, in'tens
intensify, ver'hogen, ver'scher-pen
intensity, intensi'teit
intensive, inten'sief
intent, ('in)ge'spannen: be'doe-ling
intention, be'doeling
intentional, op'zettelijk
inter, ter aarde be'stellen
interaction, wisselwerking
intercede on behalf of, voor-spraak zijn van
intercept, onder'scheppen, de pas afsnijden
interchange, ver'wisselen, afwis-selen
interchangeable, ver'wisselbaar
intercourse, omgang, ver'keer *n*
interest, be'lang(stelling) (*n*);
aandeel *n*; rente: interes'seren
to be interested in, be'lang stellen in (*or* hebben bij)
interfere, tussen'beide komen; zich mengen in
interference, be'moeienis; stoor-nis; storing
interim, tussentijd(s)
interior, in'wendig(e *n*), binen-(lands); binnenhuis(*or* land) *n*
interlock, interlock: in el'kaar grijpen

interlude, pauze, tussenperiode; tussenspel *n*
intermarry, onder el'kaar huwen
intermediary, be'middelaar; be'middeling
intermediate, tussen–
interminable, eindeloos
intermingle, (zich) ver'mengen
intermittent, bij vlagen, af en toe onder'broken
intern, inter'neren
internal, in'wendig; binnenlands
international, internatio'naal
interplay, wisselwerking
interpolate, interpo'leren
interpose, in het midden breng-en; tussen beide komen
interpret, ver'tolken, uitleggen
interpreter, tolk
interrogate, onder'vragen
interrupt, onder'breken, in de rede vallen; be'lemmeren
intersect, door'snijden; el'kaar snijden
intersperse, door'spekken; ver'spreiden
interval, pause, tussentijd (*or* ruimte)
intervene, tussen'beide komen; liggen (tussen)
intervention, tussenkomst
interview, inter'view(en) (*n*)
interweave, door'eenweven
intestine, darm
 intestines, ingewanden
intimate, in'tiem, ver'trouwd: laten merken
intimation, aanduiding
intimidate, intimi'deren
into, in, tot (in)
intolerable, onver'draaglijk
intolerant, onver'draagzaam
intonation, into'natie
intoxicant, be'dwelmend (mid-del *n*)
intoxicate, dronken maken
intoxication, dronkenschap; roes
intractable, on'handelbaar; hard'nekkig
intransigent, intransi'gent
intrepid, onver'saagd
intricate, inge'wikkeld

intrigue, in'trige, ge'konkel *n*; amou'rette: intri'geren

intrinsic, intrin'siek

introduce, introdu'ceren; brengen in; indienen

introduction, invoeren *n*; inleiding

intrude, (zich) in(*or* op)dringen; storen

intuition, intu'ïtie; ingeving

intuitive, intuï'tief

inundate, onder water zetten; over'stromen

inure, harden

invade, binnenvallen

invalid, zieke, inva'lide; on'geldig

invaluable, on'schatbaar

invariable, con'stant

invariably, zonder uitzondering

invasion, inval; inbreuk

invective, scheldwoorden

inveigle, ver'lokken

invent, uitvinden, ver'zinnen

invention, uitvinding, ver'zinsel *n*

inventive, vindingrijk

inventor, uitvinder

inventory, inven'taris

inverse, omgekeerd

invert, omkeren, omzetten

invest, be'leggen; ver'lenen

investigate, navorsen, nasporen

investigation, onderzoek *n*

investment, (geld)be'legging

inveterate, ver'stokt

invidious, hatelijk

invigorate, kracht geven

invincible, onover'winnelijk

invisible, on'zichtbaar

invitation, uitnodiging

invite, uitnodigen; vragen om

inviting, aan'lokkelijk

invoice, fac'tuur

invoke, aan(*or* op)roepen; een be'roep doen op

involuntary, onwille'keurig

involve, met zich meebrengen, be'trekken

involved, (in)ge'wikkeld

invulnerable, on'kwetsbaar

inward, naar binnen; innerlijk

irate, woedend

Ireland, Ierland *n*

Irish, Iers (*n*)

irksome, ver'velend, lastig

iron, (strijk)ijzer *n*: ijzeren: strijken

ironic(al), i'ronisch

ironmongery, ijzerwaren

irony, iro'nie

irreconcilable, onver'zoenlijk

irrefutable, onweer'legbaar

irregular, onregel'matig.; tegen de regel

irrelevant, niet ter zake dienend

irreparable, onher'stelbaar

irrepressible, onbe'dwingbaar

irreproachable, onbe'rispelijk

irresistable, onweer'staanbaar

irresolute, be'sluiteloos

irrespective of, afge'zien van, ongeacht

irresponsible, onverant'woordelijk

irretrievable, onher'stelbaar; reddeloos

irreverent, oneer'biedig

irrevocable, onher'roepelijk

irrigate, be'vloeien

irrigation, irri'gatie

irritable, prikkelbaar

irritate, prikkelen; irri'teren

irritation, ge'prikkeldheid; branderigheid

island, eiland *n*; vluchtheuvel

isle, eiland *n*

isolate, iso'leren

issue, uitgifte, nummer *n*; uitstroming; uitkomst; kwestie: ver'strekken; uitgeven; (voort)komen uit

it, het

Italian, Itali'aan(s) (*n*)

italic, cur'sief

Italy, I'talië *n*

itch, jeuk(en); er om zitten te springen

item, stuk *n*, punt *n*; be'richt *n*

itinerant, rondtrekkend

itinerary, reisplan *n*

its, zijn

itself, (zich')zelf

ivory, i'voor *n*; i'voren

ivy, klimop

J

jab, steek: steken

jabber, kakelen

jack, (op)krik(ken); boer

jacket, jasje *n*; omslag

jade, ne'friet: knol: afjakkeren

jagged, ruw, ge'tand, puntig

jam, jam: opstopping: (samen) duwen, klemmen; storen

January, janu'ari

Japanese, Ja'pans (*n*); Ja'panner

jar, pot: schok: krassen; een schok geven

jargon, vaktaal

jaundice, geelzucht

jaunt, uitstapje *n*

jaunty, zwierig

javelin, werpspies

jaw, kaak: kletsen

jazz, jazz

jealous, ja'loers; angst'vallig be'zorgd

jeer, schimpen

jelly, ge'lei, gela'tinepudding

jellyfish, kwal

jeopardize, in ge'vaar brengen

jerk, ruk(ken), schok(ken)

jersey, trui(tje *n*)

jest, scherts(en)

jester, nar

jet, straal(buis), gaspit: git *n*

jettison, over'boord werpen

jetty, havenhoofd *n*, pier

Jew, Jood

jewel, (edel)steen, ju'weel *n*

jeweller, juwe'lier

jewellery, ju'welen

Jewish, Joods

jib, kluiver; arm; weigeren, er niet van ge'diend zijn

jig, horlepijp: dansen

jigsaw puzzle, legpuzzel

jilt, de bons geven

jingle, (laten) rinkelen

job, kar'wei, werk(je) *n*, baan(tje *n*)

jockey, jockey: manoeu'vreren

jocular, schertsend

jocund, vrolijk

jog, stoten; wippen; sukkelen; opfrissen

join, ver'binding, naad: ver'binden, ver'enigen, samenkomen, in el'kaar slaan; zich voegen bij, meedoen, komen bij

joint, ge'wricht *n*: ver'binding, naad; groot stuk vlees *n*: ge'zamenlijk

joke, grap(pen maken)

joker, grappenmaker; joker

jolly, jolig; reuze

jolt, schok: hotsen

jostle, (ver')dringen

jot, jota: vlug no'teren

journal, dagboek *n*; tijdschrift *n*

journalism, journalis'tiek

journalist, journa'list

journey, reis (maken)

joust, steekspel *n*

jovial, jovi'aal

joy(ful), vreugde(vol)

jubilant, jubelend, in de wolken

jubilee, jubi'leum *n*

judge, rechter, jurylid *n*, kenner: (be')oordelen

judgement, uitspraak, oordeel *n*, vonnis *n*

judicial, ge'rechtelijk

judicious, oordeel'kundig

jug, kan

juggle, goochelen

juice, sap *n*

juicy, sappig

July, juli

jumble, warboel: door el'kaar gooien

jump, sprong: springen; opschrikken

jumper, jumper: springer

junction, knooppunt *n*, kruispunt *n*

juncture, stadium *n*, ogenblik *n*

June, juni

jungle, rimboe

junior, junior, jonger(e)

junk, (oude) rommel: jonk

junket, met leb ge'stremde melk

jurisdiction, juris'dictie

jury, jury

just, recht'vaardig; welverdiend; ge'grond: pre'cies: net: maar; even: een'voudig

justice, recht('vaardigheid) (n), ge'rechtigheid; jus'titie; recht-er
   to do justice, billijk be'handelen; eer aandoen, goed doen uitkomen
justifiable, gerecht'vaardigd; ver'dedigbaar
justification, grond, recht'vaardiging
justify, recht'vaardigen
jut out, uitsteken
jute, jute
juvenile, jeugd(ig), jong(eling)

K

kangaroo, kangoeroe
keel, kiel
keen, scherp('zinnig); enthousi'-ast
keep, kost; slottoren: (on-der')houden, be'waren; weer'-houden; (goed)blijven
   to keep away, wegblijven
   to keep on, blijven, door-; aan (or op)houden
   to keep up, volhouden; on-der'houden
   to keep up with, bijhouden
keeper, oppasser, opzichter
keeping, hoede; over'eenstemming
keg, vaatje n
ken, ge'zicht(skring) (n)
kennel, hondehok n, kennel
kerb, trot'toirband
kernel, kern
kettle, ketel
key, sleutel(-); toets; toonaard
keyboard, toetsenbord n
keynote, grondtoon
khaki, kaki n
kick, schop(pen); te'rugstoot: trappen; stoten
kid, geitje n; glacé n; kind n: voor de gek houden
kidnap, ont'voeren
kidney, nier
kill, doden
   to be killed, sneuvelen, omkomen

kiln, oven
kilt, kilt
kin, fa'milie
kind, soort: vriendelijk
kindergarten, fröbelschool
kind-hearted, goed'hartig
kindle, aansteken
kindly, goe'daardig, vriendelijk
   kindly leave off, wees zo goed op te houden
kindness, vriendelijkheid
kindred, ver'want(en)
king, koning
kingdom, koninkrijk n
kink, slag, kink; kronkel
kinship, ver'wantschap
kinsman, bloedverwant
kiosk, ki'osk
kipper, bokking
kiss, kus(sen)
kit, uitrusting; ba'gage; ge'reed-schap n
kitchen, keuken
kite, vlieger; wouw
kitten, katje n
knack, slag, kneep
knapsack, ransel, rugzak
knave, schurk; boer
knavish, schurken-
knead, kneden
knee, knie
kneel, knielen, ge'knield liggen
knell, doodsklok
knickers, broek(je n)
knife, mes n: door'steken
knight, (tot) ridder (slaan)
knighthood, ridderorde, ridder-schap
knit, breien; samengroeien
knitting, breiwerk n
knob, knop; knobbel
knock, slag, klop(pen), slaan, stoten
   to knock down, om'vergooien, aanrijden; toeslaan
   to knock off, afslaan; ophouden; schaften
   to knock out, uitkloppen; be'wusteloos slaan
   to knock over, om'vergooien
knocker, klopper
knoll, heuveltje n
knot, knoop; kwast: knopen

knotty, vol knopen; vol kwasten; lastig
know, (het) weten; (her')kennen
knowing, schrander; veelbe'tekenend
knowledge, (voor)kennis; wetenschap
knuckel, knokkel

L

label, eti'ket *n*, label: van (een) eti'ket(ten) voor'zien
laboratory, labora'torium *n*
laborious, ar'beidzaam; zwaar
labour, arbeid(en); werkkrachten; weeën: doorzagen over
labourer, arbeider
labour-exchange, arbeidsbureau *n*
labyrinth, doolhof *n*
lace, kant; veter; ga'lon *n*: vastrijgen
lacerate, (ver')scheuren
lack, ge'brek (hebben aan) *n*
to be lacking, ont'breken
laconic, laco'niek
lacquer, lak(werk *n*)
lad, knaap
ladder, ladder
laden, be'laden; be'zwangerd
ladle, scheplepel: opscheppen
lady, dame
lag, achterblijven; be'kleden
lagoon, la'gune
lair, hol *n*
laity, leken
lake, meer *n*
lamb, lam(svlees) *n*: lammeren
lame, kreupel, zwak
lament, weeklacht: be'treuren
lamentable, jammerlijk
lamentation, weeklacht
lamp, lamp, lan'taren
lamp-post, lan'tarenpaal
lance, lans; lan'ceren
land, land(e'rij) (*n*): neerkomen; (doen) be'landen; aan land zetten
landed, land-, grond-
landing, landing; overloop
landing-stage, steiger
landlady, hospita

landlord, huisbaas, landheer; hospes, waard
landmark, baken *n*, be'kend punt *n*; mijlpaal
land-owner, grondbezitter
landscape, landschap *n*
landslide, (aard)ver'schuiving
lane, landweg(getje *n*); rijbaan; vaargeul
language, taal
languid, loom, flauw
languish, ver'slappen; wegkwijnen; smachten (naar)
languor, slapte; matheid
lank, schraal; sluik
lanky, slungelachtig
lantern, lan'taren
lap, schoot; ronde: (op)leppen; kabbelen
lapel, re'vers
lapse, a'buis *n*; ver'val(len) (*n*); ver'loop *n*
larceny, diefstal
larch, lariks
lard, reuzel
larder, pro'visiekamer (*or* -kast)
large, groot
largely, grotendeels
lark, leeuwerik; pretje *n*: lol maken
larva, larve
larynx, strottehoofd *n*
lascivious, wel'lustig
lash, zweepkoord *n*; zweepslag: geselen; (doen) zwiepen; vastsjorren
lass, meisje *n*
lassitude, matheid
last, (het) laatst; ver'leden: leest: duren, het uithouden
last straw, laatste druppel
at last, ten'slotte; eindelijk
lasting, blijvend; duurzaam
lastly, ten'slotte
latch, klink, slot *n*
late, (te) laat; re'cent; wijlen, ge'wezen
lately, (in de) laatst(e tijd)
latent, la'tent
lateral, zij(delings)
lath, lat
lathe, draaibank
lather, schuim(en) (*n*)

Latin, La'tijn(s) (*n*), Ro'maans
latitude, breedte; speling
latter, laatst(genoemd)(e)
latterly, tegen het eind; in de laatste tijd
lattice, traliewerk *n*
laud, loven
laudable, lof'waardig
laugh, lach(en)
  to laugh at, lachen om; uitlachen
laughable, lach'wekkend
laughter, ge'lach *n*
launch, (zware) sloep: te water laten; insturen; afschieten; op touw zetten, ont'ketenen
laundry, wasse'rij; was(goed *n*)
laurel, lau'rier; lauwer-
  laurels, lauweren
lava, lava
lavatory, W.C., toi'let *n*
lavender, la'vendel
lavish, kwistig; over'laden
law, recht(en) (*n*); wet
law-abiding, orde'lievend
law-court, rechtbank
lawful, wettig, recht'matig
lawless, los'bandig
lawn, ga'zon *n*; ba'tist *n*
lawsuit, pro'ces *n*
lawyer, advo'caat
lax(ity), laks(heid)
laxative, la'xeermiddel *n*
lay, lied *n*: leke(n)-: leggen; dekken
  to lay down, voorschrijven; geven; neerleggen
  to lay in, inslaan
layer, laag
layette, kinderuitzet
layman, leek
lay-out, plan *n*, aanleg
laze, luieren
lazy, lui
lead, leiding; eerste plaats, voorsprong; riem; voorbeeld *n*: lood *n*: leiden, ertoe brengen; voor('op)gaan; aanvoeren
leaden, loodzwaar
leader, leider; hoofdartikel *n*
leadership, leiding; leiderschap *n*
leading, voor'aanstaand, hoofd-

leaf, blad *n*
leaflet, blaadje *n*, folder
leafy, be'bladerd
league, (ver')bond (*n*): drie mijl
leak, lek(ken) (*n*)
leakage, lek *n*; uitlekking
lean, mager; schraal: overhellen; leunen; zetten
leaning, neiging
lean-to, afdak *n*
leap, sprong: springen
leap-year, schrikkeljaar *n*
learn, leren; ver'nemen
learned, ge'leerd
learner, leerling
learning, ge'leerdheid, wetenschap
lease, huurcon'tract *n*, pacht; huurtijd: (ver')huren
leasehold, pacht(goed *n*)
leash, riem
least, minst
  at least, tenminste, minstens
leather, leer *n*: leren
leave, ver'lof *n*; afscheid *n*: ver'trekken (uit), weggaan; (ver')laten; achter(*or* na)laten; overlaten
  to leave alone, afblijven van; met rust laten
  to leave off, ophouden (met)
  to leave out, weglaten; er buiten laten
leaven, zuurdeeg *n*
lecture, lezing (houden), col'lege (geven) (*n*); de les lezen
lecturer, spreker, lektor
ledge, richel, rand
ledger, grootboek *n*
lee, lij
leech, bloedzuiger
leek, prei
leer, gluren
left, linker(hand); links
left-handed, links
leg, been *n*, poot; (broeks)pijp; e'tappe
legacy, le'gaat *n*; erfenis
legal, rechts'kundig, rechterlijk; wettig; wettelijk; rechts'geldig
legation, ge'zantschap *n*
legend, le'gende; onderschrift *n*
legendary, legen'darisch

legible, leesbaar
legion, legi'oen *n* : legio
legislation, wetgeving
legislative, wetgevend
legitimate, wettig ; gerecht'vaardigd ; recht'matig
leisure, vrije tijd
leisurely, be'daard
lemon(ade), ci'troen(limo'nade)
lend, (uit)lenen ; ver'lenen
length, lengte, duur ; eind(je) *n*
  at length, eindelijk ; uit'voerig
lengthen, ver'lengen ; langer worden
lengthwise, in de lengte
lengthy, lang('durig)
lenient, cle'ment
lens, lens
Lent, Vasten(tijd)
leopard, luipaard *n*
leper, me'laatse
leprosy, me'laatsheid
less, min(der)
lessen, ver'minderen, (doen) afnemen
lesser, minder
lesson, les ; schriftlezing
lest, voor het ge'val dat ; opdat . . . niet ; dat
let, laten, toestaan ; ver'huren
  to let down, neerlaten ; uitleggen ; du'peren, in de steek laten
  to let go, loslaten ; laten gaan
  to let in, binnen laten
  to let off, laten gaan
lethargic, slaperig, loom
letter, brief ; letter
lettuce, (krop)sla
level, vlak, ge'lijk (met) : hoogte ; ni'veau *n* : ge'lijk maken
level-headed, ver'standig, nuchter
lever, hefboom
levy, heffing, lichting : heffen, werven
lewd, on'tuchtig, ob'sceen
liability, aan'sprakelijkheid, ver'antwoording ; blok aan het been *n*
liable, licht ge'neigd ; vatbaar ; aan'sprakelijk
  to be liable to, (licht) kunnen ; last hebben van

liaison, ver'binding(s-) ; liai'son
liar, leugenaar
libel, smaadschrift *n* : op schrift be'lasteren
liberal, vrij('gevig) ; ruim ; libe'raal
liberate, be'vrijden
liberty, vrijheid
librarian, bibliothe'caris
library, biblio'theek
licence, ver'gunning ; vrijheid
licentious, los'bandig
lichen, korstmos *m*
lick, (af)likken
lid, deksel *n*
lie, leugen : liegen ; (gaan) liggen
  to lie down, gaan liggen ; liggen te rusten
liege, soeve'rein, leen-
lieutenant, luitenant
life, leven(sbeschrijving) (*n*)
life-belt, reddingsgordel
life-boat, reddingsboot
lifeless, levenloos
lifelike, na'tuurgetrouw
lifelong, levenslang
lifetime, leven(sduur) (*n*)
lift, lift : (op)tillen ; optrekken ; gappen
ligament, band, pees
light, licht (*n*) ; vuurtje *n* : aansteken ; ver'lichten ; ver'helderen
lighten, lichter worden ; ophelderen ; weerlichten ; ver'lichten
lighter, aansteker : lichter
light-hearted, luchtig
lighthouse, vuurtoren
lighting, ver'lichting
lightly, zachtjes ; licht('vaardig) ; luchtig
lightning, bliksem(snel)
lightship, lichtschip *n*
lightweight, (van) licht (ge'wicht)
like, (zo)als : houden van, aardig vinden ; graag willen
  it is just like him, het is echt iets voor hem ; het lijkt sprekend op hem
  nothing like, lang niet
  something like, onge'veer, zo(iets) als

likeable, prettig
likelihood, kans
likely, waar'schijnlijk
  he is likely to, het is aan'nemelijk dat hij
likeness, ge'lijkenis
likewise, even'eens; insge'lijks
liking, voorliefde, zin
lilac, se'ring; lila (n)
lilting, zwierig
lily, lelie
limb, lid n; tak
limbs, ledematen
lime, kalk: li'moen: linde
limelight, voorgrond
limit, grens: be'perken
limitation, be'perking; grens, te'kortkoming
limited company, naamloze vennootschap
limp, slap: mank lopen
limpid, helder
line, lijn; linie; rij; regel; spoor n: lini'ëren; voeren, be'kleden
linen, linnen(goed) n
liner, lijnboot, lijnvliegtuig n
linger, dralen
linguistic, taal('kundig)-
lining, voering, be'kleding
link, schakel(en); inhaken; ver'binden; met elkaar in ver'band brengen
linoleum, li'noleum n
linseed, lijnzaad n
lint, pluksel n
lintel, bovendrempel
lion(ess), leeuw('in)
lip, lip; rand
lipstick, lippenstift
liqueur, li'keur
liquid, vloeibaar: vloeistof
liquidate, liqui'deren
liquor, (sterke) drank
liquorice, drop
lisle, fil d'écosse
lisp, ge'lispel n: lispelen
list, lijst; slagzij: overhellen
listen, luisteren
listless, lusteloos
lists, strijdperk n
literal, letterlijk
literary, lite'rair

literature, litera'tuur
lithe, lenig
litre, liter
litter, afval, rommel; nest n, worp: (met rommel) be'zaaien
little, klein; weinig: beetje n
  a little late, wat laat
liturgy, litur'gie
live, levend(ig); ge'laden, scherp: (blijven) leven; wonen
livelihood, kost, be'staan n
lively, levendig, be'drijvig, druk
liver, lever
livery, li'vrei
livestock, vee n
livid, doodsbleek; wit
living, levend, levens-: kost; leven n; predi'kantsplaats
living-room, huiskamer
lizard, hage'dis
load, vracht, lading: (in)laden, be'laden; over'laden
loaf, brood n: lummelen
loam, leem
loan, lening: (uit)lenen
loath, onge'negen
loathe, walgen van
loathsome, walgelijk
lob, hoog slaan
lobby, hal, fo'yer
lobe, lel
lobster, kreeft
local, plaatselijk; lo'kaal
locality, om'geving
localize, lokali'seren
locate, opsporen, thuisbrengen; vestigen
location, ligging; plaatsbepaling
lock, slot n; sluis: lok: op slot doen (or gaan), (op)sluiten; vastraken
locker, kastje n
locket, medail'lon n
locomotive, locomo'tief: be'wegings-
locust, sprinkhaan
lodge, (por'tiers)woning: lo'geren, in de kost zijn, onderbrengen; blijven steken; indienen
lodger, kostganger
lodgings, (ge'huurde) kamers
loft, zolder; gale'rij

lofty, hoog; ver'heven

log, blok hout *n*; log(boek *n*): blok-: no'teren; afleggen

loggerheads: to be at —, over'hoop liggen

logic, logica

logical, logisch

loin, lende(stuk *n*)

loiter, omhangen

loll, hangen

London, Londen(s) (*n*)

lone(ly), eenzaam, ver'laten

long, lang: door: ver'langen

longing, ver'langen *n*

longitude, lengte

longitudinal, in de lengte

long-sighted, vèrziend

long-suffering, lank'moedig

long-winded, lang'dradig

look, (aan)blik; voorkomen *n*: kijken; er uitzien

looks, uiterlijk

to look after, zorgen voor

to look at, be'kijken, kijken naar

to look back, omzien; te'rugzien

to look for, zoeken (naar); ver'wachten

to look forward to, zich ver'heugen op

to look into, onder'zoeken

to look like, lijken op, er uitzien als

to look on, toekijken

to look out, uitkijken

to look up, opkijken; opzoeken; opknappen

lookout, uitkijk

to keep a lookout for, uitkijken naar

loom, weefgetouw *n*: opdoemen

loop, lus

loophole, (schiet)gat *n*; uit-vlucht

loose, los, vrij

loosen, los(ser) maken

loot, buit: plunderen

lop, (af)snoeien

lop-sided, scheef

loquacious, praatziek

lord, heer, lord

lordly, vorstelijk, voor'naam

lore, kunde, kennis

lorgnette, face-à-main

lorry, vrachtauto

lose, (doen) ver'liezen, kwijtra-ken; missen; voor'bij laten gaan

loss, ver'lies *n*

lost, ver'loren; ver'dwaald; ver'ongelukt

to get lost, ver'dwalen

lot, lot *n*; per'ceel *n*; stel *n*: heel wat

lotion, huid-(wond- *or* haar-)water *n*

lottery, lote'rij

loud, luid('ruchtig)

lounge, sa'lon, conver'satiezaal: leunen, liggen

louse, luis

lout, pummel

lovable, lief

love, liefde; liefje *n*: nul: houden van; dolgraag (willen)

lots of love, veel liefs

(to fall) in love with, ver'liefd (worden) op

to make love, het hof maken

lovely, prachtig, mooi; heerlijk

lover, ge'liefde; liefhebber

loving, aan'hankelijk; liefheb-bend

low, laag; bijna op (*or* leeg): loeien

lower, laten zakken; strijken: dreigend kijken

lowland, laagland *n*

lowly, nederig

loyal(ty), trouw

lubricant, smeermiddel *n*

lubricate, smeren

lucid(ity), helder(heid)

luck, ge'luk *n*

bad luck, pech

good luck, ge'luk *n*: suc'ces!

lucky: to be —, boffen; ge'luk brengen

lucrative, winstgevend

ludicrous, be'lachelijk

lug, slepen

luggage, ba'gage

lugubrious, lu'guber

lukewarm, lauw

lull, stilte: sussen

lullaby, wiegeliedje *n*
lumber, ge'kapt hout *n*; rommel: dreunen
luminous, lichtgevend
lump, klomp, brok, klontje *n*, knobbel: rond
lunacy, krank'zinnigheid
lunar, maan-
lunatic, krank'zinnig(e)
lunch, lunch(en)
lung, long
lunge, uitval (doen); dres'seren
lurch, stoot: steek: voor'uit(*or* op'zij)schieten, slingeren
lure, lokstem: (ver')lokken
lurid, gloeiend; gruwelijk
lurk, zich schuil houden, ver'borgen zijn, loeren
luscious, heerlijk sappig
lush, mals
lust, (wel)lust, zucht: be'geren
lustre, glans; luister
lusty, fors
lute, luit
luxuriant, welig; weelderig
luxurious, weelderig
luxury, weelde, luxe
lying, leugenachtig
lynch, lynchen
lyre, lier
lyric, lyrisch (ge'dicht *n*)
lyrical, lyrisch

M

mace, staf: foelie
machination, kuipe'rij
machine, ma'chine; organi'satie
machinery, machine'rieën; mecha'nisme *n*; organi'satie(s)
mackerel, ma'kreel
mad, gek; dol
madam, me'vrouw, juf'frouw
madden, gek maken; gruwelijk ergeren
madman, gek
madness, krank'zinnigheid; gekkigheid
madrigal, madri'gaal *n*
magazine, tijdschrift *n*; maga'zijn *n*
maggot, made

magic, toverkunst, tove'rij: tover(achtig)
magician, tovenaar
magistrate, magis'traat
magnanimous, groot'moedig
magnate, mag'naat
magnet, mag'neet
magnetic, mag'netisch
magnificence, luister, pracht
magnificent, luisterrijk, groots
magnify, ver'groten
magnitude, grootte
magpie, ekster
mahogany, ma'honie(hout) *n*
maid, meisje *n*
maiden, maagd(elijk): onge'trouwd, meisjes-; eerste
mail, post(-): maliënkolder
maim, ver'minken
main, hoofd-, voor'naamste
mains, hoofdleiding, net *n*
mainland, vaste'land *n*
mainly, hoofd'zakelijk
mainsail, grootzeil *n*
mainstay, grote stag; steunpilaar
maintain, handhaven; onder'houden; be'weren
maintenance, onderhoud *n*
maize, maïs
majestic, majestu'eus
majesty, majesteit
major, groot(ste), hoofd-: ma'joor; majeur
majority, meerder('jarig)heid
make, merk *n*: maken; dwingen, laten; ver'dienen; schatten, denken; halen; opmaken (*a bed*); zetten (*tea*); doen (*a promise*)
to make out, opstellen; be'weren; snappen, ont'cijferen; onder'scheiden
to make up, maken; ver'zinnen; ver'goeden, aanvullen; het weer goedmaken; (zich) opmaken
to make up for, goedmaken; inhalen
make-believe, een spelletje *n*: ver'zonnen
maker, schepper, fabri'kant
makeshift, geimprovi'seerd (lapmiddel *n*)

make-up, geestesgesteldheid; schmink, make-up
malady, kwaal
malaria, ma'laria
male, mannelijk (per'soon *or* dier *n*), mannen-
malevolent, boos'aardig
malice, boos opzet *n*, haat
malicious, boos'aardig
malign, be'lasteren
malignant, kwaad'aardig
malleable, smeedbaar; kneed-baar
malnutrition, onder'voeding
malt, mout(en)
mammal, zoogdier *n*
mammoth, mammoet: reu-zen-
man, man; (de) mens: be'mannen, be'zetten
manage, aankunnen; leiden; klaarspelen
management, be'heer *n*; di'rek-tie, be'stuur *n*
manager, direk'teur, chef
mandate, opdracht; man'daat-(gebied) *n*
mane, manen
manger, voerbak, kribbe
mangle, mangel(en); ver'scheur-en
manhandle, ver'sjouwen, toe-takelen
manhood, mannelijke leeftijd
mania, waanzin; ma'nie
maniac, waan'zinnige
manicure, mani'cure
manifest, duidelijk; mani'fest *n*: tonen
manifestation, uiting
manifesto, mani'fest *n*
manifold, veel'vuldig
manipulate, han'teren; be'werk-en; knoeien met
manipulation, han'tering; manipu'latie
mankind, mensdom *n*
manly, man'haftig
mannequin, manne'quin
manner, ma'nier (van doen); soort
mannerism, hebbelijkheid, ge-manië'reerdheid

manoeuvre, ma'noeuvre; manoeu'vreren
manor, ambachtshuis *n*
mansion, herenhuis *n*
manslaughter, doodslag
mantelpiece, schoorsteenmantel
mantle, mantel; gloeikousje *n*
manual, hand(en)-: manu'aal *n*
manufacture, fabri'kage, fabri'-kaat *n*: fabri'ceren
manure, mest: be'mesten
manuscript, handschrift *n*
many, veel; velen
 a good many, heel wat
 a great many, heel veel, heel wat
map, (land)kaart, platte'grond
maple, esdoorn
mar, ont'sieren; be'derven
maraud, plunderen
marble, marmer(en) (*n*); knikker
march, mars: (doen) mar'che-ren; oprukken
March, maart
mare, merrie
margarine, marga'rine
margin, kant(lijn); speling
marginal, kant-
marigold, goudsbloem
marine, zee-; scheeps-: mari'-nier
mariner, zeeman
marital, echtelijk
maritime, zee(vaart)-
mark, plek, streep, vlek, spoor; moet, put; merk *n*; stempel, (ken)teken *n*; doel *n*; peil *n*: een vlek (*etc*) achterlaten; aan-duiden; (ken)merken; prijzen; corri'geren; letten op
 to mark time, de pas mar'keren
marked, duidelijk; ver'dacht
market, markt: aan de markt brengen
market-place, markt(plein *n*)
marksman, scherpschutter
marmalade, marme'lade
maroon, paarsrood (*n*)
 to be marooned, stranden
marquis, mar'kies
marriage, huwelijk *n*
marrow, merg(pompoen) (*n*)

marry, trouwen (met); uit-huwelijken

marsh(y), moe'ras(sig) (n)

marshal, maarschalk: ordenen; ge'leiden

martial, krijgs('haftig)

martyr, martelaar: de martel-dood doen sterven

martyrdom, martelaarschap n; marteling

marvel, wonder n: zich ver'won-deren

marvellous, wonder'baarlijk, fan'tastisch; heerlijk

masculine, mannelijk

mash, pap: (fijn)stampen

mask, masker(en) (n); mas'ke-ren

mason, steenhouwer, metselaar

masquerade, maske'rade: zich ver'mommen

mass, massa: mis

massacre, massamoord; slacht-ing

massage, mas'sage: mas'seren

massive, mas'saal

mast, mast

master, (jonge) heer; ge'zag-voerder; leraar; meester(-): hoofd-: meester worden

masterful, bazig

masterly, meesterlijk

masterpiece, meesterstuk n

mastery, overhand; meester-schap n

mat, mat(je n), kleed(je) n; ver'warde massa: plakkerig maken

mat(t), mat

match, lucifer: par'tij, com-bi'natie; wedstrijd; huwelijk n: eve'naren; bij el'kaar pas-sen

matchless, onverge'lijkelijk

mate, maat; levensgezel('in); stuurman: (zich) paren

material, stof(felijk), materi'aal (n), materi'eel (n); essenti'eel

materialist(ic), materia'list(isch)

materialize, ver'wezenlijkt wor-den; ver'wezenlijken; ver'-schijnen

maternal, moederlijk, moeder-

maternity, moederschap n; kraam-

mathematical, wis'kundig

mathematician, wis'kundige

mathematics, wiskunde

matins, metten

matrimonial, huwelijks-

matrimony, huwelijk(se staat) n

matron, ma'trone; moeder; direc'trice

matter, stof; kwestie; pus: van be'lang zijn

as a matter of fact, eigenlijk; overigens

as a matter of course, als van-zelf'sprekend

for that matter, wat dat be'treft, trouwens

it does not matter, het geeft niets, het doet er niet toe

what is the matter? wat scheelt er aan?

matter-of-fact, zakelijk

mattress, ma'tras

mature, rijp(en); ver'vallen

maturity, rijpheid; ver'valtijd

maul, toetakelen

mauve, lichtpaars

maxim, stelregel

may, meidoorn: mei: mogen, misschien kunnen

maybe, mis'schien

mayonnaise, mayon'naise

mayor, burge'meester

maze, doolhof n

me, mij, me

mead, mee: dreef

meadow, weide

meagre, schraal

meal, maal(tijd) (n): meel n

mean, ge'meen, krenterig; ge'ring, schriel: middenweg, ge'middelde n: be'doelen, me-nen; be'tekenen

meander, kronkelen; dolen

meaning, be'tekenis; be'doeling: veelbe'tekenend

meaningless, niets'zeggend

means, middel(en) n

by all means, ge'rust

by no means, geenszins

meantime: in the —, in'tussen

meanwhile, onder'tussen

measles, mazelen

measure, maat(regel) : (op)meten ; zijn

measurement, maat

meat, vlees *n* ; kost

meat-safe, vliegenkast

mechanic, mecani'cien

mechanical, machi'naal, werktuig'kundig ; werk'tuiglijk

mechanics, werktuigkunde

mechanism, mecha'nisme *n*, mecha'niek *n*

mechanize, mechani'seren

medal, me'daille

meddle with, zich be'moeien met ; komen aan

meddlesome, be'moeiziek

mediaeval, middel'eeuws

mediate, als be'middelaar optreden

medical, medisch : keuring

medicinal, genees'krachtig

medicine, ge'neeskunde ; ge'neesmiddel *n*, drankje *n*

mediocre, middel'matig

mediocrity middel'matigheid

meditate, be(*or* over)'peinzen

meditation, over'peinzing ; medi'tatie

Mediterranean, Middellandse Zee

medium, middel('matig) (*n*) ; medium *n*

medley, mengelmoes *n* ; potpour'ri

meek, zacht'moedig

meet, (el'kaar) ont'moeten ; (aan)treffen ; samenkomen ; afhalen ; vol'doen aan

meeting, ver'gadering, samenkomst ; ont'moeting

megaphone, mega'foon

melancholy, zwaar'moedig(heid)

mellow, zacht (en sappig) ; rijp ; zoet'vloeiend

melodious, wel'luidend

melodrama, melo'drama *n*

melody, melo'die

melon, me'loen

melt, (doen) smelten

member, lid(maat) (*n*)

membership, lidmaatschap *n* ; ledental *n*

membrane, vlies *n*

memento, aandenken *n*

memoirs, me'moires

memorable, gedenk'waardig

memorandum, memo'randum *n* ; nota

memorial, ge'denkteken *n* ; her'denkings-

memorize, uit het hoofd leren

memory, ge'heugen *n* ; her'innering ; nagedachtenis

menace, (voort'durende) be'dreiging

menagerie, menage'rie

mend, repa'reren ; beteren

mendicant, bedel(end) : bedelaar

menial, nederig, onderge'schikt

mental, geestelijk, geest(es)- ; hoofd-

mental arithmetic, hoofdrekenen *n*

mentality, mentali'teit

mention, (ver')melding : ver'melden

mentor, mentor

menu, me'nu *n*

mercantile, handels-

mercenary, geld'zuchtig : huurling

merchandise, koopwaar

merchant, koopman : koopvaar'dij-

merciful, ge'nadig ; ge'zegend

merciless, mee'dogenloos

mercury, kwik(zilver) *n*

mercy, ge'nade ; zegen

mere, louter

a mere (nothing), maar een (kleinigheid)

merely, alleen maar

merge, overgaan(in) ; samensmelten

meridian, meridi'aan

meringue, schuim(gebak) *n*

merit, ver'dienste : ver'dienen

mermaid, zeemeermin

merriment, vrolijkheid

merry, vrolijk

merry-go-round, draaimolen

merry-making, pret(make'rij) : pretmakend

mesh, maas

mess, rommel, bende; lelijke toestand; me'nage, (offi'ciers)-tafel: vuil maken
to mess about, friemelen, klungelen
to mess up, ver'knoeien
message, boodschap, be'richt *n*
messenger, (voor)bode
Messiah, Mes'sias
Messrs., de Heren; Firma
messy, slordig, vuil
metal, me'taal *n*: me'talen
metallic, me'talen, me'taalachtig
metamorphosis, ge'daanteverwisseling
metaphor, beeldspraak
metaphorical, fi'guurlijk
mete out, toemeten
meteor, mete'oor
meteorological, meteoro'logisch
meter, meter
method, me'thode; sys'teem *n*
methodical, syste'matisch
Methodist, Metho'dist
meticulous, (al te) zeer nauwge'zet
metre, meter; metrum *n*
metropolis, wereldstad
metropolitan, hoofd'stedelijk, Londense: metropo'liet
mettle, tempera'ment *n*
to put a person on his mettle, een uitdaging voor iemand zijn, uitdagen
mew, stal(woning): mi'auwen
mica, mica *n*
microbe, mi'crobe
microphone, micro'foon
microscope, micros'coop
mid, midden
midday, twaalf uur: middagmiddel
middle, middel(ste) (*n*), midden(-) (*n*)
middle-classes, middenstand
middle-aged, van middelbare leeftijd
middle-ages, middeleeuwen
middleman, tussenpersoon
middling, middel'matig
midge, mug
midget, dwergje *n*: minia'tuur
midnight, midder'nacht(elijk)
midriff, middenrif *n*

midshipman, adelborst
midst, (te) midden (van)
midsummer, mid'zomer
midway, halver'wege
midwife, vroedvrouw
mien, voorkomen *n*
might(y), macht(ig)
migrate, trekken
migration, trek
mild, zacht('aardig); licht
mildew, (be')schimmel(en)
mile, mijl
mileage, afstand in mijlen
milestone, mijlpaal
militant, strijdend; strijd'lustig
militarism, milita'risme *n*
military, mili'tair, krijgs-
militate, (tegen)werken
militia, mi'litie
milk, melk(en)
milkman, melkboer
Milky Way, Melkweg
mill, molen; fa'briek: malen; kartelen; kri'oelen
miller, molenaar
millet, gierst
milliner's (shop), hoedenzaak
million, mil'joen *n*
millionaire, miljo'nair
mime, ge'barenspel *n*: met ge'baren uitbeelden
mimic, mimicus: nabootsen
mince, ge'hakt *n*: fijnhakken
mind, geest, ver'stand *n*, ge'dachte; zin: er iets op tegen hebben; letten op; oppassen
to make up one's mind, be'sluiten
mindful, ge'dachtig (aan)
mine, van mij, het (*or* de) mijne: mijn; bron: delven
miner, mijnwerker
mineral, delfstof: mine'raal *n*
mingle, (zich) mengen; omgaan
miniature, minia'tuur (*n*)
minimize, zo klein mogelijk maken; ge'ringschatten
minimum, minimum *n*
mining, mijn(bouw)
minion, gunsteling
minister, predi'kant; mi'nister; ge'zant: ver'zorgen

ministry, predi'kantschap *n*; minis'terie *n*

mink, nerts *n*

minor, klein, minder (be'langrijk); mi'neur: minder'jarige

minority, minder('jarig)heid

minstrel, min'streel

mint, kruize'munt: munt(en)

minus, min; zonder

minute, mi'nuut; ogenblik *n*; notule: mi'niem; minuti'eus

miracle, wonder *n*

miraculous, wonder'baarlijk

mirage, fata mor'gana; zinsbegoocheling

mire, slijk *n*

mirror, spiegel: weer'kaatsen

mirth, vrolijkheid

misadventure, ongeluk *n*; onge'lukkig voorval *n*

misapprehension, mis'vatting

misbehave, zich mis'dragen

misbehaviour, wangedrag *n*

miscalculate, zich ver'rekenen; misrekenen

miscarriage, mis'lukking; miskraam

miscarry, mis'lukken; ver'loren gaan

miscellaneous, veel'soortig

miscellany, ge'mengde ver'zameling

mischief, (katte)kwaad *n*; on'deugendheid

mischievous, on'deugend; kwaa'daardig

misconception, dwaalbegrip *n*, mis'vatting

misconduct, wangedrag *n*; wanbeheer *n*: slecht be'heren

misconstrue, ver'keerd opvatten

miscreant, laag: onverlaat

misdeed, misdaad

misdemeanour, wangedrag *n*

miser, vrek

miserable, diep onge'lukkig; naar'geestig; el'lendig

misery, el'lende

misfire, ketsen; overslaan

misfit: to be a —, niet passen; uit de toon vallen

misfortune, ongeluk *n*

misgiving, bang ver'moeden *n*

misguided, ver'doold; onver'standig

mishap, ongeluk(je) *n*

misinform, ver'keerd inlichten

misinterpret, ver'keerd uitleggen

misjudge, ver'keerd (be')oordelen

mislay, kwijtraken

mislead, mis'leiden

mismanagement, wanbeheer *n*

misnomer, ver'keerde be'naming

misplace, ver'keerd plaatsen

misplaced, mis'plaatst

misprint, drukfout: ver'keerd drukken

misrepresent, een ver'keerde voorstelling geven van

miss, (me')juffrouw: misslaan; mislopen; missen; ver'zuimen

misshapen, mis'vormd

missile, projec'tiel *n*

mission, missie; zending

missionary, zendeling(s-)

missive, schrijven *n*

mist, nevel, lage wolk; waas *n*

mistake, ver'gissing; fout: aanzien, veer'keerd be'grijpen, mis'kennen

to be mistaken, zich ver'gissen; mis'plaatst zijn

mistress, me'vrouw; juffrouw, lera'res; mai'tresse

mistrust, wantrouwen (*n*)

misty, nevelachtig, wazig; be'slagen

misunderstand, ver'keerd be'grijpen

misunderstanding, misverstand *n*

misuse, misbruik *n*: mis'bruiken; mis'handelen

mite, dreumes; mijt

mitigate, ver'zachten, ver'lichten

mitre, mijter; ver'stek *n*

mitt(en), want, vuisthandschoen

mix, (ver')mengen; zich laten mengen; omgaan met

to mix up, ver'warren

mixture, mengsel *n*, mengeling

moan, ge'kerm *n*; ge'jammer *n*: kermen, suizen; jammeren

moat, gracht

mob, (mensen)massa; ge'peupel *n*; bende: zich ver'dringen om, als één man te lijf gaan

mobile, be'weeglijk, rondtrekkend

mobilize, mobili'seren

mock, schijn-, kunst-: (be')spotten; be'spottelijk maken; na-äpen

mockery, spotter'nij; aanfluiting

mode, mode; ma'nier

model, mo'del *n*: model'leren, boet'seren

moderate, (ge')matig(d): matigen; be'daren

moderation, matigheid

in moderation, met mate

modern(ize), mo'dern(i'seren)

modest, be'scheiden; zedig

modification, wijziging

modify, wijzigen; matigen

moist(en), vochtig (maken)

moisture, vocht(igheid) (*n*)

molasses, me'lasse

mole, mol: pier: moedervlek

molecule, mole'cule

molest, lastig vallen

mollify, ver'tederen

moment, ogenblik *n*; be'lang *n*

momentarily, voor een ogenblik

momentary, kort'stondig

momentous, ge'wichtig

momentum, arbeidsvermogen van be'weging *n*, vaart

monarch, vorst('in)

monarchy, monar'chie

monastery, klooster *n*

monastic, klooster(achtig)

Monday, maandag

monetary, munt-, geldelijk

money, geld *n*

mongrel, bastaard(hond)

monk, monnik

monkey, aap

monocle, mo'nocle

monogram, mono'gram *n*

monologue, al'leenspraak

monopolize, monopoli'seren

monopoly, mono'polie *n*

monotonous, een'tonig

monotony, een'tonigheid

monsoon, moesson

monster, monster *n*; ge'drocht *n*

monstrosity, monstrum *n*

monstrous, monsterachtig

month(ly), maand(elijks)

monument, monu'ment *n*

monumental, monumen'taal

mood, stemming, hu'meur *n*: wijs

moody, hu'meurig; ont'stemd

moon(light), maan(licht *n*)

moor, heide: Moor: meren

moorings, meertouwen; ligplaats

moot, be'twistbaar

mop, zwabber; (afwas)kwast: dweilen, zwabberen; afvegen

mope, mokken

moral, zedelijk, zeden-, mo'reel: mo'raal

morals, zeden

morale, mo'reel *n*

morality, zedelijke be'ginselen; zedelijkheid; morali'teit

moralize, morali'seren

morbid, ziekelijk; patho'logisch

more, meer, nog (meer)

some more, nog wat

more or less, min of meer

moreover, boven'dien

morgue, morgue

morning, morgen, ochtend

in the morning, 's ochtends; morgenochtend

morose, gemelijk

morsel, bete; stukje *n*

mortal, sterfelijk; dodelijk, doods-: sterveling

mortality, sterfte(cijfer *n*)

mortally, dodelijk

mortar, metselkalk; mor'tier; vijzel

mortgage, hypo'theek (nemen op)

mortify, diep ver'nederen; kas'tijden

mortuary, lijkenhuis *n*

mosaic, moza'iek (*n*)

mosque, mos'kee

mosquito, mus'kiet

moss, mos *n*

most, meest; bij'zonder: het (*or* de) meeste

at the most, op zijn hoogst (*or* meest)

to **make the most of,** zoveel mogelijk profi'teren van

mostly, groten'deels; meestal

moth, nachtvlinder, mot

mother, moeder

motherly, moederlijk

mother-or-pearl, paarle'moer-(en) (*n*)

motif, mo'tief *n*

motion, be'weging; motie; stoelgang: wenken

motionless, onbe'weeglijk

motivate, moti'veren

motive, be'weegreden

motley, bont

motor, motor: rijden

motor-cycle, motorfiets

motorist, automobi'list

mottle, vlekken

motto, motto *n*

mould, vorm(en); schimmel; teelaarde: boet'seren

mouldy, be'schimmeld; snert

moult, ruien

mound, wal, terp

mount, berg: rijdier *n*: (be')stijgen

mountain(eer), berg(beklimmer)

mountainous, bergachtig

mourn, (be')treuren

mourner, rouwdrager

mournful, treurig; droevig

mourning, rouw

mouse, muis

mouse-trap, muizeval

moustache, snor

mouth, mond(ing); opening

mouthful, hapje *n*

mouthpiece, mondstuk *n*; woordvoerder

movable, be'weegbaar; ver'anderlijk

move, zet; stap; ver'huizing: (zich) be'wegen; ver'huizen; ont'roeren

movement, be'weging

moving, roerend

mow, maaien

much, veel; zeer; verreweg; vrijwel

muck, drek, vuil *n*

mud, modder

muddle, warboel: in de war

brengen, door el'kaar gooien; scharrelen

muddy, modderig

mudguard, spatbord *n*

muff, mof: be'derven

muffle, instoppen; dempen

muffler, bouf'fante

mug, kroes: sul: smoel

mulberry, moerbei

mule, muildier *n*

multifarious, veel'soortig

multiple, veel'voudig; veelvoud *n*

multiplication, vermenig'vuldiging

multiply, (zich) vermenig'vuldigen

multitude, menigte; groot aantal *n*

mum: to keep —, stilzwijgen

mumble, mompelen

mummy, mummie: mammie

mumps, de bof

munch, (hoorbaar) k(n)auwen (op)

mundane, werelds

municipal, ge'meente-, stedelijk, stads-

municipality, ge'meente

munition, krijgsvoorraad

mural, muurschildering

murder, moord: ver'moorden

murderer, moordenaar

murderous, moord'dadig

murky, zwart, somber

murmur, ge'murmel *n*: murmelen; mopperen

muscle, spier

muscular, ge'spierd; spier-

muse, muze: mijmeren

museum, mu'seum *n*

mush, moes *n*; ge'wauwel *n*

mushroom, champi'gnon

music, mu'ziek

musical, muzi'kaal; mu'ziek-

musician, musicus; muzi'kant

muslin, neteldoek *n*

mussel, mossel

must, moet(en), moest(en)

mustard, mosterd

muster, monstering: monsteren; ver'zamelen

musty, muf, schimmelig

mute, stom; sour'dine: dempen
mutilate, ver'minken
mutineer, muiter
mutiny, muite'rij, opstand
mutter, mompelen, prevelen
mutton, schapevlees n
mutual, onderling, weder'zijds;
weder'kerig
muzzle, muil(band); mond
my, mijn
myriad, on'telbaar; tien'duizend-
tal n
myself, me('zelf), (ik')zelf
mysterious, geheim'zinnig
mystery, ge'heim n; raadsel n
mystic, mysticus
mystic(al), ver'borgen; mys'tiek
mysticism, mys'tiek
mystify, ver'bijsteren
myth, mythe; ver'dichtsel n
mythical, mythisch; ver'dicht
mythology, mytholo'gie

N

nag, hit; vitten
nail, spijker; nagel; vastspijk-
eren
naïve, na'ïef
naked, naakt; bloot
name, naam; (be')noemen; opnoemen; thuisbrengen
nameless, onbe'kend; ano'niem,
naamloos
namely, namelijk
namesake, naamgenoot
nap, dutje n: nop; dutten
nape, nek
napkin, ser'vet n; luier
narcissus, nar'cis
narcotic, slaap'wekkend middel
n: ver'dovend
narrate, ver'halen
narrative, ver'haal n; ver'halend
narrow, smal, nauw; klein
narrow-minded, klein'geestig
nasal, na'saal, neus-
nasty, akelig; smerig; naar,
lelijk
nation, volk n, natie
national, natio'naal; volks-,
staats-
nationalist(ic), nationa'list(isch)

nationality, nationali'teit
nationalize, nationali'seren
native, inboorling: ge'boorte-,
moeder-; aangeboren; in'heems
nativity, ge'boorte
natural, na'tuurlijk, na'tuur-
natural history, na'tuurlijke
his'torie
naturalist, natura'list
naturalize, naturali'seren
naturally, na'tuurlijk; van
na'ture
nature, na'tuur; aard
naught, nul; niets
naughty, on'deugend
nausea, misselijkheid; walging
nauseate, misselijk maken
nautical, zee(vaart'kundig)
naval, ma'rine-, zee-
nave, schip n
navel, navel
navigable, be'vaarbaar
navigate, be'sturen
navigation, stuurmanskunst,
navi'gatie
navigator, navi'gator
navy, ma'rine, vloot
nay, neen; ja (zelfs)
near, dichtbij, na'bij
nearly, bijna
not nearly, lang niet
neat, net(jes); handig; puur
necessarily, nood'zakelijk-
(erwijs)
necessary, nood'zakelijk: be'-
hoefte
necessitate, nood'zakelijk maken
necessity, nood(zaak); be'hoefte
neck, hals(stuk n)
necklace, (hals)ketting, (hals-)
snoer n
necktie, (strop)das
nectar, nectar
need, be'hoefte, nood(zaak): nodig hebben; hoeven, moeten
there is no need . . . het is niet
nodig . . .
needful, nodig
needle, naald
needless, on'nodig
needlework, naaiwerk n, hand-
werk(en) n
needy, be'hoeftig

negation, ont'kenning, ver'looch-ening

negative, ont'kennend; negatief (*n*)

neglect, ver'zuim(en) (*n*), ver'-waarlozing: ver'waarlozen

negligence, ver'waarlozing, on'-achtzaamheid

negligent, achteloos

negligible, niet noemens'waard

negotiate, onder'handelen

negotiation, onder'handeling

negro, neger(-)

neigh, hinniken

neighbour, buurman (*or* vrouw); naaste

neighbourhood, buurt, om'-geving

neighbouring, na'burig

neighbourly, vriendelijk

neither, geen van beide: even'min

neither . . . nor, noch . . . noch

nephew, neef

nerve, zenuw; geestkracht; (bru'tale) moed: ver'mannen

nervous, zenuw(achtig); bang

nest, nest *n*; (zich) nestelen

nestle, zich nestelen

net, net *n*; tule, vi'trage: met een net vangen

nether, onder-

Netherlands, Nederland(s) (*n*)

netting, gaas *n*

nettle, (brand)netel: pi'keren

network, net(werk) *n*

neurotic, zenuw(patient), zenuwziek

neuter, on'zijdig

neutral, neu'traal (land *n*)

neutralize, neutrali'seren; neu'-traal ver'klaren

never, nooit; niet eens

nevertheless, desondanks

new, nieuw, vers

newborn, pasgeboren

newcomer, nieuweling

new-fangled, nieuwer'wets

newly, pas, opnieuw

news, nieuws(berichten) (*n*), be'richt *n*

newspaper, krant

newsreel, jour'naal *n*

next, volgend, aan'staande: daar'na

next door, hier'naast

next (door) to, naast

nib, pen

nibble, knabbelen

nice, aardig; lekker; net(jes); fijn

nicety, nauwge'zetheid; fi'nesse

niche, nis, hoekje *n*

nick, keep: inkepen

nickname, bijnaam

nicotine, nico'tine

niece, nicht

niggard(ly), vrek(kig)

night, nacht, avond

at (*or* in the) night, 's nachts

nightdress, nachtjapon

nightfall, het vallen van de avond

nightingale, nachtegaal

nightmare, nachtmerrie

nimble, kwiek

nine(teen), negen(tien)

ninety, negentig

nip, kneep: halfje *n*: knijpen

nipple, tepel

nitrogen, stikstof

nitwit, domoor

no, neen: niet, geen

no one, niemand

nobility, adel(stand)

noble, edel(man), adellijk; groots

nobody, niemand: nul

nocturnal, nachtelijk, nacht-

nod, knik(ken); knikkebollen

noise, la'waai *n*, ge'luid *n*

noiseless, ge'ruisloos

noisy, luid'ruchtig, druk

nomad, no'made; zwerver

nominal, in naam; nomi'naal

nominate, be'noemen; kan-di'daat stellen

nomination, be'noeming; kandi'-daatstelling

nonchalant, onver'schillig

non-committal, (op'zettelijk) vaag

nonconformist, afgescheiden(e)

nondescript, onbe'paald; on-op'vallend

none, geen (één), niemand, niets: geenszins

nonentity, nul

nonsense, onzin

nook, hoekje *n*, plekje *n*

noon, twaalf uur ('s middags)

noose, strop, strik

nor, noch, en . . . ook niet

normal, nor'maal

normally, ge'woonlijk

north, (naar het) noorden; noord(en)-

northerly, northern, noordelijk

Norway, Noorwegen *n*

Norwegian, Noor(s) (*n*)

nose, neus

nosegay, ruiker

nostril, neusgat *n*

not, niet

notable, op'merkelijk, aan'zienlijk: no'tabele

notably, met name, voor'al

notation, schrijfwijze

notch, kerf: kerven

note, aantekening, no'titie; briefje *n*; nota; toon, noot; be'tekenis: no'teren; opmerken

notebook, aantekenboekje *n*

noted, be'kend, be'roemd

noteworthy, opmerkens'waardig

nothing, niets

notice, aandacht; aankondiging: (op)merken

  to give notice, de dienst (*or* huur) opzeggen; kennis geven

  to take notice of, aandacht schenken aan

noticeable, merkbaar

notification, kennisgeving

notify, ver'wittigen; be'kend maken

notion, i'dee *n*

notorious, be'rucht

notwithstanding, (des)ondanks

nought, niets; nul

nourish, voeden; koesteren

nourishment, voeding, voedsel *n*

novel, ro'man: nieuw

novelist, ro'manschrijver

novelty, nieuwigheid

November, november

novice, nieuweling

now, nu

nowadays, tegen'woordig

nowhere, nergens

noxious, schadelijk

nozzle, tuit

nucleus, kern

nude, naakt (*n*); naaktstudie

nudge, duwtje *n*: zachtjes aanstoten

nugget, (goud)klomp

nuisance: to be a —, lastig zijn

null and void, van nul en gener waarde

nullify, nietig ver'klaren; opheffen

numb, ver'kleumd, ver'doofd: ver'doven

number, ge'tal *n*; aantal *n*; nummer(en) (*n*); tellen, rekenen

numeral, cijfer *n*; telwoord *n*

numerical, nume'riek

numerous, talrijk

nun, non

nunnery, nonnenklooster *n*

nuptial, huwelijks-

nurse, ver'pleegster; kindermeisje *n*: ver'plegen; zogen; ver'zorgen; koesteren

nursery, kinderkamer; kweke'rij

nurture, (op)voeden; koesteren

nut, noot; moer

nutmeg, nootmus'kaat

nutrition, voeding(s'waarde)

nutritive, voedzaam

nymph, nimf

O

oaf, pummel

oak, eik(enhout *n*) (en)

oar, riem

oasis, o'ase

oats, haver

oath, eed; vloek

oatmeal, havermeel *n*, havermout

obdurate, onver'murwbaar, ver'stokt

obedience, ge'hoorzaamheid

obedient, ge'hoorzaam

obeisance, diepe buiging

obese, zwaar'lijvig

obey, ge'hoorzamen

obituary notice, in Me'moriam

object, voorwerp *n*; doel *n*: be'zwaar hebben (*or* maken) (tegen)

objection, be'zwaar *n*, tegenwerping
objectionable, on'aangenaam,
afkeurens'waardig
objective, objec'tief (*n*)
obligation, ver'plichting
obligatory, ver'plicht
oblige, ver'plichten; ge'noegen
doen
obliging, voor'komend
oblique, schuin; zijdelings
obliterate, uitwissen
oblivion, ver'getelheid
oblivious, onbe'wust
oblong, lang'werpig: rechthoek
obnoxious, aan'stotelijk
oboe, hobo
obscene, on'zedelijk
obscure, ob'scuur; onbe'kend;
ver'borgen; on'duidelijk:
on'zichtbaar maken; be'lemmeren; ver'doezelen
obscurity, on'duidelijkheid;
onbe'kendheid
obsequious, kruiperig
observance, in'achtneming
observant, op'merkzaam
observation, waarneming, obser'vatie; opmerking
observatory, sterrenwacht
observe, (op)merken, waarnemen; in acht nemen
obsess, (ge'heel) ver'vullen
obsession, ob'sessie
obsolete, ver'ouderd
obstacle, hindernis; be'letsel *n*
obstetrics, ver'loskunde
obstinate, hard'nekkig
obstreperous, wild, luid'ruchtig
obstruct, ver'sperren, be'lemmeren
obstruction, hindernis, be'letsel
n; be'lemmering
obtain, ver'krijgen, ver'werven,
be'halen; gelden
obtainable, ver'krijgbaar
obtrude, (zich) opdringen
obtuse, stomp('zinnig)
obviate, uit de weg ruimen
obvious, overduidelijk
occasion, ge'legenheid; aanleiding (geven tot)
occasionally, nu en dan

occult, oc'cult
occupant, be'woner, inzittende
occupation, be'roep *n*, bezigheid;
be'zetting
occupy, be'zetten, innemen;
be'wonen
occur, voorkomen; opkomen (bij)
occurrence, voorval *n*, ge'beurtenis
ocean, oce'aan
ocean-going, zee-
o'clock, uur
octagonal, acht'hoekig
octave, oc'taaf
October, oc'tober
octopus, achtarm
oculist, oogarts
odd, on'even; los; over; vreemd
odd job, kar'weitje *n*
odd moment, ver'loren ogenblik *n*
oddity, eigen'aardigheid, vreemde
snuiter
oddment, res'tant *n*
odds, kans; (alle) nadelen;
ver'schil *n*
ode, ode
odious, ver'foeilijk
odorous, kwalijk (*or* wel')riekend
odour, reuk; lucht(je *n*)
of, van, uit; met; over
off, van (. . . af); weg; af; vrij
offal, afval
offence, over'treding; aanstoot,
be'lediging; aanval
offend, be'ledigen, ergeren
offensive, be'ledigend; on'aangenaam; aanval(s-)
offer, (aan)bod *n*: (aan)bieden;
aanvoeren; zich voordoen
offering, gift
offhand, op het eerste ge'zicht
office, kan'toor *n*, ambt *n*,
functie; zorg
officer, offi'cier; functio'naris
official, offici'eel; ambtenaar,
be'ambte
officiate, dienst doen; de dienst
leiden
officious, be'moeiziek
offing, ver'schiet *n*
offset, (laten) opwegen tegen
offspring, kroost *n*

often, vaak
ogle, (toe)lonken
ogre, boeman
oil, olie, pe'troleum : smeren
oilcloth, zeildoek *n*
oil-painting, schilde'rij in olie-
verf
oilskin, oliegoed *n* ; oliejas
oily, olieachtig
ointment, zalf
old, oud
old-fashioned, ouder'wets
oligarchy, oligar'chie
olive, o'lijf(boom)
omelet, ome'let
omen, voorteken *n*
ominous, onheil'spellend
omission, ver'zuim *n*, weglating
omit, weglaten ; nalaten
omnipotent, al'machtig
omniscient, al'wetend
on, op ; aan ; bij, met ; over : verder ;
aan de gang
once, eens, één keer ; eenmaal
at once, on'middellijk
once in a while, zo nu en dan
once or twice, een paar keer
one, één : men
onerous, zwaar
oneself, (zich')zelf, zich
one-sided, een'zijdig
onion, ui
onlooker, toeschouwer
only, slechts, (al'leen) maar ;
pas, nog : enig
only too, maar al te
onset, aanval ; aanvang
onslaught, woeste aanval
onto, op
onus, last
onward(s), voorwaarts
ooze, (door)sijpelen
opal, o'paal
opaque, ondoor'schijnend
open, open('baar) ; open'hartig ;
blootgesteld : openlucht : opengaan ; opendoen
opening, opening ; be'gin *n* ;
kans : inleidend
opera, opera
opera-glasses, to'neelkijker
operate, ope'reren ; werken ;
be'dienen

operation, ope'ratie ; handeling
operator, telefo'nist(e) ; be'dien-
er
opinion, oordeel *n*, mening
opium, opium *n*
opponent, tegenstander
opportune, gunstig
opportunist, opportu'nist
opportunity, ge'legenheid
oppose, tegenwerken ; stellen
tegen'over
opposite, tegen'over (gesteld)
opposition, tegenstand ; oppo'-
sitie
oppress, (onder')drukken
oppression, onder(*or* ver)'drukking
oppressive, drukkend
optic, ge'zichts-, oog-
optical, ge'zichts-
optimistic, opti'mistisch
option, keus
optional, faculta'tief
opulence, rijkdom
or, of
oracle, o'rakel *n*
oral, mondeling ; mond-
orange, sinaasappel : o'ranje
oration, rede
orator, redenaar
oratorio, ora'torium *n*
oratory, wel'sprekendheid ; ka'pel
orb, bol
orbit, baan ; kring
orchard, boomgaard
orchestra(l), or'kest(-) (*n*)
orchid, orchi'dee
ordain, voorschrijven ; wijden
ordeal, be'proeving, proef
order, (volg)orde ; stand ;
be'vel(en) (*n*) ; be'stelling :
ordenen ; be'stellen
in order that, opdat
in order to, om te
out of order, niet op volgorde ;
niet in orde
orderly, ordelijk ; ordon'nans ;
zaalmeisje (*or* knecht) (*n*)
ordinance, ver'ordening
ordinarily, ge'woonlijk
ordinary, ge'woon
ordnance, ge'schut *n* ; staf-
ore, erts *n*

organ, orgel; *n* or'gaan *n*
organic, or'ganisch
organism, orga'nisme *n*
organist, orga'nist
organization, organi'satie
organize, organi'seren
orgy, baccha'naal *n*
Orient, Oosten *n*
Oriental, Oosters: Oosterling
orientate, orien'teren
orifice, opening
origin, oorsprong; afkomst
original, oor'spronkelijk; origi'-neel (*n*)
originate, ont'staan (uit); in het leven roepen
ornament, sieraad *n*, ver'siersel *n*
ornamental, sier-
ornate, zwierig; bloemrijk
ornithologist, vogel'kundige
orphan, wees(-), ouderloos
orphanage, weeshuis *n*
orthodox, ortho'dox; ge'brui-kelijk
oscillate, slingeren; oscil'leren
osier, rijs *n*
ossify, ver'benen; ver'stenen
ostensible, ogen'schijnlijk
ostentation, uiterlijk ver'toon *n*
ostentatious, praalziek
ostracize, doodverklaren
ostrich, struisvogel
other, ander; nog
 the other day, onlangs
otherwise, anders
otter, otter
ought, moest(en)
ounce, (approx.) kwart ons *n*
our(selves), ons(zelf)
ours, de (*or* het) onze, van ons
oust, ver'dringen
out, (er')uit; (naar) buiten; weg
 out and out, door en door
 out of, uit; buiten; zonder
outbreak, uitbarsting; oproer *n*
outbuilding, bijgebouw *n*
outburst, uitbarsting
outcast, ver'stoteling
outcome, resul'taat *n*
outcry, luid pro'test *n*
outdoor, openlucht-
outer, buiten-
outfit, uitrusting, uitzet

outgoing, uitgaand, aftredend: uitgave
outgrow, groeien uit; ont'groeien
outhouse, bijgebouw *n*, schuurtje *n*
outing, uitstapje *n*
outlandish, vreemd'soortig
outlaw, banneling; vogel'vrij ver'klaren
outlay, uitgave(n)
outlet, afvoer(kanaal *or* buis) *n*; uitweg
outline, omtrek; schets(en): aftekenen
outlive, over'leven
outlook, (voor')uitzicht *n*; op-vatting
outlying, afgelegen
outnumber, (in aantal) over'tref-fen
out-of-date, ver'ouderd
out-of-the-way, afgelegen; bui-te'nissig
outpost, buiten(*or* voor)post
output, opbrengst
outrage, annranding; schande
outrageous, schan'dalig
outright, in'eens; rond'uit
outset, begin *n*
outside, buiten(kant)
outsider, buitenstaander
outskirts, buitenkant
outspoken, open'hartig
outstanding, voor'treffelijk
outstrip, achter zich laten; over'treffen
outward, uit-, naar buiten
 (to all) outward appearances, uiterlijk (*n*)
outwardly, uiterlijk
outweigh, zwaarder wegen dan
outwit, ver'schalken
oval, o'vaal (*n*)
ovation, o'vatie
oven, oven
over, boven; over('heen); door; meer dan: om
 over again, nog eens
overall, huishoudschort *n*: to'taal
overalls, ove'rall
overbearing, aan'matigend
overboard, over'boord
overcast, be'trokken

overcharge, te veel vragen

overcoat, overjas

overcome, over'stelpt, be'vangen: over'winnen

overcrowded, over'vol

overdo, te veel doen; over'drijven

overdue, achter'stallig, te laat

overflow, overloop: over'stromen, overlopen

overgrown, over'woekerd

overhang, uitstekende rand: overhangen

overhaul, nakijken en repa'reren; inhalen

overhead, boven (het hoofd): boven'gronds, lucht-

overheads, vaste uitgaven

overhear, horen; afluisteren

overjoyed, dolblij

overlap, ten dele be'dekken, ge'deeltelijk samenvallen

overlook, over'zien; over het hoofd zien

overnight, in één nacht; de avond te'voren

overpower, over'weldigen

overrate, over'schatten

overrule, ver'werpen

overrun, over'stromen, over'woekeren

overseas, over'zee(s)

overseer, opzichter

overshadow, over'schaduwen

oversight, a'buis *n*

oversleep, zich ver'slapen

overstep, over'schrijden

overtake, inhalen

overtax, te veel vergen van

overthrow, ten val brengen

overtime, overwerk *n*

overture, voorstel *n*; ouver'ture

overturn, om'verwerpen, om-slaan

overwhelm, over'stelpen

overwork, zich over'werken

overwrought, over'spannen

owe, schuldig zijn

owing to, dank zij

owl, uil

own, eigen(dom *n*): be'zitten; er'kennen

owner, eigenaar

ownership, eigendom(srecht *n*)

ox, os

oxygen, zuurstof

oyster, oester

P

pace, pas, tempo *n*: stappen

pacific, vrede'lievend

Pacific, Stille Oce'aan

pacifist, paci'fist

pacify, tot be'daren brengen

pack, pak(ken) (*n*); hoop; spel *n*: ver'(*or* in)pakken; proppen

package, pak *n*

packet, pakje *n*

packing, ver'pakking

pact, ver'drag *n*

pad, kussen(tje) *n*; blok *n*: capiton'neren; opvullen

paddle, pa'gaai(en); pootje baden

paddock, paddock

padlock, hangslot *n*

pagan, heiden(s)

page, bladzijde: page

pageant, ver'toning; optocht

pail, emmer

pain, pijn (doen)

to take **pains,** moeite doen

painful, pijnlijk

painstaking, nauwge'zet

paint, verf: verven; schilderen

paint-brush, verfkwast, pen'seel *n*

painter, schilder

painting, schilde'rij *n*; schilderkunst

pair, paar *n*

pal, maat

palace, pa'leis *n*

palatable, smakelijk

palate, ge'hemelte *n*; smaak

palatial, vorstelijk

palaver, samenspreking; ge'klets *n*

pale, bleek, licht: paal: ver'bleken

palette, pa'let *n*

paling, om'heining

palisade, palis'sade

pall, lijkkleed *n*; mantel; gaan tegenstaan

pallid, bleek
pallor, bleekheid
palm, palm(tak)
 to palm off on, aansmeren
palpable, in het oog springend
palpitate, snel kloppen; trillen
paltry, nietig
pamper, ver'wennen
pamphlet, pam'flet *n*
pan, pan
panacea, pana'cee
pancake, pannekoek
pandemonium, pande'monium *n*
pane, ruit
panegyric, lofrede
panel, pa'neel *n*, vak *n*
pang, steek; plotseling ge'voel, *n*
panic, pa'niek: het hoofd ver'liezen
panic-stricken, ver'lamd van schrik
panorama, pano'rama *n*
pansy, vi'ooltje *n*
pant, hijgen; snakken (naar)
pantomime, sprookjesvoorstelling; panto'mime
pantry, pro'visiekast
pants: (pair of) —, onderbroek
papal, pauselijk
paper, pa'pier(en) (*n*); krant; ver'handeling; (e'xamen)opgave: be'hangen
par, pari
 on a par, ge'lijk
parable, ge'lijkenis
parachute, para'chute
parade, pa'rade; ap'pel *n*; ver'toon *n*; para'deren; aantreden; pronken met
paradise, para'dijs *n*
paradox, para'dox
paraffin, pe'troleum
paragon, toonbeeld *n*
paragraph, a'linea
parallel, paral'lel, even'wijdig: eve'naren
paralyse, ver'lammen
paralysis, ver'lamming
paramount, hoogst
parapet, borstwering, leuning
paraphernalia, spullen

parasite, para'siet
parasol, para'sol
parcel, pakje *n*, pak'ket *n*
parch, ver'dorren, uitdrogen
parchment, perka'ment *n*
pardon, ver'giffenis; gratie (ver'lenen): ver'geven: par'don!
pare, schillen; (af)snijden; be'knotten
parent, ouder
parentage, afkomst
parental, ouder(lijk)
parenthood, ouderschap *n*
parish, pa'rochie
park, park('eren) (*n*)
parley, onder'handeling: onder'handelen
parliament, parle'ment *n*
parliamentary, parlemen'tair
parlour, sa'lon
parochial, parochi'aal; klein'-burgerlijk
parody, paro'die
parole, erewoord *n*
paroxysm, hevige aanval
parrot, pape'gaai
parry, afweren
parsimonious, karig
parsley, peter'selie
parsnip, pasti'naak
parson, dominee
part, deel *n*, ge'deelte *n*; rol; stem; steek: scheiden
partake, ge'bruiken
partial, ge'deeltelijk; par'tijdig; ge'steld(op)
partially, ten dele
participant, deelnemer
participate, deelnemen (aan)
particle, deeltje *n*
particular, bij'zonder(heid); kies'keurig, pre'cies
 that particular one, die ene daar; die be'paalde
 in particular, in het bij'zonder
particularly, (in het) bij'zonder, voor'al
parting, afscheid *n*; scheiding
partisan, aanhanger; par'tijdig
partition, ver'deling; tussenschot *n*; vak *n*: ver'delen
partly, ge'deeltelijk, deels
partner, partner, compa'gnon

partnership, ven'nootschap
partridge, pa'trijs
part-time job, niet-vol'ledige
be'trekking
party, ge'zelschap n, krans;
par'tij (tje n)
pass, pas; stand van zaken:
pas'seren, voor'bijgaan; aangeven; slagen; vellen (judgement); doorbrengen; goed-
keuren; ge'beuren; ermee door-
kunnen
passable, redelijk; be'gaanbaar
passage, (door)gang; pas'sage;
voor'bijgaan n
passenger, passa'gier
passer-by, voor'bijganger
passing, voor'bijgaand; over'-
lijden n
in passing, ter'loops
passion, hartstocht(elijke liefde);
Lijden(sverhaal) n
passionate, harts'tochtelijk
passive, pas'sief
passport, paspoort n
password, wachtwoord n
past, voor'bij; ver'leden (n);
vorig; over
paste, kleefpasta (or pap);
pas'tei: plakken
pastel, pas'tel(tekening)
pastime, tijdverdrijf n
pastor, (zielen)herder
pastoral, herderlijk, herders-,
landelijk; ziel-
pastry, korstdeeg n; ge'bakje n
pasture, weide; gras n
pat, tikje n; kluitje n: zachtjes
kloppen
patch, lap(je n); plek(je n):
oplappen
pate, bol
patent, pa'tent (n); duidelijk
paternal, vader(lijk)
path, pad n; baan
pathetic, aan'doenlijk; zielig
pathology, patholo'gie
pathos, pathos
pathway, pad n
patience, ge'duld n; pa'tience n
patient, ge'duldig: pa'tient
patriarch, patri'arch
patriot, patri'ot

patriotic, vaderlands'lievend
patrol, pa'trouille: patroui'lleren
patron, vaste klant; be'scherm-
heer(or vrouw); be'scherm-
patronage, klan'dizie; be'gun-
stiging
patronize, be'gunstigen, vaste
klant zijn van
patronizing, neer'buigend
patter, ge'kletter n, ge'trippel
n; ge'babbel n: kletteren,
trippelen
pattern, pa'troon n; voorbeeld n
patty, pas'teitje n
paunch, buik,
pauper, arme
pause, rust, onder'breking:
pau'seren, (even) wachten
pave, pla'veien; banen
pavement, trot'toir n
pavilion, pavil'joen n
paw, poot: krabben; aanraken
pawn, pi'on; werktuig n: pand
n: ver'panden
pay, loon; n, sol'dij: (uit-)
be'talen; schenken (attention); maken (compliments);
afleggen (visit); lonen
it does not pay, het loont de
moeite niet; het heeft geen zin
payment, be'taling; loon n
pea, erwt
peace, vrede; rust
peaceable, vrede'lievend, vreedzaam
peaceful, rustig; vreedzaam
peach, perzik
peacock, pauw
peak, piek; klep; hoogtepunt n
peal, ge'rommel n; ge'lui n;
ge'schater n: luiden
peanut (butter), pinda(kaas)
pear, peer
pearl, parel
peasant, boer
peat, turf
pebble, kiezelsteen
peck, kwart schepel: pikken
peculiar(ity), eigen'aardig(heid)
pecuniary, geldelijk, geld-
pedagogue, peda'goog
pedal, pe'daal n: peddelen
pedant(ic), pe'dant

peddle, venten
pedestal, voetstuk n
pedestrian, voetganger: alle'-
daags
pedigree, stamboom, ras-
pedlar, marskramer
peek, kijkje n: gluren
peel, schil (len)
peep, gluren
peer, edelman; weerga: turen
peerage, adelstand
peerless, weergaloos
peeved, gepi'keerd
peevish, korzelig
peg, pen, haak, knijper, haring
to peg away, ploeteren
pelican, peli'kaan
pellet, propje n, klontje n, korrel,
balletje n
pelt, vel n: be'kogelen; kletteren
pen, pen: kooi
penal, straf-, strafbaar
penalize, straffen
penance, boete (doening)
pencil, potlood n
pendant, hanger; luchter
pending, hangend; in afwachting
van
pendulum, slinger
penetrate, doordringen, door'-
boren
penetrating, scherp ('zinnig)
penguin, pinguïn
peninsula, schiereiland n
penitence, be'rouw n
penitent, be'rouwvol; boeteling
penknife, zakmes n
penniless, straat'arm
penny, 4 cent; stuiver
pension, pen'sioen n, uitkering
pensioner, gepensio'neerde
pensive, peinzend
penthouse, afdak n
pent-up, opgekropt; opgesloten
penury, armoede
people, mensen; volk n; fa'milie
pepper, peper
peppermint, peper'munt
per, per
perambulator, kinderwagen
perceive, waarnemen, be'merken

percent, pro'cent n
percentage, percen'tage n
perceptible, waar'neembaar,
merkbaar
perception, waarneming (svermogen n)
perch, stok (je n), zitplaats:
baars: gaan zitten
percolate, fil'treren; doorsijpelen
percussion, slag (-)
peremptory, ge'biedend, be'slissend
perennial, overblijvend; altijd
durend
perfect, vol'maakt, vol'slagen:
perfectio'neren
perfection, vol'maaktheid, per'-
fectie
perfectly, vol'maakt, vol'komen
perfidious, trouweloos
perforate, perfo'reren
perform, doen; opvoeren, ten
beste geven, uitvoeren
performance, opvoering, uitvoering; optreden n; pres'tatie
perfume, par'fum; geur
perfunctory, noncha'lant, vluchtig
perhaps, mis'schien
peril(ous), ge'vaar (lijk) (n)
perimeter, omtrek
period, peri'ode, uur n
periodical, perio'diek: tijdschrift n
periodically, van tijd tot tijd
periphery, omtrek
periphrasis, om'schrijving
periscope, peri'scoop
perish, omkomen, ver'gaan
perishable, aan be'derf onder'hevig; ver'gankelijk
perjure oneself, een meineed
doen
perjury, meineed
perk up, opkikkeren
perky, par'mantig
permanent, vast, perma'nent
permeate, (door')dringen,
(door')trekken
permissible, ge'oorloofd
permission, ver'lof n
permit, ver'gunning: toestaan

pernicious,   ver'derfelijk;
  kwaa'daardig
perpendicular, loodrecht: loodlijn
perpetrate, be'gaan
perpetual,   aan'houdend,
  eeuwig('durend)
perpetually, con'stant
perpetuate, ver'eeuwigen
perplex, ver'bijsteren
perplexity, ver'bijstering
persecute, ver'volgen
perseverance, vol'harding
persevere, vol'harden
Persian, Per'zisch (n); Pers
persist, hard'nekkig doorgaan,
  volhouden
persistent, hard'nekkig
person, per'soon, mens
personal, per'soonlijk
personality, per'soonlijkheid
personally, per'soonlijk; wat
  mij be'treft
personification,   verper'soon-
  lijking
personnel, perso'neel n
perspective, perspec'tief n
perspiration, transpi'ratie
perspire, transpi'reren
persuade, over'reden, over'tuig-
  en
persuasion, over'reding (skracht)
persuasive, over'redend
pert, vrij'postig
pertain, be'horen (tot), be'trekking hebben (op)
pertinent, ter zake dienend
perturb, veront'rusten
perusal, studie
peruse, bestu'deren
pervade, ver'vullen, trekken door
perverse, weer'barstig, dwars;
  ver'draaid; ver'dorven
pervert, be'derven; ver'draaien
pessimism, pessi'misme n
pessimist(ic), pessi'mist (isch)
pest, plaag
pester, plagen; lastig vallen
pestilence, dodelijke epide'mie
pet, lieveling (sdier n); lievelings-:
  ver'troetelen
petal, bloemblad n
petite, klein en tenger

petition,   ver'zoek (schrift) n,
  smeekbede
petrify, ver'lammen
petrol, ben'zine
petticoat, onderjurk
petty, klein, nietig
petulant, kribbig
pew, kerkbank
pewter, tin (nen) (n)
phantom, schim
phase, fase; stadium n; schijngestalte
pheasant, fa'zant
phenomenal, fenome'naal
phenomenon,   ver'schijnsel n;
  wonder n
philanthropist, filan'troop
philosopher, filo'soof
philosophic(al), filo'sofisch
philosophy, filoso'fie
phlegm, slijm n
phlegmatic, flegma'tiek
phosphorescent, fosfores'cerend
photograph, foto (gra'feren)
photographer, foto'graaf
photography, fotogra'fie
phrase, frase; uitdrukking: uitdrukken
physical, li'chamelijk, lichaams-;
  na'tuur ('kundig)
physician, dokter, inter'nist
physicist, natuur'kundige
physics, na'tuurkunde
physiology, fysiolo'gie
physique, lichaamsbouw
pianist, pia'nist
piano, pi'ano
pick, keus; beste n; hou'weel
  n: plukken; peuteren; uitzoeken
  to pick up, oprapen; op de kop
  tikken; oppikken; ophalen
pickaxe, hou'weel n
picket, paal; pi'ket, post
pickle, tafelzuur n; lastpost;
  pekelen; inmaken
pickpocket, zakkenroller
picnic, picknick (en)
pictorial, in beeld: geillus'treerd
  tijdschrift n
picture, schilde'rij n; plaat;
  (toon) beeld n: zich voorstellen

picturesque, schilderachtig

pie, pas'tei, taart

piebald, bont (paard *n*)

piece, stuk(je) *n*

piecemeal, bij stukken en brok-
ken

pier, pier

pierce, door'boren; door'zien

piercing, door'dringend

piety, vroomheid

pig, varken *n*

pigeon, duif

pigeon-hole, vak(je) *n*

pig-headed, eigen'wijs

pigment, pig'ment *n*

pigsty, varkenskot *n*

pigtail, vlecht

pike, piek; snoek

pile, stapel; hoop: aambei:
nop: heipaal: (op)stapelen,
ophopen

pilfer, ont'futselen

pilgrim(age), pelgrim(stocht)

pill, pil

pillage, plunderen

pillar, (steun)pi'laar, zuil

pillory, schandpaal: aan de kaak
stellen

pillow, (hoofd)kussen *n*

pillow-case, kussensloop

pilot,   loods(en);   pi'loot:
be'sturen

pimple, puistje *n*

pin, speld(en); pen; vastgekneld
houden

pinafore, schortje *n*

pincers, nijptang; schaar

pinch, kneep; snuifje *n*; nood:
knijpen, klemmen; gappen

pine, pijnboom; pijnhout *n*:
smachten (naar), kwijnen

pine-apple, ana'nas

pinion, klein tandrad *n*: binden

pink, roze (*n*); kleine anjer

pinnace, pi'nas

pinnacle, (berg)spits, torentje
n; toppunt *n*

pint, (*approx*) halve liter

pioneer, pio'nier(en)

pious, vroom

pip, pit

pipe, pijp, buis; fluit(en)

piper, doedelzakspeler

piping, ge'fluit *n*: buizen(net *n*):
kokend

piquant, pi'kant

pique, pi'keren; prikkelen

pirate, zeerover(sschip *n*)

pistil, stamper

pistol, pis'tool *n*

piston, zuiger

pit, kuil; mijn, groeve; par'terre

pitted, vol kuiltjes; pok'dalig

pitch, pek *n*: toonhoogte; graad:
pik-: gooien; opslaan; stam-
pen; storten

pitcher, kan

pitchfork, hooivork

piteous, beklagens'waardig

pitfall, val(strik)

pith, pit *n*

pitiable, pitiful, beklagens'waardig; jammerlijk

pitiless, mee'dogenloos

pittance, schijntje *n*

pity, medelijden (hebben met)
(*n*)

  what a pity, wat jammer

pivot, spil: draaien

placard, plak'kaat *n*: re'clame
maken voor, be'plakken

place, plaats(en); thuisbrengen

  to take place, plaatsvinden

placid, kalm

plague, pest; plaag: plagen;
lastig vallen

plaid, ge'ruite stof

plain, duidelijk; een'voudig;
effen; onaan'trekkelijk: vlakte

plaintiff, aanklager

plaintive, klaaglijk

plait, vlecht(en)

plan, plan *n*, platte'grond:
ont'werpen, uitwerken, op touw
zetten; van plan zijn

plane, vlak *n*; peil *n*; vliegtuig
n: schaaf: pla'taan: schaven

planet, pla'neet

plank, plank

plant, plant(en); instal'latie

plantation, plan'tage

planter, planter

plaque, pla'quette

plasma, plasma *n*

plaster, pleister(en) (*n*); be'-
smeren

plastic, plastic *n*: plastisch

plate, bord *n*; plaat; goud en zilver *n*, pleet *n*

plateau, hoogvlakte

platform, per'ron *n*, podium *n*

platinum, platina *n*

platitude, ge'meenplaats

platoon, pelo'ton *n*

platter, schotel

plausible, geloof'waardig

play, spel(en) (*n*); to'neelstuk *n*; speling

player, (to'neel)speler

playful, speels, schertsend

playground, speelplaats

playmate, speelmakker

play-pen, box

plaything, stuk speelgoed *n*; speelbal

playwright, to'neelschrijver

plea, (dringend) ver'zoek *n*; veront'schuldiging; pleit *n*

plead, aanvoeren; smeken; (be')pleiten

pleasant, prettig, aardig

pleasantry, geestigheid

please, een ple'zier doen (*n*), be'hagen; ver'kiezen: alstublieft

be pleased to . . ., met ge'noegen . . .

pleasing, aangenaam; in'nemend

pleasure, ge'noegen *n*, ple'zier *n*

pleat, plooi(en)

plebeian, ple'bejer; ple'bejisch

plebiscite, plebis'ciet *n*

pledge, ge'lofte; pand *n*, teken *n*: be'loven, ver'binden

plenipotentiary, gevol'machtigd(e)

plenteous, plentiful, over'vloedig

plenty (of), ruim vol'doende, veel

pliable, pliant, buigzaam; plooibaar

pliers, buigtang

plight, toestand

plod, zwoegen

plop, plons: plonzen

plot, kom'plot *n*, in'trige; stukje grond *n*: be'ramen, samenspannen; in kaart brengen

plough, ploeg(en)

pluck, moed: plukken; tokkelen

plucky, flink

plug, stop(contact *n*), prop: (dicht)stoppen

plum, pruim

plumage, ge'vederte *n*

plumb, loodrecht; pre'cies: peilen

plumber, loodgieter

plumbing, loodgieterswerk *n*

plume, pluim

plump, mollig: (neer)ploffen

plunder, buit: plunderen

plunge, sprong: indompelen; (zich) storten

plural, meervoud *n*

plus, plus

plush, pluche

plutocrat, pluto'craat

ply, han'teren; uitoefenen; over'laden (met); ge'regeld rijden, be'varen

pneumatic, lucht-, pneu'matisch

pneumonia, longontsteking

poach, stropen: po'cheren

pocket, zak(-): in de zak steken; (in)slikken

pock-marked, pok'dalig

pod, peul

poem, ge'dicht *n*

poet(ic), dichter(lijk)

poetry, poëzie, dichtwerk *n*, ge'dichten

poignant, schrijnend; scherp; aan'grijpend

point, punt (*n*); zin; wissel: wijzen, richten

point of view, ge'zichtspunt *n*

to point out, aanwijzen; er op wijzen

point-blank, à bout por'tant, bot'weg, op de man af

pointed, puntig; scherp: ad rem

pointer, wijzer; aanwijzing

pointless, zinloos

poise, houding

poised, in evenwicht

poison, ver'gift(igen) (*n*)

poisonous, ver'giftig

poke, (op)por(ren); steken

poker, pook: poker

poky, benepen en slonzig

polar, pool-

pole, paal, stok; pool

police, po'litie
policeman, (po'litie)a'gent
policy, poli'tiek; polis
polish, was, smeerpoets; glans:
Pools (n): wrijven, poetsen;
be'schaven, opknappen
polite, be'leefd
political, poli'tiek; staats-
politician, po'liticus
politics, poli'tiek, staatkunde
poika, polka
poll, stemming; aantal stemmen
(n): stemmen (ver'krijgen)
pollen, stuifmeel n
pollinate, be'stuiven
pollute, be'zoedelen, veront'reinigen
polo, polo n
polygamy, polyga'mie
pomp, praal
pompous, praalziek, hoog'dravend
pond, vijver
ponder, (be')peinzen
ponderous, zwaar'wichtig;
zwaar op de hand
pontifical, pauselijk; pontifi'-
caal
pontoon, pon'ton: vingt-et-'un
pony, pony
poodle, poedel
pool, plas; pot: bij el'kaar doen
poop, achterdek n, achtersteven
poor, arm('zalig); slecht
poorly, arm('zalig); niet lekker,
minnetjes
pop, knallen; wippen; puilen
pope, paus
poplar, popu'lier
poppy, klaproos
poppycock, larie
populace, ge'peupel n
popular, popu'lair; volks-
populate, be'volken
population, be'volking
populous, dichtbevolkt
porcelain, porse'lein(en) (n)
porch, por'tiek
porcupine, stekelvarken n
pore, porie: zich ver'diepen
(in)
pork, varkensvlees n
porous, po'reus

porridge, havermoutpap
port, haven: bakboord n: port
portable, koffer-, draagbaar
portend, voor'spellen
portent, voorteken n
porter, kruier; por'tier
portfolio, porte'feuille
porthole, pa'trijspoort
portico, zuilenportiek (or gale'rij)
portion, deel n, portie
portly, welgedaan
portmanteau, va'lies n
portrait, por'tret n
portray, (af)schilderen
pose, houding; aanstelle'rij:
po'seren; zich voordoen als;
stellen
position, po'sitie; houding; stelling
positive, posi'tief; stellig
positively, abso'luut
possess, be'zitten
possession(s), be'zit(tingen) (n)
possessive, hebberig; be'zittelijk
possibility, mogelijkheid
possible, mogelijk
possibly, mis'schien
not possibly, on'mogelijk
post, stijl, paal: post; be'trekking: op de post doen; (over)-
plaatsen; aanplakken
postage, port; post-
postal, post-
postcard, briefkaart
poster, aanplakbiljet n
posterior, achter-; later
posterity, nageslacht n
posthumous, pos'tuum
postman, postbode
post-mortem, lijkschouwing
postpone, uitstellen
postscript, post'scriptum n
postulate, postu'leren
posture, houding
post-war, na-oorlogs
posy, tuiltje n
pot, pot(ten); fuik; bom (duit-
en): inmaken
potash, potas
potato, aardappel
potent, krachtig
potentate, poten'taat

potential, potenti'eel (*n*); po-tenti'aal

potion, drank

potter, pottenbakker: prutsen

pottery, aardewerk *n*; potten-bakkerij

pouch, zak, buidel

poultice, kom'pres *n*, pap

poultry, pluimvee *n*

pounce, zich storten

pound, (*approx*) half kilogram, pond *n*: schutstal: beuken (op); bonzen (op); fijnstampen

pour, gieten, schenken; stromen

pout, pruilen

poverty, armoede

poverty-stricken, arm('oedig)

powder, poeier(en), (be')poeder-(en); buskruit *n*

power, macht, kracht; mogend-heid

powerful, machtig, krachtig

powerless, machteloos

power-station, elektrici'teits-centrale

practicable, uit'voerbaar

practical, praktisch

practically, nage'noeg

practice, oefening; prak'tijk; ge'woonte

practise, (be')oefenen; (prak'-tijk) uitoefenen

prairie, prairie

praise, lof: prijzen, loven

praiseworthy, loffelijk, lof'waar-dig

prance, dansen, steigeren; trots stappen

prank, (dolle) streek

prate, wauwelen

prattle, babbelen

prawn, steurgarnaal

pray, ge'lieve: bidden

prayer, ge'bed *n*

preach, preken, prediken

preacher, predilker

preamble, inleiding

precarious, hachelijk

precaution, voorzorg(smaatregel)

precede, voor('af)gaan

precedence, voorrang

precedent, prece'dent *n*

precept, grondregel, voorschrift *n*

precinct, ter'rein *n*

precious, kostbaar, dierbaar; edel; ge'wild

precipice, hoge rotswand

precipitate, plotseling; over-ijld, onbe'zonnen: neerslag: ver'haasten

precipitous, zeer steil

precise, juist, pre'cies

precision, nauw'keurigheid

preclude, uitsluiten

precocious, voorlijk

preconceived, voor'opgezet

precursor, voorloper

predatory, roof-

predecessor, voorganger

predicament, hachelijke po'sitie

predict, voor'spellen

predominant, over'heersend, over'wegend

predominate, over'heersen

pre-eminence, superiori'teit

pre-eminent, uit'blinkend

pre-eminently, bij uitstek

preen, gladstrijken

preface, voorbericht *n*: inleiden

prefer, de voorkeur geven aan, liever willen

preferable, wenselijker, beter

preferably, bij voorkeur

preference, voorkeur

pregnancy, zwangerschap

pregnant, zwanger; ge'laden

prehistoric, voorhistorisch

prejudice, voor'oordeel *n*: be-voor'oordelen

prejudicial, schadelijk

prelate, pre'laat

preliminary, voor'afgaand(e for-mali'teit)

prelude, voorspel *n*; pre'lude

premature, vroeg'tijdig, voor'-barig

premeditated, voor'opgezet

premier, eerste (mi'nister)

premise, pre'misse: voor'op-stellen

premises, pand *n*, per'ceel *n*

premium, premie

premonition, voorgevoel *n*

preoccupation, af'wezige ge'-dachten

preoccupy, in be'slag nemen

preparation, (voor)bereiding
preparatory, voorbereidend
prepare, (zich) voorbereiden, be'reiden
preponderance, overwicht *n*
preposterous, ab'surd
prerogative, (voor)recht *n*
presage, voor'spellen
Presbyterian, Presbyteri'aan(s)
prescribe, voorschrijven
prescription, re'cept *n*; voorschrift *n*
presence, aan'wezigheid
present, aan'wezig, tegen'woordig: heden *n*: ca'deau *n*: schenken; presen'teren; ver'tonen; opvoeren; voorstellen
at present, op het ogenblik
presentable, presen'tabel
presentation, schenking; uitreiking; opvoering
present-day, heden'daags
presentiment, voorgevoel *n*
presently, straks
preservation, be'houd *n*; con'ditie
preserve, wildpark *n*; ge'bied *n*: redden; be'waren, goedhouden, conser'veren
preserves, con'serven
preside, presi'deren, de leiding hebben
presidency, presi'dentschap *n*
president, presi'dent; voorzitter
press, pers(en); drukken; (aan)dringen; pressen
pressing, dringend
pressure, druk(ken *n*); drang; pressie
prestige, pres'tige *n*
presumably, ver'moedelijk
presume, veronder'stellen; zo vrij zijn; ge'bruik maken (van)
presumption, veronder'stelling; aanmatiging
presumptuous, aan'matigend
pretence, voorwendsel *n*; aanstelle'rij
pretend, doen alsof; aanspraak maken (op)
pretension, pre'tentie
pretentious, pretenti'eus

pretext, voorwendsel *n*
pretty, lief, knap: nogal
prevail, heersen; zegevieren
to prevail upon, overhalen
prevalent, heersend; veel'voorkomend
prevent, voor'komen, ver'hinderen
prevention, voor'komen *n*
preventive, prevent'ief
previous, voor'afgaand, vorig
previously, vroeger; van te voren, al eerder
pre-war, voor'oorlogs
prey, prooi
price, prijs: prijzen
priceless, on'schatbaar; kostelijk
prick, prik(ken)
prickle, stekel(tje) *n*; prikkel
prickly, stekelig; kriebelig
pride, trots, hoogmoed
to pride oneself, prat gaan
priest, priester
prig, pe'dante kwezel
prim, stijf, preuts
primarily, in de eerste plaats
primary, pri'mair
prime, eerst: bloei(tijd): voorbereiden
primeval, oor'spronkelijk, oer-
primitive, primi'tief
primrose, sleutelbloem
prince, prins, vorst
princely, vorstelijk
princess, prin'ses
principal, voor'naamst; hoofd(-) (*n*)
principally, voor'namelijk
principle, prin'cipe *n*
print, druk(ken); prent; afdruk; afdrukken; be'drukken; prenten
printer, drukker
prior, voor'afgaand, eerste: prior
priority, voorrang
priory, prio'rij
prism, prisma *n*
prison, ge'vangenis
prisoner, ge'vangene
privacy, vrijheid; ge'heimhouding
private, vrij, pri'vé, per'soonlijk; particu'lier; ge'heim: sol'daat

privateer, kaper(schip *n*)
privation, ont'bering
privilege, voorrecht *n* : be'voor-rechten
prize, prijs : be'kroond
probability, waar'schijnlijkheid
probable, waar'schijnlijk, ver'-moedelijk
probation, proef(tijd)
probe, peilen; doordringen; son'deren
problem, pro'bleem *n*, vraag-stuk *n*
problematic(al), twijfelachtig
procedure, handelwijze
proceed, voortgaan; voortkomen
he proceeded to tell me, hij ver'telde me ver'volgens
proceedings, handelingen; ma'nier van doen
proceeds, opbrengst
process, pro'ces *n*, procédé *n* : be'handelen
procession, stoet, optocht, pro'cessie
proclaim, af(*or* ver')kondigen; uitroepen tot
proclamation, procla'matie
procrastinate, talmen
procure, (zich) ver'(*or* aan)-schaffen
prod, (aan)porren
prodigal, ver'kwistend
prodigious, ge'weldig
prodigy, wonder *n*
produce, pro'dukten: pro-du'ceren, opleveren, voortbreng-en; te voorschijn halen; aan-voeren; opvoeren; ver'lengen
producer, regis'seur; produ'cent
product, pro'dukt *n*, voort-brengsel *n*
production, pro'duktie
productive, produk'tief
profane, pro'faan: ont'heiligen
profess, be'weren, be'tuigen, be'-lijden
profession, be'roep *n*; be'tuig-ing, be'lijdenis
professional, be'roeps(speler); vak'kundig
professor, pro'fessor
proffer, aanbieden

proficiency, be'kwaamheid
profile, pro'fiel *n*
profit, winst: zijn voordeel doen (met)
profitable, winst'gevend, voor'-delig, nuttig
profiteer, o'weeër: woekerwinst maken
profound, diep ('zinnig *or* gaand)
profuse, over'vloedig, over'dadig
profusion, overvloed
progeny, kroost *n*
programme, pro'gramme *n*
progress, voor'uitgang, voort-gang; loop; vorderingen: vor-deren, voor'uitgaan, vordering-en maken
progressive, progres'sief (per'-soon)
prohibit, ver'bieden
prohibition, ver'bod *n*
prohibitive, schrik'wekkend hoog
project, plan *n*, onder'neming: uitspringen; slingeren; pro-jec'teren; ont'werpen
projectile, projec'tiel *n*
projection, uitsteeksel *n*; pro'jec-tie
projector, pro'jectietoestel *n*
proletariat, proletari'aat *n*
prolific, zeer vruchtbaar
prologue, pro'loog; inleiding
prolong, ver'lengen, rekken
prolongued, lang'durig
promenade, prome'nade
prominence, be'lang *n*; ver'-hoging, uitsteeksel *n*
prominent, voor'aanstaand; in het oog vallend; hooggelegen
promise, be'lofte: be'loven
promising, veelbe'lovend
promontory, voorgebergte *n*
promote, be'vorderen
promoter, oprichter
promotion, pro'motie; be'vor-dering
prompt, on'middellijk, stipt: nopen (tot); souf'fleren, voor-zeggen
promulgate, afkondigen; ver'-breiden
prone, ge'neigd: languit voor'-over

prong, tand

pronoun, voornaamwoord n

pronounce, uitspreken; uitspraak doen

pronunciation, uitspraak

proof, be'wijs n; proef: be'stand

prop, stut(ten); steunpilaar: zetten, (onder')steunen

propaganda, propa'ganda

propagate, zich voortplanten; ver'spreiden, propa'geren

propel, voortdrijven

propeller, schroef

propensity, ge'neigdheid

proper, juist; ge'past

properly, op de juiste ma'nier, netjes, goed; eigenlijk

property, eigendom n, bezit n; eigenschap

prophecy, voor'spelling

prophesy, voor'spellen

prophet, pro'feet

propitious, gunstig

proportion, (juiste) ver'houding; deel n : proportion'neren

proportions, pro'porties

proportional, even'redig

proposal, voorstel n; aanzoek n

propose, voorstellen; zich voornemen; een aanzoek doen

proposition, voorstel n; stelling; ge'val n

propound, opperen

proprietary, pa'tent-, merk-, eigendoms-; eigenaars-

proprietor, eigenaar

propriety, goede vorm

propulsion, stuwkracht

pros and cons, voor en tegen n

prosaic, pro'zaïsch

proscribe, ver'bieden; ver'bannen

prose, proza n

prosecute, ver'volgen; uitvoeren

prosecutor, aanklager

prospect, (voor')uitzicht n: zoeken

prospective, eventu'eel; aan'staande

prospector, pros'pector

prosper, ge'dijen

prosperity, voorspoed, welvaart

prosperous, voor'spoedig

prostitute, prostitu'ée

prostrate, voor'overliggend; ver'slagen: neerwerpen

protect, be'schermen

protection, be'scherming

protective, be'schermend

protectorate, protecto'raat n

protein, eiwit(stof) (n)

protest, pro'test('eren) (n)

Protestant, Protes'tant(s)

protestation, aan'houdende be'tuiging

prototype, prototype n

protract, ver'lengen, rekken

protracted, langge'rekt

protrude, (voor')uitsteken; zich opdringen

proud, trots (op); groot

prove, be'wijzen; blijken

proverb, spreekwoord n

proverbial, spreek'woordelijk

provide, voor'zien; zorgen

provided (that), mits

providence, (de) voor'zienigheid

provident, zorgzaam

province, pro'vincie; ge'bied n

provincial, provinci'aal; pro'vincie-

provision, voor'ziening; voorwaarde; voorzorg(smaatregel): provian'deren

provisions, levensmiddelen

provisional, voor'lopig

proviso, voorbehoud n

provocation, aanleiding

provocative, provo'cerend

provoke, (op)wekken, uitlokken; tergen

prow, voorsteven

prowess, dapperheid; vaardigheid

prowl, rondsluipen

proximity, na'bijheid

proxy, volmacht; gevol'machtigde

prudence, voor'zichtigheid, be'leid n

prudent, be'dachtzaam, ver'standig

prudish, preuts

prune, pruime'dant: (be')snoeien
pry, snuffelen: (open)breken
psalm, psalm
pseudo(nym), pseudo('niem *n*)
psychiatrist, psychi'ater
psychic, spiri'tistisch
psychological, psycho'logisch
psychology, psycholo'gie
pub, kroeg
puberty, puber'teit
public, open'baar, pu'bliek (*n*): volk *n*
  in public, in het open'baar
publication, publi'katie
publicity, publici'teit
publish, uitgeven; be'kend maken
publisher, uitgever
pucker, rimpelen, zich samentrekken
pudding, pudding, toetje *n*
puddle, plas
puerile, kinderachtig
puff, wolkje *n*, stoot; soes: puffen; opblazen
pugilist, bokser
pugnacious, strijd'lustig
pull, ruk(ken); trek(ken) (aan)
  to pull up, uit(*or* op)trekken; stilhouden
pullet, jonge kip
pulley, ka'trol
pullover, slipover
pulp, vruchtvlees *n*; pap
pulpit, preekstoel
pulsate, kloppen; trillen
pulse, pols(slag)
pulverize, ver'brijzelen
pumice-stone, puimsteen
pump, pomp(en); uithoren
pun, woordspeling
punch, stomp(en); pons(en), drevel; punch: knippen
Punch-and-Judy, Jan Klaassen en Ka'trijn
punctilious, nauwge'zet
punctual, punctu'eel, stipt
punctuate, interpun'geren; onder'breken
puncture, lekke band, gaatje *n*: (door)prikken
pungent, scherp, prikkelend
punish, straffen

punishment, straf
punt, punter(en)
puny, nietig
pup, jong(e hond) (*n*)
pupil, leerling: pu'pil
puppet, mario'net; speelpop
purchase, (aan)koop; houvast *n*: (aan)kopen
pure, zuiver, rein; louter
purgatory, vagevuur *n*
purge, zuiveren
purify, zuiveren
Puritan, Puri'tein(s)
purity, zuiverheid, reinheid
purple, paars, purper (*n*)
purport, strekking: heten
purpose, doel *n*, be'doeling
purposely, on purpose, op'zettelijk
purr, spinnen; snorren
purse, beurs: samentrekken
pursue, (achter')volgen
pursuit, achter'volging: jacht; bezigheid
purveyor, leveran'cier
pus, pus
push, duw(en), zetje *n*: dringen
puss(y), poes(je *n*)
put, zetten, leggen; brengen; zeggen; doen
  to put down, neerzetten; onder'drukken; opschrijven; toeschrijven (aan)
  to put off, uitstellen; van zijn stuk brengen, afschrikken; uitdoen
  to put on, aantrekken
  to put out, uitsteken; uitdoen; blussen; lastig vallen
  to put up, ophangen; opsteken; (aan)bieden; maken, bouwen; ver'hogen; bergen, lo'geren; aanpraten
  to put up with, dulden
putrefy, ver'rotten
putrid, rot
putty, stopverf
puzzle, (een) raadsel (zijn) (*n*): piekeren
pygmy, dwerg
pyjamas, py'jama
pyramid, pira'mide

Q

quack, kwak(en): kwakzalver
quadrangle, binnenplein
quadrilateral, vierhoek(ig)
quadruped, vier'voetig (dier *n*)
quaff, met grote teugen drinken
quail, kwartel: (te'rug) sckrikken
quaint, typisch, eigen'aardig
quake, beven
Quaker, Kwaker
qualification, kwalifi'catie; re'strictie
qualified, be'voegd
qualify, ge'schikt maken; de be'voegdheid ver'werven; kwalifi'ceren
quality, kwali'teit; eigenschap
qualm, onbe'haaglijk ge'voel *n*; scru'pule
quandary, lastig par'ket *n*
quantity, (grote) hoe'veelheid; grootheid
quarantine, quaran'taine
quarrel, (reden tot) twist, ruzie: twisten
quarrelsome, twistziek
quarry, wild *n*, prooi; slachtoffer *n*: steengroeve: (uit)graven
quart, (approx.) liter
quarter, kwart('aal) *n*; windstreek; wijk; ge'nade: in vieren delen; inkwartieren
quarter of an hour, kwar'tier *n*
quarters, kwar'tier(en) *n*; kringen
quarterdeck, achterdek *n*
quarterly, drie'maandelijks
quartet, kwar'tet *n*
quartz, kwartz *n*
quasi, kwasi
quaver, trilling; achtste noot: trillen
quay, kaai, kade
queen, koning'in; vrouw
queer, raar: be'derven
quell, onder'drukken
quench, lessen; blussen
querulous, knorrig
query, vraag(teken *n*); twijfel: in twijfel trekken; een vraagteken zetten achter

quest, zoeken *n*
in **quest of,** op zoek naar
question, vraag; kwestie; sprake; twijfel: onder'vragen; be'twijfelen
questionable, twijfelachtig
queue, rij: in de rij staan
quibble, spits'vondigheid: haarkloven
quick, vlug
quicken, ver'haasten; sneller worden
quicksand, drijfzand *n*
quicksilver, kwikzilver *n*
quick-tempered, op'vliegend
quiet, rust(ig), stil; vrede
quieten, sussen, be'daren
quill, schacht; ganzepen
quilt, gewat'teerde deken: wat'teren, doorstikken
quinine, ki'nine
quintessence, kwintessens
quip, geestigheid; steek
quit, ver'trekken (uit); ophouden
to be **quit of,** af zijn van
quite, helemaal; verreweg; vrij: juist, ja
quits, kiet
quiver, peilkoker: trillen
quoit, werpring
quota, (even'redig) deel *n*
quotation, aanhaling(s-), ci'taat *n*; no'tering
quote, aanhalen

R

rabbit, ko'nijn *n*
rabble, ge'spuis *n*
rabid, dol
race, wedloop, wedren: ras *n*: racen; om het hardst lopen; rennen
racial, ras(sen)-
racing, wedrennen *n*
rack, rek *n*; pijnbank: folteren; afpijnigen
racket, racket *n*: herrie; afzette'rij
racketeer, afzetter
radiance, straling
radiant, stralend

radiate, (uit)stralen; straals-gewijs uitlopen
radiator, radi'ator
radical, radi'caal
radio, radio(-)
radish, ra'dijs
radium, radium *n*
radius, straal; cirkel
raffle, ver'loting: ver'loten
raft, vlot *n*
rafter, dakspar
rag, lapje *n*, vod *n*; jool: keet maken, te grazen nemen
ragamuffin, schooier
rag-and-bone man, vodden-koopman
rage, woede; rage: tieren
ragged, haveloos
raid, in(*or* over)val (doen)
rail, stang, spaak; rail; spoor *n*: uitvaren (tegen)
railing(s), hek *n*
railway, spoorweg, spoorbaan
raiment, ge'waad *n*, tooi
rain, regen(en)
rainbow, regenboog
rainfall, regenval
rainy, regenachtig
raise, oplichten; ver'heffen; ver'hogen; bij'eenbrengen, op-brengen; fokken; ver'wekken
raisin, ro'zijn
rake, hark(en); losbol: enfi'leren
rally, bij'eenkomst: (zich) ver'-zamelen; bijkomen
ram, ram(men)
ramble, zwerftocht: zwerven; zich slingeren; bazelen, af-dwalen
ramp, ta'lud *n*; afzette'rij
rampant: to be —, woekeren; hoogtij vieren
rampart, wal; bolwerk *n*
ramshackle, gammel
ranch, (vee)fokke'rij
rancid, ranzig
rancour, wrok
random, luk'raak
  at random, op goed ge'luk
range, ruimte, veld *n*, kring; draagwijdte; baan; keten; for'nuis *n*: vari'eren; zwerven (over); (zich) opstellen

rank, ge'lid *n*; rang, stand: geil; grof: be'horen (tot)
rankle, iemand dwars zitten
ransack, plunderen
ransom, losgeld *n*
rant, te keer gaan
rap, tik(ken): duit: gooien
rape, ver'krachting; roof: ver'-krachten
rapid, snel
rapids, stroomversnelling
rapidity, snelheid
rapt, opgetogen, ver'rukt
rapture, ver'voering
rapturous, opgetogen, ver'ruk-kelijk
rare, zeldzaam; ijl
rarely, zelden
rarity, zeldzaamheid; ijlheid
rascal, schelm
rash, onbe'zonnen: uitslag
rasp, rasp(en)
raspberry, fram'boos
rat, rat; onderkruiper: over-lopen
rate, koers, cijfer *n*, snelheid, prijs; klas; plaatselijke be'las-ting; ge'val *n*: schatten: be'ris-pen
rather, liever, eerder: nog'al: nou en of!
ratify, be'krachtigen
ratio, ver'houding
ration, rant'soen('eren) (*n*)
rational, ratio'neel, redelijk
rattle, rammelaar, ratel; ge'klet-ter *n*; rammelen, ratelen; van streek brengen
raucous, schor, rauw
ravage, ver'woesting: teisteren
rave, raaskallen, razen, ijlen; dwepen
raven, raaf
ravenous, uitgehongerd
ravine, ra'vijn *n*
ravishing, be'toverend
raw, rauw; ruw; groen; guur
  raw materials, grondstoffen
ray, straal: rog
rayon, kunstzijde
raze, uitwissen; slechten
razor, scheerapparaat(*or* mes) *n*
razor-blade, scheermesje *n*

re-, op'nieuw

reach, be'reik(en) (*n*); ge'-deelte *n*: (zich) uitstrekken; reiken; er (bij) komen

react, rea'geren

reaction, re'actie

reactionary, reactio'nair

read, (voor)lezen; zeggen, aan-wijzen; stu'deren; opvatten

readily, ge'makkelijk; gaarne

readiness ge'reedheid; be-reid'willigheid

reading, lezen *n*, lezing; stand; interpre'tatie; lec'tuur: lees-

ready, klaar; be'reid('willig); ge'makkelijk

ready-made, con'fectie, pas-klaar

real, werkelijk, echt

realism, rea'lisme *n*

realist(ic), rea'list(isch)

reality, werkelijkheid

realization, be'sef *n*; ver'wezen-lijking

realize, be'seffen; ver'wezen-lijken; opbrengen

really, (in) werkelijk(heid)

realm, (konink)rijk *n*

reap, maaien; oogsten

reappear, op'nieuw ver'schijnen

rear, achter-: achterhoede, achterkant

reason, rede(n): (be)rede'neren (with)in reason, redelijk-(erwijs)

it stands to reason, het spreekt van'zelf

reasonable, redelijk

reasoning, rede'nering

reassurance, ver'zekering

reassure, ver'zekeren; ge'rust-stellen

rebate, korting

rebel, oproerling: in opstand komen

rebellion, opstand

rebellious, op'standig

rebound, te'rugstoot: te'rug-stuiten

rebuff, koude douche: voor het hoofd stoten

rebuke, be'risping: be'rispen

recalcitrant, weer'spannig

recant, her'roepen; er van te'rug-komen

recapitulate, recapitu'leren

recapture, her'overen, op'nieuw ge'vangennemen; weer op-roepen

recede, te'rugwijken, te'ruglopen

receipt, re'cu *n*, kwi'tantie; ont'vangst: kwi'teren

receive, ont'vangen

receiver, hoorn, ont'vangtoestel *n*

recent, re'cent

recently, on'langs, in de laatste tijd

receptacle, (ver'gaar)bak

reception, ont'vangst; re'ceptie

receptive, ont'vankelijk (voor)

recess, re'ces *n*; nis; schuil-hoek

recipe, re'cept *n*

recipient, ont'vanger

reciprocal, weder'kerig; omge-keerde *n*

reciprocate, be'antwoorden; heen en weer gaan

recital, voordracht; opsomming

recite, voordragen; opsommen

reckless, roekeloos

reckon, (be')reken en; be'schouw-en

reclaim, her'winnen, droogleg-gen, redden

recline, achter'over liggen

recluse, kluizenaar

recognition, (h)er'kenning: waar'dering

recognizable, her'kenbaar

recognize, (h)er'kennen

recoil, te'rugloop: te'rugdeinzen; te'ruglopen

recollect, zich her'inneren

recollection, her'innering

recommend, aanbevelen; aan-raden

recommendation, aanbeveling: ad'vies *n*

recompense, be'loning: be'-lonen; schadeloosstellen

reconcile, ver'zoenen; over'een-brengen

reconciliation, ver'zoening

reconnaissance, ver'kenning(s-)

reconnoitre, ver'kennen

reconstruct, weder opbouwen; reconstru'eren

reconstruction, weder'opbouw; recon'structie

record, offici'ele ver'melding; no'titie; (grammo'foon)plaat: re'cord *n*; repu'tatie: ongeëve'naard: optekenen; opnemen, te boek stellen

recount, nieuwe telling: ver'halen

recourse: to have — to, zijn toevlucht nemen tot

recover, te'rugkrijgen; inhalen; her'stellen

recovery, her'stel *n*

recreation, ont'spanning

recrimination, tegenbeschuldiging

recruit, re'kruut, nieuweling: rekru'teren

rectangle, rechthoek

rectangular, recht'hoekig

rectify, her'stellen

rector, dominee; rector

rectory, pasto'rie

recumbent, liggend

recuperate, her'stellen

recur, te'rugkeren

recurrence, her'haling

recurrent, steeds te'rugkerend

red(den), rood (maken *or* worden)

reddish, roodachtig

redeem, aflossen; ver'vullen; ver'lossen; ver'zachten

red-handed, op heter daad

red-hot, rood'gloeiend

redouble, ver'dubbelen

redoubtable, ge'ducht

redress, ver'goeding: weer goedmaken

reduce, ver'minderen; brengen

reduction, afname, ver'mindering; korting

redundant, over'bodig

re-echo, weer'galmen

reed, riet *n*

reef, rif *n*: reef *n*: reven

reek, stinken

reel, klos(je *n*): duizelen, wankelen

refer, ver'wijzen; zinspelen (op); be'trekking hebben (op); raadplegen

referee, scheidsrechter

reference, ver'wijzing; be'trekking; toespeling; ge'tuigschrift *n*: hand-

refine, raffi'neren

refined, geraffi'neerd; be'schaafd

refinement, raffi'nering; fi'nesse

refinery, raffinade'rij

reflect, te'rugkaatsen; weer'spiegelen; weergeven; nadenken

reflection, weer'spiegeling; spiegelbeeld *n*;

on reflection, bij nader inzien

reflector, re'flector

reflex, re'flex(-)

reform, ver'betering: ver'beteren; (zich) beteren

reformation, her'vorming; Refor'matie

refraction, breking

refractory, weer'barstig

refrain, re'frein *n*: zich ont'houden (van)

refresh, ver'kwikken; opfrissen

refreshing, ver'kwikkend; op'wekkend

refreshment, ver'kwikking, restau'ratie; con'sumptie

refrigerator, ijskast

refuge, toevlucht(soord *n*)

refugee, vluchteling

refund, te'rugbetaling: te'rugbetalen

refusal, weigering

refuse, vuilnis *n*: weigeren

refute, weer'leggen

regain, her'winnen; weer be'reiken

regal, koninklijk

regale, ont'halen

regard, aandacht; achting: be'schouwen; in acht nemen; be'treffen

regards, groeten

regardless of, ongeacht

regent, re'gent('es)

regime, re'gime *n*

regiment, regi'ment *n*; dres'seren

region, streek, ge'west *n*, ge'bied *n*

regional, ge'westelijk

register, re'gister *n*: registreren; inschrijven; aangeven, te kennen geven; (laten) aantekenen

registration, regis'tratie

regression, achter'uitgang

regret, spijt: be'treuren

regretfully, met leedwezen

regrettable, betreurens'waardig

regular, ge'regeld, regel'matig, vast; echt: be'roeps(sol'daat)

regularity, regelmaat

regulate, regelen

regulation, voorschrift *n*, be'-paling *n*; regeling

rehabilitation, rehabili'tatie

rehearsal, repe'titie

rehearse, repe'teren, instuderen

reign, re'gering; be'wind *n*

reimburse, ver'goeden

rein, teugel: inhouden; be'teugelen

reindeer, rendier(en) *n*

reinforce, ver'sterken

reinforcement, ver'sterking

reinstate, her'stellen

reiterate, her'halen

reject, afgekeurd voorwerp *n*; afkeuren, van de hand wijzen

rejoice, ver'heugd zijn

rejoicing, vreugde(betoon *n*)

rejoin, zich weer voegen bij

rejoinder, re'pliek

rejuvenate, ver'jongen

relapse, instorting, te'rugval: weer instorten, weer ver'vallen

relate, ver'halen; in ver'band brengen (met)

related, ver'want

relation, be'trekking, ver'houding; fa'milielid *n*

relationship, ver'wantschap; ver'houding

relative, fa'milielid *n*: be'trekkelijk; respec'tief

relax, (zich) ont'spannen; ver'slappen

relaxation, ont'spanning; ver'slapping

relay, ploeg; re'lais *n*: relay'eren; weer leggen

release, vrijlating; be'vrijding: vrij (*or* los)laten; bevrijden; vrijgeven

relegate, te'rugzetten; ver'bannen

relent, zich laten ver'murwen

relentless, mee'dogenloos

relevant, van toepassing (op), toe'passelijk

reliable, be'trouwbaar

reliance, ver'trouwen *n*

relic, reli'kwie ; overblijfsel *n*

relief, ver'lichting; opluchting; hulp, aflossing (sploeg); reli'ëf *n*: extra

relieve, ver'lichten; ont'lasten; ont'zetten; aflossen; afwisselen

religion, godsdienst

religious, godsdienst-, gods'dienstig; klooster-; plichtsgetrouw

relinquish, opgeven; afstand doen van

relish, smaak; pi'kante lekker'nij: ge'nieten van

reluctance, tegenzin

relunctant, on'willig

rely, ver'trouwen (op)

remain, (over)blijven

remains, overblijfselen

remainder, rest

remark, opmerking: opmerken

remarkable, merk'waardig; op'merkelijk

remedy, (hulp)middel *n*: ver'helpen

remember, zich her'inneren; ont'houden, denken om; de groeten doen van

remembrance, nagedachtenis

remind, her'inneren (aan)

reminder, (vriendelijke) aanmaning

reminiscent: to be — of, her'inneren aan

remiss, na'latig

remission, kwijtschelding

remit, overmaken; kwijtschelden

remnant, res'tant *n*

remonstrate, protes'teren

remorse, wroeging

remorseless, onbarm'hartig

remote, afgelegen; ver; ge'ring
remotely, in de verte, enigs'zins
removal, ver'wijderen *n*; ver'huizing
remove, ver'wijderen, afnemen, uittrekken; afzetten
remuneration, ver'goeding
remunerative, winst'gevend
Renaissance, Renais'sance
rend, (ver')scheuren
render, geven; be'tuigen; maken; ver'tolken; klaren
renegade, af'vallig(e)
renew, ver(*or* her)'nieuwen; ver'lengen
renounce, afstand doen van; ver'stoten
renovate, ver'nieuwen, opknappen
renown, ver'maardheid
renowned, ver'maard
rent, huur, pacht: scheur: huren, pachten
rental, huur
renunciation, afstand doen *n*; ver'werping, ver'loochening
reopen, her'openen; her'vatten
reorganize, reorgani'seren
repair, repar'atie; con'ditie: her'stellen
reparation, schadeloosstelling
repartee, puntigheid, ge'vatheid
repast, maaltijd
repatriation, repatri'ëring
repay, te'rugbetalen
repeal, afschaffing: her'roepen, afschaffen
repeat, her'haling: her'halen; nazeggen, navertellen; opzeggen
repeated(ly), her'haald(elijk)
repel, te'rug(*or* af)slaan; afstoten
repellent, af'stotend
repent, be'rouw hebben
repentance, be'rouw *n*
repentant, be'rouwvol
repercussion, re'actie, te'rugslag
repertoire, reper'toire *n*
repetition, her'haling
replace, ver'vangen, ver'nieuwen; te'rugzetten
replacement, ver'vanging; nieuwe

replenish, aan(*or* bij)vullen
replica, ko'pie
reply, antwoorden
report, ver'slag (*n*) (doen), rap'port *n*, be'richt *n*; knal: rappor'teren; (zich) melden
reporter, ver'slaggever
repose, rust(en)
repository, opslagplaats; schatkamer
reprehensible, laakbaar
represent, voorstellen; vertegen'woordigen
representation, voorstelling; vertegen'woordiging
representative, vertegen'woordiger: representa'tief; typisch
repress, onder'drukken
reprieve, uitstel *n*, gratie
reprimand, be'risping: be'rispen
reprint, herdruk: her'drukken
reprisal, repre'saille
reproach, ver'wijt(en) (*n*): schande
reprobate, onverlaat
reproduce, reprodu'ceren; (zich) voortplanten
reproof, be'risping
reprove, be'rispen
reptile, rep'tiel *n*
republic, repu'bliek
republican, republi'kein(s)
repudiate, ver'werpen; niet er'kennen; ver'stoten
repugnant, weerzin'wekkend
repulse, afslaan; afwijzen
repulsive, weerzin'wekkend
reputable, respec'tabel
reputation, (goede) naam
repute, aanzien *n*: houden voor
request, ver'zoek(en) (*n*), aanvraag: vragen om
require, nodig hebben; ver'langen
requirement, be'hoefte, ver'eiste *n*; eis
requisite, ver'eist(e *n*): be'hoefte
requisition, vordering: vorderen
requite, ver'gelden
rescind, intrekken
rescue, redding: redden
 to come to the rescue, te hulp komen

research, weten'schappelijk on-derzoek *n*

resemblance, ge'lijkenis; over'-eenkomst

resemble, ge'lijken (op)

resent, aanstoot nemen aan

resentful, ge'belgd

resentment, wrevel

reservation, voorbehoud *n*; re-ser'vatie

reserve, re'serve; reser'vaat *n*; gereser'veerdheid: be'waren, re-ser'veren

reserved, gereser'veerd; te'rug-houdend

reservoir, reser'voir *n*

reside, woon'achtig zijn

residence, woonplaats, woning; ver'blijf *n*

resident, inwoner; gast; resi'-dent: inwonend

residential, woon-

residue, overschot *n*; resi'du *n*

resign, aftreden: neerleggen

to resign oneself to, be'rusten in

resignation, ont'slag *n*; be'rus-ting

resilience, veerkracht

resin, hars

resist, zich ver'zetten, weerstand bieden; zich weer'houden (van); weer'staan

resistance, ver'zet *n*; weer-stand(svermogen *n*)

resolute, vastbe'raden

resolution, be'sluit *n*, voor-nemen *n*; voorstel *n*; vast-be'radenheid

resolve, be'sluit(en) (*n*); vast-be'radenheid: (zich) oplossen

resonance, reso'nantie

resonant, reso'nerend

resort, (va'kantie)oord *n*; red-middel *n*; zijn toevlucht nemen (tot)

resound, weer'galmen; weer'-kaatsen

resource, (red)middel *n*, rijk-dom, (hulp)bron

resourceful, vindingrijk

respect, eerbied; opzicht *n*; be'trekking: respec'teren, eer'biedigen

respectable, fat'soenlijk; re-spec'tabel

respectful, eer'biedig

respecting, aan'gaande

respective, respec'tief

respectively, respec'tievelijk

respiration, ademhaling

respite, ver'ademing; uitstel *n*

resplendent, glansrijk, schit-terend

respond, rea'geren (op); be'antwoorden

response, antwoord *m*, weer-klank; tegenzang

responsibility, verant'woorde-lijkheid

responsible, verant'woordelijk

responsive, ont'vankelijk (voor)

rest, rust (geven); steun: rest: (uit)rusten, liggen; leunen (met); be'rusten

restaurant, restau'rant *n*

restful, rustig, kal'merend

restitution, resti'tutie, ver'goed-ing

restive, on'rustig

restless, onge'durig, on'rustig, rusteloos

restoration, restau'ratie; her'stel *n*, te'ruggave

restore, restau'reren; her'stel-len, te'ruggeven, terug'zetten

restrain, be'dwingen, in be'-dwang houden

restrain, be'dwingen, in be'-dwang houden

restrict, be'perken

restriction, be'perking; voor-behoud *n*

result, resul'taat *n*, uitslag, ge'volg *n*; uitkomst: uitlopen (op); komen

resume, her'vatten

resumption, her'vatting

resurrection, opstanding

retail, klein(handel), en de'tail

retailer, detail'list, leveran'cier

retain, (vast *or* ont')houden

retaliate, re'vanche nemen

retaliation, wraak

retard, tegen(*or* op)houden

reticent, terug'houdend

retina, retina

retinue, ge'volg *n*

retire, met pen'sioen gaan, aftreden; naar bed gaan; (zich) te'rugtrekken

retired, gepensio'neerd; afgelegen

retirement, ont'slag *n*; pensio'nering; afzondering

retiring, te'ruggetrokken

retort, vinnig (*or* ge'wiekst) antwoord(en) (*n*); re'tort

retrace, te'rugkeren op

retract, her'roepen

retreat, te'rug (*or* af)tocht; a'siel *n*: zich te'rugtrekken

retribution, ver'gelding

retrieve, te'rugvinden; her'stellen

retrograde, achter'uit

retrospect: in —, achter'af be'schouwd

return, te'rugkomst, te'rugkeer; te'rugbrengen (*or* geven *or* zenden) (*n*); opbrengst; rap'port *n*: re'tour-: te'ruggaan (*or* keren *or* komen)

by return, per omgaande

in return, in ruil

many happy returns, nog vele jaren!

reunion, her'eniging; reü'nie

reunite, (zich) her'enigen

reveal, ont'hullen, open'baren; aan het licht brengen; kenbaar maken

revel, zich ver'lustigen; feestvieren

revelation, open'baring

revelry, pretmake'rij

revenge, wraak(zucht)

to revenge oneself, to be revenged, zich wreken (op)

revenue, (rijks)inkomsten

reverberate, weer'galmen

reverberation, nagalm

revere, (ver')eren

reverence, eerbied; buiging

Reverend: The —, De Weleerwaarde Heer Ds., De Weleerwaarde Pater

reverent, eer'biedig

reverie, mijmering

reverse, omgekeerd(e *n*); tegendeel *n*; keerzijde; tegenslag;

nederlaag: omkeren; her'roepen; achter'uitrijden

reversion, te'rugkeer

revert, weer te'rugkeren; ver'vallen (in)

review, re'visie; te'rugblik; re'censie: op'nieuw in ogenschouw nemen; te'rugzien op; her'zien; recen'seren

revile, (be')schimpen

revise, nazien; her'zien

revision, repe'teren *n*; her'ziening

revival, opleving; weder'opvoering

revive, weer bijbrengen; (doen) bijkomen; weer opvoeren

revoke, her'roepen; niet be'kennen

revolt, opstand: in opstand komen; doen walgen

revolting, walgelijk

revolution, revo'lutie; omwenteling

revolutionary, revolution'nair

revolutionize, een ommekeer te'weegbrengen

revolve, (om)wentelen

revolver, re'volver

revulsion, ommekeer; walging

reward, be'loning: be'lonen

rhapsody, rapso'die

rhetoric, re'torica; reto'riek

rhetorical, re'torisch

rheumatic, reu'matisch

rheumatism, reuma'tiek

rhinoceros, ri'noceros

rhubarb, ra'barber

rhyme, rijm(pje *n*): rijmen

rhythm, ritme *n*

rhythmic, ritmisch

rib, rib(stuk *n*); ba'lein; nerf

ribald, liederlijk

ribbon, lint *n*; flard

rice, rijst

rich, rijk; machtig, extra fijn warm

riches, rijkdom(men)

richly, rijkelijk

rickety, wankel

rid, af: afhelpen

to get rid of, kwijt raken, ver'drijven

riddle, raadsel *n*: grove zeef: door'zeven

ride, rit(je *n*), tocht(je *n*): (paard)rijden

rider, ruiter, be'rijder

ridge, kam; nok; rug

ridicule, spot: be'spotten

ridiculous, be'lachelijk

rife, wijd ver'spreid

riff-raff, uitschot *n*

rifle, ge'weer *n*: plunderen

rift, scheur, kloof

rig, tui'gage; plunje: optuigen; in el'kaar draaien

rigging, tui'gage, want *n*

right, juist; goed; in orde; vlak, helemaal; pre'cies; recht (*n*); rechterzijde: rechtzetten
 to be right, ge'lijk hebben
 on the right, rechts
 to the right, aan de rechter- kant; rechts('af)
 right away, on'middellijk

righteous, recht'schapen; (ge)- recht'vaardig(d)

rightful, recht'matig

right-hand, rechter-

rightly, te'recht; goed

rigid, vast, stijf; star

rigmarole, ge'klets *n*

rigorous, zeer streng

rigour, strengheid

rim, rand, velg

rime, rijp

rind, korst, zwoerd *n*, schil

ring, ring; piste; kliek; tele'foontje *n*: luiden; bellen; weer'galmen

ringleader, belhamel

rink, baan

rinse, (om)spoelen

riot, oproer *n* (maken)

riotous, op'roerig; los'bandig

rip, scheur(en)

ripe, rijp; be'legen

ripen, rijp worden (*or* maken)

ripple, golfje *n*; lichte golfslag: kabbelen

rise, stijgen (*n*); stijging; op- komst; opslag; toename: op- staan; opstijgen; om'hoog- lopen; stijgen; opkomen
 to give rise to, ver'oorzaken

risk, ge'vaar *n*, risico *n*: wagen, ris'keren

risky, ris'kant

rissole, cro'quet

rite, plechtigheid

ritual, ritu'eel (*n*)

rival, mededinger; mededingend: concur'reren met; wedijveren met

rivalry, wedijver; concur'rentie

river, ri'vier

riverside, oever

rivet, klinknagel: klinken

rivulet, beekje *n*

road, weg, straat

roadside, (aan de) kant van de weg, berm

roadway, rijweg

roam, dwalen

roar, ge'brul *n*, ge'raas *n*: brul- len, bulderen; ronken

roast, ge'braden: braden

rob, be'roven

robber(y), rover('ij)

robe, toga, mantel

robin, roodborstje *n*

robust, fors

rock, rots, klip: schommelen; wiegen; schudden

rocket, ra'ket, vuurpijl

rocky, rotsachtig: wankel

rod, roe(de); 5 meter

rodent, knaagdier *n*

rogue, schelm

roguish, schalks

rôle, rol

roll, rol(len); roffel(en); lijst; broodje *n*; slingeren (*n*)

roller, rol, wals; zware golf

rollicking, uitgelaten, dol

Roman, Ro'mein(s); Rooms- (Katho'liek)

romance, liefdesgeschiedenis; ro'mance: fanta'seren

romantic, roman'tisch: ro'man- ticus

romp, stoeipartij: stoeien

roof, dak *n*; ge'welf *n*; ver'- hemelte *n*

rook, roek

room, kamer; ruimte; aan- leiding

roomy, ruim

roost, roest : op stok gaan
root, wortel (schieten) ; oorzaak : wortelen ; omwroeten
  to root up (or out), uitroeien
rooted, vastgegroeid ; ingeworteld
rope, touw *n*, koord *n*
rosary, rozenkrans
rose, roos
rosette, ro'zet
rostrum, spreekgestoelte *n*
rosy, roze, blozend ; roos'kleurig
rot, ver'rotting ; be'derf *n* ; larie : (doen) ver'rotten
rotate, (doen) draaien
rotation, (om)wenteling ; afwisseling
  in rotation, om beurten
rotten, (ver')rot ; be'roerd ; ge'meen
rotund, kort en dik
rouge, rouge
rough, ruw, on'effen ; ruig ; vaag ; hard
roughly, onge'veer ; in het klad
round, rond('om) ; om(-) : ronde ; reeks : omgaan
  to round off, afronden ; afmaken, vervol'maken
roundabout, om-: draaimolen ; circu'latieplein *n*
rouse, wakker maken ; prikkelen
rout, wilde vlucht : op de vlucht drijven ; snuffelen ; opdiepen
route, route
routine, rou'tine : ge'bruikelijk
rove, zwerven
row, rij : herrie : roeien
rowdy, la'waaierig
royal, koninklijk ; vorstelijk
royalty, vorstelijke per'sonen, oplagecommissie
rub, wrijven ; schuren
  to rub out, uitstuffen
rubber, rubber ; stuf *n* : robber
rubbish, afval, vuilnis *n* ; rommel ; klets
rubble, puin *n*
ruby, ro'bijn(rood)
rudder, roer(blad) *n*
ruddy, blozend
rude, onbe'leefd ; grof

rudiment(ary), rudi'ment('air) (*n*)
rue, be'treuren
ruff, (plooi)kraag
ruffian, woesteling
ruffle, in der war brengen, rimpelen ; ver'storen
rug, reisdeken ; kleedje *n*
rugged, fors en hoekig ; stoer
ruin, ru'ïne ; ondergang : be'derven ; ruï'neren
ruinous, ver'derfelijk ; ruï'neus
rule, regel ; heerschap'pij ; lini'aal : be'slissen ; be'heren, re'geren ; lini'ëren
  as a rule, in de regel
ruler, re'geerder ; lini'aal
ruling, be'slissing : re'gerend ; heersend
rum, rum : raar
rumble, ge'rommel *n* : rommelen
ruminate, her'kauwen ; be'peinzen
rummage, snuffelen
rumour, ge'rucht *n*
rumple, kreuken
rump-steak, biefstuk
run, wedloop ; reis ; ritje *n*; run ; peri'ode : (hard)lopen ; rennen ; kruipen ; raken ; doorlopen ; laten (vol)lopen ; drijven
  in the long run, op de lange duur
  to run down, stil gaan staan ; opsporen ; over'rijden ; uitgeput raken ; afkammen
  to run into, tegenkomen ; oprijden (or lopen) tegen
  to run out, aflopen ; opraken
  to run out of, door . . . heen raken
  to run over, over'rijden ; overlopen
  to run through, er door'brengen ; door'steken ; doorlezen
runaway, op hol ge'slagen
rung, sport
runner, hardloper ; bode ; loper
running, door'lopend : achter el'kaar
runway, groef ; startbaan
rupture, breuk

rural, landelijk, platte'lands-
ruse, krijgslist
rush, drukte, haast; toeloop:
bies: rennen, vliegen; storten;
zich haasten
russet, roodbruin (n)
Russia, Rusland n
Russian, Rus(sisch (n))
rust, roest: (ver')roesten
rustic, boers; rus'tiek: platte'lander
rustle, ge'ritsel n: (doen) ritselen
rusty, roestig
rut, wagenspoor n; sleur
ruthless, mee'dogenloos
rye, rogge

S

sable, sabelbont n
sabotage, sabo'tage
sabre, sabel
sack, zak; plundering: (de) bons
(geven); plunderen
sacrament, sacra'ment n
sacred, heilig; ge'wijd
sacrifice, offer(ande) (n), op-
offering: (op)offeren
sacrilege, heiligschennis
sad, be'droefd; droevig
saddle, zadel(en) (n); opschepen
sadness, be'droefdheid
safe, veilig; zeker: brandkast;
vliegenkast
safeguard, waarborg(en)
safety, veiligheid
sag, doorbuigen; (af or door)zak-
ken
saga, sage
sagacious, schrander
sage, wijze: salie
sail, zeil(en) (n); ver'trekken,
varen
sailor, ma'troos, zeeman
saint, heilig(e); sint
sake: for the — of; ter wille
van; om . . . te
salad, sla
salary, sa'laris n
sale, (uit)verkoop, ver'koping
salesman, be'diende; handels-
reiziger

salient, op'vallend; treffend
saliva, speeksel n
sallow, ziekelijk (geel)
sally, uitval (doen)
salmon, zalm
saloon, sa'lon; bar; zaal
salt, zout (n): zouten
salutary, heilzaam
salutation, groet
salute, sa'luut n; salu'eren
salvage, berging; bergloon;
afval: bergen; redden
salvation, ver'lossing; zaligheid
salve, zalf: sussen; redden
salvo, salvo n
same, zelfde
all the same, deson'danks:
allemaal het'zelfde (or eender)
sample, monster n; staal(tje) n;
voorproefje n: keuren
sanatorium, sana'torium n; ziek-
enzaal
sanctify, heiligen
sanctimonious, schijn'heilig
sanction, sanctie: sanctio'neren
sanctity, heiligheid
sanctuary, sanctu'arium n; re-
ser'vaat n; a'siel n
sand, zand n
sands, strand n
sandal, san'daal
sand-paper, schuurpapier n:
schuren
sandpit, zandgroeve; zandbak
sandwich, sandwich, be'legde
boterham
sandy, zandig, zand-
sane, ge'zond van geest, ver'standig
sanguine, opgewekt; blozend
sanitary, ge'zondheids-
sanitation, sani'tair n
sanity, ge'zond ver'stand n
sap, sap n: uitputten
sapling, jonge boom; jong'mens n
sapphire, saf'fier(blauw (n))
sarcasm, sar'casme n
sarcastic, sar'castisch
sardine, sar'dine
sardonic, smalend
sash, sjerp: schuifraamkozijn n
Satan, Satan
satchel, schooltas

satellite, satel'liet

satiate, (over)ver'zadigen

satin, sa'tijn(en) (*n*)

satire, sa'tire

satiric(cal), sa'tirisch

satirize, be'vredigend

satisfaction, vol'doening; ge'-
noegdoening

satisfactorily, naar ge'noegen

satisfactory, be'vredigend

satisfy, vol'doen aan; be'vredig-
en, te'vreden stellen

  to be satisfied with, te'vreden
  zijn over (*or* met)

saturate, ver'zadigen; door'trekken; door'weken

satyr, sater

sauce, saus; brutali'teit

saucepan, (steel)pan

saucer, schoteltje *n*

saucy, bru'taal; vlot

saunter, slenteren

sausage, worst(je *n*)

sausage-roll, sau'cijzebroodje *n*

savage, wild(e), woest

save, redden; sparen; voor'komen

savings, spaarpenningen

saviour, redder, heiland

savour, smaak: smaken (naar);
ge'nieten van

savoury, smakelijk; pi'kant
(schoteltje *n*)

saw, zaag: zagen

sawdust, zaagsel *n*

saxophone, saxo'foon

say, zeggenschap: (op)zeggen;
luiden

  that is to say, dat wil zeggen

  it says . . . , er staat . . .

saying, ge'zegde *n*

scab, roofje *n*; schurft

scabbard, schede

scaffold, scha'vot *n*

scaffolding, stel'lage, steiger

scald, met kokend water be'gieten, met stoom branden; uitkoken

scale, schub; schilfer; ketelsteen:
schaal; graadverdeling; (toon)-
ladder: be'klimmen

scales, weegschaal

scallop, kammossel; schelp;
schulp

scalp, scalp('eren)

scaly, ge'schubd; schilferig

scamp, rakker

scamper, rennen

scan, afzoeken; een vluchtige
blik werpen in (*or* op); (zich
laten) scan'deren

scandal, schan'daal *n*, schande;
lasterpraat

scandalize, aanstoot geven

scandalous, schandelijk; lasterlijk

Scandinavian, Scandi'navisch;
Scandi'naviër

scant, schraal; karig (zijn met)

scanty, spaarzaam, onvol'doende,
dun

scapegoat, zondebok

scar, litteken *n*: rotswand

scarce, schaars

scarcely, nauwelijks

scarcity, schaarste

scare, schrik('barend be'richt *n*);
bang maken

scarecrow, vogelverschrikker

scarf, das

scarlet, schar'laken (*n*)

  scarlet fever, roodvonk

scathing, bijtend

scatter, (zich) ver'strooien;
uit'eendrijven

scavenger, opruimer; aasdier *n*;
scharrelaar

scene, tafe'reel *n*; scène

scenery, decor *n*; landschap *n*,
na'tuur(schoon *n*)

scenic, na'tuur-; toneel-

scent, geur, o'deur; reuk(zin);
spoor *n*: ruiken; snuffelen

sceptic, scepticus

sceptical, sceptisch

sceptre, scepter

schedule, ta'bel; ceel; schema *n*

scheme, plan *n*; schema *n*:
intri'geren

schism, scheuring

scholar, leerling; ge'leerde

scholarly, ge'leerd, weten'schappelijk

scholarship, ge'leerdheid;
studiebeurs

school, school

schooling, schoolopleiding

schoolmaster, leraar

schoolroom, schoollokaal *n*

school-teacher, onder'wijzer-('es)

schooner, schoener

science, (na'tuur-)wetenschap

scientific, weten'schappelijk

scientist, ge'leerde

scintillate, fonkelen

scissors, schaar

scoff at, spotten met

scold, een uitbrander geven

scone, droog theegebak *n*

scoop, schoep, schep(pen); pri'meur

scooter, autoped

scope, be'stek *n*; vrij spel *n*

scorch, schroeien

score, stand, aantal punten *n*; twintig(tal *n*); parti'tuur: maken, be'halen; tellen; krassen

scorn, hoon: ver'smaden, het be'neden zich achten

scornful, minachtend

scorpion, schorpi'oen

Scot(ch), Schot(s)

scoundrel, schurk

scour, schuren: afzoeken

scourge, gesel(en)

scout, ver'kenner; padvinder: op zoek gaan

scowl, dreigend kijken

scraggy, mager

scramble, ge'jakker *n*; jachten (*n*): klauteren; zich ver'dringen

scrambled egg, roerei *n*

scrap, stukje *n*: kloppartij: oud: afdanken

scrapbook, plakboek *n*

scrape, knel: schrappen; schuren, krabben; schrapen

scratch, kras(sen), schram(men): krabben

scrawl, ge'krabbel *n*: krabbelen

scream, gil(len)

screech, ge'krijs *n*: krijsen

screen, scherm *n*; koorhek *n*: be'schermen, mas'keren

screw, schroef: schroeven

screwdriver, schroevedraaier

scribble, ge'krabbel *n*: krabbelen

scribe, schrijver, schriftgeleerde

script, schrift *n*; tekst

Scripture, Schrift

scroll, rol; krul

scrounge, (in)pikken; klaplopen

scrub, schrobben

scruple, scru'pule, ge'wetensbezwaar *n*

scrupulous, angst'vallig; nauwge'zet

scrutinize, nauw'keurig onder'zoeken

scrutiny, kritisch onderzoek *n*

scud, jagen

scuffle, handgemeen *n*

scullery, bijkeuken

sculptor, beeldhouwer

sculpture, beeldhouwkunst(*or* werk *n*): beeldhouwen

scum, schuim *n*

scurf, roos

scurry, ritsen

scurvy, scheurbuik: ge'meen

scuttle, bak: luik(gat) *n*: doen zinken: snellen

scythe, zeis: maaien

sea, zee

seafaring, zeevarend

seal, zeehond: zegel(en) (*n*): ver(*or* be)'zegelen, sluiten

sea-level, zeespiegel

sealing-wax, zegellak *n*

seam, naad; laag

seaman, zeeman, ma'troos

sear, ver'schroeien

search, zoeken; foui'lleren

in search of, op zoek naar

searching, onder'zoekend, diep'gaand

searchlight, zoeklicht *n*

seashore, zeeoever

seaside, zee(oever)

season, sei'zoen *n*, tijd: kruiden; drogen

seasonal, sei'zoen-

seasoning, kruide'rij

seat, (zit)plaats; bank; zetel

seaweed, zeewier *n*

secede, zich afscheiden, zich te'rugtrekken

secluded, afgezonderd

seclusion, afzondering

second, tweede: se'conde: steunen

secondary, secun'dair; middelbaar

second-hand, tweede'hands; uit de tweede hand

secondly, ten tweede

second-rate, tweede'rangs

secrecy, ge'heimhouding

secret, ge'heim (*n*); heimelijk; ge'sloten

secretary, secre'taris, secreta'resse

secrete, afscheiden; ver'bergen, ver'duisteren

secretive, ge'sloten

secretly, in het ge'heim

sect, sekte

section, (onder)deel *n*, afdeling; sectie; doorsnee; para'graaf; tra'ject *n*

sector, sector

secular, wereldlijk

secure, veilig; ver'zekerd; vast(maken): zich ver'zekeren van

security, veiligheid; waarborg; ef'fect *n*

sedate, be'zadigd, waardig

sedative, pijnstillend (*or* kal'merend) (middel *n*)

sedentary, zittend

sedge, zegge

sediment, be'zinksel *n*

sedition, opruiing

seduce, ver'leiden

see, (aarts)bisschopszetel, (aarts)-bisdom *n*: (in)zien; ervoor zorgen; ont'vangen, be'zoeken, spreken, raadplegen; brengen

to see off, uitgeleide doen, wegbrengen

to see through, door'zien; doorzetten

to see to, zorgen voor

seed, zaad *n*

seeing that, aange'zien

seek, zoeken; trachten

seem, (toe)schijnen

seemingly, ogen'schijnlijk

seemly, be'tamelijk

seep, sijpelen

seer, ziener

seesaw, wip

seethe, zieden; gisten

segment, seg'ment *n*, partje *n*

segregate, (zich) afzonderen

seize, pakken; nemen; aangrijpen

seizure, nemen *n*; be'slaglegging; aanval

seldom, zelden

select, uitgelezen; chic: (uit)-kiezen

selection, keus

self, zelf

self-assured, zelfbe'wust

self-centred, ego'centrisch

self-confidence, zelfvertrouwen *n*

self-conscious, ver'legen

self-contained, vrij; een'zelvig

self-control, zelfbeheersing

self-defence, zelfverdediging

self-denial, zelf'verloochening

self-evident, vanzelf'sprekend

self-government, zelfbestuur *n*

self-interest, eigenbelang *n*

selfish, zelf'zuchtig

selfless, onbaat'zuchtig

self-pity, zelfbeklag *n*

self-preservation, zelfbehoud *n*

self-respect, zelfrespect *n*

self-righteous, eigenge'rechtigd

self-sacrifice, zelfopoffering

selfsame: the —, pre'cies de (*or* het)'zelfde

self-satisfied, zelfvol'daan

self supporting: to be —, in eigen be'hoefte kunnen voor'zien

self-willed, eigen'zinnig

sell, ver'kopen

semblance, schijn, voorkomen *n*

semicircle, halve cirkel

semi-detached, twee onder één dak

senate, se'naat

senator, se'nator

send, sturen, zenden

to send for, laten komen

senile, se'niel

senior, oudste, ouder

sensation, ge'voel *n*, ge'waarwording; sen'satie

sensational, opzien'barend; sensatio'neel

sense, zin(tuig *n*); ge'voel *n*; ver'stand *n*: (aan)voelen

in a sense, in zekere zin
senses, ver'stand n
senseless, be'wusteloos; on'zinnig
sensible, ver'standig, praktisch
sensitive, ge'voelig (voor)
sensual, sensuous, zinnelijk
sentence, zin; vonnis n: ver'oordelen
sentiment, ge'voel(en) n
sentimental, sentimen'teel
sentinel, sentry, schildwacht
separate, af'zonderlijk: (af)schei-
den
separation, scheiding
September, sep'tember
septic, septisch
sepulchre, graf n
sequel, ver'volg n; ge'volg n
sequence, op'eenvolging, volgorde
seraph(im), sera'fijn(en)
serenade, sere'nade (brengen)
serene, kalm
serenity, vreedzaamheid
serf, lijfeigene
serge, serge
sergeant, ser'geant
serial, volg-: feuilleton n
series, serie, reeks, op'eenvolging
serious, ernstig: ge'wichtig
seriously, ernstig, in alle ernst,
au séri'eux
sermon, preek
serpent, slang
serrated, ge'karteld
serum, serum n
servant, be'diende; knecht,
dienstmeisje n; dienaar
serve, (be')dienen; opscheppen;
ser'veren
service, dienst; strijdkracht; service; ser'vies n
serviceable, nuttig
servile, slaafs, kruipend
servitude, slaver'nij; dwangarbeid
session, zitting
set, (toe)stel n: vast, strak: zetten; vast worden
to set about, te werk gaan
to set against, ophitsen tegen;
afwegen tegen

to set off, ver'trekken; af laten
gaan
to set on fire, in brand steken
set-back, tegenslag
settee, bank
setting, zetting; (tijd en) plaats,
om'geving
settle, regelen; zich vestigen;
gaan zitten; ver'zakken
to settle down, tot rust komen
settlement, schikking; ver'effen-
ing; nederzetting
settler, kolo'nist
seven(teen)(th), zeven('tien)(de)
seventy, zeventig
sever, scheiden, ver'breken;
doorsnijden
several, ver'scheiden; af'zonderlijk
severe, streng; ernstig; sober;
hevig; zwaar
sew, naaien
sewage, ri'oolslijk n
sewer, ri'ool n
sewing, naaien n, naaiwerk n
sex, ge'slacht n
sexual, ge'slachts-, seksu'eel
shabby, haveloos; min
shack, keet
shackle, boei(en)
shade, schaduw; achtergrond;
scherm n, kap; tint; tikje n,
nu'ance: be'schutten; be'schaduwen
shadow, schaduw(en); zweem
shadowy, schaduwrijk; vaag
shady, lommerrijk; ver'dacht
shaft, schacht; straal; pijl
shaggy, ruig
shake, schudden (n)
shaky, on'vast, wankel
shale, leisteen
shall, zal, zullen
shallow, on'diep; opper'vlakkig
sham, namaak; schijn: voorwenden
shamble, schuifelen
shame, schaamte; schande:
be'schaamd maken; te schande
maken
a shame, jammer
shameful, schandelijk

shanty, keet
shape, ge'daante; vorm(en); zich ont'wikkelen
shapeless, vormeloos
shapely, goed ge'vormd
share, (aan)deel *n*; samen delen, ver'delen
shark, haai; oplichter
sharp, scherp; bijde'hand; pre'cies: kruis *n*
sharpen, slijpen
shatter, ver'brijzelen; ver'nietigen
shave, (zich) scheren
shaving, krul; scheren *n*
shawl, sjaal, omslagdoek
she, zij
sheaf, schoof; bundel
shear, scheren
shears, schaar
sheath, schede
shed, hok *n*, schuur(tje *n*): ver'gieten, storten; afwerpen; ver'spreiden
sheen, glans
sheep, schaap *n*, schapen
sheepish, schaapachtig
sheer, ragfijn; klinkklaar; loodrecht
sheet, laken *n*; vel *n*, plaat, vlak *n*: schoot
shelf, plank; platte rand
shell, schaal, schelp, schil(d *n*); huls; ge'raamte *n*: doppen; be'schieten
shellfish, schelpdier *n*
shelter, schutting, schuilplaats: be'schermen; schuilen
shelve, van zich afschuiven: glooien
shepherd, herder: ge'leiden
sheriff, drost
sherry, sherry
shield, schild *n*: be'schermen
shift, ploeg, werktijd: ver'schuiven
shilling, shilling
shimmer, glinsteren
shin, scheen
shindy, herrie
shine, glans: (laten) schijnen; glimmen; uitblinken
shingle, grint *n*

shiny, glimmend, blinkend
ship, schip *n*; in(*or* ver')schepen
shipbuilding, scheepsbouw
shipment, ver'scheping; zending
ship-owner, reder
shipping, scheepvaart, schepen
shipwreck, schipbreuk
to be shipwrecked, schipbreuk lijden
shipyard, werf
shirk, zich ont'trekken aan
shirt, (over)hemd *n*
shiver, rilling: rillen
shoal, on'diepte: school
shock, schok (geven); shock: bos: aanstoot geven
shocking, aan'stotelijk; gruwelijk; schan'dalig
shoddy, prul-, snert-
shoe, schoen
shoot, uitloper: (dood)schieten; afschieten; storten
shop, winkel(en)
shopkeeper, winke'lier
shore, kust, oever: stut(ten)
short, kort; krap; bros
to cut short, onder'breken
in short, kort'om
to run short, opraken
to be short of, ge'brek hebben aan; te'kort komen
shortage, te'kort *n*
short-circuit, kortsluiting (ver'oorzaken)
shortcoming, te'kortkoming
shorten, (ver')korten
shorthand, stenogra'fie
short-lived, kort'stondig
shortly, (binnen)kort
shorts, korte broek
short-sighted, bij'ziend; kort'zichtig
short-tempered, prikkelbaar
shot, schot *n*; schroot *n*; poging; kiekje *n*; slag
shotgun, jachtgeweer *n*
should, moest(en); be'horen; zou(den); mocht(en)
shoulder, schouder(stuk *n*): op zich nemen
shout, schreeuw(en); brullen
shove, schuiven
shovel, schop: scheppen

show, ver'toon *n*, schijn; ten'toonstelling, amuse'ments-voorstelling, schouwspel *n*, show: (ver')tonen; te zien zijn; laten zien; (be')wijzen; blijk geven van

to show off, zich aanstellen; pronken met

to show up, aan de dag brengen; uitkomen

shower, bui; douche; regen; over'stelpen

shrapnel, gra'naatscherven

shred, flard; schijn

shrew, feeks

shrewd, schrander

shriek, gil(len)

shrill, schel

shrimp, gar'naal

shrine, schrijn; heilige plaats

shrink, (doen) krimpen; te'rugdeinzen (voor)

shrivel, (doen) ver'schrompelen

shroud, doodskleed *n*; sluier: staand want *n*: hullen

shrub, heester

shrubbery, heesterbosje *n*

shrug, ophalen

shudder, huiveren; schudden

shuffle, schuifelen; wassen

shun, schuwen

shunt, ran'geren

shut, dicht (doen); sluiten

to shut up, (op)sluiten; zijn mond houden

shutter, luik *n*; sluiter

shuttle, schietspoel: pendel-

shy, ver'legen, schuw: schrikken: keilen

sick, ziek(en); misselijk; beu

to be sick, overgeven

sickening, walgelijk; ver'velend

sickle, sikkel

sickly, ziekelijk; onge'zond

sickness, ziekte; misselijkheid

side, (zij)kant; zij(de); par'tij (kiezen)

side by side, naast el'kaar

sideboard, buf'fet *n*

side-track, zijspoor *n*: van zijn onderwerp afbrengen *or* af-dwalen;

sideways, zijdelings

siding, zijspoor *n*

sidle up to, schuchter be'naderen

siege, be'leg *n*

sieve, zeef: zeven

sift, zeven; ziften

sigh, zucht(en)

sight, ge'zicht *n*; beziens'waar-digheid; vi'zier *n*: (in) zicht *n* (krijgen)

at sight, op het eerste ge'zicht; van het blad

to catch sight of, in het oog krijgen

sign, (uithang)bord *n*; wenk, teken *n*: (onder')tekenen; een teken geven

signal, sein(en) (*n*); een teken geven

signature, handtekening

signet(-ring), zegel(ring), (*n*)

significance, be'tekenis; be'lang *n*

significant, veelbe'tekenend; be'langrijk

signify, be'tekenen; te kennen geven

signpost, handwijzer

silence, stilte; stilzwijgen *n*: tot zwijgen brengen

silent, stil (zwijgend), zwijgzaam; stom

to be silent, zwijgen

silently, in stilte, ge'ruisloos

silhouette, silhou'et

silk, zij(den)

silky, zijdeachtig

sill, vensterbank, drempel

silly, on'nozel, dwaas, flauw

silt, slib *n*: dichtslibben

silver, zilver(werk) *n*: zilveren

similar, ge'lijk, dergelijk

similarity, over'eenkomst

simile, verge'lijking

simmer, zachtjes (laten) sud-deren; pruttelen; gisten

simper, meesmuilen

simple, een'voudig; enkel'voud-ig; simpel; on'nozel

simpleton, on'nozele hals

simplicity, eenvoud

simplify, vereen'voudigen

simply, een'voudig; ge'woon-weg, al'leen

simulate, voorwenden; nabootsen

simultaneous, gelijk'tijdig

sin, zonde: zondigen

since, sinds('dien), na'dien; van'af: daar

sincere, op'recht

sincerity, op'rechtheid

sinecure, sine'cuur

sinew, pees

sinful, zondig

sing, zingen

singe, (af)schroeien; fri'seren

singer, zanger('es)

singing, zingen n; suizen n

single, enkel; eenpersoons-; onge'trouwd

  to single out, uitpikken

singly, af'zonderlijk; al'leen

singular, bij'zonder: enkelvoud n

sinister, si'nister

sink, gootsteen: (ver')zinken, ondergaan; tot zinken brengen

sinner, zondaar

sinuous, kronkelend

sip, teugje n: met teugjes drinken

siphon, hevel(en); si'fon

sir, mijnheer; sir

  Dear Sir, Mijne Heren, Zeer geachte Heer

sire, (voor)vader; sire

siren, si'rene

sister, zusje n; zuster

sit, (gaan) zitten; zitting houden; po'seren

  to sit down, gaan zitten

  to sit up, rech'top (gaan) zitten; opblijven

site, bouwgrond, ('bouw)ter'rein n; ligging

sitting-room, zitkamer

situated, ge'legen

situation, ligging; situ'atie; be'trekking

six(teen)(th), zes(tien)(de)

sixpence, kwartje n, halve shilling

sixty, zestig

sizable, flink

size, grootte, omvang; maat; lijmwater n

sizzle, sissen

skate, schaats(enrijden): vleet

skein, streng

skeleton, ske'let n; ge'raamte n

sketch, schets(en)

skewer, vleespen

ski, ski(ën)

skid, slippen

skilful, be'kwaam, knap

skill, be'kwaamheid, vaardigheid

skilled, ge'schoold

skim, afscheppen, afromen; scheren over; doorbladeren

skimp, zuinig zijn (met)

skin, huid; vel n; pels: villen

skinny, broodmager

skip, springen; overslaan

skipper, schipper

skirmish, scher'mutseling

skirt, rok; trekken (om)

skulk, lijntrekken; laf'hartig schuilen; sluipen

skull, schedel; doodskop

skunk, skunk

sky, lucht, hemel

skylark, veldleeuwerik; pret

sky-scraper, wolkenkrabber

slab, plak, plaat

slack, slap; laks; stil: gruis n

slacken, ver'slappen; laten vieren

slacks, lange broek

slag, slak

slake, lessen; blussen

slam, bons; slem n: dichtslaan

slander, (be')laster(en)

slanderous, lasterlijk

slang, slang n

slant, helling: hellen

slap, klap (geven): par'does: kwakken

slapdash, noncha'lant

slash, houw, jaap: (er'op los) maaien (or slaan); drastisch ver'minderen

slat, lat, reep

slate, lei(steen n): leien: ervan langs geven

slaughter, slachting: slachten: afmaken

slave, slaaf: zich afbeulen

slavery, slaver'nij

slavish, slaafs

slay, doodslaan

sledge, slede: voorhamer: sleeën

sleek, glanzig, glad

sleep, slaap: slapen
sleeper, slaper; slaapwagen; dwarsligger
sleeping, slapen n; slapend: slaap-
sleepless, slapeloos
sleepy, slaperig; doods; melig
sleet, natte sneeuw
sleeve, mouw
sleigh, arreslee
sleight of hand, goochela'rij
slender, slank, dun; karig, zwak, klein
slice, snee(tje n): snijden
slick, vlot, glad
slide, glijbaan; glijkoker; plaatje n: glijden
slight, ge'ring, licht; tenger: klei'nering: klei'neren
slightly, iets; opper'vlakkig
slim, slank
slime, slijk n, slijm n
slimy, slijmerig
sling, slingerverband n; leng; slinger(en); gooien
slink, sluipen
slip, sloop n; onderjurk; ver'gissing; strookje n; helling: (uit)-glijden; wippen; uitschieten; schuiven; laten glijden; aan(or uit)doen; voor'bijgaan; ont'-schieten
slipper, pan'toffel
slippery, glibberig, glad
slipshod, slordig
slit, spleet, scheur(en); snijden
slobber, kwijlen
slogan, leus
sloop, sloep
slop, morsen
slope, helling: hellen, schuin lopen
sloppy, drassig; dun; slordig; zoetelijk
slot, gleuf
sloth, luiheid; luiaard
slouch, slungelen, hangen
slough, moe'ras n: afgeworpen vel n
slovenly, slonzig, slordig
slow, langzaam, traag; achter
  to slow down, ver'tragen, ophouden; vaart ver'minderen

slug, slak; hagelkorrel
sluggish, traag
sluice, sluis, ver'laat: spoelen
slum, slop, achterbuurt
slumber, sluimering: sluimeren
slump, ma'laise
slur, vlek, smet: in el'kaar laten lopen
slush, half ge'smolten sneeuw; bagger
slut, slet
sly, sluw
smack, klap, smak, pats: bij-smaak: zweem: een klap geven; smakken met: zwemen naar
small, klein
smallpox, pokken
smart, vinnig; flink; bijde'hand, handig; chic, keurig: zeer doen
smash, botsing; cata'strofe: ver'pletteren; stukslaan; breken; botsen (tegen)
smattering, mondjevol n
smear, veeg: (be')smeren; be'smeuren
smell, reuk, lucht: ruiken (naar); rieken (naar)
smelt, smelten
smile, (glim)lach(en)
smirk, grijns (or grijnzen) van vol'doening
smite, (hard) slaan; kwellen
smith, smid
smithereens, gruzele'menten
smithy, smidse
smock, kiel: smokken
smoke, rook: roken; walmen
smoky, rokerig
smooth, glad, vlak; kalm; vlot: gladstrijken
smother, smoren; stikken; be'delven; doven
smoulder, smeulen
smudge, vlek(ken)
smug, zelf'ingenomen
smuggle, smokkelen
smut, roetdeeltje n; schunnig-heden
snack, hapje n
snack-bar, cafe'taria
snag, uitsteeksel n; moeilijkheid
snail, huisjesslak
snake, slang

snap, klap, krak; drukknoop; kiekje *n*: knappen; happen; snauwen; pikken

snapshot, kiekje *n*

snare, (val)strik; (ver')strikken

snarl, grauw(en); snauw(en)

snatch, brokstuk *n*: grissen

sneak, klikspaan: klikken; sluipen; gappen

sneer, schimplach: be'schimpen; smalen (op)

sneeze, niezen (*n*)

sniff, snuiven; de neus ophalen (voor); snuffelen; ruiken aan

snigger, grinniken

snip, snipper; knip(pen)

snipe, snip: ter'sluiks één voor één neerschieten

snob, snob

snooze, dutje *n*: dutten

snore, snurken

snort, snuiven

snout, snuit

snow, sneeuw(en)

snowdrift, sneeuwbank

snowflake, sneeuwvlok

snowy, sneeuw-

snub, brute afwijzing: bits afwijzen

 snub nose, mopneus

snuff, snuif: snuiven: snuiten

snug, knus

snuggle, (zich) nestelen

so, zo: dus: ook

 or so, onge'veer

 so that, zodat; opdat

soak, (door')weken; in de week zetten (*or* staan);| (laten) trekken

 to soak up, (op)slorpen

soap, zeep

soap-suds, zeepsop *n*

soar, om'hoogvliegen; de hoogte invliegen

sob, snik(ken)

sober, nuchter; sober: ont'nuchteren

so-called, zoge'naamd

soccer, voetbal *n*

sociable, soci'aal; ge'zellig

social, soci'aal

socialism, socia'lisme *n*

society, ver'eniging; maatschap'pij; ge'zelschap *n*; deftige stand

sock, sok

socket, gat *n*, kas, holte

sod, zode

soda, soda

sodden, doornat

sofa, sofa

soft, zacht; week

soften, zacht maken (*or* worden); ver'zachten

soggy, door'weekt, drassig, klef

soil, grond, bodem: vuil maken

sojourn, ver'toeven

solace, troost

solar, zonne-, zons-

solder, sol'deersel *n*: sol'deren

soldier, sol'daat; mili'tair

sole, enig: zool: tong

solely, al'leen

solemn, ernstig; plechtig

solemnity, plechtigheid

solicit, ver'zoeken om

solicitor, rechts'kundig advi'seur, procu'reur

solicitous, be'zorgd; ver'langend

solid, vast (lichaam *n*); mas'sief; stevig; soli'dair

solidarity,   saam'horigheidsgevoel *n*

solidify, mas'sief (doen) worden

soliloquy, al'leenspraak

solitary, eenzaam

solitude, eenzaamheid

solo, solo

soluble, op'losbaar

solution, oplossing

solve, oplossen

solvent, sol'vent; oplossend: oplosmiddel *n*

sombre, somber

some, sommige; enige; (er) wat (van); een (of ander); onge'veer

 some such, een dergelijk, zo'n

 some day, weleens

somebody, (een zeker) iemand

somehow, op de een of andere ma'nier; hoe dan ook

someone, iemand

somersault, buiteling, salto mortale

something, iets

sometime, wel eens

sometimes, soms

somewhat, enigs'zins; iets, wat

somewhere, ergens; een plaats (waar)

son, zoon

sonata, so'nate

song, lied *n*; appel en een ei

sonnet, son'net *n*

sonorous, diepklinkend; weids

soon, spoedig, vroeg; lief
  as soon as, zo'dra
  no sooner ... than, nauwe- lijks ... of
  I would sooner, ik zou liever

soot, roet *n*

soothe, sussen; ver'zachten

soothsayer, waarzegger

sophisticated, mon'dain

sophistication, ge'kunsteldheid

soporific, slaap'wekkend

sopping wet, drijfnat

soprano, so'praan

sorcerer, tovenaar

sorcery, tovena'rij

sordid, vuil; on'smakelijk

sore, zeer; gepi'keerd; teer: zere plek

sorrow, smart: treuren

sorrowful, droevig

sorry, treurig
  I am sorry, het spijt me

sort, soort: sor'teren

soul, ziel; sterveling

soul-destroying, geest'dodend

sound, ge'luid *n*, klank: zeeëngte: degelijk, gaaf, ge'zond, be'- trouwbaar; flink, vast: (doen) klinken: peilen; polsen

sounding, klinkend: peiling

soup, soep

sour, zuur

source, bron

south, zuid(er-), zuiden(-) (*n*), naar het zuiden, ten zuiden van

southerly, zuidelijk

southern, zuidelijk, zuider-

souvenir, souve'nir *n*

sovereign, vorst: soeve'rein

sovereignty, soevereini'teit

Soviet, Sovjet

sow, zeug: (be')zaaien

space, (tijd)ruimte; spatie: spati'ëren, ver'delen

spacious, ruim

spade, schop

span, spanwijdte; spanne

spangle, lovertje *n*: be'zaaien

spaniel, spaniël

spank, voor zijn broek geven; patsen

spanner, moersleutel

spar, rondhout *n*: (oefenend) boksen; redetwisten

spare, vrij; re'serve; schraal: (re'serve)onderdeel *n*; sparen: missen; ont'zien

spark, vonk(en); greintje *n*

sparkle, vonken schieten; fonk- elen; tintelen; mous'seren

sparrow, mus

sparse, dun(ge'zaaid)

spasm, kramp('achtige be'- weging); vlaag

spasmodic, kram'pachtig; bij vlagen, intermit'terend

spats, slobkousen

spate, stroom, vlaag, hoop

spatter, spatten; plassen (tegen)

spawn, kuit (schieten)

speak, spreken; uitdrukken

speaker, spreker; voorzitter

spear, speer

special, bij'zonder, speci'aal

specialist, specia'list

specialize, speciali'seren

specially, in het bij'zonder, voor'al

species, soort(en), ge'slacht(en) *n*

specific, be'paald; uit'drukke- lijk; speci-fiek

specification, specifi'catie

specify, specifi'ceren; ver'melden

specimen, proef; staaltje *n*

specious, schoonschijnend

speck, spikkel; vuiltje *n*

speckle, (be')spikkelen

spectacle, schouwspel *n*

spectacles, bril

spectacular, groots, grandi'oos

spectator, toeschouwer

spectre, spook *n*; schim

spectrum, spectrum *n*

speculate, be'spiegelingen hou- den; specu'leren

speculation, be'spiegeling; specu'latie

speculator, specu'lant

speech, (toe)spraak

speechless, sprakeloos

speed, vaart; snelheid; ver'snelling: snel rijden

speed(il)y, spoedig

spell, beurt; peri'ode: be'tovering: spellen; be'tekenen

spend, uitgeven; be'steden, doorbrengen; uitputten

spew, (uit)braken

sphere, bol; hemellichaam *n*; ge'bied *n*, sfeer

spherical, bol'vormig

spice, spece'rij

spicy, ge'kruid; pi'kant

spider, spin

spike, (ijzeren) punt; stekel

spill, fidibus: morsen; overlopen

spin, ritje *n*; vrille: spinnen; draaien

spinach, spi'nazie

spinal, ruggegraats-

spindle, klos; spil

spine, ruggegraat; stekel

spinney, bosje *n*

spinster, ongetrouwde vrouw

spiral, spi'raal(vormig)

spire, torenspits

spirit, geest; fut

  spirits, stemming; levenslust; sterke drank

spirited, vurig; geani'meerd

spiritual, geestelijk (lied *n*)

spit, spuug *n*: spit *n*; landtong: spuwen; druppelen

spite, kwaa'daardigheid: ergeren

spiteful, hatelijk

splash, spat: be'spatten; plassen; uit el'kaar spatten; natmaken

spleen, milt; gal

splendid, schitterend, prachtig

splendour, pracht

splice, splitsen; lassen

splint, spalk(en)

splinter, splinter

split, spleet; scheuring: splijten; splitsen; (ver')delen

splitting, barstend

splutter, sputteren

spoil, buit: be'derven; ver'wennen

spoil-sport, spelbreker

spoke, spaak; sport

spokesman, woordvoerder

sponge, spons; mos'covisch ge'bak *n*: sponzen; klaplopen

sponsor, borg en stichter; peet; op touw zetten

spontaneous, spon'taan; zelf-

spool, spoel

spoon(ful), lepel

sporadic, spo'radisch

spore, spoor

sport, sport; grap, spot; fi'dele vent (*or* meid): spelen

sporting, sport-; spor'tief; aardig

sportsman, sportliefhebber

spot, vlek; stip(pelen); plek; scheutje *n*: in de gaten krijgen

spotless, smetteloos; brandschoon

spotlight, zoeklicht *n*

spouse, gade

spout, tuit; straal: spuiten

sprain, ver'stuiken

sprawl, uitgestrekt (gaan) liggen; wijd uit'eenlopen, zich wan'orderlijk ver'spreiden

spray, sproeiregen; sproeier: takje *n*: (be')sproeien

spread, wijdte; ont'haal *n*: (zich) (uit)spreiden; (zich) ver'spreiden; (be')smeren

spree, pretje *n*; braspartij

sprig, twijgje *n*

sprightly, opgewekt

spring, veer(kracht); lente; bron: springen; ont'staan(uit); (uit de grond) schieten

sprinkle, (be')sprenkelen, strooien

sprint, sprint(en)

sprout, spruit(en)

spruce, spar(rehout *n*): keurig: opknappen

spry, kwiek

spur, spoor; uitloper; prikkel: de sporen geven; aansporen

  on the spur of the moment, in de eerste opwelling

spurious, on'echt

spurn, ver'smaden

spurt, guts; vlaag: spuiten (met); spurten

sputter, sputteren, spatten

spy, spi'on; (be)spio'neren; be'speuren
squabble, ge'kibbel *n*: kibbelen
squad, troep
squadron, eska'dron *n*; es'kader *n*
squalid, vuil en ar'moedig
squall, (wind)vlaag: schreeuwen
squalor, vuile armoede
squander, ver'spillen
square, vierkant (*n*); plein *n*; kwa'draat *n*: recht('hoekig); quitte; eerlijk: in het kwa'draat brengen; afrekenen
squash, kwast: platdrukken, platgedrukt worden
squat, ge'drongen: neerhurken
squawk, krijsen
squeak, piepen
squeal, gillen
squeamish, overdreven ge'voelig
squeeze, ge'drang *n*: knijpen, uitpersen; bijstoppen;· afpersen
squelch, ploeteren
squint, scheelkijken; pinkogen
squire, landjonker
squirm, zich in allerlei bochten wringen; in el'kaar kruipen
squirrel, eekhoorn
squirt, spuiten
stab, steek(wond): (door)steken
stability, stabili'teit
stabilize, stabili'seren
stable, stal(len): sta'biel, vast
stack, stapel: opstapelen
stadium, stadion *n*
staff, staf, stok
stag, mannetjeshert *n*
stage, e'tappe, stadium *n*; to'neel *n*; tra'ject *n*: ten to'nele brengen; op touw zetten
stage-coach, dili'gence
stagger, (doen) wankelen; ver'bijsteren; spreiden
stagnant, stilstaand
stagnation, stilstand; stremming
staid, be'zadigd
stain, (be')vlek(ken): smet; beits(en); kleurstof: afgeven; brandschilderen
stainless, smetteloos; roestvrij

stair, trede: trap-
staircase, stairs, trap
stake, paal: brandstapel; inzet(ten); staken
  at stake, op het spel
stale, oud('bakken), ver'schaald, muf; suf
stalk, stengel: (be')sluipen
stall, stal(letje n); koorstoel: (laten) afslaan
stallion, hengst
stalwart, stoer
stamen, meeldraad
stamina, uithoudingsvermogen *n*
stammer, ge'stamel *n*: stamelen, stotteren
stamp, (post)zegel; stempel(en): fran'keren; stampen
stampede, pa'niek; stormloop: stormlopen
stand, standard, voet, stel *n*; tri'bune; plaats: (gaan *or* blijven) staan; liggen; zetten; ver'dragen, uitstaan; van kracht blijven; trak'teren; zijn
  to stand back, achter'uitgaan; (van . . .) af liggen
  to stand out, uitsteken; opvallen
standard, standaard; maatstaf; vaandel *n*
standardize, standaardi'seren
stand-by, re'serve, steun
standing, aanzien *n*: permanent; (stil)staand
standpoint, standpunt *n*
standstill, stilstand
stanza, vers *n*, strofe
staple, hoofd-: kram, niet
star, ster; ge'sternte *n*
starboard, stuurboord
starch, zetmeel *n*; stijfsel: stijven
stare, (aan)staren
stark, stapel-, spier-
starling, spreeuw
starry, sterren-
start, be'gin(nen) (*n*); start(en); schok: ver'trekken; aanzetten, aanslaan; opschrikken
startle, doen schrikken
startling, verbazing'wekkend; ont'stellend

starvation, ver'hongering

starve, (laten) ver'hongeren

state, staat, toestand; staatsie: staats-: mededelen, uit'eenzetten, consta'teren

stated, ge'noemd; vastgesteld

stately, statig

statement, ver'klaring

statesman, staatsman

statesmanship, staatkunde

static, statisch

station, sta'tion *n*; stand- (plaats): plaatsen

stationary, stilstaand; statio'nair

stationer, kan'toorboekhandel(aar)

stationery, schrijfbehoeften

statistic, sta'tistisch

statistics, statis'tiek(en)

statue, standbeeld *n*

stature, ge'stalte; ge'halte *n*

status, toestand; po'sitie

statute, landswet, sta'tuut *n*

staunch, trouw: stelpen

stave, duig; staaf: inslaan

to stave off, afwenden

stay, ver'blijf *n*: stut: stag: (ver')blijven; lo'geren

steadfast, stand'vastig

steady, stevig, vast; so'lide; stand'vastig; kalm: vasthouden

steak, lap

steal, stelen; sluipen

stealthy, heimelijk

steam, stoom: dampen; stomen

steamer, stoomboot; stomer

steed, ros *n*

steel, staal *n*: stalen

steep, steil; kras: (in)dompelen

steeple, toren(spits)

steer, jonge os: sturen

steering-wheel, stuur *n*

stem, stengel, steel; (voor)steven: stuiten

stench, stank

stencil, stencil(en) (*n*)

stenographer, steno'graaf

step, stap(pen); pas; trede, stoep

step-, stief-

step-ladder, trapleer

stereotyped, stereo'tiep

sterile, ste'riel; on'vruchtbaar

sterilize, sterili'seren

sterling, sterling: recht'schapen

stern, achtersteven: streng

stevedore, stuwa'door

stew, stoofschotel: stoven

steward, hofmeester; rentmeester; be'diende

stick, stok: plakken; (blijven) steken; volhouden

sticky, kleverig

stiff, stijf, stroef; stevig; moeilijk

stiffen, stijver (*or* moeilijker) maken

stifle, (ver')stikken; onder'drukken

stigma, brandmerk *n*

stile, overstap

still, stil(te): distil'leerketel: nog (al'tijd): toch: kal'meren

stillness, stilte

stilt, stelt

stilted, hoog'dravend

stipend, be'zoldiging

stipulate, be'dingen

stipulation, voorwaarde

stir, ophef: (be')roeren, zich ver'roeren; aanzetten

stirring, veelbe'wogen; op'windend

stirrup, stijgbeugel

stitch, steek, hechting: stikken, hechten

stock, voorraad; ef'fecten; afkomst; boui'llon: standaard, cou'rant: voor'zien(van), voorraad inslaan; in voorraad hebben

stockade, palis'sade

stockbroker, e'fectenmakelaar

stocking, kous

stodgy, onver'teerbaar; zwaar

stoic(al), stoï'cijns

stoke, stoken

stolid, stomp'zinnig

stomach, maag: ver'duwen

stone, (edel)steen; pit; 6·35 kilo: stenen: stenigen; ont'pitten

stone-deaf, stokdoof

stony, steenachtig; steenhard; doods, koud

stool, kruk; stoelgang

stoop, ronde rug: bukken; zich ver'lagen

stop, oponthoud *n*; halte; re'gister: (dicht)stoppen; blijven (staan); stilstaan; ophouden (met); stopzetten; stelpen

to put a stop to, een eind maken aan

stoppage, oponthoud *n*; op-stopping

stopper, stop

storage, opslaan *n*; bergruimte: opslag-

store, warenhuis *n*; ba'zaar; voorraad; maga'zijn *n*: op-slaan; opbergen

to lay in a store of, inslaan

storeroom, bergruimte, pro'visie-kamer

stork, ooievaar

storm, storm, (flinke) bui, on-weer *n*: razen; stuiven; be'stormen

stormy, stormachtig, onweers-achtig

story, ver'haal *n*, ge'schiedenis: ver'dieping

stout, ge'zet; stevig; flink: stout *n*

stove, kachel, for'nuis *n*

stow, stouwen; opbergen

stowaway, ver'stekeling

straddle, schrijlings staan (*or* zitten); spreiden over

straggle, zich ver'spreiden; ach-terblijven

straight, recht; eerlijk; in orde; puur

straight away, di'rect

straighten, rechttrekken (*or* zet-ten); in orde brengen

straightforward, op'recht; een'voudig

strain, (in)spanning: toon: af-komst; trek: (over' *or* in)-spannen; (ver')rekken; af-gieten

strained, ge'dwongen

strainer, ver'giet, zeefje *n*

straits, zee'ëngte, Straat; ver'legenheid

strand, streng: stranden

to be stranded, stranden; hulpeloos staan

strange, vreemd

stranger, vreemde; onbe'kende

strangle, worgen; onder'druk-ken

strap, riem, band: vastmaken (met een riem)

strapping, potig

stratagem, (krijgs)list

strategic, stra'tegisch

strategy, strate'gie

stratum, (aard)laag

straw, stro(otje) *n*; zier

strawberry, aardbei

stray, afgedwaald (dier *n*): (af)-dwalen

streak, streep; straal: strepen

stream, stroom: stromen

streamer, serpen'tine, wimpel

streamline(d), (ge')stroom-lijn(d)

street, straat

strength, kracht(en); sterkte; ge'halte *n*

strengthen, (ver')sterken

strenuous, inspannend

stress, aandrang; spanning; nadruk; klemtoon: de nadruk (*or* de klemtoon) leggen op

stretch, uitge'strektheid: (zich) (uit)rekken; spannen; uit-steken

at a stretch, achter el'kaar

stretcher, bran'card

strew, strooien; be'zaaien

stricken, ge'troffen

strict, streng; pre'cies; strikt

stride, schrede: schrijden

strident, krassend

strife, twist, strijd

strike, staking: slaan; aan-steken; (toe)schijnen, opkomen bij; treffen; staken; door-halen

striking, treffend

string, touw *n*; snoer *n*; snaar; file; strijkinstrument *n*: (aan'een)rijgen

stringent, streng

strip, strook: (af)stropen; (zich) uitkleden; ont'doen; afhalen

stripe, streep: strepen

stripling, jonge borst

strive, streven (naar); worstelen

stroke, slag; haal; be'roerte; zet: strelen

stroll, wandeling: kuieren; trekken

strong, sterk

stronghold, bolwerk *n*

structure, struc'tuur, (ge')bouw (*n*); samenstelling

struggle, strijd; krachtsinspanning: vechten; strompelen

strum, trommelen

strut, stijl: trots stappen

stub, stomp, stronk, peukje *n*

stubble, stoppels

stubborn, hard'nekkig, hals'starrig

stud, knop; (boorde)knoopje *n*: stoete'rij: be'zaaien

student, onder'zoeker, leerling(-), stu'dent

studied, welover'wogen

studio, atel'ier *n*, studio

studious, leer'gierig

study, studie; stu'deerkamer: (be)stu'deren

stuff, stof, materi'aal *n*; goedje *n*; spul(len) *n*: volproppen; opzetten, vullen

stuffy, be'nauwd

stumble, struikelen, strompelen

stump, stomp, stronk: stommelen

stun, wezenloos slaan; ver'bluffen

stunt, stunt: be'lemmeren

stupefy, ver'stomd doen staan

stupendous, over'weldigend, machtig

stupid, dom, on'zinnig

stupor, ver'doving

sturdy, fors

stutter, stotteren

sty, hok *n*: strontje *n*

style, stijl

stylish, stijlvol; deftig

suave, minzaam

subconscious, onderbe'wust- (zijn *n*)

subdivision, onderverdeling; onderafdeling

subdue, onder'werpen; onder'drukken; dempen

subject, onderwerp *n*; vak *n*; onderdaan: onder'hevig (aan): onder'werpen; blootstellen (aan)

subjection, onder'werping; onder'worpenheid

subjective, subjec'tief

subjugate, onder'werpen

sublime, su'bliem

submarine, onder'zeeboot

submerge, over'stromen, ver'zwelgen

submission, onder'werping; onder'danigheid; be'wering

submissive, onder'danig

submit, (zich) onder'werpen; overleggen; zou(den) naar voren willen brengen; voorleggen

subordinate, onderge'schikt(e)

subscribe, tekenen voor; onder'schrijven; zich abon'neren (op)

subsequent, later

subservient, onderge'schikt; onder'danig

subside, zakken; afnemen; zinken

subsidiary, dochter-, bij('komstig)

subsidize, subsidiëren

subsidy, sub'sidie

subsist, be'staan; leven

subsistence, be'staan *n*

substance, stof; hoofdzaak; wezen *n*; sub'stantie

substantial, aan'zienlijk; so'lide

substantially, in wezen

substantiate, be'wijzen

substitute, plaatsver'vanger, surro'gaat (*n*): in de plaats stellen

substitution, substi'tutie

subterfuge, uitvlucht

subterranean, onderaards

subtle, sub'tiel, fijn, spits'vondig

subtract, aftrekken

suburb, voorstad

suburban, fo'renzen-, voorstads-

succeed, slagen; (op)volgen
success, suc'ces n
successful, ge'slaagd; ge'lukkig
succession, op'eenvolging;
  suc'cessie
  in succession, achter el'kaar
successive, opeen'volgend
successor, opvolger
succinct, kort en bondig
succulent, sappig
succumb, be'zwijken
such, zulk; zo('n); zo'danig
  such as, zo'als; wat
suck, zuigen (op)
suckle, zogen
suction, zuiging: zuig-
sudden, plotseling
sue, ge'rechtelijk ver'volgen;
  smeken
suede, peau de suède
suet, niervet n
suffer, lijden; boeten
suffering, lijden n
suffice, vol'doende zijn
sufficient, vol'doende
suffocate, (doen) stikken
suffocation, ver'stikking
suffrage, kiesrecht n
sugar, suiker(en)
suggest, doen denken aan; voorstellen; sugge'reren
suggestion, voorstel n; sug'-
  gestie; spoor n
suggestive, sugge'rerend; sug-
  ges'tief
suicide, zelfmoord
suit, pak n; kleur; huwelijksaanzoek n: (aan)passen;
  ge'schikt zijn voor; schikken;
  goed staan(bij)
suitable, ge'schikt
suitcase, (hand)koffer
suite, ge'volg n; ameuble'ment
  n; aparte'menten
suitor, minnaar; eiser
sulk, mokken
sulky, gemelijk
sullen, stuurs; somber
sully, be'zoedelen
sulphur, zwavel
sultan, sultan
sultana, sul'tanarozijn
sultry, zwoel

sum, som
  to sum up, samenvatten; opsommen
summarize, resu'meren
summary, samenvatting:
  sum'mier
summer, zomer
summerhouse, tuinhuisje n
summit, top(punt n)
summon, ont'bieden, bij'eenroepen; ver'zamelen
summons, dagvaarding
sumptuous, weelderig
sun, zon(ne-)
sunbeam, zonnestraal
sunburn, zonnebrand
sunburnt, ver'brand
Sunday, Zondag
sundial, zonnewijzer
sundown, zons'ondergang
sundry, di'vers
sunken, blind; ingevallen
sunlight, zonlicht n
sunny, zonnig
sunrise, zons'opgang
sunset, zons'ondergang
sunshine, zonneschijn
sunstroke, zonnesteek
super, machtig
superb, groots, schitterend
supercilious, hoog'hartig
superficial, opper'vlakkig
superfluous, over'tollig
superhuman, boven'menselijk
superintend, toezicht houden
  op
superintendent, inspec'teur
superior, superi'eur, hoger;
  arro'gant
superlative, van de hoogste
  graad: superlatief
supernatural, bovenna'tuur-
  lijk(e n)
supersede, ver'vangen
superstition, bijgeloof n
superstitious, bijge'lovig
supervise, toezicht hebben op;
  survei'lleren
supervision, toezicht n
supper, (avond)eten n, avondmaal n, sou'per n
supplant, ver'dringen
supple, soepel, buigzaam

supplement, supple'ment *n*: aanvullen

supplementary, aanvullend

suppliant, smekend: smekeling

supplication, smeekbede

supply, voorraad; voor'ziening:
ver'schaffen; vol'doen (aan)

support, steun: (onder')steunen;
onder'houden; staven

supporter, aanhanger, sup'porter

suppose, veronder'stellen
I am not supposed to, ik mag
(eigenlijk) niet

supposed, ver'meend; aangenomen

supposing (that), stel dat

supposition, veronder'stelling

suppress, onder'drukken; ver'-
bieden

supremacy, oppermacht

supreme, opper-, uiterste

surcharge, toeslag

sure, zeker
to make sure, contro'leren

surely, (toch) zeker

surety, borg

surf, branding

surface, oppervlak (te) (*n*), vlak *n*

surfeit, overdaad

surge, opwelling: golven, storten; stuwen; zwellen

surgeon, chi'rurg

surgery, chirur'gie; spreekkamer

surly, nors

surmise, ver'moeden (*n*)

surmount, be'kronen; over'-
winnen

surname, achternaam

surpass, over'treffen

surplice, koorhemd *n*

surplus, overschot *n*: over-
('tollig)

surprise, ver'rassing, ver'bazing:
ver'rassen; ver'wonderen, ver'-
bazen

surprising, ver'wonderlijk, ver'-
bazend

surrender, overgave: (zich)
overgeven

surround, om'ringen, om'singelen

surroundings, om'geving

surveillance, toezicht *n*

survey, in'spectie; overzicht *n*;
opmeting: inspec'teren;
over'zien; opmeten

surveyor, ex'pert; opzichter;
landmeter

survival, leven *n*, voortbestaan
n; overblijfsel *n*

survive, over'leven; blijven
be'staan

survivor, over'levende

susceptible, vatbaar, ge'voelig
(voor)

suspect, ver'dacht(e): ver'moed-
en; ver'denken

suspend, staken; schorsen; opschorten
to be suspended, hangen

suspenders, sokophouders; jarre'telles

suspense, spanning

suspicion, ver'moeden *n*; achterdocht; ver'denking; schijntje *n*

suspicious, ver'dacht; achter'-
dochtig

sustain, staande houden; voed-
en; schragen; lijden

sustenance, voedsel *n*; onderhoud *n*

swab, zwabber (en): prop

swagger, zeilen; opscheppen

swallow, zwaluw: (door *or*
in)slikken; ver'zwelgen

swamp, moe'ras *n*: over'spoelen;
over'stelpen

swampy, moe'rassig

swan, zwaan

swank, opsnijde'rij: opsnijden

swap, (ver')ruilen

swarm, zwerm (en): wemelen

swarthy, donker

sway, heerschap'pij: schommelen
ervan afbrengen

swear, zweren; vloeken

sweat, zweet *n*: zweten

sweater, trui

Swedish, Zweeds (*n*)

sweep, zwaai; schoorsteenveger: (op)vegen; voeren;
schrijden

sweeping, wijds; ver'strekkend

sweet, zoet; lief; fris: snoepje
n; toespijs

sweeten, suiker doen in

sweetheart, liefje *n*, vrijer

swell, deining : (aan *or* op) zwellen ; toenemen

swelling, zwelling, ver'dikking

swerve, zwenken

swift, snel : gierzwaluw

swill, draf : (uit)spoelen

swim, zwemmen ; duizelen

swindle, oplichte'rij : oplichten

swine, zwijn(en) *n*

swing, zwaai(en) ; schommel ; animo ; swing : slingeren

swirl, (doen) warrelen

swish, ge'ruis *n* : ruisen

Swiss, Zwitser(s)

switch, schakelaar, wissel ; teen : schakelen ; overplaatsen

swoon, flauwte : be'zwijmen

swoop, zich storten

sword, zwaard *n*

syllable, lettergreep

symbol, sym'bool *n*

symbolic(al), sym'bolisch

symbolize, symboli'seren

symmetrical, sym'metrisch

symmetry, symme'trie

sympathetic, vol medeleven ; wel'willend

sympathize, meevoelen

sympathy, sympa'thie

symphony, symfo'nie

symptom, symp'toom *n*

synagogue, syna'goge

synchronize, (doen) samenvallen ; ge'lijkzetten

syncopate, synco'peren

syndicate, syndi'caat *n*

synod, sy'node

synonym(ous), syno'niem (*n*)

synopsis, sy'nopsis

syntax, syn'taxis

synthesis, syn'these

synthetic, syn'thetisch

syringe, spuit(je *n*) : uitspuiten

syrup, stroop, si'roop

system, sys'teem *n* ; stelsel *n* ; net *n* ; lichaam *n*

systematic, syste'matisch

T

tab, label ; lus

table, tafel ; ta'bel

table-spoon, eetlepel

tablet, ta'blet(je) *n* ; ge'denkplaat

taboo, ta'boe (ver'klaren)

tabulate, classifi'ceren

tacit, stil'zwijgend

taciturn, zwijgzaam

tack, kopspijker ; spoor *n* : rijgen ; toevoegen ; la'veren

tackle, tuig *n* ; takel : aanpakken ; tekkelen

tact(ful), tact(vol)

tactical, tac'tisch

tactics, tac'tiek

tactless, tactloos

taffeta, tafzij

tag, eti'ketje *n* ; eindje *n*, bandje *n*

to tag on to, zich aansluiten bij

tail, staart ; pand : achter-

tailor, kleermaker

taint, smet : be'derven

take, (aan, in, mee *or* op)nemen ; brengen ; kosten

to take down, opschrijven

to take for, houden voor

to take in, herbergen ; innemen ; in zich opnemen ; beetnemen

to take off, uittrekken ; opstijgen ; naäpen

to take on, aannemen ; op zich nemen

taken aback, van zijn stuk ge'bracht

takings, ont'vangsten

talc(um), talk

tale, ver'haal *n* ; praatje *n*

talent(ed), ta'lent(vol) (*n*)

talk, ge'sprek *n* ; cause'rie ; sprake ; be'spreking : praten, spreken

to talk over, be'spreken, be'praten

talkative, praatziek

tall, lang, hoog

tallow, talk

tally, eti'ket *n* : kloppen

talon, klauw

tame, tam : temmen

tamper with, knoeien met

tan, (geel)bruin : tanen ; bruinen

tang, scherpe smaak

tangerine, manda'rijn

tangible, tastbaar

tangle, knoop, war: in de war raken (or maken)

tank, tank, bak

tankard, drinkkan

tannin, looizuur n

tantalize, tantali'seren

tantamount: to be — to, neerkomen op

tantrum, driftbui

tap, kraan: tik(ken), kloppen: (af)tappen

tape, band n

taper, waspit: taps toelopen

tapestry, tapisse'rie; wandtapijt n

tapioca, tapi'oca

tar, teer; pikbroek: teren

tardy, traag

target, schietschijf; mikpunt n, doel n

tariff, ta'rief n

tarnish, be'slaan, aantasten; be'zoedelen

tarpaulin, zeil(doek) n

tarry, (ver')toeven

tart, taart: slet; wrang

tartar, wijnsteen: driftkop: Tar'taar

task, taak

tassel, kwast(je n)

taste, smaak(je n), proefje n: proeven, smaken (naar)

tasteful, smaakvol

tasteless, smakeloos

tasty, smakelijk

tattered, haveloos

tatters, flarden

tattoo, taptoe: schouw(spel n): tatoe'ëren

taunt, schimpscheut: schimpen op

taut, strak

tavern, herberg

tawdry, op'zichtig, prullig

tawny, vaalgeel

tax, be'lasting: veel vergen van; be'schuldigen

to be taxed, be'lasting be'talen, onder'hevig zijn aan be'lasting

taxation, be'lasting

taxi, taxi(ën)

tea, thee

teach, onder'wijzen, les geven, leren

teacher, onder'wijzer('es), leraar, lera'res

teaching, onderwijs n, leer

team, elftal n; ploeg; span n

teamwork, samenspel n, samenwerking

tea-pot, theepot

tear, traan: scheur(en); vliegen

tease, plagen

teat, tepel; speen

technical, technisch, ambachts-

technicalities, tech'niek; formali'teiten

technically, technisch; strikt ge'nomen

technician, technicus

technique, tech'niek

tedious, ver'velend

teem, wemelen (van)

teetotaller, ge'heelonthouder

telegram, tele'gram n

telegraph, tele'graaf: telegra'feren

telephone, tele'foon: telefo'neren

telephone-box, tele'fooncel

telescope, teles'coop: in el'kaar schuiven

television, tele'visie

tell, (het) ver'tellen, (het) zeggen; onder'scheiden

telling, raak

temper, aard, hu'meur n; drift(bui); hardheid: ver'zachten; harden

temperament, aard; tempera'ment n

temperamental, tempera'mentvol, vol kuren

temperance, matigheid; ont'houding

temperate, ge'matigd, matig

temperature, tempera'tuur; ver'hoging

tempest, hevige storm

tempestuous, stormachtig, on'stuimig

temple, tempel: slaap

temporal, tijdelijk; wereldlijk

temporary, tijdelijk, voor'lopig

tempt, ver'leiden; lokken

temptation, ver'leiding; aan-vechting
tempting, ver'leidelijk
ten, tien
tenable, ver'dedigbaar
tenacious, vast'houdend; hard'nekkig
tenant, huurder, pachter
tend, ge'neigd zijn; lopen; over-hellen; (licht) kunnen: passen op
tendency, neiging
tender, mals; te(d)er; ge'voelig: of'ferte; be'taalmiddel n: ten-der: aanbieden
tendon, pees
tendril, rank
tenement, e'tagewoning
tenet, leerstuk n
tennis(-court), tennis(baan) (n)
tenor, te'nor; loop; strekking
tense, strak; ge'spannen, span-nend: tijd
tension, spanning
tent, tent
tentacle, voelhoorn; vangarm
tentative, bij wijze van proef-ballon
tenterhooks: on —, op hete kolen
tenth, tiende
tenuous, ijl, schraal
tenure, be'zit n; tijd
tepid, lauw
term, term('ijn); kwar'taal n: noemen
terms, be'woording(en); con'-dities; voet
terminal, eind('standig): pool-(klem)
terminate, (be')eindigen, af-lopen; opzeggen
terminology, terminolo'gie
terminus, eindstation(or punt) n
terrace, ter'ras n; huizenrij
terrestrial, aard-; land-
terrible, vreselijk, ver'schrik-kelijk
terrier, terrier
terrific, ge'weldig
terrify, schrik aanjagen
to be terrified, in doodsangst ver'keren, zich doodschrikken

territorial, territori'aal
territory, (grond)gebied n
terror, schrik, angst
terse, kort en bondig
test, proef(werk n), e'xamen n; be'proeving: testen, exami'-neren; op de proef stellen
testament, testa'ment n
testify, ge'tuigen (van); onder ede ver'klaren
testimonial, ge'tuigschrift n, ver'klaring
testimony, ge'tuigenis n
text, tekst
text-book, leerboek n
textile, tex'tiel
texture, weefsel n; samenstel n, bouw
than, dan
thank, (be')danken
thanks, be'dankt: dank
thankful, dankbaar
thankless, on'dankbaar
thanksgiving, dankzegging
that, dat; die; wat; daar-
thatch(ed roof), riet(en dak) n
thaw, dooi(en); (doen) ont'-dooien
the, de, het
the . . . the, hoe . . . hoe
theatre, schouwburg; to'neel n; ter'rein n; zaal
theatrical, to'neel-; thea'traal
thee, U
theft, diefstal
their, hun
theirs, (die or dat) van hun
them, hen, ze
theme, onderwerp n; thema n
themselves, zich(zelf), zelf
then, toen('malig); dan; boven'dien
by then, tegen die tijd
but then, maar . . . (dan ook)
then and there, on'middel-lijk
thence, van'daar; daaruit
theologian, theo'loog
theological, theo'logisch
theology, godge'leerdheid
theoretical, theo'retisch
theory, theo'rie
there, daar('heen); er

thereabouts, daar in de buurt; daarom'trent

therefore, daarom

thermometer, thermometer

these, deze; hier-

thesis, stelling; disser'tatie

they, zij

thick, dik; dicht

thicken, dikker worden; binden

thicket, struikgewas *n*

thickness, dikte; laag

thick-set, ge'drongen

thick-skinned, dik'huidig

thief, dief

thieve, stelen

thigh, dij

thimble, vingerhoed; dopmoer

thin, dun; mager; ijl: ver'dunnen

thine, de (*or* het) Uwe: Uw

thing, ding *n*
  a thing, iets
  the thing that, wat
  things, spullen; (de) dingen

think, denken (aan *or* over); nadenken; ge'loven; een i'dee hebben; vinden

thinnish, vrij dun

third, derde: terts

thirdly, ten derde

thirst, dorst(en); zucht (naar)

thirsty: to be —, dorst hebben; dorstig zijn

thirteen (th), dertien (de)

thirty, dertig

this, deze, dit; hier-

thistle, distel

thither, derwaarts

thong, riem

thorn, doorn

thorny, doornig; netelig

thorough, grondig; echt

those, die; de'genen; er; daar-

thou, gij

though, hoe'wel; al (. . . ook); (ja) maar, (en) toch
  as though, als'of

thought, i'dee *n*, ge'dachte; (na)denken *n*; at'tentie

thoughtful, in ge'dachten ver'zonken; at'tent

thoughtless, onbe'zonnen; onat'tent

thousand, duizend

thrash, afranselen; woelen

thread, garen *n*; draad: de draad steken door; zich (een weg) banen

threadbare, kaal; afgezaagd

threat, be'dreiging

threaten, dreigen met; be'dreigen

three, drie

thresh, dorsen

threshold, drempel

thrice, driemaal

thrift, zuinigheid

thrifty, spaarzaam

thrill, sen'satie: aangrijpen; ver'rukken

thrilling, aan'grijpend; (erg) op'windend

thrive, ge'dijen; bloeien

throat, keel

throb, bonzen, kloppen

throne, troon

throng, ge'drang *n*: (zich ver')dringen (op)

throttle, smoorklep: smoren

through, door('heen): doorgaand

throughout, door heel
  throughout the day, de hele dag door

throw, worp: werpen; (toe *or* af)gooien; gooien met

thrush, zanglijster

thrust, stoot, steek: stoten, steken; werpen

thud, plof

thug, ban'diet

thumb, duim: be'duimelen

thump, bons; stomp(en); bonken (op), bonzen (op)

thunder, donder(en (*n*)), onweer *n*

thunderbolt, dondersteen; bliksemstraal

thundercloud, onweerswolk

thunderous, daverend

thunder-storm, onweer(sbui) (*n*)

Thursday, donderdag

thus, (al')dus; zo

thwart, doft; dwarsbomen, ver'ijdelen

thy, Uw

tick, tik(ken); streepje *n*; ogen- blikje *n*: teek: tijk: aftekenen

ticket, kaartje *n*

tickle, kietelen; jeuken; amu'- seren

ticklish, kietelig; netelig

tidal, ge'tij-, vloed-

tide, ge'tij *n*. stroom: helpen

tidings, nieuws *n*

tidy, net(jes); flink: opruimen

tie, das; band; onbesliste wed- strijd: (vast)binden; strikken, knopen; ge'lijkstaan, ge'lijk aankomen

tier, rang, ver'dieping

tiger, tijger

tight, vast; dicht op el'kaar; strak; kachel

tighten, strakker aanhalen; ver'scherpen

tile, tegel; dakpan: be'tegelen

till, tot(dat): geldlade: be'- ploegen

up till, tot (aan)

not . . . till, pas

tilt, overhellen; kantelen; schuinhouden (or zetten)

full tilt, met volle vaart

timber, timmerhout *n*; balk

time, (de) tijd; keer; ge'legen- heid; maat, tempo *n*: de tijd opnemen van; uitrekenen

at the same time, tege'lijker- tijd: desondanks

for the time being, voor'lopig

in time, op tijd; op den duur; in de maat

timely, tijdig

timid, timorous, schuchter

tin, tin *n*; blik(ken) (*n*); bus, trommel

tinge, tint(en); tikje *n*

tingle, tintelen

tinker, ketellapper: prutsen

tinkle, tingelen

tinned, in blik

tinsel, klatergoud *n*

tint, tint(en)

tiny, heel klein

tip, punt, top: (een) fooi (geven); wenk, foefje *n*: optillen, kan- telen; storten

tipsy, aangeschoten

tiptoe : on —, op de tenen; in spanning

tire, band: ver'moeien; moe (or beu) worden

tired, moe; beu

tireless, onvermoeid

tiresome, ver'velend

tissue, weefsel *n*: vloei-

tit, mees

titbit, lekker hapje *n*

tithe, tiende

title, titel; aanspraak (op): be'titelen

titled, adellijk

titter, giechelen

to, naar; tot (aan); (om) te; in; aan: dicht

to and fro, heen en weer

toad, pad

toadstool, paddestoel

toast, ge'roosterd brood *n*; toost: roosteren: drinken op

tobacco, ta'bak

tobacconist, si'garenhandelaar

toboggan, slee(ën)

today, van'daag; tegen'woordig

toddle, dribbelen

toe, teen

toffee, toffee

together, samen; tege'lijk

toil, arbeid: strik: zwoegen; zich slepen

toilet, toi'let *n*

token, (ken)teken *n*

tolerable, draaglijk; redelijk

tolerance, ver'draagzaamheid

tolerant, ver'draagzaam

tolerate, dulden

toll, tol: luiden

tomato, to'maat

tomb, graftombe

tombstone, grafsteen

tome, zwaar boekdeel *n*

tomorrow, morgen

tom-tom, tam'tam

ton, ton

tone, toon, klank; tint: har- moni'ëren

tongs, tang

tongue, tong; taal; klepel

tonic, ver'sterkend middel *n*

tonight, van'avond, van'nacht

tonnage, tonnenmaat
tonsil, a'mandel
too, ook (nog); (al) te
tool, ge'reedschap n, werktuig n
toot, ge'toeter n: toeteren
tooth, tand, kies
toothache, kiespijn
toothbrush, tandenborstel
tooth-paste, tandpasta
toothpick, tandestoker
top, top: tol: bovenste, bovenaan
topic, onderwerp n
topical, actu'eel
topography, topogra'fie
topple, tuimelen
topsy-turvy, op zijn kop
torch, zaklantaren; fakkel
torment, foltering: kwellen
tornado, wervelstorm
torpedo, tor'pedo: to pe'deren
torrent, (berg)stroom; stortvloed
torrential, stort-
torrid, heet
torso, torso, romp
tortoise, schildpad
tortuous, kronkelend; draaiend
torture, foltering; kwelling: folteren; kwellen
toss, toss: opgooien; slingeren;
de lucht in gooien
tot, peuter; oorlam n
total, to'taal (n): be'dragen
totally, vol'komen
totter, wankelen
touch, aanraking; con'tact n;
tikje n; trekje n; aanslag:
(aan)raken; el'kaar raken;
(aan)roeren
touching, roerend
tough, taai; zuur; hard;
moeilijk: ruwe klant
tour, (rond)reis; rondtoer; (op)
tour'nee (zijn); (af)reizen
tourist, toe'rist
tournament, toer'nooi n
tourniquet, drukverband n
tousle, ver'fomfaaien
tow, sleeptouw n: slepen
toward(s), naar ... toe, in de
richting van; jegens; tegen
towel, handdoek

tower, toren: zich torenhoog
ver'heffen
town, stad
townhall, stad'huis n
toxic, ver'giftig
toy, (stuk) speelgoed n; speelbal:
spelen
trace, spoor n; tikje n: opsporen, vinden: overtrekken,
schetsen
tracery, tra'ceerwerk n
track, spoor n; pad n; baan:
opsporen
tract, uitge'strektheid, streek:
trak'taatje n
tractor, tractor
trade, handel(en); vak n; zaken:
handeldrijven
trade-mark, handelsmerk n
trader, handelaar; handels-
vaartuig n
tradesman, leveran'cier
trades-union, vakvereniging
tradition, tra'ditie
traditional, traditio'neel
traffic, ver'keer n; handel(en)
tragedy, treurspel n; trage'die
tragic, treurspel-; tragisch
trail, spoor n; nasleep; pad n:
(laten) slepen; kruipen; opsporen;
to trail off (or away), wegsterven
trailer, kruipplant; aanhangwagen
train, trein; sleep; ge'volg n;
reeks: opleiden; trainen:
(af)richten
trainer, trainer
training, opleiding; training
trait, trek
traitor(ous), ver'rader(lijk)
tram, tram
tramp, landloper; wilde boot;
wandeling: sjouwen; lopen;
trappen
trample, trappen
trance, trance; geestvervoering
tranquil, rustig
tranquillity, rust
transact, doen, sluiten
transaction, trans'actie; ver'-
richten n

transcend, te boven gaan

transcribe, overbrengen

transfer, overplaatsing; overdruk : overdragen, overbrengen, over (*or* ver')plaatsen

transfigure, een andere ge'daante geven

transfix, door'steken : aan de grond nagelen

transform, (ge'heel) ver'anderen; transfor'meren

transgress, over'treden; te buiten gaan

transient, kort'stondig

transit : in —, onder'weg

transition (al), overgang (s-)

transitory, ver'gankelijk

translate, ver'talen; omzetten

translation, ver'taling

translucent, door'schijnend

transmission, trans'missie; overbrengen *n*; gangwissel

transmit, overbrengen; uitzenden

transparent, door'zichtig

transpire, blijken; zich voordoen

transplant, ver'planten

transport, ver'voer *n*, trans'port *n* : ver'voeren

transpose, ver'wisselen; transpo'neren

transverse, dwars

trap, val (strik), hinderlaag; sjees : in de val laten lopen; opsluiten

trap-door, valluik *n*

trappings, sja'brak; opschik

trash, prullen, prul'laria

travail, barensnood

travel, reizen (*n*) : zich voortplanten

traveller, reiziger

traverse, dwars : doortrekken

travesty, traves'tie; aanfluiting

trawler, treiler

tray, blad *n*; bak

treacherous, ver'raderlijk; vals

treachery, ver'raad *n*

tread, tred (en); loopvlak *n*: be'treden; trappen

treason, landverraad *n*

treasure, schat (ten); ju'weel *n*:

hoogschatten; angst'vallig be'waren

treasurer, penningmeester

treasury, schatkist; minis'terie van fi'nanciën *n*

treat, trak'tatie, feestje *n*: be'handelen; trak'teren

treatise, ver'handeling

treatment, be'handeling

treaty, ver'drag *n*

treble, drie'voudig : so'praan : verdrie'voudigen

tree, boom; leest

trek, trek (ken)

trellis, latwerk *n*

tremble, beven

tremendous, e'norm

tremor, trilling

trench, loopgraaf; voor

trenchant, snijdend; krachtig

trend, neiging; loop, richting

trepidation, schroom, beven *n*

trespass, op ver'boden ter'rein zijn (*or* komen); be'slag leggen

tress, lok

trestle, schraag

trial, ver'hoor *n*; proef (neming); be'proeving; lastpost

triangle, driehoek; tri'angel

triangular, drie'hoekig

tribe, stam

tribulation, be'proeving

tribunal, rechtbank; tribu'naal *n*

tributary, zijrivier; bij-

tribute, hulde (blijk *n*); schatting

trice, wip : trijsen, sjorren

trick, truc; kunstje *n*; streek; slag : be'driegen

trickle, straaltje *n*: sijpelen, biggelen; druppelen

tricky, lastig, netelig

tricycle, driewieler

trifle, kleinigheid; klein beetje *n*; fruit en cake met custard en room : spotten

trifling, onbe'duidend

trigger, trekker

trill, triller : trillend zingen

trim, net (jes) : con'ditie : bijwerken, bijknippen; gar'neren

trimming, gar'nering, ver'siering
Trinity, Drie'ëenheid
trinket, kleinood *n*
trip, tocht(je *n*): (doen) struikelen; trippelen
 to trip up, struikelen; zich in de
vingers snijden
tripe, pens
triple, drie'delig; drie'dubbel
tripod, drievoet
trite, afgezaagd
triumph, tri'omf: zegevieren
triumphal, tri'omf-
triumphant, zegevierend, triom'-
fantelijk
trivet, treeftje *n*
trivial, onbe'duidend
trolley, trolley; rolwagen(tje *n*),
ser'veerboy
trombone, trom'bone
troop, troep; pelo'ton *n*: zich
scharen; allen (tege'lijk) gaan
trooper, cavale'rist
trophy, zegeteken *n*
tropics, tropen
tropical, tropisch
trot, draf: draven
trouble, zorg; moeite (nemen):
hinderen; lastig vallen
troublesome, lastig
troublous, veelbewogen
trough, trog; dal *n*
troupe, troep
trousers, broek
trousseau, uitzet
trout, fo'rel(len)
trowel, troffel; schopje *n*
truant: to play —, spijbelen
truce, wapenstilstand
truck, vrachtauto; (goederen)-
wagen
trudge, sjokken
true, waar; echt; (ge')trouw;
zuiver
truism, afgezaagde waarheid
truly, heus
trump, troef: troeven
 to trump up, ver'zinnen
trumpet, trom'pet(ten)
truncheon, stok
trundle, rollen
trunk, stam, romp; hutkoffer;
slurf: interlo'kaal

truss, bundel, spant: (vast)bin-
den
trust, ver'trouwen (op) (*n*);
be'waring; trust: hopen
trustee, execu'teur; gevol'-
machtigde
trustful, goed van ver'trouwen
trustworthy, be'trouwbaar
trusty, trouw
truth, waarheid
truthful, eerlijk
try, poging: pro'beren; be'-
proeven; op de proef stellen;
ver'horen
trying, moeilijk
tub, kuip, ton
tube, buis, slang; (binnen)band;
tube; onder'grondse
tuber, knol
tuberculosis, tubercu'lose
tuck, plooi: stoppen
Tuesday, dinsdag
tuft, bosje *n*
tug, ruk(ken); sleepboot: trekken
tuition, onderwijs *n*
tulip, tulp
tumble, tuimelen
tumbledown, bouw'vallig
tumbler, (limo'nade)glas *n*
tumor, tumor
tumult, tumult *n*
tumultuous, on'stuimig, ru'-
moerig; stormachtig
tune, wijsje *n*, melo'die: stemmen
tuneful, wel'luidend
tunic, overgooier; tu'niek
tunnel, tunnel (maken)
turban, tulband
turbid, troebel
turbine, tur'bine
turbulent, woelig
turf, zode(n), gras *n*; rensport
turkey, kal'koen: Tur'kije *n*
turmoil, be'roering
turn, draai; bocht; ommekeer;
beurt; dienst; kunstje *n*:
(om)draaien; omslaan; om-
keren; worden; ver'anderen;
omzetten; wenden
 to turn down, om'vouwen;
afwijzen

to **turn out**, uitdraaien; aantreden, opstaan; (er) uitzetten;
produ'ceren; aflopen; blijken
to **turn over**, omslaan; (zich)
omkeren; overdragen; over'-
denken
to **turn to**, overgaan op; zich
wenden tot; aanpakken
to **turn up**, omslaan, optrekken;
opdraaien; ver'schijnen
turnip, knol
turnover, omzet
turnpike, tolhek n
turpentine, terpen'tijn
turquoise, tur'koois
turret, torentje n; ge'schuttoren
turtle, zeeschildpad
tusk, slagtand
tussle, worsteling: worstelen
tut tut, nou nou
tutor, huisonderwijzer; pri've-
leraar
twaddle, ge'wauwel n: wauwelen
twang, ping: tingelen
tweed, tweed
tweezers, pin'cet n
twelve, twaalf
twenty, twintig
twice, tweemaal
twiddle, draaien
twig, twijgje n
twilight, schemering
twin, tweeling
twine, twijn(en): zich slingeren
twinge, steek
twinkle, fonkelen
twirl, (rond)draaien
twist, kromming; (ver')draaien;
zich slingeren; ver'trekken
twitch, zenuwtrekking: trekken
twitter, tjilpen
two, twee
twofold, twee'voudig
type, type n; letter(type n):
tikken
typewriter, schrijfmachine
typhoid, tyfus
typhoon, ty'foon
typical, typisch
typify, ty'peren
tyrannical, tiran'niek
tyranny, tiran'nie
tyrant, ti'ran

U

ubiquitous, alomheersend
udder, uier
ugly, lelijk
ulcer, zweer
ulterior, heimelijk, bij-
ultimate, laatste; uit'eindelijk;
essen'tieel, grond-
ultimatum, ulti'matum n
ultra-violet, ultravio'let
umbrella, para'plu; tuinparasol
umpire, scheidsrechter
un-, on-
unable, niet in staat
unaccompanied, zonder bege'-
leiding; a-ca'pella
unaccountable, onver'klaarbaar
unaccustomed, niet ge'wend
unanimous, een'stemmig, eensge'zind
unassuming, be'scheiden
unattended, onbe'heerd
unauthorized, onbe'voegd
unavailing, ver'geefs
unavoidable, onver'mijdelijk
unaware, niet be'wust
unawares, onbe'wust; onver'-
hoeds
unbearable, on'draaglijk
unbelievable, onge'looflijk
unbound, niet ge'bonden
unbroken, onver'broken; on'-
afgebroken
unbutton, losknopen
uncalled-for, onge'vraagd;
mis'plaatst
uncanny, griezelig, onge'looflijk,
geheim'zinnig
uncertain, on'zeker
unchecked, onbe'lemmerd
uncle, oom
uncommon, onge'woon
uncompromising, on'buigzaam
rotsvast
unconcerned, onver'schillig; onbe'kommerd
unconditional, onvoor'waardelijk
unconquerable, onover'winnelijk
unconscious, be'wusteloos; onbe'wust

uncontrollable, onbe'dwingbaar, onbe'daarlijk

uncork, ont'kurken

uncouth, lomp

uncover, ont'bloten; aan het licht brengen

unction, zalving, oliesel *n*

unctuous, zalvend

undaunted, onver'saagd

undecided, onbe'slist; in dubio

undeniable, ontegen'zeglijk, onbe'twistbaar

under, onder(-)

undercurrent, onderstroom; ver'borgen stroming

underdone, on'gaar

undergraduate, stu'dent

underground, onder de grond; onder'gronds(e)

undergrowth, kreupelhout *n*

underhand, onder'hands

underlying, grond-,

undermine, onder'mijnen

underneath, onder, be'neden: onderkant

understand, be'grijpen; horen; aannemen

understanding, be'grip *n*; ver'standhouding: sympa'thiek

undertake, onder'nemen; op zich nemen

undertaker, be'grafenisondernemer

undertaking, onder'neming; be'lofte

undertone, ge'dempte stem; grondkleur; ondergrond

underwear, ondergoed *n*

undesirable, onge'wenst

undo, los(*or* open)maken; onge'daan maken

undoing, ondergang

undoubtedly, onge'twijfeld

undress, (zich) uitkleden

undue, over'matig

undulate, golven

unearth, opgraven; aan het licht brengen

unearthly, boven'aards; on'mogelijk

uneasy, onge'rust, on'rustig

uneducated, onont'wikkeld

unemployed, werkloos

unemployment, werk'loosheid

unending, eindeloos

unequal, onge'lijk; niet opgewassen (tegen)

unerring, on'feilbaar

uneven, on'effen; onge'lijk; on'even

uneventful, onbe'wogen

unexpected(ly), onver'wacht(s), onvoor'zien

unfailing, nimmer falend; onuit'puttelijk; zeker

unfamiliar, onbe'kend; niet op de hoogte

unfasten, los(*or* open)maken

unfathomable, ondoor'grondelijk

unfeeling, onge'voelig

unfetter, ont'ketenen

unfinished, onvol'tooid

unfit, onge'schikt

unfold, ont'vouwen, (zich) ont'plooien

unforgettable, onver'getelijk

unforgivable, onver'geeflijk

unfortunately, jammer ge'noeg, he'laas

unfounded, onge'grond

unfurl, (zich) ont'plooien

ungainly, lomp, onbe'vallig

ungodly, goddeloos

ungovernable, on'tembaar

ungracious, on'hoffelijk

unhappiness, ver'driet *n*

unharmed, onge'deerd, onbe'schadigd

unheard-of, onge'kend; onge'hoord

unheeded, on'opgemerkt; onge'merkt, ver'waarloosd

unholy, goddeloos; heidens

unicorn, eenhoorn

uniform, ge'lijk('matig): uni'form

unify, ver'enigen

unimaginative, zonder fanta'sie

unimpaired, on'aangetast

uninformed, niet op de hoogte, on'wetend

uninhabitable, onbe'woonbaar

unintelligent, dom

unintelligible, onver'staanbaar, onbe'grijpelijk

uninvited, onge'nood

union, ver'eniging, unie; ver'bintenis

unique, u'niek

unison : in —, een'stemmig; tege'lijk

unit, eenheid; afdeling

unite, (zich) ver'enigen

unity, eenheid; eensge'zindheid

universal, univer'seel; alge'meen

universe, heel'al *n*

university, universi'teit

unkempt, onver'zorgd

unkind, on'aardig

unknown, onbe'kend (e *n*)

unless, ten'zij

unlike, ver'schillend, anders dan
it is unlike him to forget, het is niets voor hem het te ver'geten

unload, ont'laden, lossen

unlock, ont'sluiten

unmanageable, on'handelbaar

unmask, (zich) demas'keren; ont'maskeren

unmistakable, onmis'kenbaar

unmitigated, onver'minderd; onver'valst

unnerve, ont'zenuwen

unobtrusive, be'scheiden

unoccupied, onbe'zet; onbe'woond; niet bezig

unofficial, niet offi'cieel

unopposed, onbe'streden; zonder tegencandidaat

unpack, uitpakken

unpalatable, on'smakelijk; on'aangenaam

unparalleled, weergaloos

unpardonable, onver'geeflijk

unpleasant, on'aangenaam

unprecedented, onge'hoord

unpredictable, onbe'rekenbaar

unprincipled, ge'wetenloos

unprofitable, on'vruchtbaar

unquestionable, onbe'twistbaar

unquestionably, onge'twijfeld

unravel, ont'warren

unreasoned, onberede'neerd

unremitting, onver'droten

unreservedly, zonder voorbehoud

unrestrained, onbe'teugeld; onge'dwongen

unrivalled, ongeëve'naard

unruly, on'ordelijk, on'handelbaar

unsavoury, smakeloos; on'smakelijk; onver'kwikkelijk

unscathed, onge'deerd

unscrew, losschroeven

unscrupulous, ge'wetenloos

unselfish, onbaat'zuchtig

unsettled, on'zeker

unsightly, on'ooglijk

unsparing, kwistig, mild; mee'dogenloos

unspeakable, onbe'schrijf(e)lijk

unsuccessful, ver'geefs
to be unsuccessful, geen suc'ces hebben

unsuspicious, argeloos

untangle, ont'warren

untenable, on'houdbaar

unthinkable, on'denkbaar

untidy, slordig, wan'ordelijk

untie, losmaken

until, tot (dat)

untimely, on'tijdig; onge'legen

untiring, onver'moeid

unto, tot (aan)

untold, onver'teld; on'telbaar

untoward, on'gunstig

unused, onge'bruikt; niet ge'wend (aan)

unusual, onge'woon, onge'bruikelijk

unutterable, onuit'sprekelijk

unvaried, unvarying, onver'anderlijk

unveil, ont'hullen; ont'sluieren

unwarranted, ongerecht'vaardigd

unwavering, stand'vastig

unwieldy, log

unwind, afwinden; (zich) ont'rollen

unwittingly, onop'zettelijk, onbe'wust

unwonted, onge'woon

unwrap, uitpakken

unyielding, onver'zettelijk

up, (verder) op; (naar) boven; om'hoog; over'eind: ver'streken

to be up to, in staat zijn; in de zin hebben, uitvoeren; zijn aan
upbraid, be'rispen
upbringing, opvoeding
upheaval, opschudding
uphill, de heuvel op, opwaarts; zwaar
uphold, hooghouden; steunen
upholstery, be'kleding
upkeep, onderhoud *n*
uplift, ver'heffen
upon, op
upper, boven(ste): bovenleer *n*
uppermost, hoogst; bovenst; op de voorgrond
upright, recht'op; op'recht
uprising, opstand
uproar, tu'mult *n*
uproarious, ru'moerig; storm-achtig
uproot, ont'wortelen; uitroeien
upset, om'verwerpen; in de war sturen; van streek maken
upshot, resul'taat *n*
upside down, onderste'boven
upstairs, (naar) boven
upstart, parve'nu(achtig); poen(ig)
upstream, stroom'opwaarts
up-to-date, mo'dern; op de hoogte
upturn, om'vergooien; opzetten
upward(s), opwaarts, naar boven; (en) hoger, (en) ouder
uranium, u'ranium *n*
urban, stedelijk, stads-, steeds
urbane, wel'levend
urchin, kwa'jongen
urge, (aan)drang: aanzetten; aandringen (op)
urgent, dringend
urn, urn
us, ons
usable, bruikbaar
usage, ge'bruik *n*; be'handeling
use, ge'bruik(en) (*n*); toepassing; nut *n*: ver'bruiken
to be used to, ge'wend zijn (aan)
it used to be, het was vroeger
useful, nuttig, handig
useless, nutteloos
usher, ou'vreuse, plaatsaanwijzer: leiden

usual, ge'bruikelijk, ge'woon
as usual, zoals ge'woonlijk
usually, ge'woonlijk
usurp, usur'peren
utensils, ge'rei
utility, nut(tigheids-) (*n*)
utilize, be'nutten
utmost, uiterste (*n*), hoogste (*n*)
utter, vol'slagen: uiten
utterance, uiting; uitspraak
uttermost, uiterst

V

vacancy, vaca'ture, leemte
vacant, va'cant; onbe'woond; wezenloos
vacate, ont'ruimen
vacation, va'cantie
vaccinate, inenten
vacillate, weifelen
vacuum, lucht'ledig *n*
vacuum-cleaner, stofzuiger
vagabond, vagebond
vagary, gril
vagrant, ronddolend
vague, vaag
vain, ijdel: ver'geefs
in vain, tever'geefs
vale, dal *n*
valet, be'diende
valiant, koen
valid, (rechts')geldig
validity, deugdelijkheid; rechtsgeldigheid
valise, va'lies *n*
valley, dal *n*
valour, koenheid
valuable, waardevol; kostbaar(heid)
valuation, ta'xatie
value, waarde: ta'xeren; **op** hoge prijs stellen
valve, klep, vén'tiel *n*; lamp
van, (be'stel)wagen: voorhoede
vandalism, vanda'lisme *n*
vane, vaantje *n*; wiek, schoep
vanguard, voorhoede
vanilla, va'nille
vanish, (spoorloos) ver'dwijnen; uitsterven
vanity, ijdelheid

vanquish, over'winnen

vantage, voorsprong: gunstig

vapour, damp

variable, ver'anderlijk; ver'stelbaar

variation, afwisseling; ver'andering; vari'atie

variety, ver'scheidenheid, afwisseling; soort: varié'té *n*

various, ver'scheiden

varnish, ver'nis(sen) (*n*)

vary, vari'eren

vase, vaas

vassal, va'zal

vast, on'metelijk, kolos'saal

vastly, e'norm

vat, vat *n*

Vatican, Vati'caan *n*

vault, ge'welf *n* kluis: sprong:
springen

veal, kalfsvlees *n*

veer, draaien; vieren

vegetable, groente(-): plant'-
aardig

vegetarian, vege'tariër: vege'-
tarisch

vegetation, plantengroei

vehement, hevig

vehicle, voertuig *n*; drager

veil, sluier(en)

vein, ader; neiging, trek; stemming

velocity, snelheid

velvet, flu'weel *n*: flu'welen

venal, om'koopbaar

vendor, ver'koper

veneer, fi'neer(hout) *n*; ver'-
nisje *n*: fi'neren

venerable, eerbied'waardig; eer'-
waard

venerate, diep ver'eren

venereal, ge'slachts-

Venetian blind, jaloe'zie

vengeance, wraak

vengeful, wraak'gierig

venial, ver'geeflijk

venison, wildbraad *n*

venom(ous), ve'nijn(ig) (*n*)

vent, opening, luchtgaatje *n*;
uitweg: luchten

ventilate, venti'leren

ventilation, venti'latie

ventriloquist, buikspreker

venture, waagstuk *n*: (het)
wagen

venturesome, venturous,
stout'moedig

veracity, waarheid

verb, werkwoord *n*

verbal, in woorden; mondeling;
werk'woordelijk

verbatim, woordelijk

verbiage, omhaal

verbose, breed'sprakig

verdict, uitspraak; be'slissing

verge, rand: grenzen (aan)

verify, verifi'ëren

veritable, waar

vermilion, vermil'joen (*n*)

vermin, ongedierte *n*

vernacular, moedertaal

versatile, veel'zijdig

verse, poë'zie; cou'plet *n*

versed, be'dreven

version, ver'taling, lezing, be'-
werking

vertibrate, ge'werveld (dier *n*)

vertical, verti'caal: loodlijn

very, zeer, erg: pre'cies; al'leen
al

vespers, vesper

vessel, vaartuig *n*; vat *n*

vest, hemd *n*; vest *n*: (be')-
kleden

vestibule, vesti'bule

vestige, spoor *n*

vestment, (priester)ge'waad *n*

vestry, sacris'tie

veteran, vete'raan: er'varen

vet(erinary), veearts(e'nij)

veto, veto *n*: ver'werpen

vex, ergeren

vexation, ergernis

viaduct, via'duct *n*

vial, flesje *n*

vibrate, vi'breren

vibration, trilling

vicar, dominee, pas'toor

vice, ondeugd: bankschroef:
vice-

viceroy, onderkoning

vice versa, omgekeerd

vicinity, na'bijheid, buurt

vicious, boos'aardig; vici'eus

vicissitude, wissel'valligheid

victim, slachtoffer *n*

victor, over'winnaar
victorious, zegevierend
victory, over'winning
victual, provi'and innemen, pro-vian'deren
victuals, levensmiddelen
vie, wedijveren
view, uitzicht *n*, ge'zicht *n*; mening: be'schouwen
in view, in het ge'zicht; voor ogen
in view of, ge'zien
viewpoint, uitzichtpunt *n*; ge'zichtspunt *n*
vigil, wacht, waken *n*, wake
vigilance, waakzaamheid
vigorous, krachtig, ener'giek
vigour, kracht, ener'gie
vile, af'schuwelijk
villa, villa
village, dorp *n*
villain, schurk
villainous, laag
vindicate, handhaven, recht'-vaardigen, zuiveren (van blaam)
vindictive, wraak'gierig
vine, wijnstok; wingerd
vinegar, a'zijn
vineyard, wijngaard
vintage, jaar *n*; wijnoogst
viola, altviool: vi'ooltje *n*
violate, schenden
violation, schennis
violence, ge'weld *n*
violent, hevig, heftig, geweld'-dadig
violet, vi'ooltje *n*: vio'let
violin, vi'ool
violinist, vio'list
violoncello, violon'cel
viper, adder
virgin, maagd(elijk); onge'-rept
virile, man'moedig, krachtig
virtual, eigenlijk
virtually, praktisch
virtue, deugd; ver'dienste
virtuous, deugdzaam
virulent, kwaad'aardig; ve'-nijnig
visa, visum *n*
viscount, burggraaf

visibility, zicht *n*
visible, zichtbaar
visibly, zienderogen
vision, ge'zicht *n*; vérziende blik; visi'oen *n*
visionary, dromer(ig); inge-beeld: ziener
visit, be'zoek(en) (*n*)
visitor, be'zoeker, gast
visual, ge'zichts-
vital, essen'tieel; vi'taal; fa'taal
vitality, vitali'teit
vitamin, vita'mine
vitiate, be'derven; on'geldig maken
vivacious, levendig
vivid, hel(-); levendig
vocabulary, woordenlijst; woor-denschat
vocal, stem-, zang-
vocation, roeping; be'roep *n*
vogue, zwang; populari'teit
voice, stem: uiten
void, on'geldig; ont'bloot: leegte
volatile, vluchtig; wispel'turig
volcano, vul'kaan
volley, regen, stroom; volley
volt(age), volt('age)
voluble, woordenrijk
volume, (boek)deel *n*; vo'lume *n*, omvang; massa
voluminous, volumi'neus
voluntary, vrij'willig; wille'-keurig; lief'dadigheids-
volunteer, vrij'williger: vrij'-willig in dienst treden; aan-bieden
voluptuous, wel'lustig; weel-derig
vomit, (uit)braken
votary, liefhebber
vote, stem(recht *n*); motie: stemmen; toestaan
voter, kiezer
vouch, instaan
vow, ge'lofte: plechtig be'-loven
vowel, klinker
voyage, reis
vulgar, vul'gair, plat
vulgarity, platheid
vulnerable, kwetsbaar
vulture, gier

W

wad, prop; pakje *n*

waddle, waggelen

wade, waden

wafer, wafel; hostie

waft, drijven, zweven

wag, grappenmaker: kwispelen

wage, loon *n*: voeren

wager, weddenschap: wedden om

wagon, wagen, wa'gon

waif, vondeling

wail, weeklagen; loeien

wainscot(ing), lambri'zering

waist, taille

waistcoat, vest *n*

wait, wachten; dienen

waiter, kelner

waiting-room, wachtkamer

waitress, kelner'in

waive, afstand doen van

wake, kielzog *n*; spoor *n*

  to wake up, wakker worden (*or* maken)

walk, wandeling, eind lopen *n*; loop; laan; sfeer: lopen, wandelen

  to go for a walk, gaan wandelen

wall, muur, wand, wal

wallet, (zak)porte'feuille

wallow, rollen; slingeren; zwelgen

wall-paper, be'hang(selpapier) *n*

walnut, walnoot; notehout(en) (*n*)

waltz, wals(en)

wan, bleek; flets

wand, toverstaf

wander, zwerven; dwalen

wane, afnemen (*n*)

wangle, klaarspelen; knoeien met

want, be'hoefte; ge'brek *n*, nood: willen (hebben); nodig hebben, moeten worden

wanton, bal'dadig; wild

war, oorlog: strijden

warble, kwelen

ward, pu'pil; zaal; stadswijk

  to ward off, afweren

warden, direc'teur

warder, ci'pier

wardrobe, klerenkast; garde'-robe

wardroom, offi'cierskajuit

ware, waar, goed *n*

warehouse, pakhuis *n*

warlike, oorlogs'zuchtig

warm, warm: (ver')warmen

warmth, warmte

warn, waarschuwen

warning, waarschuwing

warp, kromtrekken; ver'-draaien

warrant, be'vel *n*: waarborgen

warren, (ko'nijnen)berg *n*

warrior, krijgsman

wart, wrat

wartime, oorlogs(tijd)

wary, voor'zichtig

wash, was; golfslag: (zich) wassen; spoelen

  to wash up, afwassen

washable, wasbaar

wash-basin, wastafel

washer, wasser; sluitring, leertje *n*

washing, was(goed *n*): was-

wasp, wesp

wastage, ver'spilling

waste, ver'spilling; afval(-); woest(e'nij): ver'spillen; (weg)kwijnen

  to lay waste, ver'woesten

wasteful, ver'kwistend

wastepaper-basket, prullenmand

watch, wacht; hor'loge *n*: uitkijken; gadeslaan; opletten

watchful, waakzaam

watchman, waker

water, water (geven) (*n*); wateren

water-colour, waterverf; aqua'rel

watercourse, bedding

waterfall, waterval

watertight, waterproof, waterdicht

watery, water(acht)ig; regen-

wave, golf: wuiven (met); watergolven, perma'nenten

waver, flikkeren; weifelen; beven

wavy, golvend

wax, was(sen): wassen; worden

way, ma'nier, wijze; opzicht *n*; kant, weg, eind *n*; zin; vaart

by the way, tussen haakjes

to give way, toegeven; weg- zakken

in a way, in zekere zin

to make one's way, zijn weg vinden; voor'uitkomen

wayfarer, reiziger, zwerver

waylay, aanranden; aanklam- pen

wayside, (aan de) kant van de weg

wayward, eigen'zinnig

we, wij

weak, zwak; slap

weaken, ver'zwakken; ver'- slappen

weakling, zwakkeling

weakness, zwakte; zwak (punt) *n*

wealth, rijkdom; schat

wealthy, rijk

wean, spenen

weapon, wapen *n*

wear, dracht, kleding; slij'- tage: dragen; slijten; zich houden

to wear out, (ver')slijten, af- dragen; afmatten

weariness, ver'moeidheid

weary, moe

weather, weer *n*: ver'weren; door'staan

weather-beaten, door stormen ge'teisterd; ver'weerd

weathercock, weerhaantje *n*

weave, weeftrant: weven; (samen)vlechten

web, web *n*; weefsel *n*

wedding, huwelijk(splechtig- heid) (*n*)

wedge, wig: vastzetten

wee, heel klein

weed, onkruid *n*: wieden

weedy, vol onkruid; spichtig

week, (over een) week

weekend, weekend *n*

weekly, wekelijks, week-

weep, wenen

weeping, wenend; treur-

weigh, (af)wegen; drukken; lichten

weight, ge'wicht *n*

weighty, zwaar; ge'wichtig

weir, stuwdam

weird, griezelig, raar

welcome, welkom (*n*), ver'- welkoming: ver'welkomen

weld, las(sen)

welfare, welzijn *n*: soci'aal, weten'schappelijk

well, goed; ver: wel: put, bron: wellen

as well, ook; even'goed; zo'- wel

well-being, welzijn *n*

well-bred, wel'opgevoed

well-known, be'kend

well-nigh, nage'noeg

well-off, welge'steld; goed'af

well-read, be'lezen

wench, deern

west, West(en) (*n*), west(waards)

west of, ten westen van

westerly, westelijk, wester-

western, westers, westelijk

wet, nat (maken)

whak, mep: slaan

whale, walvis

wharf, kaai

what, wat (voor (een)), welk; waar-

what is the time? hoe laat is het?

what is it called? hoe heet het?

whatever, wat (*or* welk) dan ook; wat ... toch

wheat, tarwe

wheedle, be'praten, aftroggelen

wheel, wiel, *n*, rad *n*: zwenken; duwen

wheelbarrow, kruiwagen

wheeze, piepen, hijgen

whelp, welp; kwa'jongen

when, wan'neer; (en) toen

whence, van'waar

whenever, wan'neer ook; telkens wan'neer

where, waar (naar toe)

whereabouts, waar onge'veer: ver'blijfplaats, ligging

whereas, ter'wijl

wherever, waar (. . . ook *or* toch); overal waar
wherewithal, middelen
whet, opwekken
whether, of
whew ! oef !
whey (cheese), wei(kaas)
which, welk, wat; die, dat; wie
whiff, vleugje *n,* wolkje *n*
while, tijd : ter'wijl : hoe'wel
    to while away, ver'slijten
whilst, ter'wijl; alhoe'wel
whim(sical), gril(lig)
whimper, grienen, janken
whine, jengelen, janken
whinny, hinniken
whip, zweep : (met de zweep) slaan; wippen, schieten; kloppen
whir, ge'snor *n* : snorren
whirl, roes : dwarrelen; tollen, slingeren, stormen
whirlpool, draaikolk
whirlwind, wervelwind
whisk, klopper : (weg)wippen
whiskers, bakkebaarden; snor
whisky, whisky
whisper, ge'fluister *n* : fluisteren
whistle, fluit(je *n*) : fluiten
whit, zier
white, wit; blank
whitewash, witkalk : witten
whither, werwaarts
Whitsun, Pinksteren
whittle down, ge'leidelijk ver'-minderen
whiz, suizen
who, wie; die
whoever, wie . . . ook; al wie
whole, (ge')heel (*n*); vol'ledig
    on the whole, over het ge'heel ge'nomen
wholesale, groothandel : inkoops-; op grote schaal
wholesome, ge'zond
wholly, to'taal
whoop, kreet : schreeuwen
whooping-cough, kinkhoest
whore, hoer
whose, wiens, wier; van wie
why, waarom : wel
wick, pit, ka'toentje *n*

wicked, slecht; on'deugend; schan'dalig
wicker, rieten
wide, breed, wijd
    wide-awake, klaar wakker
widely, wijd en zijd; zeer
widen, (zich) ver'wijden
widespread, uitgestrekt; wijd ver'spreid
widow, weduwe
widower, weduwnaar
width, breedte, wijdte
wield, zwaaien; uitoefenen
wife, vrouw
wig, pruik
wiggle, wiebelen met
wild, wild : woest
wilderness, wildernis
wile, list : lokken
wilful, eigen'zinnig; moed'-willig
will, wil(len); testa'ment *n* : zal, zult, zullen; kunnen
willing, be'reid('willig), ge'willig
willow, wilg
wilt, ver'leppen
wily, slim, sluw
win, winnen, be'halen
wince, in'eenkrimpen, zijn ge'-zicht ver'trekken
winch, windas
wind, wind : blaas- : kronkelen; winden
windfall, afgewaaide vrucht; buitenkansje *n*
window, raam *n*
window-pane, ruit
window-sill, vensterbank
windscreen, voorruit
windward, loefzijde
windy, winderig
wine, wijn
wing, vleugel; cou'lisse; spatbord *n*
wink, knipoogje *n* : knipogen
winner, winnaar
winning, winnend; in'nemend
winter, winter(-)
wintry, winters
wipe, (af)vegen
wire, (ijzer)draad (*n*); tele'-gram *n*
    wire netting, kippegaas *n*

wireless, radio: draadloos
wisdom, wijsheid
wise, wijs, ver'standig: wijze
wish, ver'langen (n); wens(en);
  I wish that you were here, ik
  wou dat je hier was
  I wish to speak to him, ik zou
  hem willen spreken
wisp, bosje n, paar losse
  (haartjes); sliert
wistful, ver'langend, wee'moedig
wit, ver'nuft n, ver'stand n;
  geest(igheid)
  at one's wits' end, ten einde
  raad
witch, heks
witchcraft, tovena'rij
with, met, bij; van
withdraw, (zich) te'rugtrekken
wither, ver'welken; ver'nietigen
withhold, ont'houden
within, binnen(in)
without, zonder; buiten
withstand, weer'staan
witness, ge'tuige(nis n): ge'-
  tuige zijn van; ge'tuigen (van)
witticism, geestigheid
witty, geestig
wizard, tovenaar
wobble, wiebelen
woe, ellende: wee!
woeful, ramp'zalig
wolf, wolf: opschrokken
woman, vrouw; mens n
womb, baarmoeder; schoot
wonder, wonder n; ver'wondering: (zich) ver'wonderen;
  zich afvragen
wonderful, wonder'baarlijk;
  prachtig
wont, ge'woon(te)
woo, het hof maken
wood, hout n; bos n
wooded, be'bost
wooden, houten; houterig
  woodland, bosland n: bos-
woodman, houthakker; boswachter
woodwork, houtwerk n; hout-
  be'werking
woody, bosrijk
wool(len), wol(len)
woolly, wollig

word, woord n; be'richt n
wording, re'dactie
work, werk(en) (n); han'teren
worker, arbeider, werker
working, werking
workmanship, vakmanschap n
workshop, werkplaats
world(ly), wereld(s)
world-wide, over de hele wereld,
  wereld-
worm, wurm(en); kruipen; indringen
worn-out, ver'sleten; uitgeput
worry, zorg: (zich) be'zorgd
  maken; lastig vallen
worse, erger, slechter
worship, aan'bidding; gods-
  dienst(oefening): aan'bidden;
  ver'eren
worst, ergst, slechtst
worsted, kamgaren n
worth, waard(e)
worth while, **worth doing**
  (**seeing** *etc*), de moeite waard
worthless, waardeloos; ver'achtelijk
worthy, (achtens')waardig,
  waard
would, zou(den) (willen);
  wilde(n); wou
would-be, zogenaamd; ge'wild
wound, wond(en)
wrangle, kijven
wrap, sjaal, cape: wikkelen, inpakken; hullen, ver'zinken
  to wrap round, omslaan
wrapping, ver'pakking
wrath(ful), toorn(ig)
wreak, koelen, oefenen
wreath, krans
wreck, wrak n: ver'nielen
wrench, ruk(ken); schroef-
  sleutel
wrest, ont'wringen, afpersen
wrestle, worstelen
wretch, stakker
wretched, el'lendig; be'roerd
wriggle, draaien, wriemelen; zich
  wringen
wring, (uit)wringen; afdwingen;
  omdraaien
wrinkle, rimpel(en)
wrist, pols

writ, (be'vel)schrift *n,* dagvaarding
write, schrijven
writer, schrijver
writhe, (zich ver')wringen
writing, (ge')schrift *n,* schrijven *n :* schrijf-
wrong, ver'keerd; on'juist; niet in orde: kwaad *n,* onrecht (aandoen) (*n*)
  what is wrong? wat man'keert eraan? wat is er?
  to go wrong, misgaan; ver'keerd gaan; de'fect raken; de ver'keerde weg opgaan
wrought iron, smeedijzer *n*
wry, zuur

X

X-ray, röntgenfoto: röntgenen

Y

yacht, jacht *n :* zeilen
yap, keffen; snauwen
yard, plaats(je *n*), erf *n :* kleine meter (91, 44 cm.); ra
yarn, garen *n :* ver'haal *n*
yawn, geeuw(en); gapen
ye, gij
yea, ja (zelfs)
year, jaar *n*
yearly, jaarlijks
yearn, vurig ver'langen (naar)
yeast, gist
yell, gil(len)
yellow, geel
yelp, janken

yes, ja
yesterday, gisteren
yet, nog; al: toch
  as yet, tot nu toe
yew, taxus
yield, opbrengst: (zich) overgeven; (be'z)wijken (voor); opleveren
yoke, juk *n ;* schouder(*or* heup)-stuk *n*
yokel, pummel
yolk, dooier
yonder, ginds
you, u; jij, je, jou; jullie
young, jong(en) (*n*): jeugd
youngster, jongeman, jong meisje *n*
your, uw; je, jouw; jullie
yours, (die *or* dat) van u, (die *or* dat) van jou, (die *or* dat) van jullie
yourself, (u')zelf, zich; je('zelf)
youth, jeugd; jongeling
youthful, jeugdig

Z

zeal, vuur *n ;* ijver
zealot, dweper
zealous, ijverig; vurig
zenith, zenit *n ;* toppunt *n*
zero, nul(punt *n*)
zest, animo
zigzag, zigzag
zinc, zink *n*
zip-fastener, ritssluiting
zodiac, dierenriem
zone, zone
zoo, dierentuin
zoological, zoö'logisch

DUTCH

H. Koolhoven

A course in the Dutch language, complete in one easy-to-follow volume.

One of the hurdles in learning any language is mastering its pronunciation: this is the first problem which this text overcomes. Chapter One deals as fully as possible with spoken Dutch, leading naturally to an examination of the technicalities of the language. Thirty chapters then introduce and practise, step by step, the various points of Dutch grammar, idiom and construction. Vocabulary is built up throughout the course and an extensive vocabulary is to be found at the end of the book.

A graded course, ideal for the beginner studying on his own or for students in the classroom.

TEACH YOURSELF BOOKS

FINNISH

ARTHUR H. WHITNEY

A lively and practical course in Finnish from which the student will emerge with a sound grasp of the language.

This course has been divided into twenty lessons, each dealing with the key points in the construction, use and grammar of modern Finnish. Exercises are to be found at the end of each lesson and also included in the text are several reading passages from modern Finnish writings.

TEACH YOURSELF BOOKS